Paton James Gloag

Introduction to the Catholic Epistles

Paton James Gloag

Introduction to the Catholic Epistles

ISBN/EAN: 9783337730048

Printed in Europe, USA, Canada, Australia, Japan

Cover: Foto ©ninafisch / pixelio.de

More available books at **www.hansebooks.com**

INTRODUCTION

TO

THE CATHOLIC EPISTLES.

BY

PATON J. GLOAG, D.D.,

MINISTER OF GALASHIELS,

AUTHOR OF 'AN INTRODUCTION TO THE PAULINE EPISTLES,' 'A COMMENTARY ON THE ACTS OF THE APOSTLES,' 'EXEGETICAL STUDIES,' 'MESSIANIC PROPHECY: BEING THE BAIRD LECTURES FOR 1879,' ETC.

EDINBURGH:
T. & T. CLARK, 38 GEORGE STREET.
MDCCCLXXXVII.

PRINTED BY MORRISON AND GIBB,

FOR

T. & T. CLARK, EDINBURGH.

LONDON,	. . . .	HAMILTON, ADAMS, AND CO.
DUBLIN,	. . . .	GEO. HERBERT.
NEW YORK,	. .	SCRIBNER AND WELFORD.

PREFACE.

THIS work is intended to form a companion volume to the *Introduction to the Pauline Epistles*, published about twelve years ago. It does not purport to treat of the Catholic Epistles critically or exegetically, to explain their meaning, or to give any commentary on their contents. It does not belong to the class of "Commentaries," but to that of "Introductions to the New Testament." It discusses topics appropriate to such Introductions, such as the authenticity of the Epistles, their authorship, the readers to whom they are addressed, the design or intention of the writings, the peculiarities which belong to them, and the time when and the place from which they were written. To each Epistle there are also attached dissertations or appendices referring to certain special difficulties, disputed questions, apostolic customs, or, as in the case of the Epistle of Jude, to apocryphal writings there referred to. Several of these dissertations, it is admitted, are not very relevant, if the work be considered as an Introduction in a restricted sense; but they are all on points of theological interest and importance, and have a certain connection with the subject treated of. Some of them, as for example the dissertations on the eschatology of St. Peter and on the Book of Enoch, may be thought to be drawn out to undue length; but the intention was to treat the subjects as fully as possible, so that each dissertation may be considered as complete in itself.

A list of the most important books read or consulted in writing this work has been appended, with references to the editions in my possession; so that the quotations made from them may be referred to and verified. In translations from the German, references have been generally made to the original when possible, as well as to the English version. After the book was completed, several recent works of importance came under my notice ; these have been carefully read and consulted, and such references as were thought desirable have been made in notes, as they could not without much inconvenience be incorporated into the body of the work. Four of these deserve special mention : Holzmann's *Einleitung in das neue Testament*, 1885 ; Spitta's *Der zweite Brief des Petrus und der Brief des Judas*, 1885 ; Mangold's edition of Bleek's *Einleitung in das neue Testament*, vierte Auflage, 1886 ; and Weiss' *Lehrbuch der Einleitung in das neue Testament*, 1886.

Introductions to the New Testament are rare in England. The only important books of the kind with which I am acquainted, are the works of the Rev. T. Hartwell Horne, Dr. Samuel Davidson, and Professor Salmon. Horne's *Introduction to the Scriptures* is a repository of information with regard to biblical criticism in general ; but the part of it which consists of a proper introduction to the different books of the New Testament is meagre and defective. A new and more valuable edition of this work has been published by Tregelles. The work has, however, in a great measure become antiquated. Dr. Davidson has two Introductions : the one entitled *Introduction to the New Testament*, published in 1848 ; and the other entitled *Introduction to the Study of the New Testament*, published in 1868 ; and a second edition, considerably altered, published in 1882. These, it need not be said, are both works of the highest interest and importance, but they can with no propriety be considered to be recensions of the same work ; they proceed from very different standpoints. In the first work Dr. Davidson belongs to the positive critical school ; while in the second work he is in close relation to the Tübingen school. Nor do I consider that the second work supersedes the first ; for although Dr. Davidson has modified several of his opinions, yet the reasons by which he supports his former opinions are of great force, and sometimes appear to me to be even more convincing than those for their alteration. Whilst differing from several of his later views, I have always treated them with that respect which his vast erudition demands. Of course Dr. Davidson's present views are to be found in the last edition of his *Introduction to the Study of the New Testament;* whilst many of the opinions advanced in the former work are no longer held by him. Professor Salmon's work, entitled *Introduction to the New Testament*, published in 1885, is an expansion of his lectures as regius professor of divinity in the University of Dublin. It is a work of considerable learning, showing much knowledge of Hellenistic Greek: his opinions are expressed with decision and perspicuity; but it may be questioned whether he always estimates adequately the objections of his opponents. Professor Salmon belongs to the positive school of exegetes, and maintains throughout the traditionary opinions. There are also English translations of important German Introductions; of these two call for special attention on account of their excellence, fulness, and erudition, Bleek's *Introduction to the New Testament*, and Reuss' *History of the Sacred Scriptures of the New Testament.*

There are frequent references in this work to the so-called Tübingen school. This is a phrase to be taken in a somewhat wide sense, but is designed to embrace all those theologians who have been influenced more or less by the celebrated Dr. F. C. Baur of Tübingen. Some may consider these references antiquated and an anachronism; as, according to their opinion, the influence of the Tübingen school is now almost extinct in Germany. I wish it were so; but on the contrary, similar views are very prevalent, although they may not be so pronounced as those of Baur. So long as such eminent theologians as Hilgenfeld, Volkmar, Keim, Holtzmann, Hausrath, and Lipsius—who, though differing in some points from each other, may be considered as belonging to the same school of theological thought—survive and influence theology, it cannot be said that the Tübingen school is extinct, or has even lost much of its power. The eminence of these theologians demands that their opinions be listened to with respect.

I have had considerable difficulty in determining the age of the writings of the apostolic Fathers. This point has been carefully examined, although I have not thought it necessary to state in the notes the process by which the conclusions were arrived at. I merely state in the text what seems to me the most probable date, differing sometimes from that adopted by the best recognised authorities. After much consideration I have come to the conclusion that the newly-discovered work, the *Didachè*, is, with the possible exception of the Epistle of Clemens Romanus, the oldest of the post-apostolic documents, and was written some time between A.D. 80 and A.D. 100. I have seldom referred to the Ignatian Epistles, as, notwithstanding all that has been written about them, I consider their authenticity still involved in uncertainty, and their value in biblical criticism to be unimportant. The quotations from the Fathers are in general taken from Kirchhofer's *Quellensammlung;* and for the translation I am indebted to Clark's *Ante-Nicene Fathers*, except where I thought the translation defective.

In the quotations from Scripture no uniform plan has been followed; in general I have quoted from the Authorized Version, except where there is a decided improvement in the Revised Version, or where extreme exactness is required; occasionally the Greek has been translated independently of both versions.

The substance of some of the articles and dissertations has already appeared in various periodicals; and I may refer to an article on the Book of Enoch in the *British and Foreign Review,* and to articles on the early Syriac versions and on St. Peter's residence in Rome in the *Monthly Interpreter.* Free use has also been made in the dissertation on the eschatology of Peter of an exposition on "the spirits in prison" (1 Pet. iii. 18–20), which appeared in my *Exegetical Studies*, published in 1884. I have pleasure in acknowledging my obligations to the Rev. W. P. Paterson, B.D., for verifying my references and for various important and valuable suggestions.

CONTENTS.

GENERAL INTRODUCTION.

I. The Term Catholic—Use of the Term by the Fathers—Four Views of its Meaning. II. Authors of the Catholic Epistles—Apostles and Apostolic Men—Their Relation to the Pauline Epistles, and to each other—Types of Doctrine. III. Number and Order of the Catholic Epistles. IV. Interpretation of the Catholic Epistles—Necessity of Candour and a Religious Spirit. V. Authenticity of the Catholic Epistles—The External Evidence—Catalogues of the Catholic Epistles—Versions—The Syriac—The Old Latin—Quotations from the Fathers—Internal Evidence, ... 1-22

THE EPISTLE OF JAMES.

I. The Authenticity of the Epistle—Dubiety concerning it—External Evidence—Internal Evidence—By whom disputed—Examination of Objections. II. The Author of the Epistle—Not James, the son of Zebedee—James, the Lord's brother—Three Opinions concerning him: 1. James, the son of Alphæus. 2. James, the son of Joseph by a previous Marriage. 3. James, the son of Mary and Joseph—Result of the Investigation—Notices of James in Scripture and in Ecclesiastical History. III. The Readers of the Epistle—Not Christians in general or Jews in general—Addressed to Jewish Christians—After history of the Jewish Christians—The Ebionites and Nazarenes. IV. The Design of the Epistle—Its Ethical Design—The Absence of Doctrine—Contents of the Epistle—Its Style and Language. V. The Time and Place of Writing—Commentaries. Dissertation I.: *The Pauline and Jacobean Views of Justification.* Different Views—Methods of Reconciliation—Different Views of Faith—Peculiar Characteristics of Paul and James—No Contradiction between them. Dissertation II.: *Resemblances in the Epistles of James.* To the Sermon on the Mount—To the Epistles of Paul—To the Epistle to the Hebrews—To the First Epistle of Peter—To the Apocrypha. Dissertation III.: *The Anointing of the Sick.* Anointing used as a Religious Ceremony—Use of Anointing in the Primitive Church—Rise and Development of Extreme Unction — Observance in the Greek Church — The Miraculous Gift of Healing, ... 23-108

THE FIRST EPISTLE OF PETER.

I. The Authenticity of the Epistle—External Evidence—Internal Evidence—Reminiscences of Christ—By whom disputed—Objections stated and examined—1. Dependence on Paul. 2. The want of Definiteness. 3. Impossibility of Peter being in Babylon. II. The Author of the Epistle—Notices of Peter in Scripture and in Ecclesiastical History—Legends concerning Peter. III. The Readers of the Epistle—Not Jewish Christians or Jewish Proselytes—Addressed to Christians in general—The Circle of Churches—Condition of these Churches. IV. The Design of the Epistle—Its design to confirm and comfort Believers—Its Contents—Its Style and Language —Its Peculiarities. V. The Time and Place of Writing—Indications of Time—The Place supposed to be Rome—According to others, Babylon on the Euphrates — Commentaries. Dissertation I.: *Peter's Residence in Rome.* Opinion that Peter was in Rome—By whom adopted—Testimonies of the Fathers—Opinion that Peter was never in Rome—Argument from Paul's Epistles—Argument from Peter's Residence in Babylon—Supposed origin of the Tradition in Peter's Encounter with Simon Magus—Result of the Examination—Period of Peter's Roman Residence—Literature on the Subject. Dissertation II.: *Petrine Theology.* Relation of Christianity to Judaism—The Nature of Sin—The Christology of Peter—The Doctrine concerning the Holy Ghost—The Eschatology of Peter — Review of Peter's System. Dissertation III.: *The Eschatology of Peter.* Eschatology a peculiarity in Peter's Writings — Derivation of Sheol and Hades — Christ's Descent into Hell. 1. Preaching to the Spirits in Prison, 1 Pet. iii. 18-20— Opinions of those who hold an actual Descent into Hades — The Spirits of the Just—Those who repented at the Deluge—Disobedient Spirits in Hades—Opinions of those who deny the actual Descent into Hades—Preaching of the Apostles—Preaching in Spirit by Noah. 2. The Preaching to the Dead, 1 Pet. iv. 6— Not the spiritually Dead—Two Views of the Passage—The Gospel preached in their Lifetime to those who are now dead—The Gospel preached to the Dead in Hades — History of Opinions — The Fathers—The Mediævalists—The Reformers—Recent Views—Conditional Immortality—Universalism—The Intermediate State a State of Probation—Mystery of the Future State, . . . 109-203

THE SECOND EPISTLE OF PETER.

1. The Authenticity of the Epistle—A purely historical Inquiry—External Evidence—Internal Evidence — Characteristics of Peter— Coincidences with Peter's Speeches in the Acts—Smilarity in Style and Sentiment to 1 Peter—Superiority to the Writings of the Fathers — By whom disputed—Objections stated and examined. 1. Difference in Style from 1 Peter. 2. Difference in Sentiment. 3. Solicitude of the Author to make himself known as Peter. 4. Mention of Paul's Epistles. 5. Mention of the Holy Mount. 6. Use of the Epistle of Jude. 7. Acquaintance with the Writings of Josephus. II. The Readers of the Epistle—The same as those of the First Epistle. III. The Design of the Epistle— Character of the Heretical Teachers—Contents of the Epistle—

Knowledge the Keynote of the Epistle—Its Language. IV. The Time and Place of Writing—Indications of Time in the Epistle—Place of Composition—Commentaries. Dissertation : *Relation between 2 Peter and Jude*. Resemblances between these two Epistles—Supposition that both Authors wrote independently—Supposition that both borrowed from the same Document—Supposition that Jude borrowed from Peter—Supposition that Peter borrowed from Jude—Examples of like Resemblances, ... 204-255

THE FIRST EPISTLE OF JOHN.

I. The Authenticity of the Epistle—External Evidence—Internal Evidence—Resemblances to John's Gospel—Impress of John's Character—By whom disputed—Objections stated and examined : 1. The Feebleness of the Epistle ; 2. Its Post-Apostolic Views ; 3. The Epistle Montanistic. II. The Author of the Epistle—Notices of John in Scripture—Notices in Ecclesiastical History—Banishment to Patmos—Residence in Ephesus—Legends concerning John. III. The Readers of the Epistle—Supposed to be a Treatise—Supposed to be addressed to the Parthians—Addressed to the Asiatic Churches—Condition of these Churches. IV. The Design of the Epistle—Supposed Relation to the Gospel—Polemical Design : Character of the Heretical Teachers—Ethical Design—Different Opinions as to the Arrangement of the Epistle—Its Contents—Its Style—Its Characteristics—Its Profoundity. V. The Time and Place of Writing—After the Destruction of Jerusalem—Indications of a late Date—Place of Composition—Commentaries. Dissertation I. : *The Heavenly Witnesses*. Critical Examination of 1 John v. 7, 8—External Evidence—The Manuscripts—The Versions—The Greek and Latin Fathers—Supposed References to the Passage in the Writings of Tertullian and Cyprian—Internal Evidence—Context supposed to be in favour of the Passage—Required by grammatical Construction—Omitted by a Homœoteleuton—General Result of the Examination—Origin of the Latin Gloss—The History of the Text. Dissertation II. : *Gnosticism as referred to in John's Epistle*. Spread of Gnosticism in the Second Century—Its Nature, Origin, and Sources—Principles common to Gnosticism—Antithesis between God and Matter—The Demiurgus or Creator—The Docetic Nature of Christ—Ethical Tendency of Gnosticism—Notices of Gnosticism in the New Testament — Docetism opposed by John — Account of Cerinthus — His Views of Creation — His Christology — His Chiliastic Eschatology—Opposition of John to him—Effects of Gnosticism on Christianity—Modern Gnosticism, . . . 256-321

THE SECOND EPISTLE OF JOHN.

I. The Authenticity of the Epistle — External Evidence — Internal Evidence—Resemblances to the First Epistle—By whom disputed—Consideration of Objections. II. The Author of the Epistle—

Ascribed to John the Presbyter—The Statement of Papias—On the Title Presbyter. III. The Person addressed—Not a Church—Different Opinions—The Lady Electa—The Elect Kyria—The Elect Lady. IV. The Design and Contents of the Epistle. V. The Time and Place of Writing—Commentaries, ... 322–338

THE THIRD EPISTLE OF JOHN.

I. The Authenticity of the Epistle — External Evidence — Internal Evidence—Objections of Baur and Hilgenfeld. II. The Person addressed — On Gaius. III. The Design of the Epistle — On Diotrephes—On Demetrius—The Reception of travelling Evangelists—Lost Epistle of John—Contents of the Epistle. IV. The Time and Place of Writing, ... 339–350

THE EPISTLE OF JUDE.

I. The Authenticity of the Epistle — External Evidence — Internal Evidence—By whom disputed—Objections stated and examined: 1. Professes to be Post-Apostolical; 2. Apocryphal References. II. The Author of the Epistle—Not Jude the Apostle, nor Judas, surnamed Barsabas, but Jude the Brother of the Lord—Notices of Jude in Scripture and in Ecclesiastical Tradition—Account of Hegesippus concerning Jude's Grandchildren. III. The Readers of the Epistle—Addressed to Christians in general—Supposed to be specially addressed to Jewish Christians—Different Localities assigned. IV. The Design of the Epistle—Opinions concerning the Persons described—Contents of the Epistle—Its Style and Character—Its Peculiarity. V. The Time and Place of Writing—Commentaries. Dissertation I. : *The Assumption of Moses.* Jude supposed to quote from it—References to the Assumption of Moses by the Fathers and Jewish Writers—Discovery of the Book by Ceriani—Its Contents—Its Authorship—Its Age—Its Relation to the Epistle of Jude—Different Opinions—Result of the Investigation—Literature on the Subject. Dissertation II. : *The Book of Enoch.* Supposed Quotation by Jude from it—References to the Book of Enoch by the Fathers and Jewish Writers—Discovery of the Book of Enoch by Bruce—Translations of it—Its Language—Its Contents—Opinions concerning its Authorship—Views of Dillmann, Ewald, and Schürer—Opinions concerning its Age—View of Dillmann—View of Volkmar—The Messianic Statements—Its Relation to the Prophecies of Daniel—The Character of the Book—The Reference to it by Jude—Different Opinions as to Jude's Information — Jude quoted from the Book of Enoch—Extensive Literature referring to it, . 351–403

LIST OF WORKS REFERRED TO.

Abbott's Articles on Second Peter, in Expositor. Vol. iii. Second Series.
Alexander (Bishop) On the Epistles of John, in Speaker's Commentary.
Alford's Greek Testament. Vol. iv. Second Edition, 1862.
Ante-Nicene Library. Edinburgh, 1867-1872.
Bassett On the Epistles of James. London, 1876.
Baur's Apostel Paulus. Zweite Auflage. Leipzig, 1861. Translated by Rev. W. Menzies. London, 1875.
Baur's Kirchengeschichte der drei ersten Jahrhunderte. Dritte Auflage. Translated by Rev. W. Menzies. London, 1878.
Bengel's Gnomon Novi Testamenti. Editio tertia. Tübingen, 1850. Translated by Fletcher. Edinburgh, 1859.
Beyschlag's Brief des Jacobus. Göttingen, 1882.
Bigg's Bampton Lectures for 1886. Oxford, 1886.
Bingham's Christian Antiquities. London (Reeves & Turner), 1878.
Bleek's Introduction to the N. T. Translated by Urwick. Edinburgh, 1869.
Braune On the Epistles of John, in Lange's Commentary.
Brückner's Petrus, Judas, und Jakobus. Leipzig, 1868.
Burgess' Tracts on the Divinity of Christ. London, 1820.
Burton's Bampton Lectures for 1829. Oxford, 1829.
Calvin's Commentaries: The Catholic Epistles: The Catholic Translation Society.
Cassiodori Opera. Geneva, 1650.
Cook On First Peter, in Speaker's Commentary.
Credner's Einleitung in das neue Testament. Halle, 1836.
Cureton's Syriac Gospels. London, 1858.
Davidson's Biblical Criticism. Edinburgh, 1852.
Davidson's Introduction to the N. T. London, 1849.
Davidson's Introduction to the Study of the N. T. London, 1868. Second Edition. London, 1882.
Deane's Article on the Assumption of Moses, in the Monthly Interpreter. Vol. i.
De Wette's Einleitung N. T. Sechste Ausgabe. Berlin, 1860. Translation. Boston, 1858.
Dillmann's Das Buch Henoch. Leipzig, 1853.
Dorner's Entwicklungsgeschichte der Lehre von der Person Christi. Berlin, 1851. Translated by Dr. L. Alexander. Edinburgh, 1884.
Drummond's Jewish Messiah. London, 1877.
Düsterdieck's Johanneische Briefe. Göttingen, 1852.
Ebrard On John's Gospel. Translated. Edinburgh, 1860.

LIST OF WORKS REFERRED TO.

Eichhorn's Einleitung in das N. T. Leipzig, 1804.
Encyclopedia Britannica. Ninth Edition.
Erdmann's Brief des Jakobus. Berlin, 1881.
Eusebii Historia Ecclesiastica.
Ewald's Abhandlung über des Buch Henoch Entstehung, etc. Göttingen, 1854.
Ewald's Geschichte des Volkes Israel. Sechster Band. Zweite Ausgabe. Göttingen, 1858. Translation, "History of Israel." Vol. vii. London, 1885, and Vol. viii. 1886.
Ewald's Jakobus Sendschreiben. Göttingen, 1870.
Ewald's Sieben Sendschreiben. Göttingen, 1870.
Fabricius' Codex Pseudepigraphus V. T. Hamburgh, 1722.
Farrar's Eternal Hope. London, 1878.
Farrar's Early Days of Christianity. London, 1882.
Farrar's Mercy and Judgment. London, 1881.
Foster's Three Heavenly Witnesses. London, 1867.
Fritzsche's Libri Veteris Testamenti Pseudepigraphii selecti. Leipzig, 1871.
Frohschammer's Romance of Romanism. Translated by Rev. W. Hastie. Edinburgh, 1878.
Fronmüller On the Epistles of Peter and Jude, in Lange's Commentary.
Gieseler's Church History. Translated by Dr. Samuel Davidson. Edinburgh, 1846.
Gloag's Exegetical Studies. Edinburgh, 1884.
Guericke's Neutestamentliche Isagogik. Dritte Auflage. Leipzig, 1868.
Haupt On the First Epistle of John. Translation. Edinburgh, 1879.
Hausrath's New Testament Times. Translation. London, 1878.
Herzog's Real-Encyklopädie. Zweite Auflage.
Hilgenfeld's Einleitung in das N. T. Leipzig, 1878.
Hilgenfeld's Evangelium und die Briefe Johannis. Halle, 1869.
Hofmann's Schriftbeweis. Nördlingen, 1882.
Hofmann: der erste Brief Petri. Nördlingen, 1875.
Holtzmann's Einleitung in das N. T. Freiburg, 1885.
Horne's Introduction to the Scriptures. Tenth Edition. London, 1875.
Horsley's Works. London, 1830.
Hug's Introduction to the N. T. Translation. London, 1827.
Huther's Brief des Jakobus. Dritte Auflage. Göttingen, 1870. Translation. Edinburgh, 1882.
Huther's Briefe des Petrus und Brief des Judas. Vierte Auflage. Göttingen. Translation. Edinburgh, 1881.
Huther's Epistles of John. Translation. Edinburgh, 1882.
Jones on the Canon. Oxford Edition, 1827.
Keil's Briefe des Petrus und Judas. Leipzig, 1883.
Keim's Jesus of Nazara. Translation. London, 1876-1883.
Kern's Der Brief Jakobi. Tübingen, 1838.
Kirchhofer's Quellensammlung. Zurich, 1842.
Kitto's Cyclopedia of Biblical Literature. Third Edition. Edinburgh, 1869.
Köstlin's Lehrbegriff des Evangeliums und der Briefe Johannis. Berlin, 1840.
Kuenen's Religion of Israel. Translation. London, 1875.
Kurtz, History of the Christian Church. Translation. Edinburgh, 1860.
Lange On the Epistle of James, in Lange's Commentary.
Lardner's Works. Quarto Edition. London, 1815.
Laurence's Book of Enoch. Third Edition. Oxford, 1838.

Lechler's Das apostolische Zeitalter. Zweite Auflage. Stuttgart, 1857. Translation of the Third Edition. By A. J. K. Davidson. Edinburgh, 1886.
Lightfoot's St. Paul's Epistle to the Galatians. Second Edition. London, 1866.
Lightfoot's St. Paul's Epistle to the Colossians. First Edition. London, 1875.
Lightfoot's (Dr. John) Works. Edited by Pitman. London, 1825.
Lipsius' Die Quellen der römischen Petrus Sage. Kiel, 1872.
Lipsius' Apostelgeschichten und Apostellegenden. Braunschweig, 1883.
Lücke's John's Epistles. Translation. Edinburgh, 1837.
Lücke's Einleitung in die Offenbarung Johannis. Göttingen, 1832.
Lumby's Articles on the Epistles of Peter, in Expositor. Vol. iv. First Series.
Lumby On Second Peter and Jude, in Speaker's Commentary.
Mangold's Edition of Bleek's Einleitung in das N. T. Vierte Auflage. Berlin, 1886.
Mansel's Gnostic Heresies. London, 1875.
Marsh's (Bishop) Lectures. London, 1838.
Mayerhoff's Petrinische Schriften. Hamburg, 1835.
Michaelis, Introduction to the New Testament. Edited by Marsh. Second Edition. London, 1802.
Murray's Enoch restitutus. London, 1836.
Neander's Church History. Bohn's Edition.
Neander's Planting of Christianity. Bohn's Edition.
Neander On the Epistle of James. Translation. Edinburgh, 1871.
Oehler's Theology of the Old Testament. Translation. Edinburgh, 1875.
Pearson On the Creed.
- Pfleiderer's Paulinism. Translation. London, 1877.
Plummer On the Epistles of John. Cambridge Bible for Schools.
Plummer On Second Peter and Jude. Bishop Ellicott's Commentary.
Plumptre On the Epistle of James. Cambridge Bible for Schools.
Plumptre On the Epistles of Peter and Jude. Cambridge Bible for Schools.
Plumptre On the Spirits in Prison. London, 1884.
Porson's Letters to Travis. London, 1790.
Pusey's Lectures on Daniel. Third Edition. Oxford, 1876.
Pusey, What is of Faith as to Everlasting Punishment? Third Edition. London, 1880.
Rawlinson's Bampton Lectures for 1859. London, 1859.
Renan's Hibbert Lectures for 1880.
Reuss' History of Christian Theology in the Apostolic Age. Translation. London, 1872.
Reuss' Geschichte der heiligen Schriften N. T. Vierte Ausgabe. Braunschweig. Translation. Edinburgh, 1884.
Ritschl's Altkatholische Kirche. Bonn, 1857.
Row's Jesus of the Evangelists. London, 1865.
Salmon's Introduction to the N. T. London, 1885.
Schaff's Encyclopedia of Biblical Theology. Edinburgh, 1883.
Schaff's History of the Christian Church. Edinburgh, 1869.
Schaff's Oldest Church Manual. Edinburgh, 1883.
Schegg's Jakobus der Bruder des Herrn und sein Brief. München, 1883.
Schmid's Biblical Theology of the N. T. Translation. Edinburgh, 1882.

Schmidt's Lehrgehalt des Jakobus Briefes. Leipzig, 1869.
Schodde, The Book of Enoch. Translated. Andover, 1882.
Schotte's Briefe des Petrus und Judas. Erlangen, 1861.
Schürer's Jewish People in the Time of Christ. Translation. Edinburgh, 1885, 1886.
Scott On the Epistle of James, in the Speaker's Commentary.
Scrivener's Introduction to the Criticism of the N. T. First Edition. Cambridge, 1861. Third Edition. Cambridge, 1883.
Sherlock On the Authenticity of Second Peter. Sherlock's Discourses. Vol. iv. Oxford, 1812.
Smith's Dictionary of Christian Antiquities.
Smith's Dictionary of Christian Biography.
Smith's Dictionary of the Bible.
Spitta, Der Zweite Brief des Petrus und der Brief des Judas. Halle, 1885.
Stanley's Jewish Church. Vol. iii. Second Edition. London, 1877.
Stanley's Sermons and Essays on the Apostolic Age. Third Edition. London, 1874.
Steiger On First Peter. Translation. Clark's Biblical Cabinet.
Stier On Epistle of James. Translation. Edinburgh, 1871.
Volkmar's Mose Himmelfahrt. Leipzig, 1867.
Warfield On the Genuineness of Second Peter. South Presbyterian Review of America, 1883.
Weiss' Petrinische Lehrbegriff. Berlin, 1855.
Weiss' Biblical Theology of the N. T. Translation. Edinburgh, 1882.
Weiss' Einleitung in das N. T. Berlin, 1881.
Westcott On the Epistles of John. London, 1883.
Westcott On the Canon of the N. T. Second Edition. London, 1866.
Westcott and Hort's N. T. in Greek. Cambridge, 1881.
White's Life in Christ. Third Edition. London, 1880.
Wieseler's Chronologie des apostolischen Zeitalter. Göttingen, 1848.
Wiesinger's Briefe des Jakobus, Petrus, und Judas. Königsberg, 1854.
Winer's Biblisches Wörterbuch. Leipzig, 1833.
Wiseman's (Cardinal) Essays on various Subjects. London, 1853.
Wolf's Briefe Johannis. Leipzig, 1881.
Wordsworth's Greek Testament : The General Epistles. London, 1875.
Zeller's Apostelgeschichte. Stuttgart, 1854. Translation. London, 1875.

THE CATHOLIC EPISTLES.

GENERAL INTRODUCTION.

I. ON THE TERM CATHOLIC.

THE group of seven Epistles, treated of in the present work, is named *the Catholic Epistles* (ἐπιστολαὶ καθολικαί). They form a distinct and important class among the books of the New Testament. The term *catholic* (καθολικός), by which they are designated, is compounded of κατὰ and ὅλος, and denotes universal or general.

This epithet, applied to epistolary writings, frequently occurs in the works of the Fathers. Thus Clement of Alexandria calls the Epistle proceeding from the Council of Jerusalem, and addressed to the Churches in Antioch, Syria, and Cilicia, "the Catholic Epistle of all the Apostles."[1] Origen applies the term to the Epistle of Barnabas. "In the Catholic Epistle of Barnabas," he observes, "it is written that Jesus selected His own apostles as persons who were more guilty of sin than all other evil-doers."[2] He speaks of the "Catholic Epistle of Peter" and the "Catholic Epistle of John," and in a passage, found in the Latin translation of his works, he uses the expression: "Jude, the apostle, says in the Catholic Epistle."[3] Dionysius of Alexandria, the pupil of Origen, applies the term to the First Epistle of John. Speaking of the Apocalypse, he says: "I do not deny that this is the writing of one John, and I agree that it was

---

[1] *Strom.* iv. 15 : Κατὰ τὴν ἐπιστολὴν τὴν καθολικὴν τῶν ἀποστόλων ἁπάντων.
[2] *Contra Celsum*, i. 63 : Γέγραπται δὲ ἐν τῇ Βαρνάβα καθολικῇ ἐπιστολῇ κ.τ.λ.
[3] *Opp.* tom. iv. p. 549 : Quomodo etiam quod Judas apostolus in epistola catholica dicit.

A

the work of some holy and inspired man. But I do not so easily consent that this was the apostle, the son of Zebedee, the brother of James, who is the author of the Gospel, and of the Catholic Epistle that bears his name."[1] It is not, however, until the fourth century that we find this epithet employed to designate the group of Epistles. In this sense it first occurs in Eusebius, who applies it to the seven Epistles, but in such a manner as to show that it had already become the ordinary appellation of these Epistles. "These accounts," he observes, "are given concerning James, who is said to have written the first of the Catholic Epistles. Not many, indeed, of the ancients have mentioned it, and not even that called the Epistle of Jude, which is also one of the seven so-called Catholic Epistles."[2] And in another part of his history he observes: "Clement (of Alexandria), in the work called *Hypotyposes*, has given us abridged accounts of all the canonical writings, not even omitting those that are disputed, I mean the Book of Jude and the other Catholic Epistles."[3] It is also to be observed that the term *catholic* is never applied by the Fathers to any of the other books of Scripture, to any of the Epistles of Paul, or even to the Epistle to the Hebrews.[4]

It is admitted that the word *catholic* denotes universal or general; but the precise reference of the adjective is disputed. It may refer to the authority of the writings, and in that case either (1) to their general acceptance as scripture (canonicity), or (2) to their conformity with generally received doctrine (orthodoxy). Or the reference may be to the nature of the Epistles, and in that case either (3) to the character of the authorship (general or joint apostolic authorship), or (4) to the description of the persons addressed (general or circular Epistles).

1. Some, applying the epithet to the authority of the Epistles, suppose that it is synonymous with *canonical*, and is used to denote those Epistles which were universally recog-

[1] Euseb. *Hist. Eccl.* vii. 25. [2] ii. 23. [3] vi. 14.
[4] The term *catholic* was not applied to the Epistle to the Hebrews, because it was included among the Epistles of Paul.

nised in the Christian Church. This is the opinion adopted by Michaelis, Eichhorn, Benson, and Horne, and, in point of fact, we find that in the Latin Church this group of Epistles is called *Epistolæ Canonicæ*. The following account is given by Michaelis of the origin of this term. At first the word καθολικός was employed by Origen with reference to the First Epistle of Peter and the First Epistle of John, to distinguish them as canonical and undisputed from the other five Epistles which were disputed. But as in process of time the doubts concerning these five Epistles gradually diminished, and at length disappeared, and as these five were written in the same manuscripts with the other two, the title became at last a common appellation for all these Epistles.[1] It is asserted that the term is used in this sense by Eusebius, as when he says: "As to that work, which is ascribed to Peter, called 'The Acts' and the 'Gospel according to Peter,' and that called 'The Preaching and the Revelations of Peter,' we know nothing of their being handed down as catholic writings; since neither among the ancient nor the ecclesiastical writers of our own day has there been one that has appealed to testimony taken from them."[2] Eusebius here certainly uses the term in the sense of authoritative, though not in the precise sense of canonical or universally received.[3] But even if we suppose that in the passage cited the word denotes "universally received," yet the term is not here applied by Eusebius to a special class of writings, but to the books of Scripture in general; he speaks not of catholic Epistles, but of catholic writings (γραφῶν). And that canonical was not the original meaning of the term is evident from the fact that Epistles which are not canonical have received this name. Thus, as already remarked, Origen calls the Epistle of Barnabas a Catholic Epistle, and Eusebius speaks of the Epistles of Dionysius of Alexandria, addressed to the Lacedæmonians and Athenians, as Catholic Epistles. "He was," he says, "useful

[1] Michaelis' *Introduction to the N. T.*, translated by Marsh, vol. vi. p. 270.
[2] *Hist. Eccl.* iii. 3.
[3] Kirchhofer supposes that Eusebius here uses the term *catholic* in the sense of being publicly read in the churches, but without any reference to the recognised genuineness of the writings.—*Quellensammlung*, p. 257.

to all in the Catholic Epistles that he addressed to the Churches."[1]

2. Others modify this view, and apply the term catholic, not to the canonicity, but to the orthodoxy of the writings. They regard the word as opposed to heretical, and as used to denote those Epistles whose doctrine and teaching were of universal authority, and in harmony with the teaching of the catholic or universal Church. This is the opinion adopted by Salmeron, Cornelius a Lapide, and Schmidt. But it is evident that such a meaning imparts no characteristic distinction to these Epistles; it is equally applicable to the other writings of the New Testament. The Epistles of Paul are in the above sense no less catholic than those Epistles to which this name is restricted. And if this be the case, no reason can be assigned why it should be exclusively used of these seven Epistles. And that there is no contrast between catholic and heretical is evident from the words of Eusebius, who employs the term *catholic* of an Epistle which he distinctly affirms to be heretical. Speaking of an Epistle written by Themison, who appears to have been a disciple of Montanus, he uses these words: "Themison dared to imitate the apostles by drawing up a certain catholic Epistle, to instruct those who had a better faith than himself." [2]

3. According to the third hypothesis, catholic is a technical term, used to distinguish these Epistles from the Epistles of Paul, denoting the Epistles of all the apostles, or, to speak more correctly, of the apostles in common. This opinion was first advanced by Hug, and adopted by Schleiermacher. "The ancients," observes Hug, "never applied the term *catholic* to other acknowledged and undoubted books of the New Testament, which certainly must have belonged to them, if it designated the idea of that which was generally acknowledged. It is a technical expression for one class of biblical writings, which possesses it exclusively, and communicates it to no other—namely, for that class which comprised in itself the didactic compositions of all the apostles collectively, with the exception of Paul (καθολικῶς, *i.e.* καθολοῦ καὶ συλλήβδην). When the Gospels and the Acts of the Apostles constituted

---
[1] Euseb. *Hist. Eccl.* iv. 23.   [2] v. 18.

one peculiar division, the works of Paul another, there still remained writings of different authors, which likewise formed a collection of themselves, and to which some name must be given. It might most aptly be called the *common collection* (καθολικὸν σύνταγμα) of the apostles, and the writings which comprised it κοιναί and καθολικαί, which are commonly used by the Greeks as synonymous. Our seven Epistles are catholic, or Epistles of *all* the apostles, who are authors."[1] But such a use of the word καθολικός, as denoting "all the apostles," is never found in any ecclesiastical writer; and although the name may in process of time have lost its original meaning, and come to be used as a mere technical appellation, yet this was evidently not its primary sense. And besides, as already remarked, the epithet is applied by Origen to the Epistle of Barnabas, and by Eusebius to the Epistles of Dionysius, and even to the heretical Epistle of Themison.

4. The fourth theory is that the term was selected in reference to the persons to whom the Epistles were addressed. In this sense the word is synonymous with exegetical or circular, and is used to denote those Epistles which are not, like those of Paul, addressed to particular Churches or individuals, but to a number of Churches or to Christians in general. This is the view adopted by Leontius Byzanticus, Oecumenius, Grotius, Credner, Neudecker, De Wette, Bleek, Holtzmann, and in general by the majority of theologians. "They are called catholic," observes Leontius, "inasmuch as they were not written to one nation, as Paul's, but generally to all."[2] "These Epistles," says Oecumenius, "are called catholic, equivalent to circular. For the company of such disciples of the Lord does not address these Epistles to one nation or city separately, as Paul to the Romans or Corinthians, but to the faithful generally; either to the Jews of the dispersion, as Peter does, or even to all Christians who hold the same faith."[3] To this opinion we subscribe. It suits the general

---

[1] Hug's *Introduction to the Writings of the New Testament*, vol. ii. pp. 537, 538; translated from the German by the Rev. D. G. Wait, LL.D., 1827.

[2] *De sectis*, c. 2.

[3] *Proleg. in Epist. Jacobi:* καθολικαὶ λέγονται αὗται οἱονεὶ ἐγκύκλιοι.

character of the address of these Epistles, though this has been disputed. It is applicable to the Epistle of the Council of Jerusalem, so called by Clement of Alexandria, as this was a circular Epistle addressed to several Churches in different countries. And in this sense the Epistle of Barnabas is called by Origen a catholic Epistle. In short, this sense appears to be the meaning of the term as employed by the Fathers in reference to epistolary writings down to the time of Eusebius.

To this view it is, however, objected that the term so employed is not characteristic of all these Epistles, but is only applicable to three out of the seven, namely, to the Second Epistle of Peter, the First Epistle of John, and the Epistle of Jude. The Epistle of James, it is pointed out, is not catholic or universal, but is limited to "the twelve tribes who are scattered abroad" (Jas. i. 1). The First Epistle of Peter is not addressed to the Church in general, but to "the strangers scattered throughout Pontus, Cappadocia, Asia, and Bithynia" (1 Pet. i. 1). And the Second and Third Epistles of John are not even addressed to a particular Church, but to private individuals (2 John 1); the former to "the elect lady and her children," and the latter to "the well-beloved Gaius" (3 John 1). But this objection is of no great weight. The Epistle of James is decidedly circular in its inscription; and if it was written at a very early period, when the Church was chiefly composed of Jewish converts, before Paul's mission to the Gentiles,—as we shall afterwards endeavour to prove,— then it is catholic in its address. The First Epistle of Peter was addressed to a large circle of Churches in five countries, and may well be considered as encyclical. And though the Second and Third Epistles of John were addressed to private individuals, and were therefore in this sense not catholic, they were attached to the larger Epistle, and may have been considered as an appendix to it. Besides, it was the opinion of many of the Fathers that "the elect lady" ($\dot{\epsilon}\kappa\lambda\epsilon\kappa\tau\dot{\eta}$ $\kappa\upsilon\rho\dot{\iota}a$), to whom the Second Epistle of John was addressed, was an appellation to denote the Christian Church, so that this Epistle was regarded by them as catholic.

The result of the investigation may be summed up in few

words. The title *catholic* was first employed to denote those Epistles which were not addressed to any particular individual or Church, but to the Church in general, or at least to a wide circle of readers. In this sense the term was first applied by Origen to the First Epistle of Peter and the First Epistle of John. Afterwards, but before the time of Eusebius, it was used to denote the whole seven Epistles as being descriptive of their nature, the Second and Third Epistles of John being considered as an appendix to the First. In process of time it became a technical term, used to designate that group of Epistles, as distinguished from the other three groups of writings in the New Testament, namely, the Gospels and the Acts, the Pauline Epistles, including the Hebrews, and the Apocalypse, and thus lost in a measure its primary meaning; but it does not appear to have been ever used in the sense in which Hug employs it, as "the writings of all the apostles." After this it was used, chiefly in the Latin Church, as synonymous with canonical. Junilius, in the sixth century (A.D. 550), appears to have been the first who employed the term in this sense.[1] These, however, were secondary uses which did not occur until after the time of Eusebius.

II. THE AUTHORS OF THE CATHOLIC EPISTLES.

The seven Catholic Epistles are ascribed to four authors—one to James, two to Peter, three to John, and one to Jude. Two of these are undoubtedly apostles, indeed the two chief apostles of our Lord,—Peter and John, who in the Acts of the Apostles are usually conjoined. This has been seldom disputed. The genuineness of the Epistles themselves has been questioned, but it has seldom been questioned that the persons to whom they have been ascribed, rightly or wrongly, are the apostles Peter and John.[2] On the other hand, the apostolic character of the other two authors has been questioned.

---

[1] *De partibus legis divinæ*, i. 6. So also Cassiodorus (A.D. 556), *De institutione divinarum litcrarium*, chap. viii. On the other hand, Jerome, in his list of canonical books, mentions these Epistles separately, and not under any common name.

[2] The Second and Third Epistles of John were ascribed by several writers to John the Presbyter. See below.

Some suppose them to be of the number of the Twelve—James the son of Alphæus, and Judas the brother of James (Acts i. 13). Others regard James as the Lord's brother and a different person from James the son of Alphæus, and Jude, who calls himself "the brother of James" (Jude 1), as a different person from Judas the apostle. The determination of these questions is reserved until we examine the special Epistles.

The Catholic Epistles possess a peculiar importance among the writings of the New Testament.[1] Without them there would be a want of completeness in the sacred writings. They bear a similar relation to the Epistles of Paul that the Gospel of John bears to the Synoptics; they form the necessary compliment to Pauline theology. Had we only the Epistles of Paul, Christianity would have a tendency to assume a purely Pauline form, and so far would be one-sided. We require other forms of Christianity,—the Jacobean, the Petrine, and the Johannine,—as exhibited in the Catholic Epistles, to impart to it its due proportion. The pre-eminence of faith as the only instrument of our salvation, according to Paul, is saved from abuse by the teaching of James concerning the importance of good works. The supposed conflict between the views of Paul and Peter, as regards Gentile and Jewish Christianity, is refuted by a careful study of the similarity of the views of Peter in his First Epistle with those of Paul, especially as these are exhibited in the Epistle to the Ephesians. And the objective side of Christian doctrine, as given chiefly by Paul, is supplemented by the subjective side, as given chiefly by John. Not that we mean that there is any modification of Pauline Christianity, but rather that a completeness or fulness is imparted to it by the Catholic Epistles. Points of doctrine and practice, on which Paul dwells only incidentally, are in these Epistles brought into prominence. Far less do we mean that there is any opposi-

[1] We do not here enter into any minute discussion on the relation of the Catholic Epistles to Biblical theology, but we would refer our readers to Neander's *Planting*; Schmid's *Biblical Theology of the N. T.*; Weiss' *Biblical Theology of the N. T.*; Immer's *Theologie des N. T.*; Farrar's *Early Days of Christianity*. There are, besides, important monographs of the theology of the different New Testament writers.

tion or antagonism in these Epistles to the views of Paul. The only appearance of opposition is between the doctrine of justification as taught by Paul and that doctrine as taught by James; but we shall afterwards endeavour to prove that this opposition is only verbal and apparent, that there is a real harmony amid seeming antagonism, and that these writers merely regard this doctrine from different points of view.[1]

There is also a close relation between several of these Epistles to each other—a relation so close and peculiar that we reserve it for future investigation.[2] We would merely observe at present that the Epistle of James and the First Epistle of Peter closely resemble each other in their contents, and that this resemblance is often not merely in ideas, but in words. There is a still greater and closer resemblance between the Epistle of Jude and the second chapter of the Second Epistle of Peter; the train of thought, the examples used for illustration, and often the words are the same, so that we might almost suppose that the one writer borrowed from the other.

It has often been observed that in the epistolary writings of the different apostles there are peculiar types of doctrine; Paul has been called the apostle of faith, James the apostle of works, Peter the apostle of hope, and John the apostle of love. And there is a certain degree of truth in this: the writings of each of these authors are thus characterized, with the possible exception of the Epistles of Peter, in which it does not appear that hope is invested with such a peculiar prominence as to be regarded as a characteristic mark. Other points of difference have been noted. Viewed with regard to the distinction between Jews and Gentiles, Paul is the apostle of Gentile Christianity, James the apostle of Jewish Christianity, Peter is intermediate, and forms the connecting link between the doctrine of Paul and that of James, and John is the apostle of universal Christianity. Viewed ecclesiastically, Peter may be regarded as the apostle of the medieval Church, Paul as the apostle of the Protestant Church, and John as the apostle of

---

[1] See dissertation on the Pauline and Jacobean views of justification, *infra*.

[2] See dissertations on the "References in the Epistle of James," and the "Relation between Second Peter and Jude," *infra*.

the Church of the future. Paul represents Christian scholasticism; James, Christian activity; and John, Christian mysticism. And so also Lange has observed that each of these sacred writers stands in a peculiar relation to Christianity, as the fulfilment of different phases of Old Testament revelation. James teaches Christianity as the fulfilment of the law of the Old Testament, hence "the royal law of love," "the law of liberty;" Peter as the fulfilment of the theocracy of the Old Testament, hence the real kingdom of God, "the royal priesthood;" Paul as the fulfilment of the old covenant, and of the sacraments of the Old Testament, hence "the new covenant," "the true circumcision," and "the true passover;" and John as the fulfilment of the symbolism of the Old Testament, hence "the true light," "the true life," and "the true love."[1] Thus do these apostles mutually support and supplement each other, and their writings constitute a full development of the religion of Christ. Of Him do the glorious company of the apostles bear witness. "To disown these phases," observes Nitzsch, "in favour of a one-sided dogmatism, is to abandon that completeness and solidity which these modes of contemplating the Christian faith impart, while they reciprocally complete one another; it is to slight that by which Scripture truth maintains its elevation above all conflicting systems."[2]

III. NUMBER AND ORDER OF THE CATHOLIC EPISTLES.

The Catholic Epistles in the Greek and Latin Churches are seven in number. In the Syrian Churches only three are inserted in the canon, namely, the Epistle of James, the First Epistle of Peter, and the First Epistle of John; the other four are regarded as apocryphal.

The order of these seven Epistles in our English Bible is as follows: the Epistle of James, the two Epistles of Peter, the three Epistles of John, and the Epistle of Jude. This is the usual order observed in the chief manuscripts, versions, and scriptural catalogues. It is apparently adopted by

---

[1] Lange's *Bibelwerk: Der Brief des Jakobus*, p. 3 [E. Tr. pp. 5, 6].
[2] Quoted in Neander's *Planting*, vol. i. p. 414, Bohn's edition. See also on this subject, Farrar's *Early Days of Christianity*, vol. i. pp. 99, 100.

Eusebius, who expressly mentions the Epistle of James as "the first of the Catholic Epistles;"[1] and it is observed in the catalogues of the Council of Laodicea, Athanasius, Epiphanius, and Jerome. Other arrangements, however, occur. In the Apostolical Constitutions and in the canon of the Third Council of Carthage the order is: two Epistles of Peter, three of John, one of James, and one of Jude. Rufinus, in his *Symbolum Apostolorum*, enumerates them as follows: "Two Epistles of the Apostle Peter, one of James the brother of the Lord and apostle, one of Jude, three of John." Augustine, in his work on *Christian Doctrine*, gives them under the following arrangement: two of Peter, three of John, one of Jude, and one of James. The arrangement given in the German Bible is peculiar. There we find the latter books of the New Testament placed in the following order: the First and Second Epistles of Peter, the First, Second, and Third Epistles of John, the Epistle to the Hebrews, the Epistle of James, the Epistle of Jude, and the Revelation of John. Such an arrangement, so far as we are aware, is found in no other catalogue ancient or modern: in all other lists the Catholic Epistles are kept as a class distinct by themselves. It seems to have arisen from the peculiar views of Luther, who placed those books about which he was doubtful at the end of the New Testament, regarding them as canonical in a secondary sense.

In the oldest manuscripts of the New Testament the Catholic Epistles do not follow the Epistle to the Hebrews as they do in our English Bible, but are placed between the Acts of the Apostles and the Pauline Epistles.[2] They occupy this place in the Greek Testaments of Scholz, Lachmann, Tischendorf, Tregelles, and Westcott and Hort.

IV. INTERPRETATION OF THE CATHOLIC EPISTLES.

With regard to the interpretation of the Catholic Epistles, we have little more to advance than what was written in our

---

[1] *Hist. Eccl.* ii. 23.
[2] In the Codex Sinaiticus (ℵ), however, they immediately precede the Apocalypse and come after the Pauline Epistles.

former treatise on the interpretation of the Pauline Epistles.[1] Although these Epistles may be inspired, yet to discover their meaning the ordinary rules of interpretation, which are employed in the translation of any other ancient work, must be adopted. First of all, we must obtain a pure text, and this, owing to the abundance of manuscripts, and to the labours of such distinguished critics as Lachmann, Tischendorf, Tregelles, and Westcott and Hort, may be considered as to all intents accomplished. An almost universal consensus of opinion has been arrived at with regard to the disputed passages in the First Epistle of John.[2] The next task is to obtain the true sense of the words; and distinguished scholars have made the peculiar dialect of Greek, contained in the New Testament generally, and in these Epistles in particular, their special study, so that the exact meaning of the words may now be regarded as ascertained. These are, however, only the preliminary steps to a true interpretation. We may possess a pure text, and know the import of the separate words, and yet not be able to understand the precise sense which the sacred writer intends to convey: as may be seen in the celebrated passage in the First Epistle of Peter concerning Christ's descent into Hades (1 Pet. iii. 18-20). We must therefore study the peculiar style of each writer, and endeavour to ascertain the train of thought pursued by him. And for this purpose we must make each Epistle a separate study, and endeavour to put ourselves into the circumstances of the author when he wrote that Epistle, and, as far as possible, into the circumstances of those to whom the Epistle was written. For example, our interpretation of the Epistle of James will differ according as we regard the persons to whom the Epistle was addressed as Christians in general, whether Jews or Gentiles, or as Jewish Christians, or as Jews in general, whether believers or unbelievers; all which views have been adopted by different commentators, giving rise to a variety of interpretations.

It is unnecessary to consider how far the element of inspiration modifies our interpretation of these Epistles. On this subject we have nothing to add to our former exposi-

[1] *Pauline Epistles*, pp. 52-64.   [2] 1 John ii. 23, v. 7, 8.

tion.¹ But, whatever opinion of inspiration we adopt, we must in our interpretation exercise a candid and honest spirit. The truth, and the truth only, ought to be the great object of our pursuit: all other considerations must yield to this. Hence we must come to the study of these Epistles without any undue prepossession. It is impossible to read them without some prepossession; but we must guard against allowing the opinions which we have formed to exercise an undue influence. We must derive our opinions from Scripture, and beware of forcing Scripture to suit our opinions. There is, we believe, a divine harmony in the books of the New Testament, because we regard them as all inspired by one Spirit; but there must be no wresting of the words of Scripture to produce this harmony. For example, the statements of Paul and James concerning justification are apparently opposite; and although we believe that the opposition is only apparent, and that there is a real harmony in their views, yet this harmony must not be sought for by forcing the statements of Paul into an agreement with those of James, or conversely: but by a patient and careful study of the meaning of the terms which they employ, and of the different views of the opponents against whom each wrote. Whatever theory of reconciliation is adopted, it must answer the statements of both writers; if no theory of reconciliation can thus be obtained, we must confess our ignorance and suspend our judgment.² "We must not," remarks Luther, "make God's word mean what we wish; we must not bend it, but allow it to bend us, and give it the honour of being better than we can make it, so that we must let it stand."

It is especially necessary that we should come to the study of these Epistles in a religious spirit. The word of God can only be truly understood by the spiritual mind. Just as the masterpieces of poetry can only be appreciated by those who are endowed with a poetic spirit; as the paintings of the great artists can only be fully understood by those who are artistic; as the oratorios of our great composers can only be relished by those who have an ear for music; as the profound

[1] *Pauline Epistles*, pp. 56-64.
[2] See dissertation on the Pauline and Jacobean views of justification, *infra*.

treatises of mathematics can only be mastered by those who have a mathematical mind; as the systems of metaphysics can only be comprehended by those who have a philosophic spirit: so the holy and spiritual truths of the Scriptures can only be fully realized and understood by those who are themselves holy and spiritual.

V. AUTHENTICITY OF THE CATHOLIC EPISTLES.

The external and internal evidences of each of these Epistles will be examined when we consider them separately. It may be generally stated that the evidence in favour of most of them is not so strong or convincing as that in favour of the Pauline Epistles.[1] The reason of this is not difficult to discover. These Epistles were directed to no particular Church, and therefore on no particular Church was the responsibility laid of preserving them. All of them have been more or less impugned. The Tübingen school, as represented by Baur, Schwegler, and Hilgenfeld, have rejected all the Epistles. Schleiermacher and Ritschl challenge the authenticity of the Epistle of James, and Luther's opposition to it, arising from his subjective views, is well known. De Wette called in question the First Epistle of Peter, and Bretschneider the First Epistle of John; whilst the other four Epistles—the Second Epistle of Peter, the Second and Third Epistles of John, and the Epistle of Jude—are ranked by Eusebius among the antilegomena, or disputed books,[2] are omitted in the Peshito,[3] and are called in question by numerous theologians both in this country and in Germany. The various objections, which have been adduced, will be stated and examined when we come to examine the authenticity of each Epistle.

[1] The First Epistle of Peter and the First Epistle of John are as strongly attested as most of the Pauline Epistles.
[2] *Hist. Eccl.* iii. 25.
[3] The name given to the earliest Syriac version, as it has come down to us; the epithet, as commonly interpreted, means *The Simple*. It was not until the revival of letters that the Peshito became known to the theologians of Europe. Manuscripts were brought from the East, and from them the Syriac editions of the Scriptures were printed; the first edition being published by Widmanstadt at Vienna in 1555.

The external evidence in favour of the Catholic Epistles as a class is founded on the catalogues of these Epistles, the various versions, and the quotations from the Fathers. The first catalogue that contains any reference to the Catholic Epistles is the Muratorian canon.[1] This celebrated fragment is by most competent critics supposed to belong to the second century, and may be proximately assigned to A.D. 170. Its genuineness has been generally acknowledged. The following is the reference in it to the Catholic Epistles: " The Epistle of Jude, however, and the three Epistles of John, who has been mentioned above, are received in the Catholic (Church);" or as has been suggested, " are received among the Catholic (Epistles)."[2] There is no mention of the Epistle of James, nor of the First and Second Epistles of Peter, and an Epistle of John is omitted. But the Muratorian canon is a fragment; there is in it, in another place, a reference to the First Epistle of John;[3] and the probability is that the other Catholic Epistles were also mentioned, as the Epistle of Jude and two Epistles of John (probably the Second and Third),[4] inferior in point of importance to the Epistles of James and the Epistles of Peter, are named. In the catalogue of Eusebius (A.D. 325) the First Epistle of Peter and the First Epistle of John are placed among the $\delta\mu o\lambda o\gamma o\acute{u}\mu\epsilon\nu a$, or those apostolic writings which were undisputed; whilst the other five Epistles are classed among the $\dot{a}\nu\tau\iota\lambda\epsilon\gamma\acute{o}\mu\epsilon\nu a$ or disputed writings. " Among the disputed books," he observes, " although they are well known and approved by many, are reputed those called the Epistles of James and Jude, also the Second Epistle of Peter, and those called the Second and Third of John, whether they are by the evangelist or some other of the same name."[5] Subsequently to the time of Eusebius the whole

[1] So called, because first published by Muratori in 1740. It was discovered in the Ambrosian Library in Milan. It is a manuscript of the seventh century, in the Latin language, but is supposed to be a translation from the Greek. It is a fragment, mutilated both at the beginning and at the end. A transcript of it is given by Westcott in his *Canon of the New Testament*, pp. 466-480. Most eminent scholars place its date not later than 170 or 180.

[2] Epistola sane Judæ et superscripti Johannis duas in catholica habentur.

[3] Quid ergo mirum si Johannes tam constanter singula etiam in Epistolis suis proferat dicens in semetipso: Quæ vidimus oculis nostris, etc.

[4] As the context tends to show. [5] *Hist. Eccl.* iii. 25.

seven Epistles were admitted into the canon, and are mentioned in the various ecclesiastical catalogues, whether promulgated by the Councils of the Church, or given in the works of the celebrated Fathers. Thus they are contained in the catalogue of Athanasius (A.D. 330), the Council of Laodicea (A.D. 363), Apostolical Constitutions (A.D. 370), Jerome (A.D. 390), Augustine (A.D. 395), the Third Council of Carthage (A.D. 397), and the authoritative catalogue of Pope Innocent I. (A.D. 405).[1]

Of the versions the earliest is the Syriac. Although the date assigned to this translation by Jones and Michaelis, toward the close of the first or at the beginning of the second century,[2] is too early, yet there are good reasons for fixing the date of the Syriac version as early as the middle of the second century (A.D. 150).[3] This version, at least as it has been transmitted to us in the form of the Peshito, omits the Second Epistle of Peter, the Second and Third Epistles of John, the Epistle of Jude, as well as the Apocalypse, and thus is a witness for the genuineness of only three of the Catholic Epistles.

Recent discoveries made in Syriac manuscripts have led several eminent critics to consider that the Peshito is not the original form of the Syriac, but a revised version. Cureton, in 1858, published a Syriac manuscript containing fragments of the Gospels found in a Syrian monastery in the valley of the Natron lakes.[4] This Syriac manuscript was found to be a different version from the Peshito, and to contain marks of high antiquity. Many of the most distinguished critics,

---

[1] Kirchhofer's *Quellensammlung*, pp. 1–26; Westcott on *The Canon*, pp. 481–520, second edition.

[2] Jones' *Canon of the New Testament*, vol. i. pp. 81–107. Michaelis, *Introduction to the N. T.*, translated by Marsh, vol. ii. pp. 29–39.

[3] The early age of the Syriac version appears to be proved from the discovery which has lately been made of Ephræm's commentary on the Diatessaron of Tatian. According to Professor Zahn, Tatian wrote his Diatessaron in Syriac, and used as the basis of his work the Curetonian Syriac. Now Tatian was a disciple of Justin Martyr, and therefore must have flourished about A.D. 160; and hence we cannot assign a later date to the Syriac version than A.D. 150. See two articles by Professor Wace in the *Expositor* for 1882.

[4] The work is entitled *Remains of a very ancient Recension of the Four Gospels in Syriac, hitherto unknown in Europe*.

among whom is to be ranked Ewald, Alford,[1] Tregelles, Hort, and apparently Bleek, consider this version as older than the Peshito; an opinion which has been controverted by Scrivener and other textual critics.[2] All, however, agree that the two versions do not represent two separate recensions, but that the one is taken from the other. Cureton has shown that although there is a marked difference in some places between the text of the Peshito and that of these Syriac fragments, yet that the general similarity and agreement between the two is so great as to preclude the possibility of their having been two altogether distinct and independent versions.[3] And this is not only admitted but asserted by Scrivener, though he considers the Curetonian to be derived from the Peshito. "Any one," he observes, "who shall compare the verses we have cited from them in parallel columns, will readily admit that the two translations have a common origin, whatever that may be; many other passages, though not perhaps of equal length, might be named where the resemblance is closer still; where for twenty words together the Peshito and the Curetonian shall be positively identical, although the Syriac idiom would admit other words and another order just as naturally as that actually employed."[4] Now those who maintain that the Curetonian is prior to the Peshito, and that they are not independent versions, draw the inference that the Peshito is a revised edition of a more ancient Syriac version, of which the Curetonian manuscript is a fragment. According to them, the Peshito bears the same relation to the ancient Syriac as the Vulgate does to the Old Latin.[5]

---

[1] Alford remarks of the Curetonian Syriac: "Perhaps the earliest and the most important of all the versions."

[2] Scrivener's *Introduction to the Criticism of the N. T.*, p. 244; third edition, p. 321.

[3] Cureton's *Syriac Gospels*, p. 67.

[4] Scrivener's *Introduction to the Criticism of the N. T.*, p. 238; third edition, p. 321.

[5] See on this point Westcott and Hort's *Greek Testament*, vol. ii. p. 84. They come to the conclusion that the Peshito is "a Syriac Vulgate, answering to the Latin Vulgate;" that "an Old Syriac must have existed as well as an Old Latin." The authoritative revision they consider to have taken place either in the latter part of the third or in the fourth century.

It has been maintained that there is evidence that the original Syriac, of which the Peshito is only a revised edition, contained the omitted books; in short, that as there was a revision of the Syriac text which resulted in the Peshito, there was also a revision of the Syriac canon, which resulted in the omission of four of the Catholic Epistles. The opinion that the omitted books were originally contained in the Syriac was first advanced by Hug. He supposes that the Peshito formerly contained all the omitted books, and that these books gradually fell out before the sixth century. The reason which he assigns for this opinion is, that Ephræm Syrus quotes from them. "Let me be pardoned for persisting in the assertion that Ephræm read in some version the disputed Epistles and the Apocalypse which he frequently quotes."[1] The same supposition has been made by Hilgenfeld. "The old Syriac version," he observes, "as it has come down to us, or the Peshito, recognises only three of the Catholic Epistles, and omits the Apocalypse of John; but Ephræm certainly made use of these writings in an older Syriac translation." "Ephræm, the oldest witness of this version (the Peshito), has read these (omitted) writings in Syriac, and their exclusion is conceivable as an act of Antiochene theology."[2]

The chief argument in proof of the assertion of the existence of the four Catholic Epistles, omitted in the Peshito, in the original unrevised Syriac version, is the fact that Ephræm Syrus quotes from these omitted books; and as Ephræm wrote in Syriac, it is supposed that in doing so he used a Syriac version. Now, with the exception of 2 Pet. iii. 10, "The day of the Lord will come as a thief in the night," and which may as well be considered as a quotation from 1 Thess. v. 2, and a doubtful reference to 2 Pet. iii. 7, the quotations of Ephræm from the omitted Catholic Epistles are found only in the Greek translations of his works, and

[1] Hug's *Introduction to the N. T.*, vol. i. pp. 348-351, translation.
[2] Hilgenfeld's *Einleitung in das neue Testament*, pp. 122, 804. This view is also maintained by Professor Warfield of Alleghany, in an able article on the Canonicity of Second Peter, in the *Southern Presbyterian Review* of America, 1882. See also on this subject, Lücke on *The Epistles of John*, pp. 300, 301, translation.

are on this account somewhat doubtful.[1] But even admitting that Ephræm quoted from these omitted Epistles, how can it be proved that he quoted from a Syriac version, and did not rather translate from the Greek? To this it is replied that Ephræm was ignorant of the Greek language, and could only converse in it through an interpreter.[2] But although Ephræm could not converse in Greek, it by no means follows that he could not read the Scriptures in Greek, and could not employ that language for critical purposes. It cannot be supposed that being so long resident in the learned city of Edessa, and exercising such a powerful influence on the Syriac Churches, he was wholly ignorant of Greek. His attention must have been directed to the acquirement of that language in which the New Testament was originally written.[3]

It has further been asserted that the early Syrian writers possessed the rejected books. Theophilus of Antioch had Second Peter and the Apocalypse, Malchion had Jude, and Pamphilus had the Apocalypse and apparently also the whole Catholic Epistles.[4] How far these Fathers can be regarded as Syrian writers is doubtful; Antioch, where Theophilus and Malchion resided, was a Greek city; and Cæsarea, the abode of Pamphilus, was the Roman capital of Judea, and also Greek. Unless it can be proved that these Fathers wrote in Syriac, whereas it is certain that they wrote in Greek, no argument can be derived from their writings as to the state of the Syriac version in their day. The Greek-Syriac Church must not be confounded with the native Syriac Church, which used the Syriac version.

[1] See Lardner's *Works*, quarto edition, vol. ii. p. 483. "How far," observes Lardner, "they are to be relied upon as genuine and uncorrupted may be hard to say. I rather think, it cannot be depended on, that Ephræm is here truly represented. For my own part, I must own that I prefer the Syriac works much before the Greek, which at best are translations only, in which, too, the translator may have inserted some of his own sentiments." "The Greek writings," observes Tregelles, "which bear the name of Ephræm, come to us with very doubtful credentials."

[2] Gregory of Nyssa, in his life of Ephræm, informs us that when Ephræm paid a visit to Basil, the celebrated bishop of Cæsarea, he conversed with him by means of an interpreter.

[3] For a discussion on Ephræm's knowledge of Greek, see the article "Ephræm," by Dean Smith, in Smith's *Dictionary of Christian Biography*.

[4] So Warfield, in the article above referred to.

The testimony of Ephræm Syrus, therefore, is not sufficient to prove that the original Syriac version or early Peshito contained these Epistles which are now omitted. Granted that the Peshito is a revised edition, yet this is no proof that the original Syriac perhaps contained the omitted books. The only remains which we have of it are fragments of the Gospels contained in the Curetonian manuscript; we have no information as to the other writings of the New Testament. And besides, if these books were formerly in the Syriac canon, it is highly improbable that they should be omitted in any subsequent critical revision,[1] and that at a time when they were almost universally acknowledged in the Greek and Latin Churches. "Had these books," observes Bleek, "formed part of the authorized Syriac version from the outset down to the time of Ephræm Syrus and after, we should be utterly unable to explain how it came to pass that they were afterwards excluded, at a time when their authority as canonical was established in the Christian Church."[2]

The next version in order of time and importance is the Old Latin, the so-called *Vetus Latina*. The date assigned by competent critics to this version is A.D. 170.[3] It is supposed that it was made, not for the Church of Rome, which was at first Greek, but for the use of Christians in Northern Africa, whose capital was Carthage. The manuscripts of the Old Latin which contain the Catholic Epistles are very few; indeed the Epistle of James is the only Epistle which is found entire. That Epistle is contained in the Codex Corbeiensis. A few verses of Third John are found in the Codex Bezæ, and fragments of James and First Peter are

---

[1] I am not aware of any instance of the omission of canonical books in the critical revision of any version. Luther, although he doubted the genuineness of some books, yet did not omit them in his canon, but translated them and marked them with a note. The First Epistle of Clemens Romanus, though found in the Codex Alexandrinus, and sometimes read in the churches, never formed part of the canon. See Lightfoot's *Clement of Rome*, p. 11.

[2] Bleek's *Introduction to the N. T.*, vol. ii. p. 338. See also Lücke on *The Epistles of St. John*, pp. 300, 301, English translation; and on the whole subject, an article on the "Early Syriac Versions" in the *Monthly Interpreter*, vol. i. pp. 424-435.

[3] Tertullian alludes to the existence of a Latin version.

contained in the Codex Bobbiensis.¹ There is also a remarkable manuscript preserved in the monastery of the Santa Croce at Rome, entitled *Speculum Augustini*. The manuscript, however, is not earlier than the eighth century. It consists of a classified list of extracts from both Testaments, the quotations being from the Old Latin. This manuscript contains fragments of James, First and Second Peter, First and Second John, and Jude. It is peculiarly interesting as containing the celebrated passage of "the heavenly witnesses" (1 John v. 7, 8). Its value has been very differently estimated by competent critics.²

The quotations of the Fathers from the Catholic Epistles are not numerous, though there are several references in their writings. Clemens Alexandrinus (A.D. 190) is said by Eusebius to have given abridged accounts of all the canonical writings, not even omitting those that are disputed, as the Book of Jude and the other Catholic Epistles.³ Tertullian (A.D. 200) quotes from the Epistle of Jude as apostolic and authoritative.⁴ Origen (A.D. 230) received the First Epistle of Peter and the First Epistle of John as undoubtedly genuine,⁵ and in the Latin translation of his works makes mention of the Epistle of Jude.⁶ Dionysius of Alexandria (A.D. 245) makes mention of the First Epistle of John.⁷ It is admitted that the quotations of the Fathers from these Epistles are few in number and somewhat distant in time, but they are not fewer or more distant than are the quotations taken from classical writers. Canon Rawlinson has shown that it is a very rare occurrence for classical works to be distinctly quoted, or for their authors to be mentioned by name within a century of the time of their publication. Herodotus is quoted but once in the century which followed the composition of his history, and only once in the next

---

¹ Davidson's *Biblical Criticism*, vol. ii. p. 247. Hilgenfeld's *Einleitung in das N. T.*, p. 801. Westcott, *On the Canon*, p. 226.

² Davidson's *Biblical Criticism*, vol. ii. p. 410. Scrivener's *Introduction to the Criticism of the N. T.*, p. 258; 3rd edition, p. 345. Wiseman's *Essays on Various Subjects*, vol. i. p. 12 ff.

³ Euseb. *Hist. Eccl.* vi. 14.   ⁴ *De Cultu fœm.* c. 3.
⁵ Euseb. *Hist. Eccl.* vi. 25.   ⁶ *Opp.* tom. iv. p. 549.
⁷ Euseb. *Hist. Eccl.* vii. 25.

century. The first distinct quotation from Thucydides is about two centuries after his death. Livy is only quoted by Quinctilian a century after he wrote. And Tacitus, though mentioned as a writer by the younger Pliny, is first cited by Tertullian nearly a century after his death.[1] If on authority, such as above, the genuineness of Herodotus, Thucydides, Livy, and Tacitus are maintained, we have the like and even greater authority arising from quotations in favour of the Catholic Epistles, with the possible exception of the Second Epistle of Peter.[2]

The internal evidences in favour of the Catholic Epistles are various. These are derived from the peculiar dialect of Greek in which the Epistles are written, from the nature of their contents, from the simplicity of their form, and from their resemblance to other remains of the same writers—as, for example, the resemblance of Peter's Epistles to his speeches as recorded in the Acts of the Apostles, and of John's Epistles to his Gospel. It has also been affirmed that the marked superiority of these Epistles to the writings of the Apostolic Fathers who lived nearest their times, as the Epistle of Barnabas, the Epistle of Clemens Romanus, the Ignatian Epistles, the Epistle of Polycarp, and the Shepherd of Hermas, is a strong proof of their inspiration and genuineness.[3] How far this superiority is founded on fact, and how far, if admitted, it is a proof of genuineness, will be afterwards considered.

[1] Rawlinson's *Bampton Lectures* for 1859, pp. 199, 460. It is observed that the first six books of the *Annals* of Tacitus are known to us only through a single manuscript discovered in the fifteenth century, and are not distinctly alluded to by any writer until the first half of the fifteenth century. Salmon's *Introduction to the N. T.*, p. 6.

[2] See, however, the remarks on the genuineness of this Epistle, *infra*.

[3] Farrar's *Early Days of Christianity*, vol. i. p. 101.

THE EPISTLE OF JAMES.

IN a special introduction to the Catholic Epistles, there are five points which merit consideration with regard to each Epistle: first, its authenticity; secondly, its author; thirdly, its readers; fourthly, its design and contents; fifthly, the time and place of writing. Any difficulties, specialities, or controversial questions arising from the Epistles are discussed in separate dissertations.

I. THE AUTHENTICITY OF THE EPISTLE.

In the early Church there was a certain degree of dubiety concerning the authenticity of the Epistle of James. It is classed by Eusebius among the *Antilegomena*, or disputed writings of the New Testament. "Among the disputed books," he observes, "although they are well known and approved by many, are to be reckoned the Epistles of James and Jude."[1] And in another place, when writing about James, the Lord's brother, he remarks: "These accounts are given concerning James, who is said to have written the first of the Catholic Epistles; but it is to be observed that it is considered spurious. Not many of the ancients have mentioned it, nor that called the Epistle of Jude, which is also one of the seven so-called Catholic Epistles. Nevertheless we know that these, with the rest, are publicly used in most of the churches."[2] It does not appear that Eusebius shared in

[1] *Hist. Eccl.* iii. 25.   [2] *Ibid.* ii. 23.

these doubts, for, as will afterwards be seen, he expressly quotes the Epistle of James as sacred Scripture; he merely states the opinion of others. The Epistle did not obtain universal acceptance until the beginning of the fifth century; for Jerome (A.D. 390) remarks concerning it: "James, the Lord's brother, surnamed The Just, wrote only one Epistle, which is among the seven Catholic Epistles; which is said to have been published by another in his name, but gradually in process of time it obtained authority."[1] It is not difficult to account for this dubiety in the early Church. Considerable uncertainty prevailed regarding the identity of the author, and consequently regarding his authority as an inspired writer. The Epistle was written to Jewish Christians, who, by reason of the views of the Ebionites,[2] were regarded with suspicion during the first two centuries; nor was it, like the Epistles of Paul, addressed to any particular Church or person, on whom the responsibility of its preservation might rest. And its contents excited suspicion; the Epistle appeared to conflict with the views of Paul concerning justification, and it was considered to be defective with regard to the peculiar facts and doctrines of Christianity. But, as has been remarked, these difficulties in the way of its reception increased the value of the ancient testimonies in its favour.

Although, for the above reasons, dubiety existed in the ancient Church concerning the authenticity of this Epistle, the external testimonies in its favour are neither few nor unimportant. The First Epistle of Peter has with some plausibility been advanced as a testimony in favour of this Epistle, on account of certain resemblances between these Epistles; but we do not at present place any stress on this, because both the reality of these resemblances[3] and the priority of the Epistle of James have been questioned. Numerous apparent references or allusions

---

[1] *Catal. Script. eccles.* cap. 2.

[2] Many of the Jewish Christians, in the second century, separated from the Catholic Church, and formed the heretical sect of the Ebionites. Their views were somewhat similar to those Judaizers who opposed Paul. See below.

[3] The resemblances between the Epistle of James and the First Epistle of Peter are discussed in a dissertation on the "References in the Epistle of James;" and it is there maintained that the First Epistle of Peter is a testimony in favour of the authenticity of the Epistle of James.

have been adduced from the Epistle of Clemens Romanus (A.D. 95) which are by no means unimportant. Thus Abraham is called "the friend of God" (chap. x., comp. Jas. ii. 23); it is said that Rahab was saved by faith and hospitality (chap. xii., comp. Jas. ii. 25); reference is made to the sacrifice of Isaac (chap. xxxi., comp. Jas. ii. 21); the rare word δίψυχοι (*double-minded*) is employed (chap. xxiii., comp. Jas. i. 8); and the quotation, "God resisteth the proud, but giveth grace to the humble," found in the Epistle of James, is used (chap. xxx., comp. Jas. iv. 6). Hermas (A.D. 110) appears to refer to the Epistle of James when he writes : "If ye resist the devil, he will be conquered, and flee from you in disgrace"[1] (comp. Jas. iv. 7). This Epistle is contained in the ancient Syriac (A.D. 150), although that version omits four of the Catholic Epistles. The following passage from Irenæus (A.D. 180) contains an evident reference to it: "That man is not justified by these things, but that they were given as a sign to the people, this fact shows that Abraham himself, without circumcision and without observance of Sabbaths, believed God, and it was counted to him for righteousness, and he was called the Friend of God."[2] The Epistle was in all probability found in the Old Latin version (A.D. 170), as it is contained in the Codex Corbeiensis. Clemens Alexandrinus (A.D. 190), according to Eusebius, gave abridged accounts of all the canonical Scriptures, not omitting those that are disputed—the Epistle of Jude and the other Catholic Epistles;[3] and Cassiodorus informs us that one of the Epistles commented on by Clement was the Epistle of James.[4] Hippolytus

---

[1] *Mand.* xii. 5 : ἐὰν οὖν ἀντιστῆς αὐτὸν (διάβολον), νικηθεὶς φεύξεται ἀπό σου κατῃσχυμμένος. Several other resemblances to this Epistle are found in the works of Hermas, as *Mand.* ii. 2, ix. 1, xi. 5, 9, xii. 1, 6. See Charteris, *Canonicity*, pp. 293-295. Credner's *Einleitung*, p. 15.

[2] *Adv. Hær.* iv. 16. 2 : Ipse Abraham credidit Deo et reputatum est illi ad justitiam, et amicus Dei vocatus est. Clemens Alexandrinus also calls Abraham by this appellation : "Abraham is found to have been expressly called the Friend (of God)." *Strom.* ii. 5.

[3] Euseb. *Hist. Eccl.* vi. 14 : Πεποίηται διηγήσεις μηδὲ τὰς ἀντιλεγομένας παρελθών, τὴν Ἰούδα καὶ τὰς λοιπὰς καθολικὰς ἐπιστολάς.

[4] *Instit. divin. Script.* cap. viii. : In epistolis autem canonicis Clemens Alexandrinus i. e. in epistola sancti Petri prima, sancti Joannis prima et secunda et Jacobi attico sermone declaravit.

(A.D. 230), in a treatise concerning the end of the world, quotes from this Epistle: "For judgment is without mercy to him that has showed no mercy"[1] (comp. Jas. ii. 13). Origen (A.D. 230) directly ascribes the Epistle to James: "For though it is called faith, if it be without works it is dead, as we read in the Epistle attributed to James."[2] And again: "As in James, As the body without the spirit is dead."[3] And the quotations from this Epistle are numerous in the Latin version of his works. And Eusebius (A.D. 325), although he classes the Epistle among the Antilegomena, yet acknowledges its genuineness, as when he says: "For the holy apostle says, Is any among you afflicted? let him pray. Is any merry? let him sing psalms"[4] (Jas. v. 13). And again: "Since the Scripture says, Speak not evil, brethren, one of another, lest ye fall into condemnation"[5] (Jas. iv. 11).

Such is the external evidence which we possess in favour of this Epistle. On the other hand, it is to be observed that it is not found in the Muratorian canon, though, on account of the fragmentary nature of that manuscript, no great importance can be attached to the omission: nor is it referred to by Tertullian, for we cannot put stress on certain supposed allusions to it in his works given by Kirchhofer.[6] Although traces of it are found at a very early period, yet Origen is the first Father who expressly attributes the Epistle to James. But the strongest external testimony in its favour is its insertion in the Syriac version, and its early reception by the Syrian Church. We shall afterwards see that it was to the Syrian Church that this Epistle was chiefly addressed: most

---

[1] Hippol., ed. Lagarde, p. 122: ἡ γὰρ κρίσις ἀνίλιώς ἐστι τῷ μὴ ποιήσαντι ἔλεος. The genuineness of this treatise of Hippolytus is doubtful.

[2] *Comm. in Joann. Opp.* iv. p. 306: ἐὰν γὰρ, λίγηται μὲν πίστις, χωρὶς δὲ ἔργων τυγχάνῃ, νεκρά ἐστιν ἡ τοιαύτη, ὡς ἐν τῇ φερομένῃ Ἰακώβου ἐπιστολῇ ἀνέγνωμεν.

[3] *Selecta in Psalm. Opp.* ii. p. 644: ὡς παρὰ Ἰακώβῳ, ὥσπερ δὲ τὸ σῶμα χωρὶς πνεύματος νεκρόν ἐστι.

[4] *In Psal.*: λίγει γοῦν ὁ ἱερὸς ἀπόστολος· Κακοπαθεῖ τις ἐν ὑμῖν; προσευχέσθω· εὐθυμεῖ τις; ψαλλάτω.

[5] *Ibid.*: τῆς γραφῆς λεγούσης· Μὴ καταλαλεῖτε ἀλλήλων ἀδελφοί, ἵνα μὴ ὑπὸ κρίσιν πίπτητε.

[6] *Quellensammlung*, p. 263. Tertullian calls Abraham "the friend of God," *Adv. Judæos*, c. 2. But this had already become a familiar appellation.

of the Christian Jews of the dispersion belonged to it, and therefore its recognition by that Church is an important evidence in its favour. It is repeatedly quoted by Ephræm Syrus and other Syrian writers.

The internal evidence in favour of this Epistle is, we consider, even stronger than the external. The simple designation of the writer: "James, a servant of God and of the Lord Jesus Christ," is a proof of genuineness. Were it a forgery, other titles would be attached to impart to it authority; as "James the apostle," "James the bishop of Jerusalem," "James the Lord's brother," or even, as he is styled in the apocryphal writings, "James the brother of God" ($\dot{a}\delta\epsilon\lambda\phi\acute{o}\theta\epsilon\iota\sigma$s). The character of the Epistle corresponds with what we know of James the Lord's brother, conservative in his views regarding the Mosaic law, and so strict in his conduct as to merit the title "The Just;" as, for example, his view of the gospel as the perfect law of liberty, his abhorrence of all pretence, and his demand that faith should approve itself by works. But, above all, the contents of the Epistle, so pure and lofty, so exalted above the writings of heathen moralists, so pervaded with the spirit of Christ's teaching, place it at an immense distance from all non-apostolic writings, and its perusal cannot fail to impress us with a sense of its inspiration. "The authenticity of this Epistle," observes Bleek, "is vouched for by its entire character and contents, which bring before us a man who, along with stedfast faith in Jesus as the Christ, and a firm hope in His return in glory, had above all at heart the moral side of the gospel, which he treated (unlike Paul, for instance) rather as a new law, the cast of his piety giving more of a legal hue to Christianity. Such a man, judging from all the historical accounts we have of him, we should suppose James the Lord's brother to have been."[1]

In recent times the Epistle of James has been called in question by many theologians. Luther's attack upon it is well known; he repeatedly questioned its genuineness, and always regarded it unfavourably. "The Epistle of James," he observes, "is a mere Epistle of straw compared with these writings (that is, those of John, Peter, and Paul), for it

[1] Bleek's *Introduction to the New Testament*, E. Tr. vol. ii. p. 150.

contains nothing of the Gospel."[1] "To express my opinion upon it, without prejudice to any one, I regard it as the work of no apostle, for the following reason, that in direct opposition to Paul and all Scripture it ascribes justification to works. This James does no more than insist on the law and its works, and he mixes one thing with another so confusedly, that it seems to me he must have been some good, pious man who had caught up some sayings of the disciples of the apostles, and put them on paper."[2] The objections of Luther are not critical, but entirely subjective; the reason why he rejected the Epistle was because it appeared to him to conflict with his fundamental doctrine of justification by faith.[3] Several of the Reformers, and even some Roman Catholic writers, shared in his doubts. Cardinal Cajetan, Erasmus, the Magdeburg Centuriators, Grotius, and Wetstein have disputed the genuineness of this Epistle. Among recent writers it has been called in question by De Wette, who thought it incomprehensible that James should have attained to such a use of the Greek language;[4] by Schleiermacher,[5] who asserted that its teaching savoured of Ebionite Christianity; and by Holtzmann, who, among other reasons, objected to the supposed use of the apocryphal writings.[6] Baur, Schwegler, Hilgenfeld, and other theologians of the Tübingen school, suppose that it was written with the purpose of reconciling Pauline and Petrine Christianity; on this

---

[1] *Preface to the N. T.* 1522: Eine rechte strohene Epistel, denn sie doch keine evangelische Art an ihr hat. It must, however, be remembered that Luther does not make this statement absolutely, but only in comparison with the writings of Paul, John, and Peter; a fact which is often forgotten when these rash words of Luther are repeated. See Hare's *Vindication of Luther*, pp. 215-217.

[2] *Preface to the Epistles of James and Jude.*

[3] Calvin, on the other hand, it would seem, with a view to these objections of Luther, observes: "There are also at this day some who do not think it entitled to authority. I am, however, inclined to receive it without controversy, because I see no just cause for rejecting it." *Preface to the Epistle of James.*

[4] That there is no ground for this objection of De Wette will be seen when we consider the language of the Epistle.

[5] In his *Einleitung in das N. T.*, herausgegeben von Wolde.

[6] Holtzmann's *Einleitung in das N. T.*, p. 482. The Epistle of James has also been called in question by Weizsäcker and Hausrath.

account there is no mention, on the one hand, of circumcision and the other rites of Judaism; and, on the other hand, the authority of the moral law is specially insisted on.

The following are the chief internal or subjective objections that have been urged against this Epistle.

1. It is affirmed to be in direct opposition to Paul's doctrine of justification by faith, as it teaches justification by works. This was the great, if not the sole reason that caused Luther to call in question the genuineness of this Epistle. "It proclaims the righteousness of works in contradiction to Paul and all other Scripture. An explanation of such righteousness of works may be found; but that the Epistle adduces the saying of Moses, which speaks only of Abraham's faith and not of his works, in favour of works cannot be defended."[1] This objection we propose minutely to examine afterwards;[2] meantime, it is only necessary to say that while there is undoubtedly an apparent opposition, yet we believe and maintain that there is no real opposition, and that the views of these two writers on justification are not antagonistic.

2. De Wette, Schwegler, Holtzmann, and others object that the Epistle bears internal marks of a late origin. It is affirmed that the author of the Epistle borrowed words and phrases from the Epistles of Paul, and that the illustration of Rahab receiving the spies is taken from the Epistle to the Hebrews; so that this Epistle must be regarded as post-apostolic.[3] The resemblances between the Epistle of James and the Epistles of Paul are few and unimportant: the most important arose out of the Jewish training of the two writers, both being deeply versed in the Scriptures of the Old Testament. The example of Abraham must readily have presented itself to every Jewish mind;[4] that of Rahab is more difficult to account for, but was a remarkable incident in the history

---

[1] *Preface to the Epistle of James.*

[2] See dissertation on the Pauline and Jacobean views of justification.

[3] De Wette's *Einleitung in das N. T.*, sechste Ausgabe, p. 371. So Schwegler urges as an objection against the Epistle, its acquaintance with the Pauline Epistles, the Epistle to the Hebrews, and the Gospel to the Hebrews (?).

[4] See Lightfoot's *Commentary on the Galatians:* dissertation on the faith of Abraham, third edition, pp. 156-163.

of the Jewish people. And even although there were some reasons for the objection, which we do not admit, yet it would only prove that the Epistle was written after these writings, not that it was post-apostolic.

3. The absence of Christian doctrine is another objection. It is affirmed that the essential doctrines of Christianity, such as the atonement by the death of Christ, His resurrection, the influences of the Spirit, the resurrection of the dead, etc., are wanting in this Epistle.[1] And certainly it must be admitted that there is a comparative want of Christian doctrine, the reason of which we shall afterwards consider; but there is no want of Christian precept; the Epistle is practical rather than doctrinal; and there is no Epistle which is so deeply imbued with the teaching of Christ as displayed to us in the Sermon on the Mount. "This short Epistle of James," observes Reuss, "alone contains more reminiscences of the discourses of Jesus than all the other writings of the New Testament put together."[2]

4. Wetstein, Holtzmann,[3] and others object to this Epistle, that it exhibits an acquaintance with the apocryphal books of the Old Testament, as is seen in its references to the Wisdom of Solomon and the Book of Ecclesiasticus. We shall afterwards examine into the truth of this assertion.[4] But in the meantime we would only remark, that admitting its truth, granting that there are references to, and even quotations from, these apocryphal books, as many divines who assert the genuineness of this Epistle affirm,[5] we cannot possibly see what objection can arise from this fact to the genuineness of the Epistle. James might freely quote from these apocryphal books, with which, as a Jew, he must have been acquainted.

---

[1] Thus Luther objects that the Epistle makes "no mention of the sufferings, the resurrection, and the Spirit of Christ."

[2] Reuss' *Geschichte der heiligen Schriften N. T.*, p. 132, vierte Ausgabe [E. Tr. p. 140].

[3] Thus Holtzmann remarks: "The author in iv. 6 cites the LXX. and has an Old Testament before him which, besides the canonical books, contains also the Apocrypha." *Einleitung in das N. T.*, p. 482.

[4] See references in the Epistle of James to the Apocrypha, *infra*.

[5] Notably Dean Plumptre.

II. THE AUTHOR OF THE EPISTLE.

The author designates himself "James, a servant of God and of the Lord Jesus Christ." This name ('Ιακώβος) is common to many in the New Testament; but there are especially three distinguished men bearing this name to whom this Epistle has been ascribed. 1. James the son of Zebedee, the brother of John, one of the three favoured apostles of Jesus. 2. James the son of Alphæus, called also James the Less, another of the twelve apostles. 3. James "the Lord's brother," who is generally regarded as identical with James the bishop of Jerusalem. By many the last two are regarded as the same person.

The Epistle has been attributed to James the son of Zebedee. This opinion appears to have been adopted by Michaelis,[1] and has recently been ingeniously supported by Bassett in his Commentary on the Epistle of James.[2] The external evidence in its favour is of the most meagre description. A manuscript of the Old Italic version, the Codex Corbeiensis, belonging to the ninth century, states, in the subscription, that the Epistle was written by James the son of Zebedee.[3] And in the early printed editions of the Peshito the same statement is made; but it is unknown to what manuscript authority the editors appealed.[4] The manuscripts of the Peshito have simply, either in the superscription or in the subscription, "The Epistle of James the apostle." In the edition of Widmanstadt, the first printed edition of the Peshito, it is stated in Syriac that "the three Epistles (James, First Peter, and First John) were written by the three apostles who were witnesses to the revelation of the Lord when He was transfigured on Mount Tabor, and who saw

[1] Michaelis, *Introduction to the N. T.*, translated by Bp. Marsh, vol. vi. p. 277 ff.
[2] Bassett's *Catholic Epistle of St. James*, pp. i.-xxxvi.
[3] Explicit Epistola Jacobi filii Zebedæi.
[4] Bassett himself observes: "The assertion, so freely made by Grotius and Pole and later writers, that the Peshito Syriac assigned this Epistle expressly to James the son of Zebedee, appears to be without any foundation so far as the authority of MSS. is concerned, and must have been derived from this general title to the three Catholic Epistles in these early editions of the printed text."

Moses and Elias speaking with Him."[1] And a similar statement is made in the subscription to these Epistles in the edition of Tremellius:[2] "The three Epistles of the blessed apostles, before whose eyes our Lord was transfigured, namely, James, Peter, and John." The internal reasons for the authorship of James the son of Zebedee—such as the supposed improbability that one who was so highly favoured by our Lord should have passed away without leaving any written memorial of his teaching, the coincidences between the contents of this Epistle and the circumstances in the life of this apostle, the supposed reference to the transfiguration, the resemblances to the Sermon on the Mount—are of no weight. They are either too vague in their character, or are equally applicable to the other two who bear the name of James. We do not indeed consider the early death of the son of Zebedee (A.D. 44) as opposed to his being the author of this Epistle; but we really know little about him, whereas there is another James, whose character we do know, and which corresponds in a remarkable degree with the characteristics of this Epistle. The opinion that the author was James the son of Zebedee does not appear to have been entertained by any of the Fathers; indeed, Jerome asserts that he greatly errs who considers that this James was the brother of John.[3]

James the Lord's brother has been almost universally regarded as the author of this Epistle. He stands out prominently in the Acts of the Apostles; he appears to have been the acknowledged head of the Church of Jerusalem, and hence has received the title of "Bishop of Jerusalem." If not an apostle, he was one of the most eminent leaders of the primitive Church; he presided at the Council of Jerusalem; and was regarded by Paul as one of the pillars of the Church (Gal. ii. 9).

There have been several opinions entertained regarding the

---

[1] This statement was prefixed as a special title to the Catholic Epistles immediately before that of James; and as Widmanstadt printed from a MS. brought by Moses of Mardin, it may be presumed that he took what he found in that MS.; but the statement is not repeated by Schaaf and the later editors, probably because it is destitute of manuscript authority. It is not in the Arabic version from the Peshito.

[2] The edition of Tremellius was published in Hebrew characters in 1569.

[3] *Comm. in Ep. ad Gal.* i. 19. See Erdmann, *Der Brief des Jakobus*, p. 3.

personality of this James. Of these there are three which have been maintained by high authorities in the Christian Church, and which have received their names from their authors or chief supporters. These are—the Hieronymian view, which regards James not as an actual brother, but as a full cousin of our Lord (the most of those who hold this view identifying him with James the son of Alphæus); the Epiphanian, which regards him as a half-brother of our Lord, being the son of Joseph, but not of Mary; and the Helvidian, which considers him as a full brother, being the son of Mary and Joseph.

It has been maintained that James the son of Alphæus and James the brother of the Lord are identical. According to this view, the word *brethren* is used in an extended sense for cousins. The line of argument by which this opinion is maintained is as follows:—We are informed in the Gospels that the brethren of Jesus were James, and Joses, and Simon, and Judas (Matt. xiii. 55; Mark vi. 3). Now a James and a Joses are mentioned as the sons of Mary the wife of Clopas, and the sister of the mother of Jesus (John xix. 25 compared with Matt. xxvii. 56; Mark xv. 40). It is further affirmed that Clopas is the same name as Alphæus,[1] Alphæus being the Hebrew name (חלפי), and Clopas being a different mode of expressing the Hebrew letters in Greek characters (Κλωπᾶς); and hence James the son of Alphæus is the same as the above-mentioned James the son of Clopas and Mary, and the cousin of our Lord. Further, in the apostolic list given by Luke in the Acts of the Apostles, Judas is called "the brother of James" (Acts i. 13). Hence the sons of Alphæus, or Clopas, and Mary, the sister of the Virgin, are James, and Judas, and Joses, being the names of three of the brethren of Jesus; so that in order to identify them we have only to suppose that the word *brethren* or *brothers* is used in an enlarged sense so as to include cousins. This opinion, which appears to have been first definitively brought forward by Jerome, and hence called the Hieronymian,[2] was supported by the authority

[1] See Winer's *Wörterbuch:* Alphæus.
[2] *Catal. Script. eccl.* ch. 2: Jacobus qui appellatur frater Domini, ut nonnulli existimant, Joseph ex alia uxore, ut autem mihi videtur Mariæ sororis matris Domini filius.

of Augustine, and has been embraced by Calvin, Pearson, Doddridge, Herder, Schneckenburger, Gieseler, Theile, Hug, Baumgarten, Guericke, Hengstenberg, Keil, Philippi, Mansel, Ellicott, Wordsworth, Tregelles, and Dean Scott, in his exposition of the Epistle of James in the *Speaker's Commentary*.

But although this opinion is so highly supported, yet it labours under so many and such great difficulties, that we are constrained to relinquish it as untenable. It is built on a series of assumptions, each of which is doubtful, and it is liable to several grave objections. 1. It is arbitrary to assume that the word *brethren* here signifies cousins. The word *brethren* is frequently used in Scripture in a metaphorical sense, but without any danger of misconception;[1] but there is nothing in the narrative here to suggest such an extended and metaphorical sense, nor is there any instance in the New Testament where the word is used in the sense of cousins. If the so-called brethren of Jesus were only cousins, we would have expected the word ἀνέψιοι and not ἀδελφοί. The objection is equally strong with regard to those who are called our Lord's sisters (Matt. xiii. 56). 2. It is doubtful if Mary the wife of Clopas was the sister of the Virgin. The words of the evangelist are: "Now there stood by the cross of Jesus His mother and His mother's sister, Mary the wife of Clopas, and Mary Magdalene" (John xix. 25). The probability is that there were four women, here mentioned in pairs, and that the sister of our Lord's mother was not Mary the wife of Clopas, but Salome the mother of John, who, we know, also stood by the cross (Matt. xxvi. 56).[2] This avoids the improbability of two sisters being called by the same name. 3. It is more than doubtful if Clopas and Alphæus are the same name. Alphæus is Semitic, and is to be referred to אלפי or חלפי, and rendered into Greek characters can only be Ἀλφαί or Χαλφαί;

---

[1] In only two instances, and both in the O. T., is the word used to denote a relationship different from that of brother. Lot is called the brother of Abraham (Gen. xiii. 8), and Jacob the brother of Laban (Gen. xxix. 15), whereas in reality they were nephews.

[2] See *Exegetical Studies*, by the author, pp. 62-65. According to this supposition, the sons of Mary the wife of Clopas were no relations to Christ; whereas James and John, the sons of Zebedee and Salome, were His full cousins.

whereas Clopas (Κλωπᾶς) is Greek, and cannot be derived from the Hebrew name.[1] In the Syriac version, which comes nearest the Hebrew, these names are regarded as different. 4. It is doubtful if Ἰούδας Ἰακώβου (Acts i. 13) is to be translated "Judas the brother of James," and not rather "Judas the son of (an unknown) James." 5. We are expressly informed that during our Lord's public ministry His brethren did not believe on Him (John vii. 5); whereas, if according to the above opinion two of them, James and Judas, were apostles, this assertion could not have been made. The force of the objection is not lessened by the supposition that the unbelief here adverted to might be some temporary wavering, for there is nothing in the context to warrant such a conjecture. 6. The brethren of Jesus are several times expressly distinguished from the apostles as belonging to a distinct and separate group (John ii. 12; 1 Cor. ix. 5; Acts i. 13, 14). For these reasons we are constrained to reject the opinion of the identity of James the son of Alphæus with James the Lord's brother.

A very ingenious opinion, which still maintains that our Lord's brother was the cousin of Jesus, but which avoids most of the above difficulties, has lately been advanced by Professor Schegg of Munich. He supposes that James is the son of Clopas and Mary, the sister of the Virgin, but he denies that the names Clopas and Alphæus are identical. Thus, then, according to him, James was not one of the apostles. This opinion avoids many of the difficulties to which the opinion of the identity of James the son of Alphæus and James the Lord's brother is exposed. It is also in favour of it that many of the Fathers asserted that James the Lord's brother was not an apostle; and the Greek Church in their calendar

[1] Wätzel in the *Studien und Kritiken*, 1883, iii. 620-626, contends that ח at the beginning of words is not translated by κ, but usually by the spiritus lenis or spiritus asper, or by χ. He further contends that not only κ, but every letter and sound in Κλωπᾶς is inexplicable as representative of חלפי. See also Sieffert in Herzog-Plitt's *Real Encyklopädie*, article "Jakobus in N. T." He observes that even Jerome, acquainted with Hebrew, although he held that Mary of Clopas was the wife of Alphæus, yet did not think of the possibility of considering these two names as identical. See also, on the impossibility of deriving Clopas from Alphæus, Mangold's edition of Bleek's *Introduction*, p. 700, and Schegg, *Jakobus der Bruder des Herrn*, p. 53.

have different days for James the apostle and James the Lord's brother. But still there is the great objection that the word *brother* is here employed for cousin, and the less objection that Mary and her sister have the same name. Certainly if the Hieronymian view is to be defended with any plausible arguments, it must be on the lines of the view advanced by Professor Schegg.[1]

Some who abandon the Hieronymian view of cousinship, and consider James the son of Alphæus and James the Lord's brother to be different persons, yet think that the author of the Epistle is not James "the Lord's brother," but James the apostle, the son of Alphæus. This opinion is adopted by Stier, Wieseler,[2] and Dr. Davidson in his *Introduction to the New Testament*. They suppose that it is the Apostle James, the son of Alphæus, who is so prominently mentioned in the Acts of the Apostles, and who by the early Church was considered bishop of Jerusalem. "It agrees better with the Acts," observes Dr. Davidson, "to conceive that the *apostle* presided over the Church at Jerusalem, occupied a prominent place in ecclesiastical matters, was present at the Council there, and gave that opinion, after other apostles, which was adopted,—than to suppose that *a brother of our Lord*, who had become a believer after His resurrection, should have attained to such influence by virtue of his relationship and personal character, especially among Jewish Christians. That one who was an apostle should never be mentioned in the Acts, while another of the same name, who was not, should be so conspicuous, is most improbable."[3] But this hypothesis constrains those who adopt it to regard James, the Lord's brother, mentioned in Gal. i. 19, and James, one of the pillars of the Church, mentioned a few verses farther on (Gal. ii. 9), as different persons—a supposition which is most improbable. The James mentioned in these passages is evidently one and the same. And the example of Paul teaches us that there is no improbability in supposing that James, who became a believer

---

[1] Schegg's *Jakobus der Bruder des Herrn*. München 1883.
[2] *Comm. zu Gal.* 1859.
[3] Davidson's *Introduction to the N. T.*, vol. iii. p. 309. Dr. Davidson, in his *Introduction to the Study of the N. T.*, abandons this opinion.

only after the resurrection, should in a short time step into prominence in the early Church, especially when we consider his relationship to the Lord and his high personal character.

We consider then that neither James the son of Zebedee, nor James the son of Alphæus, was the author of this Epistle, but James the Lord's brother. Concerning him, however, there are several opinions. Some suppose that he was the son of Joseph, our Lord's reputed father, by a previous marriage, and was on account of this connection called "the Lord's brother."[1] This opinion avoids all the difficulties attending the supposition that James was merely the cousin of our Lord, and, moreover, does no violence to the general sentiment of the Christian Church concerning the perpetual virginity of Mary. It is also the best supported by ecclesiastical authority, as it appears to have been the favourite opinion of the early Greek Fathers, being held by Origen, Eusebius, Epiphanius,[2] Chrysostom, Gregory of Nyssa, and Cyril of Alexandria; and among the Latin Fathers, by Hilary and Ambrose, and has become the generally received opinion of the Greek Church. It has been maintained by Vossius, Cave,[3] and Thiersch, and has recently been revived by Renan, Bishop Lightfoot, and apparently adopted by Dean Plumptre.[4] Still, however, it must be regarded as a compromise. It savours too much of a mere arbitrary supposition adopted to avoid difficulties, and is destitute of any positive arguments in its favour. There is not the slightest indication in the Gospels that Joseph, previous to his marriage with the Virgin, was a widower. The idea appears to have had its origin in an old tradition contained in the apocryphal literature—in the Gospel of Peter and the Protevangelium of James,

---

[1] Lange takes another view; he supposes that James and his brothers were the sons of Clopas, the brother of Joseph, and that after the death of their father they were adopted by Joseph. *Introduction to the Epistle of James.* Theophylact held the same view.

[2] Hence called the Epiphanian, because Epiphanius was one of its chief supporters.

[3] In his *Lives of the Apostles.*

[4] See Bishop Lightfoot's dissertation attached to his *Commentary on the Epistle to the Galatians.* Plumptre's *Commentary on the Epistle of James*, p. 15.

that Joseph was an old man when he was married to the Virgin, and had children by a previous marriage.[1]

We arrive then at the conclusion that the preponderance of evidence is in favour of the opinion that James was the real brother of our Lord, being the son of Mary and Joseph. This view avoids the difficulties attached to the other views, and gives to the word *brother* its natural meaning. According to it, Mary, after the birth of Jesus, bore Joseph four sons—James, Joses, Simon, and Judas, besides daughters. This opinion was first advocated by Helvidius,[2] whose followers were called Helvidians or Antidicomarianitæ,[3] and were universally regarded as heretics: it was condemned by the Sixth Œcumenical Council. It has been embraced by De Wette, Meyer, Ewald, Neander, Bleek, Oertel, Lechler, Wieseler, Stier, Credner, Huther, Sieffert, Reuss, Wiesinger, Beyschlag, Mangold, Brückner, Erdmann, Kern, C. Schmid, Keim, Schaff, W. Schmidt, Weiss, Alford, Farrar, and Eadie.

The opinion, however, is open to various objections. 1. It is opposed to the doctrine of the perpetual virginity of Mary. This doctrine has been the sentiment of the universal Church until comparatively recent times. Both the Western and the Eastern Churches clung to the idea that the Virgin remained always a virgin; hence the name ἀειπάρθενος among the Greeks, and *semper virgo* among the Latins.[4] And it cannot be denied that there is a feeling of repugnance at the supposition that the Virgin, the mother of our Lord, should ever afterwards have been the mother of other children. But, on the other hand, it is contended that the question is not

---

[1] In the Protevangelium of James, Joseph is represented as objecting to marry Mary, saying, "I have children, and I am an old man."

[2] Helvidius was a Roman Christian who lived toward the close of the fourth century. Jerome wrote against him: *Contra Helvidium de beatæ Mariæ virginitate perpetua* (Ep. xlviii.). Helvidius appealed to the writings of Tertullian.

[3] Antidicomarianitæ appellati sunt hæretici, qui Mariæ virginitati usque adeo contradicunt, ut affirment eam post Christum natum viro suo fuisse commixtam (Augustine).

[4] The grounds of this opinion are thus stated by Bishop Pearson in his *Exposition of the Creed:* "We believe the mother of our Lord to have been, not only before and after His nativity, but also for ever, the most immaculate and blessed virgin. For although it may be thought sufficient as to the mystery of the incarnation, that when our Saviour was conceived and born His mother was a virgin; though whatever should have followed after could

one of sentiment, but of fact; and the Gospels assert that our Lord had brothers and sisters. The idea of the perpetual virginity of Mary is considered as arising from a false notion of the superior sanctity of celibacy, and has no authority in the word of God (Luke ii. 1 ; Matt. i. 23). 2. It is asserted that James, the Lord's brother, is expressly called an apostle by Paul. Thus, in enumerating the appearances of our Lord after His resurrection, Paul says: "After that He was seen of James, then of all the apostles" (1 Cor. xv. 7). But these words do not necessarily imply that James was an apostle, but merely emphasize the appearance of Christ to the apostles as a body. So also, in the Epistle to the Galatians, Paul writes: "After three years I went up to Jerusalem to see Peter, and abode with him fifteen days. But other of the apostles saw I none, save James the Lord's brother" (Gal. i. 18, 19). Now, although it is admitted that the most natural interpretation of these words is that James is included among the apostles, yet the restrictive clause ($\epsilon i\ \mu\dot{\eta}$) may refer not to the word apostles, but to the whole sentence, in the sense that Paul on this occasion saw no apostle except Peter, but that he also saw that important individual James the Lord's brother.[1] 3. It is further objected that, if Mary had children of her own, Jesus would not when dying have recommended her to the care of John (John xix. 25-27). But we do not know the circumstances of the case. John was present with Mary at the cross, while the brethren of Jesus were absent. Besides, it would appear from various incidental notices that John was in a better social position than our Lord's brothers,

have no reflective operation upon the first-fruit of her womb ; though there be no further mention in the Creed than that He was 'born of the Virgin Mary ;' yet the peculiar eminency and unparalleled privilege of that mother, the special honour and reverence due unto that Son, and ever paid by her, the regard o that Holy Ghost who came upon her, and the power of the Highest which overshadowed her, the singular goodness and piety of Joseph, to whom she was espoused, have persuaded the Church of God in all ages to believe that she still continued in the same virginity, and therefore is to be acknowledged 'the ever-Virgin Mary.'" In the Helvetic Confession Jesus is spoken of as *natus e.c Maria semper virgine*.

[1] For a similar use of $\epsilon i\ \mu\dot{\eta}$, see John xvii. 12. Others suppose that the word ἀπόστολος is here used in a wide sense, and not as restricted to the Twelve ; being applied in the Acts of the Apostles not only to Paul, but also to Barnabas (Acts xiv. 14).

and that he had a residence in Jerusalem. As Dr. Bushnell remarks: "Why Jesus committed Mary to John, and not to the four brothers, it is not difficult to guess; for John has a home, as they certainly have not, and are not likely soon to have." [1]

James the Lord's brother is frequently mentioned in Scripture. Like the other brethren of our Lord, he was at first unbelieving (John vii. 4), but appears to have been converted by a special appearance of our Lord to him after His resurrection (1 Cor. xv. 7). From the very first, probably on account of his high moral character and his relationship to Jesus, he occupied a distinguished position in the Christian Church. When Peter was miraculously delivered from prison, he ordered that special intelligence should be sent to James: "Go show these things to James and to the brethren" (Acts xii. 7). James presided at the council of Jerusalem, and pronounced the decree of the assembled Church (Acts xv. 19). To him, as the head of the Church of Jerusalem, Paul on his last journey to that city repaired with the offerings of the Gentiles (Acts xxi. 20). In the Epistle to the Galatians Paul gives him the honourable appellation of the Lord's brother (Gal. i. 19), and ranks him along with Peter and John among the pillars or leaders of the Church (Gal. ii. 19). Mention is made of certain who came from James who found fault with Peter for his free intercourse with the Gentile converts (Gal. ii. 21). And in the short Epistle of Jude the writer commends himself to his readers as "Jude the brother of James" (Jude 1).

[1] The interesting question concerning the personality of James the Lord's brother is discussed more or less fully in Winer's *Biblisches Wörterbuch*, article "Jacobus." Lange's *Life of Christ*, vol. i. 421-437, Clark's translation. Neander's *Planting*, vol. i. 350-354. Schaff's *Apostolic History*, vol. ii. 35-38; and in his *Das Verhältniss des Jakobus Bruders des Herrn zu Jak. Alphei*, Berlin 1842. Alford's *Greek Testament*, introduction to the Epistle of James. Lardner's *Works*, vol. iii. 368-384. Davidson's *Introduction to the Study of the N. T.*, 1st ed. vol. i. 281-284; 2nd ed. vol. i. 304-309. Lightfoot's *Commentary on the Epistle to the Galatians:* dissertation, "The Brethren of the Lord." Herzog-Plitt's *Real-Encyklopädie*, article "Jacobus," by Sieffert. Schegg's *Jakobus der Bruder des Herrn*. Farrar's *Early Days of Christianity*, vol. i. p. 489 ff. Wiesinger's *Der Brief des Jakobus*, Introduction, pp. 1-12. Holtzmann, "Jacobus der Gerechte und seine Namensbruder," in Hilgenfeld's *Zeitschr.* 1880, Nr. 2. Gloag's *Commentary on the Acts of the Apostles*, vol. i. pp. 422-429. Weiss' *Einleitung in das N. T.*, pp. 387-396.

The Lord's brother occupied a prominent position in the traditions of the Church. The same general character is given to him: he is described as a man of legal strictness, universally esteemed, who earned for himself the title of "The Just," and who continued to the last an observer of the Mosaic law. A long and interesting account of his character and martyrdom, written by Hegesippus, who lived about the middle of the second century, is preserved by Eusebius.[1] He informs us that to distinguish him from others of the same name he was called The Just, and Oblias, which signifies "the bulwark of the people." He lived as a Nazarite. He was consecrated from his mother's womb; he drank neither wine nor strong drink, and no razor came upon his head. He was in the habit of entering the temple alone, and was often found on his knees interceding for the forgiveness of his people, so that his knees became as hard as camels' in consequence of his habitual supplication and kneeling before God. He was put to death by the fanatical Jews a few years before the destruction of Jerusalem. "Thus," concludes Hegesippus, "he suffered martyrdom, and they buried him on the spot where his tombstone still remains near the temple. He was a faithful witness to the Jews and to the Greeks, that Jesus is the Christ. Immediately after this, Vespasian invaded and took Jerusalem."[2] Josephus, in a remarkable passage, gives a similar account of the martyrdom of James. He was put to death by the high priest Ananus, during a vacancy in the Roman procuratorship, after the death of Festus, and before the arrival of Albinus. "Ananus," he writes, "assembled the Sanhedrim, and brought before them the brother of Jesus who is called Christ, whose name was James, and some of his companions; and when he had formed the accusation against them as breakers of the law, he delivered them to be stoned."[3]

[1] *Hist. Eccl.* ii. 23.
[2] Although the narrative of Hegesippus is partially mythical, yet the main features appear to be founded on fact. It may be regarded as a certain fact that James was martyred at the temple by the fanatical Jews shortly before the fall of their city. See Lechler's *Apostolic and Post-apostolic Times*, translated from the 3rd edition, vol. i. pp. 59-66. 1886.
[3] *Ant.* xx. 9. 1. The narrative of Josephus has without good reason been suspected by Credner, and recently by Schürer and Sieffert; it is inserted by

According to this account, James was martyred in the year 63, shortly before the commencement of the Jewish war.

In the *Clementine Homilies* and other apocryphal writings, James occupies a conspicuous place, and is exalted above all the apostles. Peter is represented as addressing him as "the lord and bishop of the holy Church;"[1] and Clement addresses him as the "bishop of bishops (ἐπίσκοπος ἐπισκόπων) who rules Jerusalem, the holy Church of the Hebrews."[2] In the *Apostolic Constitutions* it is affirmed that he was appointed bishop of Jerusalem by the Lord Himself and His apostles.[3] Eusebius informs us of the tradition that James received the dignity of the episcopate at Jerusalem from the Saviour Himself, and that his episcopal seat, which was preserved until the present time, was held in veneration by his successors.[4] In the *Liturgy of James* he is called ἀδελφόθεος, "the brother of God."[5] Epiphanius affirms that he went yearly into the holy of holies, and wore the diadem of the high priest; and he mentions the tradition of his ascension into heaven.[6]

From these scriptural statements, and from the traditionary accounts, though mixed with fable and exaggeration, it appears that James "the Lord's brother" was considered even more than Peter as the apostle of the circumcision. He was regarded as the chief of the Church of Jerusalem, and when all the apostles were dispersed he made the holy city his residence. He was evidently looked up to by the Jewish converts, and exercised authority over them. Even those Jewish Christians who did not reside in Jerusalem, but belonged to the Diaspora, would come into frequent contact with him in their yearly visits at the Passover, and would greatly esteem him on account of his high moral character and strict observance of the Mosaic law. Although a Christian, he did not cease to be a Jew; he was a regular wor-

Eusebius in his account of the death of James. See the reasons against the genuineness of this passage in Josephus stated by Credner in his *Einleitung in das N. T.*, pp. 580-582.

[1] The Clementines: *Epistle of Peter to James*.
[2] *Epistle of Clement to James*.   [3] *Apost. Const.* viii. 35.
[4] *Hist. Eccl.* vii. 19. See also ii. 1.   [5] Trollope's *Liturgy of James*, p. 25.
[6] *Hær.* xxx. 16.

shipper in the courts of the temple. The description given by Paul of Ananias, "a devout man according to the law, having a good report of all the Jews" (Acts xxii. 12), was equally applicable to the Lord's brother. He did not dissever Christianity from Judaism, but regarded Christianity as the development and perfection of Judaism; and although he was strongly opposed to the opinions of those Judaizers who wished to impose the yoke of the Mosaic law on the Gentile converts, yet he saw no reason why the Jewish Christians should separate themselves from the worship of their fathers and renounce their national religion. "Had not," observes Schaff, "the influence of James been modified and completed by that of a Peter and especially a Paul, Christianity perhaps would never have cast off entirely the envelope of Judaism and risen to independence. Yet the influence of James was necessary. He, if any, could gain the ancient chosen nation in a body. God placed such a representative of the purest form of Old Testament piety in the midst of the Jews, to make their transition to the faith of the Messiah as easy as possible, even at the eleventh hour. But when they refused this last messenger of peace, the divine forbearance was exhausted, and the fearful, long-threatened judgment broke upon them. And with this the mission of James was fulfilled. He was not to outlive the destruction of Jerusalem and the temple."[1]

III. THE READERS OF THE EPISTLE.

The Epistle is inscribed ταῖς δώδεκα φυλαῖς ταῖς ἐν τῇ διασπορᾷ, "to the twelve tribes which are in the Dispersion;" but this inscription, plain and simple as it appears, has given rise to different and contradictory interpretations. Some suppose that it is written to Jewish Christians; others assert that the phrase includes all believers, whether Jews or Gentiles; and others, all Jews, whether believers or unbelievers.[2] This variety of interpretation arises, not so much from any obscurity in the inscription, as from the preconceived opinions of the interpreters.

---
[1] Schaff's *Apostolic History*, vol. ii. p. 38.
[2] See Beyschlag, *der Brief des Jakobus*, p. 7.

Some suppose that the Epistle was addressed to *Christians in general*—that it is, in the fullest sense of the term, a catholic Epistle addressed to the catholic Church. "A correct interpretation of the inscription," observes De Wette, "and a proper apprehension of the whole Epistle, show it to be addressed to all Christians outside of Palestine, and intended to rebuke the faults of their condition as Christians, as these were manifested to the author in silent contrast with the simple, uncorrupted state of the mother Church."[1] This opinion has been adopted by Hengstenberg, Hofmann, Schwegler, Schenkel, Hilgenfeld,[2] Neudecker, Lücke, Philippi, and Lange.[3] They take the expression "twelve tribes" in a figurative sense to denote the "Israel of God" (Gal. vi. 16), in contrast to "Israel after the flesh" (1 Cor. x. 18). The Church of Christ is the true Israel, the chosen generation, the royal priesthood, the peculiar people (1 Pet. ii. 9). All believers belong to the Dispersion, being "strangers and pilgrims upon earth" (Heb. xi. 13). But such an opinion is inadmissible and without support in the Epistle. There is not the slightest indication given that the words "the twelve tribes" are to be understood in a metaphorical sense. On the contrary, the Epistle is throughout addressed to the Jews. James speaks of Abraham as "our" father (Jas. ii. 21), thus indicating that as a Jew he wrote to the Jews;[4] he assumes that his readers know of Job, Elijah, and Rahab (Jas. v. 11, 17); he uses the Old Testament names of God, as Lord and "the Lord of Hosts" (Jas. v. 4); he speaks of their place of worship as a synagogue (Jas. ii. 2, εἰς τὴν συναγωγήν); and the faults which he censures, such as swearing, quarrelling, sycophancy, worldliness, and formality, are such as characterized the Jews of that period.

[1] De Wette's *Einleitung in das N. T.*, p. 368 [E. Tr. p. 329].

[2] Hilgenfeld observes: "James writes to the twelve tribes of the Dispersion, that is, to the Israel of Christianity outside of Palestine, and we are as little necessitated as in the Apocalypse (Rev. vii. 4, xxi. 12) to think only of Christians of Jewish birth." *Einleitung in das N. T.*, p. 529.

[3] Lange adopts the strange and fanciful opinion that by the rich man in the Epistle is meant the Ebionitizing Jewish Christian, and by the poor the Gentile Christian. Lange's *Commentary*, p. 27, E. Tr.

[4] This taken by itself is no proof of the Jewish descent of the readers, as such language is common to early Christian writers whether Jewish or Gentile; its force consists in its combination with other considerations.

As some consider the Epistle as addressed to Christians in general, so others, more plausibly, considered it as addressed to *Jews in general*—to non-Christian as well as to Christian Jews. This opinion is maintained by Grotius, Macknight, Theile, Lardner, Credner,[1] Hug, Wordsworth, and Bassett. A modified view is adopted by Michaelis: he supposes that James wrote to persons who were already converted from Judaism to Christianity, but that it was his wish and intention that unbelieving Jews should also read it and be converted, and that this wish and intention influenced his choice of materials.[2] The Epistle, it is affirmed, is addressed to the "twelve tribes of the Dispersion," without any recognition of the Christian faith of the readers; they are described according to their nationality. The Jews at this time were a mixed community: the Christian faith had been embraced by many of them; and this accounts for the different tone of the Epistle; sometimes stern and severe, and at other times consolatory and conciliatory; at one time full of invective, and at another time commendatory. Certain statements, it is observed, are of such a nature that they can only be true of unconverted Jews (Jas. ii. 6, 7, v. 6). In consistency with this there is no salutation to "the saints" or "the elect" in the preface of the Epistle, and no mention of the distinctive doctrines of the gospel.[3] But the general contents of the Epistle refute this hypothesis. The readers, whoever they were, were at least Christians. James rests his authority upon being a servant of God and of the Lord Jesus Christ (Jas. i. 1); he speaks of his readers as having been begotten again by the word of God, and as possessing the faith of the Lord Jesus Christ, the Lord of glory (Jas. ii. 1); he mentions those who blasphemed that worthy name by which they were called (Jas. ii. 7); and he

---

[1] "The contents of the Epistle bring before us at one time believing and at another time unbelieving Jews, but always only readers who have sprung from Abraham." *Einleitung*, p. 595.

[2] Michaelis' *Introduction to the N. T.*, by Marsh, vol. vi. p. 295.

[3] The reasons in favour of the opinion that the Epistle was addressed to Jews in general are fully given by Bassett in his *Commentary on James*, pp. 41–45. Surely the absence of "the distinctive doctrines of the gospel" is not *for* but *against* the hypothesis that the Epistle was addressed to Jews in general. It would be strange conduct in missionaries to suppress the doctrines of the Christian faith in preaching to the heathen.

exhorts them to await in patience the advent of Christ (Jas. v. 7). Besides, it does not appear to have been the custom of the apostles to write Epistles to those who were not Christians;[1] and if they did so, it could only be with the intention of converting them to Christianity; but in this Epistle no attempt at conversion is made.[2] Those few passages, which are addressed to the enemies of Christianity, are so expressed that they may be regarded as apostrophes, introduced in the spirit of the Old Testament prophets, denouncing the oppressors of the Jewish Christians.

We consider, then, that the Epistle was addressed to *Jewish Christians*. This opinion, with various modifications, is held by Beza, Beyschlag, Brückner, Bleek, Huther, Wiesinger, Lechler, Schaff, Schmidt, Schegg, Sieffert, Mangold, Weiss, Davidson, Alford, Salmon, and the majority of critics. The readers of the Epistle were Jews: it is addressed to the "twelve tribes;" and this phrase was a usual appellation of Jews in general. Thus Paul, in his speech before Agrippa, says, "Unto which promise our twelve tribes hope to come" (Acts xxvi. 7). The twelve tribes were now blended together, and constituted the nation of the Jews. They were "Jews in the Dispersion" (ἐν τῇ διασπορᾷ), that is, Jews residing beyond the limits of the Holy Land, or perhaps Jews residing outside of Jerusalem. They were Christian Jews of the Dispersion, Jews who had recognised Jesus as the Messiah, on whom His goodly name had been invoked, and who are enjoined to look forward in patience and hope to His second advent.

The Jews were then, as now, dispersed throughout the world. In all the large cities of the Roman Empire, especially in Cyrene,[3] Alexandria, and Rome, and in all countries subject to Rome, especially in Syria, Proconsular Asia, and Cyprus,

[1] "The object of the apostolic Epistles," observes Bishop Prettyman, "was to confirm and not to convert: to correct what was amiss in those who did believe, and not in those who did not believe." *Elements of Christian Theology*, third edition, vol. i. 467.

[2] Credner, so far as we are aware, is alone in asserting that James wrote his Epistle with a direct design to convert the unbelieving Jews. *Einleitung*, p. 597.

[3] Josephus remarks, "There were four classes of men among those of Cyrene: that of citizens, that of husbandmen, that of strangers, and the fourth of Jews." *Ant.* xiv. 7. 2.

numerous Jews were to be found.[1] We read that on the day of Pentecost there were assembled at Jerusalem "Jews of every nation under heaven" (Acts ii. 5). There were several great dispersions of the Jews. The first was when the kings of Assyria led the ten tribes captive, and settled them in Assyria and in the cities of the Medes (2 Kings xvii. 6). Nebuchadnezzar afterwards transported the Jews to Babylon; and although permission was given them by Cyrus to return, yet the majority remained in their adopted country. Ptolemy Lagus caused the Jews to emigrate to Alexandria in such numbers, that one-fourth of the population of that city is said to have been Jewish.[2] The kings of Syria settled numbers of them in the cities of their empire. And Pompey carried vast numbers of captive Jews to Rome, where they regained their freedom, and colonized a portion of the imperial city. In many places the Jews of the Dispersion enjoyed peculiar privileges and had their own governors. In Babylon, for example, the chief of the Jews was called "the prince of the captivity;" and in Alexandria he received the title of Alabarches.[3]

But it has been asked, Where were those Churches in the Diaspora to whom this Epistle was addressed? Where do we find congregations composed of Jewish Christians?[4] All the Churches, with the sole exception of the Church of Jerusalem, mentioned in the Acts of the Apostles, were mixed Churches, where the Gentile element predominated. Now, in answer to this question, it is to be observed that the Christian Church, before the call of the Gentiles, was for ten years after Pentecost (until A.D. 43) composed entirely of Jews and proselytes. And we have undoubted evidence that during that period it was not confined to Jerusalem nor to the limits of Judea. We read of Jews belonging to fourteen nation-

[1] On the diffusion and commercial influence of the Jews at this time, see Herzfeld, *Handelsgeschichte der Juden*.

[2] Josephus, *Ant.* xii. 1. 1. His successor, Ptolemy Philadelphus, was a great patron of the Jews. A large portion of Alexandria was assigned to the Jews. *Ant.* xiv. 7. 2.

[3] Josephus, *Ant.* xiv. 7. 2.

[4] The difficulty of accounting for the existence of these Jewish Christian Churches is urged as an objection by De Wette and Davidson (*Introduction to the Study of the N. T.*, second edition, p. 311) against the authenticity of the Epistle, and by Wiesinger against its early date.

alities—Parthians, Medes, Elamites, the dwellers of Mesopotamia, and in Judea and Cappadocia, in Pontus, and Proconsular Asia, Phrygia, Pamphylia, in Egypt, and in the parts of Libya about Cyrene, and strangers of Rome, Cretes and Arabians—being present at Jerusalem on that remarkable Pentecost when the Holy Spirit was visibly poured out upon the apostles, and when thousands of Jews and proselytes were converted to the faith (Acts ii. 9–11). Many of these converts would carry the seeds of Christianity to their native lands, and in many of these lands the Jews of the Dispersion were numerous. A few years afterwards, in consequence of the persecution that arose on the death of Stephen, the disciples were all scattered abroad throughout the regions of Judea and Samaria (Acts viii. 1); and some of those dispersed "travelled as far as Phœnicia, and Cyprus, and Antioch, preaching the word to none but to Jews only" (Acts xi. 19). And, before the call of the Gentiles, numerous Christians were in Damascus (Acts ix. 2); mention is made of Christian teachers belonging to Cyprus and Cyrene (Acts xiii. 1); and at an early period the Christian Church must have been planted at Rome. The numbers of Jewish Christians are stated in various parts of the Acts to have been very considerable, and James could say to Paul: "Thou seest, brother, how many myriads of Jews there are which believe; and they are all zealous of the law" (Acts xxi. 20). Thus Christianity was diffused among the Jews of the Dispersion at an early period; and if we suppose that this Epistle was written before the gospel was preached to any extent among the Gentiles, as we shall afterwards show to be the case, there must have been numerous Churches composed of Jewish Christians beyond the limits of Judea. It is to these Churches of the Dispersion that the Epistle of James is addressed; and as this Epistle was written in Greek, it would be primarily addressed to the Greek Jews or Hellenists, who had embraced Christianity, and who in all probability were chiefly congregated in the countries in closest proximity to Judea, namely Phœnicia, Syria, Cilicia, and Proconsular Asia.

But it will be asked, What has become of these Jewish Christian Churches? Although all the writers of the New

Testament, with the possible exception of Luke, were Jews; yet it is a remarkable fact that none of the great Fathers of the early Church belonged to that nation. Almost the only one of the early Fathers who was of Jewish origin, and the fragments of whose writings are preserved in the Church History by Eusebius, is Hegesippus.[1] The after history of the Jewish Christians is very interesting. Until the call of the Gentiles, the Christian Church was entirely Jewish; but, after that call, it became preponderantly Gentile. Many of the converted Jews would renounce Judaism, regarding the Jewish law as abolished. It would, however, appear that most of them, and among them the original apostles (at least at first), and especially James the Lord's brother to the end of his life, continued in the practice of the Jewish rites.[2] Many of the Christian Jews looked with suspicion on the Gentile converts, and taught the necessity of circumcision and the observance of the law of Moses for salvation (Acts xv. 1). Among these were those Judaizing teachers who everywhere opposed the preaching of Paul, and sought to turn away the disciples from the faith. During the lives of the apostles the views of these bigoted Jewish Christians would be kept within bounds; but still they formed a distinct class in the Church. The destruction of Jerusalem by Titus gave a great blow to Jewish Christianity, as it rendered the performance of many of their rites impossible; and it is probable that in consequence of this many of the Jewish Christians renounced their distinctive customs, and became absorbed among the Gentile Christians. Still, however, even after the Jewish war, the Church of Jerusalem continued for some time to be Jewish Christian, presided over by bishops of the circumcision.[3] The revolt of the

[1] Even the Jewish origin of Hegesippus has been questioned. Eusebius expressly calls him "a convert from the Hebrews" (*Hist. Eccl.* iv. 22). Bishop Lightfoot, with considerable plausibility, conjectures that Clemens Romanus was a man of Jewish parentage, on the ground chiefly of his knowledge of the O. T., as seen in the numerous quotations from it in his Epistle. *The Epistles of St. Clement of Rome,* pp. 263-265.

[2] It is an interesting problem to inquire to what extent the Christian Jews practised the rites of Judaism. They practised circumcision, avoided unclean meats, kept the Sabbath, attended the Jewish festivals, but we do not see how they could continue to offer sacrifices.

[3] James was succeeded by Simeon the son of Cleophas, who is represented as

Jews under Barcocheba in the reign of Hadrian (A.D. 132) was another blow to Jewish Christianity. After the suppression of this revolt the Jews were forbidden under pain of death to reside in the Roman colony Aelia Capitolina,[1] which was erected on the ruins of Jerusalem; and consequently the Church in that city became Gentile.[2] Eusebius informs us that "when the Church was collected there of the Gentiles, the first bishop after those of the circumcision was Marcus."[3] Thus Gentile Christianity possessed the seat of the mother Church of Jewish Christianity.

Justin Martyr (A.D. 150) states that in his time there were numerous Jewish Christians who still preserved their national distinctions. Of these he mentions two classes: the one moderate Jewish Christians, who observed circumcision and other rites of Judaism, but did not seek to impose them on the Gentiles, nor regarded them as essential to salvation; the other, the strict Jewish Christians, who held no intercourse with the Gentile Christians unless they were circumcised, and who may be regarded as the successors of the Judaizing Christians, the opponents of Paul. "Some," he remarks, "wish to observe such institutions as were given by Moses, from which they expect some virtue, but live with other Christians, not inducing them either to be circumcised like themselves, or to keep the Sabbath, or to observe other such ceremonies; but others wished to compel those Gentiles who believe in Christ to live in all respects according to the law given by Moses, or do not choose to associate with them."[4]

It is evident that the strict Jewish Christians, holding such extreme views and refusing to hold communion with the Gentile Christians, could not long remain connected with the catholic Church; and hence toward the close of the second century they either separated from the Church of their own

---

the cousin of our Lord. Eusebius gives a list of fifteen bishops of Jerusalem to the time of Hadrian. All these, he states, were of the circumcision (*Hist. Eccl.* iv. 5). It is doubtful whether these bishops resided at Jerusalem or at Pella, to which the Christian Jews retired after the destruction of their city.

[1] So called in honour of the Emperor Aelius Hadrian.
[2] Ritschl, *Entstehung der altk. Kirche*, p. 257.   [3] *Hist. Eccl.* iv. 6.
[4] *Dial. cum Tryph.* chap. xlvii.

accord or were cast out. They are known in Church history as Ebionites.[1] The first who mentions this sect is Irenaeus (A.D. 180): "Those who are called Ebionites agree that the world was made by God; but their opinions with respect to the Lord are similar to those of Cerinthus and Carpocrates.[2] They use the Gospel according to Matthew only, and repudiate the Apostle Paul, maintaining that he was an apostate from the law. As to the prophetical writings, they endeavour to expound them in a somewhat singular manner; they practise circumcision, persevere in the observance of those customs which are enjoined by the law, and are so Judaic in their style of life that they even adore Jerusalem, as if it were the house of God."[3] The Ebionites, when they separated from the Christian Church, adopted various heretical opinions. They not only maintained that the Mosaic law was binding on all Christians alike, but they held low views of the person of Christ, denied His divinity, regarding Him as the Son of Mary and Joseph, and rejected all the Epistles of Paul. Still, however, there seems to have been a diversity of opinion among them. Origen (A.D. 230) observes that among the Ebionites there were two classes, those who acknowledged, with Christians in general, that Jesus was born of a virgin; and those who denied this, and maintained that He was begotten like other human beings.[4] And the same distinction among the Ebionites is made by Eusebius (A.D. 325). "The Ebionites," he observes, "cherish low and mean opinions of Christ; for they consider Him a plain and common man, superior to others only by His advances in virtue. Others, however, of the same name, avoid the absurdity of these opinions, not denying that the Lord was born of a virgin."[5]

[1] According to Tertullian, the Ebionites were the disciples of a heretic named Ebion. But it is much more probable that the word is derived from אֶבְיוֹן, *poor*, and that it is an appellative. Eusebius observes: "They are properly called Ebionites, as those who cherished low and mean opinions of Christ." But it is more probable that they received their name on account of the poverty of their condition, or because they practised voluntary poverty.
[2] Both of these heretics asserted that Christ was a mere man.
[3] *Adv. hær.* i. 26. 2. So also Hippolytus, *Refutat. Omn. hær.* vii. 22.
[4] *Contra Celsum*, v. 61.
[5] *Hist. Eccl.* iii. 27. Gieseler identifies Eusebius' two classes of Ebionites with the Ebionites and Nazarenes.

Several of the Ebionites seem also to have adopted Gnostic views; and some of the Gnostic sects are clearly connected with Ebionism.[1] In the time of Epiphanius (A.D. 348), the Ebionites are represented as very numerous, not confined to Palestine and the neighbouring countries, but found in Cyprus, Asia Minor, and even Rome. After this they gradually diminished in numbers, until in the middle of the fifth century they became extinct, having, it is probable, relapsed into pure Judaism, with which they had more affinities than with Christianity.[2]

The moderate Jewish Christians, who still retained their Jewish customs inside of the Christian Church, were, as may be imagined, few in number. They are known in ecclesiastical history under the name of Nazarenes.[3] Justin Martyr represents them as weak Christians who still held to Jewish customs, and had not attained to the liberty of the gospel.[4] These Jewish Christians cherished no antipathy to Paul, and acknowledged his Epistles as part of the word of God; they regarded Christ as a divine being, born of a virgin; they lamented the unbelief of their fellow-countrymen, and looked forward to their conversion, and to the millennial reign of Christ on earth. Accordingly they were not properly heretics, but stunted Christians. Little notice is taken of them in the writings of the Fathers, probably on account of the smallness of their numbers. The name Nazarenes is first mentioned by Epiphanius, who ranks them as heretics;[5] whilst Jerome and other Christian Fathers considered them as orthodox, though

---

[1] Cerinthus appears to have been a Jew; and the Elchasaites, mentioned by Hippolytus (*Refutat. Omn. hær.* ix. 9), were a Jewish Gnostic sect. The Ebionites are distinguished by ecclesiastical writers as Ebionites proper or Pharisaic Ebionites, and Essene or Gnostic Ebionites.

[2] For an account of the Ebionites, see art. "Ebionism" in Smith's *Dictionary of Christian Biography*. Lechler's *Das apostolische Zeitalter*, pp. 449-473 [translation of 3rd ed. vol. ii. pp. 260-292]. Lightfoot's dissertation on "Paul and the Three" in his *Commentary on the Galatians*. Schaff's *Church History*, vol. i. pp. 210-218. Gieseler's *Church History*, vol. i. pp. 133 ff., E. Tr. Mansell's *Gnostic Heresies*, pp. 110-128.

[3] This name appears at first to have been applied to Christians in general (Acts xxiv. 5), and was afterwards restricted to the Jewish Christians.

[4] *Dial. cum Tryph.* chap. xlvii. Jerome observes of them, "that wishing to be Jews and Christians alike, they were neither the one nor the other."

[5] *Hær.* xxix. 7.

imbued with Jewish notions.[1] According to Epiphanius, they resided in Syria and Decapolis, about Pella, and in the land of Bashan; here they lived among the Jews entirely cut off from the Gentile Christian Churches, and Augustine remarks that their number in his time was very insignificant.[2]

IV. THE DESIGN AND CONTENTS OF THE EPISTLE.

The design of this Epistle has been variously understood. Some have assigned to it a *polemical* design. They suppose that it was written with direct reference to the views of Paul concerning justification, either in opposition to these or to correct their perversion. If the teaching be anti-Pauline, then this is a presumption of the spuriousness of the Epistle; but, as we shall afterwards maintain, this opinion is unfounded.[3] If the aim of the Epistle be to correct the perversion of Paul's views, then the design is polemical. "This Epistle," observes Bishop Wordsworth, "is in some respects supplementary to the Epistles of Paul to the Galatians and the Romans."[4] But this is a mistaken notion. The polemical section of the Epistle occupies only a small space (Jas. ii. 14–26), whilst throughout there is a remarkable absence of doctrine.—Others maintain that the design of the Epistle was *political.* This is the view entertained by Lange. According to him, the primary object of the Epistle was to warn the Jewish Christians against the fanatical and revolutionary spirit of the Jews, and its secondary object was to warn the Jews against being drawn into revolt by the hostility and oppression of the Romans.[5] But although undoubtedly there are in the Epistle warnings against a revolutionary spirit,—protests against wars and fightings,—yet these constitute but a small portion of the

---

[1] Hieronym. *ep. ad Augustin.* 89.
[2] Lechler supposes that the Nestorian Christians in Kurdistan, described by Dr. Grant, may be the representatives of the Nazarenes, *Das apostolische Zeitalter,* p. 472.
[3] See dissertation on the Pauline and Jacobean views of justification.
[4] *Preface to the Epistle of James.* The view also of Ewald, *Geschichte des Volkes Israel,* sechster Band, pp. 610, 611 [E Tr. vol. vii. p. 453].
[5] Lange's *Commentary on James,* p. 20, E. Tr.

Epistle.—Others hold that the design of the Epistle was *ascetic*—the inculcation of the superior sanctity of poverty. According to Kern, the keynote of the Epistle is found in the distinctions drawn between the rich and the poor; on the one side there is the love of the world, the lust of the flesh, the struggle for earthly riches, and the oppression of the poor; on the other side the consciousness of inward dignity which Christianity confers on the poor, and their exaltation in the sight of God. Throughout the Epistle the rich are denounced and threatened, whilst the poor are praised and comforted.[1] Certainly there are throughout the Epistle severe denunciations against the rich oppressors, but these are accounted for from the condition of the readers of the Epistle; there is no denunciation of the rich on account of their riches, nor any commendation of the poor on account of their poverty.

The design of the Epistle was neither polemical, nor political, nor ascetic, but *ethical*, and was occasioned by the circumstances in which the readers were placed. The Jewish Christians were as a class poor; not many rich men among the Jews had embraced the gospel. As Christians they were exposed to much persecution from their fellow-countrymen; they would be regarded as apostates, members of the hated sect of the Nazarenes. Accordingly they were dragged before the judgment-seat; they were imprisoned; they were deprived of their goods. On account of their trials, they were strongly tempted to renounce Christianity, and to relapse into their former Judaism. They carried the spirit of Jewish covetousness with them into the Christian Church; they were eagerly desirous of riches, showed even in their religious assemblies an obsequious attention to the rich, and by their actions declared that they preferred the friendship of the world to the friendship of God. This worldly spirit was the occasion of bitter strife among themselves; and that charity, which is

---

[1] Kern's *Brief Jakobi*, p. 61. So also, somewhat similarly, Reuss observes: "The fundamental thesis of the Epistle of James is the antagonism between the friendship of the world and the friendship of God: the one procuring an illusive and momentary good, but predoomed and certainly fatal to those who seek it; the other inseparable from suffering and tribulation in the time present, but happy in hope and secure of reward." *History of Christian Theology in the Apostolic Age*, vol. i. p. 416, E. Tr.

the spirit of the gospel, was in a great measure absent. Accordingly the Epistle is adapted to this condition of the readers. It seeks to comfort them amid the trials to which they were exposed, but especially to correct the errors of practice into which they had fallen, and to admonish them of the faults to which they were addicted. James presupposes the great truths and facts of Christianity as known, and builds upon them practical Christianity. He dwells upon the government of the tongue, the sin of worldliness, the observance of the moral law; he shows the utter worthlessness of a faith which is destitute of works, and of a love which expends itself in benevolent wishes; and he inculcates the principles of that pure and undefiled religion which consists in doing good to others, and in keeping ourselves pure in this world.

There is in this Epistle a singular absence of dogma, which has prejudiced many against it. Luther, in particular, adduces this feature as an objection to the Epistle. James does not insist on the resurrection of Christ, on the atonement, or on the promise of the Spirit. Our Lord's sufferings are hardly alluded to; even the name of our Saviour only occurs twice (Jas. i. 1, ii. 1). And generally the name Lord, when it occurs in this Epistle, does not apply to Christ, as it does in the Epistles of Paul, but is the translation of Jehovah.[1] There are, however, no germs of Ebionism in this Epistle; there is nothing at variance with the exalted and divine nature of Christ. James calls himself "the servant of God and of the Lord Jesus Christ" (Jas. i. 1), thus maintaining a union between God and Christ; he speaks of Him as "the Lord of glory" (Jas. ii. 1), exalted above all human power and majesty; he mentions the worthy name, namely that of Christ (Jas. ii. 7), which is invoked upon Christians; he adverts to the second coming of the Lord (Jas. v. 7, 8), and evidently designates Him as the Judge of the world (Jas. v. 9). And, as has been already remarked, although there may be a comparative want of Christian dogma, there is no want of Christian ethics; for there is no writing

---

[1] Jas. v. 7, 8, 14 are exceptions to this remark, for κύριος in these verses evidently applies to Christ.

of the New Testament which is more deeply pervaded with the moral teaching of Christ.[1]

The absence of Christian dogma may be accounted for in two ways, either from the character of those to whom James wrote, or from the views which James himself possessed of Christianity at the time when he wrote. Both reasons, we consider, co-operated. Those to whom James wrote were already instructed in Christian doctrine; their Christianity throughout the Epistle is presupposed, nor do they appear to have been affected by doctrinal errors. But their character was defective and their conduct wrong. James endeavours to supply what was defective and to rectify what was wrong. Hence the practical tendency of this Epistle.—On the other hand, as this Epistle was written, as we shall afterwards endeavour to prove, at a very early stage of Christianity, certainly before the Council of Jerusalem, and perhaps even before the founding of the Gentile Church at Antioch, the Christian views of the apostles themselves were not fully developed on many points. They were ignorant, for example, of the fact that the Gentiles were to be admitted into the Christian Church without becoming proselytes to Judaism, until it was revealed to Peter by a miraculous vision. The "many things," which Christ during His life had not told His disciples (John xvi. 12), were only gradually revealed to them, and therefore at an early stage in the history of the Church there was not a full disclosure of Christian truth.[2] There is truth in the observation of Neander: "Christianity appears to James as true Judaism. The Spirit of Christ glorifies the forms of the Old Testament, and leads them to their true fulfilment. The standing-point which we perceive in the teaching of Christ, as set forth in the Sermon on the Mount, which contains the germs of everything essentially Christian, but where the abolition of the law is not explicitly declared, where everything proceeds from the idea of the kingdom of God, and the references of each of its principles to the Person of Christ, though everywhere implied as the basis and central

---

[1] "So wesentlich noch Lehre Christi, und so wenig noch Lehre von Christo," Beyschlag, *Der Brief des Jakobus*, p. 18.
[2] Salmon's *Introduction to the N. T.*, p. 583.

point, is not so expressed in the letter; this is the peculiar standpoint of James. In the development of the kingdom of God, where, as in all His works, equally in those of nature as of grace, there is no sudden abrupt transition; but where the law of gradation prevails throughout, he forms an important transition from the Old Testament to the New."[1]

Contents.—It is not easy to trace a connected train of thought in this Epistle. It resembles the Book of Proverbs in being a somewhat unconnected collection of maxims. James commences his Epistle by alluding to the trials and persecutions to which his readers were exposed, and exhorts them to patience under them, because if patiently endured they would be to them a means of moral improvement and a source of joy. He exhorts them to practical religion; he insists that they be not mere hearers, but doers of the word. Worship does not consist in the performance of ceremonies, but in active benevolence and personal purity (chap. i.). They must not envy the rich nor despise the poor, but practise religion without respect of persons, observing the royal law of love. Faith without love expressed in acts of benevolence is dead. To no purpose do they believe in God, unless their faith is accompanied with holiness (chap. ii.). They must cultivate all the parts of holiness—the government of the tongue, the subjection of the irascible passions, purity of heart, humility before God, and the resistance of evil (chap. iii., iv.). Their rich oppressors are then warned, and in a stern apostrophe James pronounces the doom that awaits them; whilst those suffering from their oppressions are exhorted to patient waiting for the coming of the Lord. In all things, and in every condition of life, they must abound in prayer and seek to reclaim the erring, for by so doing they will hide a multitude of sins (chap. v.).

The *style* of the Epistle is peculiar; it bears no resemblance to any other writing in the New Testament; it might be described as the Christian book of Proverbs. It is strikingly

[1] Neander on the *Epistle of James*, pp. 71, 72. See also Neander's *Planting*, vol. i. p. 366. This subject is afterwards more fully treated in the dissertation on "The References in the Epistle of James," particularly the relation of this Epistle to the Sermon on the Mount.

fresh and vivid; the writer is rich in illustrations which are always appropriate and impressive. A vein of poetry pervades it, so that it may almost be considered as a prose poem.[1] There is a remarkable vividness in his address; the persons whom James addresses are brought forward and spoken to as if present. The denunciations are uttered in the spirit of the Old Testament prophets.[2] With James practical religion is everything; no profession, no faith, no assertion is of any value without purity of heart and holiness of life. The writer of the Epistle answers to the character of James the Just.

De Wette objects to the Epistle on account of the purity of its Greek. "How," he asks, "could James write such Greek?"[3] And the same objection is made by Dr. Davidson. "The style of writing," he observes, "is too good for James, being pure, elevated, poetical, betraying the influence of Greek culture. All we know of him, and all that can reasonably be inferred from his education, training, and cast of mind, make it highly improbable that he could write *such* Greek as that of the Epistle."[4] And it is admitted by many that the Greek of this Epistle is remarkably pure, and beyond what could be expected from a Galilean Jew. "The Greek style of this Epistle," observes Alford, "must ever remain, considering the nature, place, and position of its writer, one of those difficulties with which it is impossible for us to deal satisfactorily."[5] Accordingly some critics, as Bolten and Bertholdt, suppose that this Epistle, being addressed to Jews, was originally written in Aramaic, and afterwards translated into Greek. But for this supposition there is no evidence; and as the

---

[1] Bishop Jebb entitles it "a prophetic poem;" and Bassett calls it "a Hebrew poem in a Greek garb."

[2] "Almost as much as the discourses of Christ in the Synoptics and in the Gospel of John, or as the sentences of the First Epistle of John, the exhortations of this Epistle have the ring of genuine prophetic utterances, conducting at once to the heart of the weighty subjects dealt with, and deciding everything from an elevation with the utmost calmness." Ewald, *History of Israel*, vol. vii. p. 454.

[3] De Wette's *Einleitung in das N. T.*, p. 272.

[4] *Introduction to the Study of the N. T.*, 1st edition, vol. i. p. 300 (2nd edition, vol. i. p. 309).

[5] *Greek Testament*, vol. iv. p. 108, 2nd edition. See also Credner's *Einleitung*, pp. 602, 603.

Epistle was addressed to Hellenists or Greek Jews, Greek would be its original language.[1] But the objection rests on mere subjective grounds. Other eminent critics, from a careful study of the language, arrive at a different opinion as to its purity and as to James' knowledge of Greek. Schleiermacher and Schmidt[2] find in James a great artificiality, which proves that the Greek language was foreign to him. And Michaelis remarks: "The language is more figurative than that of a Greek Epistle written by a classical author would be. There occur words which a correct Greek writer would not have used in those places. This perhaps may be ascribed to the circumstance that the author was not much accustomed to write Greek."[3] It is to be observed that the country of Galilee was bilingual, and that its inhabitants could speak both Greek and Aramaic. From the passage in Hegesippus we learn that the Jews wished James to address the people at the Passover in Greek: "Stand therefore upon a wing of the temple that thou mayst be conspicuous on high, and thy words may be easily heard by all the people; for all the tribes have come together on account of the Passover, with some of the Gentiles also."[4] The Apostles John and Peter wrote in Greek; and granting that the Greek of James is purer than that of these apostles, we have no means of ascertaining to what degree of perfection any writer attained.

V. TIME AND PLACE OF WRITING.

There is an extreme diversity of opinion concerning the date of the Epistle, but only two views need here be considered: that which fixes it after the composition of Paul's Epistles, and that which places it before the Council of Jerusalem.

[1] Ewald observes: "Though James might not himself be able to write good Greek, there could not be wanting Christians in Jerusalem who could put his thoughts and words into a good Grecian dress," *Geschichte des Volkes Israel*, zweiter Ausgabe, sechster Band, p. 610 [E. Tr. vol. vii. p. 452].

[2] W. Schmidt, *Der Lehrgehalt des Jacobus Briefes*, p. 33.

[3] Michaelis, *Introduction to the New Testament*, by Marsh, vol. vi. pp. 300, 301.

[4] Euseb. *Hist. Eccl.* ii. 23.

Those who suppose that the Epistle was designed to correct certain perversions of Paul's doctrine of justification by faith must assign to it a late date. They affirm that the language and the illustrations employed by James intimate an acquaintance with the writings of Paul, and that therefore his Epistle was written after the Epistles to the Romans and the Galatians. Such is the view adopted by Hug, De Wette, Credner, Bleek, Ewald, Lange, Guericke, Wiesinger, Pfleiderer, W. Schmidt, Reuss, Kern, Schmid, Lardner, Farrar, and Wordsworth. But there is no necessity for supposing that James was acquainted with Paul's doctrine of justification, any more than of supposing that Paul was acquainted with the Epistle of James. The expressions justification, faith and works, were not peculiarly Pauline ideas, but current in the Jewish schools, and the subject of justification was a matter frequently discussed by them.[1] The error which James corrects may not have been a doctrinal perversion of justification by faith, but the practical error of the Pharisees introduced into the Christian Church—that their external privileges as Jews, an orthodox creed and the performance of certain religious ceremonies, would procure salvation independently of personal holiness; that faith, unproductive of works, would justify.[2]

On the other hand, there are strong indications that this Epistle was written at an early period of the Christian Church. It is addressed to the Jewish Christians in the Dispersion; and it was only at an early period that Churches composed of Jewish Christians existed beyond the limits of Judea. There is no mention or indication of the existence of Gentile Christians: the impression left on reading the Epistle is that the Christian Church was then predominantly Jewish. There is not the slightest allusion to the great controversy concerning

[1] "Let us recollect," observes Neander, "that the Pauline phraseology formed itself from Judaism, from the Jewish-Greek diction; that it by no means created new modes of expression, but often only appropriated the old Jewish terms, employed them in new combinations, and animated them with a new spirit." Neander's *Planting*, vol. i. p. 362.

[2] Those who call in question the genuineness of the Epistle in general suppose the date of its composition to be post-apostolic. Thus Davidson, in his *Introduction to the Study of the N. T.*, places it about 69; Schenkel, between 70 and 80; Scholten and Blom, about 80; Hilgenfeld, about 90; Baur, Schwegler, and Zeller, in the second century.

circumcision, or to the question whether the Gentiles were obliged to observe the Mosaic law; from which it may be inferred that the circumstances which gave rise to the controversy and evoked this question had not arisen. Further, those to whom James wrote were suffering persecution; and we know that a great persecution arose among the Jewish Christians after the death of Stephen, which was not confined to Jerusalem, but extended beyond the boundaries of Judea to Damascus, to which city Saul was sent to persecute the disciples of the Lord. After this another persecution arose, when Herod Agrippa "stretched forth his hand to vex certain of the Church, and killed James the brother of John with the sword." The Jewish Christians would be fined and imprisoned by their fellow-countrymen, by whom they would be regarded as apostates from the religion of their fathers. For these reasons we consider that the Epistle was written before the Council of Jerusalem, about twelve years after the ascension (A.D. 45). An early date is assigned to the Epistle by Michaelis, Theile, Neander, Thiersch, Schneckenburger, Eichhorn, Hofmann, Erdmann,[1] Huther, Beyschlag, Schwegg, Ritschl, Schaff, Mangold,[2] Weiss, Lechler,[3] Davidson (*Introduction to N. T.*), Alford, Plumptre, Eadie, Lumby, and Salmon.

Several objections have been brought against this view. 1. It is asserted that the Epistle presupposes the development of the organization of the Church, which only occurred at a later period. Mention is made of a regularly organized congregation (ἐκκλησία), with elders (πρεσβύτεροι) attached to it (Jas. v. 14). But "elders" was the name given to office-bearers

[1] Erdmann supposes that the Epistle was written before the formation of the Gentile Christian Church at Antioch, when consequently almost all the Christians would be Jews and Jewish converts. *Der Brief des Jakobus*, p. 49.

[2] Mangold, in a long note, combats the opinion of Bleek, who held that the Epistle was composed not long before the death of James. *Einleitung*, pp. 706–708.

[3] Lechler formerly advocated a late date for the Epistle; but in the last edition of his *Das apostolische Zeitalter* he has changed his opinion. "The date of the Epistle," he observes, "belongs to the beginning of the apostolic Church. Though we once thought that the influence of the Pauline doctrine might be perceived in it, we have come to retract that opinion in consequence of continual converse with the work." E. Tr. vol. i. p. 290.

of the Jewish synagogue,[1] and our Lord Himself makes mention of the Christian community as an ἐκκλησία (Matt. xviii. 17). 2. Wiesinger objects to an early date of the Epistle, because the readers are treated "as those who are mature in doctrine," and because "the faults censured in their conduct are such as can only be understood on the supposition of a lengthened continuance of Christianity among the readers."[2] But it is to be remembered that the converts were not ignorant Gentiles, but Jews who had the advantage of a previous revelation; and the faults censured are the very faults of which we should antecedently conjecture that those Jewish converts would be guilty, being the faults of their previous unconverted Jewish state. 3. It is asserted that in the Epistle the name *Christian* is applied to believers as the worthy name by which they were called (Jas. ii. 7); but that name was not bestowed upon them until after the conversion of the Gentiles (Acts xi. 26). But this objection arises from a mistaken exegesis of the passage. James does not refer to the name *Christian* as an appellation of believers, but to the name *Christ* which was invoked upon them at their baptism.[3] 4. It is further objected that beyond the limits of Palestine there could have been few Jewish Christian Churches at such an early period to whom James could address his Epistle.[4] Whereas we have seen that it was precisely at this period, before the gospel was preached to any considerable extent to the Gentiles, that such Jewish Christian Churches existed: then the Jewish element was predominant; afterwards it was the Gentile element.

At the time when James wrote his Epistle, the Christian Church would be almost entirely composed of Jewish converts. The preaching to the Gentiles had just commenced. No dispute concerning circumcision had arisen. It may be that Paul and Barnabas had not set out on their first great missionary journey. The name *Christian* had not been coined to dis-

[1] The elders in the Christian Church are mentioned before the mission of Paul to the Gentiles, Acts xi. 30.

[2] Wiesinger's *Der Brief des Jakobus*, p. 38.

[3] The correct translation of the verse is, "Do they not blaspheme that goodly name which was named on you?" that is, which was invoked upon you, namely, at your baptism, when baptized into the name of Christ.

[4] Wiesinger, *Der Brief des Jakobus*, p. 39.

tinguish believers from Jews. Believers would still be regarded by the Gentiles as a Jewish sect, distinguished from their countrymen by their belief that Jesus was the Messiah, the Son of God. There was sufficient time for the formation of Churches or communities of Jewish Christians among the Jews of the Dispersion. Twelve years had elapsed since the outpouring of the Spirit at Pentecost; and Christian teachers had, at a very early period, carried the gospel to Phœnicia, Syria, Cilicia, and Cyprus. We regard this Epistle, then, as one of the earliest, if not, as Schneckenburger remarks, the very earliest writing of the New Testament. We have here an inspired document of primitive Christianity—allied to the simple teaching of the Master—before the religion of Christ was developed by the doctrinal statements of Paul and the profound intuitions of John.

The place of composition was Jerusalem. Here James, the Lord's brother, resided as the head of the mother Church; and from this, as from a centre, he wrote his Epistle to the Jewish Christians of the Dispersion. In this Epistle the mother Church addresses her offspring. Hug observes that the physical notices observable in the Epistle correspond to the environment of the author;[1] and the same remark is made by Dean Plumptre, who observes that the local colouring of the Epistle indicates with sufficient clearness where the author lived.[2]

The Epistle of James has been often commented on. The most important commentaries are those of Pott (Göttingen 1810), Schneckenburger (Stuttgart 1832), Theile (Leipsic 1833), Kern (Tübingen 1838), Stier (1845: translated Edinburgh 1871), Neander (translated Edinburgh 1851), Wiesinger (Königsberg 1854: translated New York 1858), Lange (in Lange's *Bibelwerk*, Bielefeld 1862: translated by Mombert, New York 1867), Brückner (Leipsic 1865), W. Schmidt (Leipsic 1869),[3] Huther (third edition, Göttingen 1870: translated Edinburgh 1882), Ewald (Göttingen 1870), Hofmann (Nordlingen 1876), Erdmann (Berlin

---

[1] *Introduction to the N. T.*, vol. ii. p. 549 ff.   [2] *Epistle of James*, p. 43.
[3] This valuable work is not so much a commentary as a monograph in Biblical theology.

1880), Beyschlag (Göttingen 1882),[1] Schwegg (Munich 1883); and in our country, Bassett (London 1876), Plumptre (in the Cambridge series: Cambridge 1878),[2] Dean Scott (in the *Speaker's Bible*, London 1881), Gloag (in Schaff's *Commentary*, Edinburgh 1883), besides the valuable notes contained in Alford's *Greek Testament*.

DISSERTATION I.

THE PAULINE AND JACOBEAN VIEWS OF JUSTIFICATION.[3]

The Jacobean doctrine of justification, as stated in the second chapter of this Epistle, is apparently at variance with the view of Paul. The instrumental cause of our justification, according to Paul, appears to be faith without the co-operation of works, whilst according to James it appears to be faith in combination with works. Paul, in the Epistle to the Romans, declares that "a man is justified by faith without the deeds of the law" (Rom. iii. 28). In his Epistle to the Galatians he makes the same declaration: "Knowing that a man is not justified by the works of the law, but by the faith of Jesus Christ, even we have believed in Jesus Christ, that we might be justified by the faith of Christ, and not by the works of the law: for by the works of the law shall no flesh be justified"

[1] Although professedly a revised edition of Huther's Commentary, yet it may be regarded as an independent work.

[2] This small manual of Dean Plumptre deserves special consideration on account of its excellence.

[3] This subject is more or less fully discussed in Baur's *Apostel Paulus* (die paulinische Rechtfertigungslehre und die des Jakobus), vol. ii. p. 322 ff. [E. Tr. vol. ii. p. 297 ff.]. Beyschlag's *Jakobus*, p. 146 ff. Brückner's *Brief des Jakobus*, p. 237 ff. Erdmann's *Jakobus*, p. 216 ff. Kern's *Brief des Jakobus*, p. 42 ff. Hofmann's *Schriftbeweis*, vol. i. pp. 556-563. W. Schmidt's *Der Lehrgehalt des Jacobus Briefes*, p. 157 ff. Hug's *Introduction to the New Testament*, vol. ii. p. 555 ff. Lechler's *Das apostolische Zeitalter*, p. 252 ff. Huther's *Brief des Jakobus*, p. 143 ff. Mangold's edition of Bleek's *Einleitung*, pp. 709-712. Neander's *Planting of Christianity*, vol. ii. p. 15 ff. Laurence's *Bampton Lectures* for 1804, Lect. v. and vi. Farrar's *Early Days of Christianity*, chap. xxiii. (St. Paul and St. James on Faith and Works). Schaff's *Popular Commentary*, vol. iv. p. 123 ff.

(Gal. ii. 16). And to the Ephesians he writes: "For by grace are ye saved through faith; and that not of yourselves: it is the gift of God: not of works, lest any man should boast" (Eph. ii. 8, 9).—James, on the other hand, affirms that faith must be combined with works to render it justifying: "What doth it profit, though a man say he hath faith, and have not works? can that faith save him?[1] Faith, if it have not works, is dead, being alone. Wilt thou know, O vain man, that faith without works is dead? Ye see then how that by works a man is justified, and not by faith only. For as the body without the spirit is dead, so faith without works is dead also" (Jas. ii. 14, 17, 20, 24, 26). And this apparent antagonism is strikingly displayed in the instance of the justification of Abraham, which both adduce as confirming or illustrating their respective statements. Paul ascribes the justification of Abraham to his faith: "If Abraham were justified by works, he hath whereof to glory, but not before God. For what saith the Scripture? Abraham believed God, and it was counted unto him for righteousness" (Rom. iv. 2, 3). Whereas James ascribes the justification of Abraham to his works: "Was not Abraham our father justified by works, when he offered Isaac his son upon the altar?" (Jas. ii. 21). The one seems to exclude works entirely in the matter of justification; the other appears to assert that works are as essential to our justification as faith. In short, these writers appear to be establishing two opposite doctrines: the one, the Protestant doctrine of justification by faith; the other, the Romish doctrine of the merit of good works.[2]

Accordingly, some suppose that there is not only an apparent, but a real contradiction between the views of these writers, so that the one affirms what the other denies: Paul maintaining the doctrine of justification by faith, and James

---

[1] *Revised Version.* So ought the words: μὴ δύναται ἡ πίστις σῶσαι αὐτόν; to be rendered. The article must receive its full force: literally, "Can the faith save him?" that is, the particular faith which such a man possesses. Faith certainly does save; but not *the* faith to which James alludes.

[2] This apparent opposition in doctrine is clearly seen by comparing the respective statements of James and Paul: ἐξ ἔργων δικαιοῦται ἄνθρωπος, καὶ οὐκ ἐκ πίστεως μόνον (Jas. ii. 24); and: λογιζόμεθα οὖν πίστει δικαιοῦσθαι ἄνθρωπον, χωρὶς ἔργων νόμου (Rom. iii. 28).

the doctrine of justification by works. According to them, James wrote for the express purpose of opposing Paul, or at least of entering his dissent from the views maintained by that apostle. Luther, as is well known, supposed that the views of James were opposed to those of Paul;[1] and in recent times this opinion has been adopted by Baur, Schwegler, Holtzmann, Hilgenfeld, Rauch, Davidson (*Introduction to the Study of the N. T.*), and to some extent by Hug.[2] Baur is comparatively moderate in his views. He supposes that the Epistle of James was written by some unknown author about the beginning of the second century, with a conciliatory design of mediating between the views of Paul and those of the Judaizing Christians. "The doctrine of this Epistle," he observes, "must be considered as intended to correct Paul. But what we have here is no longer the original harsh and rigid opposition of Judaism to Christianity, as we meet it in the Epistles of Paul; the opposition has softened down, the harsher demands of the law are now departed from. There is nothing here to remind us of the Judæo-Christianity of James, a man whom we know from Gal. ii. to have been impregnated with all the obstinacy of traditionary Judaism, and to have been the uncompromising upholder of every Jewish institution, even of circumcision.... The main point is now to maintain Judaism on its spiritual side as the religion of practical conduct or moral action."[3] Others, however, and

---

[1] "Many," he observes, "have endeavoured to reconcile the Epistles of James and Paul. Philip Melancthon refers to it in his *Apology*, but not with earnestness; for 'faith justifies,' and 'faith does not justify,' are plain contradictions." Quoted by Huther from Luther's *Table Talk*, Plochmann's edition, vol. lxii. p. 127.

[2] Hug, in his *Introduction to the New Testament*, contradicts himself. In one place he says: "The Epistle of James was therefore written intentionally against Paul, and against the doctrine that faith effects justification and divine grace in man" (vol. ii. p. 557); whilst in another place he says: "If James attacked the erroneous interpretations which they (the Jews) made of Paul and his proofs, can it be laid to his charge that he was one who did not comprehend or understand Paul? James did not raise himself up against Paul." "Each, on his side, has seen and judged correctly, and neither assails the notions and representations, nor disparages the doctrine of the other" (vol. ii. p. 583). We have not been able to compare these statements with the original, and are inclined to suspect that the translation is faulty.

[3] Baur's *Apostel Paulus*, vol. ii. p. 338 [E. Tr. vol. ii. pp. 309, 311].

especially the disciples of Baur, go much farther, and affirm that in this Epistle Jewish Christianity, as taught by the apostles of the circumcision, finds its full expression in opposition to Gentile Christianity as taught by Paul; in short, that the doctrinal systems of these two writers (James and Paul) are in sharp antagonism, and that two distinct phases of Christianity were taught in the apostolic Church. Dr. Davidson, who may be considered the English representative of the Tübingen school, remarks: "The Pauline doctrine of justification is combated in this Epistle. Doubtless it had been abused by many. James opposes the thing itself, not its abuse. Instead of attacking erroneous interpretations which the Jewish converts deduced from Paul's writings, he attacks the real doctrine. The Pauline doctrine of justification was unacceptable to Jewish Christians, whose modes of thinking could not be readily reconciled to it."[1] If this were the case, if there were not only an apparent but an actual contradiction, if there were two gospels,—the one "the gospel of the circumcision" as taught by James, and the other "the gospel of the uncircumcision" as taught by Paul,—this discovery would seriously impair the authority of Scripture, and shake the very foundations of Christianity.[2]

Others affirm that there is no contradiction in the views of Paul and James; that the difference is one of expression only; that the one sacred writer supplements the other, and that thus there is a fuller development of Christian doctrine. Such was the view adopted by Calvin[3] and the Reformed Church; and the same opinion has in modern times been

[1] Davidson's *Introduction to the Study of the New Testament*, vol. i. (1st edition) pp. 293, 294. Dr. Davidson does not enter into any examination of this difference of view, but merely asserts that the contradiction is self-evident. "It is," he observes, "unnecessary to show that the doctrine of justification by faith which Paul preached, and that of justification by works which James sets forth, are irreconcilable" (p. 292). But in his *Introduction to the New Testament*, vol. iii. p. 330, he asserts that "James's doctrine of justification by works, and Paul's by faith, are quite reconcilable." Credner, although he defends the genuineness of the Epistle, yet supposes that the views of Paul are combated in it. *Einleitung*, p. 601.

[2] Of course there is another alternative, supposing the contradiction proved, namely, that the Epistle of James is uncanonical.

[3] Calvin in *Jacobi Ep.* ii. 21.

maintained by Neander, Hofmann,[1] Wiesinger, Lange, Hengstenberg, Philippi, Bleek, Huther, Theile, Beyschlag, Sieffert, Reuss,[2] Erdmann, Guericke, Schaff, Brückner;[3] and among English theologians by Alford, Plumptre, Bishop Lightfoot, Dean Scott, Salmon, and Farrar. According to some of these theologians, James wrote for the purpose of correcting the perversions which had been made of Paul's doctrine; but according to most of them, the Epistle was written without any reference to the views of Paul. The Epistle is by most conceived to have been an earlier phase of Christianity than that which was afterwards developed by the great apostle of the Gentiles; and the terms justification, faith and works are considered not to have been taken from the Pauline Epistles, but to be technical terms employed by Jewish writers.[4]

There is a third class of theologians who adopt a middle view. They suppose that there is a certain diversity of doctrine in the writings of Paul and James, but that this does not exclude a higher unity. The sacred writers view the doctrine of justification in different lights and from different standpoints, and hence the diversity of expression; but there underlies this diversity of expression a harmonizing principle, or at least the points of deviation in the statements of these writers are unimportant. Such are the views adopted by Kern, Woldemar Schmidt, Ch. F. Schmid, Weizsäcker, Lechler,[5]

---

[1] For Hofmann's peculiar views, see his *Schriftbeweis*, vol. i. p. 556 ff.

[2] "The two apostles," observes Reuss, "are on totally different grounds, not opposed to each other; and this the less, as there are plenty of passages to be found in Paul where he speaks just as James does." *Geschichte d. heil. Schrift. N. T.* p. 133.

[3] Brückner's views are not clear; in one part of his commentary he asserts that there is a reconciling principle between the views of Paul and James, whilst in another part he would appear to assert that Luther and others have correctly recognised a contradiction between James and Paul. *Brief des Jakobus*, p. 239.

[4] See on this point Lightfoot's *Commentary on the Galatians:* "On the faith of Abraham," p. 156 ff. 3rd edition. Weber, *Alt-palästinische Theologie.*

[5] Lechler observes: "We recognise an opposition between the statements of these two writers; but, at the same time, we are convinced that this is only subordinate and unessential, whilst the points of agreement between these two doctrinal statements are much more important than the points of difference." *Das apostolische Zeitalter*, p. 256, zweite Auflage [E. Tr. of 3rd edition, vol. ii. p. 243].

and Delitzsch.¹ Thus Kern observes: "The relation between Paul and James with reference to this doctrinal point is clear. With Paul faith, because it justifies, is the source of good works; with James faith, because it is the source of good works, and proves in them its own vitality, is the faith that justifies. With Paul, justification is conditioned by faith, or justification and faith are both present in the man who is justified by faith, and works proceed from justification by faith. With James, justification is conditioned by the moral conduct produced by faith; justification proceeds from works in which faith proves itself a living faith."² And still more clearly Woldemar Schmidt thus states the points of difference: " 1. According to James, faith is only made perfect by works; but according to Paul, faith, even without works, as the self-surrender of the man to God's grace in Christ, as the apprehension of the atonement accomplished in the death of Christ, is perfect faith. 2. According to James, therefore, justification is conditioned by faith and works; but according to Paul, a man is justified by faith without the works of the law."³ Similarly also Ch. F. Schmid observes: " The deepest ground of difference between them is that James looks upon faith without works as dead, and that Paul most fully recog-

---

¹ Delitzsch almost goes the length of asserting that the view of James is opposed to that of Paul, and does not admit of reconciliation. "In Paul's system," he says, "πίστις and δικαίωσις precede ἔργα, while for James πίστις and ἔργα precede δικαίωσις. Paul knows of no works pleasing to God before justification; James makes justification depend on antecedent good works." He adds: "In comparing the doctrines of each with the other, we must not forget that James the Lord's brother was not an apostle, and acknowledge that his most precious Epistle is on this doctrine of justification one-sided." *Commentary on the Ep. to the Hebrews*, vol. ii. pp. 273, 274, E. Tr.

² Kern's *Jakobus-Brief*, p. 47.

³ Schmidt's *Lehrgehalt des Jacobus-Briefes*, p. 182. Along with these two points of difference Schmidt mentions the three following points of agreement:— 1. Both recognise the same idea in justification; with both, justification is a judicial act of God, in which God declares the sinner as righteous. 2. Both consider faith, so far as it is living, as combined with works; according to James, works serve for the completion of faith; according to Paul, for the evidence of faith. 3. Both deny entirely a justification by works. James, as well as Paul, refers salvation exclusively to the grace of God (i. 17, δώρημα), recognising regeneration as the creative act of God in man (i. 18). We would recommend this work of Schmidt to the theological student as the most suggestive work we have met with on the theology of James.

nises the vitality of faith in itself, even before it has produced works, that it may be and is a principle of life so far as it embraces Christ, and exactly so far a condition of justification, apart from the fact whether it has been developed in works."[1]

Various methods of interpretation have been adopted to reconcile the apparent discrepancy in the views of Paul and James. These methods differ according to the different meanings attached to the three principal terms—justification, works, and faith.

Some, as Calvin, Calovius, and in recent times Michaelis, Hofmann, Thiersch, Wiesinger, Lange, and Philippi, suppose that the word *justification* is employed in different senses by the two apostles. Thus Calvin observes: "We must take notice of the twofold meaning of the word *justified;* Paul means by it the gratuitous imputation of righteousness before the tribunal of God; James, the manifestation of righteousness by the conduct, and that before men."[2] According to this view, Paul speaks of justification by faith in the sight of God, whilst James speaks of justification by works in the sight of man; the one referring to the justification of our persons, the other rather to the justification of our faith. Paul speaks of justification properly so called—the declaration of righteousness by God; James speaks of the manifestation or proof of that declaration. But it is evident from an attentive perusal of the passage that James speaks of justification in the sight of God: he is discussing the condition of the professed believer, not before men or before the Church, but before God; and thus he uses the term justification in the same sense as Paul does. To speak of justification in the sight of man, would be to assign a meaning to the term which it never has in the writings either of Paul or of James.

---

[1] Schmid's *Biblical Theology of the New Testament*, p. 346, E. Tr.

[2] *Jacobi Ep.* ii. 21. Similarly Lange observes that the term δικαιοῦν is used by Paul to describe an act "which transpires solely between God and the sinner in the tribunal of his consciousness;" but by James as "the declaration of righteousness in the consciousness of the theocratic congregation." *Commentary on James*, p. 85, E. Tr. Similarly Michaelis, *Introduction to the N. T.*, by Marsh, vol. vi. p. 305. Hofmann's *Schriftbeweis*, vol. i. p. 560 ff. Wiesinger on Jas. ii. 21.

Hengstenberg rightly recognises that the term δικαιοῦν has with Paul and James the same meaning; but he supposes that justification is a gradual process, and that Paul speaks of the commencement of justification which is by faith only, and James of the continuance or development of justification which is by faith confirmed or made perfect by works. As faith must prove and perfect itself by works, so justification is not imparted to man at once, but gradually; it is conditioned by the increase of faith, and the stages of justification correspond to the stages of our faith.[1] But this is to adopt the Romish notion of justification, and to confound it with sanctification. According to this view, our justification would be ultimately assigned to our works, which is in evident contradiction with the doctrine of Paul. Besides, it is to be observed that according to James, works do not perfect our justification or advance it from an imperfect to a more perfect stage, but make perfect our faith, which as a subjective feeling is capable of increase. Even justification at the last judgment is not more perfect than that by which God in this life absolves the sinner from his sins; his forgiveness is already complete, and he is already in a saved condition.

Huther, on the other hand, distinguishes between justification and salvation. He supposes that Paul intends a restoration to the favour of God, a full forgiveness, which is bestowed in this life whenever a man believes on Christ; whereas James intends the complete realization of this forgiveness, and that in all its fulness, by the bestowal of salvation at the day of judgment. "James," he observes, "has in view the justification that places believers at the last judgment in the full enjoyment of salvation; whereas Paul denotes by δικαιοῦσθαι the justification that even here in this world puts believers in a gracious relation toward God."[2] This opinion has also

---

[1] "Brief des Jakobus" in the *Evang. Kirchenz.* 1866, Nos. 93, 94. Hengstenberg affirms: "If by faith is understood genuine living faith, and by works genuine works proceeding from faith, justification by faith and justification by works can be taught without contradiction." This is evidently erroneous, because the justification of which Paul speaks is the cause, and in no sense the effect of works.

[2] Huther's *Der Brief des Jakobus*, p. 145, dritte Auflage [E. Tr. p. 142].

been adopted by Dean Scott.[1] According to this view, Paul by justification denotes that act of God by which forgiveness is adjudged to the sinner for the sake of Christ; and James, that act of God by which the believer is justified or acquitted at the day of judgment. James, it is asserted, uses the word justified (δικαιοῦν) in the sense of saved (σώζειν), as when he says: "What doth it profit, my brethren, though a man say he hath faith and have not works? Can that faith save him?" (Jas. ii. 14). And in this sense the term is also used by our Lord when He says, with evident reference to the day of judgment: "By thy words thou shalt be justified, and by thy words thou shalt be condemned" (Matt. xii. 37). Now, if this be the true meaning of the language of James, certainly there is not the slightest difference between his view and that of Paul; for whilst Paul always asserts that we shall be justified by faith, he is no less emphatic in declaring that we shall be judged by our works (2 Cor. v. 10). But the theory is untenable. The whole argument of James, and his use of the present δικαιοῦται (Jas. ii. 24), prove that he is speaking not of acquittal in the next world, but of justification in this life. Besides, the example of Abraham's justification, which was certainly in this life, is a refutation of the above opinion.[2]

A second class of theologians, as Theophylact, Oecumenius, and in recent times Knapp and Gebser, affirm that whilst the justification, about which the sacred writers discourse, is the same, namely, a declaration of righteousness in the sight of God, the *works*, which Paul excludes from justification, and which James combines with faith in justification, are different. Among this class there is a variety of views. Some consider that Paul speaks of works wrought in obedience

---

[1] Dean Scott in the *Speaker's Commentary*. "James's subject," he observes, "is not so much *justification*, as it is *judgment* by works."

[2] Huther endeavours to remove the objection to his view, derived from Abraham's justification, by remarking: "When James appeals to what happened to Abraham there is nothing unsuitable, for why should not that which God has done in a definite instance be regarded as a type and testimony of what He shall do at the future judgment? Moreover, this is completely appropriate, since to Abraham, by the address to him after the offering of Isaac, the promise which was before made to his faith was *rendered unchangeably firm at the close of his theocratic life.*" *Der Brief des Jakobus*, p. 140.

to the ceremonial law, whilst James speaks of works done in obedience to the moral law. Others think that Paul speaks of the works of the law (ἔργα τοῦ νόμου), which were unnecessary for justification, and James of the works of faith (ἔργα τῆς πίστεως), which were necessary. Others assert that Paul speaks of the works of the unregenerate done in an unconverted state, and James of the works of believers done in a state of grace. And undoubtedly there is a difference in their use of the term *works*. The works, of which Paul speaks, are legal works done without faith; whereas the works, of which James speaks, are evangelical works which arise from faith. But this cannot be the true solution of the difficulty. Paul excludes from his idea of justification not merely legal, but evangelical works; according to him, by no works whatever can a man be justified. Besides, evangelical works presuppose the previous existence of justifying faith, and can only be done by a man who is already in a state of justification; they do not precede, but follow justification.

A third class of theologians think that the *faith*, about which these sacred writers discourse, describes two different conceptions. Paul speaks of genuine faith, an active principle which manifests its reality by works, the consent of the will to the truths of the gospel; whereas James speaks of a mere speculative, inoperative faith, the assent of the understanding, a dead faith which is unaccompanied by works. This is the opinion which is adopted by most of those theologians who consider that there is a real harmony between the statements of Paul and James concerning justification; and it is on the lines of this opinion that we consider the true solution of the question is to be obtained.

In any solution we must not forget the peculiar characteristics of Paul and James, and the difference in their relations and characters. They stand in different relations to the law of Moses. Paul regarded the Mosaic law as abolished; and although he himself kept it and occasionally joined in its ceremonies, yet he does not appear to have been a strict observer of the law; he felt himself freed from its restrictions, and lived as a Gentile among the Gentiles. James, on the other hand, continued to the last a strict observer of the law of Moses; he was regular in his attendance as a worshipper in the temple; and whilst he taught that the Gentiles were freed from the Mosaic law, he appears to have considered that the Jews were under no obligation to separate themselves from the religion of their fathers.[1] Hence Paul would regard Christianity as the deliverance from the law; James would look upon it as the transfiguration of the law. The circumstances of their conversions also necessarily affected their views and characters. Paul was suddenly arrested and converted to the faith; a mighty crisis convulsed his soul; in three days he was transformed from a bitter persecutor to an ardent defender of Christianity. James, on the contrary, was gradually won over to the faith; with him the Spirit of the Lord was not in the earthquake, but in the still small voice; no sudden revolution appears to have taken place in his personal history; when he became a Christian there was no marked change in his outward conduct; the moral law became to him "the perfect law of liberty" (Jas. i. 25). Besides, their characters were different. Paul was ardent and zealous, he required faith in Christ as essential to salvation; James was calm and collected, he demanded holiness of all those who professed to be Christians. Paul was eminently doctrinal, and therefore faith occupied a prominent place in his theology; James was eminently practical, and therefore works occupied a prominent place in his teaching. Both agreed in ascribing justification to faith, and both asserted that the faith which justifies must be active; but they contemplated the subject from different points of view, and accordingly there is a difference in their expressions where there is no difference in their opinions. "James would hardly assert with Paul that a man is justified by faith without the works of the law, because he regarded faith as only efficacious when it is productive of works; and Paul would hardly assert with James that by works a man is justified and not by faith only, because he admitted of

---

[1] James even seems to indicate that if Paul had "taught the Jews which are among the Gentiles to forsake Moses, saying that they ought not to circumcise their children, neither to walk after the customs" (Acts xxi. 21), he would have acted imprudently.

no other kind of faith than one that was living and active."[1]

We must also attend to the difference of design in their discussions. They are arguing with different persons, and combating different errors. Paul is arguing against those who supposed that they could be justified by their works. His opponents were self-righteous Pharisees, who trusted in their own righteousness, and looked upon the observance of the law as the ground of their acceptance with God. He tells them that the only ground of justification by the law is perfect obedience, and that as this was unattainable, the law, instead of justifying, condemns them. On this ground he affirms that "by the deeds of the law there shall no flesh be justified in His sight" (Rom. iii. 20). He hence infers that the only method of justification is by faith in the righteousness of Christ. "Therefore we conclude that a man is justified by faith without the deeds of the law" (Rom. iii. 28). But by faith he evidently means genuine faith— not a mere profession of belief—not a passive assent of the understanding, but an active principle, such a faith as involves reliance on Christ, and leads a man to act as he believes—a faith which, as he elsewhere says, "works by love" (Gal. v. 6). James, on the other hand, is arguing against those professing Christians who supposed that they were justified by a bare orthodox profession. His opponents were those Jewish Christians who prided themselves on their external privileges, and considered that the mere profession of Christianity would ensure their justification. He tells them that the mere assent to the truths of Christianity will save no man; that faith if destitute of works is spurious and useless; and that, unless it be productive and living, it will be unavailing. The question which James discusses is not whether a man is justified partly by works and partly by faith, but whether a man who professes to be justified by faith, but whose faith is unaccompanied by good works, is really in a justified state. Faith alone justifies the sinner, but it must be a true faith, a faith which is proved, or rather

[1] Schaff's *Popular Commentary on the N. T.*, vol. iv. 124: The Epistle of James, by the author.

proves itself, to be genuine by good works. And therefore on this ground James affirms: "Ye see then how that by works a man is justified, and not by faith only" (Jas. ii. 24). Thus the designs of these two writers are different. Paul opposes Pharisaical legalism, the error of those who trusted for salvation to their works; James opposes Pharisaical antinomianism, the error of those who trusted to their religious knowledge and speculative faith.

Paul and James view justification from different standpoints. Paul discusses the question how a guilty sinner may be justified before God; James teaches us that no man living in sin can be justified whatever his profession may be. Paul answers the question of the awakened sinner, "What must I do to be saved?" James exhorts professing Christians to walk worthy of their calling. Paul, arguing with Pharisaical legalists, shows the worthlessness of their works; James, arguing with Pharisaical formalists, shows the worthlessness of their faith. Paul views justification from the divine standpoint, and teaches that God will only justify us by faith in the merits of His Son; James views it from the human standpoint, and teaches that the faith which justifies must be active and embody itself in good works.

Hence the true solution of the difficulty is that James and Paul employ the term *faith* in different senses; the former gives it a wider meaning than the latter. The faith to which Paul ascribes justification is represented by him as an active principle—a faith which not only supposes the assent of the understanding to the revelation of the gospel, but an acting upon that assent; in short, a reception of the gospel, an exercise of the will as well as of the understanding. Faith must prove that it is real, living, and sincere, by putting in practice the truths which it believes. And hence the apostle, in the same passage in which he excludes works from any concern in our justification, asserts their importance and indispensable obligation. "By grace are ye saved through faith; and that not of yourselves, it is the gift of God: not of works, lest any man should boast. For we are His workmanship, created in Christ Jesus unto good works, which God hath before ordained that we should walk in them"

(Eph. ii. 8–10). In the matter of justification Paul knows no other kind of faith than that which is genuine and active; an inactive faith is with him not faith, but faithlessness. His writings abound with precepts addressed to those who believe, thus connecting the faith which justifies with obedience to the law of God (Tit. iii. 8). It is by this faith, productive of works, that Paul says we are justified; and in this he is perfectly at one with James, who lays great stress on good works as a necessary accompaniment of saving faith.

James uses the term *faith* in a somewhat different sense. Whilst with Paul the term is limited to genuine and active faith, James uses it in a more general acceptation, so as to include theoretical as well as active faith. He speaks not only of genuine faith,—a firm confidence in God as the hearer of prayer (Jas. i. 6),—but also of a faith which is dead and unproductive, and consequently incapable of justifying. He compares such a faith to an inactive love which expends itself in good words and kind wishes, but never proceeds to works of benevolence (Jas. ii. 14–17). As this love is of no value, so neither is the faith of him who professes to believe the gospel, and yet does not walk up to his profession. James compares such a faith to that which the devils possess: "Thou believest that there is one God; thou doest well: the devils also believe and tremble. But wilt thou know, O vain man, that faith without works is dead" (Jas. ii. 19, 20). It is to this dead, inactive faith that James denies justification; it is wholly unproductive; it cannot profit. And indeed, on one occasion, Paul uses faith in the same sense, and in as strong language as James denies to it any saving or justifying efficacy: "Though I have all faith, so that I could remove mountains, and have not charity, I am nothing" (1 Cor. xiii. 2). The faith which justifies is a faith which worketh by love—this is the doctrine of Paul; not a faith which is destitute of love—this is the doctrine of James.[1]

We shall now proceed to test our solution by the example of Abraham's justification, which both Paul and James adduce

---

[1] See excursus "James and Paul" in my commentary on the Epistle of James in Schaff's *Popular Commentary*, vol. iv. pp. 123–125.

in support of their views, especially as here the difference in their expressions is conspicuous. Paul assigns the justification of Abraham to that faith which he displayed when it was revealed to him that he should have a son. "What saith the Scripture? Abraham believed God, and it was counted unto him for righteousness. Now to him that worketh is the reward not reckoned of grace, but of debt. But to him that worketh not, but believeth on him that justifieth the ungodly, his faith is counted to him for righteousness" (Rom. iv. 3, 5). Faith, then, and not works, was the efficient cause of his justification; Abraham simply believed the testimony of God, and that was counted to him for righteousness. James takes a different view of the matter; he appears to assign Abraham's justification to that great proof which he gave of his obedience when he offered up Isaac. "Was not Abraham our father justified by works, when he had offered Isaac, his son, upon the altar? Seest thou how faith wrought with his works, and by works was faith made perfect? And the Scripture was fulfilled which saith, Abraham believed God, and it was imputed to him for righteousness" (Jas. ii. 21–23). Abraham's real justification in the sight of God occurred twenty years before his offering up Isaac; God, who sees the hearts of men, saw that his faith was genuine; but his offering up Isaac was an outward manifestation of the truth and reality of his faith; thereby the declaration, which was made to him so many years before, received its fulfilment and confirmation. His justification was complete and certain whenever his faith was counted to him for righteousness; but its truth was confirmed by his works. It is to be observed that James does not say that by works Abraham's justification was made perfect, but that his faith was so perfected. Faith co-operated with his works, his works flowed from his faith—without faith they would never have been wrought, and thus by works his faith was made perfect—proved to be that genuine faith to which the promises of the gospel are annexed. If his faith had not been active, it would not have been justifying.

There are two distinct parts in the doctrine of justification: the one, that a man is justified by faith in the merits of Christ, and the other, that the faith which justifies must be active. Paul dwells chiefly on the first part, and James on the second; so that, instead of a contradiction in their views, there is a development of the truth.[1] "The relation between these two apostles, as well their difference as their agreement," observes Schaff, "may be thus stated: James proceeds from without inward, from phenomenon to principle, from periphery to centre, from the fruit to the tree. Paul, on the contrary, proceeds from within outward, from principle to phenomenon, from centre to circumference, from the root to the blossom and the fruit."[2]

DISSERTATION II.

RESEMBLANCES IN THE EPISTLE OF JAMES.

The Epistle of James forms the link of connection between the Jewish and the Christian Church. Writing exclusively to Jewish Christians, James was led to express himself according to Jewish modes of thought. But this arose not merely from the circumstances of those whom he addressed, but also from the idiosyncrasy of the writer; for, as we have already had occasion to remark, James, when he became a Christian, did not cease to be a Jew; he resided in Jerusalem, attended the worship of the temple, and practised the rites and ceremonies of Judaism. Besides, he wrote his Epistle at a very early stage of the development of Christianity, when Christians were hardly distinguished from the Jews, and were regarded as a Jewish sect. By James, at the period when he wrote, Christianity would be regarded as a development of Judaism; the Mosaic law was not so much abolished as trans-

[1] Since writing the above, I have found the same view expressed by Mangold in his edition of Bleek's *Introduction:* "Both are agreed that faith justifies, and that it must prove and perfect itself by works. Paul emphasizes the first proposition, and James brings prominently forward the second." *Einleitung,* p. 710.

[2] Schaff's *History of the Apostolic Age,* vol. ii. p. 328.

figured. We have in this Epistle primitive Christianity in a more peculiar sense than in any of the other writings of the New Testament: the teaching *of* Christ rather than the teaching *concerning* Christ. We meet here with what may be called, in a true and unobjectionable sense, Jewish Christianity in its purest and original form.[1] There is no book of the New Testament which is so pervaded with the spirit of the Old. James writes rather like a Jewish prophet than a Christian apostle. And yet notwithstanding there is no book which contains fewer quotations from the Old Testament: the spirit is preserved, but not the letter. There are only two passages which can be considered as references: the one is a direct quotation, and the other a somewhat doubtful allusion. In the one James gives the words as a citation: "Wherefore he saith, God resisteth the proud, but giveth grace to the humble" (Jas. iv. 6). The quotation is from the Book of Proverbs, and follows not the original Hebrew, but the Septuagint version,[2] which is easily accounted for by the fact that the Epistle was written in Greek, and addressed to the Hellenists or Greek Jews. The Septuagint here differs materially from the Hebrew, where the words are: "Surely he scorneth scorners, but he giveth grace to the lowly" (Prov. iii. 34). The other passage is: "He shall save a soul from death, and shall hide a multitude of sins" (Jas. v. 20);[3] where it is possible there may be an allusion to another passage from the Proverbs: "Love covereth all sins"[4] (Prov. x. 12).

But whilst there are only these two references in the Epistle of James to the Old Testament, expositors have discovered, or think they have discovered, numerous references or resemblances to the books of the New Testament, especially to our Lord's Sermon on the Mount, to the Pauline Epistles,

---

[1] There are some excellent remarks on this subject in Beyschlag's *Der Brief des Jacobus*, pp. 16–18.

[2] In the Septuagint the words are: κύριος ὑπερηφάνοις ἀντιτάσσεται, ταπεινοῖς δὲ δίδωσι χάριν. The only variation is that James has ὁ θεός instead of κύριος, a variation which also occurs in the same quotation in 1 Pet. v. 5.

[3] Καλύψει πλῆθος ἁμαρτιῶν.

[4] Here, however, the Septuagint differs from the Hebrew: "Love covers all that do not love strife;" πάντας δὲ τοὺς μὴ φιλονεικοῦντας καλύπτει φιλία.

to the Epistle to the Hebrews, to the First Epistle of Peter, and to the Apocalypse; and also to the apocryphal books, especially the Book of Ecclesiasticus and the Wisdom of Solomon. In this dissertation it is proposed to examine the nature of these references or resemblances, to consider to what extent they are real, and, if real, to inquire into their causes.

I. It is affirmed that there are in the Epistle of James numerous references to, or reminiscences of, the words of Christ, as given in the synoptic Gospels, and especially in the Sermon on the Mount. Some even go the length of affirming that the Epistle was written on its model. Thus Schmid observes: "James not only agrees in numerous separate passages with Matthew's Gospel, which (passages) appear to be but the echo of the discourses of Jesus with reference to the moral life in God's kingdom, but also in that great body of precepts which Matthew gives as a whole, the Sermon on the Mount, which, in its whole spirit, may be looked upon as the model of James' Epistle."[1] Lists of these references or points of resemblance are given by Theile, Kern, Huther,[2] Schmid, Beyschlag, Reuss, Erdmann,[3] Alford, Davidson, Bassett, Plumptre, and Salmon. If we compare these parallels, we shall find many of them far-fetched and fanciful, but still enough remains to show an undoubted and striking simi-

[1] Schmid's *Biblical Theology of the New Testament*, p. 364, E. Tr.
[2] We give the following list of parallelisms from Huther's commentary, because they are there most fully given, and the list has been generally adopted. Huther's *Der Brief des Jakobus*, p. 20 [E. Tr. p. 19]:—

Jas. i. 2 compared with Matt. v. 10–12.
„ i. 4 „ „ v. 48.
„ i. 5, v. 15 „ „ vii. 7–12.
„ i. 9 „ „ v. 3.
„ i. 20 „ „ v. 22.
„ ii. 13 „ „ vi. 14, 15, v. 7.
„ ii. 14–16 „ „ vii. 21–23.
„ iii. 17, 18 „ „ v. 9.
„ iv. 4 „ „ vi. 24.
„ iv. 10 „ „ v. 3, 4.
„ iv. 11 „ „ vii. 1, 2.
„ v. 2 „ „ vi. 19.
„ v. 10 „ „ v. 12.
„ v. 12 „ „ v. 33–37.

[3] For a different and even longer list, see Erdmann's *Jacobus*, p. 29.

larity. But these points of resemblance are by no means confined to the Sermon on the Mount; these are the most numerous only because that Sermon contains the most considerable collection of the words of Jesus in the synoptic Gospels; they extend to the other sayings of Christ scattered throughout the Gospels; and although chiefly found in the Gospel of Matthew, are not restricted to it.

We subjoin a list in parallel columns of those passages in which the resemblances are the most striking:—

Be ye doers of the word, and not hearers only, deceiving your own selves.—Jas. i. 22.	Blessed are they that hear the word of God and keep it.—Luke xi. 28.
If ye fulfil the royal law according to the Scriptures, Thou shalt love thy neighbour as thyself, ye do well.—Jas. ii. 8.	And the second is like unto it, Thou shalt love thy neighbour as thyself.—Matt. xxii. 39.
Can the fig-tree bear olive berries? either a vine, figs?—Jas. iii. 12.	Ye shall know them by their fruits. Do men gather grapes of thorns, or figs of thistles?—Matt. vii. 16.
Your riches are corrupted, your garments are moth-eaten. Your gold and your silver is cankered.—Jas. v. 2, 3.	Lay not up for yourselves treasures upon earth, where moth and rust doth corrupt.—Matt. vi. 19.
But above all things, my brethren, swear not, neither by heaven, neither by the earth, neither by any other oath; but let your yea be yea, and your nay, nay: lest ye fall into condemnation.—Jas. v. 12.	But I say unto you, Swear not at all: neither by heaven; for it is God's throne: nor by the earth; for it is His footstool. . . . But let your communication be, Yea, yea; Nay, nay: for whatsoever is more than these cometh of evil.—Matt. v. 34-37.

From these examples it is evident that there are references to, or reminiscences of, the words of Christ, and that they are not confined to the Sermon on the Mount. But these similarities are not so clear and decided, or so plain and direct, as to warrant us regarding the passages as quotations. They are too independent in form, and too free in the terms employed, to be referred to a direct connection with the Sermon on the Mount.[1] The only one which seems a direct citation

---

[1] The nearest resemblance to the Epistle of James is the Didachè, or "Teaching of the Twelve Apostles," probably the most ancient post-apostolic document, assigned by the most learned authorities to A.D. 70-100. Its teaching, especially in the doctrine of "The Two Ways," agrees with that of James; as Dr. Schaff observes: "These writings represent the early Jewish-Christian type of teaching before the universalism and liberalism of the great Apostle of the

is the prohibition against swearing. Hence, then, these resemblances do not prove that the Sermon on the Mount was written before the Epistle of James, nor do they militate against the early date which we have assigned to this Epistle. Even admitting that the Gospel of Matthew may have been written at an early period, even before the Epistle of James, there is no evidence from the similarities in these writings to show that the author of the Epistle ever saw the Gospel. The teaching of Christ would be diffused among Christians before it was committed to writing. There was an oral before there was a written Gospel. It is probable that the early preaching of the apostles was composed of the sayings of our Lord and of records of His actions. And this is perfectly sufficient to account for the coincidences between the Epistle of James and the synoptic Gospels.[1] We have endeavoured to prove that this Epistle was written at a very early period, when the Church was chiefly composed of Jewish Christians, before the great controversy concerning circumcision arose, and probably before Paul's mission to the Gentiles. The words of Christ would then be fresh and vivid to the minds of the disciples, and hence James reminds his readers of the sayings of the Lord, and presses them on their attention and practice; and, just because this Epistle was the earliest writing of the New Testament, it is most pervaded with the teaching of Christ.

Indeed, the moral teaching of the Epistle of James resembles in a remarkable manner our Lord's teaching in the Sermon on the Mount. This is seen not so much from any striking resemblance in words, as from the spirit which pervades both. There is in both a similar absence of doctrinal statements and a preponderance of the ethical element. Both writings insist chiefly on the moral precepts of the law, whilst

Gentiles had penetrated the Church" (*The oldest Church Manual*, p. 26). The Didachè also abounds with reminiscences of the words of Christ as given in Matthew's Gospel; in the Didachè these are generally supposed to be references to the written Gospel; but Lechler supposes that, as in the case of the Epistle of James, they may be taken from the oral Gospel as preached by the apostles (*Urkundenfunde zur Geschichte des Christlichen Alterthums*, p. 17).

[1] See Weiss' *Einleitung in das N. T.*, p. 407, where the same remark is made. So also Beyschlag, *Brief des Jakobus*, p. 17.

the ceremonial precepts, including circumcision and the other rites of Judaism, are in a great measure passed by.[1] Both insist, not so much on the performance of external duties, as on the spirituality of the law. Both dwell on the law of love as the fulfilment of the moral law. Both regard sin as having its seat in the heart, and manifesting itself outwardly from within. In both the blessing is pronounced on the poor in spirit, on the merciful, on those who mourn, and on those who are persecuted for righteousness' sake. According to the Sermon on the Mount, God is the source of all good, who causeth His sun to rise on the evil and on the good, and sendeth rain on the just and on the unjust; according to the Epistle, He is the Father of lights from whom cometh every good and perfect gift. According to the Sermon on the Mount, the law is elevated and spiritualized; according to the Epistle, it is the perfect law of liberty, the word of truth by which Christians are begotten, the implanted word which is able to save our souls. According to the Sermon on the Mount, the impossibility of serving both God and the world is strongly asserted; according to the Epistle, the friendship of the world is declared to be enmity with God. According to the Sermon on the Mount, we must not judge others, lest we ourselves be judged; according to the Epistle, he that speaketh evil of his brother speaketh evil of the law, and judgeth the law. By the Sermon on the Mount, we are warned against the profession of religion without the practice of it, against calling Christ "Lord, Lord," without doing the things which He commands; by the Epistle, the doing of the word is emphasized above the mere hearing of it. In the Sermon on the Mount, the rich are warned of the danger to which their riches expose them; in the Epistle, the judgments of God are denounced against those who make an unlawful use of their riches, and who thus heap treasure together for the last days. In short, the teaching of Christ in the Sermon on the Mount is embodied in this Epistle.[2]

---

[1] The same remarks apply to the doctrine of "The Two Ways" in the Didachè, though the Didachè comes far behind the spirituality and elevation of the teaching of James.

[2] One may judge of the extent to which the spirit of the Sermon on the Mount pervades the Epistle of James from the following quotation from

II. Some expositors suppose that there are references in the Epistle of James to the Epistles of Paul, and especially to his Epistles to the Romans and Galatians, where the doctrine of justification is discussed. Of course, if this be the case, the early date of the Epistle must be relinquished, and we must either assign to it a later date or call in question its authenticity. That the Pauline writings are presupposed by our Epistle, is maintained by Hug, Baur, Schwegler, De Wette, Kern, Wiesinger, Holtzmann, Dr. Davidson (*Introduction to the Study of the N. T.*), and generally by all those who consider the Epistle of James either as an attack on Paul's view of justification, or as a correction of the perversion of it. Thus Wiesinger, who considers the Epistle of James written with a design to correct the erroneous views entertained of Paul's doctrine, observes that "any unbiassed writer will see in chapters i. 3, iv. 1, 12, allusions to Rom. v. 3, vi. 13, vii. 23, viii. 7, xiv. 4."[1] And Dr. Davidson gives the following list of parallelisms, or, as he expresses it, of "borrowed Pauline ideas and words:" "The phrase *the transgressor of the law* is both in Rom. ii. 25, 27, and Jas. ii. 11; the single term *transgressor* being used absolutely in Gal. ii. 18 and Jas. ii. 9; *to fulfil the law* is

---

Schmid's *Biblical Theology of the N. T.*, pp. 365, 366: "Among these points of similarity are: the joy in temptation (Jas. i. 2; Matt. v. 12); prayer for wisdom (Jas. i. 5; Matt. vii. 7, 11); God's liberal and loving giving (Jas. i. 5; Matt. vii. 11); the warning against wrath (Jas. i. 19, 20; Matt. v. 22); the commendation of gentleness (Jas. i 21, iii. 13; Matt. v. 4); the earnest injunction to be doers of the divine word (Jas. i. 22; Matt. vii. 24, 26); the taming of the tongue (Jas. i. 26; Matt. v. 22); the utterance, that the poor are heirs of the kingdom (Jas. ii. 5; Matt. v. 3); the royal law of love (Jas. ii. 8; Matt. vii. 12); mercy in connection with God's judgment (Jas. ii. 13; Matt. v. 7, 9, 13), and the judgment on the unmerciful (Jas. ii. 13; Matt. vii. 2); the tree and its fruits (Jas. iii. 12; Matt. vii. 16); the importance of peaceableness (Jas. iii. 18; Matt. v. 9); a true prayer being heard (expressed negatively, Jas. iv. 3; positively, Matt. vii. 8); the friendship of the world is enmity to God (Jas. iv. 4; Matt. vi. 24); the purification of the heart (Jas. iv. 8; Matt. v. 8); mourning for sin (Jas. iv. 9; Matt. v. 4); judgment of brethren (Jas. iv. 11, 12; Matt. vii. 1-3); dependence on God (Jas. iv. 13-16; Matt. vi. 25); the perishableness of earthly treasures (Jas. v. 2, 3; Matt. vi. 19, 20); the unresisting spirit of the righteous (Jas. v. 6; Matt. v. 39-42); the expectation of our Lord's second coming (Jas. v. 7-9; Matt. vii. 21-23); the persecution of the prophets (Jas. v. 10; Matt. v. 12); and the warning against oaths (Jas. v. 12; Matt. v. 33-37)."

[1] Wiesinger's *Brief des Jacobus*, p. 37.

alike in Rom. ii. 27 and Jas. ii. 8; *doer of the law, hearer of the law*, are common to Rom. ii. 13 and Jas. iv. 11, etc.; *fruit of righteousness* is found in Phil. i. 11 and Jas. iii. 18; *be not deceived* is in 1 Cor. vi. 9, xv. 33, Gal. vi. 7, and Jas. i. 16; *but some one will say* is common to 1 Cor. xv. 35 and Jas. ii. 18; the word *entire* is in 1 Thess. v. 23; the term *members* in Jas. iii. 6, iv. 1, is frequent in Paul's Epistles to the Romans and Corinthians; the verb translated *deceiving* in Jas. i. 22 is in Col. ii. 4; and the word of God is termed *the perfect law of liberty* in Jas. i. 25, a phrase apparently derived from Paul's ideas of freedom. The apostle of the Gentiles was the first to bring the idea of law over into the department of Christianity in connection with freedom of conscience; and James applies it to the word of God, because such transference has been made."[1] A similar list of resemblances is given us by Baur[2] and Holtzmann.[3] And, besides these verbal phrases, it is strongly insisted on that the theological terms justification, faith, and works, and the argument built upon them, have reference to Paul's doctrine of justification as expounded in his Epistles to the Romans and Galatians.

Every careful reader must see that the examples adduced by Dr. Davidson as resemblances are some of them faint, others fanciful, and others familiar phrases. That both Paul and James censure the hearing of the word without the doing, only proves that this practical error was general. The terms "transgressors" and "members," and the phrases "be not deceived" and "some one will say," are too common to admit of any inference from them. Liberty, as applied to the law, is used in a very different sense by Paul and James; when used by Paul, it denotes freedom from the ceremonial law; whereas, when James speaks of "the perfect law of liberty," he denotes the word of truth, the gospel of Christ, "the moral law transfigured by love."[4] The only passages where

[1] Davidson's *Introduction to the Study of the New Testament*, vol. i. pp. 290, 291; 2nd ed. vol. i. p. 317.

[2] Baur's *Apostel Paulus*, vol. ii. p. 335, note [E. Tr. vol. ii. p. 308].

[3] Holtzmann's *Einleitung*, p. 480.

[4] For the difference in the views of Paul and James concerning ἐλευθερία as applied to the law, see Brückner's *Jakobus*, p. 198.

there is a remarkable resemblance in the language of these two writers, and which, strange to say, are not adverted to by Dr. Davidson, are Jas. i. 3, where James says: "The trying of your faith worketh patience" (τὸ δοκίμιον ὑμῶν τῆς πίστεως κατεργάζεται ὑπομονήν); and Rom. v. 3, 4, where Paul says: "Tribulation worketh patience, and patience experience" (ἡ θλίψις ὑπομονὴν κατεργάζεται· ἡ δὲ ὑπομονὴ δοκιμήν); but even here the idea is not the same: according to James, it is experience (δοκίμιον) that produces patience (ὑπομονή); whereas according to Paul, it is the reverse, it is patience (ὑπομονή) which produces experience (δοκιμή). As regards the employment of the theological terms—justification, faith, and works, and the citation of the instance of Abraham by both writers in illustration of their argument, we have already shown that the coincidence can be quite naturally explained, apart from the theory of mutual dependence.[1] Even Baur observes: "As for the use made of the example of Abraham, this, as De Wette remarks, cannot be held to prove that James was referring to Paul's Epistles to the Galatians and the Romans."[2] In short, we fail to see in the writings of these apostles any indications that would cause us to believe or suspect that the one borrowed from the other; the few resemblances between them are what we would expect from authors writing on similar subjects; whereas the differences both in thought and diction are many and striking. "The conceptions," observes Reuss, "forms of speech, characteristic words, and proofs of the views of Christian truth current in the apostolic age, have not, as has been objected, been learned from writings only, but have come from living intercourse and the scriptural proofs from the Old Testament, which had been long in use for this purpose." And again he observes: "The numerous cases of use of the Pauline Epistles, of the Epistle to the Hebrews, of the Gospel of the Hebrews, of Hermas, of Philo, exist only in the imagination of the critics."[3]

---

[1] See dissertation on the Pauline and Jacobean views of Justification.
[2] *Apostel Paulus*, vol. ii. 335.
[3] Reuss' *Geschichte der heiligen Schriften N. T.*, pp. 134, 136 [E. Tr. pp. 142, 143.]

III. The example of Rahab, referred to both by James and by the author of the Epistle to the Hebrews, has led to the assertion that there is a reference by James to the Epistle to the Hebrews. James asks: "Was not Rahab the harlot justified by works, when she had received the messengers, and had sent them out another way?" (Jas. ii. 25); whilst in the Epistle to the Hebrews it is written: "By faith the harlot Rahab perished not with them that believed not, when she had received the spies with peace" (Heb. xi. 31). This opinion is especially insisted upon by Hilgenfeld,[1] who adduces other supposed resemblances to the Epistle to the Hebrews. "The author," he observes, "is acquainted not only with the Epistles of Paul, but with the Epistle to the Hebrews, which was written after the death of Paul. In contrast to dead works (Heb. vi. 1, 9, 14), James speaks of a dead faith (Jas. ii. 17, 20, 26). In Heb. xi. 17 f., Abraham's offering up Isaac is adduced in favour of justification by faith, whilst in Jas. ii. 21 it is urged in favour of justification by works. In Heb. xi. 31 the harlot Rahab is an example of justification by faith, whilst in Jas. ii. 25 she is an example of justification by works. In Heb. xii. 11 there is the expression καρπὸς εἰρηνικὸς δικαιοσύνης; and in Jas. iv. 18 the similar expression καρπὸς δικαιοσύνης ἐν εἰρήνῃ."[2]

It may be difficult to assign the reason why James should adduce the harlot Rahab as an example of justification by works;[3] but there is not the slightest ground for the supposition that he took this example from the Epistle to the Hebrews; for no reason can be assigned why out of so many examples of faith mentioned in the 11th chapter of that Epistle, he should have precisely fixed upon this one, perhaps the least remarkable. The other resemblances adduced by

---

[1] It is also dwelt upon by Baur, De Wette, and Holtzmann.
[2] Hilgenfeld's *Einleitung*, p. 540.
[3] The reason which Alford assigns is fanciful: "What more probable than that Rahab, a Canaanite and a woman of loose life, who became sharer of the security of God's people simply because she believed God's threatenings, should be exalted into an instance, on the one hand, that even a contact with Israel's faith sufficed to save, and that the apostle, on the other, should show that such faith was not mere assent, but fruitful in practical consequences?" Alford's *Greek Testament*, vol. iv. p. 102, 2nd edition.

Hilgenfeld are not of much importance,—that the one writer speaks of a dead faith, and the other of dead works, would prove rather a dissimilarity than a similarity; that the one adverts to the peaceable fruits of righteousness, and the other to the fruit of righteousness as sown in peace, is merely an accidental resemblance. In short, as Bleek remarks, "There is not the slightest ground for the assumption that the author had the Epistle to the Hebrews in view."[1]

IV. The resemblances between the Epistle of James and the First Epistle of Peter have been adverted to by almost all expositors of these Epistles, but especially by Credner and Hug. There are phrases and expressions common to each, and sometimes the same train of thought may be traced. The following are the most remarkable of these parallel passages, but the list might be increased by others more or less minute:—

To the twelve tribes in the dispersion (ἐν τῇ διασπορᾷ).—Jas. i. 1.	Peter, an apostle of Jesus Christ, to the strangers of the dispersion (διασπορᾶς).—1 Pet. i. 1.
Count it all joy when ye fall into divers temptations (πειρασμοῖς ποικίλοις).—Jas. i. 2.	Wherein ye greatly rejoice, though now for a season ye are in heaviness through manifold temptations (ποικίλοις πειρασμοῖς).—1 Pet. i. 6.
But the rich, in that he is made low: because as the flower of the grass (ὡς ἄνθος χόρτου) he shall pass away.—Jas. i. 10.	For all flesh is grass, and all the glory of man is as the flower of the grass (ὡς ἄνθος χόρτου). The grass withereth, and the flower thereof falleth away.—1 Pet. i. 24.

---

[1] Bleek's *Introduction to the N. T.*, vol. ii. p. 148. Hilgenfeld further asserts that there are, in the Epistle of James, references to the Apocalypse. "Further," he observes, "our author was acquainted with the Apocalypse. When he observes, 'Blessed is the man that endureth temptation, for when he is tried he shall receive the crown of life' (στέφανον τῆς ζωῆς, Jas. i. 12), the reference, as Zeller has remarked, is to Rev. ii. 10: 'Be thou faithful unto death, and I will give thee the crown of life.' So also in Jas. i. 18, 'a kind of first-fruits (ἀπαρχήν) of His creatures,' there is a reference to Rev. xiv. 4. 'These are the redeemed among men, being the first-fruits (ἀπαρχή) unto God and to the Lamb'" (*Einleitung*, p. 540). But such resemblances are far-fetched, as if single words occurring in two different writings were sufficient to prove a connection between these writings, unless indeed the words were rare and peculiar, which in the present case they are not. The "crown of life" was probably a phrase common among Christians to denote future bliss; and "first-fruits" was a very obvious and familiar metaphor among the Jewish Christians.

Wherefore, laying aside all filthiness, and superfluity of naughtiness, receive with meekness the engrafted word, which is able to save your souls.—Jas. i. 21.	Wherefore, laying aside all malice, and guile, and hypocrisies, and envies, and evil speakings, as new-born babes, desire the sincere milk of the word, that ye may grow thereby.—1 Pet. ii. 1, 2.
From whence come wars and fightings among you? Come they not hence, even of your lusts that war (τῶν στρατιυομένων) in your members?—Jas. iv. 1.	I beseech you as strangers and pilgrims, abstain from fleshly lusts that war (αἵτινες στρατεύονται) against the soul.—1 Pet. ii. 11.
Wherefore he saith, God resisteth the proud, but giveth grace to the humble.—Jas. iv. 6.	God resisteth the proud, but giveth grace to the humble.—1 Pet. v. 5.
Resist (ἀντίστητε) the devil, and he will flee from you.—Jas. iv. 7.	Your adversary the devil, as a roaring lion, walketh about, seeking whom he may devour: whom resist (ἀντίστητε) stedfast in the faith.—1 Pet. v. 8, 9.
Humble yourselves (ταπεινώθητε) in the sight of the Lord, and He shall lift you up (ὑψώσει).—Jas. iv. 10.	Humble yourselves (ταπεινώθητε) therefore under the mighty hand of God, that He may exalt you (ὑψώσῃ) in due time.—1 Pet. v. 6.
Let him know, that he which converteth a sinner from the error of his way shall save a soul from death, and shall hide a multitude of sins (καλύψει πλῆθος ἁμαρτιῶν).—Jas. v. 20.	Charity shall cover a multitude of sins (καλύψει πλῆθος ἁμαρτιῶν).—1 Pet. iv. 8.

It is evident from this list that the resemblances of this Epistle to the First Epistle of Peter are nearly as numerous as the resemblances to the Sermon on the Mount, and that they are much more direct and striking. Sometimes the same words are given, as Jas. i. 2 comp. 1 Pet. i. 6; Jas. iv. 6 comp. 1 Pet. v. 5; and Jas. iv. 10 comp. 1 Pet. v. 6. It is true that both Jas. iv. 6 and 1 Pet. v. 5 are quotations from Prov. iii. 34; but the singularity is that both quote from the Septuagint with the same variation, using the word God (ὁ θεός), whereas in the Septuagint the word is Lord (κυριός). But although there is a close similarity between these two writers, there is a remarkable independence. The temptations (πειρασμοί), to which both refer, are somewhat different; Peter has in view chiefly bodily sufferings, whilst James has in view chiefly tests of character; the one using the word chiefly in the sense of afflictions, the other chiefly in the sense of trials. The ethical nature of the Epistles is also different; James draws his motives for the performance of moral duties chiefly from the relation in which we stand to God, whereas Peter does so chiefly from the relation in which we stand to Christ.

There are two ways by which the resemblance between these two Epistles may be accounted for. Some assert that it is not necessary to suppose that either apostle read the Epistle of the other, but that they wrote within the same circle of thought, and thus inadvertently used the same forms of expression. Both were intimately acquainted with the words of Jesus, and both wrote chiefly to Jewish Christians; the practical errors which they had to correct were similar, and hence the similarity in their exhortations. "The coincidence," observes Dr. Davidson, "may be accounted for without supposing that Peter read and followed the Epistle of James. The intercourse which existed between the writers, their touching on like particulars, above all, the one divine source of their knowledge and guide of their writing, may explain all the likeness observable. In one of the examples it is not surprising that their language is alike, because both quote the same passage from the Proverbs. Although, therefore, the similarity of tone in the two cases is striking, it is hardly necessary to assume that Peter read the production of his fellow-apostle, to account for it. Even if he did so, it is not probable that he would imitate the ideas and language."[1] The resemblances are, however, too close and verbal to be thus explained. Similar coincidences to the words of James, found in the works of the Fathers, would justly have been considered as allusions to the Epistle. It would rather seem that Peter had read the Epistle of James, and had referred to it. And certainly this supposition is not only not impossible, but is even probable, as the Epistle of James was written at a very early period, and the First Epistle of Peter much later;[2] and both Epistles were addressed to a similar circle of readers, with this difference, that James wrote exclusively to Jewish

---

[1] Davidson's *Introduction to the New Testament*, vol. iii. p. 332. He has since altered his opinion.

[2] See *infra*. On the other hand, Weiss supposes that the First Epistle of Peter was written first, and that James referred to it. *Einleitung*, p. 401.

Christians, and Peter to Christians in general. "We must suppose," observes Credner, "Peter's acquaintance with the Epistle of James. The personal relations of Peter and James do not suffice to explain the resemblance."[1] "If," says Hug, "as was really the case, James composed his Epistle first, the parts alluded to (in Peter's Epistle) must certainly have been drawn from James."[2] If this be so, the earliest testimony in proof of the authenticity of the Epistle of James is the First Epistle of Peter.

V. It is further asserted that not only are there references in the Epistle of James to the other writings of the New Testament, but even to the apocryphal writings, and especially to the Book of Ecclesiasticus and to the Wisdom of Solomon. This assertion has been maintained by Wetstein, Theile, Kern, Huther, Beyschlag, Schwegg, Schmidt, Holtzmann,[3] and Dean Plumptre. We quote from Dean Plumptre's *Commentary*, where the subject is most fully discussed, and where a list of parallel passages is given: "The Holy Scriptures are naturally the chief object of his (James') studies, but his early knowledge as a Galilean, and his frequent intercourse with the Hellenistic pilgrims of the Dispersion, who came up to keep their Pentecost or other feasts at Jerusalem, made him familiar with the Greek version of these Scriptures, and so with the books which the Alexandrian Jews had added to the Hebrew volume. His Epistle shows how much he valued the practical teaching of one of those books, how he found in the son of Sirach one who, like himself, had sought for wisdom, and had not sought in vain. The parallelisms with that book are, as the following table will show, nearly as numerous as those with the Sermon on the Mount: Jas. i. 5, Ecclus. xx. 15, xli. 22; Jas. i. 8, Ecclus. i. 28, ii. 12; Jas. i. 12, Ecclus. i. 11, 16, 18; Jas. i. 12, Ecclus. xv. 11;[4] Jas. i. 19, Ecclus. v. 11, xx. 7; Jas. i. 23, Ecclus. xii. 11; Jas. i. 25, Ecclus. xiv. 23,

---

[1] Credner's *Einleitung in das N. T.*, p. 606.

[2] Hug's *Introduction to the N. T.*, vol. ii. p. 588.

[3] Kern, *Der Brief Jakobi*, p. 85. Beyschlag's *Jakobus*, p. 19. Schwegg's *Jakobus*, p. 10. Schmidt's *Lehrbegriff des Jacobus*, p. 32. Holtzmann's *Einleitung*, p. 48.

[4] Probably a mistake for Jas. i. 13, Ecclus. xv. 11, 12.

xxi. 23; Jas. iii. 5, Ecclus. xxviii. 10; Jas. iii. 6, Ecclus. xxviii. 19. Yet another book, the work probably of a contemporary, written, as some have thought, by the Jew of Alexandria, eloquent and mighty in the Scriptures, to whom many critics, from Luther onwards, have assigned the authorship of the Epistle to the Hebrews, must have attracted him by its very title, the Wisdom of Solomon, and with this also we find not a few interesting and suggestive parallelisms: Jas. i. 11, Wisd. ii. 8; Jas. i. 12, Wisd. v. 7; Jas. i. 17, Wisd. vii. 17–20; Jas. i. 20, Wisd. xii. 10; Jas. i. 23, Wisd. vii. 26; Jas. ii. 21, Wisd. x. 5; Jas. iv. 14, Wisd. iii. 16, v. 9–14."[1]

We have here certainly a large number of supposed parallelisms, and if they were clear they would certainly prove the truth of the statement affirmed. But if any one will take the trouble of comparing them, he will be astonished to find that in the great majority of instances the resemblances are exceedingly faint, fanciful, and strained, often restricted to a single word or turn of thought, without any regard to the context, and proving only the ingenuity of the expositor. Passing entirely over those where there is either no resemblance or where the resemblance is so faint as hardly to be appreciable, we select those which appear the most plausible; and even among them it will be seen how slender is the foundation on which to base the assertion that James refers in his Epistle to the apocryphal books—

If any of you lack wisdom, let him ask of God, that giveth to all men liberally, and upbraideth not.—Jas. i. 5.	After thou hast given, upbraid not.—Ecclus. xli. 22.
Let every man be swift to hear, slow to speak, slow to wrath.—Jas. i. 19.	Be swift to hear; and let thy life be sincere, and with patience give answer.—Ecclus. v. 11.

---

[1] Plumptre on *The Epistle of James*, pp. 32, 33. According to Holtzmann, Ecclesiasticus is referred to fifteen times and the Book of Wisdom five times; but he gives no list of parallel passages. *Einleitung*, p. 482. On the other hand, the relation of the Epistle of James to the Book of Wisdom is so slight that the Rev. W. Deane, in his commentary on the Wisdom of Solomon, does not even allude to it.

If any man offend not in word, the same is a perfect man.—Jas. iii. 2.	He that ruleth his tongue shall live without strife. There is one that slippeth in his speech, but not from his heart, and who is he that hath not offended with his tongue?—Ecclus. xix. 6, 16.
Even so the tongue is a little member, and boasteth great things. Behold how great a matter a little fire kindleth!—Jas. iii. 5.	Many have fallen by the edge of the sword; but not so many as have fallen by the tongue.—Ecclus. xxviii. 18.
Whereas ye know not what shall be on the morrow. For what is your life? It is even a vapour, that appeareth for a little time, and then vanisheth away.—Jas. iv. 14.	And our names shall be forgotten in time, and no man shall have our works in remembrance, and our life shall pass away as the trace of a cloud, and shall be dispersed as a mist that is driven away with the beams of the sun, and overcome with the heat thereof.—Wisd. ii. 4.[1]

These examples are the best that we can find, and certainly they show that the resemblances between this Epistle and the apocryphal books are extremely faint, and that the references of James to them are imaginary. Certain similarities are unavoidable in all writings which treat upon ethical subjects, and especially, as in the present case, where the authors were Jews, whose minds moved in the same circle of thought. Indeed, applying the same criterion, it might be asserted that almost every ethical book had references to the Apocrypha, for similar coincidences would be found. We consider that there is no trace of any knowledge by James of the apocryphal writers: indeed, there are more obvious traces of such knowledge in other books of the New Testament.[2] It is not improbable that James may have read them, but there is no proof that he employed them in the composition of his Epistle.[3] Quotations from, and references to, the Apocrypha would certainly affect neither the authenticity of the Epistle nor its value and inspiration, as some critics maintain; but we merely affirm, that it is not demonstrated that such quotations and references occur.

[1] It will be observed that some of those examples differ from those given by Dean Plumptre.
[2] As, for example, Heb. xi. 25 is in all probability an allusion to the martyrdom of the widow and her seven sons recorded in the Second Book of Maccabees.
[3] See Weiss' *Einleitung*, p. 407.

DISSERTATION III.

THE ANOINTING OF THE SICK.

Among the many passages of interest in this Epistle of James there is one which merits special consideration, as having given rise to numerous opinions regarding its interpretation, and to various ceremonial practices in the early Church, which ultimately culminated and took definite shape in the sacrament of extreme unction in the Romish Church: we allude to the passage regarding the anointing of the sick: "Is any among you sick? Let him call for the elders of the Church, and let them pray over him, anointing him with oil in the name of the Lord: and the prayer of faith shall save the sick, and the Lord shall raise him up; and if he have committed sins, it shall be forgiven him" (Jas. v. 14, 15).[1]

The medicinal use of oil was exceedingly common in the East, especially in the case of wounds. Thus, in our Lord's parable, the good Samaritan is represented as pouring into the wounds of the traveller wine and oil (Luke x. 34); Isaiah, in describing the wretchedness of his people, represents them as full of wounds and bruises which have not been closed, neither bound up, nor mollified with ointment (Isa. i. 6); and Josephus informs us that Herod the Great in his last illness was bathed in a vessel full of oil, and that by means of this remedy his life was for a short period prolonged.[2] We are also informed that among the Rabbis it was a question of casuistry whether it was lawful to anoint the sick on the Sabbath: a question which the distinguished Rabbi Simeon decided in the affirmative.[3] Now it is supposed that it is to

---

[1] There is no difficulty in the exegesis of the passage. The elders are evidently the presbyters or office-bearers of the Church. The Lord is most probably Christ, in whose name miracles of healing were performed. The verb σώσει is often used in the New Testament of bodily healing (Matt. ix. 21, 22, etc.). The last clause admits of the translation, "even if (κἂν) he have committed sins, it shall be forgiven him." So Huther, Lange, etc.

[2] Joseph. *Antiq.* xvii. 6. 5; *Bell. Jud.* i. 33. 5. See also Pliny, *Hist. Nat.* xxxi. 47. Winer's *Biblisches Wörterbuch*, article "Oel."

[3] Dr. John Lightfoot's *Works*, vol. iii. p. 315.

this custom of anointing with oil as a medicinal remedy that James here refers. This ordinary medicinal remedy was to be applied to the sick man with a view to recovery; and it was enjoined to be administered in the name of the Lord, because the divine blessing was to be implored on the means employed; and there was good ground to hope for restoration to health, resulting from the use of proper remedies, and given in answer to believing prayer. "The prayer of faith shall save the sick," that is, restore him to health.[1] But the great objection to this view is that it is contrary to the whole spirit of the passage. The whole description leaves the impression that this anointing with oil was a religious service, and that the recovery of the sick was not the result of natural means, but a supernatural effect resulting from the prayer of faith.[2] If the anointing were a mere medicinal remedy, it would have been performed by the physician rather than by the elders of the Church.

In the Jewish law, anointing with oil was much employed in religious ceremonies. Oil formed a principal part of all the meat-offerings of the Jews (Lev. ii. 1–9; Num. xxviii. 12). All their sacred things—the tabernacle and all its contents, the altar of burnt-offering, the holy laver, and all the vessels of the sanctuary—were anointed with oil (Ex. xl. 9-11). This was the emblem of consecration: by this ceremony these articles were separated from a common, and devoted to a sacred use. But especially were persons, who were solemnly set apart for some special religious service, consecrated by being anointed with oil. Aaron the high priest was thus solemnly set apart as the appointed medium between God and the people (Ex. xxix. 7); and it would appear that the oil was used in such profusion that his whole body, or at least his sacred vestments, were thus anointed (Ps. cxxxiii. 2). So also it is probable that every subsequent high priest was thus consecrated to his office (Lev. xvi. 32). Kings, as being the vicegerents of God, and thus occupying a religious office, were consecrated with holy oil, and hence were called the

---

[1] So Bassett, *Epistle of James*, p. 78. See also Kern's *Brief Jacobi*, p. 232. Huther's *Jakobus*, p. 223.

[2] See Wiesinger's *Jakobus*, p. 202.

"Lord's anointed" (1 Sam. xxiv. 6; Ps. ii. 2). We have also the example of a prophet being so consecrated, when Elijah anointed Elisha as his successor in the prophetic office (1 Kings xix. 16). Hence, also, originated the term Messiah or the Anointed, the usual designation of the great future Deliverer of Israel. The oil of consecration was the emblem of the Holy Spirit, by whom the Messiah was anointed for the performance of the functions of His divine office: "The Spirit of the Lord God was upon me, because the Lord hath anointed me" (Isa. lx. 1). The only example of anointing in the case of sickness was on the recovery of the leper; but here also it was not a medicinal remedy, but a religious rite, intimating that the future life of the recovered leper was to be consecrated to the Lord (Lev. xiv. 15–18).

Dr. John Lightfoot informs us that among the Jews anointing was used along with certain superstitious rites in the case of sickness. Here the anointing with oil was not a medicinal remedy, but a religious ceremony degraded by superstition. The Jerusalem Talmud says: "The charmer putteth oil on the head of the man whom he charmeth." And hence Lightfoot supposes that it was to rescue the wholesome practice of anointing the sick from superstition, that James directs the Jewish Christians as to the proper method of performing this rite. "This being," he observes, "a common, wretched custom to anoint some that were sick, and to use charming with the anointing, this apostle directs them better; namely, to call the elders or ministers of the Church to come to the sick, and to add to the medicinal anointing of him their fervent prayers for him, far more valuable and comfortable than all charming and enchanting, as well as far more warrantable and Christian."[1]

Anointing with oil was also much used as a religious rite among the early Christians.[2] We have numerous traces of such a custom in the writings of the Fathers. Catechumens,

---

[1] Dr. John Lightfoot's *Works*, vol. iii. p. 316.
[2] On unction as a religious rite in the Christian Church, see Bingham's *Christian Antiquities*, Herzog's *Real-Encyklopädie*, and a valuable article on "Unction," by the Rev. William Scudamore, in Smith's *Dictionary of Christian Antiquities*.

before they were regularly admitted into the Church by baptism, were anointed. Thus we are informed in the *Apostolic Constitutions*, that after the catechumen had made a confession of his faith, and previous to his baptism, he was anointed with oil.[1] But especially anointing formed an important part in the administration of baptism, which, in the early Church, was not the simple rite of sprinkling with water, as with us, but was accompanied with a great number of ceremonies.[2] Thus Tertullian observes: "When we have issued from the font, we are thoroughly anointed with the blessed unction, a practice derived from the old procedure wherein, on entering the priesthood, men were wont to be anointed with oil from a horn, ever since Aaron was anointed by Moses. Thus, too, in our case, the unction runs down our flesh carnally, but profits spiritually, in the same way as the act of baptism itself is carnal, in that we are plunged in water; the effect, spiritual, in that we are freed from sins."[3] And in another passage he thus mentions the different rites employed in baptism: "The flesh is washed, that the soul may be cleansed; the flesh is anointed, that the soul may be consecrated; the flesh is signed by the cross, that the soul may be fortified; the flesh is shadowed by the imposition of hands, that the soul may be illuminated by the Spirit; the flesh feeds on the body and blood of Christ, that the soul may be nourished in God."[4] And so also Cyprian says: "It is necessary that he should be anointed who is baptized, so that having received the chrism, that is, the anointing, he may be anointed of God and have in him the grace of Christ. The baptized are anointed with oil sanctified on the altar."[5]

---

[1] *Apost. Const.* vii. 22 and vii. 41. According to the *Constitutions*, the rite of anointing was also administered after baptism: "After this, when the (priest) has baptized him in the name of the Father and of the Son and of the Holy Ghost, he shall anoint him with ointment" (vii. 43).

[2] No mention is made in the *Didache* of the application of oil at baptism, which is a presumption that its use did not commence until the middle of the second century, and that it was not of apostolic origin.

[3] *De Bapt.* chap. vii. See also *Clementine Recognitions*, iii. 67.

[4] *De Resurr.* chap. viii.

[5] *Ep.* lxix., Oxford ed. *Ep.* lxx. In the Greek Church infants are anointed with oil at baptism, accompanied with the words: "This child is baptized with the oil of gladness."

Heretics, also, when they retracted and returned to the Church, if they had formerly been baptized, were not rebaptized, but were anointed with oil.[1] And as in the case of the Jewish religion, so among the early Christians, the sacred vessels employed in worship were consecrated by being anointed.

It was also the custom in the East, at least among the Jews, to anoint the dead. We have allusions to this custom in the case of our Lord. When Mary, the sister of Lazarus, anointed our Lord immediately before His passion, He commended the action, saying, "In that she hath poured this ointment upon my body, she did it for my burial" (Matt. xxvi. 12). And after His death and burial we are informed that "Mary Magdalene, and Mary the mother of James, and Salome had bought sweet spices that they might come and anoint Him" (Mark xvi. 1). This anointing of the dead was probably a species of embalming; but still we learn from the Fathers that it was a religious rite, as perhaps was also the case with embalming, being an emblem of the resurrection. The body by being anointed was consecrated; it was devoted to the Lord; it was consigned to the grave in the hope of the resurrection. This religious rite is mentioned by Clemens Alexandrinus, who, adverting to the anointing of our Lord, gives the following mystical interpretation: "The oil (ἔλαιον) is the Lord Himself, from whom comes the mercy (ἔλεος) which reaches us; for the dead are anointed."[2] We learn from Irenæus that certain Gnostic heretics anointed persons at the point of death as a charm to defend them against evil spirits, which practice may be regarded as a species of extreme unction: "Others still there are who continue to redeem persons, even up to the moment of death, by placing on their heads oil and water, using at the same time certain invocations that the persons referred to may become incapable of being seized or seen by the principalities and powers, and that their inner man may ascend on high in an invisible manner, as if their body were left among the created things in this world, whilst their soul is sent for-

---

[1] Cyprian, Ep. lxix.
[2] *Pædag.* ii. 8. See also Tertullian, *De Resurr.* 27.

ward to the Demiurge."[1] By anointing those at the point of death these Gnostic heretics supposed that whilst the body was left in the earth, the soul was rescued from evil spirits, and introduced into the presence of the Demiurge or the world's Creator.[2]

But although anointing was so extensively employed as a religious rite in the early Church, and especially in the administration of baptism, yet, except in the solitary instance of these Gnostic heretics, alluded to by Irenæus, there is no trace in the writings of the Fathers of the first three centuries of its being employed in reference to the sick; there is mention of the anointing of the dead, but no mention of the anointing of the sick. And yet it is to this that James alludes in his Epistle; nay, it would seem that he lays it as an injunction on the sick man to send for the elders of the Church, in order that they should anoint him with oil and pray over him. And even in our Lord's lifetime there is mention of this anointing of the sick in order to their recovery. We read that the disciples, whom our Lord sent endowed with the miraculous powers of healing, "anointed with oil many that were sick and healed them" (Mark vi. 13). Whether the disciples did this of their own accord or by the injunction of Christ we cannot tell. When, then, we think on the practice of the disciples in the days of our Lord and on the injunction of the apostle, we cannot suppose that the religious rite of anointing the sick was unpractised in the early Church, even although there are no discoverable references to it in the writings of the early Fathers.[3] Certain it is that toward the close of the fourth century it was employed in the Christian Church. The oil used was consecrated oil, that is, oil that had been solemnly blessed, and set apart by the presbyters of the Church for sacred purposes. Thus we are informed that oil was taken from the lamps in the

---

[1] Irenæus, *Hær.* i. 21. 5.

[2] On this custom of the Gnostics, see Neander's *Church History*, vol. ii. p. 155.

[3] The first ascertainable mention of it is by Ephræm Syrus (A.D. 370): Ἐὰν οἰκονομίαν πληρῶν ἀλείφῃς ἐλαίῳ τὸν κάμνοντα: "If in discharge of thy office thou anointest the sick with oil." Quoted in Bengel's *Gnomon*, *in loco*.

churches to anoint the sick. We meet with frequent traces of this religious rite in the writers of the sixth and seventh centuries. Thus Cæsarius of Arles (A.D. 502) says: "Let him who is sick receive the body and blood of Christ, and then let him anoint his body;" and in an epidemic he recommends a person to "anoint both himself and his family with the consecrated oil."[1] And St. Eligius (A.D. 640) says: "Let him faithfully seek the blessed oil from the Church wherewith to anoint his body in the name of Christ."[2]

The first intimation which we have of the rite as a sacrament is contained in the letter of Innocent I. to Decentius, bishop of Eugubium (A.D. 416), where it is spoken of as a kind of sacrament (*genus sacramenti*).[3] Decentius wrote to Innocent I. to ask his opinion on two points, whether the sick ought to be anointed with chrism,[4] that is, with consecrated oil, and whether this oil might be used not merely by the bishops and presbyters, but by Christians in general. To this question Innocent replies, that the words of James refer only to the faithful who were sick, and that they are to be anointed with the consecrated oil which had been blessed by the bishop; but that this oil might be used not merely by bishops and presbyters, but by all Christians both for themselves and their friends. Here we have certainly the germs of the sacrament of extreme unction, but as yet far removed from the Romish doctrine and practice.[5]

---

[1] *Serm.* 66, § 3, and *Serm.* 89, § 5.

[2] Smith's *Dictionary of Antiquities*, vol. ii. p. 2004. From these testimonies it would appear that at first the sick man anointed himself, and did not require the intervention of others.

[3] The genuineness of this Epistle has been called in question.

[4] The chrism or consecrated oil used by the Romish Church is not simple olive oil, but olive oil mixed with balsam, designed to typify the union of the sacerdotal and the regal functions. In the Greek Church it is said that thirty-six different kinds of aromatics are used to form the sacred chrism.

[5] According to Kurtz, Innocent represented this custom as a sacrament intended for the *spiritual* benefit of the sick. But he adds, "centuries intervened before it was generally introduced as the *sacrament of extreme unction.*" *History of the Christian Church*, vol. i. p. 241, E. Tr. According to Innocent, the rite might be performed by Christians in general, and not by the presbyters of the Church exclusively.

Soon, however, the practice of anointing with oil was restricted to the bishops and presbyters of the Church; and, indeed, for this restriction there appeared to be some authority; for James expressly enjoins the sick man to send for the elders of the Church. At first anointing was employed with a view to restoration to health; and this is certainly the obvious meaning of the words of James and of the rite as practised by the disciples of Christ. When, however, the rite failed to bestow health on the sick man, it was regarded as emblematical of spiritual blessings; the saving of the sick (σώσει τὸν κάμνοντα) was looked upon as referring not to bodily recovery, but to spiritual salvation. Hence the rite came to be regarded as a sacrament. According to Cornelius a Lapide, it had all the characteristics of a sacrament; it was instituted by Christ in the command given to His disciples; the outward sign employed was the use of holy oil in the anointing of the sick; the things signified were the salvation of the soul and the forgiveness of sins; and the sacramental words were contained in the prayer of faith.[1] Hence in the twelfth century the expressions extreme or last unction (*extrema unctio*), and the sacrament of the dying (*sacramentum exeuntium*), occur. Thomas Aquinas developed at length the sacramental nature of the rite; Peter the Lombard gave it the fifth place among the seven sacraments; and at length the Council of Trent authoritatively decreed it to be one of the seven sacraments of the Catholic Church, on the ground that it was recommended (suggested) by Christ in the Gospel of Mark and commended and promulgated by James:[2] "Whosoever shall affirm that extreme unction is not truly and properly a sacrament, instituted by Christ our Lord and published by the blessed Apostle James, but only a ceremony received from the Fathers or a human invention, let him be accursed." And it pronounces a similar anathema

---

[1] Oratio fidei, id est, sacramentum et forma sacramentalis extremæ unctionis, salvabit infirmum, hoc est, conferet ei gratiam qua salvetur anima. Quoted by Alford, *Greek Testament*, vol. iv. p. 326.

[2] Instituta est hæc unctio infirmorum tanquam vere et proprie sacramentum, a Christo Domino nostro apud Marcum quidem insinuatum, per Jacobum commendatum et promulgatum. *Conc. Trid.* Sess. xiv. See Schwegg's *Jakobus*, p. 255 ff.

upon all those who call in question its sacramental efficacy: "Whosoever shall affirm that the sacred unction of the sick does not confer grace, nor forgive sin, nor relieve the sick, but that its power has ceased, as if the gift of healing existed only in past ages, let him be accursed."

The oil employed in extreme unction is olive oil mixed with balsam; it is blessed by the bishop on what is called Maunday Thursday,[1] and delivered to the parochial clergy to be used by them during the course of the year. As the sacrament is now administered, extreme unction is performed on persons, who apparently are hopelessly sick, with a view to prepare them for death; the idea of recovery from sickness is now ignored.[2] When recovery is despaired of, the priest administers to the patient the holy communion, and afterwards the sacrament of extreme unction. He anoints with the sacred oil the organs of the five senses—the eyes, the ears, the nostrils, the mouth, the hands, and feet, using at each anointing the following words: "By this holy unction and through His great mercy Almighty God forgive thee whatever sins thou hast committed by sight" (or hearing, smell, taste, and touch).[3] The anointing is supposed to represent the grace of God poured into the soul, so that the dying man is prepared to enter into the eternal world.

The uses or purposes intended by extreme unction are variously stated. Thus the Synod of Pavia (A.D. 850) calls the rite "a healthful sacrament of which one must partake by faith, in order thereby to secure forgiveness of sins and restoration to health." The original design of anointing the sick,—restoration to health,—however, gradually disappeared, and an entirely spiritual efficacy was ascribed to the rite[4]—

---

[1] The Thursday of the passion week, so called with reference to the words of our Lord, "Mandatum novum do vobis, ut diligatis invicem" (John xiii. 34).

[2] The Council of Trent decreed that the anointing is not to take place except when recovery is not to be looked for: qui tam periculose decumbunt ut in exitu vitæ constituti videantur.

[3] Per hanc sacram unctionem, et suam piissimam misericordiam indulgent tibi Deus quicquid peccaste, per visum, auditum, olfactum, gustum et tactum.

[4] The Council of Mayence (A.D. 847) limited its administration to those who were on the point of death.

restoration to spiritual health; it was viewed as designed for the benefit, not of the body, but of the soul: "It saves the sick." "The Lord shall raise him up." "If the man have committed sins, they shall be forgiven him." According to the catechism of the Church of Rome, two benefits result from the observance of this sacrament: it removes the guilt of all venal sins, not possessing sufficient efficacy for the forgiveness of mortal sins; and it removes all spiritual infirmity resulting from sin, and all the other remains of sin. And, according to the decrees of the Council of Trent, it confers the pardon of any faults that may previously have been unexpiated, and it removes the remains of sin; it strengthens the soul, and enables it the better to bear up under pain, and more successfully to resist the assaults of the devil.

The Romish Church appeals for the observance of extreme unction to the authority of Christ as implied in Mark xvi. 13, and to the authority of the apostles as implied in Jas. v. 14, 15. With regard to the authority of Christ this is a mere conjecture; and even if Christ did enjoin the anointing of the sick, it was conjoined with their miraculous recovery, and not with their death. And with regard to the authority of the apostles, the practice is a manifest perversion of the words of James. The anointing which he recommends has reference not so much to spiritual as to bodily healing. It is administered with a view to recovery from sickness; not, as is the practice of the Romanists, when humanly speaking all hope of recovery is over. This is the obvious meaning of the words of the apostle: "And the prayer of faith shall save the sick" —that is, shall restore him to health; for it follows: "And the Lord shall raise him up"—namely, from his bed of sickness. It is indeed added: "And if he have committed sins, they shall be forgiven him." This addition is designed to show the extension of the promise even to the case of those who have committed sins; these sins shall be forgiven them. The sins are here regarded as the cause of the sickness. The causal connection between moral evil and disease is one of the most obvious phenomena of human life, and in the apostolic age appears to have been illustrated even more strikingly than now; then it would appear that sickness was often inflicted by God as the direct punishment for sin.[1] In such a case the removal of the sickness would be the removal of the punishment, and a proof of forgiveness. Cardinal Cajetan himself admits that the words of James do not speak of the sacrament of extreme unction.[2]

The Greek Church have also founded on these words of James one of their sacraments, which they call Εὐχέλαιον or Ἅγιον ἔλαιον — *prayer-oil* or *the holy oil;* but it bears little resemblance to the extreme unction of the Romish Church. It is not administered in anticipation of death, but in all cases of sickness. The idea of restoration to health, as taught by James, is preserved, though the rite is regarded as productive chiefly of spiritual benefit to the sick. It is defined as "a sacrament in which the body is anointed with oil, God's grace is invoked on the sick to heal him of spiritual and bodily infirmities."[3] The Greek ritual properly requires seven priests to perform the rite; and the number must not be less than three, because James uses the plural: "If any is sick among you, let him send for the elders of the Church."

In the Anglican Church the rite was at first retained, as the Romish customs were only gradually abolished; but it was purified from the errors of extreme unction, and employed in accordance with the design stated in the words of James. Thus, in the first prayer-book of Edward VI., it is stated that if any sick person desire it, he might be anointed with oil, accompanied with the prayer that "our heavenly Father vouchsafe for His great mercy, if it be His blessed will, to restore thee thy bodily health." The rite, however, soon disappeared from the ritual of the English Church.

The words of James refer to the miraculous gifts which were present in the apostolic Church, and especially to the miraculous gift of healing (χάρισμα ἰαμάτων). We learn from the First Epistle to the Corinthians that the gift of healing

---

[1] Thus it is said concerning those who profaned the Lord's Supper among the Corinthians: "For this cause many are weak and sickly among you, and many sleep" (1 Cor. xi. 30). See also 1 Cor. v. 5.

[2] Hæc verba non loquuntur de sacramentali unctione extremæ unctionis. Quoted in Wordsworth's *Greek Testament, in loco.*

[3] In general, this sacrament is administered in the church, and only in extreme cases in private houses.

was conferred by the Spirit upon many of the early Christians (1 Cor. xii. 9); and from the practice of the disciples of Christ that they combined the anointing of oil with the exercise of that gift (Mark vi. 13). Of course, we cannot suppose that this miraculous gift of healing was a permanent power to be exercised on all occasions; for if so, there would have been neither sickness nor death in the primitive Church; but it was conditioned by the will of God, and the result was determined according to His pleasure. Paul undoubtedly possessed and exercised the gift of healing, as in the case of the cripple at Lystra (Acts xiv. 8–10); but Epaphroditus, one of his fellow-companions, was sick unto death (Phil. ii. 27); he had to leave Trophimus at Miletum sick, without laying his hands on him that he might recover (2 Tim. iv. 20); nor could he cure himself of the thorn in the flesh (2 Cor. xii. 7–9). In the performance of a miracle there must have been a peculiar impulse of the Spirit—a faith which causes a man to feel that he was called upon to effect a work of healing. Hence, then, we give what we believe is the meaning of the passage: the elders of the Church being sent for, anointed the sick man with oil in the name of the Lord, and by the prayer of faith miraculously restored him to health. Oil was employed as an external symbol, in a similar manner as our Lord in His miracles sometimes made use of external signs (Mark vii. 33; John ix. 1). "The anointing," observes Meyer, "is to be looked upon as the conductor of the supernatural healing power, analogous to the laying on of hands, so that the faith was the *causa apprehendens*, the miraculous power the *causa efficiens*, and the oil was the *medians*, therefore without independent power of healing, and not even necessary, when the way of immediate operation was, probably in accordance with the susceptibility of the persons concerned, adopted by the healer."[1] These external signs would be of special use in arresting the attention of those who were to be cured, and of exciting faith within them; for it would appear that faith was necessary, not only in the person who performed the miracle, but also in the person cured (Acts xiv. 9). Oil, as we have seen, had a sacred import among the Jews,

[1] On *The Gospel of Mark*, p. 94, translation.

being the emblem of consecration, and perhaps was here employed to denote that the person cured was consecrated to the Lord.

One great objection to this meaning of the passage is that it would imply that the gift of healing was inherent in the elders of the Church. The sick man was enjoined to call, not for those favoured Christians on whom the gift of healing was conferred, but for the presbyters. To this objection it has been answered, that it is most probable that those who were most highly endowed with miraculous gifts would be selected as presbyters. Still, however, we cannot suppose that all the presbyters were thus endowed. It is possible that these miraculous gifts were not so much conferred on individuals, to be exercised according to their pleasure, as on the Church; they were a sacred deposit committed to the Christian Church as a body, and were exercised by the presbyters as the representatives of the Church.[1] And further, it is to be observed that although the promise of recovery is here stated as unconditional, yet, as we have remarked above, we must consider it as conditioned by the will of God; but under what conditions the anointing of the sick was exercised we cannot determine.[2] And further, as the miraculous gift of healing has now been withdrawn from the Church, so this rite of anointing, having lost its purpose in the recovery of the sick, is now no longer serviceable to the Church, and thus should cease to be observed; its retention tending only to superstition. "Whatever," observes Bishop Wordsworth, "was instituted by Christ or by His apostles, under His guidance and that of the Holy Ghost, for the purpose of conveying grace to the soul, and for the attainment of everlasting glory, is of perpetual and universal obligation; for all men need grace, and all men desire glory. But things which were practised and prescribed by Christ and His apostles are not of perpetual obligation, unless they are con-

[1] "James," observes Neander, "regards the presbyters as organs, acting in the name of the Church." *Commentary on the Epistle of James*, p. 120.

[2] "Every one," observes Bishop Burnet, "that was sick was not to be anointed, unless an authority and motion from Christ had been secretly given for doing it; but every one that was anointed was certainly healed." *On the Thirty-Nine Articles.*

ducive to an end which is of perpetual necessity, namely, to the bestowal of spiritual grace to the soul, and to its everlasting salvation. If such is not their character, they are mutable, and may be omitted or foregone by the Christian Church, according to the wisdom and discretion with which God has endued her."[1]

[1] Wordsworth's *Greek Testament: the Catholic Epistles*, p. 33.

THE FIRST EPISTLE OF PETER.

I. THE AUTHENTICITY OF THE EPISTLE.

THE First Epistle of Peter is as strongly attested by external evidence as any other writing of the New Testament; it has been transmitted to us by an unbroken chain of testimony from the apostolic times. Hardly any writing is so frequently quoted by the early Fathers. Eusebius expressly mentions it among the ὁμολογούμεναι or universally acknowledged books of the New Testament.[1] Renan, no partial judge, observes: "This First Epistle of Peter is one of the writings of the New Testament which are most anciently and most unanimously cited as authentic."[2] And even De Wette, although he questioned the authenticity of the Epistle on purely subjective grounds, yet admits that some of the apostolic Fathers knew and used it, and that "it is supported by the whole mass of ancient ecclesiastical authorities." "The testimonies," he observes, "of the most important Fathers down to Eusebius, who reckons it among the universally accepted writings, support it; and, if we set aside its omission in the ancient catalogue of Muratori, and its rejection by the Paulicians, there is no opposition to it."[3]

The earliest testimony in its favour is the Second Epistle of Peter, which, whether genuine or not, is generally admitted to be a document of a very early date. In that Epistle the author designates his writing as his "Second Epistle" (2 Pet.

---

[1] *Hist. Eccl.* iii. 25: αἷς ἑξῆς τὴν φερομένην Ἰωάννου προτέραν, καὶ ὁμοίως τὴν Πέτρου κυρωτέον ἐπιστολήν.

[2] *Antichrist*, p. 7.

[3] *Einleitung in das N. T.*, p. 385, E. Tr. p. 345. The rejection of the Epistle for dogmatic reasons by the Paulicians, who arose in the seventh century, is no objection.

iii. 1).[1] A passage occurs in the Didaché (A.D. 70–100) which is by many regarded as an allusion or quotation from this Epistle: "Abstain from fleshly and bodily lusts" (1 Pet. ii. 11).[2] Eusebius informs us that Polycarp (A.D. 116)[3] in his Epistle to the Philippians makes use of certain testimonies taken from the First Epistle of Peter.[4] Polycarp does not name Peter as the author of the Epistle, but we have only to glance at his Epistle to the Philippians to see that his quotations from it are direct and numerous. Thus in the first chapter he writes: "In whom though now ye see him not, ye believe, and believing, ye rejoice with joy unspeakable and full of glory (1 Pet. i. 8); into which joy many desire to enter;"[5] in the second chapter: "Wherefore, girding up your loins (1 Pet. i. 13), serve the Lord in fear and truth, as those who have forsaken the vain, empty talk and error of the multitude, and believed in Him who raised up Jesus from the dead, and gave Him glory (1 Pet. i. 21), and a throne at His right hand;"[6] and in the eighth chapter: "Let us continually persevere and in the earnest of our righteousness, which is Jesus Christ, who bore our sins in His own body on the tree (1 Pet. ii. 24), who did no sin, neither was guile found in His mouth (1 Pet. ii. 22), but who endured all things that we might live in Him."[7] Eusebius also informs us that Papias (A.D. 116) "made use of testimonies from the First Epistle of John and likewise from that of Peter."[8] In the Epistle to Diognetus (A.D. 150) we have the following reference: "He delivered up His own Son a ransom for us, the holy for the transgressors, the innocent

---

[1] ταύτην ἤδη ἀγαπητοὶ δευτέραν ὑμῖν γράφω ἐπιστολήν.

[2] Didaché i. 4: ἀπέχου τῶν σαρκικῶν καὶ σωματικῶν ἐπιθυμιῶν.

[3] The date of the Epistle of Polycarp is disputed. There is reference in it to the martyrdom of Ignatius, which, according to the best authorities, occurred A.D. 115.

[4] *Hist. Eccl.* iv. 14.

[5] *Ad Philip.* c. 1 : εἰς ὃν οὐκ ἰδόντες πιστεύετε, πιστεύοντες δὲ ἀγαλλιᾶσθε χαρᾷ ἀνεκλαλήτῳ καὶ δεδοξασμένῃ.

[6] *Idem*, c. 2 : διὸ ἀναζωσάμενοι τὰς ὀσφύας ὑμῶν πιστεύσαντες εἰς τὸν ἐγείραντα τὸν κύριον ἡμῶν Ἰησοῦν Χριστὸν ἐκ νεκρῶν καὶ δόντα αὐτῷ δόξαν.

[7] *Idem*, c. 8 : . . . ὃς ἀνήνεγκεν ἡμῶν τὰς ἁμαρτίας τῷ ἰδίῳ σώματι ἐπὶ τὸ ξύλον, ὃς ἁμαρτίαν οὐκ ἐποίησεν, οὐδὲ εὑρέθη δόλος ἐν τῷ στόματι αὐτοῦ.

[8] *Hist. Eccl.* iii. 29 : Κέχρηται δ' ὁ αὐτὸς (ὁ Παπίας) μαρτυρίαις ἀπὸ τῆς Ἰωάννου προτέρας ἐπιστολῆς καὶ τῆς Πέτρου ὁμοίως.

for the guilty, the just for the unjust (1 Pet. iii. 18)."[1] Irenæus (A.D. 180) is the first who expressly ascribes this Epistle to Peter: "And Peter says in his Epistle, "Whom having not seen, ye love; in whom, though now ye see Him not, ye believed; ye will rejoice with joy unspeakable" (1 Pet. i. 8).[2] And again: "On this account Peter says that we have not liberty as a cloak of maliciousness, but for the proof and manifestation of the faith" (1 Pet. ii. 16).[3] Clemens Alexandrinus (A.D. 190) frequently quotes from this Epistle, and expressly attributes it to Peter: "Knowing then the duty of each, pass the time of your sojourning here in fear; forasmuch as ye know that ye were not redeemed with corruptible things from your vain conversation, received by tradition from your fathers; but with the precious blood of Christ, as of a lamb without blemish and without spot (1 Pet. i. 17–19). For as Peter says, the time past of our life may suffice us to have wrought the will of the Gentiles, when we walked in lasciviousness, lusts, excess of wine, revellings, banquetings, and abominable idolatries" (1 Pet. iv. 3).[4] And again: "One aim and one end as regards perfection being demonstrated to belong to the man and the woman, Peter in his Epistle says: Though now for a season, if need be, ye are in heaviness through manifold temptations" (1 Pet. i. 6–9).[5] Tertullian (A.D. 200) writes: "Peter says to the Christians of Pontus, How great indeed is the glory if ye suffer patiently without being punished as evil-doers! For this is acceptable, for even hereunto were ye called, since Christ also suffered for us, leaving us an example that we should follow His steps" (1 Pet. ii. 20, 21).[6] In like

---

[1] Justin. *Opp.* p. 500: αὐτὸς τὸν ἴδιον υἱὸν ἀπέδοτο λύτρον ὑπὲρ ἡμῶν τὸν ἅγιον ὑπὲρ ἀνόμων, τὸν ἄκακον ὑπὲρ τῶν κακῶν, τὸν δίκαιον ὑπὲρ τῶν ἀδίκων.

[2] *Adv. Hær.* iv. 9. 2: Et Petrus ait in epistola sua: Quem non videntes diligitis, in quem nunc non videntes credidistis gaudebitis gaudio inenarrabili.

[3] *Adv. Hær.* iv. 16. 5: Et propter hoc Petrus ait non velamentum malitiæ habere nos libertatem, sed ad probationem et manifestationem fidei.

[4] *Pædagog.* iii. 12.

[5] *Strom.* iv. 20: ὁ Πέτρος ἐν τῇ ἐπιστολῇ φησί κ.τ.λ. See also *Strom.* iv. 7, and *Pæd.* i. 6, quoted by Kirchhofer.

[6] *Scorpiace*, c. 12: Petrus quidem ad Ponticos. "Quanta enim gloria, si non ut delinquentes puniamini, sustinetis? Hæc enim gratia est in hoc et vocati estis," etc.

manner Origen frequently refers to this Epistle: "They do not read what is written respecting the hope of those who were destroyed in the deluge; of which hope Peter himself thus speaks in his First Epistle, that Christ was put to death in the flesh, but quickened in the Spirit" (1 Pet. iii. 18, 19).[1] And again: "Concerning the journey in spirit to prison in Peter's catholic Epistle, being put to death in the flesh, he says, but quickened in the spirit" (1 Pet. iii. 18–20).[2] Cyprian (A.D. 248) often appeals to this Epistle: "Peter also, upon whom by the Lord's condescension the Church was founded, lays it down in his Epistle, and says: Christ suffered for us, leaving us an example that we should follow His steps" (1 Pet. ii. 21).[3] And again: "Peter also, in his Epistle, has taught that persecutions occur for the sake of our being proved, and that we also should, by the example of righteous men who have gone before us, be joined to the love of God by death and sufferings. For he wrote in his Epistle and said, Beloved, think it not strange concerning the fiery trial which is to try you" (1 Pet. iv. 12).[4] Eusebius (A.D. 325) always speaks of this Epistle as undisputed: "In what provinces Peter also proclaimed the doctrine of Christ appears from his own writings, and may be seen from that Epistle which we have mentioned as admitted in the canon."[5] We have only further to remark that this Epistle is found in the Peshito, the old Latin, and all the most ancient versions. Its apparent omission in the Muratorian canon may be accounted for from the fragmentary nature of that manuscript,

---

[1] *De Principiis*, ii. 5. 3 : Non legunt quid scriptum sit de spe illorum qui in diluvio perempti sunt, de qua spe Petrus ipse in prima epistola sua ita ait, etc.

[2] *Comment. in Joan. Opp.* vol. iv. p. 135 : καὶ περὶ τῆς ἐν φυλακῇ πορείας μετὰ πνεύματος παρὰ τῷ Πέτρῳ ἐν τῇ καθολικῇ ἐπιστολῇ· θανατωθεὶς γὰρ, φησι, σαρκὶ, ζωοποιηθεὶς κ.τ.λ.

[3] *De bono patient.* 9: Item Petrus, super quem ecclesia Domini dignatione fundata est, in epistola sua ponit et dicit : Christus passus est pro nobis, relinquens nobis exemplum ut sequamini vestigia ejus, etc.

[4] *Epist.* 55, Oxford ed. 58 : Petrus quoque apostolus ejus docuerit, ideo persecutiones fieri, ut probemur et ut dilectioni Dei, justorum præcedentium exemplo, nos etiam morte et passionibus computemur. Posuit enim in epistola sua dicens, etc.

[5] *Hist. Eccl.* iii. 4. See also vi. 25, in the catalogue of Origen, preserved by Eusebius.

and from the difficulty of translating the passage where reference is made to the writings of Peter.[1]

The Epistle, then, could not be more strongly attested by external evidence. It is admitted that the internal evidence is not so strong; this arises from the nature of the case, because such evidence depends greatly on subjective considerations. Still, however, it is by no means defective. Thus it has been remarked, that the Epistle bears the impress of that strongly marked individuality of Peter which is portrayed in the Gospels and in the Acts of the Apostles. The sanguine spirit of the Epistle, the reference to the hopes of futurity, the consolation imparted to its readers, the exhortations to prepare for trial and suffering, the prominence given to the love of Christ, and the frequent representation of Christ as an example, all remind us of the eager nature of the apostle, of his intense love for the Saviour, and of the command of the Lord: "When thou art converted, strengthen thy brethren" (Luke xxii. 32). "This Epistle," observes Grotius, "has the vehemence agreeable to the disposition of the chief of the apostles."

It has also been remarked, that there are in the Epistle many personal recollections of the author's intercourse with Christ. The tone of the Epistle with reference to the earthly ministry of our Lord is very different from that of the Epistles of Paul. Paul refers to the actions of Christ as matter of report; whereas the author of this Epistle speaks of them from personal observation. He himself had seen and conversed with Christ when upon earth. Thus, when referring to the love of his readers toward Christ as a love to an unseen Saviour, he expressly excludes himself: "Whom having not seen, ye love" (1 Pet. i. 8); and yet this fact is not prominently brought forward, but introduced in an incidental manner.[2] So also there are in the Epistle many indirect

---

[1] The passage is as follows: Et Sapientia ab amicis Salomonis in honorem ipsius scripta. Apocalypsis etiam Joannis et Petri, tantum recipimus, quam quidam ex nostris legi in ecclesia nolunt. The text is evidently corrupt. Thiersch proposes to change *tantum* into *unam epistolam*, and *quam quidem* into *alteram quidam*.

[2] Schleiermacher finds in this a proof of the genuineness of the Epistle. Paul would have said, "Whom having not seen, we love."

references to Peter's experiences. Christ had named him a rock; and the author of the Epistle speaks of believers as living stones, built up into a spiritual house (1 Pet. ii. 5), and Christ as the rock on which the Church is built (1 Pet. ii. 6). Peter was solemnly warned by his Master of the attempt which would be made upon him by Satan; and the author warns his readers to beware of their adversary the devil, who as a roaring lion goeth about seeking whom he may devour (1 Pet. v. 8). Peter had denied Christ, and the Epistle abounds in exhortations to stedfastness (1 Pet. i. 13). Peter had been a witness of the sufferings of Christ, and these are continually referred to in the Epistle (1 Pet. v. 1). Peter had especially marked the spotless character of Christ, and the wonderful forbearance with which He endured His unparalleled sufferings; and to this example and this forbearance there is a marked allusion in the Epistle (1 Pet. ii. 21–23). Peter had made a noble profession of his love to Christ, and on this the author of the Epistle dwells with special affection (1 Pet. i. 8).[1]

It has been asserted that there are undesigned coincidences between the Epistle and the speeches of Peter recorded in the Acts. In the early part of the Acts, Peter was the spokesman of the apostolic community, and numerous discourses given by him are recorded.[2] Of course these discourses are not given in full, but merely extracts from them, or the substance of them; but still they exhibit Peter's mode of reasoning, and give indications of his peculiar diction. Now, in the Epistle we find traces of the same spirit and method as are displayed in the discourses. In both Peter is spoken of as a witness of the sufferings and resurrection of Christ (Acts ii. 32; 1 Pet. v. 1). The connection of the predictions of the prophets with the sufferings of Christ is alluded to in both (Acts iii. 18; 1 Pet. i. 10). In his speech before the Sanhedrim Peter refers to Christ as the stone set at nought of the builders which has become the head of the corner (Acts

---

[1] For numerous examples of these reminiscences of Christ, see Farrar's *Early Days of Christianity*, vol. i. pp. 124-127.

[2] Acts i. 16-22, ii. 14-39, iii. 12-26, iv. 8-18, v. 29-32, viii. 20-23, x. 34-43, xi. 5-18, xv. 7-11.

iv. 11), and the same reference is contained in the Epistle (1 Pet. ii. 7, 8). The remarkable expression descriptive of the crucifixion of Christ, "being hanged on a tree," is found alike in Peter's address (Acts v. 30) and in Peter's Epistle (1 Pet. ii. 24). And the phrase " the Judge of the quick and the dead," which Peter used in his address to Cornelius (Acts x. 42), occurs in this Epistle (1 Pet. iv. 5).[1]

But although this Epistle is so strongly attested by external and internal evidence, yet it has not escaped the attacks of opponents. Among the first who disputed it was Eichhorn,[2] but he only went the length of affirming, that whilst Peter furnished the leading ideas, Mark, or some disciple of Paul, gave them literary expression; as, according to his opinion, there are Pauline views in the Epistle which do not suit the character of Peter.[3] Bertholdt brings forward the same opinion in another form: he supposes that Peter wrote his Epistle in Aramaic, but that Mark or Silvanus translated it into Greek.[4] De Wette directly called in question its genuineness, but solely for subjective reasons. As already remarked, he admits the force of the external evidence, but asserts that the Epistle is defective in originality, and bears too close a resemblance to the Epistles of Paul.[5] Similar objections have also been made by Reuss, who speaks of the genuineness of this Epistle in hesitating terms: "Ecclesiastical tradition," he observes, "from the earliest times is unanimous in favour of Peter as the author. But many of the phenomena discussed are surprising in an apostle whom authentic history names as a pillar of Jewish Christianity, and whose name served as the standard of a party. It is not easy to reconcile the theological complexion and geographical horizon of the

[1] For further examples of parallelisms between the speeches of Peter contained in the Acts and the First Epistle of Peter, see Farrar's *Early Days of Christianity*, vol. i. pp. 127-129; Plumptre's *Commentary*, p. 71; Schmid's *Theology of the N. T.*, p. 376; and Wieseler's *Der erste Brief des Apostel Petrus*, pp. 28, 29.

[2] Cludius was the first who called in question the genuineness of this Epistle, *Uransichten des Christenthums*, 1808, pp. 296-311.

[3] Eichhorn's *Einleitung in das N. T.*, pp. 606, 609, 616. This opinion has been revived by Wilibald Grimm in the *Studien und Kritiken*, 1872.

[4] *Einleitung*, vi. p. 667.

[5] *Einleitung in das N. T.*, p. 381 [E. Tr. p. 311].

author as obtained from the Epistle with the other data of history; and its dependence upon the Pauline Epistles, whose general dissemination during the lifetime of Peter is scarcely conceivable, will always throw an adverse weight into the scale."[1] The Tübingen school, as represented by Baur,[2] Schwegler, Hilgenfeld, Pfleiderer, Zeller, Holtzmann, and Volkmar, are unanimous in their rejection of the Epistle. These critics in general suppose that this Epistle was written with a design to reconcile Pauline and Petrine Christianity. Thus Schwegler observes: "Our Epistle is an attempt of a follower of Paul to reconcile the divided parties of Paul and Peter, by putting into the mouth of Peter a testimony to the orthodoxy of his brother apostle Paul, together with a statement of Paul's doctrinal system somewhat coloured by the views of Peter."[3] Schwegler, Pfleiderer,[4] and Mangold[5] think that the notices of persecution contained in the Epistle point not to the persecution under Nero, but to that under Trajan, —an hypothesis wholly extravagant, and contradicted by the early testimonies of Polycarp and Papias.[6]

1. De Wette objects to the Epistle on account of its want of originality, and especially because it is full of Pauline ideas and phrases. "One," he observes, "seeks in vain in this supposed work of Peter, that head of Jewish Christianity, for a definite distinctness such as is seen in the writings of Paul and John. There are not only to be found in it reminiscences of the Pauline Epistles which the author without doubt read, but also the doctrine and the phraseology are essentially Pauline."[7] In proof of this assertion, De Wette gives a list of parallelisms between this Epistle of

[1] Reuss' *Geschichte der heil. Schriften N. T.*, pp. 138, 139 [E. Tr. pp. 146, 147].
[2] "Peter," observes Baur, "cannot possibly have written an Epistle which the general opinion of scholars declares to be so Paulinizing and so strikingly dependent upon the Epistles of Paul. This writing can only be regarded as an additional evidence of the desire to obtain positive demonstrations of the agreement of the two apostles." *Kirchengeschichte*, p. 144 [E. Tr. vol. i. p. 151].
[3] *Nachapost. Zeitalter*, vol. ii. p. 22.
[4] Pfleiderer, *Paulinismus*, vol. ii. p. 150.
[5] Mangold, *Einleitung in das N. T.*, p. 747.
[6] See *infra* on the date of the Epistle.
[7] *Einleitung in das N. T.*, p. 381 [E. Tr. p. 341].

Peter and the Pauline Epistles;[1] and a further list of Pauline views, formulæ, and terms, which, according to him, were incorporated in this Epistle of Peter: as, for example, the view of Christ's death (ii. 24 comp. Rom. vi. 8–14), the ideas of calling (i. 15 comp. Gal. i. 6, 15), election (i. 2), hope (i. 3, iii. 15), obedience (i. 2 comp. Rom. vi. 16, xvi. 19), freedom and its abuse (ii. 16 comp. Gal. v. 13), the gifts of grace (iv. 10), recompense (i. 7 comp. Rom. ii. 7 ; 1 Cor. iv. 5), inheritance (i. 4 comp. Gal. iii. 18).[2]

Many theologians admit in general terms the fact here stated, that there are in the First Epistle of Peter undeniable traces of acquaintance with the Pauline Epistles, and especially references to the Epistles to the Romans and Ephesians; and long lists of these references are given in several commentaries.[3] This admission has been made by Hug, Bleek, Credner, Weiss, Schmid, Ewald, Wiesinger, Lechler, Hofmann, Reuss, Schott, Sieffert, and Mangold among German theologians; and by Alford, Davidson (*Introduction to the Study of the N. T.*), Plumptre, Cook, Salmon, and Farrar among English exegetes. Most of them suppose the acquaintance of Peter with the Pauline Epistles; whilst Weiss is alone in maintaining that it was Paul who made use of the First Epistle of Peter in his writings.[4] Michaelis had previously asserted that either

[1] They are as follows:—1 Pet. i. 1 f. comp. Eph. i. 4-7 ; 1 Pet. i. 3 comp. Eph. i. 3 ; 1 Pet. i. 14 comp. Rom. xii. 2 ; 1 Pet. ii. 1 comp. Col. iii. 8 ; 1 Pet. ii. 6 comp. Rom. ix. 33 ; 1 Pet. ii. 10 comp. Rom. ix. 25 ; 1 Pet. ii. 13, 14 comp. Rom. xiii. 1-4 ; 1 Pet. ii. 16 comp. Gal. v. 13 ; 1 Pet. ii. 18 comp. Eph. vi. 5 ; 1 Pet. iii. 1 comp. Eph. v. 22 ; 1 Pet. iii. 9 comp. Rom. xii. 17 ; 1 Pet. iv. 9 comp. Phil. ii. 14 ; 1 Pet. iv. 10 f. comp. Rom. xii. 6 f. ; 1 Pet. v. 1 comp. Rom. viii. 18 ; 1 Pet. v. 5 comp. Eph. v. 21 ; 1 Pet. v. 8 comp. 1 Thess. v. 6 ; 1 Pet. v. 14 comp. 1 Cor. xvi. 20.

[2] De Wette's *Einleitung in das N. T.*, p. 384 [E. Tr. p. 314]. Seufert goes the length of asserting that the coincidences between First Peter and the Epistle to the Ephesians are so strong as to prove an identity of authorship. Hilgenfeld's *Zeitschrift*, 1881.

[3] See Eichhorn's *Einleitung*, vol. iii. pp. 610, 611. Credner's *Einleitung*, pp. 634-637. Schott, *Der erste Brief Petri*, pp. 338, 339. Holtzmann's *Einleitung*, pp. 488, 489. Alford's *Greek Testament*, vol. iv. p. 131. Farrar's *Early Days of Christianity*, vol. i. p. 129. Plumptre's *Commentary on the Epistles of Peter*, pp. 68-70. Davidson's *Introduction to the Study of the N. T.*, vol. i. pp. 414-418 (2nd ed. vol. i. pp. 508-511).

[4] Weiss, *Der petrinische Lehrbegriff*, pp. 406-425. *Einleitung in das N. T.*, p. 426 ff.

Peter had read Paul's Epistle to the Romans or Paul the First Epistle of Peter; and, as the latter is not probable, he concludes that the former is true.[1] And this opinion of Michaelis has been followed by others. But whilst these theologians admit a resemblance or familiarity with the Pauline Epistles, and a certain dependence on them, most of them deny the inference which De Wette and others draw from this admission, and assert that no objection can be drawn from it to invalidate the authenticity of this Epistle of Peter. For, on the one hand, it is affirmed that this dependence is confined to the earlier Epistles of Paul, which Peter might well have read before the composition of his Epistle, and does not extend to the later or the Pastoral Epistles; and, on the other hand, that it is limited in extent, for this Epistle of Peter is distinguished by marked peculiarities of its own, both in its representation of doctrine and in its phraseology.

Other theologians call in question this dependence on the Pauline Epistles, and affirm that whatever resemblances there may be, these can be accounted for on different grounds. This denial has been made by Rauch,[2] Mayerhoff,[3] Brückner,[4] Steiger, Ritschl,[5] Davidson (*Introduction to the N. T.*), Eadie,[6] and partially by Huther.[7] And, indeed, if we take the trouble of comparing the list of parallelisms which are given, we shall find that many of them consist of quotations from the Septuagint translation of the Old Testament, that some of

---

[1] Michaelis, *Introduction to the New Testament*, by Bishop Marsh, vol. vi. p. 323 f.

[2] Defence of the originality of First Peter in Winer and Engelhardt's *Krit. Jour.* viii. 396.

[3] Mayerhoff, *Einleitung in die petrinischen Schriften*, pp. 104-115.

[4] Brückner examines the subject at great length and with great minuteness. *Der erste Brief des Petrus*, pp. 10-17.

[5] Ritschl's *Altkatholische Kirche*, p. 116. "The many coincidences with Paul's circle of thoughts," he observes, "are either only apparent or refer to general Christian ideas."

[6] Article on Peter's Epistle in Kitto's *Encyclopedia*.

[7] Huther wavers in his opinion. In one place he observes: "The similarity between particular passages of Peter's Epistle and Paul's other Epistles is not of such a nature as to warrant the conclusion that there is a dependence of the former upon the latter;" whilst elsewhere he appears to admit such a dependence. *Der erste Brief des Apostel Petrus*, pp. 21, 24.

them agree only in a single word, and that there are few which are striking, and that even these may be accounted for by the fact that the two apostles were writing on the same subjects, and moving in the same circle of Christian thought.[1] And, further, it is erroneous to affirm that there is an adoption of Pauline views, for we meet in almost every clause of this Epistle marks of individuality and independence. There is hardly any mention in this Epistle of the great Pauline doctrine of justification by faith; and, on the other hand, the views of Peter concerning the relation of prophecy to Christianity, and his peculiar eschatological views, are but slightly dwelt upon in the Pauline Epistles. Hence, then, we regard the opinion of those theologians as nearer the truth who hold that there is no necessity for supposing, as regards this Epistle, a previous acquaintance of Peter with the writings of Paul, or at least a designed reference to them. "An attentive consideration of the subject," observes Dr. Davidson, "has not convinced us of the fact that the parallelisms in question should be attributed to Peter's perusal of Paul's Epistles. Ideas and expressions are sometimes alike; but whether the likeness proceeded from the cause assigned admits of grave doubt. It is obvious that Peter has not literally transcribed Paul's language in any one passage. There is a diversity in the midst of coincidence—a diversity which far exceeds the similarity. The nature of the parallelism is unlike what might have been expected from the circumstances alleged. Reminiscences would have been better marked. They would have been less ambiguous. In a writer so dependent on Paul as the author is represented to have been, they would have been more formal."[2]

2. Others object to the Epistle on account of its want of definiteness. Thus Schwegler urges the following reasons for its rejection: the want of any definite occasion, and the

---

[1] Steiger reduces the list to a very few examples: 1 Pet. i. 3 comp. Eph. i. 3; 1 Pet. ii. 1 comp. Col. iii. 8; 1 Pet. ii. 18 comp. Eph. v. 5; 1 Pet. iii. 1 comp. Eph. v. 22; 1 Pet. v. 5 comp. Eph. v. 21. *Commentary on First Peter*, vol. i. p. 10, in Clark's *Biblical Cabinet*.

[2] Davidson's *Introduction to the N. T.*, vol. iii. pp. 381, 382. No doubt Dr. Davidson, in his *Introduction to the Study of the N. T.*, has altered his views; but this does not diminish the value of the above argument.

general character of its contents and aims; the want of any literary or theological characteristics bearing the impress of individuality; and the want of any close connection and evolution of thought.[1] These subjective reasons are strained and without weight. The absence of any special occasion, if admitted, is no objection; to comfort believers in trial, and to exhort them to perseverance and stedfastness, were in themselves sufficient reasons. So far from there being no special peculiarities in the Epistle it is full of them, and in particular its statements regarding "the last things" have given rise to more speculations on the future life than perhaps any other book of the New Testament. And the Epistle, being entirely hortative, did not admit of that close connection of thought which is discernible in the Epistles of Paul. All such subjective reasons, even admitting their truth, are of no value when set against the strong external evidence in favour of the Epistle. If the Epistle has been strongly attested to have been written by Peter, no reasonable objection can be founded on any arbitrary opinion about the nature of its contents, so far as these do not directly contradict the opinions of the apostle as elsewhere ascertained. And besides, as we have already shown, the internal evidence is not against, but in favour of the authenticity of the Epistle.

3. Another objection is the improbability, or rather the impossibility, of the residence of Peter in Babylon. The Epistle professes to have been written from Babylon: "The Church that is in Babylon, elected together with you, saluteth you" (1 Pet. v. 13). Now it is asserted that it is very improbable that Peter would go beyond the limits of the Roman Empire into the kingdom of Parthia, to which Babylon belonged; and that as he wrote this Epistle in the midst of the persecution under Nero, it is impossible that he could have journeyed in so short a period to Rome, where he suffered martyrdom during the same persecution. Thus Schwegler, as another objection, adduces the "impossibility, on the assumption of the Epistle having been composed in Babylon, of harmonizing the Neronian persecution, presupposed

---

[1] See Huther's *Der erste Brief des Apostel Petrus*, pp. 36, 37, vierte Auflage. Schwegler's *Das Nachapostolische Zeitalter*, vol. ii. p. 7.

in the Epistle, with the martyrdom of Peter at Rome during that persecution."[1] Now, in answer to this objection, it is to be observed that its whole force depends on three disputed assumptions; first, that by Babylon is meant the celebrated city on the banks of the Euphrates, and not imperial Rome; secondly, that the persecution to which Peter refers was the persecution under Nero, and not the general trials to which Christians in the early ages were exposed from the heathen; and thirdly, that Peter suffered martyrdom at Rome during the Neronian persecution, and not at a time and in a locality which are undetermined. We shall afterwards particularly examine these three points; but meanwhile would remark that whilst an uncertainty rests on Babylon as denominating the city on the Euphrates, and on the fact of Peter's martyrdom at Rome, yet, granting that the preponderance of evidence is in favour of these points, there is no evidence whatever for the second assumption, that in the trials and sufferings mentioned in the Epistle there is an allusion to the persecution under Nero; and, consequently, if a sufficient interval be supposed to elapse between the writing of this Epistle and the death of the apostle, the fancied contradiction, in the supposition that he might have written the Epistle at Babylon and died as a martyr at Rome, disappears.[2]

II. THE AUTHOR OF THE EPISTLE.[3]

Peter, the author of this Epistle, is familiar to every reader of the Gospels and of the Acts of the Apostles. He was a native of Bethsaida on the Sea of Galilee; his father's name was Jonas ('Ιωνᾶς), or John ('Ιωάννης);[4] and he was by

---

[1] Huther's *Der erste Brief des Apostel Petrus*, p. 37 [E. Tr. p. 38].

[2] A fourth objection, that the persecution referred to in the Epistle is that which occurred under Trajan, will be examined when we consider the date of the Epistle.

[3] For the biography of Peter, see excellent articles in Winer's *Biblisches Wörterbuch*, *Encyclopedia Britannica*, Kitto's *Encyclopedia*, and Herzog and Plitt's *Real-Encyklopädie*. See also Keil's *Der erste Brief der Petrus*, and Plumptre's *Commentary on the Epistle of Peter*.

[4] The reading to be preferred in John i. 42, xxi. 15, 16, and adopted in the Revised Edition of the N. T.

occupation a fisherman. His original name was Simon (the Hebrew שִׁמְעוֹן),[1] and he received from the Lord Himself the name of Peter (Πέτρος), or Cephas (כֵּיפָא), to denote his strong and marked character. He was, like many ardent youths of Galilee, a disciple of John the Baptist, and was brought to Jesus by his brother Andrew (John i. 41).[2] Peter appears in the Gospels as a married man, and his house in Capernaum was frequented by our Lord (Matt. viii. 14). He received his direct call to the apostleship, when following his occupation as a fisherman at the Lake of Gennesareth (Mark i. 16-18). He followed Jesus in all His wanderings; he was the most zealous of His disciples, and on several occasions acted as the leader and spokesman of the apostles. On account of his noble confession of Jesus as the Messiah, he received a special benediction (Matt. xvi. 16); a confession which he afterwards renewed when His disciples threatened to desert Him (John vi. 68, 69). His conceptions, however, of the Messiahship of his Master were at this time defective, as is evident from his venturing shortly after the confession to rebuke Christ when He spoke of His sufferings and death (Matt. xvi. 22). He was one of the most highly favoured of our Lord's apostles, being privileged, along with John and James, to be with Him when He was transfigured on the holy mount, to be present when He raised the daughter of Jairus, and to be an eye-witness of His agony in Gethsemane. But although bold and impetuous, ardent in his attachment to his Master, and confident in his resolution to lay down his life for His sake, yet like many impulsive men he did not stand the test of the hour of danger. He thrice denied his Lord in the hall of Caiaphas. But although he sinned deeply, he repented sincerely. After His resurrection our Lord honoured him with a special appearance (Luke xxiv. 34; 1 Cor. xv. 5); and as Peter had thrice denied Him, so Jesus thrice restored him to his apostolic office (John xxi. 15-17).

Peter is the most prominent character in the first part of

[1] The name Simeon occurs in Acts xv. 14 and 2 Pet. i. 1.
[2] It was then that he first received the name Peter, an appellation which was renewed on his confession of Christ.

the Acts of the Apostles (Acts i.-xii.). He came forward as the leader and spokesman of the apostles in the election of a successor to Judas (Acts i. 15). On the day of Pentecost, he addressed the multitude of Jews of various nations assembled at the feast with such effect that three thousand were converted to the faith (Acts ii. 14, 38, 41), and thus the diffusion of Christianity was commenced by him. He and John preached the gospel in Samaria, where he encountered Simon Magus, afterwards converted by legend into his great opponent (Acts viii. 14–24). And as he was the first to preach the gospel to the Jews, so he was also the first to preach it to the Gentiles. Guided by a divine vision, he opened the Church of Christ to the whole world by the conversion of Cornelius (Acts x.). "God made choice," he observes, "among us that the Gentiles by my mouth should hear the word of the gospel and believe" (Acts xv. 7). He was the special object of that persecution which Herod Agrippa raised against the Church, and only by a miracle escaped the death designed for him (Acts xii.). He took a prominent part in the Council of Jerusalem, and stood forward as the advocate for the freedom of the Gentiles from the restrictions of the Mosaic law (Acts xv. 7). After this he is no more mentioned in the Acts; the missionary labours of Paul occupy the remainder of that book, and James, the Lord's brother, occupies the place of Peter as the recognised head of the Church in Jerusalem (Acts xxi. 10).

In the Epistles Peter is rarely mentioned. We are informed that at Antioch, then the capital of Gentile Christianity, he showed for a second time an unsteadiness of character. He had come down to that city from Jerusalem, and had freely mixed with the Gentile Christians; but, on the arrival of certain bigoted Jews, he temporized, and thus brought upon himself the merited reproof of Paul (Gal. ii. 11). In the First Epistle to the Corinthians, mention is made of a section of the Church of Corinth who designated themselves as the party of Cephas (1 Cor. i. 12), probably those extreme Jewish converts who wished to impose the observance of the Mosaic law on the Gentiles, and who regarded Peter as their leader, though such sentiments were not entertained by him.[1] There is nothing in Scripture to show that Peter, as Paul and Apollos, the other leaders mentioned in that Epistle, made a personal visit to Corinth, though the fact of such a visit is attested by ecclesiastical tradition.[2] We are also informed that Peter, being a married man, was accustomed in his missionary journeys to be accompanied by his wife (1 Cor. ix. 5). We have, however, no record in Scripture of these journeys. His Epistle is addressed to Christians belonging to certain countries in Asia, but we cannot gather from that Epistle that he himself personally visited these countries. If Babylon, from which he wrote this Epistle (1 Pet. v. 13), be the well-known city on the Euphrates, which, however, is by no means certain, Peter must have travelled beyond the boundaries of the Roman Empire into the distant East.

The character of Peter may be distinctly traced from the incidents recorded in Scripture. The same characteristic features are discernible throughout; the Peter, who denied Christ in the hall of Caiaphas, is the same who temporized at Antioch; and so also the Peter, who nobly confessed Christ at Cæsarea Philippi, is the same who denounced the Sanhedrim to their face with being the betrayers and murderers of their Messiah. He excelled all the apostles in zeal, boldness, and impetuosity. Naturally sanguine and impulsive, he was ever ready to come forward and take the lead. Ardent in his attachment to the Lord, it was no vain boast, but the expression of deep affection, when he declared his willingness to die for Him. But like most impulsive men, he was deficient in steadiness, and on two occasions he showed a want of moral courage. Of all the apostles Peter appears the most human, the most liable to be affected with the frailties and infirmities of humanity; and this human element of his character, ennobled as it was by high aspirations and aims, renders him attractive and lovable. He had not the calm contemplativeness of John, nor the spiritual insight and moral grandeur of Paul, and was better fitted for the task of founding than for that of building up the Church.

---

[1] The difference between Petrine and Pauline Christianity, so much insisted upon by the Tübingen school, we consider to be a baseless assumption.

[2] Euseb. *Hist. Eccl.* ii. 25.

The notices of Peter in the traditions of the Church are numerous and somewhat inconsistent; it is impossible to unravel them. His visit to Antioch (Gal. ii. 11) probably led to the tradition that he was the founder of the Church in that city, and presided there as bishop for several years. Thus Eusebius informs us that Ignatius is celebrated by many even to this day as the successor of Peter at Antioch.[1] Dionysius, the bishop of Corinth (A.D. 170), informs us that Peter along with Paul was the founder of the Church of Corinth: "Thus, likewise, you by means of this admonition have mingled the flourishing seed that had been planted by Paul and Peter at Corinth; for both of these have planted us at Corinth, and likewise instructed us,"[2]—a tradition which probably arose from the existence of the Cephas party in Corinth (1 Cor. i. 12). Origen tells us that Peter preached the gospel in Pontus, Galatia, Cappadocia, Asia, and Bithynia;[3] but the apparent ground for this statement is the mention of these countries in this Epistle.[4] When released from prison in the reign of Herod Agrippa, we are informed that he went to another place (Acts xii. 17), which "other place" tradition tells us was Rome. Here he is said to have continued for several years, and only to have returned to Jerusalem in time to take part in the council of the Church in that city (Acts xv.). It is the general tradition of the Church that he again repaired to Rome, and suffered martyrdom in the great Neronian persecution.[5] That he died a martyr's death may be considered as an undoubted fact, as such a fate was foretold him by his Master (John xxii. 18, 19), and is attested by his contemporary Clemens Romanus (A.D. 97), though the place of martyrdom is not recorded. "Peter," writes Clement, "through unrighteous envy endured, not one or two, but numerous labours; and when he had at length suffered martyrdom, departed to the place of glory due to him."[6]

The legends concerning Peter are numerous. The most

---

[1] *Hist. Eccl.* iii. 36. [2] *Ibid.* ii. 25. [3] *Ibid.* iii. 1.

[4] See, however, *infra*, where the probability of Peter's journey in these quarters is maintained.

[5] The question regarding Peter's residence and martyrdom at Rome is reserved for a separate dissertation.

[6] *Epist. ad Corinthos*, chap. v.

noted of these is his encounter with Simon Magus. Indeed, a whole literature grew up in the primitive Church around this idea, a species of Christian romance.[1] Simon Magus is represented as a hero among heretics, the personification of the antichristian principle. According to Eusebius, in the reign of Claudius, Peter encountered him at Rome, and confounded him by his miracles and prayers.[2] According to the *Clementines*, Peter disputed with Simon Magus at Cæsarea, Tyre, Sidon, and Berytus. The final encounter took place at Rome in the reign of Nero. Simon Magus had gained the favour of Nero by working miracles before him. By the aid of demons he flew up toward heaven; when Peter, by his prayers and commands laid on these wicked spirits, caused him to fall headlong with such violence that he was killed on the spot.[3]

A few other legends deserve a brief notice. Clemens Alexandrinus informs us that Peter, seeing his wife led out to martyrdom, rejoiced on account of the honour conferred on her in receiving the martyr's crown, and addressing her by name, called upon her to remember her Lord.[4] According to tradition, the name of his wife was Concordia or Perpetua, and their daughter was called Petronella. Connected with his death, there is the following beautiful legend: Peter, escaping out of prison and flying from Rome, met the Lord outside the gates, whom he asked, "Lord, whither goest Thou?" and the Lord replied, "I go to Rome to be crucified afresh."

---

[1] The *Clementine Homilies*, the *Clementine Recognitions*, the *Apostolic Constitutions*, the *Acts of Peter and Paul*, the *Passion of Peter and Paul*, the *Acts of the Holy Apostles*, etc. See also Cureton's *Ancient Syriac Documents*.

[2] *Hist. Eccl.* ii. 14.

[3] *Apostolic Constitutions*, vi. 9. The death of Simon Magus is also described at great length in the *Acts of Peter and Paul*. It is not only in the *Clementines* that this legend of Peter's encounter with Simon Magus is found, but also in the works of the early Fathers. A curious mistake is committed by Justin Martyr (*Apol.* i. 26), who informs us that Simon Magus was honoured as a god at Rome, and had a statue erected on the Tiber, between the two bridges, with the inscription Simoni Deo Sancti. Near the very spot mentioned by Justin a stone was dug up in 1574, in the popedom of Gregory XIII., with the inscription Semoni Sanco Deo—an inscription which applies to the Sabine god Semo-Sancus (Ovid, *Fast.* vi. 213), whom Justin must have confounded with Simon Magus. For further remarks on this Simon Magus legend, see *infra*.

[4] Euseb. *Hist. Eccl.* iii. 30. Clemens Alex. *Strom.* vii. 11.

On hearing this, Peter returned to prison, and submitted to that martyrdom which the Lord had formerly announced to him;[1] a legend which the Roman Catholic Church has perpetuated by the erection of the Church *Domine-quo-vadis* at Rome. According to Origen, Peter was crucified by his own desire with his head downwards, esteeming himself unworthy to suffer the same kind of punishment as his Master;[2] a tradition which is repeated by Chrysostom and Jerome.[3] Such a mode of crucifixion was sometimes practised by the Romans in their ingenuity to increase the sufferings of a death in itself one of the cruellest; but the earliest writers who attest the martyrdom of Peter make no mention of it, merely stating that whilst Paul was slain by the sword, Peter was crucified.

III. THE READERS OF THE EPISTLE.

The Epistle bears the inscription: "To the strangers scattered throughout Pontus, Galatia, Cappadocia, Asia, and Bithynia, elect;" or, as it is more correctly rendered in the *Revised Version*: "To the elect, who are sojourners of the Dispersion" (ἐκλεκτοῖς παρεπιδήμοις διασπορᾶς).

These words taken by themselves, without reference to the contents of the Epistle, or to the state of the Churches in the countries named, would seem to imply that the First Epistle of Peter was, like the Epistle of James, addressed to Jewish Christians, to the Jews of the Dispersion (διασπορᾶς), who had been converted unto Christianity. Thus Eusebius says: "In what provinces Peter also proclaimed the doctrine of Christ appears from his own writings, and may be seen from that Epistle we have mentioned as admitted into the canon, and which he addressed to the Hebrews in the Dispersion."[4] Accordingly this opinion has been adopted by Epiphanius, Jerome, Calvin, Erasmus, Beza, Grotius, Bengel, Hug, Lange,

---

[1] This legend is contained in the *Acts of Peter and Paul*, and is related by Ambrose, *Epist.* 33.

[2] Euseb. *Hist. Eccl.* iii. 1. Some think that Origen's language may have been misunderstood, and that κατὰ κεφάλης may denote merely capitally, or upon the head: "He was put to death by crucifixion."

[3] Lardner's *Works*, vol. iii. p. 408.

[4] *Hist. Eccl.* iii 4.

Weiss,[1] Beyschlag, Schenkel, Fronmüller, and Dean Plumptre. The following are the chief reasons assigned for it :—
1. The designation of the readers, "sojourners of the Dispersion," is similar to that found in the Epistle of James, which was addressed to Jewish Christians (Jas. i. 1). 2. The Epistle abounds with references and quotations from the Old Testament, presupposing that the readers were acquainted with the Jewish Scriptures. 3. Several passages occur which presuppose that those addressed were not Gentile, but Jewish Christians; as, for example, "Having your conversation honest among the Gentiles" (1 Pet. ii. 12). "Even as Sarah obeyed Abraham, calling him Lord; whose daughters ye are as long as ye do well" (1 Pet. iii. 6). 4. Peter was the apostle of the circumcision, and therefore his ministry was chiefly confined to the Jews.[2] But these reasons are insufficient. The terms of the inscription are not so definite as in the Epistle of James, "to the twelve tribes of the Dispersion," where "the twelve tribes" denote the Jewish nation. Here it is to "the strangers of the Dispersion" (παρεπιδήμοις διασπορᾶς),—a phrase which admits of a figurative sense, being an allusion to Christians as strangers dispersed throughout the world; and as such Peter addresses his readers : " I beseech you, as strangers and pilgrims (παρεπιδήμους), abstain from fleshly lusts which war against the soul" (1 Pet ii. 11). As to the quotations from the Old Testament, these also occur in the Epistles to the Romans and Galatians, which were addressed chiefly to Gentile Christians. The passages adduced do not prove that the readers were Jewish Christians; for simply as Christians they were to have their conversation honest among the Gentiles; and the words referring to Sarah, " whose daughters ye are," ought rather to be rendered, " whose daughters ye are become."[3] Besides, as we shall see, there are other passages which indicate the Gentile origin of the readers. Although Peter was the apostle of the circumcision,

---

[1] *Einleitung*, p. 424.

[2] These reasons are stated at great length and with much force by Weiss in his *Der Petrinische Lehrbegriff*, p. 99 ff. See also Fronmüller in Lange's *Bibelwerk* [E. Tr. p. 7].

[3] ἧς ἐγενήθητε τέκνα ; the phrase is so rendered in the margin of the Revised Version.

yet this does not necessitate the restriction of his ministry to the Jews.

Some suppose that the readers are called "sojourners of the Dispersion," because they were chiefly composed of Jewish proselytes. This is supposed to be indicated by the word παρεπιδήμοις joined to διασπορᾶς. This opinion has been adopted by Michaelis, Credner,[1] Neudecker, Benson, and Reuss.[2] Thus Michaelis observes: "The expression 'strangers scattered throughout Pontus,' etc., may very properly denote Jewish proselytes who had embraced the Christian religion, or persons who were born heathens but were become converts, first to Judaism and then to Christianity."[3] But this is an opinion which cannot be sustained; for although it is highly probable that many of the early converts were Jewish proselytes, yet there were no churches composed of such; when converted to Christianity they ceased to be Jewish proselytes, and were incorporated in the general body of Christians.

We consider, then, that the Epistle was addressed to Christians in general, whether converted Jews, Jewish proselytes, or Gentiles. This opinion has been adopted by Augustine, Cassiodorus, Luther, Calovius, Steiger, Mayerhoff, Hofmann, Guericke, Huther, Schott, Brückner, Lechler, Wiesinger, Thiersch, Sieffert, De Wette, Keil, Schaff, Alford, Davidson, and the vast majority of modern commentators. The Churches in several of the countries mentioned, especially in Galatia and Proconsular Asia, were founded by Paul, and, as we learn from the Acts and the Pauline Epistles, were chiefly composed of Gentile Christians, or at least were mixed congregations, composed of Jews and Gentiles. Nor is there the slightest intimation that in the apostolic times the Jewish and Gentile Christians formed separate congregations; they were united in one body. Besides, there are several references in this Epistle which suggest the predominant Gentile element; as, for example, "As obedient children, not fashioning yourselves according to the former lusts in your ignorance" (1 Pet. i. 14),—

---

[1] See especially Credner's *Einleitung*, pp. 639, 640.
[2] "Members of the Israelitish nation by religious faith, but not by birth and ascetic rites." Reuss' *Christian Theology*, vol. ii. p. 272, E. Tr.
[3] Michaelis, *Introduction*, by Marsh, vol. vi. p. 320.

words which receive their most probable meaning when applied to the former heathenism of the readers. And again: "For the time past of our life may suffice us to have wrought the will of the Gentiles, when we walked in lasciviousness, lusts, excess of wine, revellings, banquetings, and abominable idolatries" (1 Pet. iv. 3), referring evidently to their former heathen life. Accordingly, the designation of the readers must be taken in a somewhat figurative sense. They are called (ἐκλεκτοί), because they were chosen of God; strangers (παρεπίδημοι), because this world was not their home; and belonging to the Dispersion (διασπορᾶς), because they were dispersed in those countries mentioned in the Epistle.[1]

Those addressed are Christians resident in Pontus, Galatia, Cappadocia, Asia, and Bithynia. The question has been asked, Why the Epistle was restricted to Christians resident in those specified countries? To this question a confession of ignorance has generally been returned. Thus Farrar observes: "Why he selected the Christians of Asia Minor, and did not include the Churches of Syria, Macedonia, and Achaia, is a question which we cannot solve, seeing that both in Greece and in Syria he was personally known."[2] But the probability is that Peter was personally related to the Christians in those countries by having preached the gospel among them. It is admitted that there is nothing in the Epistle which implies this; but there is nothing that contradicts it. It has indeed been affirmed that the words, "which are now reported unto you by them that preached the gospel unto you" (1 Pet. i. 12), militate against the idea of Peter's personal acquaintance with his readers; but so much cannot be inferred from this general expression.[3] The very fact that Peter wrote to them presupposes his acquaintance with them. And accordingly this is the opinion adopted

---

[1] Salmon supposes that by "the sojourners of the Dispersion" are meant those members of the Roman Church whom Nero's persecution had dispersed to seek safety in the provinces in Asia Minor. *Introduction to the N. T.*, p. 551.

[2] Farrar's *Early Days of Christianity*, vol. i. p. 146.

[3] That Peter himself visited these countries is maintained by Credner, Neudecker, and Weiss, and denied by Bleek. "As to Peter's personal relations towards his readers," observes Bleek, "we have no trace in the Epistle of his

by the early Church; it is asserted by Origen, Eusebius,[1] Jerome, and Epiphanius. It is true that the only ground for this assertion may have been the address at the commencement of the Epistle; but it may also have been a matter of fact.

The first country named is Pontus, lying along the shores of the Black Sea. We do not know how the gospel penetrated into that distant land; Jews from Pontus are mentioned among the number of those present at Jerusalem on the day of Pentecost (Acts ii. 9); and Aquila, one of Paul's fellow-travellers, was a native of that country (Acts xviii. 2). Galatia received the gospel by the direct preaching of Paul (Acts xvi. 6, xviii. 33), and to the Christian inhabitants of that country he wrote his celebrated Epistle. Cappadocia probably received the gospel from "Jews, dwellers in Cappadocia," who were converted at Pentecost by the preaching of Peter (Acts ii. 9); some centuries later it derived fresh lustre from the fame of its Churches and the vigorous orthodoxy of its bishops.[2] Asia is the celebrated province of Proconsular Asia, including the districts of Pisidia, Mysia, Lycaonia, and Phrygia, embracing, along with Ephesus, its capital, some of the most notable cities mentioned in the Acts, as Pisidian Antioch, Lystra, Derbe, Miletus, in which Paul preached the gospel; and the Apocalypse is addressed to "the seven Churches which are in Asia." Bithynia is only once mentioned in the Acts, where we are informed that Paul and his company assayed to go into Bithynia, but the Spirit suffered them not (Acts xvi. 7). When and by whom the gospel was first preached in Bithynia, we do not know.

We have in this list of countries a remarkable proof of the rapid diffusion of Christianity. At this early period the gospel was spread throughout the East in countries far distant from Jerusalem, where it originated. At a very

having been among them himself. Many texts, on the contrary, make it probable that the gospel had not long been known and received by them, and that it had not been preached by the writer." *Introduction to N. T.*, vol. ii. p. 166.

[1] *Hist. Eccl.* iii. 1. 4.
[2] As Gregory Nazianzen and his brother Basil, and Gregory, bishop of Nyssa.

early period there were flourishing Churches in the chief cities of Syria and Proconsular Asia. The Christians must have been very numerous in Antioch and Ephesus. Whilst the Jews as a nation rejected the gospel, the Greeks were peculiarly susceptible to its influences. The Greek mind was dissatisfied with the rites and superstitions of heathenism, and with the sceptical philosophy of the schools, and longed for a system of living religion and of positive truth. Besides, at this period there was a great spirit of unrest,—a longing for some truths on which men could rely,—a desire for something on which they could rest some hope of immortality. Christianity supplied this void in the Greek mind; and perhaps in no countries, if we except Macedonia and Achaia, did Christianity spread more rapidly than in those mentioned in this Epistle. We know from Pliny's celebrated letter to Trajan (A.D. 108), written not long after this Epistle of Peter, that Christianity had taken such a firm hold on the inhabitants of Bithynia that men of all ranks and ages embraced the gospel, that the temples were deserted and the sacrifices discontinued; and that this was the case not only in the cities, but in the villages and in the open country.[1]

Regarding the condition of the readers of this Epistle, it is manifest that they were threatened with persecution. We meet in the Epistle with continual references to trial. The time was come when judgment must begin at the house of God (1 Pet. iv. 17); Christians were exposed to false accusations as malefactors (1 Pet. iii. 16); they were liable to be dragged before the heathen tribunals; they were called upon to give an answer ($ἀπολογία$) for their faith (1 Pet. iii. 15); they were reproached for the name of Christ, and were made partakers with Him in His sufferings (1 Pet. iv. 13, 14); their Christianity was regarded as a crime (1 Pet. iv. 16). At its very commencement Christianity aroused the hostility of the world, and as time elapsed this hostility increased; and therefore it is not surprising that Christians in these countries were exposed to persecution. Christianity was everywhere spoken against (Acts xxviii. 22); and the Christian teachers

[1] *C. Plin. Trajano Imp.* lib. x. ep. xcviii. See Paley's *Evidences of Christianity*, chap. ix., on "The Propagation of Christianity."

were regarded as the disturbers of the peace, turning the world upside down (Acts xvii. 6). Still, however, it is unnecessary to suppose that any special or authorized persecution against the Church had as yet arisen; either, with Eichhorn,[1] Mayerhoff, Ewald, Schott, and Salmon, to consider that the allusion is to the persecution under Nero, or, with Baur, Schwegler, Hilgenfeld, Mangold, and Pfleiderer, to assert that the persecution under Trajan is adverted to.[2] The expressions are general, and it would rather appear that persecution was threatened than that it had actually broken out. Believers had to be forewarned of the trials that awaited them, and to be encouraged and confirmed in the faith. "Beloved, think it not strange concerning the fiery trial which is to try you, as though some strange thing happened unto you. The time is come that judgment must begin at the house of God" (1 Pet. iv. 12, 17). "It seems clear," observes Canon Cook, "that no regular systematic persecution conducted under imperial authority had broken out at that time, either in the city where this Epistle was written, or in the districts to which it was addressed. The mutterings of the storm were heard, and there were frequent anticipations of impending woes; but the great judgment had not yet begun from ($\grave{a}\pi\acute{o}$) the house of God."[3]

IV. THE DESIGN AND CONTENTS OF THE EPISTLE.

The design of this Epistle is not *doctrinal* or *polemical;* the apostle does not aim at the instruction of his readers in the doctrines of Christianity, or at the refutation of those errors which had sprung up among them; he assumes their knowledge, and builds his exhortations upon it. Nor is the design *conciliatory* — to reconcile, as the Tübingen school suppose, Pauline with Petrine Christianity:[4] there is nothing

[1] *Einleitung in das N. T.*, vol. iii. p. 619.
[2] Hilgenfeld's *Einleitung*, p. 679. Mangold's *Einleitung* (edition of Bleek's *Introduction*), p. 748.
[3] *Speaker's Commentary*, vol. iv. p. 160. See also Wiesinger, *Der Brief des Petrus*, p. 33. So also Credner, Wieseler, Reuss, Huther, Bruckner.
[4] Davidson's *Introduction to the Study of the N. T.*, vol. i. p. 518, 2nd ed. He remarks: "The Epistle bears evidence of a mediating or conciliatory stand-

in the Epistle to support this idea. The Epistle is mainly *hortatory*—designed to exhort Christians to the practice of the duties of Christianity. We find the occasion of the Epistle in the condition of the Churches to which Peter wrote—the approach of that fiery trial which was to try them.[1] The hatred of their enemies was increasing; if open and systematic persecution had not commenced, many particular instances of persecution had occurred. In accordance with this state of matters, the design of the Epistle is thus stated by the author himself: "By Silvanus I have written briefly, exhorting and testifying ($παρακαλῶν$ $καὶ$ $ἐπιμαρτυρῶν$) that this is the true grace of God wherein ye stand" (1 Pet. v. 12). Thus the design of Peter in his Epistle was twofold: First, to confirm his readers ($ἐπιμαρτυρῶν$) in the faith. Peter knew from his own sad experience that the approaching day of persecution would test their faith, and therefore he seeks to confirm them in their profession of Christianity, to show them the reality of the grace of God wherein they were established, to prove to them that they had not followed cunningly-devised fables, and to enable them to give an answer to those who asked a reason of the hope that was in them. Secondly, to exhort and comfort them ($παρακαλῶν$) in their trials. They were not to be astonished at these as unlooked-for events, but rather to rejoice that they were called upon to suffer for the name of Christ. They were to remember the sufferings of Christ for them, and to consider it a privilege to be made partakers in these sufferings. And especially they were to look forward to that happy issue out of all their troubles, when they would receive the crown of life which God had promised to them that love Him. But they were carefully to guard against giving any reasonable cause for these sufferings; they were to live blameless lives, so that no crime could be laid to their charge; if it was only as Christians, on account of their religion, that they were called upon to suffer,

---

point. . . . The sharp points of antagonism between the Petrines and Paulines give place to a mild statement, in which the Ebionitic James is used along with the liberal Paul."

[1] This is well stated by Ewald in his *Sieben Sendschreiben des neuen Bundes*, p. 4 f.

they had no cause to be ashamed, but rather to glorify God on this behalf (1 Pet. iv. 15, 16). The design of the Epistle is thus stated with tolerable correctness by Pfleiderer: "an exhortation to patience under persecution from without, and to a blameless life, by which the Christian community might avoid every occasion for a justifiable persecution."[1]

Contents.—The Epistle, being wholly hortatory, does not demand a logical sequence of ideas. The precepts are somewhat detached; Peter passes from one exhortation to another without any discernible continuity of thought. It resembles in this respect the Epistle of James, though there the connection is even less discernible. The apostle, having saluted his readers, renders thanks unto God for the living hope with which they were inspired by the resurrection of Christ. Though they were for a season exposed to manifold temptations, yet these trials would only serve to strengthen their faith and to increase their love to Christ. They must stand fast in that faith which had been foretold by the holy prophets, and was now manifested to them. Hence it becomes them to live holy lives, to remember their high calling, to consider that they had been purchased by the precious blood of Christ, and born again by the word of God (chap. i.). Thus begotten again, as new-born babes, they must lay aside their former evil nature, and live lives of innocence and sincerity; they are a holy priesthood, a peculiar people; they are called upon to show forth the glory of the Lord; once they were not a people, but now they are the people of God. They must submit with patience to all the sufferings to which they will be inevitably exposed, and in this respect they must follow the example of their divine Lord and Master (chap. ii.). In all the relations of life they must show themselves examples of holiness; the same rules apply to the man and to the woman, to husbands and to wives. Their best defence against their enemies will be their forbearance toward them and the holiness of their lives; and if called upon to suffer for righteousness' sake, they ought to esteem it an honour and a privilege, it being better to suffer for well-doing than for evil-doing. Christ Himself suffered for sins; but though put to death in

[1] Pfleiderer's *Paulinism*, vol. ii. p. 150.

the flesh He was quickened in the spirit, in which He preached to the disobedient spirits before the flood (chap. iii.). As, then, Christ had suffered for them in the flesh, so it becomes them to arm themselves with the Spirit of Christ. They had already lived too long to the lusts of the flesh; the past must now be abandoned. Judgment was at hand, and therefore they must be sober and watchful unto prayer. They must be armed and prepared; the fiery trial which is to try them was near: they must be made partakers of the sufferings of Christ; but this to them should be the cause of joy and not of dismay (chap. iv.). The apostle next proceeds to address the elders of the Church, and exhorts them to feed the flock of Christ; he admonishes the younger among them to submit to the elder, and all to be humble, sober, and watchful. He then concludes his Epistle with a doxology; he recommends to them Silvanus as the bearer of the Epistle, and sends salutations from Mark and from the Church, or, as others think, from a female disciple at Babylon (chap. v.).

The style of the Epistle is suited to its hortatory design; it is earnest and pressing, warm and affectionate. The whole Epistle being designed to comfort and strengthen believers under the sufferings to which they were exposed, the apostle especially dwells upon the sufferings of Christ, as at once their example and encouragement. There is nothing of despondency in the Epistle; on the contrary, its character is sanguine; it looks forward to a happy issue out of all these trials, and holds out the eternal glory to which they are called by Jesus Christ (1 Pet. v. 10). "This Epistle," observes Erasmus, "is full of apostolic authority and dignity, sparing in words and fertile in thought." With regard to its diction there is a certain want of logical connection; the writer appears to be hurried on by the thoughts which successively suggest themselves. Alford observes that "the word οὖν occurs only in connection with imperatives introducing practical inferences; ὅτι and διότι only as substantiating motives to Christian practice by Scripture citation or by sacred facts; γάρ mostly in similar connections. The link between one idea and another is found not in any progress of unfolding thought or argument, but in the last word of the foregoing sentence, which is taken up and followed out in the new one." [1]

Baronius supposes that the Epistle was originally written in Aramaic; and Bertholdt thinks that it is a translation into Greek by Silvanus or Mark. But for these opinions there is no foundation. The numerous quotations from the Old Testament are taken from the Septuagint, and not from the original Hebrew. It is not improbable that Silvanus acted as Peter's amanuensis, but there is nothing to indicate that he was the translator.[2] The country of Galilee, of which Peter was a native, was bilingual; without doubt Peter was early accustomed to speak Greek as well as Aramaic, and his subsequent intercourse with the Greeks would improve his knowledge of their language. There is nothing incredible or surprising in the fact that the Galilean apostles, James, Peter, and John, could write Greek.[3]

The Epistle, far from being dependent on the thoughts of others, as some affirm, is full of marked peculiarities. Peter has with some reason been styled "the Apostle of Hope." This has indeed been somewhat exaggerated, but still hope may be regarded as the keynote of the Epistle.[4] It commences with blessing God that He had called its readers unto a lively hope; it holds forth the rewards of the faithful as their comfort and support amid the trials of life; it speaks of the salvation of their souls as the end of their faith; it describes them as but strangers and pilgrims in this world; it looks forward to the appearance of Jesus Christ as at hand, and alludes to the hope that is in them. The apostle is continually looking forward to the future; the present is dark and gloomy, but the future is full of hope. Another peculiarity is that the Epistle, more than any other writing of the New Testament, bears upon it the impress of the Old Testament. Not only are there proportionately more quota-

---

[1] Alford's *Greek Testament*, vol. iv., Prolegomena, pp. 137, 138. For remarks on the style and diction of the Epistle, see Davidson's *Introduction to the Study of the N. T.*, vol. i. pp. 432-434 (2nd ed. vol. i. pp. 526, 527).

[2] So Schenkel, *Christusbild*, p. 48.

[3] See Mayerhoff's *Petrinische Schriften*, p. 136.

[4] So Mayerhoff and Weiss. Weiss calls Peter, Der Apostel der Hoffnung. *Der Petrinische Lehrbegriff*, p. 25.

tions from the Old Testament, but much of the phraseology of the Epistle is Old Testament phraseology. Christians are the heirs to the privileges of God's ancient people; they are a royal priesthood, a holy nation, a peculiar people; their works are spiritual sacrifices; once they were not a people, but now they are the people of God. There are also, both in this and in the Second Epistle, frequent references to the prophecies of the Old Testament as predicting the sufferings and glory of Christ, and foreshadowing the salvation which is revealed in the gospel (1 Pet. i. 10–12; 2 Pet. i. 19–21). And a further peculiarity of this Epistle, as of the Second, is its eschatology. There are in it statements regarding a future life, disclosures of the unseen world which distinguish it from the other writings of the New Testament, such as Christ preaching in spirit to the spirits in prison (1 Pet. iii. 18–20), and the preaching of the gospel to the dead (1 Pet. iv. 6).[1]

V. TIME AND PLACE OF WRITING.

Various dates have been assigned to this Epistle. Weiss and Fronmüller rank it among the earliest writings of the New Testament, and suppose it to be written about the year 53 or 54.[2] Michaelis, Steiger, Guericke, Brückner,[3] Wieseler, Davidson (*Introduction to N. T.*), Alford, and Cook, supposing that the trials alluded to did not point to the Neronian persecution, think that it was written before that event, between the years 60–63. Hug, Neander, Thiersch, De Wette, and Mayerhoff, adopting the opinion that the apostle alludes to the persecution under Nero, suppose that it was written toward the close of the year 64, when that persecution was raging. Eichhorn, Credner, Schott, Bleek, Sieffert, Wiesinger, Huther, and Farrar think that it was written when the Church was suffering from the after-effects of that persecution, between the years 65–67. And, as already mentioned, the Tübingen

---

[1] See *infra*, "Dissertation on the Eschatology of Peter."
[2] Weiss's *Biblical Theology of the N. T.*, vol. i. p. 163 ff. *Einleitung in das N. T.*, p. 434. Fronmüller in Lange's *Bibelwerk*, p. 9.
[3] Brückner supposes that the Epistle was written during the later activity of Paul, but before his imprisonment in Jerusalem.

school[1] affirm that it was written about the year 112, during the persecution under Trajan.

In the Epistle itself there are few indications of time. The gospel was already diffused in the countries of Pontus, Galatia, Cappadocia, Asia, and Bithynia, and time must be allowed for this extension of Christianity. Silvanus is mentioned as the bearer of this Epistle (1 Pet. v. 13);[2] and if he is the same as the companion of Paul, the Epistle must have been written after Paul's second missionary journey (A.D. 54), because it was not until then that Silvanus left him. If there are in the Epistle references to Paul's Epistle to the Ephesians, as many suppose, it must have been written after that Epistle (A.D. 63); but if, as we believe, these references are imaginary, this argument is baseless. An argument has been drawn from the presence of Mark (1 Pet. v. 13). It is generally supposed that this is the same as John, whose surname was Mark, who accompanied Paul on his first missionary journey. Now, Mark was with Paul when he wrote the Colossians (Col. iv. 10) during his first Roman imprisonment (A.D. 63), but was absent from Rome during Paul's second Roman imprisonment (A.D. 67); for, writing to Timothy, the apostle says: "Take Mark, and bring him with you: for he is profitable to me for the ministry" (2 Tim. iv. 11). Hence it is supposed that in the interval (A.D. 63–67) Mark may have been with Peter. But no inference can be drawn from this, for it might as reasonably be argued that Mark was with Peter during the interval between Paul's first missionary journey, when Mark left him, and Paul's first Roman imprisonment (A.D. 46–63); and indeed this is more probable, as according to tradition Mark is regarded rather as the disciple of Peter than of Paul.[3] Another argument has been drawn

---

[1] So Baur, Pfleiderer, Lipsius, Keim, Holtzmann, Schwegler, and Hilgenfeld. Zeller goes the length of supposing that it was written in the reign of Hadrian. Dr. Davidson, in his *Introduction to the Study of the N. T.*, vol. i. p. 427, fixes the date between A.D. 75 and 80; but in his second edition of that work he adopts the opinion of Baur, that it was written in the reign of Trajan, perhaps A.D. 113 (vol. i. p. 524).

[2] Or the words may denote that Silvanus was Peter's amanuensis.

[3] According to ecclesiastical tradition, Mark journeyed with Peter as his interpreter, and it was chiefly at Peter's dictation, or on the information given

from the improbability that Peter would have written to Paul's converts in Galatia and Proconsular Asia during that apostle's lifetime, or at least before his imprisonment, and whilst he was at liberty to take the personal superintendence of those Churches which he had founded. But not much can be made of this alleged improbability; it is a mere gratuitous supposition; the apostles must have been free to write to whom they pleased. Taking all the circumstances of the case into consideration, giving time for the diffusion of the gospel probably by Peter and Silvanus in the countries mentioned, although it is admitted that there are slight grounds for a definite decision, we would assign the year 59 or 60 as the date of this Epistle.

But if there is an uncertainty regarding the date of this Epistle, there is still greater uncertainty regarding the place of writing. In the Epistle that place is denominated Babylon (1 Pet. v. 13); but there is a variety of opinion as to what is to be understood by this name. The following opinions may be rejected, as too plainly erroneous to merit examination. Harduin and Semler suppose that Babylon is a figurative designation of Jerusalem. Michaelis thinks that Seleucia is meant, as that city is sometimes, though, as he himself admits, rarely, called Babylon.[1] Calovius, Le Clerc, Pearson, Pott, and Burton suppose that Babylon in Egypt is meant, on the ground that Mark, who was with Peter, was the founder of the Church of Alexandria: but the Egyptian Babylon was not a city, but a military fort.[2]

There are two opinions which merit consideration. The first is that Babylon is a metaphorical designation of Rome—the successor of Babylon as the grand centre of power and vice. This opinion is maintained, not only by almost all Roman Catholic, but by numerous Protestant theologians. It has been adopted by Grotius, Lardner, Whitby, Macknight, Dietlein, Olshausen, Wiesinger, Hitzig, Sieffert, Thiersch, Schott, Hofmann, Hengstenberg, Baur, Ewald, Schaff, Horne,

---

by Peter, that he wrote the Gospel which bears his name. Eusebius, *Hist. Eccl.* iii. 39; Irenæus, *Hær.* iii. 10, 6.

[1] Michaelis, *Introduction to the N. T.*, by Marsh, vol. vi. p. 331.

[2] Strabo, xvii. 1.

Davidson, Salmon, Cook, and Farrar.[1] The testimony of antiquity is in its favour. Rome was then in the Christian Church known by the name of Babylon, and is so called in the Apocalypse (Rev. xiv. 8, xvii. 5, 18). Eusebius, in a passage where he apparently gives the opinion of Clemens Alexandrinus and Papias, observes: "Peter makes mention of Mark in the First Epistle, which he is also said to have composed at the same city of Rome, and that he shows this fact by an unusual metaphor, Babylon; thus, 'The Church at Babylon elected together with you saluteth you.'"[2] So also Jerome observes: "Peter mentions this Mark in his First Epistle, figuratively denoting Rome by the name of Babylon;"[3] and Oecumenius: "He calls Rome Babylon on account of the pre-eminence which of old had belonged to Babylon."[4] So also the subscription to the Epistle in several ancient manuscripts mentions Rome: ἐγράφη ἀπὸ Ῥώμης. Nor is there any trace in the writings of the Fathers, or in the traditions of the Church, of Peter's residence in Babylon; nor any mention of a Christian Church in that city. It is also urged that it is highly improbable that Peter should undertake so great a journey, that he should pass beyond the limits of the Roman Empire and go to Babylon, which then belonged to Parthia. And, lastly, it is asserted that Peter's residence in Babylon, if it occurred, as is generally supposed about the period of the Neronian persecution, does not admit of his journey to Rome, where, according to the general tradition of the Church, he suffered martyrdom.

These arguments, however plausible, are by others considered as insufficient to prove that by Babylon is here meant Rome, and that for the following reasons. It is by no means proved that in the days of Peter, Babylon was a current designation for Rome. It might have been so in apocalyptic literature, but this is a very different thing from ordinary usage. Eusebius does not give his own opinion, but merely

[1] See especially Farrar's *Early Days of Christianity*, vol. ii. p. 514 ff. Excursus iii., "Use of the name Babylon for Rome" in 1 Pet. v. 13. See also Cook's commentary on 1 Pet. in the *Speaker's Bible*: Schott's *Der erste Brief Petri*, p. 347; and Hofmann's (of Erlangen) *Der erste Brief Petri*, pp. 201-203.
[2] *Hist. Eccl.* ii. 15.   [3] *Catal. Script. Eccl.* 668.   [4] *In loco.*

states a report; nor is it evident from the context that he quotes from Clemens Alexandrinus or Papias. Jerome and Oecumenius lived at too late a date. The mere negative testimony, that Peter's residence in Babylon is not mentioned by the Fathers, is not conclusive. Peter's residence at Rome is itself doubtful; but, even if an ascertained fact, he would have ample time to travel from Babylon to Rome between the years 59 or 60, the probable date of the Epistle, and 64, when the Neronian persecution broke out. But the great objection adduced against the view of supposing Rome to be intended is that in writing an epistle Peter would not add an allegorical designation in his salutation. As Reuss observes: "A doctrinal epistle is not an apocalypse. Nor is it either demonstrable or probable that in later times the apocalyptic language without intimation was generally accepted among Christians." [1]

The other opinion is, that the celebrated Babylon on the Euphrates is meant. This is the view adopted by Calvin, Bengel, Credner, Neander, De Wette, Brückner, Wieseler,[2] Guericke, Weiss,[3] Steiger, Bleek, Lange, Frommüller, Huther, Reuss, Hug, Keil, Mangold, Lipsius, Alford, and Wordsworth. An argument in its favour has been derived from the order in which the different provinces are mentioned. They are enumerated from east to west, as one would do in writing from Babylon, and not from west to east, as one would do in writing from Rome. A reason for Peter's journey to Babylon is to be found in the fact that Babylon was the chief centre of the Jews of the Dispersion.[4] Peter was the apostle of the circumcision; he felt that it was his primary duty to preach the gospel to the Jews, and he could not find a larger number of them than at Babylon. "To the east of Syria," observes Merivale, "the dispersion of the Jews was still greater than to the west. . . . After the fall of Babylon and the desolation of its population, the Jews, if we may believe their own writers, took the place of the native races throughout the

---

[1] Reuss' *Geschichte der Schrift. N. T.*, p. 140 [E. Tr. p. 148].
[2] Wieseler's *Chronologie des apost. Zeitalter*, p. 578.
[3] Weiss' *Einleitung*, p. 433.
[4] Josephus, *Ant.* xv. 2. 2, xv. 3. 1, xvii. 2. 1-3.

surrounding districts."¹ "This Babylonian settlement," observes Dean Milman, "was so numerous and flourishing, that Philo more than once intimated the possibility of their marching in such force to the assistance of their brethren in Palestine, as to make the fate of the war with Rome very doubtful."²

But to this opinion it has been objected, that Babylon was at this period in ruins and deserted; and that some years before this the Jews were persecuted by the Parthians and expelled from Babylon. Josephus gives us an account of the calamities which befell the Jews in Babylon. He tells us that in the reign of Caligula they were so assaulted by the Babylonians that most of them fled to Seleucia; that shortly afterwards a pestilence carried off many of those who still remained, and occasioned new removals from the city; that in Seleucia the fugitives were attacked by the Greeks and Syrians, so that fifty thousand were slain; and that the Jews betook themselves to Nearda and Nisibis, and obtained security there by the strength of these cities.³ But to this it is replied, that Babylon is not merely the name of a city but of a province; and that it is an undoubted fact that it formed a great centre of Jewish population. Besides, twenty years had elapsed since these calamities had befallen the Jews in Babylon; and there is no reason to doubt that during that period they would again return and inhabit their old quarters. The Jews, though frequently expelled from Rome, as frequently returned; and doubtless this would be the case at Babylon, where they were more numerous and influential. The whole question as to the locality of Peter when he wrote the Epistle must accordingly remain doubtful. Nothing definite can be asserted; there are plausible arguments on both sides.

It is to be observed that in the salutation: "The Church which is at Babylon elected together with you saluteth you;" the word *Church* is not in the original,⁴ the phrase is

---

¹ *History of the Romans under the Empire*, vol. iii. 359.

² Milman's *History of the Jews*, vol. ii. 152.

³ Josephus, *Ant.* xviii. 9. 9. Milman's *History of the Jews*, vol. ii. pp. 152-155. Cook's *Commentary* in *Speaker's Bible*.

⁴ To this the Codex Sinaiticus is a notable exception; it contains the word ἐκκλησία.

ἡ συνεκλεκτή; and hence the "Revised Version" more correctly renders the passage: "She that is in Babylon elect together with you." Accordingly, some suppose that a Christian lady resident at Babylon is alluded to, like "the elect lady" in the Second Epistle of John. Eichhorn, Neander, Bengel, Mayerhoff, Credner, Rauch, Alford, Stanley, and Plumptre suppose that the lady alluded to by ἡ συνεκλεκτή is the apostle's wife, an opinion extremely fanciful, as it is most improbable that the apostle would, in his Epistle to a circle of churches, designate his wife as the co-elect lady at Babylon.[1] It is much more natural to supply the word ἐκκλησία, as is done in our Authorized Version.

The most important commentaries on this Epistle are those of Pott (Göttingen, 1810), Steiger (1832, translated Edinburgh 1836), Theile (Leipzig 1833), Mayerhoff (Hamburg 1835), Wiesinger (1854, translated in New York 1858), Weiss (*der Petrinische Lehrbegriff*, Berlin 1855), Schott (Erlangen 1863), Fronmüller (Lange's *Bibelwerk*, 1862, translated by Dr. Mombert, 1867), Brückner (dritte Auflage, Leipzig 1865), Huther (vierte Auflage, Göttingen 1877; translated Edinburgh 1881), Plumptre[2] (in the Cambridge series, Cambridge 1880), Cook (in the *Speaker's Bible*, London 1881), Keil (Leipzig 1883).

DISSERTATION I.

PETER'S RESIDENCE IN ROME.

The residence of Peter in Rome has been, and still is, disputed by theologians of every shade of opinion. Formerly it was the great subject of debate between Romanists and Protestants, but it was then discussed too much in a sectarian

---

[1] A still more fanciful opinion is to suppose that the person called "Marcus, my son," was not the spiritual, but the real son of the apostle. So Dean Stanley, *Sermons and Essays on the Apostolic Age*, p. 91.

[2] The commentary of Dean Plumptre, although brief, is perhaps one of the best.

spirit, each party aiming at victory rather than the ascertainment of the truth.¹ The result was that the subject was gradually allowed to drop, and, in general, Peter's Roman residence was acquiesced in as a historical fact. In recent times the question has been reopened and discussed, not from *à priori* conclusions, but from a historical and critical point of view. Baur, in his celebrated work *Der Apostel Paulus*, critically examined the testimony of the Fathers in favour of Peter's Roman residence, and pronounced the proof invalid, asserting that the foundation of this almost universal tradition was the romance or myth of the encounter of Peter with Simon Magus at Rome, which in various forms was circulated in the primitive Church.² In still more recent times this view has been maintained and wrought out in an exhaustive manner by Lipsius in his *Quellen der römischen Petrus-Sage*.³ It is to be observed that the point of dispute is not the *fact* but the *place* of Peter's martyrdom. Nearly all theologians agree that Peter's life terminated in martyrdom; this is a fact attested by evidence too strong to be disputed.⁴ Indeed, as we learn from John's Gospel, this was foretold by our Lord Himself, for, addressing Peter, He says: "Verily, verily, I say unto thee, When thou wast young, thou girdedst thyself, and walkedst whither thou wouldest; but when thou shalt be old, thou shalt stretch forth thy hands, and another shall gird thee, and carry thee whither thou wouldest not. This," adds the evangelist, "spake He, signifying by what death he should glorify God" (John xxi. 18, 19). From these words it is evident that Peter had ended his life by martyrdom before John wrote his Gospel;⁵ but there is in them no intimation as to the place of martyrdom, nor can any inference be drawn

---

¹ On the Protestant side, the subject was discussed by Matthias Flacius, Salmasius, and Friedrich Spanheim, and on the Catholic side by Foster, bishop of Rochester.

² Baur's *Apostel Paulus*, vol. i. p. 243 ff., and vol. ii. p. 316 ff. [E. Tr. vol. i. 227 ff., and vol. ii. 291 ff.], also the *Tübingen Zeitschrift für Theologie*, 1831, p. 136.

³ Kiel, 1872.

⁴ Testified by Clemens Romanus, A.D. 95, the earliest of the Fathers.

⁵ The words are a prediction, but it is evident from the language of the evangelist that that prediction had received its fulfilment.

K

from them in favour of Rome.¹ Accordingly on this point theologians have differed. Whilst Schott, the Protestant divine, goes the length of affirming that "the residence of Peter at Rome is one of the best attested facts of the later New Testament times,"² Ellendorf, the Roman Catholic theologian, sums up his critical investigations in the following terms: "Peter may have been at Rome; it is possible that he was there about the year 65 or 66. But it is nothing more than possible, and the opposite is equally likely, or even more likely. Nor can we take it ill of Protestants, if they follow the proofs offered by Holy Scripture and by the earliest Fathers, Clement and Justin, and hold Peter's residence at Rome, and all that is connected with it, to be a story drawn from the Apocrypha. Peter's residence at Rome can never be proved."³

Most theologians have adopted the opinion that the residence of Peter at Rome is a fact sufficiently established by the testimony of the Fathers. This is the view adopted by Bertholdt, Lardner, Ewald,⁴ Credner,⁵ Bleek, Olshausen, Gieseler,⁶ Huther, Keil, Schaff, Wieseler, Schott, Sieffert, Delitzsch, Wiesinger, Rothe, Fronmüller, Renan, Hilgenfeld, Weizsäcker, Weiss,⁷ Mangold, Farrar, Cook, Bishop Lightfoot,⁸ and by Windischmann⁹ and most of the Roman Catholic theologians.

The following are the testimonies of the Fathers on which

---

[1] We have no right to affirm, with Renan: "It is not to be supposed that Peter suffered martyrdom elsewhere than in Rome."

[2] *Der erste Brief des Petrus*, p. 348. So also Olshausen observes: "The presence of Peter in Rome, and his martyrdom there, are facts so well attested by historical evidence that they ought never to have been questioned." *Der Brief an die Römer*, p. 40.

[3] *Ist Petrus in Rom gewesen?* 1841. Quoted by Baur in the *Apostel Paulus*, vol. ii. p. 322, zweite Auflage [E. Tr. vol. ii. p. 296].

[4] *Geschichte des Volkes Israel*, vol. vi. p. 616 ff. [E. Tr. vol. vii. pp. 459–470].

[5] *Einleitung*, pp. 628–630.

[6] Gieseler, the great Church historian, discusses the subject in a valuable note, and comes to the conclusion that Peter suffered martyrdom in Rome A.D. 67. *Ecclesiastical History*, vol. i. p. 77, E. Tr.

[7] *Einleitung in das N. T.*, pp. 623, 624.

[8] See *Epistles of St. Clement of Rome*, p. 46.

[9] *Vindiciæ Petrinæ*, published at Ratisbon in 1836.

this opinion is founded: Clemens Romanus (A.D. 95), in the notable passage in which he mentions the martyrdom of Peter and Paul, observes: "Peter who by reason of unrighteous jealousy endured not one nor two but many labours, and thus having borne his testimony, went to his appointed place of glory;"[1] and then follows the account of the martyrdom of Paul before the rulers at Rome.[2] It is to be observed that Clement does not inform us where the martyrdom of Peter occurred, probably because the place was well known to his readers. Some infer that this must have been Rome, because Paul's martyrdom at Rome is mentioned immediately afterwards;[3] whilst others, from the same reason, draw an opposite conclusion.[4] Ignatius (A.D. 115), in his Epistle to the Romans, classed among his genuine Epistles, writes: "I do not, as Peter and Paul, issue commandments unto you."[5] From this it has been inferred that Peter as well as Paul preached the gospel to the Romans, to whom Ignatius wrote; whilst others assert that Peter and Paul are mentioned because they were the two chief preachers of Christianity. Papias (A.D. 116), as quoted by Eusebius, is supposed to testify to the presence of Peter in Rome, though others maintain that Eusebius does not, in the passage referred to, quote the words of Papias, but states what was the current tradition of his own day.[6] Dionysius, bishop of Corinth (A.D. 170), in his Epistle to the Romans, writes: "Thus likewise you, by means of this admonition, have mingled the flourishing seed that had been planted by Peter and Paul at Rome and Corinth. For both of these have planted us at Corinth, and likewise instructed

---

[1] *Ep. ad Corinth.* chap. v. The translation here given is that of Bishop Lightfoot.

[2] In describing Paul's martyrdom, Clement does not mention Rome, but merely states "that he came to the extreme limits of the west, and suffered martyrdom under the prefects." It is, however, generally agreed that Rome is here meant.

[3] So Sieffert, Bleek.

[4] Thus Froschammer observes: "If Peter had laboured and died at Rome as well as Paul, why does not Clement say also of him, that having preached in the east and west, he also died in the west? Manifestly Clement meant in these words to say something special about Paul, which could not be ascribed to Peter." *Romance of Romanism*, p. 20.

[5] *Ep. ad Rom.* chap. iv.   [6] Euseb. *Hist. Eccl.* ii. 15.

us; and having in like manner taught in Italy, they suffered martyrdom about the same time."[1] Irenæus (A.D. 180) gives the same testimony. "Matthew," he observes, "issued a written Gospel among the Hebrews, whilst Peter and Paul were preaching at Rome, and laying the foundation of the Church there."[2] And again: "We put to confusion all those who assemble in unauthorized meetings by indicating the tradition derived from the apostles of the very great, the very ancient, and universally known Church founded and organized at Rome by the two most glorious apostles, Peter and Paul."[3] Clement of Alexandria (A.D. 190) asserts that "Peter proclaimed the word publicly at Rome."[4] Tertullian (A.D. 200) says: "Let us see what utterance the Romans give, so very near to the apostles, to whom Paul and Peter conjointly bequeathed the gospel, and sealed it with their own blood."[5] And again, addressing the Church of Rome, he writes: "Happy Church, on which the apostles poured forth their doctrine along with their blood; where Peter's sufferings resembled those of our Lord, where Paul is crowned with the death of John (the Baptist), and where John was first plunged unhurt into boiling oil and sent to his island exile."[6] Eusebius gives the following quotation from Caius, the Roman presbyter (A.D. 212): "I can show the trophies (τὰ τρόπαια) of the apostles; for if you will go to the Vatican or to the Ostian Road, you will find the trophies of those who have laid the foundations of this Church."[7] Caius evidently alludes to Peter and Paul, and by the trophies of those apostles he, in all probability, means the places of their martyrdom, as, according to tradition, Peter was crucified on the Vatican and Paul was beheaded on the way to Ostia. Origen (A.D. 230) observes: "Peter appears to have preached through Pontus, Galatia, Bithynia, Cappadocia, and Asia, to the Jews of the Dispersion; finally, coming to Rome, he was crucified with his head downward, having requested to suffer in this way."[8] Lactantius (A.D. 306) gives the following account of the martyrdom of

---

[1] Euseb. *Hist. Eccl.* ii. 25.   [2] *Adv. Hær.* iii. 1.
[3] *Adv. Hær.* iii. 3.   [4] Euseb. *Hist. Eccl.* vi. 14
[5] *Adv. Marcion.* iv. 5.   [6] *De Præscript. Hæreticorum*, cap. 36.
[7] Euseb. *Hist. Eccl.* ii. 25.   [8] Euseb. *Hist. Eccl.* iii. 1.

Peter at Rome: "While Nero reigned, the Apostle Peter came to Rome, and, through the power of God committed to him, wrought certain miracles, and, by turning many to the true religion, built up a faithful and stedfast temple to the Lord. When Nero heard of these things, and observed that not only in Rome, but in other places, a great multitude revolted daily from the worship of idols, and, condemning their old ways, went over to the new religion, he hastened to destroy the heavenly temple, and to abolish the true faith. He it was who first persecuted the servants of God; he crucified Peter and slew Paul."[1] Eusebius (A.D. 325) gives the same account: "Thus Nero, publicly announcing himself as the chief enemy of God, was led on in his fury to slaughter the apostles. Paul is therefore said to have been beheaded at Rome, and Peter to have been crucified. And this account is confirmed by the fact that the names of Peter and Paul still remain in the cemeteries of that city even to this day."[2] It is needless to pursue the subject farther. The same account is repeated by Jerome, Athanasius, Chrysostom, and Augustine, and was received by the Church as an undoubted fact of history.

We have certainly an unbroken chain of patristic authorities testifying to the fact of Peter's residence and martyrdom at Rome. But, on these testimonies of the Fathers, it has been remarked that the earliest—those nearest to the fact attested—are not conclusive. Clement, although he mentions the martyrdom of Peter, yet gives no intimation as to the place where it occurred, and it is only by a doubtful inference that this is supposed to be Rome. The words of Ignatius certainly favour the idea that Peter preached the gospel to the Romans; but as this is not directly asserted, nothing certain can be inferred. The testimony of Papias is very doubtful; whereas the testimonies of the other Fathers are far removed in time from the fact attested. The earliest of them, Dionysius of Corinth, lived a hundred years after the martyrdom of Peter, and during that period there was ample

[1] *De morte persecut.* chap. ii.
[2] *Hist. Eccl.* ii. 25. So also in his *Demonstratio Evang.* iii. he writes: "Peter was crucified at Rome with his head downward, and Paul beheaded."

time for the rise and growth of the legend concerning his death at Rome. Besides, these testimonies are mixed with errors and legendary fables; as when Dionysius testifies that Peter and Paul both founded the Church at Corinth, whereas, according to the Acts, Paul was the sole founder; as when Irenæus asserts that both these apostles laid the foundation of the Church at Rome, whereas Christianity must have been planted there before either of these apostles visited the imperial city;[1] and as when Tertullian unites with the martyrdom of Peter and Paul at Rome the story that John was cast unhurt into a caldron of boiling oil, which is now generally regarded as a myth.

On the other hand, it is to be observed that the belief in Peter's martyrdom at Rome was extensively diffused throughout the whole Christian Church; we meet with it not only in the writings of the Latin Fathers, but also in the writings of the Alexandrian and Asiatic Fathers; so that its origin cannot be attributed to the hierarchical ambition of the Roman Church. The tradition also is virtually unanimous; there are no contrary traditions; no other place has been assigned for the martyrdom of Peter. There is no trace in the Fathers of Peter's martyrdom at Babylon, mentioned as the place from which he wrote his First Epistle, nor in any of the Asiatic countries where he preached the gospel. Rome has been fixed upon by the unanimous and unbroken tradition of the primitive Church.

Notwithstanding this apparently strong testimony of the early Church, the other opinion, that Peter was never at Rome, has been maintained by theologians of great eminence and learning. This is the view adopted by Spanheim,[2] Eichhorn,[3] Mayerhoff,[4] De Wette,[5] Schleiermacher, Ellendorf, Baur, Zeller, Schwegler, Hase, Holtzmann,[6] Lipsius, Frosch-

---

[1] At the same time, if Peter preached the gospel at Rome and was a principal cause in the diffusion of Christianity there, Irenæus might well in a general sense describe him as one of the founders of the Church of Rome.

[2] The full title of Spanheim's work is, *Dissertatio de ficta profectione Petri Apostoli in urbem Romam, deque non una traditionis origine*, 1679.

[3] *Einleitung in das N. T.*, vol. i. p. 554 ff.

[4] *Petrinische Schriften*, pp. 73–95.   [5] *Einleitung in das N. T.*, p. 376.

[6] Article "Petrus" in Schenkel's *Bibellexicon*.

ammer, Winer, Pfleiderer, Hausrath,[1] and Davidson;[2] whilst the great Church historian Neander wavers, but rather leans to the opinion that Peter was never in Rome.[3]

There is not the slightest indication in the Acts of the Apostles that Peter was ever at Rome. He is stated to have been at Jerusalem, Samaria, Joppa, and Cæsarea, but there is no mention of Rome. Several Roman Catholic theologians, indeed, assert that when it is said that Peter, after his return from prison, into which he was cast by Herod Agrippa, "went to another place" (Acts xii. 17), the reference is to Rome. But this is an assertion for which there is not the slightest foundation, and which is against all probability, because a short time afterwards Peter was present at the Council of Jerusalem. It is true that after that Council there is no mention of the missionary travels of Peter in the Acts; but that he was not at Rome when Paul arrived in that city as a prisoner (A.D. 61), is evident from the account of that apostle's reception. Mention is made of the brethren coming to meet him as far as Appii Forum and Tres Tabernæ (Acts xxviii. 15), but there is not the slightest hint of Peter's presence; indeed this is excluded, not only by the omission of his name, but by the inadequate views which the Roman Jews entertained of Christianity (Acts xxviii. 21, 22), which they could not have had, had Peter laboured among them at Rome. "The last chapter of the Acts of the Apostles," observes Renan, "is unintelligible if Peter was at Rome when Paul came there. We may take it as absolutely certain that Peter did not come to Rome before Paul, that is to say, before the year 61, as nearly as we can fix it."[4]

In those Pauline Epistles which have reference to Rome there is no indication of the presence of Peter in that city. There are annexed to the Epistle to the Romans (A.D. 58) numerous salutations to Christians in Rome, but among them Peter's name does not occur, which undoubtedly would have been the case had that apostle been at Rome when Paul wrote

---

[1] *Das Neutestamentliche Zeitalter*, vol. iii. p. 344.
[2] *Introduction to the Study of the N. T.*, 2nd ed. vol. i. pp. 504–506.
[3] Neander's *Planting of Christianity*, vol. i. pp. 377–381, Bohn's edition.
[4] *Hibbert Lectures* for 1880, p. 65.

his Epistle. So also in the four Epistles of the captivity—the Epistles to the Ephesians, Philippians, Colossians, and Philemon, written from Rome (A.D. 62, 63)—there is no mention of Peter, nor the slightest indication of his presence. In three of these Epistles salutations are sent by Christians resident in Rome, but here also Peter's name is wanting. And in Paul's last Epistle, the Second Epistle to Timothy, written from Rome shortly before his martyrdom (A.D. 68), there is no reference to Peter, although in that Epistle salutations are sent from various Roman Christians. It is true that this is mere negative testimony; but it is negative testimony of such a nature as amounts to a demonstration that Peter was not in Rome when Paul wrote his Epistle to the Romans, or when Paul himself was at Rome during either his first or his second imprisonment.[1]

Another argument, opposed to Peter's residence in Rome, is drawn from the mention of Babylon as the place from which he wrote his First Epistle (1 Pet. v. 13). Of course if Babylon here is a metonymy for Rome itself, as many eminent theologians suppose, then this is an assertion of his residence in that city.[2] But if the celebrated Babylon on the Euphrates is meant, then we have a presumption against Peter's Roman residence. It is argued that it is highly improbable that Peter would take so long a journey from Babylon to Rome, especially as in the neighbourhood of Babylon he would have an ample sphere of labour as the apostle of the circumcision among the Jews of the Dispersion. But much cannot be made of this argument, as we are ignorant of the circumstances of the case, and as there was ample time to admit of a journey from Babylon to Rome in the interval between the writing of his Epistle (A.D. 60)[3] and his martyrdom, according to the testimony of the Fathers, in the great persecution under Nero (A.D. 64). As Neander

---

[1] We here presuppose the fact of Paul's twofold imprisonment. See this subject fully discussed in the author's *Commentary on the Acts of the Apostles*, vol. ii. p. 451 ff.

[2] See *supra*, p. 141.

[3] Of course, those who fix the date of the Epistle later than A.D. 60 will have greater difficulty in finding a place for Peter's journey from Babylon to Rome; and accordingly many fix the date of Peter's martyrdom at A.D. 67.

remarks: "So many circumstances unknown to us might conspire to bring about such an event (a journey from Babylon to Rome), that with our defective knowledge of the Church history of these times, what we have stated cannot be considered a decisive evidence against the truth of the tradition, if it can be sufficiently supported on other grounds." [1]

Those who reject Peter's residence in Rome are bound to furnish some explanation for the existence of so extensive, unanimous, and uncontradicted tradition of his martyrdom in that city. Accordingly, Baur and Lipsius attempt to account for the origin of this tradition from the romance or legend of Peter's encounter with Simon Magus. The subject is one of interest and importance with reference to early Christianity. Simon Magus, whose encounter with Peter in Samaria is related in the Acts of the Apostles (Acts viii. 9–24), occupies an important place in ecclesiastical tradition, and a far larger space in the legends of the Church is allotted to him than we should have expected from the short notice in the Acts.[2] His travels and actions, his magical arts and the temporary success of his imposture, are recorded not merely in the apocryphal writings, but in the writings of the early Fathers. Thus Justin Martyr relates that "at Rome, in the reign of Claudius Cæsar, he did mighty acts of magic, by virtue of the art of the devils operating in him. He was considered as a god, and was honoured with a statue erected on the river Tiber, which bore the inscription, Simoni Deo Sancto."[3] Irenæus writes: "Such was his procedure in the reign of Claudius Cæsar, by whom also he is said to have been honoured with a statue on account of his magical power. By many he was glorified as if he were a god."[4] And Tertullian, in his Apology to the Romans, says: "You install in your Pantheon Simon Magus, giving him a statue and the title of holy god."[5] Eusebius expands the legend, and

---

[1] Neander's *Planting of Christianity*, vol. i. pp. 377, 378, Bohn's edition.

[2] Irenæus calls him "magister et progenitor omnium hæreticorum." *Adv. Hær.* i. 27.

[3] *Apol.* ii. 26. For the curious mistake of Justin Martyr, see note on p. 126. It is probably from this mistake of Justin that the references in the Fathers to a statue erected in Rome to Simon Magus arose.

[4] *Adv. Hær.* i. 23. 1.   [5] *Apol.* 13.

expresses his belief in the encounter of Simon Magus with Peter in the reign of Claudius: "Entering the city of Rome, by the co-operation of that malignant spirit which had fixed its seat there, his attempts were soon so far successful as to be honoured as a god with the erection of a statue by the inhabitants of that city. This, however, did not long continue; for under the reign of Claudius, by the benign and gracious providence of God, Peter, that powerful and great apostle, who by his courage took the lead of all the rest, was conducted to Rome against this pest of mankind."[1]

Lipsius, in his *Sources of the Petrine Myth*, has carefully examined into the rise and development of this legend. It appears in early ecclesiastical history under two forms—an Ebionite or anti-Pauline form, and a Catholic or Petro-Pauline form.[2] The original form, according to him, is the Ebionite.[3] In this form it is expanded in the Clementine works, and is a species of Christian romance. Three works of this nature have been transmitted to us. Of these the oldest is the *Clementine Homilies*, to which the date A.D. 140 has been assigned, and which are extant in the original Greek.[4] The *Recognitions* are considered to be a replication of the *Homilies*; the Greek of this work has been lost, and it has come down to us in an incomplete Latin translation. The *Apostolic Constitutions* is the latest of the three works, and is supposed to have been written toward the close of the fourth century. In all these works Simon Magus and Peter play a prominent part. It has been maintained by Baur and Lipsius, that these works originated among the Judaizing Christians who were strongly opposed to Paulinism. According to them, Simon Magus is but a mask to represent Paul; it is Paul who is attacked in these works; Paul is the heretic whom

[1] *Hist. Eccl.* ii. 14.

[2] Besides these two forms, Lipsius mentions a third form—the Gnostic; but this form is not so apparent. Irenæus certainly in his list of heretics enumerates the Simonians or the disciples of Simon Magus. See Mansel's *Gnostic Heresies*, Lecture VI. "Precursors of Gnosticism—Simon Magus and Menander."

[3] Hilgenfeld, on the contrary, asserts that the Catholic form was the original. *Einleitung*, p. 623.

[4] The *Clementine Homilies* are considered to be a compilation of earlier writings, at the basis of which, according to Hilgenfeld and Lipsius, lies a work entitled the κήρυγμα Πέτρου, mentioned by Clemens Alex. *Strom.* vi. 5. 42.

Peter follows from place to place, disputes with, and finally vanquishes at Rome.¹ And it must be acknowledged that, on carefully reading the Clementine works, much may be said in support of this view.² Peter is represented as following Simon Magus step by step from Cæsarea, Tyre, Sidon, Berytus, Antioch, and at length to Rome, refuting his errors and finally accomplishing his ruin. Peter is the representative of pure Christianity, which is combined with the observance of Judaism, whereas Simon Magus is the heretic who teaches apostasy from the faith. Peter is represented as saying: "You may perceive to what class Simon belongs who came before me to the Gentiles, and to what class I belong who have come in upon him as light upon darkness, as knowledge upon ignorance, as healing upon disease."³ Peter is the preacher of the true, and Simon Magus the expounder of the false gnosis. These writings are undoubtedly of an Ebionite and anti-Pauline character, and were written for the purpose of opposing Pauline Christianity.

The second form of the legend is the Catholic or Petro-Pauline. Here the identity of Paul and Simon Magus is lost sight of, and the victory over Simon is represented as the joint triumph of Peter and Paul. This form of the legend is to be found in the *Acts of Peter and Paul*.⁴ According to Lipsius, this work was written toward the close of the second century.⁵ It describes the arrival of Paul at Rome, the encounter of Simon Magus with Peter and Paul before Nero, the victory of the apostles, the death of the sorcerer accom-

---

¹ See Baur's *Apostel Paulus*, vol. i. p. 248 ff. Baur's *Church History*, vol. i. p. 91, E. Tr. Lipsius, *Die Quellen*, etc., pp. 20-29. Froschammer's *Romance of Romanism*, p. 26. Zeller's *Acts of the Apostles*, vol. i. p. 250.

² See, for a discussion on the whole subject, Bishop Lightfoot's *Epistle to the Galatians*, Dissertation III. "St. Paul and the Three," pp. 313-355. According to him, the allusions to Paul in the *Clementines*, especially in the *Homilies*, are clear and undeniable. "Among other false teachers," he observes, "who are covertly denounced in his person (Simon Magus), we cannot fail to recognise the lineaments of St. Paul."

³ *Clementine Homilies*, ii. 17.

⁴ This book was first published in a complete form by Thilo in 1838. The work is entitled, *Acta SS. Apostolorum Pauli et Petri*. See Tischendorf's *Acta Apostolorum Apocrypha*, pp. 1-39. It is translated in Clark's *Anti-Nicene Library*.

⁵ Lipsius, *Die Quellen*, etc., p. 51.

plished by their prayers, and the martyrdom of Peter and Paul in consequence of Nero's anger on account of the death of Simon. Lipsius traces throughout the work a connection with the Clementines; it is the same romance in an altered form, and written for a different purpose.[1] There is no longer the antagonism between Paul (under the mask of Simon Magus) and Peter, which is perhaps rightly suspected in the Clementines, but both are represented as united in the conflict with Simon. "Peter and Paul," observes Froschammer, "are now represented in a friendly relation, but Peter is put completely in the foreground, whereas Paul plays only a subordinate part, and in particular is silent in the (final) struggle against Simon Magus."[2] The work certainly appears to be of a conciliatory character. On the one hand, Paul is represented as approaching Judaism: "The Jews came to Paul and said, Vindicate the faith in which thou wast born; for it is not right that thou, being a Hebrew of the Hebrews, shouldst call thyself a teacher of the Gentiles and vindicator of the uncircumcised; and, being thyself circumcised, that thou shouldst bring to nought the faith of the circumcision. And Paul answering said, By this you can prove that I am a true Jew; because also you have been able to keep the Sabbath and to observe the true circumcision. What does Peter preach in the kingdom of the Gentiles? If he shall wish to bring in any new teaching, send him word, that we may see, and in your presence I shall convict him. But if his teaching be true, supported by the book and testimony of the Hebrews, it becomes all of us to submit to him."[3] And, on the other hand, Peter is represented as welcoming Paul to Rome, and acknowledging before Nero his apostolic authority: "Nero said, What sayest thou, Peter? He answered and said: All that Paul said is true. For when he was a persecutor of the faith of Christ, a voice out of heaven called him, and taught him the truth; for he was not an adversary of our faith from hatred, but from ignorance."[4]

Now, it is asserted that this romance or legend of Peter's encounter with Simon Magus at Rome, divested of its anti-

---

[1] Lipsius, *Die Quellen*, etc., pp. 72–78.   [2] *Romance of Romanism*, p. 27.
[3] *Acts of Peter and Paul*, chap. xxii.   [4] *Ibid.* chap. lx.

Pauline teaching, was accepted by the Fathers as authentic history, namely, that Peter actually encountered Simon Magus at Rome, and consequently must have been in Rome. This legendary theory to account for the tradition of the presence of Peter in Rome is plausible and extremely ingenious, but it is not proven. It has been observed that in the early forms of the legend there is no mention of the encounter of Peter with Simon Magus at Rome. In the *Clementine Homilies* and in the *Recognitions*, Peter is represented as following Simon Magus from Cæsarea to Antioch, but there the journey ends. Peter's martyrdom at Rome is indeed mentioned in the Epistle of Clement to James which precedes the *Homilies*, but this, as Lipsius admits, was probably of later origin. There is also in the *Recognitions* an intimation that Peter followed Simon to Rome; Simon is represented as saying that he was going to Rome, and that there he should be reckoned as a god and receive divine honours; and Peter expresses his resolution to follow Simon: "It is necessary that I also should follow upon his track, so that whatever disputations he raises may be corrected by us."[1] But it is only in the *Apostolic Constitutions* and in the *Acts of Peter and Paul*, later productions, that we read of Peter's encounter with Simon at Rome.[2] Besides, in the earliest accounts of Simon Magus in the writings of the Fathers, there is no mention of Peter at all. The oldest information concerning Simon Magus in Rome in the reign of Claudius is given by Justin Martyr, who informs us that he was there honoured as a god; but in all Justin Martyr's writings there is no mention of Peter's residence in Rome. Irenæus speaks both of Simon Magus and Peter being at Rome, but he does not bring them into connection: this is only done by Arnobius and Eusebius[3] in the fourth century. It would appear, then, that the romance of Simon Magus cannot account for the tradition of Peter's Roman residence; it would rather seem that the historical fact of

[1] *Recognitions*, iii. 63-65.
[2] See Keil's *Der erste Brief des Petrus*, p. 8, and Sieffert's article on "Peter" in Herzog's *Encyklopädie*, vol. xi. p. 525.
[3] Arnobius (A.D. 306), *Adv. Gentes*, ii. 12. Eusebius (A.D. 325), *Hist. Eccl.* ii. 14. There is also a reference to it in the *Refutation of all Heresies*, a work ascribed to Hippolytus, *Ref. omn. Hær.* vi. 15.

Peter's residence in Rome was the foundation of the myth of his encounter with Simon Magus in that city. "It seems difficult to suppose," observes Renan, "that an Ebionite author at so early a date would have made Peter's journey to Rome of so much importance, if that journey had had no foundation in fact."[1]

Such are the arguments for and against Peter's residence in Rome; on the one hand, we have the unanimous testimony of the Fathers in its favour; and, on the other hand, various indications in Scripture that seem to preclude Peter's residence at Rome. Accordingly, several theologians consider the question as doubtful; as being one of those historical problems of which it is impossible to arrive at any satisfactory solution. Thus Alford observes: "On the whole, it seems safest to suspend the judgment with regard to Peter's presence and martyrdom at Rome."[2] And Professor Hatch concludes his able article on Peter in the *Encyclopedia Britannica* in the following terms: "The probabilities of the case are evenly balanced; on the one hand, it is difficult to account for the complete silence as to Peter in the Pauline Epistles, and it is impossible with those Epistles in sight to regard Peter as the founder of the Roman community; on the other hand, it is difficult to suppose that so large a body of tradition had no foundation in fact; such a supposition, besides its general improbability, would assume that the extreme form of Judæo-Christianity which the *Clementines* reflect had a much greater influence over the conceptions of the second century than the evidence warrants."[3] We think, however, that the evidence in favour of Peter's Roman residence preponderates. The testimony of the Fathers is too extensive and unanimous not to be founded on fact; and

---

[1] Renan's *Hibbert Lectures*, p. 69. The theory of Baur and Lipsius is ably shown to be inadmissible by Hilgenfeld in his *Einleitung*, pp. 623–625, by Mangold in a note to his edition of Bleek's *Einleitung*, pp. 733, 734, and by Sieffert in his article "Petrus" in Herzog's *Encyklop*.

[2] Alford's *Greek Testament*, vol. iv. "Prolegomena," 121.

[3] Dean Plumptre, in his *Commentary on First Peter*, also observes: "The most that can be said of this evidence is that it leaves it fairly probable that St. Peter ended his life at Rome," p. 58. So also Reuss: "That Peter met his death in Rome is a bare possibility."

although it is admitted that it is often inaccurate with regard to concomitant circumstances and sometimes mixed with fable, yet we judge that there is a kernel of truth in the story of Peter's Roman residence which is attested by all the Fathers, and of which the romance of the encounter of Simon Magus with Peter forms a very inadequate explanation.

We consider, then, that the probability is in favour of Peter's residence in Rome; that Peter ended his life by martyrdom in the imperial city. If Peter actually came to Rome, the period of his residence may be determined with some degree of probability. It could not have been before Paul's arrival there, when sent as a prisoner from Cæsarea; nor could it have been during that apostle's two years' imprisonment, mentioned in the Acts (A.D. 61–63); nor could it have been on Paul's return to Rome, when he suffered martyrdom (A.D. 67). Hence, then, the only period admissible is the interval between Paul's first and second imprisonment, that is, between A.D. 63 and A.D. 67. There is nothing incredible in the hypothesis that Peter travelled preaching the gospel from Babylon to Rome,[1] that he reached the city about A.D. 64, and that he perished in the great Neronian persecution which broke out in the month of July in that year. We thus agree with the remark of Wiesinger: "What remains then as the kernel of ecclesiastical tradition is this: that toward the end of his life Peter came to Rome, that he there laboured for the propagation of the gospel, and that he suffered martyrdom under Nero."[2] This hypothesis suits the conditions of the question, and reconciles the testimony of the Fathers with the omission of all reference to Peter in the Pauline Epistles.[3]

This subject is fully discussed on the negative side by Baur in his *Apostel Paulus*, by Froschammer in his *Romance of Romanism*, by Ellendorf in his work entitled *Ist Petrus in*

---

[1] Assuming that the Babylon mentioned in 1 Pet. v. 13 is Babylon on the Euphrates.

[2] Wiesinger's *Der erste Epistel des Petrus*, pp. 11, 12.

[3] See also Bleek's *Introduction to the N. T.*, vol. ii. p. 161. Lardner's *Works* vol. iii. p. 405, quarto edition.

Rom gewesen, and especially by Lipsius in the work frequently alluded to, *Die Quellen der römischen Petrus-Sage*. It is also more or less discussed on the same side by Mayerhoff in his *Petrinische Schriften*, by Winer in the article "Petrus" in his *Biblisches Realwörterbuch*, and by De Wette in his *Einleitung in das N. T.* The affirmative side of the question has been advocated by Credner in his *Einleitung in das N. T.*, by Ewald in his *Geschichte des Volkes Israel*, by Sieffert in his article "Petrus" in Herzog's *Encyklopädie*, by Huther in his *Commentary on Peter*, by Schott in his *Der erste Brief Petri*, by Keil in his *Commentar über die Briefe des Petrus*, by Hilgenfeld in his *Einleitung in das N. T.*, by Olshausen in his *Römerbrief*, by Wieseler in his *Chronologie des apostolischen Zeitalter*, by Schaff in his *History of the Apostolic Church*, by Renan in his *Hibbert Lectures*, and by Windischmann in his *Vindiciæ Petrinæ*.

DISSERTATION II.

THE PETRINE THEOLOGY.

The type of Christian doctrine elaborated by Peter is the connecting link between the theology of James and that of Paul. In its ethical statements this First Epistle of Peter resembles the Epistle of James, whilst in its doctrinal statements it resembles the Epistles of Paul. This arises partly from the idiosyncrasy of the writer; as a Hebrew Christian, Peter was different from Paul, who was a Hellenist, and, unlike James, he had travelled much in Gentile countries. And it arises partly from the class of readers to whom he wrote; Peter wrote to mixed churches, composed of Jews and Gentiles; James, to Jewish Christians; and Paul, chiefly to Gentile Christians. Peter resembles James in dwelling on the Old Testament, the spirit of which pervades the writings of both; and in the practical character of his Epistle, aiming not so much at the instruction of his readers in Christian doctrine, as at the inculcation of Christian duty and the formation of a Christian character. But in both respects a difference is observable between them; whilst James regards Christianity as the development of Judaism, being "the perfect law" (Jas. i. 25), Peter looks upon it as the realization of Judaism, being the fulfilment of prophecy; and whilst in the Epistle of James there is a comparative absence of the peculiar doctrines of Christianity, Peter draws his motives from such Christian topics as the sufferings, the resurrection, and the glory of Christ. On the other hand, in his doctrinal statements Peter resembles Paul.[1] Some, indeed, have unwarrantably exaggerated the degree of resemblance, affirming that Peter's Epistle is but modified Paulinism. Thus Pfleiderer calls it "a popularized, and for that very reason a diluted and faded Paulinism."[2] Both Paul and Peter place the greatest stress on the sufferings of Christ, and regard them as procuring for us a deliverance from sin. But, when closely examined, there is in this Epistle little trace of a direct influence of Paul. It will be seen that whilst both apostles assert the supreme importance of the sufferings of Christ, they view them in a somewhat different light. They emphasize different results arising from these sufferings. Peter never once alludes to Paul's fundamental doctrine of justification by faith; and whilst Paul dwells chiefly on the legal, Peter dwells chiefly on the moral efficacy of the death of Christ.[3] To the differences apparent in these sacred writers, we owe a fulness of Christian truth which we should not otherwise possess; and in the absence of all discrepancy, we have a proof that they all wrote under the inspiration of one Spirit.

Before discussing the theology of Peter, it is further necessary to observe that this First Epistle—to which we restrict our remarks—was addressed to believers. Those to

[1] For the Pauline character of the doctrine of this Petrine Epistle, drawn out into details, see especially Davidson's *Introduction to the Study of the N. T.*, vol. i. pp. 510, 511, 2nd edition; and Reuss' *History of Christian Theology in the Apostolic Age*, vol. ii. pp. 265-267, E. Tr.

[2] Pfleiderer's *Paulinism*, vol. ii. p. 162, E. Tr. See also Baur's *N. T. Theol.*, p. 287.

[3] For the relation of Peter to James and Paul, and the distinctions between them, see remarks in Lechler's *Das apostolische Zeitalter*, p. 260 f. [E. Tr. of the 3rd edition, vol. ii. pp. 246-249]; and Schmid's *Biblical Theology of the New Testament*, p. 409 f.

whom the apostle wrote were already instructed in the faith, nor, so far as is apparent from the Epistle, were they disturbed by the errors of false teachers,[1] like many of the churches to which Paul wrote. Peter's object in writing was not to impart to them further instruction in Christian doctrine, but to comfort and support them under the persecutions to which they were exposed. Hence the Epistle is not dogmatic, but hortatory. But still the hortatory and ethical teaching reposes on a definite system of Christian dogma, in which the apostle finds the sole spring of a Christian life.

I. *Relation of Christianity to Judaism.*

In adverting to the peculiarities of this Epistle, we remarked that the whole Epistle, more than any other writing of the New Testament, bears upon it the impress of the Old Testament. Its theology might almost be described as a study of the new in its relations to the ancient economy.[2] The death of Christ is described as that of "a lamb without spot," with an evident reference to the paschal lamb, and Christ Himself is described as "the corner-stone" of His spiritual temple, with an allusion to the prophecies of Isaiah. But especially is Christianity regarded as the fulfilment of prophecy.[3] This view pervades not only the writings, but the oral teaching of the apostle. On this point chiefly he dwells in his discourses transmitted to us in the Acts of the Apostles. "All the prophets," he observes, "from Samuel and those that follow after, as many as have spoken, have likewise foretold of these days" (Acts iii. 24). And in his Epistle he observes that the Spirit of Christ was in the apostles, "testifying beforehand of the sufferings of Christ and the glory that should follow" (chap. i. 10–12). All the leading facts of the Gospel history—the sufferings and the resurrection of Christ, and His exaltation to the right hand of God, are regarded by Peter as

---

[1] There is a remarkable difference in this point between the First and Second Epistles of Peter.

[2] See Lechler's *Das apostolische Zeitalter*, p. 189 [E. Tr. vol. ii. p. 156].

[3] "Peter," observes Dorner, "sees in Christianity the fulfilling of Old Testament prophecy," *Entwicklungsgeschichte der Lehre von der Person Christi*, vol. i. p. 103, zweite Auflage. Schmid's *Biblical Theology*, p. 376.

the fulfilment of prophecy; in short, according to him, the Old Testament is a prophecy of the Gospel. Christianity is the development of Judaism, only in the sense of being its fulfilment; so that there is truth in Dr. Schaff's remark: "Christianity, according to Peter, does not exist for the sake of Judaism, nor as a product of it; rather is Judaism a product of Christianity." [1]

Nor is Christianity merely the *fulfilment* of prophecy, but it is, according to Peter, the *realization* of Judaism. What Judaism was in idea, Christianity is in reality.[2] The Jews never attained to the ideal set before them, of being the theocratic people of God; they were throughout their whole history a disobedient and rebellious people; but this ideal is realized in believers. Hence the Old Testament descriptions of the Jewish people are applied by Peter to Christians. They are the elect nation, chosen out of all the nations of the world (chap. i. 2). They are the lively stones, built up into a living temple, dedicated to the worship of God (chap. ii. 4). Their actions are spiritual sacrifices acceptable to God by Jesus Christ (chap. ii. 5). They are a royal priesthood, in whom the kingly and priestly offices of Judaism are combined (chap. ii. 9). They are a chosen generation, a holy nation, a peculiar people—what Israel was to God in idea, they are in reality (chap. ii. 9, 10). They are God's spiritual offspring—the true Israel of God. And yet, notwithstanding the Hebrew dress of the Epistle, there is not the slightest trace of Jewish legalism, nothing resembling those opinions which have been attributed by the Tübingen school to Peter, as the apostle of the circumcision. There is no mention of circumcision or the other rites of Judaism; the Jewish law is not once alluded to; the word νόμος does not even occur.[3] On the contrary, whilst Christians occupy the place of the Jews, the Jews themselves, as they continued unbelieving, are rejected. They are the disobedient people unto whom

---

[1] Schaff's *History of the Apostolic Church*, vol. ii. pp. 329, 330.

[2] For the development of this statement, see Weiss' *Der petrinische Lehrbegriff*, p. 116. "The O. T.," observes Dorner, "in its highest functions is a product of that which is the principle of Christianity."

[3] See Pfleiderer's *Paulinism*, vol. ii. pp. 148, 149.

the precious corner-stone has become a stone of stumbling and a rock of offence (chap. ii. 7). So that the Jews and Christians change places; in times past Christians were not a people, but now they are the people of God (chap. ii. 10).

II. *The Nature of Sin.*[1]

According to the theology of Paul, the gospel is a remedy for sin; he proceeds from the disease to the remedy. Man is guilty, and as such has come under the condemnation of the law, and is exposed to the wrath of God. He cannot justify himself; the law condemns him, and no subsequent obedience to it can remove his guilt. Thus sin is regarded in a forensic point of view as the transgression of the law, and entailing punishment. Peter, on the other hand, whilst he does not entirely omit this view of sin, regards it chiefly in an ethical point of view, as that which corrupts and pollutes the soul. Like James, he dwells on sin as having its seat in the soul, in the form of evil desires and lusts ($\epsilon\pi\iota\theta\upsilon\mu\acute{\iota}\alpha\iota$). These he designates as fleshly lusts, which war against the soul (chap. ii. 11), as in opposition to the higher principles and powers of our nature. These lusts take outward shape and form in vain conversation ($\mu\alpha\tau\alpha\acute{\iota}\alpha$ $\dot{\alpha}\nu\alpha\sigma\tau\rho o\phi\acute{\eta}$, chap. i. 18), and show themselves in all the various branches of sin, against which Peter warns his readers. Before the preaching of the gospel, these sinful lusts and actions arose from ignorance ($\check{\alpha}\gamma\nu o\iota\alpha$); hence he warns his readers against "the former lusts in their ignorance" (chap. i. 14). But after the promulgation of the gospel, they become wilful transgressions—disobedience to the gospel. Hence sin not merely polluted the soul, but it exposed to punishment; there was not only defilement, but guilt; but still the chief element in sin, according to Peter, is its defiling nature. Whilst James gives the genealogy of sin—lust, sin, and death—Peter dwells upon its existence, and urges his hearers to guard against it. Nor does he omit the mention of the evil one, whom he regards as the great adversary, and, in language similar to that employed by James, he exhorts his

[1] See Weiss, *Der petrinische Lehrbegriff*, p. 173 f.: Die Lehre vor der Sünde.

readers to be on their guard against his attacks (chap. v. 8, comp. Jas. iv. 7).

III. *The Christology of Peter.*

The Christology of Peter is not nearly so fully developed as that of Paul and John. Weiss, indeed, goes the length of affirming that Peter dwells almost exclusively on the human nature of Christ; that he does not mention His pre-existence, and that he only alludes to His divinity in connection with His exaltation and session at the right hand of God; and he considers this Epistle as a remarkable document, forming a transition to a fuller development of Christology in the writings of Paul and John.[1] But this account is obviously defective. It is true that Peter nowhere calls Christ the Son of God;[2] but what is nearly the same, he speaks of "the God and Father of our Lord Jesus Christ" (chap. i. 3); and in the opening of his Epistle he mentions the Father, the Spirit, and Jesus Christ as co-operating in our salvation (chap. i. 2). The pre-existence of Christ is, according to the most reasonable interpretation, asserted when he speaks of the Spirit of Christ as influencing the prophets in their predictions[3] (chap. i. 11), and of Christ as being fore-ordained before the foundation of the world, but manifested in these last days (chap. i. 20). But especially does Peter frequently emphasize the sinlessness of Christ, both in reference to His character as an example for our imitation, and in reference to the efficacy of those sufferings which He endured for our sakes. "He did no sin, neither was guile found in His mouth," and thus has left us an example that we should follow His steps (chap. ii. 22); and we are redeemed "with the precious blood of Christ, as of a lamb without blemish

---

[1] See Weiss' *Biblical Theology of the New Testament*, vol. i. p. 226, and *Der petrinische Lehrbegriff*, pp. 241, 255.

[2] So also in his discourses Peter speaks of Christ under the Old Testament title as " the Servant of Jehovah," παῖς θιοῦ.

[3] See Huther's *Der erste Brief Petri, in loco*, and Alford's *Greek Testament, in loco*. Alford explains " the Spirit of Christ " as " the Spirit which Christ has and gives." Weiss, on the other hand, calls this interpretation in question (*Biblical Theology of the N. T.*, p. 225), and also Schmid, on the ground that the Spirit proceeds from the exalted Christ. *Biblical Theology of the N. T.*, p. 382.

and without spot" (chap. i. 19). It was because He was the Just One that He could give His life as a sacrifice for the unjust (chap. iii. 18). The exaltation of Christ also occupies a prominent place in this Epistle. It is the exalted Christ who is held forth as the object of our faith. He is raised to the highest dignity, and constituted the Lord of the most exalted intelligences. He is gone into heaven, and is seated at the right hand of God, angels and authorities and powers having been made subject unto Him (chap. iii. 22); and He shall again appear in this world as the judge of the quick and the dead (chap. iv. 5). Divine worship is paid to Him, and a doxology, which can only be applied to the Supreme Being, is applied to Him: "To whom be praise and dominion for ever and ever"[1] (chap. iv. 11). Thus, then, though not so prominently brought forward as in the Epistles of Paul and John, the divinity of Christ is presupposed in this Epistle of Peter.

As we have already observed, Peter agrees with Paul in assigning supreme importance in our redemption to the sufferings of Christ. The great doctrine which lies at the foundation of Pauline theology is that the death of Christ was an atonement for our sins. Christ suffered in our room and stead; His death was an expiatory sacrifice, by means of which the guilt of our sins was removed, and forgiveness was bestowed upon all those who believe. Now it has been asserted that this view of the sufferings of Christ is not exhibited in Peter's Epistle. "We find no allusion," observes Pfleiderer, "to a vicarious expiatory sacrifice for the reconciliation of our guilt and for our liberation from the punishment of sin, from the anger of God, from the sentence of death, and from the curse of the law."[2] And certainly it must be admitted that the expiatory nature of Christ's sufferings is not so much dwelt upon as their purifying nature. Peter does not insist so much on our deliverance from guilt as on our deliverance from sin. Still there are several passages wherein the doctrine of the

---

[1] It is, however, doubtful to whom this ascription of praise is to be applied. It is referred to God by Brückner, Weiss, Schott, Huther, and Alford; and to Christ by Grotius, Calovius, and Steiger.

[2] Pfleiderer's *Paulinism*, vol. ii. p. 152.

vicarious sufferings of Christ is stated or implied. Thus Peter says: "Christ also once suffered for sin, the just for the unjust (δίκαιος ὑπὲρ ἀδίκων), to bring us to God" (chap. iii. 18). It is true that the preposition ὑπέρ, *for*, is different from ἀντί, *instead of*, and properly denotes "for the benefit of," but here the contrast of the just and the unjust gives it a substitutionary force; the just one could only suffer on account of sins for the benefit of the unjust in the way of expiation.[1] Thus the death of Christ is the objective ground of our forgiveness. Again, Peter speaks of "the sprinkling of the blood of Jesus Christ" (chap. i. 2); the allusion being to the expiatory legal act of sprinkling the blood of the victim as the blood of atonement. So, also, he mentions our being redeemed with the precious blood of Christ as of a lamb without blemish and without spot (chap. i. 19), a statement which implies that the death of Christ was an expiatory sacrifice for our sins, like the sacrifices under the law. And he speaks of Christ bearing our sins in His own body on the tree (chap. ii. 24), so that His sufferings were endured for our sins. In all these passages the expiatory nature of Christ's sufferings is implied.

At the same time, it must be admitted that Peter gives still greater prominence to the purifying efficacy of Christ's sufferings, a view which is also directly stated by Paul, when he says that "Christ gave Himself for us, to redeem us from all iniquity, and to purify unto Himself a peculiar people zealous of good works" (Titus ii. 14). As Peter viewed sin chiefly on its ethical side, so he was led to dwell chiefly on the sufferings of Christ as designed to free us from the power of sin and to make us holy.[2] In most of those passages, where the sufferings of Christ are alluded to, this purpose of them is stated. His readers were redeemed from their vain conversation, received by tradition from their fathers, by the precious blood of Christ (chap. i. 18, 19); the death of Christ

---

[1] This is admitted by Weiss. See *Der petrinische Lehrbegriff*, pp. 260, 261. Huther observes: "ὑπέρ is not in itself equal to ἀντί; but the contrast here drawn between δίκαιος and ἀδίκων suggests that in the general relation the more special idea of substitution is implied," *in loco*.

[2] Hence there is no mention in this Epistle of the doctrine of justification.

rescued them from the slavery of their sinful life. Christ bore our sins in His own body on the tree, for the express purpose that we, being dead to sins, should live unto righteousness (chap. ii. 24). Thus, then, though there is no discrepancy, yet there is a difference in the views which Peter and Paul respectively take of the sufferings of Christ. Peter regards sin chiefly as a moral evil from which we must be delivered, and the sufferings of Christ as effecting our deliverance; Paul regards sin chiefly as the transgression of the law rendering us liable to punishment, and the death of Christ as the expiatory sacrifice on the ground of which our sins are forgiven. Both of these aspects of Christ's sufferings are contained in the writings of these two apostles, but the one gives peculiar emphasis to the one view, and the other to the other view. "Paul," observes Archdeacon Farrar, "dwells most on deliverance from *guilt*, Peter on deliverance from *sin*. With Paul the death of Christ is the means of expiation, with Peter it is more prominently a motive of amendment. Paul, in Rom. vi. 1–15, writes like a profound theologian; Peter, in chap. iv. 1–4, is using the language of a practical Christian." [1]

Peter regards the sufferings of Christ as affording an example to believers. Christ, by reason of His sinlessness, is our great example; in all that He has done and suffered, He has left us an example that we should follow His steps, but especially has He afforded us a perfect example for our imitation in the manner in which He endured His sufferings. Certainly His sufferings were something far more than an example, but still this is a quality in them that ought not to be overlooked, and this quality is especially dwelt upon in this Epistle. As Christ suffered for us in the flesh, we are to arm ourselves with the same mind, with the same disposition with which Christ endured His sufferings (chap. iv. 1). "Christ suffered for us, leaving us an example that we should follow His steps:" we must imitate Him in His forbearance toward His enemies, and in His resignation to the will of His heavenly Father (chap. ii. 21–23). If we suffer for well-doing, we are to derive comfort and encouragement from the

[1] Farrar's *Early Days of Christianity*, vol. i. p. 136.

fact that Christ in like manner also suffered for our sins, the just for the unjust (chap. iii. 17, 18). We are not to be depressed under our sufferings, but ought rather to take comfort from the thought that we are thus conformed to the example of our Master, and to rejoice inasmuch as we are partakers of Christ's sufferings—actual sharers with Him in sufferings similar to those which He endured (chap. iv. 13). The reason, why the apostle thus dwells so frequently on the sufferings of Christ as an example, is obvious. Those to whom he wrote were then exposed to trials for the sake of Christ; they were called upon to suffer as Christians, and one great design of this Epistle was to support and comfort them under these trials; and the apostle could adduce no brighter example for their imitation, and hold out no stronger reason for their consolation under suffering, than the sufferings of Christ; it was no reproach to them, but a glory, that they were called upon to tread the same path of suffering which was trodden by their Lord.

As Peter was writing to believers who were uncontaminated with the errors of Judaistic heretics, faith in Christ is rather presupposed than demanded. It is true that the specific object of saving-faith is not defined in this Epistle, and the phrase "faith in Christ" does not occur; but Christ is throughout the Epistle represented as the supreme and only Saviour, and it is evident that the readers could only be Christians by believing on Christ. So, also, when God is spoken of as the object of faith, it is as He who "raised up Christ from the dead and gave Him glory" (chap. i. 21). On the other hand, faith is much dwelt upon in the sense in which it is employed in the Epistle to the Hebrews, as confidence in God (Heb. xi. 1). It is a firm persuasion that God will fulfil all those precious promises which He has made to believers. Thus with Peter faith is similar to hope; for hope is but the expectation of the fulfilment of the divine promises, and faith is confidence that these promises will be fulfilled. "With Peter," observes Reuss, "the object of faith is identical with that in the Epistle to the Hebrews, namely, things to come; it is trust in the promises of God, a trust which shall be rewarded by the fulfilment of its hope, if it remains stedfast and immovable. It is thus fixed upon God, and is almost a synonym for hope."[1] This constitutes Peter the apostle of hope; believers are begotten again into a lively hope (chap. i. 3); they are kept by the power of God through faith unto salvation (chap. i. 5); they are enabled to hope to the end for the grace that is to be brought unto them at the revelation of Jesus Christ (chap. i. 13); and they are exhorted to give a reason of the hope that is in them (chap. iii. 15).

It is also to be observed that Peter lays almost as much stress on the resurrection of Christ as he does on His sufferings and death.[2] He commences his Epistle by rendering thanks to God that they were begotten again unto a lively hope by the resurrection of Jesus Christ from the dead (chap. i. 3). He speaks of God as having raised up Jesus from the dead (chap. i. 21). And he asserts that we are saved by the resurrection of Jesus Christ (chap. iii. 21). And the reason of this is obvious; for although the death of Christ is the primary cause of our salvation, inasmuch as He suffered for our sins, the just for the unjust, yet the resurrection of Christ was the necessary confirmation of the work of redemption. The death of Christ enabled God to forgive, His resurrection enabled man to believe in forgiveness; divine forgiveness was made possible by the former, saving faith on the part of man was made possible by the latter. As long as Christ remained in the grave, there could be no ground for hope that His sufferings were efficacious; but by His resurrection we are, as Peter says, begotten again unto a lively hope. And so also Paul, whilst he gives prominence to the fact that Christ died for our sins, adds that He rose again for our justification. Besides, the resurrection of Christ was the first stage of His exaltation; He rose from the dead in order that He might ascend into heaven, and as the exalted Christ promote the salvation of His people.

In accordance with the view which Peter takes of the

---

[1] *History of Christian Theology in the Apostolic Age*, vol. ii. p. 268. See also Pfleiderer's *Paulinism*, vol. ii. p. 156.

[2] In Peter's discourses in the Acts the same importance is assigned to Christ's resurrection, Acts i. 22, ii. 24–32, iii. 15, iv. 10, x. 40, 41.

sufferings of Christ as our redemption from the power of sin, or with what theologians call "the application of the remedy," he dwells upon the agency of Christ in His state of exaltation. His resurrection was followed by His ascension and session at God's right hand; He is constituted the Ruler over angels, and authorities, and powers (chap. iii. 22); He is the Shepherd and Bishop of the souls of His people (chap. ii. 25), and thus is actively engaged in defending and ruling them; He shall again appear in this world, when He shall reward His people for their patient endurance of trial (chap. i. 7); and He shall be constituted the Judge of the quick and the dead (chap. iv. 5). Everywhere He is the exalted Christ, held out as the object of His people's faith and hope.

IV. *The Agency of the Spirit.*

The work of the Holy Spirit is not overlooked in this Epistle, though it does not occupy the same prominent position as it does in Paul's Epistle to the Romans. Peter calls Him "the Holy Spirit" (chap. i. 12), "the Spirit of God" (chap. iv. 14), and "the Spirit of Christ" (chap. i. 11). His personality and divinity are necessarily implied. In one passage the three divine persons in the Trinity—the Father, the Spirit, and Jesus Christ—are mentioned together as effecting our salvation. The Father is God, according to whose foreknowledge we are elected; the Spirit is the Author of our sanctification; and it is by the blood of Jesus Christ that we are sprinkled (chap. i. 2). The Spirit inspired the prophets, when they testified beforehand of the sufferings of Christ and the glory that should follow (chap. i. 11). The Spirit assisted the apostles in preaching the gospel, accompanying their ministrations by a divine agency (chap. i. 12). Through the Spirit believers are enabled to purify their souls in obeying the truth unto unfeigned love of the brethren (chap. i. 22), so that He is the source of all those holy virtues which actuate believers. The Spirit, as the Spirit of glory and of God, rests on believers (chap. iv. 14), so that they are actuated by His sacred influences.

Regeneration, or the commencement of the spiritual life in

the soul, is attributed by Peter, as it is by James, to the word of God. "Being born again, not of corruptible seed, but of incorruptible, by the word of God (διὰ λόγου θεοῦ) which liveth and abideth for ever" (chap. i. 23; comp. Jas. i. 18).[1] By the λόγος θεοῦ we are not to understand the Logos of John, for this is an appellation of Christ entirely restricted to John's writings, but the word preached by the apostles. It receives the epithets "living" and "abiding," inasmuch as it is the word of our salvation—the truth of the gospel. Still the word is not the efficient agent in our regeneration, but only the instrumental cause; it is "through (διά) the word of God" that we are born again. The Author of this new birth is God Himself, in virtue of His redeeming mercy (chap. i. 3), and, more specifically considered, the direct agent is the Holy Spirit; we are saved through sanctification of the Spirit (ἐν ἁγιασμῷ Πνεύματος, chap. i. 2). This union of the agency of the Spirit with the instrumentality of the word in our regeneration, and as that is developed in our sanctification, pervades all Scripture.

V. *The Eschatology of Peter.*

As we have already observed, the eschatological views of Peter form the chief peculiarity of this Epistle. There are statements and disclosures regarding the unseen world which are not found elsewhere in Scripture, and which have given rise to much discussion concerning the nature of the future state. Those passages which refer to Christ preaching to the spirits in prison (chap. iii. 18-20), and to the preaching of the gospel to the dead (chap. iv. 6), are of such importance that they are reserved to form a separate dissertation.

Peter looks forward to a future state of blessedness as the great source of comfort and support to his readers exposed to sufferings and persecution.[2] The night was dark, but it would be followed by a glorious morning. The Epistle is full of joy

---

[1] λόγος is also used for the *word* in the Epistle of James. Comp. Heb. iv. 12.
[2] "Another peculiar feature of the Epistle," observes Alford, "is its constant reference and forward look to the future. . . . Wherever we consult this Epistle, it is always the future to which the exhortations point; whether we

and consolation. There was a world beyond the grave, where believers would be abundantly recompensed for all the sufferings they now endured for the sake of religion. They were called to an inheritance, incorruptible and undefiled, and that fadeth not away (chap. i. 4). They would receive the end of their faith, even the salvation of their souls (chap. i. 9). When the chief Shepherd shall appear, they would receive the crown of glory that fadeth not away (chap. v. 4). After they had endured temporary sufferings, the God of all grace would make them perfect, and call them to His eternal glory by Christ Jesus (chap. v. 10). Hope is the centre of all his exhortations.[1]

It is also to be observed that throughout this Epistle sufferings and glory are combined, both in the life of Christ and in that of believers. Sufferings come first, to be succeeded by glory; the cross and the crown are inseparably united. The prophets testified beforehand of the sufferings of Christ and of the glory that should follow (chap. i. 11). And as was the case with the Master, so is it with His disciples; they are to rejoice if they are partakers of Christ's sufferings, inasmuch as when His glory shall be revealed they may be glad also with exceeding joy (chap. iv. 13, v. 1, iii. 17, 18).[2]

Such is a brief statement of Petrine Theology. It is less logical, less dogmatic, less complete, less developed than that of Paul. Let us briefly recapitulate. There is no trace in Peter of an opposition between the law and the gospel. There is no mention of justification by faith. There is no allusion to the resurrection of the dead. Peter looks upon sin, not so much in a legal aspect as the transgression of the law, but in an ethical aspect as that which depraves the soul: and hence the sufferings of Christ are regarded, not so much as an atonement to satisfy the divine justice, but as the mode of our redemption from the power of sin, and as an example

regard the sufferings of Christ Himself as pointing on to future glory, i. 11, iv. 13; or those of His followers, i. 6, 7, 9." *Greek Testament*, vol. iv., Prolegomena, p. 136.

[1] See *supra:* Weiss, *Biblical Theology of the N. T.*, vol. i. p. 243.
[2] Lechler's *Das apostolische Zeitalter*, p. 175.

for our imitation when exposed to suffering. The resurrection of Christ, as much as His death, is the ground of our hope, and hence faith is confidence in God's grace, seen chiefly in the fulfilment of His promises, and is thus equivalent to hope. Peter does not attain to the fulness which is in Paul, nor to the spirituality which is in John; there is no mention in his Epistle of the union which subsists between Christ and His people: its object is entirely practical, and hence the higher truths of Christianity are only touched upon. Besides, we must remember that the Epistle is short compared with the writings of Paul and John, and therefore to expect the same fulness of gospel truth is unreasonable. We conclude with the words of Dr. Schaff, which fitly express the phase of doctrine as given by Peter: "According to the Petrine type of doctrine, objective Christianity is at once the fulfilment of Old Testament prophecy, and itself a precious promise; subjective Christianity is at once faith in the revealed Messiah, and lively hope in His glorious reappearance."[1]

DISSERTATION III.

ESCHATOLOGY OF PETER.

By eschatology is meant the doctrine (λόγος) of the last things (τὰ ἔσχατα). The expressions "the last days" (ἐσχάται ἡμέραι, 2 Tim. iii. 1; Heb. i. 1; 2 Pet. iii. 3), "the last time" (ἔσχατος χρόνος, 1 Pet. i. 20; Jude 18), and "the last hour" (ἐσχάτη ὥρα, 1 John ii. 18), occur frequently in the New Testament, not because the sacred writers supposed that the world was then near its dissolution, but probably because the Jews regarded the age of the Messiah as the last dispensation of religion. But the phrase "the last things" (τὰ ἔσχατα) occurs only once, and that in a passage (Matt. xii. 45) which has no reference to the topics included in eschatology. The "last things," comprised in eschatology, are generally reckoned as four—death, judgment, heaven, and hell; but other subjects are also included in systematic

[1] Schaff's *History of the Apostolic Church*, vol. ii. p. 331.

theology under this division, such as Christ's descent into Hades (*descensus ad inferos*),[1] the coming of Antichrist, the millennial reign of Christ, the restitution of all things in the new heavens and the new earth, and especially the intermediate state, or the condition of the soul in the interval between death and the resurrection.

There are both in the speeches and in the Epistles of Peter disclosures of a future state, or at least statements which have been so interpreted, which are not to be found elsewhere in the writings of the New Testament. Especially the condition of souls in Hades, or the nature of the intermediate state, and the descent of Christ into Hades, are, or are supposed to be, alluded to by this apostle. These eschatological allusions are peculiar to Peter among the writers of the New Testament, and are to be found in his addresses as well as in his Epistles.[2] Thus, in his address to the Jews on the day of Pentecost, he speaks of Christ's soul being in Hades, from which it was delivered by His resurrection (Acts ii. 31). In his First Epistle there is a passage which, according to eminent interpreters, refers to the actions of Christ, when His soul was in Hades, in the interval between His death and resurrection, and affirms that He then went in spirit and preached to the spirits in prison (1 Pet. iii. 18–20). Mention is also made of the gospel being preached to the dead (1 Pet. iv. 6). And in the Second Epistle the same peculiarity is found; the writer dwells upon "the last things," the destruction of the world by fire (2 Pet. iii. 5–10), and the renovation of all things in the new heavens and the new earth (2 Pet. iii. 11). We, however, restrict ourselves to the eschatological views promulgated in the First Epistle, taken in combination with the apostle's declaration on the day of Pentecost, which are supposed to refer to the descent of Christ into Hades, and to the end or purpose of that descent.

[1] This does not properly belong to eschatology, but to Christology. It, however, bears directly upon the doctrine of the intermediate state and the condition of departed spirits. For this reason we include the subject in the department of eschatology.

[2] Peter is the only sacred writer, if we exclude certain passages in the Apocalypse, and the parable of the rich man and Lazarus, who directly alludes to the intermediate state.

The descent of Christ into Hades constitutes one of the articles of the Apostles' Creed: "He descended into hell." This article was incorporated into the Creed at a comparatively late period. The earliest mention of it is by Rufinus (A.D. 400), who found it in the creed of his Church at Aquileia;[1] and he tells us that it was not contained in the Roman and Oriental creeds. Its original reference was to the burial of Christ, as appears from the fact that the word "buried" was not in the creed of Aquileia, which contained the article, whilst it was in those creeds which wanted it.[2] In the third article of the Church of England, as first published in the reign of Edward VI., the doctrine of Christ's descent into Hades was stated with special reference to the words of Peter in this Epistle: "The body of Christ lay in the grave until His resurrection; but His Spirit, which He gave up, was with the spirits which were detained in prison or in hell, and preached to them, as the place in St. Peter testifieth."[3] Afterwards, according to Dr. Hey, in deference to Calvin, and in accordance with Calvinistic theology, the article was modified and abbreviated, and the reference to the passage in Peter's Epistle, concerning Christ's preaching to the spirits in prison, was omitted; and now the third article reads as follows: "As Christ died for us and was buried, so also is it to be believed that He went down into hell."[4]

---

[1] According to Rufinus, the words of the Creed were: Crucifixus sub Pontio Pilato, descendit in inferna.

[2] On the history of this article, see Pearson's *Exposition of the Creed*, Article V., and Bishop Browne's *Exposition of the Thirty-Nine Articles*, Article III.

[3] The subject is again stated at greater length in the Church Catechism, published in the same reign: "That He truly died and was truly buried, that by His most sure sacrifice He might pacify His Father's wrath against mankind, and subdue him by His death who had the authority of death, which is the devil; forasmuch as not only the living but the dead, were they in hell or elsewhere, they all felt the power and force of His death, to whom lying in prison, as Peter saith, Christ preached, though dead in body, yet relieved in spirit."

[4] In the Westminster Confession, which is still more in accordance with Calvinistic theology, there is no reference to Christ's descent into hell; the eighth article merely states that Christ "was crucified and died, was buried, and remained under the power of death, yet saw no corruption." In Article IX. of the *Formula Concordia*, the descent of Christ into hell is stated merely in general terms; the mode of descent being asserted to be a mystery.

Hades is in the Septuagint the translation of the Hebrew Sheol (שְׁאוֹל or שְׁאֹל). According to Cocceius and Buxtorf, Sheol is derived from שָׁאַל, *to ask*, the reference being to its insatiableness (Prov. xxx. 15, 16). But most modern Hebrew scholars now concur with Gesenius and Boettcher in deriving it from an unused Hebrew verb שָׁעַל, "*to be hollow*," referring to its supposed subterraneous location, as under the earth. So also the German *Hölle* and the English *hell* are probably of similar derivation, being derived from Höhle, *a cavity*. Sheol occurs sixty-five times in the Old Testament; thirty-one times it is rendered in the Authorized Version *hell*, thirty-one times the *grave*, and three times the *pit*. Ἅδης, the Greek rendering of and substitute for Sheol, is derived from ἀ privative and ἰδεῖν, *to see;* hence that which is not and cannot be seen—the invisible state, the world beyond death. In the New Testament ᾅδης occurs eleven times;[1] in ten of these it is translated in the Authorized Version *hell*, and in one place the *grave* (1 Cor. xv. 55). The translation *hell*, a term which is now used to denote the place of future punishment, is peculiarly unfortunate, as it is very questionable if Sheol or Hades ever bears that meaning.[2] There is no appropriate word in English to denote what is meant by Hades; and it would have been better to have left it untranslated, as is done in the Revised Version.[3] As already observed, ᾅδης is the Greek translation in the Septuagint of the Hebrew Sheol, though on two occasions that word is rendered by θάνατος (2 Sam. xxii. 6 ; Prov. xxiii. 14). In the Vulgate the words *infernus* and *inferus* (mostly *inferi*) are employed, which are tolerable translations.[4] In German, Luther has the inappropriate rendering *Hölle;* De

[1] Matt. xi. 23, xvi. 18 ; Luke x. 15, xvi. 23 ; Acts ii. 27, 31 ; 1 Cor. xv. 55 Rev. i. 18, vi. 8, xx. 13, 14.

[2] Ps. ix. 17 is the only possible exception. In Luke xvi. 23, where it is said that the rich man lifted up his eyes in Hades, being in torments, it is not hell that is meant, but the state of separate spirits, which to the wicked is a place of torment, namely, Tartarus.

[3] In the Revised Version of the O. T. it had also been better that Sheol had been left untranslated, as is done in several places, but not in all.

[4] In the O. T. Sheol is rendered forty-eight times by *infernus*, and seventeen times by *inferus* or *inferi;* in the N. T. *infernus* is employed, except in Matt. xvi. 18, where it is *portæ inferi*.

M

Wette suggests *Unterwelt;* and others, more appropriately, render it *Todtenreich*—the kingdom of the dead.

The meaning of Hades, in the New Testament, approximates to the Greek conception of the word, and denotes the state of the dead in general, where righteous spirits are happy and wicked spirits are miserable. According to the Greeks, Hades was divided into two regions; that which constituted the abode of the good was called Elysium, and that which constituted the abode of the wicked Tartarus. In the New Testament the former word does not occur, but it finds its equivalents in "Abraham's bosom" (ὁ κόλπος Ἀβραάμ), to which the soul of Lazarus was conveyed (Luke xvi. 22); and in Paradise (παράδεισος), as when our Lord said to the penitent thief: "To-day shalt thou be with me in Paradise" (Luke xxiii. 43).[1] The other word, Tartarus, is employed by Peter in a verbal form in his Second Epistle, when he says: "God spared not the angels that sinned, but cast them down to hell" (2 Pet. ii. 4). The word rendered "cast them down to hell" is ταρταρώσας—"having thrust them into Tartarus." And so also the abode of the disobedient spirits is called φυλακή, *a prison* (1 Pet. iii. 19), denoting a place of penal detention, and an equivalent to Tartarus.[2] Sheol or Hades, then, denotes the abode of the dead, the separate state, where the souls of the dead abide between death and the resurrection. The souls, both of the righteous and the wicked, are in Hades, though considered as in different regions; the former inhabiting Paradise, or the region of the blessed, and the latter confined in Tartarus, or the abode of the wicked. The word used in the New Testament for hell, properly so called, the place of final punishment, is γέεννα,[3] and ought

---

[1] When, however, Paul says that he was caught up into Paradise (2 Cor. xii. 4), and when in the Apocalypse mention is made of the Paradise of God (Rev. ii. 7), heaven, the final abode of the blessed, must be meant.

[2] The place where the angels, which kept not their first estate, are reserved in everlasting chains under darkness unto the judgment of the great day. Jude 6.

[3] The meaning of the word is "the Valley of Hinnom," a narrow valley in the neighbourhood of Jerusalem. It was used to denote the place of future punishment, because it was there that the bloody sacrifices to Moloch were offered, and the execution of criminals was carried out. According to Jewish tradition, it was the common sewer of the city. The valley was also called Tophet.

in our version to have been carefully distinguished from Hades. It is a remarkable fact that this word is used by our Lord only, with the exception of a single passage in the Epistle of James (Jas. iii. 6).[1]

In Peter's address to the Jews on the day of Pentecost, we are informed that the soul of Christ after death descended into Hades, unhappily rendered in our version *hell*. "He (David), seeing this before, spoke of the resurrection of Christ, that His soul was not left in hell, neither His flesh did see corruption" (Acts ii. 31). The evident meaning of this remarkable passage is that on His death Christ's flesh or body was laid in the grave, there preserved from corruption until the morning of the resurrection, whilst His soul was in Hades, or the abode of separate spirits. There are supposed to be other allusions to the same descent into Hades, as when Paul says: "Now that He ascended, what is it but that He also descended first into the lower parts of the earth ? He that descended is the same also that ascended up far above all heavens, that He might fill all things" (Eph. iv. 9, 10).[2] To this descent also it is supposed by many that Peter alludes when he says that "Christ was put to death in the flesh, but quickened in the spirit; in which also He went and preached to the spirits in prison" (1 Pet. iii. 18, 19). It is especially from this utterance of Peter on the day of Pentecost, combined with the above declaration in his Epistle, that the article in the Apostles' Creed, "He descended into hell," as distinct from His burial, is derived;

---

[1] Hades is represented as situated in the lower parts of the earth (Matt. xi. 23 ; Luke x. 15). It is also regarded as an abode: hence we read of the house of Hades, the gates of Hades (Matt. xvi. 18), the keys of Hades (Rev. i. 18). It is the inseparable companion of death (Rev. vi. 8) ; and after the judgment Hades shall be no more ; it and its companion Death shall be cast into the lake of fire (Rev. xx. 13, 14). For discussions on the nature of Hades, see Smith's *Biblical Dictionary*, art. "Hell;" Trench, *On the Parables*, "Parable of the rich man ;" and especially Principal Campbell's valuable dissertation in his work, *On the Gospels*.

[2] It is very doubtful if these words refer to the descent into Hades, and not merely to the humiliation of Christ in His incarnation. Meyer, in his commentary, defends the explanation of the descent into Hades : and in this he is supported by the Fathers in general, but opposed by Beza, Calvin, Grotius, De Wette, Hofmann, Schmid, Beyschlag, who understand merely the descent to earth.

and, undoubtedly, we are here taught this much at least, that at death the human soul of Christ (in Acts ii. 27, 31, ψυχή, and in 1 Pet. iii. 18, πνεῦμα) was separated from His body (σάρξ); and that whilst His body was in the grave, His soul was in Hades.

Now it has been asserted that Peter, in his First Epistle, not only confirms what he had formerly stated at Pentecost concerning the descent of Christ into Hades, but further explains it, and mentions the end or purpose of that descent. There are especially two passages which demand our attentive consideration; the one regarding Christ's preaching to the spirits in prison (1 Pet. iii. 18-20), and the other regarding the preaching of the gospel to the dead (1 Pet. iv. 6).

I. *Christ's Preaching to the Spirits in Prison.*

The passage, literally translated, is as follows: "Being put to death in the flesh, but quickened in the spirit; in which also He went and preached to the spirits in prison; which aforetime were disobedient, when the long-suffering of God was waiting in the days of Noah, while the ark was preparing" (1 Pet. iii. 18-20).[1]

Very different and even opposite interpretations have been given to these words. These interpretations may be conveni-

---

[1] Θανατωθεὶς μὲν σαρκὶ ζωοποιηθεὶς δὲ πνεύματι, ἐν ᾧ καὶ τοῖς ἐν φυλακῇ πνεύμασιν πορευθεὶς ἐκήρυξεν, ἀπειθήσασίν ποτε ὅτε ἀπεξεδέχετο ἡ τοῦ θεοῦ μακροθυμία ἐν ἡμέραις Νῶε κατασκευαζομένης κιβωτοῦ. Tischendorf's *Text.* The exegesis of the passage is as follows. The two datives σαρκί and πνεύματι can only be understood adverbially: that as regards His flesh Christ was put to death, and as regards His spirit He was quickened. Hence the translation in the Authorized Version is wrong, and that of the Revised Version is correct. The verb ζωοποιηθεὶς does not mean preserved or remained alive, but made alive, the antithesis to θανατωθείς. ἐν ᾧ is not, as in the Authorized Version, *by which*, but, as in the Revised Version, *in which:* in which spirit, made alive, Christ went. πορευθεὶς certainly suggests a local transference. ἐκήρυξεν is here equivalent to εὐηγγελίσατο, *went and preached,* namely, the gospel, for so only can the word be understood with reference to Christ. τοῖς ἐν φυλακῇ πνεύμασιν are the disembodied spirits in Hades, who were shut up, as in a prison, waiting their final doom. These spirits are further described as ἀπειθήσασίν ποτε, "*sometime,* or, formerly, *disobedient,*" unbelieving. And the period of their disobedience is described as that when "the long-suffering of God was waiting in the days of Noah," namely, during the hundred and twenty years (Gen. vi. 3) while the ark was preparing.

ently arranged in two classes: that which affirms, and that which denies, that this passage teaches an actual descent of Christ into Hades. According to the one class of interpretations Christ preached in person in Hades, whilst according to the other class He preached mediately by His Spirit, and that not in Hades, but in this world.

1. Those who hold that this passage teaches an actual descent of Christ into Hades, differ both as to the time when this descent occurred and as to its purpose. Some maintain that Christ descended into Hades during the period which intervened between His death and resurrection, and that He then preached to the spirits in prison; the same descent being alluded to which Peter mentions in his address at Pentecost: Being released from the flesh, His liberated spirit received a fresh animation; Christ was quickened or made alive ($\zeta\omega\pi o\iota\eta\theta\epsilon i\varsigma$) in spirit—was freed from the trammels of the flesh. This view is adopted by Bengel, Weiss, Lechler, Schmid, Fronmüller, Keil, Alford, and Wordsworth. "This passage," observes Schmid, "speaks of something which took place after Christ's death in the flesh. Being in possession of the full energy of life, and only as a $\pi\nu\epsilon\hat{\upsilon}\mu a$ set free from the $\sigma\acute{a}\rho\xi$, He went and preached, not in hell, where the condemned are under judgment, but in Hades."[1] Others assert that the word $\zeta\omega\pi o\iota\eta\theta\epsilon i\varsigma$, *made alive*, can only refer to the resurrection of Christ. "He was put to death in the flesh:" He laid aside for ever His $\sigma\acute{a}\rho\xi$; "but He was made alive in the spirit:" He entered upon His spiritual resurrection-life. This is the view adopted by De Wette, Brückner, Schott, Huther, Wiesinger, and Zezschwitz. "Christ," observes Huther, "entered into an actual state of death, in so far as the $\sigma\acute{a}\rho\xi$ pertained to Him, so that His life in the flesh came to an end; but from death He was brought back again to life, that is, was raised up, as far as the $\pi\nu\epsilon\hat{\upsilon}\mu a$ pertained to Him, so that the new life was purely pneumatical. But the new life began by His reuniting Himself as $\pi\nu\epsilon\hat{\upsilon}\mu a$ to His $\sigma\hat{\omega}\mu a$, so that thus this $\sigma\hat{\omega}\mu a$ itself became pneumatical." "This passage says nothing as to Christ's existence between

---

[1] Schmid's *Biblical Theology of the N. T.*, p. 387. Similarly also Weiss, *Der petrinische Lehrbegriff*, pp. 231, 232.

His death and resurrection."[1] According to the one view, Christ went in His human spirit, during His disembodied state, to Hades; according to the other view, it was the glorified Christ, soul and body, after His resurrection.

And as expositors differ as to the time when this descent into Hades took place, so they also differ materially as to the persons on whose account Christ descended. Some suppose that He went to Hades to announce to the Old Testament saints that He had completed for them the great work of redemption, that they were completely free from the penalty of sin, and that they were no longer prisoners to divine justice.[2] Such appears to have been the view which the early Fathers in general adopted of this passage. Traces of this opinion are to be found in the writings of Justin Martyr, Irenæus, Clemens Alexandrinus, Origen, and Tertullian;[3] and the same view is adopted by most of the Roman Catholic theologians, in conformity with their notion of the *Limbus Patrum*. It is now, however, almost universally rejected by Protestant interpreters. The word φυλακή denotes a prison, a place of detention, where those confined in it are awaiting their trial or doom;[4] and it cannot with any propriety be said of the saints, belonging to the Old Testament dispensation, that they were in prison, like criminals awaiting their doom. Nor is there any mention in the passage of the Old Testament saints, but only of those who were disobedient (ἀπειθησάσι) in the time of Noah; the

---

[1] Huther's *Brief des Petrus*, pp. 176, 186 [E. Tr. pp. 178, 188]. So also Wiesinger: "He ceases to live in the flesh, in order that He might live pneumatically, and that both according to soul and body." *Die Briefe des Petrus*, pp. 334, 335.

[2] See Bishop Browne's *Exposition of the Thirty-Nine Articles*, 4th ed. pp. 95, 96. "If," he observes, "angels joy over one sinner that repenteth, may we not suppose Paradise filled with rapture, when the soul of Jesus came among the souls of His redeemed, Himself the herald (κῆρυξ) of His own victory?"

[3] See *infra*.

[4] Some, to suit their peculiar views, have attempted to modify and soften the word φυλακή. Thus Calvin observes: "It seems to me that φυλακή means a watch-tower, in which watchmen stand for the purpose of watching; and the meaning would be very appropriate that godly souls were watching in hope of the salvation promised them, as though they saw it afar off." *In loco*. And so also Bishop Horsley says: "The original word imports merely a place of safe keeping, for so this passage may be rendered with great exactness: He went and preached to the spirits in safe keeping." Horsley's *Works*, vol. i. p. 312.

reference is not to saints but to sinners. And, besides, the preaching of Christ to them in Hades would have effected no change upon them; for they must still remain there during their separate state until the resurrection.

Others, to avoid those difficulties attending the supposition that the Old Testament saints are intended, suppose that by the spirits in prison are meant those who repented at the deluge. They suppose that during the deluge many who were excluded from the ark repented when the rain was descending; and although they perished in the flood, yet their repentance availed for their salvation, and to them Christ came into Hades and announced deliverance. This is the view of Bengel, and Bishop Horsley in his famous discourse on the spirits in prison.[1] Thus Bengel observes: "It is probable that some out of so great a multitude repented when the rain came; and although they had not believed while God was waiting, and while the ark was building, afterwards, when the ark was completed, and punishment assailed them, they began to believe; and to these, and all like them, Christ afterwards presented Himself as a preacher of grace."[2] And the opinion advanced by Bishop Horsley is similar, as appears from the following quotation: "The expression 'sometime were disobedient' implies that they were recovered from that disobedience, and before their death had been brought to repentance and faith in the Redeemer to come. To such souls Christ went and preached. But what did He preach to departed souls, and what could be the end of His preaching? Certainly He preached neither faith nor repentance, for the preaching of either comes too late to the departed soul. These souls had believed and repented, or they had not been in that part of the nether regions which the soul of the Redeemer visited."[3] But this is evidently a supposition made to escape the difficulty of admitting that Christ preached repentance and faith to the impenitent after death. It may

[1] So also Suarez, Estius, Bellarmine, and, according to Bengel, Luther. For Luther's opinion, see *infra*.

[2] Bengel's *Gnomon of the N. T.*, *in loco*.

[3] Horsley's *Theological Works*, vol. i. p. 317. It is to be observed that Horsley denies that Christ came and preached faith and repentance to those who died disobedient; on the contrary, he affirms that, whilst in this world, they

be that those who perished in the deluge are the souls in prison alluded to; but there is no mention of their previous repentance; on the contrary, their disobedience is the fact that is emphasized.

Others affirm that Christ went in His disembodied state to Hades to announce to the wicked confined there, as in a prison, their condemnation. According to this view, the subject of His preaching or proclamation in Hades was not the gospel, not a call to repentance, but the announcement of condemnation on impenitent spirits. This opinion is adopted by Calovius, Hollaz,[1] Zezschwitz, Schott, and Keil. Thus Keil observes: "Accordingly, $\dot{\epsilon}\kappa\acute{\eta}\rho\nu\xi\epsilon$ cannot have been an $\epsilon\dot{\nu}a\gamma\gamma\epsilon\lambda\acute{\iota}\zeta\epsilon\iota\nu$, such as is taught in 1 Pet. iv. 6, but only a *prædicatio damnatoria*, which indeed consisted more in the real appearance of the Lord and Judge of death and life than in any verbal announcement of condemnation."[2] The reason for the adoption of this supposition is that the passage must mean that Christ made an announcement ($\dot{\epsilon}\kappa\acute{\eta}\rho\nu\xi\epsilon$) to the spirits in prison; and as it was considered to be contrary to Scripture to believe that that announcement was a message of grace, it was inferred that it could only be the declaration of the sentence of condemnation. But this notion is too horrible to be entertained. The word $\dot{\epsilon}\kappa\acute{\eta}\rho\nu\xi\epsilon$, in connection with Christ and His apostles, can only denote the preaching of the gospel. Such a condemnatory announcement would be superfluous to spirits already in a state of condemnation. And how derogatory to Christ to suppose that He, the most compassionate Saviour, should in the hour of His triumph exult over the misery of the lost! As Dean Plumptre well says: "We have not so learned Christ as to think of that as possible." Besides, such a meaning is forbidden by the con-

had renounced their disobedience, and repented and believed. He is certainly not to be cited, as has been done, as an advocate of the *eternal hope*. The same view of this passage is adopted by Pusey, *What is of Faith as to Everlasting Punishment?* p. 97.

[1] Hollaz, quoted by Huther, remarks: Fuit prædicatio Christi in inferno non evangelica quæ hominibus tantum in regno gratiæ annunciatur, sed legalis elencthica, terribilis, eaque tum verbalis, qua ipsos æterna supplicia promeritos esse convincit, tum realis, qua immanem terrorem iis incussit.

[2] Keil's *Commentar über die Brief des Petrus*, p. 131. So also Schott, *Der erste Brief Petri*, p. 238.

text. The apostle is encouraging Christians to bear persecution with patience, from the example of the similar sufferings of Christ, and of the blessed consequences arising from these sufferings: "Christ once suffered for sin, the just for the unjust, being put to death in the flesh, and quickened in the spirit, in which He went and preached;" and therefore the announcement made must not be one of wrath, but one of grace and consolation.[1]

Others affirm that the natural and obvious meaning of the passage is that Christ preached the gospel to the disobedient spirits in Hades. Those who were disobedient in the days of Noah, and who died in their disobedience, had another opportunity of grace and salvation afforded them. This opinion, with some variations, is adopted by Pott, De Wette, Brückner, Huther, Weiss, Wiesinger, Reuss,[2] and Frommüller among German theologians, and by Alford, Wordsworth, Plumptre, Farrar, and Cook among English commentators. "With the great majority of commentators, ancient and modern," observes Alford, "I understand these words to say, that our Lord, in His disembodied state, did go to the place of detention of departed spirits, and did there announce His work of redemption, preach salvation in fact to the disembodied spirits of those who refused to obey the voice of God when the judgment of the flood was hanging over them."[3] "Christ," observes Bishop Wordsworth, "who before had preached on earth to men in bodily presence, now, after His removal from them by death, preached also to human spirits in the region under the earth, in the time between His death and resurrection."[4] "After death," observes Canon Cook, "our Lord, in His own human spirit, went forth and preached to the spirits in prison, that is, to certain spirits, specified afterwards, who, when He thus came and preached to them, were not in bonds or penal durance as condemned

---

[1] See *Exegetical Studies*, by author, pp. 252, 253.
[2] Brückner's *Katholische Briefe*, pp. 75, 76. Huther's *First Epistle of Peter*, p. 183. Weiss' *Der petrinische Lehrbegriff*, p. 239. Wiesinger, *Die Brief des Petrus*, p. 230. Reuss' *History of Christian Theology*, vol. i. pp. 274, 275.
[3] Alford's *Greek Testament*, vol. iv. p. 368, 2nd ed.
[4] Wordsworth's *Greek Testament*, *in loco*.

criminals, but in custody, as prisoners awaiting their doom."[1] The result of this preaching of Christ in Hades is not told us, but it is usually supposed that many of the disobedient would avail themselves of this new offer of forgiveness, and would be brought to repentance and to the acceptance of the Saviour; whilst it may be that others would continue hardened and impenitent, as no limit can be assigned to human depravity. Why this preaching is limited in the text to the disobedient in the time of Noah has been variously explained; some suppose that this is only specified, being an extreme case, as an example of a like gracious work on all the disobedient in Hades;[2] others, that the deluge is introduced as a type of the judgment of God; and others, that it is mentioned with special reference to its baptismal import, to which the apostle immediately alludes.

The opinion here advanced is extremely plausible, and gives a good interpretation to the passage; but still two grave objections have been stated. 1. It is said to be inconsistent with the general doctrine of Scripture. If we adopt the above interpretation, it would follow that the condition of the intermediate state is not final, that death does not fix our future condition, and that there is repentance beyond the grave; whereas it is argued, the doctrine of revelation would seem to be that this present life is the only state of probation, and that the future life is a state of retribution: "after death the judgment" (Heb. ix. 27). In accordance, then, with the rule that difficult passages of Scripture are to be interpreted according to the analogy of faith, the above opinion, although in seeming accordance with the sense of the words, is to be rejected. To this it is answered, that the doctrine of the intermediate state is involved in designed obscurity, and the

---

[1] *The Speaker's Bible: Canon Cook's Commentary on First Peter*, vol. iv. p. 204. In a note he adds: "It is clear that it (this passage) tells us nothing of the effect of the announcement, and affords no ground for speculation as to the present or future condition of those who now await their judgment in the intermediate state, having rejected or not having known the gospel of Christ." But if not for their advantage, for what purpose did Christ come and preach to them?

[2] So Farrar: "If," he observes, "language has any meaning, this language means that Christ, when His spirit descended into the lower world, proclaimed the message of salvation to the once impenitent dead." *Early Days of Christianity*, vol. i. p. 140.

assertion of revelation may be that the final state is entered upon at the judgment and not at death. 2. It is argued that there is no mention elsewhere in Scripture of what appears in itself to be a most improbable fact, that Christ after death went to the prison of the disobedient, and there preached the gospel. The article in the Apostles' Creed: " He descended into hell," does not imply this. The Hades into which He descended was not Tartarus, the prison of impenitent spirits, but Paradise, the abode of the spirits of just men made perfect. "To-day," said our Lord to the penitent thief, "shalt thou be with me in Paradise." To this it is answered, that a single scriptural assertion, provided it be sufficiently plain and not contradicted by other inspired statements, is sufficient to establish a doctrine.[1] "Isolated ideas," observes Huther, "are to be found expressed here and there in Scripture, and the reconciliation of the idea of a salvation offered to the spirits ἐν φυλακῇ, with the other doctrines of Scripture, can at most be termed a problem difficult of solution; nor must it be forgotten that the eschatological doctrines comprehend within them very many problems."[2]

2. There is another class of interpreters who deny that there is any allusion to an actual descent of Christ into Hades. They suppose that the passage does not allude to Christ's preaching in person to the spirits in Hades, but to His preaching in spirit to the disobedient in this world. Those who adopt this opinion differ as to the time when Christ thus preached, and as to the persons to whom He preached.

Some suppose that the preaching alluded to is that of the apostles to the unbelieving world. "The spirits in prison" is considered to be a metaphorical phrase to denote either Jews or Gentiles, or both, who were in a state of spiritual bondage; and by Christ's preaching in spirit to them is meant the preaching of the Spirit of Christ through His apostles. The gospel, it is observed, is frequently described

---

[1] Here, however, there is a begging of the question; for it is maintained that the assertion is not plain, and that it is at variance with other inspired statements.

[2] Huther's *Die Epistel des Petrus*, p. 178 [E. Tr. p. 181].

as an announcement of deliverance to captives confined in a dungeon (Isa. xlii. 7, lxi. 1). And whereas it is objected that there is no mention in the passage of the preaching of the gospel either to Jews or Gentiles, but only to the spirits who were disobedient in the days of Noah, it is replied that these are adduced as a type of the disobedient in all ages; the preaching of Noah before the flood was a type of the preaching of the apostles before the judgment. This view is adopted by Socinus, Vorstius, Schöttgen, Grotius, and Bishop Burnet.[1] But it is evident that such an opinion is a mere fancy; the words are forced into a meaning most unnatural, which is supported by no philological or doctrinal consideration, and which one feels must be remote from the true interpretation. Surely to affirm that Christ went in spirit, and preached to the spirits in prison who were disobedient in the days of Noah, would be a most extraordinary method of expressing the simple fact that Christ was preached by the apostles to the Gentiles.

A more numerous class of writers suppose that the preaching alluded to is that of the Spirit of Christ through Noah to the disobedient or unbelieving at the time of the deluge, and who are now, in consequence of their disobedience, confined in the prison of Hades. This is the opinion, with some modifications, adopted by Augustine,[2] Thomas Aquinas, Beza, Scaliger, Leighton, Pearson, Barrow; and in recent times by Besser, Wichelhaus, Schweizer, and Hofmann. Beza thus paraphrases the passage: "Christ, whom I have said to be vivified by the power of the Godhead, formerly, in the days of Noah, when the ark was preparing, going forth, not in a bodily form, but in the self-same power through which He afterwards rose from the dead, and by inspiration whereof the

---

[1] "The place of St. Peter," observes Bishop Burnet, "seems to relate to the preaching to the *Gentile* world, by virtue of that inspiration which was derived from Christ, which was therefore called *His Spirit;* and the *spirits in prison* were the Gentiles who were shut up in idolatry as *in prison,* and so were under the *Prince of the power of the air* (Eph. ii. 2), who is called the *God of this world* (2 Cor. iv. 4), that is, of the *Gentile* world: it being one of the ends for which Christ was anointed of His Father to open the prisons to them that were bound" (Isa. lxi. 1). *Exposition of the Thirty-Nine Articles,* Article III.

[2] *Ep.* 99 ad Euodiam.

prophets spoke, preached to those spirits who now suffer deserved punishment in prison, as having formerly refused to listen to the admonitions of Noah." According to this view, the πνεῦμα is not the human spirit of Christ, but His divine Spirit. Christ preached in Spirit, that is, not in His human but in His divine nature; not personally, as in the days of His flesh, but through the instrumentality of others. The direct preacher was Noah; and those to whom he preached were the spirits now in prison, who were formerly when in this world disobedient, when the long-suffering of God waited in the days of Noah. And the period of preaching was the hundred and twenty years when the ark was preparing; during all which period the long-suffering of God waited. In like manner, as Peter formerly said that the Spirit of Christ was in the prophets (1 Pet. i. 11), so He was in Noah when he preached to the antediluvians. "Every announcement of salvation," observes Hofmann, "which preceded His incarnation was a preaching of Christ who had come in Spirit to man, and those who were not obedient to the same fell into a condition similar to criminals who are kept in prison awaiting their doom."[1]

The following are the objections which have been brought against such an interpretation:[2]—1. It is opposed to the exegesis of the passage. Πνεύματι is used without the article, and is opposed to σαρκί, and therefore can only denote the human spirit of Christ as opposed to His flesh, not the Holy Spirit, nor the divine nature of Christ. To this it has been replied, that σαρκί may refer to the human, and πνεύματι to the divine nature of Christ. "He was put to death in His human nature, but quickened in His divine nature." His human nature (σάρξ) rendered Him capable of suffering and death; His divine nature (πνεῦμα) was the source and sphere of His eternal life. In a similar manner Paul, in the Epistle to the Romans, says that "Christ was made of the seed of David

---

[1] Hofmann's *Der erste Brief Petri*, p. 134. See also the *Schriftbeweis*, ii. 335-341. *Exegetical Studies*, pp. 261, 262.

[2] For full statements of the objections to this opinion, see Alford's *Greek Testament*, vol. iv. pp. 366, 367, and Fronmüller on "First Peter" in Lange's *Bibelwerk*, p. 69.

according to the flesh (κατὰ σάρκα), but declared to be the Son of God with power, according to the Spirit of holiness (κατὰ πνεῦμα ἁγιωσύνης," Rom. i. 2, 3).[1] 2. The words indicate a local transition, the passage of Christ in person from one locality to another: "He went (πορευθείς) and preached." To this it has been answered, that a local transition is not necessarily implied. Thus, as Paul says that Christ came (ἐλθών) and preached peace (Eph. ii. 17), the meaning being that He came in Spirit, and preached through His apostles; so here "He went and preached" admits of a similar explanation. 3. There is no mention of Noah's preaching,[2] but merely the statement that those who were disobedient lived in his days. But the allusion to Noah is a difficulty which belongs to both classes of interpretation, and Peter in his Second Epistle expressly calls Noah a preacher of righteousness (2 Pet. ii. 5). 4. The word *now*[3] has to be inserted; the spirits now in prison, which formerly were disobedient in the time of Noah.[4] But to this it has been replied, that the introduction of this explanatory particle offers no violence to the passage, as it is admitted by all that the spirits were then in prison. The words indicate the locality of the spirits at the time Peter wrote. 5. Such a meaning interrupts the sequence of the passage.[5] Ἀπειθήσασίν ποτέ separates the time of Christ's preaching from the time of their disobedience; Christ preached to the spirits who formerly were disobedient. Whereas, according to the above view, they were disobedient when the gospel was

---

[1] It is opposed to this, however, that this would give to πνεῦμα two different meanings in the same passage; in ver. 18, πνεύματι would denote the divine nature or Spirit, whereas in ver. 19 πνεύμασι signifies disembodied spirits.

[2] "Not a word is indicated by St. Peter on the very far-off lying allusion to the fact that the Spirit of Christ preached in Noah; not a word here on the fact that Noah himself preached to his contemporaries." Alford, *in loco*.

[3] Nunc in carcere. Beza.

[4] "It cannot be doubted that we thus put force on the apostle's words, and that τοῖς ἐν φυλακῇ πνεύμασιν must denote the local condition of the πνεύματα at the time when the preaching took place." Alford.

[5] The whole passage contains evidently a sequence of events,—Christ suffered for sins, was put to death in the flesh, and quickened in the spirit, went and preached to the spirits in Hades, went into heaven, and sat down on the right hand of God. "The subject, Χριστός, runs through the whole without a hint that we are dealing with historical matter of fact in παθών, θανατωθείς, ζωοποιηθείς, and with recondite figure in πορευθεὶς ἐκήρυξεν." Alford.

preached. "If," observes Bengel, "he was speaking of preaching by Noah, the word *formerly* (ποτέ) would either be altogether omitted, or be joined with the word preached."[1] But to this it has been answered, that the meaning of the passage is that those spirits now in prison were the same as those who were formerly disobedient in the time of Noah. 6. If the clause had stopped with ἐκήρυξε, and if there had been no reference to the disobedient in the days of Noah, we should have been constrained to adopt the interpretation, that Christ actually went to Hades and preached to disobedient spirits. But to this objection the answer is obvious, that such a reference has been made by the apostle. On the whole, however, the feeling remains that the above interpretation is somewhat far-fetched and somewhat forced.[2] The meaning of the passage must be left in uncertainty. It is one of those obscure statements of Scripture on which it is impossible to dogmatize, and any inference derived from which must be extremely problematical.[3]

II. *The Gospel preached to the Dead.*

The second passage has reference to the preaching of the gospel to the dead; and literally translated is as follows: "Who shall give account unto Him who is ready to judge the living and the dead. For to this end also was the gospel preached to the dead, that they might be judged according to man in the flesh, but live according to God in the spirit" (1 Pet. iv. 5, 6).[4]

[1] Bengel's *Gnomon of the New Testament, in loco*. Accordingly Hofmann joins ποτέ with ἐκήρυξιν, contrary to all linguistic rules.

[2] To express this meaning we would require to read: Christ by the Spirit formerly preached to those who were disobedient in the days of Noah.

[3] For the literature on the subject, see the article on "Eschatology" in the *Encyclopedia Britannica*, by the Rev. A. S. Aylen. Fronmüller's "Commentary on First Peter" in Lange's *Bibelwerk*. Gloag's *Exegetical Studies*, xiv. Horsley's *Sermon on the Spirits in Prison*. Pearson, *On the Creed*. Plumptre's *Spirits in Prison*. Schmid's *Biblical Theology of the N. T.* Steiger's *Commentary on First Peter*. Weiss' *Der petrinische Lehrbegriff;* and Zezschwitz, *Petri ap. de Christi ad inferos descensu sententia*. The subject is also discussed more or less fully in all the chief commentaries on the Epistle.

[4] Ὅ, ἀποδώσουσιν λόγον τῷ ἑτοίμως ἔχοντι κρῖναι ζῶντας καὶ νεκρούς. Εἰς τοῦτο γὰρ καὶ νεκροῖς εὐηγγελίσθη, ἵνα κριθῶσιν μὲν κατὰ ἀνθρώπους σαρκί, ζῶσιν δὲ κατὰ θεὸν πνεύματι.

The apostle here assigns the reason why Christ can be the righteous Judge of the dead as well as of the living, because the gospel was preached to the dead; they, as well as the living, had the opportunity of accepting or rejecting it. The dead (νεκροῖς, ver. 6) to whom the gospel was preached must belong to the same category as the dead (νεκρούς, ver. 5) whom Christ will judge. Hence, then, the passage cannot possibly apply to the spiritually dead; the words do not mean that the gospel was preached to the dead in trespasses and sins,—an opinion adopted by Augustine, Oecumenius, Luther, Erasmus, Whitby, Benson, Macknight, and recently by Bishop Wordsworth.[1]

Dismissing, then, this view as wholly untenable, there are only two other opinions which are admissible, either that the gospel was preached during their lifetime to those who are now dead, or that it was preached in Hades to the dead.

A numerous class of theologians suppose that the meaning of the passage is that the gospel had been preached in their lifetime to those who are now dead. This opinion, with some modifications, is adopted by Calvin, Grotius, Bengel,[2] Hofmann, Schott, and Keil. The apostle is vindicating the justice of Christ in judging the dead; and this because the offers of salvation had been made to them in their lifetime. They were not dead, but alive, when the gospel was preached to them. With Tischendorf's text. The exegesis is as follows: The apostle is reminding his readers that their persecutors would render an account to Christ, the Judge of the living and the dead. γάρ, *for*, evidently assigning a reason for the statement that Christ shall judge the dead as well as the living. εἰς τοῦτο, "for this cause," or, "*to this end.*" εὐηγγελίσθη denotes the preaching of the gospel as an accomplished fact, "*the gospel was preached.*" νεκροῖς, "*to the dead.*" The dead in this verse must be the same as the dead (νεκρούς) in the preceding verse, namely, those who are literally dead; the want of the article does not alter the case, as the article is also awanting in the preceding verse. Thus the apostle's argument is: Christ can righteously judge the dead, because to the dead the gospel has been preached.

[1] "Νεκροῖς, *dead* in sins. No valid objection to this interpretation is to be found in the allegation that in the preceding verse νεκρούς means men *physically* dead." Wordsworth, *in loco*. Whereas to us the objection appears insuperable.

[2] Thus Bengel observes: "It is evident that the preaching of the gospel which is meant is before death, and not subsequent to it. When the body is put off in death, the condition of the soul is altogether fixed, either for evil or for good. The gospel is preached to no one after death." *In loco.*

regard to the heathen and the vast multitudes who lived before the coming of Christ, who never heard the gospel, nothing is said; they are beyond the scope of the apostle's argument; he is speaking solely of those to whom the opportunity of salvation had been afforded. Different views have been entertained concerning the persons here meant by the dead. Some (Hofmann, etc.) suppose that by the dead are specially meant the persecutors of the Christians, and that the apostle comforts his readers under persecution by the thought that their wicked persecutors cannot escape the justice of God;[1] but it is evident that many of these persecutors never had an opportunity of hearing the gospel. Others (Calvin, etc.), on the contrary, affirm that by the dead are meant the persecuted Christians who had died before the second advent, and that the design of the apostle was to console their friends by the thought that these also would be partakers of the blessings conferred at the coming of the Lord; although put to death by men in the flesh, yet they shall live according to God in the spirit; they are not lost, but saved. Others (Bengel, etc.), more in accordance with the context, recognise that by νεκροῖς the apostle does not denote unbelievers only or Christians only, but those of the dead to whom during their lifetime the gospel has been preached.—But to this opinion that the passage refers to those who were alive when the gospel was preached, but are now dead, it has been objected that this is a forced interpretation, and that the words naturally refer to those who were already dead at the time when the gospel was preached to them. "If," observes Alford, "καὶ νεκροῖς εὐηγγελίσθη may mean 'the gospel was preached to some during their lifetime who are now dead,' exegesis has no longer any fixed rule, and Scripture may be made to prove anything."[2] But notwithstanding the statement of so high an authority, we do not see the force of the objection; the words mean simply "the gospel was preached to the dead," but they do not affirm whether the persons were alive or dead at the time when this occurred. It is undoubtedly true that the latter view is at first sight the more natural interpretation, that

---

[1] Hofmann's *Schriftbeweis*, ii. 339-341.
[2] Alford's *Greek Testament*, vol. iv. p. 373.

which would most readily suggest itself; but the former alternative is also admissible, and philologically legitimate.

The other class of interpreters suppose that the words mean that the gospel was preached to those who were actually dead; they are not only dead now, but were dead at the time when the gospel was preached to them. This opinion, with some variations, is adopted by Clemens Alexandrinus, Huther, Steiger, Wiesinger, Weiss, De Wette, Brückner, Fronmüller, Schmid, Alford, Plumptre, Cook,[1] and Farrar. Thus Clemens Alexandrinus observes: "Did not the same dispensation obtain in Hades, so that even there all the souls, on hearing the proclamation, might either exhibit repentance, or confess that their punishment was just, because they believed not? For it is not right that these should be condemned without trial, and that those alone who lived after the advent should have the advantage of the divine righteousness."[2] Some suppose that by the dead here are meant the same as those formerly mentioned, namely, the spirits in prison to whom Christ in spirit preached, and that the passage is a continuation of the subject there discussed.[3] Others, in better accordance with the argument of the apostle, refer νεκροῖς to all the dead, seeing that Christ is the Judge of the dead and living. Hence they give the following meaning to the passage: For this cause, in order that Christ might righteously judge the dead, the gospel is preached to them, so that although they have been judged according to men as regards the flesh, inasmuch as they have suffered death, the penalty of sin, they might live according to God as regards the spirit—be endowed with a spiritual and divine life.[4] This apparently gives a

---

[1] "We may assume," observes Canon Cook, "as certain that the word (νεκροῖς) refers to physical and not, as some have held, to spiritual death. The announcement was made not to the quick but to the dead: those dwellers in Hades who, whether as 'prisoners of hope,' or so to speak as 'prisoners of fear,' awaited the coming of Christ." *Speaker's Commentary N. T.*, vol. iv. p. 210.

[2] *Stromata*, vi. 6.

[3] So Brückner: "To this end the gospel was preached even to the dead, to those named in iii. 19." *Katholische Briefe*, p. 87; so also White, *Life in Christ*, pp. 320, 321.

[4] "Christ," observes Weiss, "has proclaimed the message of salvation even to the spirits of these disobedient ones in Hades (iii. 19), nay, even to all

good sense to the passage, but still it is not free from objection. The apostle is here asserting a past event—the gospel was preached to the dead; whereas, according to this interpretation, a continuous preaching is supposed—the gospel is being preached to the dead. It assumes that as already accomplished which will not be accomplished until the end of the world; for to make the apostle's argument conclusive, the term *dead* must be taken to denote all the dead before the judgment.

The opinions of the Fathers on these statements of Peter on Christ's descent into Hades, and on His preaching to the spirits in prison, are various and somewhat contradictory. The general idea, however, seems to have been that the saints of the Old Testament were those to whom Christ preached, and announced salvation as an accomplished fact, and whom He delivered from the prison of hell. Several believed that the gospel is preached to the dead in the intermediate state, and that death does not fix our condition. Origen,[1] Gregory of Nyssa,[2] and others went the length of believing in universal restoration, extending even to the devil and his angels. Eusebius, in his account of the introduction of the gospel into Edessa by the Apostle Thaddeus, informs us that Thaddeus taught how Christ was crucified, and descended into Hades, and burst the bars which had never yet been broken, and rose again, and also raised with Himself the dead who had slept for ages; how He descended alone, but ascended with a great multitude to His Father.[3] Justin Martyr quotes a saying from Jeremiah, which he asserts was expunged by the Jews on account of its testimony to our Lord, but which was found in some copies in the synagogues: "From the sayings of the same Jeremiah these have been cut out: The Lord God remembered His dead people of Israel

---

the dead (iv. 6), in order that not only the living but also the dead might be judged in the final Messianic judgment." *Biblical Theology*, vol. i. p. 241.

[1] Origen, *De Princip.* iii. 6. 6.

[2] Gregory of Nyssa, *Orat. Catechet.* 26, where he speaks of freeing mankind from their wickedness and healing the very inventor of wickedness. For the views of Gregory, see Farrar's *Mercy and Judgment*, p. 256 ff., and of Origen, p. 298 ff.; see also Bigg's *Bampton Lectures* for 1886, p. 293.

[3] *Hist. Eccl.* i. 13.

who lay in their graves, and He descended to preach to them His own salvation."[1] The same reference is made by Irenæus, who adds: "The Lord descended into the lower parts of the earth, to behold with His eyes the state of those who were resting from their labours."[2] And in another passage he says: "The Lord descended into regions beneath the earth, preaching His advent there, and declaring the remission of sins received by those who believe in Him."[3] Clemens Alexandrinus extends this preaching of Christ in Hades to those heathens who walked up to the light of nature and lived virtuous lives: "Wherefore (that He might bring them to repentance) the Lord preached also to those in Hades. But how? Do not the Scriptures declare that the Lord has preached to those that perished in the deluge, and not to those only, but to all that are in chains and that are kept in the ward and prison of Hades. . . . Those who were outside the law having lived rightly in consequence of the particular nature of the voice (of God in them), though they are in Hades and in prison, on hearing the voice of the Lord, whether that of His own person or that acting through His apostles, with all speed turned and believed."[4] Tertullian writes: "With the same law of His being He fully complied by remaining in Hades in the form and condition of a dead man; nor did He ascend into the heights of heaven before descending into the lower depths of the earth, that He might there make the patriarchs and prophets partakers of Himself."[5] And similarly Origen, replying to Celsus, says: "Whether Celsus likes it or not, we assert not only while Jesus was in the body did He win over numerous souls to Himself; but also when He became a soul, without the covering of the body, He dwelt among those souls which were without bodily covering, converting such of them to Himself as were willing, or those whom He saw, for reasons known to Himself alone, to be better adapted to such a course."[6]

[1] *Dial. cum Tryph.* chap. lxxii. The passage from Jeremiah is undoubtedly spurious; it is found in no MSS. or versions of the O. T.
[2] *Adv. Hær.* iv. 22. 1. In another passage Irenæus cites the words as those of Isaiah, *Adv. Hær.* iii. 20. 4.
[3] *Adv. Hær.* iv. 27. 2.
[4] *Strom.* vi. 6.
[5] *De Anima*, chap. vi.
[6] *Adv. Celsum*, ii. 43.

During the Middle Ages the doctrine of purgatory was gradually developed. Cyprian had held that souls in the prison of Hades might be liberated after they were purified and cleansed by fire.[1] Augustine, although he rejected the views of Origen, yet spoke of a purgatorial fire by which souls might be purified and prepared for admission into heaven.[2] Jerome also speaks of Christians who are saved by fire after having undergone punishment.[3] And at length, in the time of Gregory the Great, purgatory was formulated as one of the doctrines of the Church. It is to be observed, however, that the doctrine of purgatory does not involve the theory that another opportunity of repentance will be given to those who were unbelieving and impenitent in this world; but that those who were believers, yet were unfit for heaven, will before their admission undergo a course of purification in the intermediate state before the day of final judgment.

The opinions of the Reformers varied. The abuses connected with the Romish doctrine of purgatory were the occasion of the Reformation, and consequently that doctrine was wholly repudiated. According to Bengel, Luther taught that Christ in the intermediate state went to Hades, delivered the souls of the patriarchs, and preached the gospel to those who were disobedient in the days of Noah: "Here Peter plainly says, not only that Christ appeared to the fathers and patriarchs who were dead, some of whom undoubtedly Christ, on His resurrection, raised with Himself to eternal life, but also preached to some who in the time of Noah did not believe, and waited for the patience of God; that is, who hoped that God would not deal so severely with all flesh, in order that they might recognise that their sins were forgiven through the sacrifice of Christ."[4] Zwinglius taught that Christ in Hades preached the gospel to the spirits of the just who had lived before the advent: "Christ departed from among men to be numbered among the *inferi*, so that

---

[1] *Ep.* lv.   [2] In Ps. xxxvii., *Opp.* iv. 295.
[3] *Dial. c. Pelag.* chap. 28.
[4] Bengel's *Gnomon of the N. T.* on 1 Pet. iii. 20 [E. Tr. vol. v. p. 71]. The passage occurs in Luther's commentary on Hosea vi. 1, *Opp.* vol. iv. p. 624.

the virtue of His redemption reached even to them, which Peter intimates, when he says that to the dead, that is, to those in the nether world who, after the example of Noah, from the commencement of the world, have believed upon God, the gospel was preached."[1] Calvin, on the other hand, appears to have explained away the doctrine of Christ's descent into Hades.[2] He affirms that the preaching to the spirits in Hades has no reference to Christ's descent. "The opinion is common," he observes, "that Christ's descent into Hades is here referred to, but the words mean no such thing."[3] And in his *Institutes* he gives the following interpretation of the passage: "The purport of the context is that believers who had died before that time (the advent) were partakers of the same grace with ourselves; for he celebrates the power of Christ's death, in that it penetrated even to the dead, pious souls obtaining an immediate view of that visitation for which they had anxiously waited; while, on the other hand, the reprobate were more clearly convinced that they were completely excluded from salvation."[4] The words are ambiguous; but it does not appear that an actual descent into Hades was taught by Calvin. In general, the Reformers seem to have overlooked the doctrine of an intermediate state, and to have regarded death as to all intents and purposes the same to every person as the judgment.[5]

In recent times the subject of the condition of men after death has been much discussed in the light of these declarations of Peter and of other statements of Scripture. The celebrated *Theological Essays* of Frederick Maurice, and the controversy occasioned by them, gave rise to a new discussion of the whole subject in England. The doctrine of everlasting punishment has been called in question by many theologians

[1] Quoted by Fronmüller in his commentary on First Peter, in Lange's *Bibelwerk* [E. Tr. p. 70].

[2] By Christ's descent into Hades, Calvin understood His endurance of the punishments of hell in the invisible anguish of His soul upon the cross. *Institutes*, ii. 16. 10.

[3] See commentary on 1 Pet. iii. 19.

[4] *Institutes*, ii. 16. 9. In another place he says: "I have no doubt that Peter speaks generally, that the manifestation of Christ's grace was made to godly spirits, and that they were thus endued with the vital power of the Spirit."

[5] Beza's view was that Christ's descent into hell is identical with His burial.

eminent for their learning and piety; and various views of a future state have been maintained.[1]

Some maintain what has been called the doctrine of *conditional immortality*. They suppose that immortality is not the natural condition of man, but the gift of Christ procured by His interposition and bestowed on believers. This opinion reckons among its supporters Olshausen, Nitzsch, and Rothe, among German theologians; and Locke, Coleridge,[2] Whitby, Bishop Law, Isaac Watts, Archbishop Whately, and Rev. E. White,[3] among English divines.

There is a variety in their opinions concerning the fate of the wicked. According to some, unbelievers, being not partakers of Christ's redemption, perish immediately at death; according to others, they pass into the intermediate state, and have other opportunities of salvation afforded them, but if these be neglected, sentence is pronounced against them at the judgment, and they are annihilated; and according to others, that salvation after death is only possible to those who have not had a proper opportunity in this world.

A larger and more influential number of scholars maintain the doctrine of *universal restoration*. According to them, future punishment is entirely remedial; all men will, after the lapse it may be of ages, be finally restored to God; and

---

[1] For the various opinions of recent eminent theologians and others on this subject, see Farrar's *Mercy and Judgment*, chap. ii. Anderson's *Human Destiny*. *Future Probation: A Symposium.* 1886.

[2] "I am confident," says Coleridge, "that this view would be a far stronger motive than the present; for no man will believe eternal misery of himself, but millions will admit that if they did not mend their lives, they would be undeserving of living for ever." Quoted by Farrar, *Mercy and Judgment*, p. 56.

[3] This view of a future state is especially treated by the Rev. Edward White in his work, *Life in Christ; or, Immortality peculiar to the Regenerate*. His view is that man is not naturally immortal; that immortal life is the gift of Christ to believers; that the souls both of the righteous and the wicked survive during the intermediate state; that the survival of sinful men is due to redemption (p. 309); that those to whom the gospel has been preached in life would not have a second offer, but that salvation or a new opportunity of salvation after death is possible for the heathen and for those in Christian lands to whom the gospel has not been properly presented; and that at the judgment the wicked will be annihilated. It is also said that the view of conditional immortality is entertained by Dr. Dale of Birmingham. Farrar's *Eternal Hope*, p. 79 *Mercy and Judgment*, p. 51.

a time will come when evil will be put an end to in the universe of God. Then will be the great restitution of all things, the extinction of moral evil, when God will be all in all. According to this view, the descent of Christ into Hades, His preaching to the spirits in prison, and the preaching of the gospel to the dead, have reference to the redemption of the souls of those who in this world had rejected the gospel, or, it may be, had never heard of it. Origen[1] and Gregory of Nyssa, among the Fathers, were the great advocates of this opinion; and in recent times it has, with some variations, been embraced or at least favoured by Bishop Newton, Macknight, Tillotson, John Foster,[2] Milman, Stopford Brooke, Cox,[3] Jukes;[4] and by Baldwin Brown, Kingsley, Erskine of Linlathen, Bishop Ewing, and most of those who belong to the same school of theology.[5]

A third class of theologians advocate what may be called the doctrine of *continued probation*—that the intermediate state may still be a state, if not precisely of probation, yet of moral discipline and purification. This opinion has been advanced with great force and eloquence by Archdeacon

---

[1] According to Bigg, neither Clement nor Origen is properly speaking a universalist. If the goodness of God drew them in one direction, the freedom of the will, their negative pole, drove them with equal force in the other. *Bampton Lectures*, p. 292. Origen, however, taught that all punishment is medicinal.

[2] This view appears in many parts of Foster's *Life and Correspondence*, edited by Ryland; but especially in letter No. 215 addressed to Rev. E. White. See vol. ii. p. 249 ff. White's *Life in Christ*, p. 61.

[3] In his work, *Salvator Mundi*.

[4] In his work, *The Restitution of all Things*, where the doctrine of universal restoration is stated with great ability.

[5] The opinion of Julius Müller in his work on Sin appears to be that all sins would be forgiven in a future world except the sin against the Holy Ghost. With these writers Tennyson appears to sympathize—

"Oh, yet we trust that somehow good
 Will be the final goal of ill,
 To pangs of nature, sins of will,
Defects of doubt, and taints of blood.

That nothing walks with aimless feet,
 That not one life shall be destroyed
 Or cast as rubbish to the void,
When God hath made the pile complete."—*In Memoriam*.

Farrar in various works,[1] and adopted by Martensen, Dorner, Fronmüller, Alford, Plumptre, Stanley, Dean Church, and others. According to them, death does not render the condition of men unchangeable; there is still repentance beyond the grave; the gospel is still preached to the dead; the offers of salvation are still made to them; their doom is not irreversible. Scripture, it is affirmed, with the exception of those passages in Peter's Epistle, which are in favour of a state of probation or purification after death, is silent with regard to the intermediate state; we are not informed how the souls of the departed are employed during those vast aeons which precede the judgment; it is not until the last day, when Christ will come to judge the quick and the dead, that the final destinies of men will be fixed; not until then will the final separation between the righteous and the wicked be made; not until then will "the wicked go away into everlasting punishment and the righteous into life eternal." Thus Alford, commenting on the passage relating to Christ's preaching to the spirits in prison, observes: "The inference drawn from the fact here announced is not purgatory or universal restitution; but it is one which throws blessed light on one of the darkest enigmas of the divine justice; the cases where the final doom seems infinitely out of proportion to the lapse which has incurred it."[2] "The Holy Scripture," observes Fronmüller, "nowhere teaches the eternal damnation of those who died as heathens or non-Christians; it rather intimates in many passages that forgiveness may be possible beyond the grave, and refers the final doom, not to death, but to the

[1] *Eternal Hope; Mercy and Judgment.* Archdeacon Farrar thus states his own views: "I believe that there is an intermediate state of the soul, and that the great separation of souls into two classes will not take place until the final judgment. I believe that we are permitted to hope that, whether by a process of discipline, or enlightenment, or purification, or punishment, or by the special mercy of God in Christ, or in consequence of prayer, the state of many souls may be one of progress and diminishing sorrow, and of advancing happiness in the intermediate state." *Mercy and Judgment,* p. 484. The views of Dean Plumptre, as stated in his recent work, *The Spirits in Prison, and other Studies on the Life after Death,* are similar; see p. 338. Dr. Pusey, in his answer to Farrar, *What is Faith as to Everlasting Punishment?* advocates a view similar to the Romish doctrine of purgatory, but denies continued probation.

[2] Alford's *Greek Testament,* vol. iv. p. 368.

day of Christ (Acts xvii. 31; 2 Tim. i. 12, iv. 8; 1 John iv. 17). But in our passage (1 Pet. iv. 6), as in chap. iii. 19, 20, Peter by divine illumination clearly affirms that the ways of God's salvation do not terminate with earthly life, and that the gospel is preached beyond the grave to those who have departed this life without a knowledge of the same."[1]

Some go the length of affirming that the departed spirits of the saints may in the intermediate state be employed by Christ as ministering spirits carrying the message of salvation to the dead, preaching the gospel in Hades to those who in this world had never heard of it, or who had died impenitent and unbelieving. We find traces of this opinion in the writings of the Fathers, especially in Hermas and Clemens Alexandrinus. Thus Clement of Alexandria, quoting from the Shepherd of Hermas, says: "The apostles and teachers who had preached the name of the Son of God and had fallen asleep, preached in power and faith to those who had fallen asleep before them."[2]

The doctrine of a future state, especially that which relates to the intermediate state, is a profound mystery; eschatology relates to the darkest enigmas of revelation; an impenetrable veil hangs over our condition after death which it has not pleased God to remove. "It doth not yet appear what we shall be." We dare not affirm anything positive concerning such a mysterious subject. We have few data to proceed upon. We cannot speak with confidence concerning an eternal hope with regard to those who have died impenitent, however anxious we may be to believe it, in the face of our Lord's strong declarations concerning the undying worm, the unquenchable fire, the impassable gulf fixed between the

[1] Fronmüller's commentary on 1 Peter, p. 75, in Lange's *Bibelwerk*. The same opinion is held by White. He asserts that those who have had no opportunity of hearing the gospel offers in this world, whether heathens or in Christian lands, will have in another world the gospel presented to them.

[2] *Stromata*, ii. 9. This opinion is founded on the assertion of the apostle that the gospel was preached to the dead. It was entertained by Maurice on his deathbed. When told that his earthly ministry was over, he replied: "If I may not preach here, I may preach in other worlds." *Life*, ii. p. 636. See also Plumptre's *Spirits in Prison*, especially the chapter on "The Activities of the Intermediate State," p. 392 f.

righteous and the wicked, and especially as the same term (αἰώνιός) is employed to denote the duration of the happiness of the righteous and the misery of the wicked. On the other hand, everlasting punishment is a subject too awful to contemplate, a full realization of which would convert this world to every benevolent mind into a scene of unparalleled woe.[1] Here dogmatism is entirely out of place. We must leave the fate of the departed with the Judge of all the earth, who must inevitably do right, and whose name and nature is Love; but whilst we fear His justice, we are still permitted to hope in His mercy.

[1] The opinion of Bishop Martensen is well worthy of thoughtful consideration: he conceives that both everlasting punishment and universal restoration are unequivocally taught in Scripture; that there is here an antinomy, that is, "an apparent contradiction between two laws equally divine, and which consequently cannot find a perfectly conclusive and satisfactory solution in the present stage, the earthly limits of human knowledge." *Christian Dogmatics*, p. 475. See a striking passage in Archdeacon Farrar's *Eternal Hope*, p. 202, which, so far from being mere declamation, as Dr. Pusey somewhat ungenerously insinuates, expresses the feelings of many earnest minds.

THE SECOND EPISTLE OF PETER.

I. THE AUTHENTICITY OF THE EPISTLE.

WE remarked that the external evidence in favour of the First Epistle of Peter is as strong as for any other writing of the New Testament, and that it is attested by an unbroken chain of testimony from the days of the apostles. We cannot make the same remark in reference to the Second Epistle; it is perhaps the least attested writing of the New Testament. Reuss observes that it is the only example, in his judgment, of a positive mistake of the Church in her final choice in the canonical collection of the sacred writings of the New Testament.[1] A minute examination may, however, show that there is sufficient external evidence to warrant its reception, and that the objections against it are insufficient to authorize its rejection. It must be remembered that this is a purely historical question; the authenticity of the Second Epistle of Peter is to be judged by the ordinary canons of literary criticism. Hence all supposed consequences, arising from its rejection, are not to be taken into account. No divine superintendence was promised to the Church in determining the canon of the New Testament; each writing must stand or fall on its own evidence. Assertions on this point have been made which are unwarranted and pernicious in their consequences. Thus Bishop Wordsworth observes: "If any book, which the Church universal propounds to us as scripture, be not scripture; if any book, which she reads as the word of God, be not the word of God, but the work of an impostor,—then, with reverence be it said,

[1] Reuss' *Geschichte der heil. Schriften N. T.*, p. 265 [E. Tr. p. 275].

Christ's promise to His Church has failed, and the Holy Spirit has not been given to guide her into all truth. . . . The testimony of the universal Church of Christ, declaring that the Epistles, which we receive as such, are the Epistles of Peter, and are the word of God, is not *her* testimony only; it is the testimony of Christ, who is present with her. It is the witness of the Spirit who is in her, therefore that witness is true."[1] The question of the authenticity of the Second Epistle of Peter is undoubtedly a matter of importance, and comprises weighty points as to the settlement of the canon; but to involve the subject with such *à priori* considerations, and to prejudge the case by dogmatic assertions, is injurious to all honest inquiry and perilous in its tendency.

Several supposed allusions to Second Peter by the apostolic Fathers have been adduced by Lardner, Kirchhofer, Dietlein, and Keil. The most striking are by Clemens Romanus and Barnabas. Clemens Romanus (A.D. 95) observes: "Noah preached repentance, and as many as obeyed him were saved" (2 Pet. ii. 5).[2] "On account of his hospitality and godliness, Lot was saved out of Sodom, when all the country round was punished by means of fire and brimstone, the Lord thus making it manifest that He does not forsake those that hope in Him, but reserves such as depart from Him to punishment and torment" (2 Pet. ii. 6–9).[3] These are possible, but by no means certain references to this Epistle.[4]

---

[1] Wordsworth's *Greek Testament: Catholic Epistles*, p. 78. There is here an evident begging of the question. The Syrian Church rejects the Second Epistle of Peter, and therefore it cannot be affirmed that its reception is "the testimony of the universal Church of Christ." A statement somewhat similar is made by Canon Cook: "The Church, which for more than fourteen centuries has received this Epistle, has either been imposed upon by what must in that case be regarded as a Satanic device, or derived from it spiritual instruction of the highest importance." Smith's *Dictionary of the Bible*, vol. ii. p. 809, art. "Peter;" so also Schaff in his *History of the Apostolic Church*, vol. ii. pp. 16, 17. This would be to rest the authenticity of the books of Scripture on the infallibility of the Church.

[2] *Ep. ad Cor.* chap. vii.: Νῶε ἐκήρυξε μετάνοιαν, καὶ ὑπακούσαντες ἐσώθησαν.

[3] *Ibid.* chap. ii.: Διὰ φιλοξενίαν καὶ εὐσέβειαν Λὼτ ἐσώθη ἐκ Σοδόμων, τῆς περιχώρου πάσης κριθείσης διὰ πυρὸς καὶ θείου. Πρόδηλον ποιήσας ὁ δεσπότης, ὅτι τοὺς ἐλπίζοντας ἐπ' αὐτὸν οὐκ ἐγκαταλείπει, τοὺς δὲ ἑτεροκλινεῖς ὑπάρχοντας εἰς κόλασιν καὶ αἰκισμὸν τίθησιν.

[4] Dr. Abbott, however, dwells on the resemblance between Second Peter and

In the Epistle attributed to Barnabas (A.D. 100) there are the words: "And He Himself testifieth, saying, For a day is with Him as a thousand years,"[1] which may possibly be a reference to the words of Peter, "One day is with the Lord as a thousand years" (2 Pet. iii. 8); but from the context it is more probable that the reference is to the rabbinical notion of the days of the Messiah being a Sabbath of a thousand years. The other references adduced from Polycarp and Hermas[2] are still more vague and indefinite. The testimony of Justin Martyr (A.D. 150) is more obvious; adverting to the age of Adam, he observes: "As Adam was told that in the day he ate of the tree he would die, he did not complete a thousand years. We perceive, moreover, that the expression, The day of the Lord is as a thousand years, has reference to this."[3] Some suppose that this is taken from Ps. xc. 4; but the allusion to 2 Pet. iii. 8 is more direct and evident. Melito (A.D. 177), in a Syrian fragment discovered by Cureton, refers to the flood and final conflagration in terms which remind us of the language of this Epistle: "At another time there was a flood of waters, and the just were preserved in an ark of wood by the ordinance of God. So also will it be at the last time; there shall be a flood of fire, and the earth shall be burned up, and the just shall be delivered from the fury, like their fellows in the ark from the waters of the deluge"[4] (2 Pet. iii. 7, 10-12). Irenæus (A.D. 180) says: "There are some who refer the death of Adam to the thousandth year; for since a day of the Lord is as a thousand years, he did not overstep the thousand years, but died within them, thus bearing out the sentence of his sin;"[5] which is probably a reproduction of the statement of Justin Martyr, though possibly a direct reference to 2 Pet. iii. 8. Eusebius informs us that Clemens Alexandrinus (A.D. 190), in a work

the Epistle of Clement, asserting that the author of the Epistle borrowed from Clement. *Expositor*, second series, vol. iii. pp. 152, 153.

[1] Barnabas, *Ep.* chap. xv. : Ἡ γὰρ ἡμέρα παρ' αὐτῷ (i.e. κυρίῳ) χίλια ἔτη.

[2] Polycarp, *Epist. ad Philip.* chaps. vi. and vii. Hermas, *Simil.* iii. 7, iv. 3.

[3] *Dial. c. Tryph.* chap. 81 : Συνήκαμεν καὶ τὸ εἰρημένον, ὅτι ἡμέρα κυρίου ὡς χίλια ἔτη, εἰς τοῦτο συνάγει.

[4] *Spicilegium Syriacum*, p. 51.   [5] *Adv. Hær.* v. 23. 2.

called the *Hypotyposeis*, has given us abridged accounts of all the canonical Scriptures, not even omitting those that are disputed, namely, the Book of Jude and the other Catholic Epistles.[1] And Photius also mentions Clement's exposition of the Catholic Epistles. From this it has been inferred that the Second Epistle of Peter was known to Clement, although there are no references to that Epistle in his extant works.[2] There appear to be numerous allusions to this Epistle in the writings ascribed to Hippolytus (A.D. 220). Thus, writing concerning the disciples of Noetus, he says: "They, abashed and constrained by the truth, have confessed their errors for a short period, but after a little time wallowed again in the same mire "[3] (2 Pet. ii. 22). In another place he says: "You shall never have to breast the boiling flood of hell's eternal lake of fire, and the eye ever fixed in menacing glare of wicked angels chained in Tartarus as a punishment for their sins "[4] (2 Pet. ii. 4). And, in a doubtful work attributed to Hippolytus, this Epistle is expressly ascribed to Peter: "First of all, Peter, the rock of faith whom Christ the Lord called blessed, has instructed us to this effect: Know this first, that there shall come in the last days scoffers walking after their own lusts "[5] (2 Pet. iii. 3). Origen (A.D. 230), in passages found in the Latin translation of his works by Rufinus, several times ascribes this Epistle to Peter: "And again Peter says, Ye are made partakers of the divine nature" (2 Pet. i. 6). "And the Scripture says in a certain place, the dumb ass speaking with man's voice forbade the madness of the prophet" (2 Pet. ii. 16). "Peter speaks aloud by the two trumpets of his Epistles."[6] Although these words are found only in the Latin translation of Origen's works,[7] yet they are a sufficient

---

[1] *Hist. Eccl.* vi. 14.

[2] There is no reference to 2 Peter in the *Adumbrationes* of Cassiodorus, supposed to be a translation of the *Hypotyposeis* of Clement.

[3] *Adv. Haer.* ix. 2.

[4] *Adv. Haer.* x. 30; see also *De Antichristo*, chap. 2.

[5] *De Consummatione Saeculi*, chap. 10. The writer here speaks as if the authenticity of Second Peter was then a generally understood and settled point.

[6] *Opp.* tom. ii. pp. 200, 321, 412.

[7] The faithfulness of Rufinus' Latin translation cannot be fully depended upon, yet the passages here quoted have no appearance of interpolation.

proof that Origen was acquainted with the Second Epistle of Peter. Eusebius also gives us the following quotation from Origen: "Peter, upon whom the Church of Christ is built, against which the gates of hell shall not prevail, has left one Epistle undisputed. Suppose also the second was left by him, for on this there is some doubt."[1] Firmilian, bishop of Cæsarea in Cappadocia, a contemporary of Origen (A.D. 250), in his Epistle to Cyprian, writes: "Abusing also the blessed apostles Peter and Paul, as if they delivered this doctrine; though they in their Epistles have anathematized heretics, and admonished us to avoid them."[2] By the term *Epistles* Firmilian may allude to only one Epistle of Peter; but what he here affirms can only refer to the Second Epistle, for only in this Epistle is there reference to heretics. This Epistle is not quoted or referred to by Tertullian or Cyprian. Methodius, bishop of Tyre (A.D. 290), most probably alludes to the description of the final conflagration given in this Epistle when he says: "For the whole world, that it may be purified and renewed, will be burned up with devouring flames." "Wherefore it is necessary that both earth and heaven exist again, after the conflagration of all things and the fervent heat"[3] (2 Pet. iii. 12, 13). Eusebius (A.D. 325) is acquainted with this Epistle, but expresses his doubts as to its authenticity. He writes: "As to the writings of Peter, one of his Epistles, called the First, is acknowledged as genuine. But that what is called the Second we have not, indeed, understood to be embodied with the sacred books (ἐνδιάθηκον), yet, as it appeared useful to many, it was studiously read with the other Scriptures. These (writings) are those that are called Peter's Epistles, of which I have understood only one Epistle to be genuine, and admitted by the ancient Fathers."[4] And, in another place, he classes it among the disputed writings: "Among the disputed books, although they are well known and approved by many, is reputed

---

[1] *Hist. Eccl.* vi. 25. Πέτρος . . . μίαν ἐπιστολὴν ὁμολογουμένην καταλίλοιπεν, ἔστω δὲ καὶ δευτέραν· ἀμφιβάλλεται.

[2] *Ep. Cyprian.* 74. Oxford ed. 75. Adhuc etiam infamans Petrum et Paulum beatos apostolos, quasi hoc ipsi tradiderint; qui in epistolis suis hæreticos execrati sunt, et ut eos evitemus, monuerunt.

[3] Epiphan. *Hær.* lxiv. 31. [4] *Hist. Eccl.* iii. 3.

that called the Epistle of James and Jude. Also the Second Epistle of Peter, and those called the Second and Third Epistles of John."[1] Eusebius does not assert its spuriousness, but only its doubtful authenticity; for he afterwards proceeds to mention the books which were spurious. Jerome (A.D. 390) maintains the genuineness of Second Peter, but mentions the doubts which existed about it: "Peter wrote two Epistles which are called catholic, the second of which is denied by many on account of its disagreement in style with the first."[2] The Epistle is not found in the Muratorian canon; and it is omitted in the Peshito.[3] Ephræm Syrus (A.D. 370), however, recognises it, and quotes from it; but the passages in which he does so, are found only in the Greek translation of his works.[4] After the time of Eusebius the Epistle was received into the canon, and is attested by Rufinus, Gregory Nazianzen, Athanasius, Augustine, Cyril, Basil, Ambrose, Chrysostom, and Hilary: it is contained in the canon of Laodicea (A.D. 363) and in that of Carthage (A.D. 397).

The internal evidence in favour of the Second Epistle of Peter is stronger than the external. The Epistle professes to have been written by Peter: "Simon Peter, a servant and an apostle of Jesus Christ, to them that have obtained like precious faith with us" (2 Pet. i. 1); and the author refers to the former Epistle which he had written to his readers (2 Pet. iii. 1). In examining this Epistle there is nothing in it which would lead us to doubt the truth of this declaration, but, on the contrary, much to confirm and support it. It is

[1] *Hist. Eccl.* iii. 25.

[2] *Catal. Script. Eccl.* chap. i. : Simon Petrus scripsit duas epistolas quæ catholicæ nominantur; quarum secunda a plerisque ejus esse negatur, propter styli cum priore dissonantiam.

[3] It is doubtful whether it was contained in the old Latin. Westcott asserts its omission. *On the Canon*, pp. 230, 231. So also Salmon, *Introduction to the N. T.*, p. 611.

[4] "The testimony of Ephræm Syrus," observes Westcott, "is unfortunately uncertain. For while he appears to use all the books of our New Testament in his works, which are preserved only in Greek, I am not aware that there is in the original Syriac text more than one quotation of the Apocalypse, and perhaps an anonymous reference to the Second Epistle of St. Peter." *Canon of the N. T.*, p. 395, 2nd edition. The Epistle is contained in the Philoxenian or later Syriac version.

such an Epistle as we would suppose Peter to have written; it bears upon it the impress of his character. The earnestness of its tone, the repeated exhortations to holiness, the solemn warnings against apostasy, the references to the last things, the joyful expectation of the new heavens and the new earth wherein dwelleth righteousness, the abundant entrance into the heavenly kingdom, all remind us of that apostle who knew by experience the danger of denial and the necessity of perseverance, whose glance was ever directed toward the future, and whose sanguine spirit caused him to anticipate a brighter order of things. Besides, there are in the Epistle references to incidents in the life of Peter. The author alludes to his presence at the transfiguration, which Peter, along with James and John, beheld (2 Pet. i. 16-18). And he refers to a special revelation imparted to him by the Lord concerning the nature of his death (2 Pet. i. 14); a revelation which, as we learn from the Gospel of John, was made to Peter (John xxi. 18, 19).

It has also been observed that there are undesigned coincidences between this Epistle and the speeches of Peter as recorded in the Acts of the Apostles. On these coincidences we do not place much weight, as they are neither numerous nor important; though the peculiar value of this kind of evidence greatly strengthens the case. In both the expression "the wages of iniquity" ($\mu\iota\sigma\theta\grave{o}s\ \tau\hat{\eta}s\ \dot{a}\delta\iota\kappa\acute{\iota}as$) is found; in the Acts, where Peter describes the treachery of Judas (Acts i. 18), and in the Epistle, where reference is made to the covetousness of Balaam (2 Pet. ii. 15). In both the second coming of Christ is described as "the day of the Lord" ($\dot{\eta}\mu\acute{e}\rho a\ \kappa\upsilon\rho\acute{\iota}o\upsilon$, Acts ii. 20; 2 Pet. iii. 10). In both $\epsilon\dot{\upsilon}\sigma\acute{e}\beta\epsilon\iota a$ is employed for holiness (Acts iii. 12; 2 Pet. i. 7). In both the enemies of the faith are accused of denying Christ; in the Acts, of denying the Holy One and the Just (Acts iii. 14), and in the Epistle of denying the Lord that bought them (2 Pet. ii. 1). And in both $\delta\epsilon\sigma\pi\acute{o}\tau\eta s$ is used, instead of $\kappa\acute{\upsilon}\rho\iota o s$, for Lord (Acts iv. 24; 2 Pet. ii. 1).[1]

---

[1] For other coincidences with Peter's speeches as recorded in the Acts of the Apostles, see Professor Lumby on Second Peter in *Speaker's Commentary*, vol. iv. p. 226.

A stronger argument is derived from the similarity in style and sentiment to the First Epistle. The two Epistles commence with the same salutation: "Grace unto you and peace be multiplied" (1 Pet. i. 2; 2 Pet. i. 2).[1] In both Epistles the word ἀναστροφή, *conversation*,[2] is employed to denote moral conduct (1 Pet. i. 15, 18, ii. 12, iii. 1, 2, 16; 2 Pet. ii. 7, iii. 11). The word ἀρετή, *virtue*, which elsewhere is restricted to man, is in both Epistles applied to God: in 1 Pet. ii. 9, "That ye should show forth the virtues of Him who hath called you;" and in 2 Pet. i. 3, according to the correct reading: "Through the knowledge of Him who hath called us through His glory and virtue." The word ἀπόθεσις, not elsewhere used in the New Testament, is found in 1 Pet. iii. 21, denoting putting off the sins of the flesh; and in 2 Pet. i. 14, denoting putting off the earthly tabernacle. The phrase "without spot and blemish" is found in both Epistles: in 1 Pet. i. 19 under the form ἀμώμου καὶ ἀσπίλου, and in 2 Pet. iii. 14 under the form ἄσπιλοι καὶ ἀμώμητοι. So also in 2 Pet. ii. 13 we have σπίλοι καὶ μῶμοι. Ἐπόπτης, an eye-witness, is used only in the New Testament in 2 Pet. i. 16, whilst the cognate verb ἐποπτεύειν occurs twice in the First Epistle (1 Pet. ii. 12, iii. 2). The adjective ἴδιος is employed in both Epistles in the sense of the possessive pronoun (1 Pet. iii. 1, 5; 2 Pet. i. 20, ii. 22).[3] So also the sentiments in both Epistles are similar. The same peculiarities which distinguish the one, distinguish the other. Both dwell upon the prophets predicting the salvation revealed in the gospel (1 Pet. i. 11; 2 Pet. i. 20, 21). Both mention the deluge, refer to Noah, and to the small number that were saved (1 Pet. iii. 20; 2 Pet. ii. 5). In both the eschatological element predominates: both refer to the second coming of Christ, in the First Epistle as a revelation (ἀποκάλυψις), and in the Second Epistle as a presence (παρουσία); and in both there are disclosures of "the last things" not elsewhere

---

[1] Χάρις ὑμῖν καὶ εἰρήνη πληθυνθείη.

[2] This word is only used five times elsewhere in the New Testament.

[3] For other points of resemblance between the two Petrine Epistles, see a learned article on the Second Epistle of Peter by Professor Lumby in the *Expositor* for November 1876, first series, vol. iv. p. 374 ff. See also Weiss' *Einleitung*, p. 445, for a list of similarities.

made in Scripture; in the First Epistle, concerning Christ preaching to the spirits in prison [1] (1 Pet. iii. 19, 20), and in the Second Epistle, concerning the conflagration of the world [2] (2 Pet. iii. 10–12).

Another line of internal evidence in favour of this Epistle, which has been often insisted on, is its marked superiority to the writings of the apostolic Fathers. In this Epistle there is nothing at variance with the spirit and dignity, the purity and high moral tone of the sacred Scriptures; there is a marked inspiration and loftiness in its sentiments; an absence of everything that is frivolous or trivial, which affords a remarkable contrast to the writings of the apostolic Fathers. The first chapter, especially, in which the apostle traces the development of faith in its various stages up to charity, bears impressed upon it the stamp of inspiration. On the other hand, the writings of the apostolic Fathers abound in trivial reflections which demonstrate their human origin.[3] Even the best of them, the Epistle of Clemens Romanus, is weak compared with this Epistle ascribed to Peter. Any one who is conversant with the writings of the apostolic Fathers must confess that the difference between their writings and the Second Epistle of Peter is immense; such a difference as one would expect between an uninspired and an inspired writing. "Who," observes Farrar, "will venture to assert that any apostolic Father—that Clement of Rome, or Ignatius, or Polycarp, or Hermas, or Justin Martyr—could have written so much as twenty consecutive verses so eloquent and so powerful as those of the Second Epistle of Peter? No *known* member of the Church of that age could have been the writer, not even the author of the Epistle to Diognetus. Would a writer so much more powerful than any of these have remained uninfluential and unknown?[4] Would one

---

[1] This, of course, is dependent on the explanation we put on this passage.

[2] Some may suppose that this argument is counterbalanced by the objection drawn from the points of difference in style and sentiment between the two Epistles. See *infra*.

[3] The writings of subsequent Fathers, such as Justin Martyr, Clemens Alexandrinus, Tertullian, and Origen, are much superior to those of the apostolic Fathers.

[4] Farrar seems here to forget that the author of the much greater Epistle to the Hebrews remains unknown.

who could wield his pen with so inspired a power have failed to write a line in his own name, and for the immediate benefit of his own contemporaries?"[1] Of course such an argument, being of a subjective nature, will affect minds differently; some may be unable to feel its force, whilst to others it may be most convincing; but it proves this much at least, that the Second Epistle of Peter, judged by its contents, is not unworthy of being classed among the inspired books of Scripture; whereas the writings of the apostolic Fathers, judged by their contents, are unworthy of that honour.

In consequence chiefly of the weakness of the external evidence, taken in combination with certain internal objections, no writing of the New Testament has been more disputed by theologians of all shades of opinion. Even Calvin, in a remarkable passage, expresses his doubts of its genuineness. "What Jerome writes," he observes, "influences me, that some, induced by a difference in the style, did not think that Peter was the author. For though some affinity may be traced, yet I confess that there is that manifest difference which distinguishes different writers. There are also other probable conjectures by which we may conclude that it was written by another rather than by Peter. At the same time, all will agree that it contains nothing unworthy of Peter, as it shows everywhere the power and dignity of an apostolic spirit. If it be received as canonical, we must allow Peter to be the author, since it has his name inscribed; and it would have been a fiction, unworthy of a minister of Christ, to have personated another individual. I therefore conclude, if the Epistle be regarded as worthy of credit, that it must have proceeded from Peter; not that he himself wrote it, but that some one of his disciples set forth in writing, by his command, those things which the necessity of the times required."[2] Among the older writers, Erasmus, Grotius,[3] Cardinal Cajetan, Salmasius, Scaliger, and Wetstein questioned the authenticity of Second Peter; and in recent times it has been

---

[1] Farrar's *Early Days of Christianity*, vol. i. p. 206.
[2] Introduction to his *Commentary on the Second Epistle of Peter*.
[3] For the view of Grotius, see *infra*.

denied by Semler, Eichhorn, De Wette, Neander,[1] Credner, Neudecker, Reuss, Mayerhoff, Lücke, Ewald, Bleek, Kern, Huther, Lechler, Sieffert,[2] Mangold, H. A. Schott, Schmid,[3] and by Baur, Schwegler, Holtzmann, Pfleiderer, and Hilgenfeld belonging to the Tübingen school, among German scholars; and by Davidson, Abbott, and Hatch[4] among English theologians. The objections to the Epistle are perhaps most fully stated by Credner. According to him, they are as follows: "The use of the Epistle of Jude, written after the death of Peter; the surprising diversity in style and expression from the First Epistle of Peter; the evident labour of the author to make himself known as the Apostle Peter; the value which is placed on γνῶσις and ἐπίγνωσις (knowledge), suitable only to a later period, whereas the apostolic time dwells on ἐλπίς (hope); and the designation of the mount of transfiguration as the holy mount;"[5] and to these are to be added the mention of the Epistles of Paul as "sacred scriptures."

1. An objection, frequently brought against this Epistle, is its difference in style and diction from the First Epistle.[6] This was first dwelt upon by Jerome, who solved the difficulty by supposing that a different interpreter was employed in writing the Second Epistle; that whereas Mark or Silvanus was Peter's interpreter when he wrote the First Epistle, he employed another person when he wrote the Second.[7] This objection is thus strongly insisted on by Bleek: "The Epistles present the greatest contrast both in thought and

---

[1] *Planting of Christianity*, vol. i. p. 376.

[2] In his article on Peter in the new edition of Herzog's *Real-Encyklopädie*, vol. xi. p. 535 ff.

[3] Schmid's *Biblical Theology of the N. T.*, p. 375.

[4] The general tendency of the article on Peter by Dr. Hatch in the *Encyclopedia Britannica* is unfavourable to the authenticity of Second Peter, although his views are not positively stated.

[5] Credner's *Einleitung in das N. T.*, p. 660.

[6] Eichhorn's *Einleitung*, vol. iii. p. 632.

[7] *Epist.* cxx. ad Hedibiam. "Paul," he observes, "had Titus for his interpreter, so also Peter had Mark, whose Gospel was composed by Peter narrating and the other writing. Also the two Epistles which are called Peter's differ from each other in style and character and structure of words. Whence we understand that he used different interpreters, according to the necessity of the case."

language; the main difference is, that the language of the First Epistle is somewhat rough and Hebraizing, whilst that of the Second is more eloquent and better Greek. The style of the Second is more periodic, while in the First the connection of sentences is simple and even clumsy."[1] Dr. Abbott differs from him, giving the decided preference in point of style to the First Epistle. "The style of the author throughout," he observes, "is that of a copyist and 'fine writer,' ignorant of ordinary Greek idiom, yet constantly straining after grandiloquent Greek, an affected and artificial style wholly unlike that of the First Epistle of Peter, a style so made up of shreds and patches of other men's writings, and so interspersed with obsolete, sonorous, and meaningless words, that it really has no claim to be called a style at all."[2] The following are given as examples of the difference of style and diction. In the First Epistle our Lord is usually called Christ or Jesus Christ, without any appellative; whereas in the Second Epistle predicates are attached to the name, such as "our Lord," or "our Lord and Saviour Jesus Christ." In the First Epistle the designation σωτήρ applied to our Lord never occurs, whereas it is of frequent occurrence in the Second Epistle. Whilst in both Epistles Christ's second coming is alluded to, the term employed for it in the First Epistle is ἀποκάλυψις, whilst in the Second it is παρουσία or ἡμέρα κυρίου.[3]

Some endeavour to remove the objection by supposing, with Jerome, that Peter employed different interpreters in writing these two Epistles.[4] But we do not see any necessity for

---

[1] Bleek's *Introduction to the N. T.*, vol. ii. pp. 179, 180. With this judgment Ewald also agrees, *Sieben Sendschreiben des neuen Bundes*, p. 110.

[2] *Expositor*, vol. iii. p. 153, second series.

[3] See Credner's *Einleitung*, vol. iii. p. 665. Huther's *Die Briefe des Petrus*, p. 323 ff. [E. Tr. p. 270 ff.]. Holtzmann's *Einleitung*, p. 496. Mayerhoff's *Petrinische Schriften*, p. 160.

[4] Even Canon Cook adopts this solution: "That the two Epistles," he observes, "could not have been composed and written by the same person is a point scarcely open to doubt." And he goes on to say: "If we admit that some time intervened between the composition of the two works, that in writing the First the apostle was aided by Silvanus, and in the Second by another, perhaps St. Mark, that the circumstances of the churches addressed by him were considerably changed, and that the Second was written in greater haste,

such an explanation; whatever force is in the above objection, we consider is more than counterbalanced by the more numerous points of similarity in style and diction which are undoubtedly presented by the two Epistles. Besides, these Epistles are too short to determine a difference of authorship from a diversity of style,[1] more especially as Peter has no such definite and well-marked style as the Apostles Paul and John. This is seen from the different views which adverse critics take of the diction of these Epistles; some (Ewald, Bleek) giving the preference to the Second, and others (Mayerhoff, Huther) to the First Epistle. Besides, most of the linguistic peculiarities are to be found in the second chapter, which bears such a remarkable resemblance to the Epistle of Jude.[2] Even Reuss, who on other grounds rejects the Epistle, admits: "We lay no stress on the linguistic differences between the two Epistles which modern criticism has so much emphasized. The two Epistles are too short, have to do with wholly different circumstances, and there are no direct contradictions to be found. Only when the spuriousness has been proved on other grounds may this point be taken into account."[3]

2. Lechler objects to the Epistle, because there are in it points which make the distinction between it and the First Epistle very evident;[4] there is not only a difference in style and diction, but also a difference in sentiment from the First Epistle. The keynote of the First Epistle is *hope* (ἐλπίς);

not to speak of a possible decay of faculties, the differences may be regarded as insufficient to justify more than hesitation in admitting its genuineness." Smith's *Dictionary of the Bible*, vol. ii. p. 809, article "Peter."

[1] Of course it may also be asserted that the Epistles are too short to determine an identity of authorship from a similarity in style; but the points of identity appear to us to be more numerous, and, besides, they are deduced in proof of an assertion made at the beginning of the Epistle, that its author was the Apostle Peter. Certainly, however, the brevity of the Epistles somewhat detracts from the force of the argument. It may be said that diversity is a stronger argument than similarity, because similarity must occur in an imitation; but the points of similarity in these Epistles are evidently undesigned.

[2] Weiss' *Einleitung*, p. 445: "The *differentia styli* remarked by Jerome is founded on the expression of chap. ii., whose phraseology is influenced by the Epistle of Jude."

[3] *Geschichte der heil. Schriften N. T.*, p. 266 [E. Tr. p. 276].

[4] Lechler's *Das apostolische Zeitalter*, p. 191 [translation of the 3rd edition, vol. ii. pp. 158, 159].

whilst the keynote of the Second is *knowledge* (ἐπίγνωσις or γνῶσις). In the First Epistle there are frequent references to the Old Testament, whilst in the Second such references are rare.[1] In the First Epistle the sufferings of Christ are dwelt upon, whilst in the Second they are not mentioned. In the First Epistle the example of Christ is frequently held forth for the imitation of believers, whilst in the Second it is not adverted to. In the First Epistle, the persecutions of the Christians are dwelt upon, whilst there is no trace of false teachers; whereas in the Second, the readers are warned against the errors of false teachers, whilst there is no mention of persecutions.

The point last stated is the cause of the diversity of sentiment. The Epistles were written with different purposes, the First being chiefly hortatory, and the Second polemical. The First was written with a design to comfort believers under the persecutions to which they were exposed; and the Second to warn them against the errors of false teachers. Hence in the First Epistle, the author dwelt upon the example of the sufferings of Christ to encourage believers in trial; whereas there was not the same necessity in the Second Epistle. And hence, also, hope was the keynote of the First Epistle, because its purpose was to sustain believers in suffering; and knowledge was the keynote of the Second Epistle, because its purpose was to establish them in the faith. But in both Epistles the sanguine and hopeful spirit of the apostle is apparent; in the Second, as well as in the First, the author leads forward the thoughts of his readers to the entrance that shall be ministered to them abundantly into the everlasting kingdom of our Lord and Saviour Jesus Christ (2 Pet. i. 11); in the Second, as well as in the First, Peter is the Apostle of Hope.

3. Mayerhoff objects to the Epistle, because the author shows a manifest solicitude to make himself appear as Peter.[2] The author is continually mentioning circumstances connected with the life of Peter, and referring them to himself, as if his

---

[1] See Bleek's *Introduction to the N. T.*, vol. ii. p. 180.

[2] Mayerhoff's *Petrinische Schriften*, p. 185. The same objection is made by Credner, De Wette, Neander, and Schwegler.

design was to impress upon his readers that it was Peter who wrote this Epistle. Thus in his address he calls himself "Simon Peter" (2 Pet. i. 1). He reminds his readers that the Lord Jesus Christ had revealed to him that he must soon put off his earthly tabernacle (2 Pet. i. 14). He alludes to his presence with Christ on the mount of transfiguration, when he heard the voice from the excellent glory, This is my beloved Son, in whom I am well pleased (2 Pet. i. 17, 18). He identifies himself with the author of the First Epistle (2 Pet. iii. 1). And he speaks of Paul as his beloved brother, thus claiming an equality with him (2 Pet. iii. 15). But these references, so far from being objections to the authorship of Peter, are internal proofs in favour of it, being references to incidents in the life of that apostle. And this is especially seen to be the case, as these references are naturally and not designedly or artificially introduced. If we attend to the context, we shall find that there are special reasons for them. Paul frequently insists upon his apostleship, and brings himself prominently forward when writing in opposition to false teachers; and the same method is here employed by Peter in writing against the heretics who infested the early Church. If he alludes to Christ having revealed his martyrdom, it is because he wished to impress upon his readers the solemn circumstances under which he wrote, as about to put off his earthly tabernacle. If he mentions the transfiguration, it is because he wished to prove that Christians had not followed cunningly devised fables. And if he refers to the Epistles of his brother apostle Paul, it is to guard against their abuse.

4. Bleek objects to the manner in which Paul's Epistles are here spoken of.[1] The words, on which this objection is

---

[1] "The manner in which St. Paul's Epistles are spoken of is somewhat strange. They are mentioned collectively, not one only, but all, as writings κατ' ἐξοχήν, not merely known and widely spread in the Church, but as already the topic of various interpretations, on account of the obscurity and difficulty of their contents, so that the unlearned wrest them to their own destruction, as they do also the other Scriptures (ὡς καὶ τὰς λοιπὰς γραφάς)." *Introduction to the N. T.*, vol. ii. p. 182. Similarly Eichhorn, *Einleitung*, vol. iii. pp. 629, 630. Davidson's *Introduction to the Study of N. T.*, vol. ii. p. 485, 1st ed.; vol. ii. p. 455, 2nd ed. Ewald's *History of Israel*, vol. viii. p. 182, E. Tr.

founded, are: "And account that the long-suffering of our Lord is salvation, even as our beloved brother Paul also, according to the wisdom given unto him, has written unto you; as also in all his Epistles, speaking in them of these things; in which are some things hard to be understood, which they that are unlearned and unstable wrest, as they do also the other Scriptures, to their own destruction" (2 Pet. iii. 15, 16). Here, it is asserted, mention is made of all Paul's Epistles (πάσαις ἐπιστολαῖς), as if a collection of them had already been made; and they are put on the same footing with the other Scriptures (τὰς λοιπὰς γραφάς), by which are probably meant the Old Testament Scriptures; both of which particulars belong to a stage in the history of the canon much later than the death of Peter. But there is no reason to suppose that the phrase "in all his Epistles" (ἐν πάσαις ἐπιστολαῖς) denotes a complete collection of Paul's Epistles, but merely those which might be known to the readers of Peter's Epistle; and we know that at least three of Paul's Epistles[1] were written to the Churches in Asia and Galatia addressed by Peter. Even if it is admitted that Peter here places the Epistles of Paul in the same rank with the Scriptures of the Old Testament, yet there is nothing objectionable in this, as Paul himself makes the same assertion, and requires that his Epistles be received as a revelation from the Lord (1 Cor. xiv. 37). The importance which Peter assigns to Paul's Epistles is the same which Paul himself claims.

5. Credner and Bleek further object that the expression "holy mount" (2 Pet. i. 18) betrays a post-apostolic age, when a degree of sacredness was imparted to the scenes of gospel history; in Peter's time the phrase "the holy mount" could only denote Mount Sion. "The passage," observes Bleek, "thus suggests the thought of a post-apostolic age, when a certain locality had come to be regarded traditionally as the place of transfiguration, and when the designation 'holy' had been given to it on that account."[2] But it does not appear that Peter, in calling the mount of transfiguration "the holy mount," describes its locality. This is so indefinitely

---

[1] The Epistles to the Galatians, to the Ephesians, and to the Colossians.
[2] *Introduction to the N. T.*, vol. ii. p. 182.

stated in the Gospels and in early Church history, that even to this day it has never been determined on what mount the transfiguration took place; the evangelists give us no particulars, or at least very indefinite ones, whereby that locality can be determined. But Peter uses the epithet "holy" merely because such an incident as the transfiguration occurred on that mount; it was holy because on it the Lord manifested forth His glory. Nor does it appear that afterward any particular mountain was ever known by the appellation "the holy mount," as being the mount of transfiguration.

6. Another objection, strongly insisted on, is the use made of the Epistle of Jude.[1] We reserve the relation between the Second Epistle of Peter and the Epistle of Jude to form the subject of a separate dissertation; but meanwhile we cannot shrink from the objection which is drawn from this relation. It is affirmed that Peter here incorporates in his Epistle the sentiments and even the words of Jude; instead of using his own apostolic authority, he employs the declarations of one who was not an apostle. "Jude," observes Dr. Davidson, "is copied or imitated by Peter; a fact inconsistent with the position and character of an apostle. The former was not an apostle. Is it likely that Peter would follow his letter as he has done? Had Jude been an apostle, Peter might perhaps have adopted his sentiments and words, but even in that case it would be improbable."[2] The resemblance between these two canonical Epistles is certainly very remarkable, and is too close to be regarded as accidental. We reserve the determination of the question as to which Epistle was written first; but let us assume that the Epistle of Jude was the earlier,—for, if otherwise, the objection falls to the ground,—the question which meets us is, Whether the incorporation of its sentiments and words is an objection to the authenticity of the Second Epistle of Peter? Now we must admit that the fact is surprising, but we cannot affirm that it forms a sufficient and valid objection. We know that Paul sometimes quotes

---

[1] Holtzmann's *Einleitung*. p. 497. Mangold's *Einleitung von F. Bleek*, p. 760. Reuss, *Geschichte des heil. Schrift. N. T.*, p. 266. Ewald's *History of Israel*, vol. viii. p. 180, E. Tr.

[2] Davidson's *Introduction to the Study of the N. T.*, vol. ii. 453, 2nd edition.

from heathen, and perhaps from rabbinical writers; we have seen that it is highly probable that Peter in his First Epistle, which is generally admitted to be genuine, quotes from the Epistle of James; and Jude himself quotes from the apocryphal book of Enoch; and therefore the use of the Epistle of Jude, though remarkable, cannot be regarded as a proof of spuriousness. Peter found that Jude expressed his sentiments with reference to the false teachers, and therefore he employs the words of Jude in his Epistle, not in a slavish manner, but modifying them to suit his purpose. He adapts them to the use, not only of the Hellenistic Jews (to whom Jude chiefly wrote), but of the Gentile Christians; and applies the description to the heretical teachers who disturbed the peace and corrupted the purity of the Christian Church.

7. An entirely new objection has recently been brought forward by Dr. Abbott in three articles in the *Expositor*,[1] namely, that the author of the Second Epistle of Peter was acquainted with the writings of Josephus, and that consequently he could not be the Apostle Peter. Dr. Abbott grounds his argument chiefly on a comparison between the Epistle and two passages from the works of Josephus; the one the preface to the *Antiquities*, and the other the account of the last words of Moses; and he endeavours to prove from the similarity of words and phrases that the author of the Epistle was acquainted with these passages. Farrar, in reviewing these articles of Dr. Abbott, admits that a resemblance, such as could not be accidental, to the words of Josephus has been proved. He observes: "What Dr. Abbott has proved in his first paper beyond all shadow of doubt is that Josephus and the author of this Epistle *could not have written independently of each other.* I must confess that it would be impossible for me to feel respect for the judgment of any critic who asserted that the resemblances between the two writers were purely fortuitous."[2] But he escapes the

---

[1] *Expositor*, vol. iii. second series; especially the first article for January 1882, entitled, "On the Second Epistle of St. Peter: Had the author read Josephus?" Ewald, in his *History of Israel*, it would appear, in a note observes: "It is remarkable that the phrase μύθοις ἐξακολουθήσαντες, Joseph. *Ant.* pref. § 4, is repeated 2 Pet. i. 16." *History of Israel*, vol. viii. p. 181, F. Tr.

[2] The *Expositor*, vol. iii. p. 403, second series. In his *Early Days of Chris-*

difficulty by affirming that the author of the Epistle may not have borrowed from Josephus, but Josephus from the author. We have not space, nor is this the place, for entering into any minute examination of this objection. Its originality and ingenuity are admitted; but, notwithstanding the strong and *ex cathedra* assertion of Archdeacon Farrar, its validity is questionable. Such a comparison of words and phrases as are there made, however plausible, fail to convey conviction. It is highly improbable and almost absurd to suppose that a Christian writer of the second century, even although acquainted with the works of Josephus, should in a short Epistle slavishly imitate particular passages contained in them; and it is wholly improbable and perfectly inconceivable to suppose that Josephus should take the trouble of studying a short Epistle of the Christians, in whose religion he did not believe, and whom he despised, with a view to the composition of his history—an Epistle also which had no possible connection with the subject he had undertaken to write upon.[1]

Some have endeavoured to remove the internal difficulties, connected with this Epistle, by calling in question, not its authenticity, but its integrity. Grotius thinks that the Epistle was written by Simeon, the bishop of Jerusalem, and that the words Πέτρος and ὁ ἀπόστολος are interpolations; and that the sentence, "This is the second Epistle which I now write to you," refers to the first two chapters, which were the first Epistle.[2] Bertholdt supposes that the second

tianity, vol. i. p. 190, he makes the same assertion: "One thing is indisputable, namely, that the resemblances between the writer and the Jewish historian cannot be accidental." Dr. Hatch also, in his article on Peter in the *Encyclopædia Britannica*, appears to admit the reality of the correspondence between Second Peter and Josephus, giving the priority to Josephus.

[1] There is an admirable article on Dr. Abbott's views in the American *Southern Presbyterian Review*, April 1883, by Professor B. Warfield, of Alleghany College. Here all the statements and objections of Dr. Abbott are met in a satisfactory manner. The subject is also discussed in a masterly manner by Professor Salmon in his *Introduction to the New Testament*, pp. 640-653. "What we are asked to believe," he observes, "is that (the author of) 2 Peter prepared himself for his task by studying one page of Josephus, and then tried how many words out of that page he could manage to introduce when writing on quite different topics."

[2] *Annot. ad secund. Petri.*

chapter is an interpolation from the Epistle of Jude, and that the Epistle was originally composed of the first and third chapters.[1] Lange thinks that the section i. 20–iii. 3 is a later interpolation.[2] Ullmann regards the first chapter only as the original Epistle of Peter, or rather as the fragment of an Epistle which has been lost. Bunsen asserts that the first twelve verses and the concluding doxology are all that is Petrine in the Epistle.[3] But all these hypotheses are arbitrary attempts to escape difficulties. There is no evidence whatever in manuscripts or versions of such interpolations, nor in the Epistle itself of mutilation or abbreviation. The Epistle must be admitted or rejected as a whole.

Let us now take a review of the whole evidence, with the object, if possible, of arriving at some positive result. It is admitted that the external evidence is weak; the supposed allusions in the writings of the apostolic Fathers are too vague to be founded on; it is possible that Justin Martyr and Irenæus refer to the Epistle; still more direct are the references in the writings of Hippolytus; perhaps Clemens Alexandrinus wrote on the Epistle; but it is not until the time of Origen, in the middle of the third century, that the authorship of the Epistle is mentioned. The internal evidence we consider is stronger, especially the undoubted similarity in style and sentiment to the First Epistle, even in the midst of differences—a similarity which cannot possibly be accounted for from a design on the part of the author to palm off his writing as an epistle of Peter, and its marked superiority in thought and style over the writings of the apostolic Fathers. Nor do we think the internal objections brought against the Epistle of much weight, with the possible exception of that arising from the use made of the Epistle of Jude. On the whole, the balance of evidence is in favour of the Epistle, although by no means so decidedly as in the case of most of the other books of the New Testament. Besides, it is to be remembered that the Fathers of the fourth

---

[1] *Einleitung in das N. T.*

[2] *Das apostolische Zeitalter*, vol. i. p. 152 ff., and article "Petrus" in the first edition of Herzog's *Encykl.* vol. xi. p. 436.

[3] *Ignatius und seine Zeit*, p. 175.

century, when the canon of the New Testament was fixed, had many more grounds to go upon than we possess; many of the works of the Fathers which are now lost were then extant; and it was only as the result of careful examination that any writing was admitted as part of the canonical Scriptures.

Although the Epistle has been disputed and rejected by theologians of great learning and authority, yet it has been defended and accepted by theologians of equal learning and authority. Among those who accept the Epistle, as a genuine work of Peter, are to be reckoned Augusti, Pott, Michaelis, Bengel, Hug, Guericke, Wiesinger, Thiersch, Th. Schott, Dietlein, Luthardt, Stier, Schaff, Fronmüller, Hofmann, Heydenreich, Keil, and Spitta among German divines; and Lardner, Alford, Plumptre, Lumby, Plummer, Tregelles, Cook, Eadie, Wordsworth, Salmon, and Warfield[1] among English divines. Others, such as Brückner, Olshausen, Weiss,[2] and Farrar,[3] remain undecided, and either waver in their opinions or find it impossible to arrive at any positive result.

II. THE READERS OF THE EPISTLE.

The Epistle bears the following inscription: "Simon Peter, a servant and an apostle of Jesus Christ, to them that have obtained like precious faith with us, through the righteousness of God and our Saviour Jesus Christ" (2 Pet. i. 1). The Epistle is therefore catholic; it is addressed to all Christians, whether Jews or Gentiles.[4] And this statement corresponds with the nature of its contents. The heretics, against whom the apostle warns his readers, were those who disturbed the peace of the Christian Church; and the exhortations it con-

---

[1] See a learned article on the canonicity of Second Peter by Professor Warfield in the American *Southern Presbyterian Review*, January 1882.

[2] Weiss observes: "The question of the genuineness of 2 Peter is not to be regarded as yet settled;" see also his *Einleitung*, p. 451.

[3] "I believe," observes Farrar, "that we have not here the words and style of the great apostle, but that he lent to this Epistle the sanction of his name and the assistance of his advice." *Early Days of Christianity*, vol. i. p. 207.

[4] So De Wette, Mayerhoff, Bleek.

tains are on the whole without any special application. Still it appears to be addressed to those to whom the First Epistle was written; namely, to "the strangers scattered throughout Pontus, Galatia, Cappadocia, Asia, and Bithynia" (1 Pet. i. 1). It professes to be a second Epistle to the same class of readers: "This second Epistle, beloved, I now write unto you" (2 Pet. iii. 1). So that, although catholic in inscription and tone, it was primarily addressed to the Churches in certain countries in Asia. Alford and others have observed that "we can discover traces in this Epistle of the same characteristics as those which marked the readers of the former one, or of others which would be probably subsequent to them."[1] The warnings addressed in the First Epistle were against the same vices which had sprung up among those addressed in the Second Epistle. There had been a development of the evils against which Peter cautioned his readers; but the germs of the sins condemned in the Second Epistle were in the Churches addressed in the First. And thus, "from the circumstances of the readers which respectively underlie the one and the other Epistle, this (Epistle) may well have been a sequel to, and consequent on, the former."[2]

Against this identification of the readers of the two Epistles several objections have been adduced. 1. It is objected that the salutation contained in the Second Epistle is universal, not restricted, as in the First Epistle, to certain Asiatic Churches. "The First Epistle," observes Bleek, "is addressed not to Christians at large, but to the Churches in the provinces of Asia Minor; while the Second is written to Christians in general of like precious faith with the writer, and there is no sign that it was to be sent only to those Churches of Asia Minor for whom First Peter was intended. Peter could not have expressed himself in this general way about his readers, had he simply meant those of the districts to which his First Epistle was sent, and had he their wants only in his mind."[3] But the force of this objection is not obvious. The circle of readers was wide, and Peter in

---

[1] Alford's *Greek Testament*, vol. iv., Prolegomena, p. 144.   [2] *Ibid.*
[3] Bleek's *Introduction to the N. T.*, vol. ii. p. 181. See also Davidson's

addressing them might well employ the general terms contained in the inscription; there is no contradiction here to the limitation afterwards stated in the Epistle (2 Pet. iii. 1). 2. It is objected that the circumstances of the readers of the two Epistles are entirely different. The readers of the First Epistle were exposed to persecution, and there is no mention in it of heretical tendencies; whereas the readers of the Second Epistle were exposed to the errors of false teachers, whilst there is no mention of sufferings for the sake of Christ.[1] But if we assume the lapse of a few years between the composition of these two Epistles, heretical tendencies might easily have sprung up in the interval; and we know, as a matter of fact, that heresies did in the later days of the apostolic era greatly disturb the Christian Church.[2] And although we cannot think that the persecutions of the Christians had ceased, yet the apostle had already written an Epistle to support and comfort his readers under persecution to which he refers them, and now in this Epistle he directs their attention to a new and more pressing evil—the errors of heretical teachers. The difference arose from the occasions of the Epistles; the design of the one being to comfort Christians under their sufferings, and the design of the other being to exhort them to contend for the faith. 3. It is further maintained that, according to the Second Epistle, the author had preached the gospel to those to whom he wrote, whereas there is no mention of this in the First Epistle. Thus in the Second Epistle he writes: "We have not followed cunningly devised fables, when we made known unto you the power and coming of our Lord Jesus Christ" (2 Pet. i. 16). "The author," observes Neander, "assumes that he is writing to the same Churches as those to whom the First Epistle of Peter is addressed, yet what he says of his relation to his readers is at variance with that assumption, for

Introduction to the Study of the N. T., vol. ii. p. 491, 1st edition; vol. ii. p. 458, 2nd edition.

[1] Brückner's *Katholische Briefe*, p. 122. Huther, *Die Briefe des Petrus*, p. 328 [E. Tr. p. 276].

[2] Hence the allusions to heretical teachers, chiefly of a Gnostic character, in Paul's later Epistles,—the Epistles to the Ephesians and Colossians, and the two Epistles to Timothy,—and particularly in the First Epistle of John.

according to the Second Epistle they must have been persons who had been personally instructed by the Apostle Peter, and with whom he stood in a close personal connection; yet this was a relation in which the Churches to whom the First Epistle was addressed could not stand."[1] But, in answer to this objection, it is to be observed, on the one hand, that the words on which it is founded may not refer to the apostle's having preached the gospel to his readers, but to what he had made known to them concerning the coming of the Lord in his First Epistle; and, on the other hand, there is nothing in the First Epistle which would forbid the idea that Peter had previously visited the Churches to which he wrote; but, on the contrary, as we have seen, there are statements which presuppose such a visit. The very fact that Peter addresses these Churches seems to presuppose some special tie between him and them.

III. THE DESIGN AND CONTENTS OF THE EPISTLE.

The author states that his intention in writing was to remind his readers of what had been foretold by the prophets and apostles, that there would arise among them heretical teachers who would seek to pervert their minds from the faith (2 Pet. iii. 1–3). But especially is the object of the Epistle stated in the two last verses: "Ye, therefore, beloved, seeing ye know these things before, beware lest ye also, being led away by the error of the wicked, fall from your own stedfastness; but grow in grace and in the knowledge of our Lord and Saviour Jesus Christ" (2 Pet. iii. 17, 18). The design, then, of this Epistle was twofold. First, the apostle wished to warn his readers against the errors of false or heretical teachers. He tells them that their coming had been foretold, he describes their character, he pronounces their doom, and he warns his readers to avoid them. Secondly, the apostle writes for the purpose of exhorting his readers to make progress in holiness. They are to resist those evil practices inculcated by the false teachers, they are to add to their faith all other Christian virtues, they are to confirm themselves in

[1] Neander's *Planting*, vol. i. p. 376.

the truth, making their calling and election sure; they are to keep themselves without spot and blameless until the coming of Christ, and they are to aim at growth in grace and in the knowledge of Jesus Christ.

Those who consider the Epistle as spurious have great difficulty in assigning any reason for its composition. Schwegler, who may be regarded as on this point the representative of the Tübingen school, considers that its design was conciliatory, to reconcile Pauline and Petrine Christianity. In Rome, he thinks, endeavours were made by carrying out a combined Petrinism and Paulinism to realize the idea of the catholic Church; and accordingly this Epistle was one of the class written with a view "to bring about from the standpoint of Petrinism a final and permanent peace between the opposing views of the followers of Peter and those of Paul."[1] But the only clause on which he founds this opinion is the verse wherein mention is made of Paul's Epistles (2 Pet. iii. 15).[2] There is absolutely nothing to warrant this hypothesis, no reference to the peculiar views of Paul concerning justification, and no mention of the legal ceremonies of the Jewish law.[3]

The false teachers referred to in chap. ii. ($\psi\epsilon\nu\delta o\delta\iota\delta\acute{a}\sigma\kappa a\lambda o\iota$, 2 Pet. ii. 1) are to be considered as identical with the scoffers mentioned in chap. iii. ($\dot{\epsilon}\mu\pi a\hat{\iota}\kappa\tau a\iota$, 2 Pet. iii. 3).[4] In all probability they are the same as those mentioned in the Epistle of Jude, as the terms by which they are described are similar. They were not so much outside as inside the Christian Church. They are described as having embraced pernicious errors of doctrine; they denied the Lord that bought them, probably disbelieving in His divine Sonship; they called in question the second advent of Christ; they disbelieved in a future judgment, and, probably like the

---

[1] *Nachapostolische Zeitalter*, vol. i. p. 303. Somewhat similarly Baur, Pfleiderer, and Hausrath.

[2] As Heydenreich remarks: "For this (conciliatory) purpose, the little which chap. iii. says in passing of Paul would not have sufficed; if the writer had been chiefly anxious to show such a union, he would have adapted the construction and contents of the whole Epistle to the conciliatory design."

[3] For a refutation of this view of Schwegler, see Huther's *Die Briefe des Petrus*, pp. 337, 338 [E. Tr. pp. 285, 286].

[4] Huther considers them as different.

Corinthian heretics, denied the resurrection of the dead. But these doctrinal errors were not mere speculative opinions, but led to vicious practices; the heretics were immoral in their conduct, they were the slaves of vice, they were entangled in the pollutions of the world, they were filled with self-conceit and presumption, they were irreverent in their words, speaking evil of dignities, they were full of lust and covetousness, they endeavoured to seduce others, and it would seem that many of them had apostatized from the faith (2 Pet. ii. 21, 22). In short, they appear to have been practical Antinomians who acted upon the maxim, "Let us continue in sin, that grace may abound."

When, however, we attempt the historical identification of these heretical teachers, we soon meet with difficulties. In all probability we see in their belief and conduct the germs of Gnosticism, which in the second century so greatly disturbed the peace and corrupted the purity of the Christian Church.[1] As yet the heresy had not formed itself into a system, but consisted generally in the denial of the eternal Sonship of Jesus Christ and in vicious practices, which two things are characteristic of most of the Gnostic sects. In short, it was incipient Gnosticism, the same heresy, but not in so developed a form, as that combated by John in his First Epistle. There is a resemblance also between it and the heretical views and practices referred to in the Epistle to the Colossians and in the Second Epistle to Timothy, but it is impossible to identify them, and all attempts to do so have ended in failure. Hug supposes that the heretical teachers were similar to those who infested the Colossian and Ephesian Churches: "They were," he observes, "apparently a branch of that theurgical and magical philosophy which was strikingly distinguished by its pneumatological speculations upon the angels and the spiritual state, and by the inferences which resulted from them."[2] Mayerhoff supposes that the persons censured by Paul in the two Epistles to the Thessalonians, and those Corinthians who denied the resurrection of the dead, resembled those heretics against whom Peter warns his

---

[1] Ewald's *Sieben Sendschreiben des neuen Bundes*, p. 105.
[2] Hug's *Introduction to the N. T.*, vol. ii. p. 619.

readers.¹ Oecumenius, Michaelis,² Vitringa, Burton,³ and Mansel⁴ consider that the Nicolaitanes, who are identified in the Apocalypse with the followers of Balaam (Rev. ii. 14, 15), are here meant, because Peter describes them as following the ways of Balaam (2 Pet. ii. 15). Bertholdt thinks that certain Christian Sadducees who had not relinquished their rationalistic opinions were intended.⁵ And Grotius supposes that the Carpocratians were described.⁶ All these are mere suppositions. The heresy had not yet taken definite shape or form; Gnosticism had not so fully developed itself as when John wrote his First Epistle. The impossibility of identifying the views and practices of the heretical teachers with any of the earlier Gnostic sects, with the Cerinthians, the Nicolaitanes, the Carpocratians, and the Valentinians, is a proof of the early date of the Epistle, showing that it must have been written before these sects had arisen, and consequently affords a presumption in favour of its authenticity.

Contents.—The Epistle is both admonitory and hortatory, and these two elements pervade it throughout. It may be divided into three parts, nearly corresponding with its three chapters: the first part is an exhortation to progress in the divine life (chap. i.); the second part is a warning against heretical teachers (chap. ii.); and the third part is a declaration of the destruction of the world, and an exhortation to be prepared for that great event (chap. iii.). The apostle, having saluted his readers, prays that grace and peace may abound to them through the knowledge of Christ. They must remember their high and holy calling; they had received great and precious promises; they were made partakers of the divine nature; they were delivered from the corruptions of the world. They must then make progress in the divine life; grace must be developed within them; they must add to their faith all the other virtues of the Christian character; and thus by the exercise of faith and holiness of life they were to make their calling and election sure, that so they

---

[1] Mayerhoff's *Petrinische Schriften*, pp. 156, 157.
[2] Michaelis, *Introduction to N. T.*, Marsh's edition, vol. vi. pp. 359-362.
[3] Burton's *Bampton Lectures* for 1829, pp. 152, 153.
[4] Mansel's *Gnostic Heresies*, p. 78.   [5] *Einleitung*, Theil vi. § 672 f.
[6] *Annotat. in 2 ep. Petri.*

might receive a joyful entrance into the heavenly kingdom. He was now aged, and his death revealed by his Lord was close at hand; but he was anxious before his decease earnestly to exhort them to persevere in the faith; they had not followed cunningly devised fables; he himself was present at the transfiguration, and heard the Lord Jesus proclaimed by an audible voice from heaven to be the beloved Son of God, and they had the predictions of the prophets on which to rely (chap. i.). From exhortation he turns to warning. False teachers had arisen among them who had introduced damnable heresies, denying the Lord that bought them, and bringing destruction on themselves and their followers. Their destruction was certain; the example of the fallen angels, of the world before the flood, and of Sodom and Gomorrah, were all proofs that vengeance followed on the footsteps of crime. These heretical teachers were spots and blemishes in their feasts, a disgrace to their community, the seducers of the unstable, the servants of corruption, the heirs of wrath. If his readers suffered themselves to be seduced by them; if they were entangled in their errors and overcome, they were in a far more perilous condition than those who had never heard of Christianity, and had never been rescued from the pollutions of the world (chap. ii.). These scoffers, who called in question the advent of the Lord, were not unforeseen; their coming had been foretold by the holy prophets and by the apostles of the Lord. The advent of Christ might, according to their view, appear to be delayed; but they must remember the vast difference between time in the eye of the Lord and time in the ideas of man; one day was with the Lord as a thousand years, and a thousand years as one day. The Lord was not in reality slack concerning the fulfilment of the promise of His coming. They must exercise patience and perseverance in the practice of a holy life. The day should assuredly come, when as the former world was destroyed by the waters of the deluge, so this present world and all that it contains would be destroyed by fire; but new heavens and a new earth would spring from the ashes of the old. They must prepare for this solemn day; the delay was an evidence of God's long-suffering, as Paul had written them. The apostle then concludes the Epistle with a brief summary of its object; and enjoins his hearers to avoid the errors of the wicked, and to grow in grace and in the knowledge of our Lord and Saviour Jesus Christ.

As the keynote of the First Epistle is Hope (ἐλπίς), so the keynote of this Epistle is Knowledge (γνῶσις or ἐπίγνωσις). Grace and peace are to be communicated to believers through the knowledge of God and of Jesus our Lord (i. 2); they are to add to their faith knowledge (i. 5); they are to be neither barren nor unfruitful in the knowledge of our Lord Jesus Christ (i. 8); they are to escape the pollutions of the world through the knowledge of Christ (ii. 20); and they are to grow in grace and in the knowledge of our Lord and Saviour Jesus Christ (iii. 18). And by knowledge here is not to be understood a mere theoretical knowledge of the truths of Christianity or the γνῶσις of the Gnostics; but a realization of these truths influencing the practice and leading to holiness of life. Especially did it consist in the acknowledgment of the power and coming (δύναμις καὶ παρουσία) of Christ, in feeling the power of Christ influencing their moral conduct, so that at His advent they might be found of Him in peace without spot and blameless (2 Pet. iii. 14).

The second chapter in this Epistle bears so marked a resemblance to the Epistle of Jude, that it is generally agreed that the one sacred writer must have borrowed from the other. It might be omitted without destroying the unity of the Epistle; and were it not for the unanimous authority of manuscripts and versions, it might be regarded as an interpolation.[1] This peculiarity will afterwards be discussed when we come to consider the relation between the Second Epistle of Peter and the Epistle of Jude.[2]

The disclosure concerning the destruction of the world forms another remarkable peculiarity in this Epistle. We are informed that the heavens and the earth, the present constitution of things, will be destroyed by fire. "The day of the Lord will come as a thief in the night, in which the heavens will pass away with a great noise, and the elements

---

[1] As Bertholdt has done.
[2] See *infra*, Dissertation on the Relation between Second Peter and Jude.

shall melt with fervent heat, the earth also and the works that are therein shall be burned up" (2 Pet. iii. 10). But out of the ruins of the old a new heaven and a new earth will spring into existence, wherein dwelleth righteousness (2 Pet. iii. 13). This declaration has been urged as adverse to the authenticity of the Epistle. Thus Neander observes: "What is said of the origin of the world from water and its destruction by fire does not correspond to the simplicity and practical spirit of the apostolic doctrine, but rather indicates the spirit of a later age, mingling much that was foreign with the religious interest."[1] But the statement concerning the origin of the world from water, or rather the previous aqueous condition of the world (2 Pet. iii. 5), is in entire conformity with the account given us of the creation of the world in Genesis (Gen. i. 9). The conflagration of the world is indeed a new statement or revelation, not elsewhere found in Scripture;[2] but it cannot be affirmed to be opposed to the simplicity and practical spirit of the apostolic doctrine, inasmuch as there are many equally wonderful disclosures in Scripture; and this revelation concerning the last days is especially in accordance with the characteristic teaching of Peter, who, in both his Epistles, makes disclosures concerning the unseen world; and he does so in a practical spirit, with a view to urge his readers to holiness and to preparation for these solemn events: "Seeing then that all these things shall be dissolved, what manner of persons ought ye to be in all holy conversation and godliness"[3] (2 Pet. iii. 11).

We have already referred to the style of this Epistle. The language in which it was written was undoubtedly Greek. Some, indeed, have attempted to prove that the Epistle was originally written in Aramaic, and that what we now have is a Greek translation from that language.[4] But this opinion

---

[1] Neander's *Planting*, vol. i. p. 376. So also Mayerhoff.

[2] It is interesting to notice that two modern hypotheses of the end of the world predict its destruction by fire—either through collision with a comet or by its disappearance in the sun.

[3] On the Petrine doctrine of the destruction of the world, see Weiss' *Biblical Theology of the N. T.*, vol. ii. p. 244 ff.

[4] Advocated by the Rev. E. C. King: *Did St. Peter write in Greek? Thoughts and Criticisms intended to prove the Aramaic origin of the Second Epistle of Peter.* Cambridge 1871.

has nothing to commend it. The Epistle was not written to Jewish Christians, but to Christians in general. The Greek language was diffused throughout the East, and there is no reason to suppose that Peter, or any of the Galilean apostles, was ignorant of it. For the same reason the tradition, proceeding from Jerome, that Peter dictated his Epistle in Aramaic, and that Mark or some other interpreter translated his words into Greek, is to be rejected.

IV. TIME AND PLACE OF WRITING.

Those who admit the authenticity of the Epistle all agree that it was written shortly before the death of Peter; but as they are not agreed when that event took place, they differ as to the precise year when the Epistle was written. Michaelis and Keil, supposing that Peter fell a victim in the great Neronian persecution, think that it was written A.D. 64; Schott and Weiss fix on A.D. 66; Macknight and Bishop Wordsworth on A.D. 67; Alford, Plummer, and Warfield on A.D. 68; and Koehler on A.D. 69. Those who deny the authorship of Peter differ widely in their opinions concerning the time of composition. Grotius thinks that it was written in the reign of Trajan, by Simeon, bishop of Jerusalem.[1] Bleek, on account of the comparatively late period when the Epistle was known to the Church, supposes that it was not written before the beginning of the second century, perhaps not before the middle of it.[2] Ewald thinks that it was written about A.D. 95, twenty years after the publication of the Epistle of Jude, when Jude himself had been long dead, and his Epistle was no longer much heeded, as the writer wished to revive the denunciations of Jude's Epistle against the Gnostics.[3] Mayerhoff, on account of the emphasis placed on γνῶσις, thinks that the author of the Epistle was a Jewish Christian who lived in Alexandria, and that it was composed about the middle of the second century.[4] Credner, arguing from various supposed

---

[1] *Annotat. in 2 ep. Petri.*
[2] Bleek's *Introduction to the N. T.*, vol. ii. p. 185.
[3] Ewald's *History of Israel*, vol. viii. pp. 180, 181.
[4] Mayerhoff's *Petrinische Schriften*, p. 193.

TIME AND PLACE OF WRITING.

indications of a late date, observes that the composition of this Epistle is to be placed at the very earliest in the beginning of the second century.[1] Hilgenfeld, Hausrath, Mangold, and Holtzmann, supposing that the Carpocratians are here referred to, place it in the middle of the second century. In Huther's opinion, it would be more appropriate to look upon the Epistle as a production of the first century, inasmuch as the description of the heretics contains no reference to the Gnostics properly so called.[2] Davidson places the date of the Epistle about A.D. 170.[3] And Schwegler, in conformity with the *à priori* scheme of his school, considers that it was written from Rome toward the close of the second century.[4]

In the Epistle itself, there are few indications of time by which its date might be determined. It was written before the destruction of Jerusalem (A.D. 70), as there is not the slightest reference to that great catastrophe which befell the Jewish nation, and which must have deeply impressed every Jew. It was written shortly before the death of Peter; as he refers to the approach of his death, and assigns this as one reason for writing (2 Pet. i. 14, 15). If the tradition of the Church is correct, that Peter perished in the Neronian persecution, which perhaps the balance of probabilities favours, then the Epistle must have been written in the year A.D. 64. But if the tradition is untrustworthy, and Peter's last days are unknown, nothing certain as to its date from this declaration can be determined. Further, we must allow a certain interval of time to have elapsed between the writing of the two Epistles, in order to permit of the growth of heretical tendencies, and the development of evil which the Second Epistle presupposes. If we consider that the First Epistle was written A.D. 59 or A.D. 60, an interval of four years is sufficient for these purposes. We have therefore no difficulty in agreeing with those who assign the date of the Epistle to A.D. 64, the period of the persecution under Nero.

The place of composition is also a matter of dispute.

---

[1] Credner's *Einleitung in N. T.*, p. 659.
[2] Huther's *Der zweite Brief des Petrus*, p. 339 [E. Tr. p. 284].
[3] Davidson's *New Introduction*, vol. ii. p. 502, 1st ed.; vol. ii. p. 408, 2nd ed.
[4] Schwegler's *Nachapostolische Zeitalter*, vol. i. p. 496 ff.

Mayerhoff, supposing that the Epistle was written by an Alexandrian Jew, fixes on Alexandria; an opinion for which there is not the slightest foundation. Others think that it was Babylon on the Euphrates, because the First Epistle was written from that city (1 Pet. v. 13), and because it is very improbable that Peter would travel from Babylon to Rome. But if we are to assume that Peter perished in the Neronian persecution, then we must assign Rome as the place of composition; an opinion which is accepted by most commentators.

The most important modern commentaries on this Epistle are those of Pott (Göttingen 1810), Dietlein (Berlin 1851), Lillie (New York 1854), Wiesinger (Königsberg 1862, translated, New York), Fronmüller (Lange's *Bibelwerk*, 1862, translated by Mombert, New York 1869), Theodor Schott (Erlangen 1863), Brückner (dritte Auflage, Leipsic 1865), Ewald (*Sieben Sendschreiben des neuen Bundes*, Göttingen 1870), Huther (vierte Auflage, Göttingen 1877, translated, Edinburgh 1881), Plummer (in the *New Testament Commentary*, edited by Bishop Ellicott), Plumptre (in the Cambridge Series: Cambridge 1880), Lumby (in the *Speaker's Commentary*, 1881), Keil (Leipsic 1883), Spitta (Halle 1885).

DISSERTATION.

RELATION BETWEEN SECOND PETER AND JUDE.

The second chapter of the Second Epistle of Peter is a section of peculiar difficulty. As has already been remarked, were it not for the indisputable evidence in favour of the integrity of the Epistle, we might regard it as a later interpolation, as it could be omitted without interfering with the train of thought. It has also been affirmed that it differs in style and diction from the other two chapters of the Epistle, and that it is here that the linguistic differences occur which chiefly distinguish the Second Epistle of Peter from the First.[1] But especially is the resemblance between this chapter and

[1] So Weiss, Huther, etc.; on the other hand, Spitta; see *infra*.

the Epistle of Jude remarkable; a resemblance so close that it is now almost universally conceded that there must be an intimate connection between these writings, pointing either to a common source or to a dependence of the one upon the other. And yet this dependence is by no means slavish; the one condenses or expands the ideas of the other, and both are marked by freshness of expression and vigour of thought. If the one sacred writer borrowed from the other, it has not been done mechanically; the thoughts of the one are so assimilated by the other as to appear quite natural and appropriate. As Weiss remarks: "In neither have we a slavish dependence or a mere copy, but the correspondence of the one with the other is carried out with literary freedom and licence."[1] The consequence of this is that very different opinions have been formed as to which of them is the original; and for this reason it has been by some considered that the resemblance may be best accounted for by regarding both as paraphrases or imitations of the same document.[2]

The passages in these Epistles related to each other are 2 Pet. ii. 1–iii. 3 and Jude 4–18. The subject treated of in these passages is the same, namely, the character of the false teachers, of an antinomian type, who at that period infested the Christian Church. Although there is some difference here, as Peter alludes to the heretical teachers themselves (2 Pet. ii. 1), and Jude describes the licentiousness of their followers (Jude 4), yet it is generally agreed that the same class of men is referred to. Their character, their maxims, and their vices are the same; they deny the Lord Jesus; they speak evil of dignities; they are given to covetousness, impurity, and pride; they are vain and impious mockers. Their destiny is the same; they are doomed to sudden judgment; they shall utterly perish in their own corruption. The references to punishment, mentioned in the

---

[1] Quoted by Huther in his *Die Briefe des Petrus*, p. 308 [E. Tr. p. 256].

[2] "One thing," observes Dr. Plummer, "is certain, that whichever author has borrowed, he is no ordinary borrower. He knows how to assimilate foreign material so as to make it thoroughly his own. He remains original even while he appropriates the words and thoughts of another. He controls them, not they him." *N. T. Commentary* (edited by Bishop Ellicott) *on Jude*, p. 266. Similarly Wiesinger, *Der zweite Brief des Petrus*, p. 24.

Old Testament as descriptive of their doom, are the same; the fall of the angels, the destruction of Sodom and Gomorrah, and the sin and fate of Balaam. And the illustrations employed to describe their character and destiny are the same; they are clouds or wells without water, spots or hidden rocks[1] in their feasts of charity, and for them the blackness of darkness is reserved for ever.

From the following list in parallel columns of the resemblances between these two writings, using the Revised Version as more strictly literal, and affording a truer text, it will be seen that the resemblance extends not merely to ideas, illustrations, and metaphors, but to words and expressions:[2]—

But there arose false prophets also among the people, as among you also there shall be false teachers, who shall privily bring in (παρεισάξουσιν) destructive heresies, denying even the Master that bought them (τὸν ἀγοράσαντα αὐτοὺς δισπότην ἀρνούμενοι).—2 Pet. ii. 1.	For there are certain men crept in privily (παρεισέδυσαν), even they who were of old set forth unto this condemnation, ungodly men ... denying our only Master and Lord, Jesus Christ (τὸν μόνον δεσπότην καὶ κύριον ἡμῶν Ἰησοῦν Χριστὸν ἀρνούμενοι).—Jude 4.
For if God spared not angels when they sinned, but cast them down to hell,[3] and committed them to pits of darkness (σειραῖς ζόφου[4]) to be reserved unto judgment (εἰς κρίσιν τηρουμένους).—2 Pet. ii. 4.	And angels which kept not their own principality, but left their proper habitation, he hath kept in everlasting bonds under darkness (δεσμοῖς ἀϊδίοις ὑπὸ ζόφον) unto the judgment (εἰς κρίσιν ... τετήρηκεν) of the great day.—Jude 6.
And, turning the cities of Sodom and Gomorrah (πόλεις Σοδόμων καὶ Γομόρρας) into ashes, condemned them with an overthrow, having made them an example (ὑπόδειγμα) unto those that should live ungodly.—2 Pet. ii. 6.	Even as Sodom and Gomorrah (Σόδομα καὶ Γόμορρα), and the cities about them ... are set forth as an example (δεῖγμα), suffering the punishment of eternal fire.[5]—Jude 7.
But chiefly them that walk after the flesh in the lust of defilement (ὀπίσω σαρκὸς ἐν ἐπιθυμίᾳ μιασμοῦ), and despise dominion (κυριότητος καταφρονοῦντας). Daring, self-willed, they tremble not to rail at dignities (δόξας ... βλασφημοῦντες).—2 Pet. ii. 10.	Yet in like manner these also in their dreamings defile the flesh (σάρκα μιαίνουσι), and set at nought dominion (κυριότητα ἀθετοῦσι), and rail at dignities (δόξας βλασφημοῦσιν).—Jude 8.

---

[1] See *infra*.

[2] Lists of parallel passages are given in Credner's *Einleitung*, pp. 662-664. Davidson's *Introduction to the Study of the N. T.*, vol. ii. pp. 438-440, 2nd edition. De Wette's *Einleitung*, pp. 388-390. Mayerhoff's *Einleitung in die petrinischen Schriften*, pp. 171-174.

[3] Marginal and more correct reading: "cast them down to Tartarus."

[4] Other MSS. read σειραῖς ζόφου: chains of darkness.

[5] Marginal reading: "As an example of eternal fire, suffering punishment."

Whereas angels, though greater in might and power, bring not a railing judgment (βλάσφημον κρίσιν) against them before the Lord.—2 Pet. ii. 11.	Yet Michael the archangel, when, contending with the devil, he disputed about the body of Moses, durst not bring against him a railing judgment (κρίσιν βλασφημίας).—Jude 9.
But these, as creatures without reason (ὡς ἄλογα ζῶα), born mere animals (φυσικά) ... railing in matters whereof they are ignorant (ἐν οἷς ἀγνοοῦσι βλασφημοῦντες), shall in their destroying surely be destroyed (καταφθαρήσονται).—2 Pet. ii. 12.	But these rail at whatsoever things they know not (ὅσα οὐκ οἴδασι βλασφημοῦσιν): and what they understand naturally (φυσικῶς), like the creatures without reason (ὡς τὰ ἄλογα ζῶα), in these things are they destroyed (φθείρονται).—Jude 10.
Spots and blemishes (σπίλοι καὶ μῶμοι), revelling in their love-feasts (ἐν ταῖς ἀγάπαις ² αὐτῶν), while they feast with you (συνευωχούμενοι). — 2 Pet. ii. 13.	These are they who are hidden rocks (σπιλάδες¹) in your love-feasts (ἐν ταῖς ἀγάπαις ὑμῶν) when they feast with you (συνευωχούμενοι).—Jude 12.
Forsaking the right way, they went astray, having followed the way (τῇ ὁδῷ) of Balaam (τοῦ Βαλαάμ), the son of Beor, who loved the hire (μισθόν) of wrong-doing.—2 Pet. ii. 15.	They went in the way (τῇ ὁδῷ) of Cain, and ran riotously in the error of Balaam (τοῦ Βαλαάμ) for hire (μισθοῦ), and perished in the gainsaying of Korah.—Jude 11.
These are springs without water (πηγαὶ ἄνυδροι), and mists driven by a storm; for whom the blackness of darkness hath been reserved (οἷς ὁ ζόφος τοῦ σκότους³ τετήρηται).—2 Pet. ii. 17.	Clouds without water (νεφέλαι ἄνυδροι), carried about by winds ... wandering stars, for whom the blackness of darkness hath been reserved for ever (οἷς ὁ ζόφος τοῦ σκότους εἰς αἰῶνα τετήρηται).—Jude 12, 13.
Uttering great swelling words (ὑπέρογκα) of vanity.—2 Pet. ii. 18.	Their mouth speaketh great swelling words (ὑπέρογκα).—Jude 16.
That ye should remember the words which were spoken before (μνησθῆναι τῶν προειρημένων ῥημάτων) by the holy prophets, and the commandment of the Lord and Saviour through your apostles (τῶν ἀποστόλων ὑμῶν⁴).—2 Pet. iii. 2.	But ye, beloved, remember the words which have been spoken before (μνήσθητε τῶν ῥημάτων τῶν προειρημένων) by the apostles of our Lord Jesus Christ (ὑπὸ τῶν ἀποστόλων τοῦ κυρίου ἡμῶν Ἰησοῦ Χριστοῦ).—Jude 17.
Knowing this first, that in the last days (ἐπ' ἐσχάτων τῶν ἡμερῶν) mockers (ἐμπαῖκται) shall come with mockery, walking after their own lusts (κατὰ τὰς ἰδίας ἐπιθυμίας αὐτῶν πορευόμενοι).—2 Pet. iii. 3.	How that they said unto you, In the last time (ἐν ἐσχάτῳ χρόνῳ) there shall be mockers (ἐμπαῖκται), walking after their own ungodly lusts (κατὰ τὰς ἑαυτῶν ἐπιθυμίας πορευόμενοι τῶν ἀσεβειῶν). Jude 18.

---

¹ Marginal reading: "spots." On the meaning of σπιλάδες, see *infra*.

² Note on margin: "Many ancient authorities read ἀπάταις, 'deceivings.'" See *infra*.

³ Many manuscripts insert εἰς αἰῶνα as in Jude 13.

⁴ The *textus receptus* reads ἡμῶν, "of us the apostles of the Lord and the Saviour;" but the reading ὑμῶν is attested by preponderating authority.

But with these points of resemblance there are also several remarkable points of difference. Peter mentions the false teachers among them (2 Pet. ii. 1); whilst Jude describes the general licentiousness that prevailed without any direct reference to heretical teachers (Jude 4). Peter states the artifices and proselytizing spirit of these false teachers, and their success in gaining followers (2 Pet. ii. 2, 3); points not referred to by Jude. Jude mentions the cause of the fall of the angels (Jude 6, 7); Peter states simply the fact that they sinned (2 Pet. ii. 4). Peter omits the destruction of the Israelites in the wilderness, to which Jude refers (Jude 5), and substitutes for it the destruction of the world by the flood (2 Pet. ii. 5). Both mention the overthrow of Sodom and Gomorrah (2 Pet. ii. 6); but Jude describes the sin of the inhabitants which caused that overthrow (Jude 7). Whilst Peter mentions the ruin of these cities, he dwells on the deliverance of Lot (2 Pet. ii. 7–9), a circumstance not alluded to by Jude. Peter speaks of these heretical teachers as not afraid to speak evil of dignities, and in this respect not imitating the example of angels, who did not bring railing accusations against them before the Lord (2 Pet. ii. 10, 11); whilst Jude specifies the forbearance of Michael the archangel in his contest with the devil concerning the body of Moses (Jude 9). Jude mentions three instances of Old Testament transgressors, Cain, Balaam, and Korah (Jude 11); Peter restricts himself to the example of Balaam (2 Pet. ii. 15, 16). Jude cites at length the prophecy of Enoch, probably an extract from the apocryphal book of Enoch (Jude 14, 15), which quotation is omitted by Peter. Peter cautions his readers against being led astray by the example of these false teachers to follow their pernicious ways (2 Pet. ii. 20–22); a caution which is not contained in Jude. Peter appears to include himself among the apostles of the Lord Jesus Christ[1] who had foretold the advent of these scoffers of the last days (2 Pet. iii. 2, 3); whilst Jude refers to the apostles in general terms (Jude 17). Both describe these scoffers as walking after their ungodly lusts (Jude 18);

---

[1] This is evident if the reading ἡμῶν be adopted, but not if ὑμῶν be the correct reading.

but Peter specifies the nature of their heresy, calling them deniers of the second advent (2 Pet. iii. 3, 4). According to some, these points of difference furnish arguments in favour of the priority of Peter; according to others, in favour of the priority of Jude; and according to others, in favour of some common source.

In explanation of this relation of Second Peter to Jude four theories have been advanced. 1. That Peter and Jude wrote independently, both being guided in their thoughts and expressions by the Holy Spirit. 2. That both writers paraphrased the same document, written in some other language than the Greek. 3. That Jude made use of the Epistle of Peter. 4. That Peter made use of the Epistle of Jude.

I. Some suppose that Peter and Jude wrote independently. This is the opinion adopted by those who have embraced a mechanical view of inspiration. Both, it is asserted, wrote under the inspiration of the Holy Ghost, and were guided by Him in their words as well as in their thoughts, and thus being directed by the same Spirit, they evinced a remarkable resemblance in their writings. Even Dr. Lardner, although no believer in the mechanical view of inspiration, appears to have adopted this supposition as the true solution of the problem. "Peter and Jude," he observes, "and all the Christians in general of their time, had before them the Scriptures of the Old Testament. Many of the cases referred to by these apostles are evidently found there, such as Cain, Korah, Balaam, the people of Sodom. Nor does the resemblance of style in Peter and Jude afford a conclusive argument that both borrowed from some one Jewish author. The similitude of the subject might produce a resemblance of style. The design of Peter and Jude was to condemn some loose and erroneous Christians, and to caution others against them. When speaking of the same sort of persons, their style and figures of speech would bear a great agreement. And certainly I think that the apostles needed not any other assistance in confuting and exposing corrupt Christians than their own inspiration, and an acquaintance with the ancient Scriptures of the Jewish Church."[1]

[1] Lardner's *Works*, vol. iii. pp. 445, 446, quarto edition.

Such a hypothesis is extremely unsatisfactory. The sacred Scriptures, though inspired, were yet written by men, each writer using his own style and diction; and these human elements are to be judged by the ordinary rules of criticism. The words and phrases in 2 Pet. ii. and Jude are so similar that it must follow that the one borrowed from the other, or that both made use of a common document. To admit the hypothesis that this resemblance arose from the direct inspiration of the Holy Spirit, without the intervention of human means, would be to place the Scriptures outside the sphere of criticism, and to render all attempts at their explanation useless and visionary. It pleased God to rest the facts of Christianity on human testimony, and to communicate the doctrines of Christianity by the instrumentality of human writing.[1]

II. A much more plausible supposition is that both Peter and Jude made use of the same document; that both made adaptations of some Aramaic writing.

This supposition was first propounded by Bishop Sherlock, and was stated by him with singular ingenuity.[2] "There is no necessity," he observes, "to suppose that Jude transcribed Peter's Epistle; it is much more probable, that both he and Peter wrote from the common plan communicated to the churches, and drew the description of the false teachers from the same apocryphal book." The fact that the writings are both translations from or paraphrases of the same document, he thinks, sufficiently accounts both for the points of resemblance and for the points of difference. "If we compare the different manners of expressing the same thing in the two Epistles, we shall hardly imagine that Peter and Jude had the same language before them to transcribe; it is much more probable that they both translated from some old Hebrew (Aramaic) book, which will account for the difference of

---

[1] "We have nothing to do here," observes Dean Alford, "with those who would maintain that each of these passages was a special revelation, wholly independent of the other. To our mind, once admit any such hypothesis, and you destroy Christianity." *How to Study the N. T.*, "The Epistles," p. 225. This is too strongly stated; for although the theory of mechanical inspiration is fatal to biblical criticism, yet it cannot be said to destroy Christianity.

[2] Sherlock's *Discourses*, vol. iv. p. 129 ff.: dissertation, "The Authority of the Second Epistle of Peter."

language between them, and the great agreement in their images and ideas." And again he observes: "If we suppose this copy (from which both took) to have been in the Jewish (Aramaic) language, and that each writer translated for himself, this will answer the whole appearance, and account as well for their difference as for their agreement." He supposes this original document to have been some ancient Aramaic writing, in which the prophecies of Enoch and Noah relating to the flood were recorded, as an explanation of the references to Noah by Peter and to Enoch by Jude. Still, however, the bishop feels that this hypothesis is insufficient to account for all points of similarity, as, for example, the prediction of these mockers by the apostles, and the Christian notions peculiar to the times of the gospel, and therefore he feels constrained to supplement it by a further supposition, that Jude had, along with this Aramaic book, the Second Epistle of Peter: "I see no inconvenience in supposing that Jude had as well the Epistle of Peter as the old Jewish book, which contained the description of the ancient false prophets, and the prophecy of Enoch concerning them, before him at the same time." A somewhat similar hypothesis was adopted by Lumby in his articles on the Second Epistle of Peter in the *Expositor*. He observes that he deems it "most probable that Jude and Peter drew the examples which they have given for illustration from some common Aramaic original."[1] So also Herder supposes that Jude, residing in Persia, drew from a Persian source, and that the author of Second Peter followed him; Hasse referred both to a Chaldeo-Persian original; and Kaiser agrees with Sherlock, that both translated a lost Aramaic document into Greek.[2]

Such a supposition does to a certain extent account for the resemblances and differences in the writings of Peter and Jude; it also accounts for the asserted difference in style between the second chapter and other portions of Peter's Second Epistle, and obviates to a certain extent the objection

[1] *Expositor*, vol. iv. 461, first series, December 1876. Lumby, in his commentary on the Second Epistle of Peter, in the *Speaker's Commentary* in 1881, appears to have departed from this hypothesis, for in that commentary he advocates the priority of Second Peter.

[2] See Mayerhoff's *Petrinische Schriften*, p. 178. Davidson's *Introduction to the N. T.*, vol. iii. p. 403.

drawn from the difference of style between Peter's First and Second Epistles. But, on the other hand, it appears derogatory to the sacred writers, and contrary to any idea of inspiration, to suppose that both should translate or copy from a writing which must be considered apocryphal, and improbable that both should fix on the same document. If a common document be supposed, that document must be the apocryphal Book of Enoch, as it is from it, as we shall afterwards see, that Jude apparently quotes.¹ But this book does not contain nearly all the passages commented on in the Epistles of Peter and Jude, but only references to the fall of the angels and to the destruction of the world by the flood. Nor can this view, as Bishop Sherlock admits, explain the Christian references and the exhortation to remember the sayings of the apostles of our Lord. The hypothesis is ingenious, but is now universally rejected as an unsatisfactory solution of the problem. "This notion," observes Eichhorn, "can never go beyond a bare supposition, as such a document is nowhere to be found, by comparing which with the passages common to both writings, the supposition could be rendered probable." ²

Instead of a common written document, Olshausen has substituted epistolary correspondence between these two writers. He imagines that Peter and Jude carried on a correspondence concerning the heretical tendencies and corrupt practices of the age. Jude communicated to Peter, in an epistle full of vigour and energy, the prevalence of vice and licentiousness in the Christian Church, in those countries with which he was acquainted. And Peter, tracing that vice and licentiousness to the doctrines of the heretical teachers prevalent in the Churches of Asia, to which his Epistles were directed, incorporated the description given by Jude in an Epistle written expressly to warn his readers against the errors and corrupt practices of those false teachers.³ Such a solution is extremely arbitrary, and is founded on a transfer of modern customs to a primitive age.⁴

---

¹ Sherlock wrote before the discovery of the Book of Enoch.
² *Einleitung in das N. T.*, vol. iii. p. 645.
³ So also Augusti accounts for the resemblance.
⁴ Olshausen's *Opuscula theologica*, pp. 62, 63.

III. A third supposition is that Jude made use of the Epistle of Peter. This was formerly the most generally approved hypothesis, and is still maintained by a few eminent recent critics. It is adopted by the following distinguished theologians: Oecumenius, Luther,[1] Michaelis, Pott, Bengel, Storr, Schülze, Th. Schott, Stier, Heydenreich, Hengstenberg, Dietlein, Thiersch, Döllinger, Hofmann, Luthardt, Fronmüller, and Spitta;[2] and among English divines by Horne, Wordsworth, Mansel, Plummer, and Lumby.

The following are the reasons assigned for the priority of the Second Epistle of Peter:—

1. In the Epistle of Peter the false teachers and scoffers are the subjects of prediction; they had not as yet arisen in the Church; whereas in the Epistle of Jude they had already appeared; what was future when Peter wrote, was present when Jude wrote.[3] Thus Peter writes in the future tense: "There were false prophets also among the people, even as there shall be ($\xi\sigma o\nu\tau\alpha\iota$) false teachers among you, who privily shall bring in ($\pi\alpha\rho\epsilon\iota\sigma\acute{a}\xi o\nu\sigma\iota\nu$) damnable heresies. And many shall follow their pernicious ways; by reason of whom the way of truth shall be evil spoken of. And through covetousness shall they with feigned words make merchandise of you" ($\dot{\epsilon}\mu\pi o\rho\epsilon\acute{v}\sigma o\nu\tau\alpha\iota$) (2 Pet. ii. 1–3). And again: "Knowing this first, that there shall come ($\dot{\epsilon}\lambda\epsilon\acute{v}\sigma o\nu\tau\alpha\iota$) in the last days scoffers, walking after their own lusts" (2 Pet. iii. 3). Whereas Jude writes in the present tense: "For there are certain men crept in unawares ($\pi\alpha\rho\epsilon\iota\sigma\acute{\epsilon}\delta\nu\sigma\alpha\nu$), who were before of old ordained to this condemnation" (Jude 4). To this it has been replied by Bleek and Davidson, that in Peter's Epistle the future and the present are mixed together; at one time the false teachers are referred to as future, but at another

[1] "No one," says Luther, "can deny that the Epistle of Jude is an abridgment or copy of the Second Epistle of Peter; the words of these Epistles are almost the same." *Works*, vol. xiv. p. 150.

[2] After this dissertation was written, the recent work of Spitta, entitled *Der zweite Brief des Petrus und der Brief des Judas*, Halle 1885, came under my notice. Reference will be made to it in the notes. It is an exhaustive work of great learning; no less than ninety pages are devoted to the question of the relation of these two Epistles.

[3] So Hengstenberg, Fronmüller, Keil, Lumby, Plummer, Wordsworth, Spitta.

time they are described as corrupting the Church and already working mischief (2 Pet. ii. 10 ff.).[1] But such a mode of description, transferring the future into the present, is in accordance with prophetic language; the pernicious influences of the false teachers are prophetically described as if they were already in operation.[2]

2. There is in the Epistle of Jude a direct reference to the prediction in the Second Epistle of Peter concerning the coming of the scoffers: "Beloved, remember ye the words which were spoken before of the apostles of our Lord Jesus Christ, how they told you that there should be mockers in the last time, who should walk after their own ungodly lusts" (ὅτι ἔλεγον ὑμῖν ὅτι ἐν ἐσχάτῳ χρόνῳ ἔσονται ἐμπαῖκται κατὰ τὰς ἑαυτῶν ἐπιθυμίας πορευόμενοι τῶν ἀσεβειῶν, Jude 17, 18). This prediction is found most fully and most plainly in the Second Epistle of Peter. Paul indeed frequently foretold that in the last days perilous times would come, that many should depart from the faith, that the man of sin would be revealed, and that even among the presbyters of the Church false teachers would arise seeking to draw away disciples after them. But words, closely approximating to those employed by Jude, are found in Peter's Epistle: "Knowing this first, that there shall come in the last days scoffers, walking after own lusts" (ὅτι ἐλεύσονται ἐπ' ἐσχάτου τῶν ἡμερῶν ἐμπαῖκται κατὰ τὰς ἰδίας αὐτῶν ἐπιθυμίας πορευόμενοι, 2 Pet. iii. 3). It is no answer to this to say that the reference of Jude is not to the writings, but to the oral teaching of the apostles, for the similarity of the words in these two Epistles is opposed to this solution; especially as it is to be observed that the word for mockers (ἐμπαῖκται) is found nowhere else in the New Testament. It would almost seem that the words of Jude are a quotation from the Second Epistle of Peter.[3]

---

[1] Bleek's *Introduction to the N. T.*, vol. ii. p. 175. Davidson's *Introduction to the Study of the N. T.*, vol. ii. p. 472, 1st ed.

[2] On the other hand, Wiesinger remarks that the opponents combated are described as actually present, the very words which they utter are stated, and not only were the first germs of corruption present, but this corruption was already in an advanced state. *Der zweite Brief des Petrus*, pp. 22-24.

[3] This argument is strongly insisted on by Spitta. He endeavours to show that there are several direct references in Jude to 2 Peter: as Jude 4 comp. with

3. In Jude's Epistle moral corruption appears to be in a more advanced stage. The errors and vices of false teachers, as stated by Peter, are more strongly marked, and are painted in darker colours by Jude: that which blossomed, when Peter wrote his Epistle, has borne fruit when Jude wrote. Jude is far more vehement in his expressions and denunciations than Peter; if Jude wrote first, Peter has toned down and moderated his expressions. Others adduce this consideration as a proof of the priority of Jude's Epistle; that the description of the evil-doers is there much more distinct and definite than in Peter's Epistle; but it seems rather to favour the priority of Peter's Epistle, as portraying an advance in iniquity.

4. Another argument, adduced by Lumby,[1] is that Jude has in many instances expanded the expressions of Peter, added to them, and adapted them to his purpose in writing. Certainly such instances of expansion do occur; but little can be made of this argument, as it is more than counterbalanced by more numerous instances of expansion in the Epistle of Peter.

It is supposed by those who assume the priority of Peter's Epistle, that Jude, about to write an Epistle concerning the common salvation, was diverted from his purpose by seeing the extreme wickedness which was corrupting the Christian Church; and therefore he felt that it was needful for him to write at once, and to exhort Christians earnestly to contend for the faith once delivered unto the saints (Jude 3). And finding a remarkable resemblance between the licentiousness of wicked Christians and the prediction of the scoffers who were to rise in the Christian Church, given in the Epistle of Peter, he felt that he could best accomplish his design by borrowing from that Epistle, and freely using the sentiments it contained.

There are several objections to this hypothesis; of these three deserve consideration. 1. It is maintained that it is

---

2 Pet. ii. 3; Jude 5 describing the familiarity of his readers with the characteristics of libertinism; and especially Jude 17, 18, comp. with 2 Pet. iii. 3. *Supra*, pp. 383-389.

[1] *Speaker's Commentary*, vol. iv. p. 232.

very improbable that Jude should only incorporate a portion of Peter's Epistle. "It was more likely," observes Dean Plumptre, "that Peter should incorporate the contents of a short Epistle like that of Jude in the longer one which he was writing, than that Jude, with the whole of Peter's Second Epistle before him, should have confined himself to one section of it only."[1] To this it has been answered, that the section to which Jude confined himself was the one appropriate to his purpose.[2] But this answer hardly suffices, as the reference to the deniers of the second advent (2 Pet. iii. 3 ff.) was appropriate to Jude's purpose in describing those wicked men who sought to corrupt the Church, and yet there is no mention of them in his Epistle. And it must also be admitted that the comparative brevity of Jude's Epistle, the unity of its conception, and the terse and sententious expression of its thoughts, are in favour of its originality. 2. It is asserted that some portions of the Epistle of Peter can only be understood by a reference to the Epistle of Jude. Thus the language of Peter concerning the forbearance of the angels, taken by itself, is unintelligible: "They are not afraid to speak evil of dignities; whereas angels, which are greater in power and might, bring not railing accusation against them before the Lord"[3] (2 Pet. ii. 10, 11). Who are the dignities of whom these wicked men are not afraid to speak evil, and against whom the angels do not bring a railing accusation? The readers of Peter's Epistle, it is asserted, could only understand this reference on the supposition that they were acquainted with Jude's Epistle, wherein they are informed that Michael the archangel did not bring a railing accusation against the devil (Jude 9). In Jude's Epistle, the phrase "to speak evil of dignities" is plain, whereas in Peter's Epistle it

---

[1] Plumptre on *The Epistles of Peter and Jude*, p. 88: Cambridge Series. The same objection is dwelt upon in Mayerhoff's *Petrinische Schriften*, p. 179 ff. Credner's *Einleitung*, pp. 664, 665.

[2] Thus Spitta replies that the object of Jude in reproducing that special section of 2 Peter was to impress upon his readers the fact that the apostles had predicted and warned them against the rise of the libertines. *Supra*, p. 468.

[3] "This (passage)," observes Dean Alford, "standing as it does thus by itself, would constitute, were it not for the original in Jude being extant, the most enigmatical sentence in the N.T." *Greek Testament*, vol. iv., Prolegomena, p. 147.

is obscure. As Hug puts it: "With Jude this is the case; he states the matter distinctly, and expressly names the dispute of Michael with the devil respecting the body of Moses. But Peter rests so much in generals, and explains himself respecting it so indefinitely, that we could not at all have guessed what he had in view in this passage if we were not in possession of Jude. The mode of treatment adopted by Peter shows that he imagined Jude to have been already in the hands of his readers; and that he thought that he could take it for granted, that they understood what he alluded to without the necessity of a greater circumstantiality, or a clearer exposition on his part."[1] 3. It is asserted that the style of Peter, in those portions which agree with Jude, differs from his style in other portions of this Epistle and in his First Epistle, thus showing that these portions must have been inserted from the Epistle of Jude. "It plainly appears," observes Weiss, "that wherever in the parallel passages the expression strikingly coincides with that of Jude, it is to be found nowhere else in Second Peter; but wherever it deviates from that of Jude, or becomes entirely independent, it is at once in surprising conformity with the form of expression in this or the First Epistle of Peter."[2] And so also Huther remarks: "The circumstance that the more the expression in Peter's Second Epistle coincides with that of Jude, the more do the other peculiarities in the Epistle disappear."[3] Now if this could be clearly made out, it would

---

[1] Hug's *Introduction to the New Testament*, vol. ii. pp. 606, 607. See also Bleek's *Introduction*, vol. ii. p. 174. Spitta, with remarkable ingenuity, rebuts this objection by maintaining that it rests on a misconception. According to him, 2 Peter does not allude to the incident of Michael's dispute with the devil, recorded in the *Assumption of Moses*, but to the procedure of the angels, recorded in the Book of Enoch, who, instead of themselves conveying the sentence of condemnation against Azazel and his companions, commissioned Enoch to do so (Enoch xiii. 1). Jude mistook Peter's allusion, and gave a less happy illustration, taken from the *Assumption of Moses*. *Supra*, pp. 433-437. *Commentary on Jude*, pp. 170-173.

[2] Quoted by Huther. See Weiss' *Einleitung*, p. 440.

[3] Huther's *Die Epistel des Petrus*, p. 308 [E. Tr. p. 255]. "How comes it," asks Sieffert, "that the marked linguistic peculiarities of Second Peter are limited to that portion to which Jude presents a parallel?" Herzog's *Encyklopädie*, art. "Petrus." So also Wiesinger, *Der zweite Brief des Petrus*, p. 23. Spitta, on the other hand, shows that the above remark of Weiss, copied by

demonstrate the priority of the Epistle of Jude. There are undoubtedly peculiar words and phrases common to Peter and Jude, and which are not found elsewhere in Peter's Epistles; but the peculiarities of style and expression which distinguish the Second from the First Epistle of Peter are not confined to this second chapter of Second Peter.

IV. The only other possible supposition is that Peter borrowed from Jude. This is the opinion most generally favoured in recent times.[1] It is adopted and defended by Bertholdt, Eichhorn, Hug, Ullmann, Neander, Mayerhoff, Credner, De Wette, Guericke, Ewald, Brückner, Harless, Lechler, Reuss, Philippi, Huther, Hilgenfeld, Bleek, Wiesinger, Weiss, C. F. Schmid, Sieffert, Holtzmann, Schenkel, Mangold; and among English theologians, by Davidson, Abbott, Alford, Farrar, Plumptre, Eadie, Salmon, and Warfield.

The following reasons for this supposition, first advanced by De Wette,[2] are adopted more or less by the generality of those who hold this opinion:—

1. "The phraseology in Jude is simpler than that of Peter, which is more artificial, rhetorical, and paraphrastic." It is asserted that there is a vigour, a terseness, a strength, a boldness about the expressions in Jude's Epistle which are modified and toned down in the Epistle of Peter; in short, that there is a more distinct impress of originality about Jude's Epistle. Numerous illustrations of this argument are given by De Wette.[3] But, as even Brückner—who agrees with De Wette in his opinion as to the priority of Jude—remarks, many of these examples are far-fetched and overdrawn.[4] And although most recent writers, is at least an exaggeration. He makes a minute examination of the vocabulary of the two writers; and gives a list of thirty-three words common to both writers, which do elsewhere occur in the Epistles of Peter, against twenty-two which do not occur. *Supra*, pp. 458-461. To this Weiss replies, that wherever Peter agrees in his instances with Jude, the expressions are peculiar; but where he changes or expands the statements of Jude, parallels to the expressions are found in the First or Second Epistle. *Einleitung*, p. 440.

[1] Holtzmann calls the other supposition, or the priority of 2 Peter, "an abandoned hypothesis."

[2] De Wette's *Einleitung in das N. T.*, pp. 390, 391 [E. Tr. pp. 350, 351].

[3] The examples given by De Wette are Jude 4 comp. 2 Pet. ii. 3; Jude 6 comp. 2 Pet. ii. 4; Jude 7 comp. 2 Pet. ii. 6; Jude 8 comp. 2 Pet. ii. 10; Jude 9 comp. 2 Pet. ii. 11; Jude 10 comp. 2 Pet. ii. 12.

[4] Brückner's *Katholische Briefe*, p. 172 ff.

undoubtedly there is a greater terseness in the Epistle of Jude, yet the Second Epistle of Peter is not wanting in freshness and marks of originality.[1]

2. "Some of the expressions in Jude's Epistle are distorted and altered in a singular manner." The instances adduced by De Wette are the following:[2] σπιλάδες (rocks, Jude 12) is changed into σπίλοι (spots, 2 Pet. ii. 13). The change here is certainly from a more difficult to a simpler word. Critics are not agreed as to the meaning of the word σπιλάδες. The usual meaning is certainly *rocks*, and these mockers may be called "rocks in your feasts of charity," because by their conduct the love-feasts were destroyed— wrecked as upon rocks. But others, as Beza, Huther, Hofmann, Stier, Fronmüller, Keil, Abbott, and all the early versions consider it as synonymous with σπίλοι (2 Pet. ii. 13), and render it, as in the margin of the Revised Version, *spots*. Ἀγάπαις (love-feasts, Jude 12) is changed into ἀπάταις (deceits, 2 Pet. ii. 13). But in 2 Pet. ii. 13 the MSS. vary in the reading: several important MSS. read ἀγάπαις, and this reading is adopted by Lachmann and Tregelles.[3] Νεφέλαι ἄνυδροι (clouds without water, Jude 12) is changed into πηγαὶ ἄνυδροι (springs without water, 2 Pet. ii. 17). But the change here is immaterial, and cannot indicate what was the original expression.

3. "The passages 2 Pet. ii. 4, 11 become clear only from Jude 6, 9, and are manifestly taken from that passage. The indefiniteness of the second passage results from the fear of using an apocryphal narrative." In Jude the cause of the fall of the angels is stated (Jude 6); but the simple statement in Peter, "God spared not the angels that sinned" (2 Pet. ii. 4), is not obscure, and requires no further statement for its elucidation, as not the cause but the fact of the fall of the angels was all that was requisite for his argument. We have already alluded to the other passage, the forbearance of the angels toward the angelic dignities (2 Pet. ii. 11),

---

[1] Spitta, in answer to this objection, maintains that literary superiority is no proof of priority. *Supra*, pp. 405-407.

[2] Jude 12, σπιλάδες, comp. 2 Pet. ii. 3, σπίλοι καὶ μῶμοι; Jude 12, ἀγάπαις, comp. 2 Pet. ii. 13, ἀπάταις; Jude 12, νεφέλαι ἄνυδροι, comp. 2 Pet. ii. 17, πηγαὶ ἄνυδροι.

[3] Tischendorf, Alford, Westcott and Hort adopt the reading ἀπάταις.

which, it is admitted, is rendered more intelligible by reference to the corresponding passage in Jude (Jude 9).[1] The omission of the apocryphal passages in Peter's Epistle is remarkable, and is supposed to indicate a post-apostolic age, when, it is asserted, the aversion to apocryphal references increased. It is, however, by others considered as a proof of the priority of that Epistle, Jude giving Midrash-like expositions to Peter's text.[2]

4. "The course of thought in Jude is firm and distinct, whilst in Second Peter it is wavering and unsteady, like that of an imitator." The examples of this which De Wette gives are Jude 4 compared with 2 Pet. ii. 1 and i. 9-21; Jude 5-8 compared with 2 Pet. ii. 4-11, where the interruption in vers. 7-9 and the change of cases in ver. 10 are to be noticed; Jude 11 compared with 2 Pet. ii. 15, 16; and Jude 17 compared with 2 Pet. iii. 1-3. This feature, however, is so entirely subjective, that it is differently appreciated by different critics; while some regard it as a mark of originality in Jude, others regard it as a mark of originality in Peter. The statements in each Epistle are expounded or condensed in the other.

5. "The opponents whom Jude combats are strongly and distinctly indicated, whereas in Second Peter the picture is quite indefinite, the *vicious* being arbitrarily converted into *false teachers*, of whom we know not whether they are present or future." But, whilst it is admitted that the description of these impious mockers is much more definite in Jude than in Peter, yet this may, as we have seen, be more appropriately employed as an argument for the priority of Peter. Peter's description is indefinite, because the doctrines and practices of these false teachers were not fully developed; whereas, during the interval between the composition of Peter's Epistle and that of Jude, wickedness had developed itself, and become more pronounced, and hence could be more distinctly portrayed. When Peter wrote, the scoffers had not come

---

[1] See, however, Spitta's ingenious solution, mentioned above.
[2] Lumby in the *Speaker's Commentary*. Spitta, on the other hand, denies the assumption, and asserts that there are as many apocryphal allusions in 2 Peter as there are in Jude.

openly forward, though their tendencies were indeed apparent; but when Jude wrote, they had openly advanced their pernicious errors.

Those who adopt the priority of Jude's Epistle suppose that when Peter wrote his Second Epistle, the Epistle of Jude came under his notice, and he was deeply impressed with its vigour, its earnestness, its inspiration; he felt that it contained the words of the Holy Ghost, and that it was most applicable to the state of the Churches to which he was writing. He therefore uses it in enforcing his own injunctions, he incorporates its sentiments into his Epistle, but he does so in no slavish manner; he makes the thoughts and words of Jude his own. Hence he omits and adds as the occasion serves.[1] The readers of the two Epistles were in some respects different. Both wrote to Christians whether Jews or Gentiles; but Jude's Epistle is chiefly addressed to Jewish Christians, and Peter's to Gentile Christians. Hence several references employed by Jude are omitted by Peter, because he adapts his writing to Gentile Christians. In particular, all the supposed apocryphal passages, such as the contest between Michael and the devil concerning the body of Moses, supposed to be taken from the "Assumption of Moses," the description of the nature of the sin of the angels, supposed to be taken from the "Book of Enoch," and the supposed quotation from that book itself, are omitted. Peter omits the unbelief of the Israelites in the wilderness, as being more appropriate to the Jewish Christians; and dwells upon the destruction by the flood and the deliverance of Noah, as being better adapted to the Gentile Christians.[2]

This view of the priority of Jude is exposed to several weighty objections. Especially is this use of the Epistle of Jude considered to be opposed to the opinion that Peter is

---

[1] According to Spitta, Jude's use of the Epistle of Peter is intelligible, while Peter's use of Jude's Epistle is unintelligible. *Supra*, p. 468 ff.

[2] See Plumptre, *On the Epistles of Peter and Jude*, pp. 79-81. All this appears fanciful. Plumptre even goes the length of saying: "It is not an improbable supposition that it (the Epistle of Jude) may have been sent to him (Peter) by James, the brother of the Lord, with whom, as his brother apostle of the circumcision, he would naturally be in communication, or even that Jude himself may have been the bearer of his own letter."

the author of the Second Epistle which bears his name, and consequently to the authority of that Epistle. It can hardly, it is asserted, be imagined that Peter, one of the three pillars of the Church, so ready in speech and action, would borrow from one who was not an apostle, and who was unknown in the Christian Church. "Those who, like ourselves," observes Fronmüller, "are profoundly impressed with the authenticity of the Second Epistle of Peter, deem it *à priori* highly improbable that Peter, the prince of apostles, that illumined and highly-gifted man, who proves his originality in the First Epistle, as well as in chapters i. and iii. of the Second Epistle, should have borrowed in a part of his Epistle the language, figures, and examples of a man evidently less gifted than himself. Especially remarkable, moreover, would be his silence concerning Jude, seeing that he made mention of Paul and his Epistles."[1] Hence it is that Th. Schott argues against the priority of Jude on the ground of the authenticity of Second Peter: "The genuineness of Second Peter, which is evidently conditioned by its being the composition of Peter, is completely unmaintainable if the author of this Epistle used the Epistle of Jude."[2] We have already adverted to this objection, when discussing the authenticity of Second Peter; but we must admit that if Jude's Epistle be prior, Peter's use of it is a peculiarity in his Epistle difficult to account for. Still the question as to which is the original Epistle is not, as Fronmüller, Th. Schott, Bleek, and Plummer assert, identical with the question as to the authenticity of Second Peter; Wiesinger, Brückner, Hug, Guericke,[3] Schülze, Alford, Plumptre, and Warfield defend its authenticity, although they call in question its priority.

[1] Fronmüller, "Exposition of the Second Epistle of Peter," in Lange's *Bibelwerk*, translated by Mombert, p. 7. So also Plummer observes: "This question cannot be kept distinct from that of the authenticity of Peter. Every argument in favour of the authenticity of 2 Peter is something in favour of its priority, and *vice versa*, although many arguments bear more upon one point than the other." *Commentary on Jude*, p. 266.

[2] Schott, *Der zweite Brief Petri*, p. 191. Bleek, on the other hand, argues against the authenticity of Second Peter on the ground of the priority of Jude. *Introduction to the N. T.*, vol. ii. p. 176.

[3] Brückner, *Katholische Briefe*, p. 129. Wiesinger, *Comm.* p. 24. Guericke's *Einleitung*, p. 461.

Although we consider that 2 Pet. ii. 1–iii. 3 and Jude are so dependent upon each other, that either Peter must have seen the Epistle of Jude, or Jude must have seen the Epistle of Peter, yet the arguments in favour of the priority of each, and the difficulties and objections which accompany the assumption of either opinion, are so nearly balanced, and the whole subject is of such an intricate and perplexing nature, that it is almost impossible to come to a distinct and definite conclusion. The predictive nature of Peter's language and the apparent reference of Jude to that prediction are in favour of the priority of Peter; whilst the brevity, terseness, and unity of Jude, and the light which his words throw on certain statements in Peter, are in favour of the priority of Jude. If it could be proved that the linguistic peculiarities in Peter's Second Epistle are chiefly found in those passages which resemble Jude, then Jude must be regarded as the original.[1] The admission of the fact that one sacred writer borrowed from another is no argument against the inspiration or the genuineness of one of these writings. There are several instances in Scripture where the sacred writers have copied from one another or drawn from a common source. Not to mention in this point of view several passages in the synoptical Gospels, the repetitions in the Pentateuch, and the same historical accounts in the Books of Samuel, the Kings, and Chronicles, the following passages are coincident in words: compare 2 Sam. xxii. with Ps. xviii.; Ps. xiv. with Ps. liii.; Ps. cxv. 4–11 with Ps. cxxxv. 16–21; 2 Kings xviii. 13–xix. with Isa. xxxvi.–xxxix.; 2 Kings xxv. 23, 24 with Jer. xl. 7–9; 2 Chron. xxxvi. 22, 23 with Ezra i. 1–3; Ezra ii. with Neh. vii.; Isa. ii. 2–4 with Micah iv. 1–3, etc. In all these passages the resemblance is far more complete and exact than that found between the Second Epistle of Peter and the Epistle of Jude.

[1] This is certainly the strongest argument for the priority of Jude, but its force is considerably weakened by the important results of Spitta's examination of the vocabulary of both Epistles. *Supra*, p. 152 ff.

THE FIRST EPISTLE OF JOHN.

I. THE AUTHENTICITY OF THE EPISTLE.

THE First Epistle of John belongs to the class of the best attested writings of the New Testament. The external testimonies in its favour are numerous and conclusive; and the internal evidence is also strong and convincing. Polycarp (A.D. 116), in his Epistle to the Philippians, evidently refers to it: "For whosoever does not confess that Jesus Christ has come in the flesh is antichrist"[1] (1 John iv. 3); where the resemblance to the language of the Epistle is too strong to be considered accidental; and Polycarp, as Irenæus informs us,[2] was a disciple of John. Eusebius informs us that Papias (A.D. 120) made use of testimonies from the First Epistle of John and likewise from that of Peter;[3] and Papias, according to Irenæus (who was himself a disciple of Polycarp), was a hearer of John, and an associate of Polycarp.[4] Eusebius also tells us that Irenæus (A.D. 180) makes mention of the First Epistle of John, extracting many testimonies from it.[5] Thus Irenæus writes: "For this reason he (John) thus testified to us in his Epistle: Little children, it is the last time, and as ye have heard that antichrist doth come, even now have many antichrists appeared, whereby we know that it is the last time"[6] (1 John ii. 18). And again: "Wherefore he (John)

---

[1] *Ad Philippens.* chap. vii.: Πᾶς γὰρ, ὃς ἂν μὴ ὁμολογήσῃ Ἰησοῦν Χριστὸν ἐν σαρκὶ ἐληλυθέναι Ἀντίχριστος ἐστι.

[2] Euseb. *Hist. Eccl.* v. 20.

[3] *Ibid.* iii. 39: Κέχρηται δ' ὁ αὐτὸς μαρτυρίαις ἀπὸ τῆς Ἰωάννου προτέρας ἐπιστολῆς καὶ τῆς Πέτρου ὁμοίως.

[4] Irenæus, *Adv. Hær.* v. 33. 4.   [5] *Hist. Eccl.* v. 8.

[6] *Adv. Hær.* iii. 16. 5: Propterea quod et in epistola sua sic testificatus est

again says in his Epistle: Every one that believeth that Jesus is the Christ is born of God"[1] (1 John v. 1). The Muratorian Çanon (A.D. 170) has the following direct reference to this Epistle; from which it would appear that the Epistle was regarded as an appendix to the Fourth Gospel: "What wonder that John makes so many references to the Fourth Gospel in his Epistle, saying of himself: That which we have seen with our eyes, and have heard with our ears, and our hands have handled, of that we have written"[2] (1 John i. 1). Clemens Alexandrinus (A.D. 190) writes: "John too manifestly teaches the differences of sins in his larger Epistle in these words: If any man see his brother sin a sin that is not unto death, he shall ask, and he shall give him life"[3] (1 John v. 16). And again: "This is the love of God, says John, that we keep His commandments, and that we should love one another: and His commandments are not grievous"[4] (1 John v. 3). Tertullian (A.D. 200) says: "Let us consider whom the apostles saw: That which we have seen, says John, which we have heard, which we have seen with our eyes, and our hands have handled of the word of life"[5] (1 John i. 1). Origen (A.D. 230) observes that John has left us an Epistle consisting of a few lines.[6] He makes frequent mention of it in his writings. Thus: "John, in his catholic Epistle, says he is of the devil, because the devil sinneth from the beginning"[7] (1 John iii. 8). Cyprian (A.D. 248) frequently refers

nobis (Joannes): filioli, novissima hora est, et quemadmodum audistis quoniam Antichristus venit, nunc Antichristi multi facti sunt, etc.

[1] *Adv. Hær.* iii. 16. 8: Διὸ πάλιν ἐν τῇ ἐπιστολῇ φησι. Πᾶς ὁ πιστεύων ὅτι Ἰησοῦς Χριστός, ἐκ τοῦ θεοῦ γεγέννηται.

[2] Quod ergo mirum, si Joannes tam constanter singula etiam in epistolis suis proferat, dicens in semetipso, Quæ videmus, etc.

[3] *Strom.* ii. 15: Φαίνεται δὲ καὶ Ἰωάννης ἐν τῇ μείζονι ἐπιστολῇ τὰς διαφορὰς τῶν ἁμαρτιῶν ἐκδιδάσκων ἐν τούτοις· Ἐάν τις ἴδῃ τὸν ἀδελφὸν αὐτοῦ ἁμαρτάνοντα ἁμαρτίαν μὴ πρὸς θάνατον, αἰτήσει καὶ δώσει αὐτῷ ζωήν.

[4] *Pædag.* iii. 11: Αὕτη δὲ ἐστιν ἡ ἀγάπη τοῦ θεοῦ, φησὶ Ἰωάννης, ἵνα τὰς ἐντολὰς τηρήσωμεν.

[5] *Adv. Prax.* chap. xv.: Denique inspiciamus, quem apostoli viderint. "Quod vidimus," inquit Joannes, "quod audivimus, oculis nostris vidimus, et manus nostræ contrectaverunt de sermone vitæ."

[6] Euseb. *Hist. Eccl.* vi. 25.

[7] *De Orat.*, Opp. tom. i. p. 233: ὥς φησίν ἐν τῇ καθολικῇ ὁ Ἰωάννης, ἐκ τοῦ διαβόλου ἐστίν, ὅτι ἀπ' ἀρχῆς ὁ διάβολος ἁμαρτάνει.

to this Epistle: "And the Apostle John, remembering the commandment, afterwards puts in his Epistle: By this we understand that we know Him, if we keep His commandments. Whosoever says I know Him, and keepeth not His commandments, is a liar, and the truth is not in him"[1] (1 John ii. 3, 4). Eusebius (A.D. 325) mentions this Epistle among those writings which are universally acknowledged as genuine;[2] and he states that, besides the Gospel of John, his First Epistle is acknowledged without dispute, both by those of the present day and also by the ancients.[3] The Epistle is contained in all the ancient versions, including the Peshito and Old Italic, and in all the catalogues of the books of Scripture. This general testimony of the Fathers was called in question only by a few early heretics, but purely from dogmatic reasons, because its teaching was opposed to their peculiar opinions. Thus the obscure sect of the Alogi rejected it, because there was a reference in it to the doctrine of the Logos; and the Marcionites rejected it, as they did all the books of Scripture except the Gospel of Luke and the Epistles of Paul, because it contradicted their peculiar anti-Judaistic-Gnostic views. In short, the external evidence in favour of this Epistle is so early, so strong, so clear, and so consecutive, that the assertion of Lücke is fully justified: "Incontestably, our Epistle must be numbered among those canonical books which are most strongly upheld by ecclesiastical tradition."[4] So also De Wette, a critic belonging to the negative school, remarks: "The doubts which have been raised in recent times against the genuineness of this Epistle rest on weak grounds."[5] And even Hilgenfeld, although he rejects the Epistle on internal grounds, yet admits that the First Epistle of John belongs to those writings of the New Testament the genuineness of which has never been disputed in the ancient Church, and that the chain of

---

[1] *Epist.* 24 (al. 28): Et Joannes apostolus mandati memor in epistola sua postmodum ponit: "In hos," inquit, "intelligimus, quia cognovimus eum, si præcepta ejus custodiamus," etc.

[2] *Hist. Eccl.* iii. 25.   [3] *Ibid.* iii. 24.

[4] Quoted by Alford, *Greek Testament*, vol. iv. Prolegomena, p. 162. Lücke, *The Epistles of John*, p. 7, E. Tr.

[5] *Einleitung in das N. T.*, p. 397 [E. Tr. p. 356].

witnesses who have made use of it commences as far back as Papias.[1]

Nor is the internal evidence in favour of the Epistle defective. There is a striking resemblance between it and the Fourth Gospel. The same style pervades both writings; the same connecting particles are used: there are similar words and phrases: there is the same method of developing ideas by parallelism or by antithesis: there is the same repetition of fundamental words and ideas, such as "walking in the truth," "God is light," "being born of God," "abiding in God;" and there is the same simplicity of construction.[2] Not only is there a similarity of expression, but no less than thirty-five passages are common to the Fourth Gospel and the Epistle.[3] Long lists of these parallels are given by Eichhorn, De Wette, Guericke, Bishop Alexander, Westcott, Plummer, and other critics.[4] We insert the list of parallelisms as drawn up by Guericke. The peculiar meaning of ζωή (John i. 4, vi. 26, 35, 48; 1 John i. 1, 2, v. 11, 20) and φῶς (John i. 4, 5, 7 ff.; 1 John i. 5, 7, ii. 8); ποιεῖν τὴν ἀλήθειαν (John iii. 21; 1 John i. 6); ἐκ τῆς ἀληθείας εἶναι (John xviii. 37; 1 John ii. 21); ἐκ τοῦ διαβόλου εἶναι (John viii. 44; 1 John iii. 8); ἐκ τοῦ θεοῦ εἶναι (John vii. 17, viii. 47; 1 John iii. 10, iv. 1); ἐκ τοῦ κόσμου εἶναι (John viii. 20; 1 John iv. 5); ἐκ τοῦ κόσμου λαλεῖν (John iii. 31; 1 John iv. 5); ἐν τῇ σκοτίᾳ, ἐν τῷ φωτὶ περιπατεῖν (John viii. 12, xii. 35; 1 John i. 6, ii. 11); γινώσκειν τὸν θεόν or Χριστόν (John xvii. 25; 1 John ii. 3, 4, 13, 14, iv. 6, 7, 8, v. 20); ὁρᾶν τὸν θεόν (John i. 18, vi. 46; 1 John iv. 20); ἔχειν ζωὴν αἰώνιον or τὴν ζωήν (John iii. 15, 16, 36, v. 24, 39, 40; 1 John iii. 15, v. 12 f.); μεταβαίνειν ἐκ τοῦ θανάτου εἰς τὴν ζωήν (John v. 24; 1 John iii. 14);

---

[1] Quoted by Huther, *The Epistles of John*, p. 257, E. Tr. Hilgenfeld's own words are, "that the First Epistle of John was almost universally recognised as a homologumenon in the ancient Church." *Einleitung*, p. 694.

[2] See Westcott, *The Epistles of St. John*, Introduction, pp. 39-43.

[3] Eichhorn's *Einleitung in das N. T.*, vol. ii. pp. 281-283.

[4] De Wette, *Einleitung in das N. T.*, p. 396 f. Guericke's *Neutestamentliche Isagogik*, p. 474. Bp. Alexander, *Speaker's Commentary*, vol. iv. p. 282. Westcott's *Epistles of St. John*, p. 11. Plummer, *On First John*, Cambridge series, pp. 37-40.

νικᾶν τὸν κόσμον (John xvi. 13 ; 1 John v. 4, 5, ii. 13, 14, iv. 4) ; ὁ μονογενὴς υἱός (John i. 14, 18 ; 1 John iv. 9).[1] These resemblances are of such a nature as to prove, not that the one writer borrowed from the other, but that the Fourth Gospel and the Epistle proceeded from the same author. The points of resemblance are inartificial and natural, and are so interwoven as to constitute the peculiar diction of the writer; they cannot be accounted for on the principle of imitation; the one writing bears as strong marks of originality as the other. This is clearly seen, by way of contrast, in comparing the spurious Epistle of Paul to the Laodiceans with the other Epistles of that apostle, where servile imitation is clearly discernible. "A comparison of this Epistle with John's Gospel," observes Bleek, "can leave no doubt on the mind that both are by the same writer; the similarity between them is so striking and so thorough in character, in thought and language, in distinctive representations and turns of expression, as to be utterly incomprehensible save on the supposition of identity of authorship."[2] And Dean Alford remarks: "To maintain a diversity of authorship would betray the very perverseness and exaggeration of that school of criticism which refuses to believe, be evidence never so strong."[3] Now, admitting the identity of authorship, it follows that all the external testimony in favour of the genuineness of the Fourth Gospel applies also to the Epistle; and conversely, which is perhaps still more important, the strong attestations of the genuineness of the Epistle are also attestations of the genuineness of the Gospel. Thus, then, both the Gospel and Epistle are attested by a twofold chain of evidence.

This identity of authorship of the Epistle and Fourth Gospel has, indeed, been disputed by several writers, especially by those belonging to the Tübingen school. Baur,[4] Zeller, Volkmar, Hilgenfeld, and Pfleiderer assert that there are dissimilarities

[1] Guericke's *N. T. Isagogik*, pp. 474, 475.
[2] *Introduction to the N. T.*, vol. ii. p. 186.
[3] Alford's *Greek Testament*, vol. iv. Prolegomena, p. 159. So also Credner observes: "The Epistle, in its language, expressions, and ideas, is so related to the Fourth Gospel, that both can only have one and the same author." *Einleitung*, p. 677.   [4] *Kanon. Evv.* p. 350.

THE AUTHENTICITY OF THE EPISTLE. 261

in the writings which prove them to be the compositions of different authors.[1] Thus they object that in the Gospel there is no reference to the second advent of Christ and to the end of the world, whereas the Epistle speaks of the advent of Antichrist as a proof that it is the last time (1 John ii. 18); in the Epistle the death of Christ is represented as a propitiation, ἱλασμός (1 John ii. 2, iv. 10), a word which does not occur elsewhere in the New Testament, and a representation which does not occur in the Gospel; and in the Gospel the Paraclete (ὁ παράκλητος) is the Holy Ghost (John xiv. 16), whilst in the Epistle He is Christ (1 John ii. 1).[2] But these points of dissimilarity are slight, and do not invalidate or weaken the argument drawn from the instances of agreement. It is true that in the Gospel the eschatological topics are not dwelt upon, but there is an allusion to the general resurrection, when the dead shall hear the voice of the Son of man (John v. 28), and to the last day (John vi. 40, 44); besides, it must be recollected that difference is not contradiction. Although the word propitiation (ἱλασμός) does not occur in the Gospel, yet the doctrine of the atonement, which that word implies, is by no means wanting; we are informed that Christ is "the Lamb of God, who beareth the sins of the world," and "the good Shepherd, who giveth up His life for the sheep." And the designation of the Paraclete as the Holy Ghost does not prevent its application also to Christ; indeed, our Lord speaks of the Holy Ghost as another Paraclete (ἄλλον παράκλητον, John xiv. 16), thus implying that He Himself was also a Paraclete.[3] Besides, it is no argument against the identity of the authorship of two writings that the one contains thoughts that are not included in the other, provided there be no contradiction of sentiment.[4] Most of the above dissimilarities,

[1] So also Dr. Davidson, *Introduction to the Study of the N. T.*, vol. ii. pp. 295-299, 1st ed. Vol. ii. pp. 235-239, 2nd ed.

[2] See Hilgenfeld, *Das Evangelium und die Briefe Johannis*, pp. 322-355. Hilgenfeld, it would seem, has modified his opinion, and now regards it as probable that the Fourth Gospel and the First Epistle of John were the productions of the same author, though not the Apostle John. See Mangold's *Einleitung*, p. 766. Holtzmann's *Einleitung*, p. 461.

[3] Westcott deals with these and similar objections in his *Commentary on the Epistles of St. John*, Introduction, p. 44 f.

[4] "There cannot be a more false canon of criticism than that a man who has

if they can be so called, can easily be accounted for by differences in the circumstances under which these writings were composed.

The Epistle bears upon it the impress of the character of John, as that is discerned in the narrative of the four Gospels. Love was the distinguishing feature of the beloved apostle, and love is the chief theme of this Epistle. That moral indignation, which was displayed when he wished to draw down fire from heaven to consume the Samaritans, is also seen in his invectives against those heretics who called in question our Lord's advent in the flesh. That contemplative disposition, which is seen in the record of our Lord's farewell address, and in his insight into our Lord's disposition, is also conspicuous in the Epistle. That calmness and composure of mind, which distinguished John from the ardent Peter, and which distinction on several occasions was manifested in the actions of these apostles when together, are noticeable as characteristics of this Epistle.

The authenticity of this Epistle remained undisputed until the time of the Reformation. The first who called it in question was Scaliger, who asserted that the three Epistles of John were not written by John the apostle.[1] He gives no reason for this rash assertion; the probability is, that he attributed them to John the presbyter, who is almost a mythical character in ecclesiastical history. Afterwards, S. G. Lange (A.D. 1797) attacked the Epistle on internal grounds, without, however, venturing to call in question its external evidence, or positively denying the authorship of John.[2] Cludius (A.D. 1808) maintained that the Epistle was the fabrication of a Jewish Christian, written in imitation of the Gospel.[3] Bretschneider (A.D. 1821) was a more formidable opponent. He considered that the contents of the Epistle proved that it must have been written at the beginning of the second century, and consequently at a date later than the lifetime of

written one work will, while writing a second, introduce no ideas and make use of no modes of expression that are not to be found in the first." Salmon's *Introduction*, p. 250.

[1] *Tres epistolæ Johannis non sunt apostoli Johannis.*
[2] *Die Schriften des Johannis übersetzt und erklärt*, vol. iii. p. 4 ff.
[3] *Uransichten des Christenthums*, p. 52 ff.

the apostle.[1] But especially was the Epistle exposed to the attacks of the Tübingen school. Köstlin admits the identity of the author of the Gospel and the Epistle, though he calls in question the authorship of John.[2] Baur, with whom Hilgenfeld[3] formerly agreed, views them, though closely connected, as the productions of different authors, though they disagree as to which author was the original writer. Baur considers the Epistle to be a weak imitation of the Gospel;[4] whilst Hilgenfeld, on the contrary, considers that the Epistle was written first, and regards it as a work of great excellence, which the author of the Fourth Gospel employed as his pattern.[5] All the objections of these writers are subjective, arising from their peculiar views, and cannot possibly destroy or weaken the external evidence in favour of the Epistle, which, indeed, they do not impugn.

1. S. G. Lange calls in question the genuineness of the Epistle on account of its supposed feebleness. He objects to it on the ground of "its lack of all individual references, its slavish imitation of the Gospel, the too great generality of the thoughts, the traces of the feebleness of old age, and the non-reference to the destruction of Jerusalem."[6] The only one of these objections which merits our attention is that the Epistle exhibits traces of the feebleness of old age. That there are traces of old age in the author of the Epistle, that it is the writing of an aged man, is admitted, and indeed must be evident to every reader; the author addresses his readers as a father does his children. But that there are traces of senile weakness is denied. On the contrary, it is the opinion of most commentators, and even of many, such as Hilgenfeld, who call in question the authorship of John, that the Epistle is full of vigour, that under the simplicity of

---

[1] *Probabilia de evangelii et epistolarum Johannis*, etc., p. 164 ff., Lipsiæ 1820.
[2] *Lehrbegriff des Evangelium und der Briefe Johannis*, pp. 27-31.
[3] On Hilgenfeld's change of opinion, see *supra*, p. 261.
[4] *Tüb. Theol. Jahrb.* 1848 : Die Joh. Briefe.
[5] Hilgenfeld's *Der Evangelium und die Briefe Johannis*, p. 323 ; also *Einleitung in das N. T.*, p. 681. "Whilst," he observes, "Baur found in the First Epistle of John an imitation of the Gospel, I have rather explained this Epistle as older than the Fourth Gospel."
[6] Given in Huther's *Commentary on First Epistle of John*, p. 252, E. Tr.

expression there is a depth of meaning demanding the exercise of our intellectual powers to fathom, and that it is the production of one who is remarkable for his spiritual insight. The more this Epistle is studied, the more is its profoundness discerned and its power felt. The traces of feebleness are in the mind of the objector, and not in the Epistle.[1] There are, indeed, apparent repetitions, a series of antithetical aphorisms, ideas represented by parallelisms or by contrasts; but these are also to be found in the Gospel of John, and are a peculiarity in the style of the author. Nor are they unmeaning repetitions; but often a series of statements in an ascending order, one idea leading up to a higher, forming a climax. And, by the method of positive and negative assertions, the lessons which the apostle desires to teach are emphasized and impressed upon the reader. Perhaps no writings in the New Testament require the exercise of higher powers for a full comprehension than those of the Apostle John.

2. Bretschneider argues that the Epistle must belong to the second century, on account of its containing post-apostolic views. The doctrine of the Logos which is there referred to, and the docetic notions of the person of Christ which are there condemned, were not known until the second century.[2] It was not until the apostles were dead that Gnosticism in the form of Docetism[3] was promulgated. A somewhat similar objection is made by Hilgenfeld, who finds traces of post-apostolic Gnosticism in the Epistle;[4] and by Dr. Davidson in his *Introduction to the Study of the New Testament*.[5] But, in answer to this objection, it is to be observed that the doctrine of the Logos is not inculcated, but only barely alluded to in the beginning of the Epistle (1 John i. 1). Nor was this doctrine, in its general features, post-apostolic;

---

[1] "If a wild Indian can find no relish in the Olympic Jupiter, the fault is not with Phidias." Ebrard, *Commentary on St. John's Epistles*, p. 9.

[2] "The logology and antidocetic tendency of the Epistle betrays an author of the second century." Bretschneider, *Probabilia*, p. 166 ff.

[3] By Docetism is meant that Christ's manifestations were only appearances — that the Christ did not come in the flesh. It was taught under various forms See *infra*.

[4] Hilgenfeld's *Einleitung in das N. T.*, p. 691 f.

[5] Vol. ii. p. 300, 1st ed. Vol. ii. p. 242.

it was not only promulgated by Philo, a contemporary of the apostles, but, as appears from the apocryphal Book of Wisdom[1] and the Targums, was not unknown to the Jews before the time of our Lord. It is true that Docetism, in a developed form, was not known until the second century, when it became an essential feature in the doctrines of the Gnostic sects; but the germs of Docetism, as of Gnosticism in general, appeared in the apostolic age, and indeed it was a necessary result of the contact of Christianity with heathen philosophy. There are allusions to Gnosticism in Paul's Epistle to the Colossians and in the Pastoral Epistles; and as this Epistle of John was written, as is generally admitted, at a later period, it would then be in a more advanced state, and appears to have taken the form of Docetism. Docetism is indeed attacked in the Epistle, but it is Docetism in a crude state, namely, the distinction drawn between Jesus and the Christ, and the denial that Jesus Christ came in the flesh (1 John iv. 3). Afterwards it was developed and systematized, and we have only to compare the rudimentary Docetism, impugned in this Epistle, with the developed system in the succeeding age to see the difference. It also appears from the statements of the Fathers that Cerinthus, who inculcated a form of Docetism, was a contemporary of the Apostle John. Indeed, the form of Docetism attacked in this Epistle, so far from proving that the author belonged to the second century, is rather a proof that he lived in the first, before Docetism was taught in a systematic form.

3. Baur considers the Epistle as Montanistic in its views, and supposes that it was composed by a disciple of Montanus, who lived in the middle of the second century. The reasons which he assigns for this opinion are that the Epistle describes some Christians as sinless and perfect; that it mentions an anointing ($\chi\rho\hat{\iota}\sigma\mu a$), by which we may know all things; and that it draws a distinction between venial and mortal sins—between those sins "which are not unto death," and those sins "which are unto death" (1 John v. 16). According to Baur, there is here an allusion to the mortal

---

[1] For an account of the doctrine of the Logos as contained in the Book of Wisdom, see Rev. William J. Deane's commentary on that book.

sins mentioned by Tertullian.[1] There are, according to this Father, seven mortal sins, and three of those, namely idolatry, murder, and adultery,[2] are alleged to be spoken of in this Epistle as "sins unto death." But these reasons adduced by Baur are weak. The apostle does not distinguish, as the Montanists do, the spiritual from other believers, but describes the ideal believer—the tendency of the new nature implanted within the Christian, which is not to commit sin. The anointing of which he speaks is not that conferred by means of oil at baptism, as was the case with the Montanists, but the indwelling of the Holy Spirit. And the distinction between sins unto death and sins not unto death has no reference to the deadly sins of the Montanists as enumerated by Tertullian, nor to any definitely named sins, as Baur asserts, but probably to the sin against the Holy Ghost mentioned by our Lord. Besides, if Montanism were taught in this Epistle, there would be more frequent mention of the agency of the Holy Spirit, which constitutes the essence of that particular system; not Christ, but the Holy Spirit, would have been mentioned as the Paraclete. Even Hilgenfeld, his disciple, repudiates this idea of Baur as erroneous and far-fetched.

II. THE AUTHOR OF THE EPISTLE.

The writer of this Epistle does not mention his name, but asserts that he was an eye-witness of the events in the life of Christ. "That which was from the beginning, which we have heard, which we have seen with our eyes, which we have looked upon, and our hands have handled, of the Word of life: that which we have seen and heard declare we unto you, that ye also may have fellowship with us" (1 John i. 1, 3). He writes with the authority of an apostle, he is the same as the author of the Fourth Gospel, the Epistle bears the impress of the character of the Apostle John, and the Fathers uniformly

---

[1] *De Pudicit.* chap. xix.

[2] How arbitrary the selection of deadly sins by Baur is, is evident from the fact that idolatry is mentioned only in 1 John v. 21, murder only in 1 John iii. 15, and adultery is nowhere alluded to.

assert that the author of this Epistle, as well as of the Gospel, was John, the beloved disciple.

John was probably, like Peter, a native of Bethsaida. His father was called Zebedee and his mother Salome, who, there is reason to believe, was the sister of Mary, the mother of the Lord (John xix. 25 comp. Matt. xxvii. 56). John was by occupation a fisherman on the Sea of Galilee; and he appears from various notices in the Gospels to have been in a better social position than the rest of the apostles. His father, Zebedee, we are informed, had hired servants (Mark i. 20); his mother, Salome, was one of those women of Galilee who followed our Lord and ministered unto Him of their substance (Matt. xxvii. 56); and it would also appear that he had a house of his own, or at least a temporary residence, in Jerusalem; for when our Lord on the cross consigned His mother to his care, we are informed that John took her to his own house (John xix. 27). We do not, however, lay any stress on the fact that he was identical with that disciple who was known to the high priest (John xviii. 16); for it is hardly to be supposed that any of our Lord's immediate disciples was in such a social position as to be acquainted with a person of such distinguished rank.[1]

John, being of an earnest and religious disposition, attached himself to the Baptist; and by him his attention was directed to Jesus in the memorable words: "Behold the Lamb of God that taketh away the sins of the world" (John i. 35, 36). He was early called by Jesus to be one of His followers, and was distinguished by Him among His disciples. He bears the dignified appellation of "the disciple whom Jesus loved, who also leant on His breast at supper" (John xiii. 23).[2] He belonged to the inner circle of the apostles, and along with Peter and James was privileged to be present at the

---

[1] Some strangely imagine that this other disciple was Judas Iscariot. So Archbishop Whately, *On Bacon's Essays*, p. 458. He might have been Nicodemus or Joseph of Arimathea. "It is not easy to imagine how a Galilean fisherman should have known anything personal of those wealthy Sadducean aristocrats, with whom he had not a single thought or a single sympathy in common." Farrar.

[2] Hence John is known in the writings of the Fathers by the title ὁ ἐπιστήθιος. Peter has been called φιλόχριστος, and John φιλοιησοῦς.

raising of the daughter of Jairus, the transfiguration, and the agony in Gethsemane. On three occasions he was rebuked by our Lord: once when, jealous of the glory of his Master, he wished to forbid a man who did not follow Christ casting out devils in His name (Mark ix. 38); at another time, when, carried away by his impetuous zeal for the honour of his Master, he wished to call down fire from heaven to consume the inhospitable Samaritans (Luke ix. 54); and a third time, when, actuated by ambition, he and his brother James desired to sit the one on the right hand and the other on the left of their Master in His kingdom (Mark x. 37). When on the day of trial all the disciples fled at the arrest of Christ, John recovered from his panic, and alone of the Twelve was present at the cross, and to his care Jesus commended His mother (John xix. 26). After the resurrection John was the first to recognise the risen Lord on the shores of the Sea of Tiberias (John xxi. 7); and on that occasion our Lord honoured him with words which gave rise to the report that he should never die (John xxi. 23).

In the Acts of the Apostles, John steps into the background before the more energetic apostles Peter and Paul. His province was not so much to diffuse the gospel by the conversion of unbelievers, as to confirm and build up believers in the faith. His character was contemplative rather than active. After the ascension he, along with the rest of the apostles, waited in the upper room, in prayer and supplication, for the bestowal of the Spirit (Acts i. 13, 14). In the Acts he is generally mentioned in company with Peter. He was with Peter when the lame man at the beautiful gate of the temple was cured (Acts iii. 1), and when Peter accused the rulers of being the betrayers and murderers of their Messiah (Acts iv. 13). He was sent along with Peter to Samaria by the Church to confirm the disciples converted by the instrumentality of Philip the deacon (Acts viii. 14). He does not appear to have been at Jerusalem during Paul's first visit to that city (Gal. i. 18, 19); but he was present, fourteen years after, at the Council of Jerusalem (Gal. ii. 9), though, from all that we are informed, he does not appear to have taken an active part in its deliberations. He seems finally to have left Jerusalem before Paul's last visit to that city, as the only mention is of James and the elders. John is only once mentioned in the Epistles of Paul, when he is named, along with Peter and James the Lord's brother, as giving to him and Barnabas the right hand of fellowship (Gal. ii. 9).

The notices of John in ecclesiastical history are numerous, some authentic, some probable, and others fabulous. Of those, two are considered by nearly all theologians as authentic, namely, John's banishment to Patmos and his residence in Ephesus.

His residence in Patmos is mentioned in the Apocalypse: "I was in the island that is called Patmos, for the word of God, and for the testimony of Jesus Christ" (Rev. i. 9). It is evidently implied that his residence in Patmos was a forced residence on account of his faith. The fact of his banishment to Patmos is attested by Irenæus, Clemens Alexandrinus, Tertullian, Origen, Eusebius, and Epiphanius. Tertullian conjoins with it the miracle of John's deliverance after being immersed in a caldron of boiling oil, which, according to him, occurred at Rome. "The Apostle John," he observes, "was first plunged unhurt into boiling oil, and thence remitted to his island home."[1] This is, however, in all probability, an apocryphal addition to the fact of his banishment. But although the banishment of John to Patmos is to be assumed as an authenticated fact, yet there is a diversity of opinion as to the time when it occurred, and as to the emperor by whom he was banished. Epiphanius said that it took place in the reign of Claudius; Theophylact, in the reign of Nero; and Irenæus, Clemens Alexandrinus, Victorinus, and Eusebius, in the reign of Domitian. The best attested opinion is that it occurred during the persecution under Domitian; and that on the death of that emperor and the succession of Nerva (A.D. 96), John was recalled from banishment. Thus Eusebius observes: "It was then (on the succession of Nerva) that the Apostle John returned from his banishment in Patmos, and took up his abode

---

[1] *De Præscript. Hær.* chap. xxxvi. See Lipsius' *Die Apokryphen Apostelgeschichten*, vol. i. p. 419.

at Ephesus, according to an ancient tradition of the Church."[1]

The other authentic fact is the apostle's residence in Ephesus. That John resided in Asia is implied in the Apocalypse. That writing is addressed to the seven churches which are in Asia (Rev. i. 11), thus implying that the apostle had some peculiar interest in or oversight of these churches, which is accounted for by assuming his residence in Ephesus. The testimony of the Fathers to this fact is so early, uniform, and constant, that it cannot be reasonably doubted. It is attested by Irenæus (A.D. 180), who is only removed by one degree from John.[2] "The Church of Ephesus," he observes, "founded by Paul, and having John remaining among them permanently until the time of Trajan, is a true witness of the tradition of the apostles."[3] And again: "John, the disciple of the Lord, who also had leaned upon His breast, did himself publish a Gospel during his residence at Ephesus."[4] Polycrates (A.D. 190), who was himself bishop of Ephesus toward the close of the second century, informs us that John was buried in that city.[5] Clemens Alexandrinus (A.D. 190) says: "After the tyrant (Domitian) was dead, John, coming from the island of Patmos to Ephesus, went also when called to the neighbouring regions of the Gentiles, in some to appoint bishops, in some to institute entire new churches, in others to appoint to the ministry those that were set apart by the Holy Ghost."[6] Apollonius (A.D. 200) relates that a dead man was raised by John at Ephesus.[7] And Origen (A.D. 230) says that John received Asia as his allotted region, where, after continuing for some time, he died at Ephesus.[8] It is thus the uniform testimony of the Fathers that John spent the last years of his life at Ephesus. It is evident that John did not come to Ephesus until after the death of Paul; for in Paul's Second Epistle to Timothy, written immediately before his martyrdom and sent to Ephesus, there is no allusion to John's presence

---

[1] *Hist. Eccl.* iii. 20.
[2] Irenæus was the disciple of Polycarp, and Polycarp the disciple of John.
[3] *Adv. Hær.* iii. 3. 4. [4] *Ibid.* iii. 1. 1. [5] Eusebius, *Hist. Eccl.* v. 24.
[6] *Ibid.* iii. 23. [7] *Ibid.* v. 18. [8] *Ibid.* iii. 1.

in that city. Probably it was not until after the destruction of Jerusalem that John fixed his permanent abode in the capital of Proconsular Asia.

Ecclesiastical history informs us that John lived to a great age, which must have been the case if he was banished to Patmos in the reign of Domitian, and released in the reign of Nerva (A.D. 96). It is stated by the Fathers that he continued until the reign of Trajan, who ascended the imperial throne A.D. 98. He was probably younger than our Lord, so that there is no reason to adopt the statement of Jerome, that he was a hundred years old when he died. He did not, like Peter and Paul, suffer martyrdom, but died a natural death.

The legends regarding John are numerous, some of them invested with an appearance of probability.[1] There are three which are remarkable for their simplicity, and their agreement with the character of John. One is the encounter with Cerinthus, mentioned by Irenæus. "There are," observes Irenæus, "those who heard from Polycarp that John, the disciple of the Lord, going to bathe at Ephesus, and perceiving Cerinthus within, rushed out of the bath-house without bathing, exclaiming, Let us fly, lest even the bath-house fall down because Cerinthus, the enemy of the truth, is within."[2] The testimony of Irenæus is of considerable weight, and there is nothing improbable in the account;[3] the incident reminds us of the temper of the same apostle, who wished to call down fire from heaven to consume the Samaritans. John's love to Christ would not suffer the honour of his Master to be attacked with impunity.[4] Another legend is the well-

---

[1] For a full account of the legends connected with St. John, the reader is directed to that exhaustive work of Lipsius, *Die Apokryphen Apostelgeschichten*, vol. i. pp. 348-542.

[2] *Adv. Hær.* iii. 3. 4. See also Eusebius, *Hist. Eccl.* iii. 28, iv. 14. Nicephorus, *Hist. Eccl.* iii. 30; and for a discussion upon it, Lipsius, *Die Apokryphen Apostelgeschichten*, vol. i. p. 348 f. Stanley's *Sermons on the Apostolic Age*, pp. 270-272.

[3] It is also to be observed that Irenæus gives it on the authority of Polycarp, the disciple of John.

[4] Dean Stanley observes, that we have here "a living exemplification of the possibility of uniting the deepest love and gentleness with the sternest denunciation of moral evil."

known story of John and the robber, recorded by Clemens Alexandrinus, and preserved for us in the history of Eusebius.[1] The narrative is too long for insertion, but it certainly bears impressed upon it the loving spirit of the aged apostle. According to the narrative, John had committed the care of a young man, in whom he was particularly interested, to the local bishop. The young man fell away, and, proceeding from bad to worse, at length became the captain of a band of robbers. John, on his next visit, addressed the bishop, "Return me my deposit which I and Christ committed to thee in the presence of the Church over which thou dost preside." He then learned the sad truth; and the aged apostle rode off to the haunts of the robbers, discovered the young man, and with tears and entreaties prevailed upon him to return with him, and restored him to the Church.[2] And the third legend is the affecting narrative recorded by Jerome.[3] "The apostle John," he observes, "tarried at Ephesus to an extreme old age, and could only be carried into the church in the arms of his disciples. He was unable to address them at length, but was accustomed to stretch forth his hands to his disciples and to exclaim, Little children, love one another. At length his hearers, being wearied with hearing him always repeat the same words, asked him, Master, why dost thou always speak thus? His reply was: It is the Lord's command, and if only this be done it is enough."

III. THE READERS OF THE EPISTLE.

Before discussing this subject a preliminary question requires to be answered, Whether this writing of John be an epistle at all? Many suppose it to be a treatise. Its form is not that of an epistle; it does not commence with an address to the readers, like the Epistles of Paul and the other Catholic Epistles; nor does it close with any individual references or salutations, such as are to be found even in the

---

[1] *Hist. Eccl.* iii. 23.
[2] See Lipsius, *Die Apokryphen Apostelgeschichten*, p. 349. Farrar's *Early Days of Christianity*, pp. 169-172. Stanley's *Sermons on the Apostolic Age*, p. 268 f.
[3] Jerome, *Comment. ad Gal.* vi. 10.

didactic Epistle to the Hebrews. This opinion, that it is a treatise and not an epistle, was first advanced by Heidegger, who observes: "This book, though it seems to bear the stamp of an epistle, may rather be regarded as a short epitome of Christian doctrine, to which have been added certain exhortations appropriate to the general state of the Christian Church."[1] A similar opinion, in different forms, has been adopted by Bengel, Michaelis, Eichhorn, Bishop Horsley, Reuss, and Westcott. Bengel calls the writing "a libellus rather than an Epistle." Michaelis terms it a treatise, and observes: "The name *Epistle* is improperly applied to it, since it has nothing which entitles it to this appellation. It does not begin with the salutation which is used in Greek Epistles, and with which John himself begins his last two Epistles; nor does it contain any salutations, although they are found in almost all the Epistles of the apostles. I consider, therefore, that which is commonly called the First Epistle of John as a book or treatise, in which the apostle declared to the whole world his disapprobation of the doctrines maintained by Cerinthus and the Gnostics."[2] Bishop Horsley says, "This Epistle is a didactic discourse on the principles of Christianity, both in doctrine and practice."[3] Reuss observes: "It is less an epistle than any other book in the New Testament, more properly a homiletical essay, at the most a pastoral letter, the readers being supposed to be present. All that belongs to the form of a letter from a distance is lacking, both at the beginning and end."[4] And Professor Westcott, in his commentary on the Epistles of St. John, uses language similar to that of Reuss: "We can best look at the writing, not as a letter called out by any particular circumstances, but as a Pastoral addressed to those who had been carefully trained, and had lived long in the faith; and, more particularly, to those who were familiar either with the teaching contained in the Fourth Gospel or with the record itself."[5]

[1] *Enchir. Bibl.* p. 986.
[2] *Introduction to the N. T.*, vol. vi. pp. 400, 401.
[3] *Works*, vol. i. p. 113. He observes that "in the composition of it, narrowly inspected, nothing is to be found of the epistolary form."
[4] *Geschichte der heil. Schriften N. T.*, p. 226 [E. Tr. p. 236].
[5] *The Epistles of St. John*, Introduction, p. 30.

Now it must be admitted that the external form of the writing is not that of an epistle. But although it has not the form, yet it has the substance of an epistle. It may be called a Pastoral, but it is a pastoral addressed to certain churches, and with direct reference to their peculiar circumstances.[1] All the early Fathers—Irenæus, Tertullian, Clemens Alexandrinus, Origen, and Cyprian—regarded it as an epistle. It abounds with direct practical addresses, all pointing to its epistolary character; thus, "I write unto you" occurs seven times; "I have written unto you," six times; and there are frequent repetitions of direct forms of address, as "little children," "young men," "fathers," "beloved." There are also references to certain forms of heresy into which those addressed were liable to fall. All which circumstances prove that it is an epistle written to a definite circle of readers. It may with propriety be termed a *circular epistle*—ἐπιστολὴ ἐγκυκλιή, as Oecumenius calls it—addressed to the Asiatic Churches. "The writer," observes Düsterdieck, "is acquainted with all the peculiar errors and temptations which threaten the spiritual life of his readers. The epistolary character is impressed upon it. With all its regularity there prevails throughout a certain easy naturalness and unforced simplicity of composition and representation which harmonize best with the immediate practical interest and tendency of an epistle."[2]

Some suppose that this Epistle is addressed to the Parthians. This opinion probably had its origin in a statement of Augustine, who styles it "the Epistle of John to the Parthians."[3] In this he has been followed by several Latin Fathers. It is so called by Vigilius Tapsensis in the fifth century; by Cassiodorus (A.D. 515), who applies the title to the three Epistles of John;[4] and by the Venerable Bede, who observes that "many ecclesiastical writers, and among them Athanasius, bishop of Alexandria, witness that the First Epistle of John was

---

[1] Eichhorn's *Einleitung*, vol. ii. p. 307.

[2] Düsterdieck, *Die drei johanneischen Briefe*, pp. 10, 11. See also Credner's *Einleitung*, p. 678. Weiss' *Einleitung*, p. 452.

[3] *Quæst. Evang.* ii. 39, where we read: "secundum sententiam hanc etiam illud est quod dictum est a Joanne in epistola ad Parthos."

[4] Cassiodorus, *De Institut. divin. Script.* c. 14, *Opera*, p. 459.

written to the Parthians."[1] Several manuscripts of the Vulgate have the same title in the superscription, and one Greek manuscript[2] of the Second Epistle has the subscription Ἰωάννου β. πρὸς Πάρθους. This opinion has been adopted in modern times by Grotius, Paulus, and Schulthess. It is undoubtedly an error which arose from the deference given by the early Church to the authority of Augustine. There is no mention in ecclesiastical history of John's mission to the Parthians, and no ground for the above opinion. Various suppositions have been formed as to the origin of the mistake. Hug supposes that the error originated from the Second Epistle of John being called in several manuscripts "the Epistle to the Virgins" (πρὸς παρθένους), and that this address, by the omission of two letters, was written in some manuscripts πρὸς πάρθους—"to the Parthians," a title which, as we have seen, actually occurs in a manuscript in the subscription of the Second Epistle.[3] Gieseler supposes that the mistake arose from the name παρθένος which was given to John himself, and which occurs in the superscription of a manuscript of the Apocalypse. "The Latins," he observes, "misunderstanding it, made out of it *Epistolam ad Parthos*."[4] Mangold, following Wegscheider, thinks that the Epistle, as being encyclical, had the title πρὸς τοὺς διασπαρσαμένους rendered in Latin *ad dispersos* or *ad sparsos*, which, being misunderstood, was changed into *ad Parthos*."[5] And Michaelis, with less probability, supposes that the frequent use in the Epistle of the terms "light" and "darkness," which occur in the Persian philosophy, gave rise to the opinion that John wrote it with the view of correcting the abuses of that philosophy, from which it was inferred that he designed it for the use of Christians in the Parthian empire.[6]

There are other suppositions which are equally groundless. Benson and Macknight suppose that this Epistle was chiefly

[1] There is no mention of this in the extant writings of Athanasius, and probably Bede mistook this Father for Origen.
[2] Codex 62 of Griesbach, cent. xii.
[3] *Introduction to the N. T.*, vol. ii. [E. Tr. p. 255].
[4] *Ecclesiastical History*, vol. i. p. 106.
[5] *Einleitung*, p. 770.
[6] *Introduction to the N. T.*, vol. vi. pp. 399, 400.

intended for the Jewish Christians in Judea and the neighbouring countries. The reason they give for this opinion is because the apostle says "that Christ is the propitiation not only for our sins (the sins of us Jews), but likewise for the sins of the whole world" (1 John ii. 2).[1] But the distinction here is not between Jews and Gentles, but between Christians and non-Christians; nor is there the slightest reference in the Epistle to Jewish Christianity. Dr. John Lightfoot thinks that it was written to the Church of Corinth, because in the Third Epistle, which was addressed to Gaius, the apostle says: "I wrote unto the Church, but Diotrephes, who loveth to have the pre-eminence among them, received us not" (3 John 9). He supposes that the apostle, in the words "I wrote unto the Church," alludes to his First Epistle, and, as one Gaius was a prominent member in the Corinthian Church (Acts xix. 29; 1 Cor. i. 14), he infers that the Epistle was addressed to it.[2] But evidently this is too slight a ground on which to build such a hypothesis, especially as the name Gaius or Caius was one of the most common among the Romans. Hug supposes that the Epistle was written from Patmos, and addressed to the Church of Ephesus.[3] He draws a comparison between it and the Epistle to the Ephesian Church in the Apocalypse; but the resemblance between these two Epistles is too vague to found an argument on.

We consider, then, that the Epistle was catholic in its destination. It was addressed to no particular Church, but to the circle of the Churches belonging to Proconsular Asia, in the centre of which was Ephesus, where John, during the last years of his life, chiefly resided. As the Apocalypse was addressed to the seven principal Churches of Asia, so in all probability this Epistle was similarly addressed.

The Church in Proconsular Asia was chiefly composed of Gentile Christians. There is no reference in this Epistle to Jewish Christianity, and no quotations from the Old Testament. The readers are specially warned against idolatry

---

[1] Macknight's *Translation of the Epistles:* Preface to 1 John, sec. 5.
[2] Lightfoot's *Works*, edited by Pitman, vol. iii. p. 330.
[3] Hug's *Introduction to N. T.*, vol. ii. p. 254.

(1 John v. 21), and against those heresies which arose from the contact of Christianity with heathen modes of thought. Nor is there any mention of persecution in the Epistle; the Church appears to have been in a state of external peace; the Neronian persecution, and perhaps also that of Domitian, were past, and that of Trajan had not yet commenced.[1] But although externally in a state of peace, yet internally the Church was perturbed by heresy; the danger came not from without, but from within. Those teachers "speaking perverse things," against whom Paul had warned the Ephesian elders, were risen up, "seeking to draw away disciples after them" (Acts xx. 30). The apostolic Church was by no means free from heresies; even in the lifetime of the apostles there were men who taught false doctrines, and who were not restrained even by apostolic authority; and this was especially the case in the Churches of Proconsular Asia, where Oriental and Greek philosophy of a Gnostic character was so prevalent. It is also to be observed, that the contest between Jewish and Gentile Christians had by this time passed away. There is no allusion in the Epistle to those Judaizing teachers who dogged the footsteps of Paul; no mention of the necessity of circumcision and other Jewish rites; no need of defending the great doctrine of justification by faith against Pharisaical legalism. The destruction of Jerusalem had put an effectual termination to all these controversies; and the Judaizing Christians had either renounced their errors, or constituted themselves into the sects of the Ebionites and the Nazarenes. Heresy had changed its form, and had entered upon a new departure; it was no longer the ground of our justification,[2] but the nature of the Person of Christ which was the object of controversy. It is also implied in the Epistle that its readers had been for a considerable time Christians, and that they were well instructed in the doctrines and duties of Christianity.

[1] There is no record of any persecution in the reign of Nerva.
[2] The controversy regarding justification subsided; but it is not meant that the primitive Church fully grasped the Pauline theology. See Ritschl, *Alt. Kath. Kirche.* The recently discovered Didache is not Pauline, but Jacobean in its sentiments.

IV. THE DESIGN AND CONTENTS OF THE EPISTLE.

It is supposed by many that this Epistle was written with a designed reference to the Fourth Gospel. Some think that it was a preface or introduction to that Gospel; others, that it was a supplement or a postscript; others, that it was a companion-document; and others, that it was a comment or dissertation on the Gospel. This opinion, in its different forms, has been maintained by Storr, Hug, Ebrard, Haupt, Bishop Alexander, Bishop Lightfoot, Plummer, and Westcott. Storr calls it "the second part or supplement of the Gospel."[1] Hug speaks of it as a supplement or concomitant to the Gospel.[2] Ebrard observes: "An attentive observation will lead to the assumption that the two documents—the Gospel and the Epistle—were strictly simultaneous; and in this case the Epistle must be considered as a companion-document to the Gospel, as it were an epistle dedicatory."[3] Haupt calls it "a postscript to the Gospel."[4] Bishop Alexander, in his exposition in the *Speaker's Commentary*, observes: "The Epistle has been looked upon as an encyclical letter accompanying the Gospel. Whether we are to look upon it as this, as a postscript, or as a preface to the Gospel, may be rather a question of words. Bishop Lightfoot, however, shows with unrivalled clearness the reasons for considering it practically a postscript."[5] Plummer, in his recent commentary (1883), says: "The Epistle appears to have been intended as a *companion to the Gospel*. . . . It is nearer the truth to speak of it as a comment on the Gospel, a sermon with the Gospel for its text. References to the Gospel are scattered thickly over the whole Epistle."[6] It has also been observed, that the Muratorian Canon favours this opinion; for in that catalogue the First Epistle of John is detached from the other Catholic Epistles, and follows immediately the Gospel of John.

---

[1] Storr, *über den Zweck der evangelischen Geschichte und Briefe Johannis*, p. 383 ff.
[2] *Introduction to N. T.*, vol. ii. p. 249.
[3] *Commentary on John's Epistles*, p. 25.
[4] *On the First Epistle of John*, p. 374.
[5] *Speaker's Commentary: N. T.*, vol. iv. p. 292.
[6] Plummer's *Commentary*, p. 34.

But although the relation between the Gospel and the Epistle is so close as to render it probable that both were composed about the same time, yet it cannot be proved that the Epistle was written with a designed reference to the Gospel. Both documents are complete in themselves.[1] The Gospel is introduced by a preface of its own (John i. 1–5), and the last chapter may be regarded as a supplement (John xxi.); while the Epistle has also its own introduction (1 John i. 1–4) and its definite conclusion (1 John v. 21). Although in the Epistle there are many references to the Gospel which demonstrate the unity of authorship, yet these references are incidental and not direct; nor is there anything which would lead to the conclusion that it was written as a companion-document to the Gospel. Besides, when these two works are compared, it will be seen that there is a certain difference in the circumstances under which they were composed. The teaching of heretics was more pronounced when John wrote his Epistle, and hence he was led to warn his disciples against them. The polemical element, hardly discernible in the Gospel, is stronger in the Epistle. There are warnings against antichrists, showing that new dangers had arisen, or at least that the evils within the Church had increased since John wrote his Gospel.[2]

The general design of the Epistle is stated both at its commencement and at its close. The Epistle begins with the words: "That which we have seen and heard declare we unto you, that ye also may have fellowship with us; and truly our fellowship is with the Father, and with His Son Jesus Christ. And these things we write unto you, that your joy may be full" (1 John i. 3, 4). And towards the close we read: "These things have I written unto you that believe on the name of the Son of God, that ye may know that ye have eternal life, and that ye may believe on the name of the Son of God" (1 John v. 13). It is to be observed that the design of the Gospel is stated in similar terms: "These things are written, that ye might

---

[1] "We observe," remarks Ewald, "from the style of the Epistle that it was written in an entirely different period, and in complete independence of the Gospel." *History of Israel*, vol. viii. p. 163 E. Tr.

[2] See *infra* on the priority of the Gospel to the Epistle.

believe that Jesus is the Christ, the Son of God; and that believing, ye might have life through His name" (John xx. 31). The difference between these two writings is that the Gospel was written with a special design to promote faith in Christ, whilst the Epistle was written to those who had already believed on Christ, with a view to confirm them in the faith, and to promote their religious life.

There is evidently a polemical design in the Epistle: it was written for the purpose of denouncing certain heretics and warning the readers against them—of refuting error and confirming believers in the belief that Jesus is the Christ, the Son of God. "Beloved, believe not every spirit, but try the spirits whether they are of God; because many false prophets are gone out into the world. Hereby know ye the Spirit of God: Every spirit that confesseth that Jesus Christ is come in the flesh is of God; and every spirit that confesseth not that Jesus Christ is come in the flesh is not of God; and this is that spirit of antichrist, whereof ye have heard that it should come; and even now already is it in the world" (1 John iv. 1–3). Tertullian observes: "In his Epistle John specially designates those as antichrists who denied that Christ came in the flesh, and who refused to think that Jesus was the Son of God. The one dogma Marcion maintains; the other Ebion."[1] Various heretical sects have been fixed upon as those whom John opposes in his Epistle. Michaelis thinks that John combats the Gnostics in general; De Wette, Lücke, Credner, Schmidt, Mangold, Reuss, Hausrath, and Holtzmann suppose that the Docetæ are particularly alluded to; Schleiermacher, Neander, Düsterdieck, Ebrard, Haupt, and Weiss, the Cerinthians; Macknight and Lünemann, the Nicolaitanes; Storr and Keil, the disciples of John the Baptist, afterwards called the Sabeans; Hilgenfeld, the Valentinians; Pfleiderer, the followers of Basilides; Semler, the Judaizers; Eichhorn and Lange, those who apostatized from Christianity to Judaism; and Paulus, the Persian doctrine.

We evidently see in the description of the heretical teachers the germs of that heresy which in the next century was developed into the various forms of Gnosticism, and

[1] Tertullian, *De Præscrip. Hær.* chap. xxxiii.

which so greatly disturbed and corrupted the Christian Church; so that what is here opposed is incipient Gnosticism.[1] The particular form of error mentioned in the Epistle, is that of those who "denied that Jesus Christ came in the flesh," which was the fundamental error of Docetism. But Docetism was not the name of a particular heresy, but an element which entered into most of the Gnostic systems;[2] it was not developed until the middle of the second century, and it here appears only in a crude and imperfect state. Some, with much probability, suppose that the opinions of Cerinthus are specially alluded to; as, according to the testimony of the Fathers, John encountered Cerinthus at Ephesus. His tenets were an imperfect and undeveloped Docetism. According to him, Jesus was a mere man, the earthly Messiah, on whom the Christ, the heavenly Messiah, descended at His baptism, but withdrew at His crucifixion.[3]

The polemical element, however, forms a small portion of the Epistle; its aim is less the confutation of error than edification. Its leading purpose was to promote fellowship with God and with His Son Jesus Christ among believers, to confirm them in the faith, to increase within them the grace of love, in order that their joy might be full; in short, to bring Christians into a living union with Christ as the source of life and light and love (1 John i. 3). The fundamental principle on which it proceeds is that there is an antagonism between Christ and the world (ὁ κόσμος). Those who belong to the world are the children of the devil, the prince of darkness; those who believe in Jesus Christ as the Son of God are born of God and have fellowship with God. The world is the rival of God: "If any man love the world, the love of the Father is not in him." And by the world John evidently means the present world—its lusts, its allurements, its principles, involved as it then was in the darkness of heathenism and in the pollutions of idolatry: "The whole world lieth in wickedness." And it is this contrast between Christ and the world, between light and darkness, between

---

[1] See dissertation, Gnosticism as referred to in John's Epistle.
[2] The Gnostics in general denied that the Christ came in the flesh.
[3] Irenæus, *Adv. Hær.* i. 26.

those who love God and those who do not love God, that pervades the Epistle (1 John ii. 15–17, iv. 4, v. 4, 5, 19).[1]

Very different opinions have been formed concerning the arrangement of the Epistle. According to some, the apostle has no regular plan; he gives a few detached sentences springing from the fulness of his love, but without connection, without method; a series of detached aphorisms. Thus Calvin says: "John at one time admonishes us to lead a pious and holy life, and at another time he expressly enjoins love. But he does none of those things in a regular order; for he everywhere mixes teaching with exhortation."[2] Reuss remarks: "We have not been able to discover any premeditated order in this Epistle. Its utterances are dictated on the one hand by personal relations, and on the other by strongly marked religious feelings; but reflection and method are not called into play."[3] And Holtzmann observes: "Exegetes have failed to trace any consecutive train of thought, any plan or arrangement in the shapeless mass, at least one that has satisfied any but its discoverer."[4] According to others, the apostle wrote according to a definite plan, though it is acknowledged that this plan is often difficult to trace; and they differ widely as to the nature of that plan and the arrangement of the Epistle. Bengel bases his arrangement on 1 John v. 7, and considers this verse as the key to the Epistle. According to him, chap. i. treats of fellowship with the Father, chap. ii. iii. of fellowship with the Son, chap. iv. of the confirmation and fruit of abiding in the Son by the Spirit, and chap. v. is a comprehensive statement of the testimony of the Father and Son and Spirit.[5] Lücke supposes that the whole Epistle is a development of the thought that the ground of all Christian fellowship is the fellowship which each individual believer has with the Father and the Son, unfolding

---

[1] On the antagonism between God and the world as developed in the Epistle, see Lücke's *Commentary*, p. 63 f., and Weiss' *Biblical Theology of the N. T.*, vol. ii. p. 393.

[2] *Preface to 1 John.* Luther says: "The main substance of this Epistle is love; the apostle will teach faith against heretics, and love against the vicious."

[3] *History of Christian Theology in the Apostolic Age*, vol. ii. p. 338.

[4] *Einleitung*, p. 462.   [5] *Gnomon*: comment on 1 John v. 7.

itself in fellowship with the brethren.[1] Düsterdieck supposes that the theme of the Epistle is fellowship with God the Father and the Lord Jesus Christ. He arranges it into two great divisions: the first, that God is light (i. 5–ii. 28); and the second, that God is righteous (ii. 29–v. 5); on which follows the conclusion (v. 6–21).[2] This is modified by Farrar, who arranges it into three sections, and finds at the commencement of each of these sections the three keynotes of the Epistle: "God is light" (i. 5), "God is righteous" (ii. 28), "God is love" (iv. 7).[3] Huther divides the Epistle into four sections: in the first section the apostle attacks the moral indifference which endangers his readers (i. 5–ii. 11); in the second he warns them of the love of the world and of antichrist (ii. 12–28); in the third he shows that only a righteous life of brotherly love corresponds to the nature of the Christian (ii. 29–iii. 22); and in the fourth he points them to faith in Jesus Christ, the Son of God, as that which is testified by God to be the basis of the Christian life.[4] Plummer divides the Epistle into two sections, corresponding with the two propositions: "God is light" and "God is love." His arrangement, which is perhaps the best that can be made, is as follows—Introduction (i. 1–4). Division I.—God is Light, subdivided into two parts. (*a*) What walking in the light involves; the condition and conduct of the believer (i. 5–ii. 11). (*b*) What walking in the light excludes; the things and persons to be avoided (ii. 12–28). Division II.—God is Love, subdivided into two parts. (*a*) The evidence of sonship; deeds of righteousness before God (ii. 29–iii. 24). (*b*) The source of sonship; possession of the Spirit as shown by confession of the incarnation (iv. 1–v. 12). Conclusion of the Epistle (v. 13–21).[5] In reading the Epistle, and endeavouring to find out the train of thought, two points have to be attended to: the main design that the apostle had in view in writing, namely, to promote fellowship with the Father

---

[1] *Commentary*, pp. 46–54.

[2] *Johanneische Briefe*, vol. i. pp. 16–25. The arrangement of Düsterdieck is adopted by Alford.

[3] *Messages of the Book*, p. 486.

[4] *Commentary on 1 John*, p. 240, E. Tr.

[5] Plummer's *Commentary*, pp. 44, 45.

and the Son; and the antagonism which is presupposed between Christ and the world.

Contents.—The apostle commences by stating his object in writing, that his readers might have fellowship with him in his fellowship with the Father and the Son; and that in this manner their joy might be full. God is light, and therefore to have fellowship with God we must walk in the light; we must cultivate holiness of life and purity of character; we must confess our sins, in order to their forgiveness through Jesus Christ our Lord (chap. i.). As there can be no fellowship between God and sin, we must render a ready obedience to His commands; and especially to that new commandment of love to the brethren which Christ taught His disciples. He that does not love his brother is not in the light, but in darkness; whereas he that loveth his brother abideth in the light. The world is our great antagonist; those who belong to it are out of fellowship with God; they are of the antichristian party; but believers have an anointing from the Holy One which preserves them from seducers, and enables them to abide in God. God is righteous, and only they who do righteousness are born of God (chap. ii.). God is love, and hence to have fellowship with God we must walk in love. The love of God is manifest in our sonship; those who commit sin are the children of the devil; those who follow after righteousness are the children of God. Hatred is of the devil; love is of God; we can thus judge from the presence or absence of love with whom we have fellowship (chap. iii.). We must cultivate the spirit of truth and avoid the spirit of error, and thus we shall walk in the light. Love especially is of God; light and love must ever be combined. The love of God is seen in sending His Son to be a propitiation for our sins; and if God thus loved us we ought to love one another (chap. iv.). He that loveth God must love the children of God, and keep His commandments. The source of this love is faith, and by this only can we overcome the world and obtain eternal life. The apostle then concludes his Epistle by repeating his design in writing it, by announcing the antagonism between God and the world, and by cautioning his readers against idolatry (chap. v.).

The style of the Epistle is peculiar. It is aphoristic—short statements are made expressing important truths; and antithetic—in general, the proposition is stated both positively and negatively, as "God is light, and in Him is no darkness at all." John is a realist. Light and Darkness, Truth and Falsehood, Love and Hatred are brought forward as having a concrete real existence; they are, so to speak, incarnated and personified, and hence a certain degree of mysticism pervades the Epistle. The apostle treats, not so much of the active life of the Christian, as of his inner life, —a life of fellowship with God. Hence also the logical connection between the different sentences is slight; there is hardly any attempt at reasoning; the appeal is to the heart rather than to the understanding. Connecting particles are very sparingly used. There is undoubtedly a certain repetition of the same thoughts for the sake of emphasis. That God is Light and that God is Love are the two pivots round which the thoughts of the apostle revolve. God is Light, and hence he that sinneth walketh in darkness. God is Love, and hence he that loveth not his brother is out of fellowship with God.

Love is the keynote of the Epistle. John is pre-eminently the apostle of love, as Paul is of faith, Peter of hope, and James of works. Love is the spirit which breathes in every section,—love to God, and, resulting from that, love to men. We can only have fellowship with God if we walk in love, for God is love. And this love is founded on redemption; it is not a mere natural feeling, but arises from union with Christ, and has its origin in regeneration. And so also the love of Christ toward us, in surrendering His life for us, is the model of our love to the brethren. Faith and love are here, as elsewhere in Scripture, inseparably conjoined. Nor is this love, which John inculcates, a weak sentimental benevolence, it is combined with sternness against that which is evil. The very love which animates the Christian manifests itself in a hatred of evil, the light excludes the darkness. Such was the love of Christ Himself, which, whilst it caused Him to sacrifice His life for us, yet manifested itself in the severest invectives against the Pharisees. Combined, then, with intense love, there is a certain tone of severity in the Epistle. In short, there is a spirituality, a purity, a heavenly repose about the Epistle which stamps it as having been written under the inspiration of the Spirit of God; it is a disclosure of the heart of the beloved disciple, the nearest approach to the heart of the Saviour. "It appears," says Ewald, "to be the tone, not so much of a father talking with his beloved children, as of a glorified saint speaking to mankind from a higher world. Never in any writing has the doctrine of heavenly love, of a love working in stillness, a love ever unwearied, never exhausted, so thoroughly proved and approved itself as in this Epistle."[1]

Although there is an apparent simplicity in the thoughts and statements of this Epistle which endears it to the most simple reader who is possessed of a spiritual mind, yet there is a real depth. Perhaps in no writer of the New Testament is there so much spiritual insight, such a profundity of thought and deep comprehension of the genius of Christianity, and hence John has been designated "the apostle of the Church of the future." "This Epistle appears," says Düsterdieck, "to the simplest reader, if only his heart has an experience of the Christian salvation, immediately intelligible, while to the most profound Christian thinker it is unfathomable. To both it is equally dear and stimulating."[2] It is not improbable that this Epistle was the latest book of Scripture, and that with it the volume of inspiration closed. An Epistle of love, inspired by the God of love, is a fit and blessed conclusion to the words of eternal life.[3]

V. TIME AND PLACE OF WRITING.

There is a variety of opinion regarding the time when John wrote this Epistle. Some suppose that it was written

[1] Quoted by Alford, *Greek Testament*, Prolegomena, vol. iv. p. 179. See also Ewald's *History of Israel*, vol. viii. p. 168.

[2] *Johanneische Schriften*, vol. i. p. 31.

[3] John's three writings—the Gospel, the Epistles, and the Apocalypse—have been compared. The Gospel exhibits Christ as in the world, the Epistle as in the heart, and the Apocalypse as in heaven. The Gospel sets forth the divine life as it is seen in the person of Christ, the Epistle as it is seen in the indi-

before the destruction of Jerusalem. This opinion was adopted by Grotius, Whitby, Benson, Hammond, Macknight Michaelis, and recently by Düsterdieck.[1] They ground this opinion on various expressions in the Epistle, and on the supposition that if written after the fall of Jerusalem such a momentous occurrence would have been alluded to in the Epistle. Thus John says, "We know that it is the last time" (1 John ii. 18), which expression they refer to the impending destruction of Jerusalem. But this phrase does not necessarily allude to that event, but either to the gospel dispensation as being the last dispensation of religion, or to the second advent of Christ. Again, it is argued that the words, "Ye have known Him that is from the beginning" (1 John ii. 13), apply better to the disciples before Jerusalem was destroyed than to a later age, when few who knew Christ from the commencement of His ministry could have been alive.[2] But this argument is founded on a misapprehension of the meaning of the apostle; he does not allude to Christ's ministry, but to His eternal existence as being from the beginning of creation. And as to the apostle not alluding to the destruction of Jerusalem, there was no necessity that he should do so, as he was writing to the Asiatic Churches, who were not directly concerned in that catastrophe, and as probably the Epistle was written twenty years after that occurrence, when time had already lessened its comparative importance.

On the other hand, there are various indications from which it may be inferred that the Epistle was written at a late period of the apostolic age. There is no allusion to persecution; the Church was in a state of outward peace; hence in all probability it was written after the Neronian persecution, when under the beneficent rule of Vespasian and Titus the Church enjoyed repose, or even after the persecution under Domitian. The heretical views alluded to show a stage of

vidual Christian, and the Apocalypse as it is seen in the Church. In the Gospel we have a summary of Christian theology, in the Epistle a summary of Christian ethics, in the Apocalypse a summary of Christian politics.

[1] *Johanneische Schriften*, vol. i. p. 101 ff.
[2] Macknight, *Translation of the Epistles:* Preface to 1 John.

development of Gnosticism more advanced than that which appears in the Epistles of Paul. The Epistle bears internal marks that it was written by an aged man; it is the outpouring of the love of an aged saint toward his beloved children. John is writing as an old man to a younger generation. And further, as already observed, the Church had advanced to that stage in her history when the contest between Jewish and Gentile Christians had ceased. Accordingly, by far the greater number of critics have assigned a late date to this Epistle. And as, according to the universal tradition of the Church, John lived to a great age, even to the reign of Trajan (A.D. 98), we may not be far wrong in fixing, with Ebrard, the time of composition at A.D. 94, or even later.

It is still a matter of dispute whether the Gospel or the Epistle was first composed. Michaelis, Bleek, Brückner, Huther, and Weiss favour the priority of the Epistle; Lücke, Ewald, Ebrard, and Haupt, the priority of the Gospel. An argument has been drawn from a comparison of John xx. 31, where it is written, "These things are written that ye might believe," with 1 John v. 13, "These things have I written unto you that believe," in favour of the priority of the Gospel; but such an argument cannot be pressed. A better reason may be assigned from the fact that from the Epistle there appears to be a further development or a fresh outbreak of heretical opinions.

As regards the place of composition, some fix on Patmos and others on Ephesus. Hug, Ebrard, and Haupt suppose that the Apocalypse, the Gospel, and the Epistle of John were all composed about the same time; and hence Patmos, where the Apocalypse was composed, is regarded by them as the place of composition. There is no reason for this supposition; ancient tradition fixes on Ephesus as the place where the Gospel was composed; and as there is reason to believe that the Epistle was written not long after, it also was probably composed in that city. The ancient tradition of the Church is in all probability true, that John spent the last twenty years of his life in Ephesus as his usual residence, and from this city proceeded the Gospel and the Epistle, the precious legacy of the beloved disciple to the Church.

The most important commentaries on this Epistle are those of Lücke (Bonn 1836; translated, Edinburgh 1837), Neander (Berlin 1851; translated, New York 1853), Düsterdieck (Göttingen 1852), Huther (Göttingen 1855; 4th Auflage, 1880; translated, Edinburgh 1882), F. D. Maurice (Cambridge 1857), Ebrard (Königsberg 1859; translated, Edinburgh 1880), Braune (Lange's *Bibelwerk*, 1862; translated, New York 1867), Haupt (Colberg 1870; translated, Edinburgh 1879), Bishop Alexander (*Speaker's Commentary*, 1881), Wolf (Leipzig 1881); Sinclair (in the *New Testament Commentary*, edited by Bishop Ellicott), Plummer (in the Cambridge series, 1883), Pope (Schaff's *Popular Commentary*, 1883), Westcott (London 1883), Lias (London 1887).

DISSERTATION I.

THE HEAVENLY WITNESSES.[1]

There are two disputed passages in the First Epistle of John. The one is 1 John ii. 23, where the last clause, "He that confesseth the Son hath the Father also" (ὁ ὁμολογῶν τὸν υἱὸν καὶ τὸν πατέρα ἔχει), is printed in *italics* in the Authorized Version, thus intimating that its genuineness was considered doubtful. It is omitted in the *textus receptus*. This hesitation as to its reception has now been removed, and the clause is printed in Roman characters in the Revised Version, without any marginal note, indicating that its genuineness is attested by preponderating authority.[2] The other passage, the testimony of the heavenly witnesses, con-

---

[1] The principal authorities referred to in this dissertation are: Burgess' *Tracts on the Divinity of Christ;* Davidson's *Biblical Criticism;* Foster's *Three Heavenly Witnesses;* Porson's *Letters to Travis;* Michaelis' *Introduction to the N. T.*, by Marsh; Scrivener's *Introduction to the Criticism of the N. T.;* and Wiseman's *Two Letters on* 1 *John* v. 7.

[2] This clause is found in the Sinaitic, the Vatican, the Alexandrian MSS., and is retained by Lachmann, Tischendorf, Tregelles, and Westcott and Hort. The omission evidently arose from a homœoteleuton, the words τὸν πατέρα ἔχει occurring twice.

T

tained in 1 John v. 7, 8, is much more celebrated, and gave rise in the last century to a voluminous controversy.[1] The disputed words are: ἐν τῷ οὐρανῷ ὁ Πατὴρ ὁ Λόγος καὶ τὸ "Ἅγιον Πνεῦμα· καὶ οὗτοι οἱ τρεῖς ἕν εἰσι· καὶ τρεῖς εἰσιν οἱ μαρτυροῦντες ἐν τῇ γῇ (" in heaven the Father, the Word, and the Holy Ghost: and these three are one. And there are three that bear witness on earth "). In the Authorized Version there is no mark indicating the doubtfulness of these words; but in the Revised Version they are expunged, without any intimation that they were ever contained in the text. Nor is there here, as is generally the case with disputed passages, any reference to them in the margin, indicating that in the opinion of the Revisers no reasonable doubt can be entertained as to the propriety of their rejection. And certainly the passage in question is so weakly attested by external authorities, and so feebly supported by internal evidence, that its retention is no longer defensible. Recent critics and commentators of all shades of opinion, from the extreme of orthodoxy to the extreme of rationalism, have united in rejecting it, and hardly any scholar of note is now to be found among its defenders.[2] The great controversy regarding it, which in a former age gave rise to such a multitude of publications, which engaged the attention of illustrious scholars, and which was carried on with so much acrimony on both sides, has now come to a close; and the spuriousness of the passage has been demonstrated. It may be considered superfluous to reopen the question and to re-examine the reasons for its rejection, but this subject can hardly be omitted in an Introduction to the Catholic Epistles; and besides, the controversy is in itself highly instructive, casts light on so many points

---

[1] Tregelles, in his edition of Horne's *Introduction*, vol. iv. pp. 384-388, gives a curious list of more than fifty volumes, pamphlets, or critical notices on this question.

[2] The late Rev. Charles Forster, Rector of Stisted, Essex, published in 1867 a book entitled, *A New Plea for the Authenticity of the text of the Three Heavenly Witnesses;* but he fails entirely to meet the objections urged against that passage; indeed, how any scholar can now defend it, we cannot comprehend. In a former age manuscripts were not so carefully examined as they are now; and therefore it was not surprising that the passage should have been defended by such eminent scholars as Bengel, Horsley, and Burgess. For the opinion of Cardinal Wiseman, see *infra*.

connected with textual criticism, exemplifies the application of the principles of that science, and is interesting in showing in what manner a passage which, without doubt, is an interpolation, gained admission, first into the Latin, and then into the Greek text, and through that into all recognised national versions.

The external evidence, arising from manuscripts, ancient versions, and quotations from the Fathers in favour of this passage, is singularly weak. It is almost entirely awanting in manuscript attestation. It is omitted in the Sinaitic, the Vatican, the Alexandrian, and all the other uncial manuscripts. It is contained in none of the numerous cursive manuscripts previous to the fifteenth century, about 190 of which containing this Epistle have been examined. It has only been found in three or at the most in five manuscripts, and those of so recent a date as to be possessed of no authority. The most celebrated of these is Codex 34, or Codex Montfortianus or Dubliensis, now in the library of Trinity College, Dublin. This manuscript was formerly in the possession of Dr. Montfort of Cambridge, from whom it received its name; from him it passed into the hands of Archbishop Ussher, who presented it to the University of Dublin.[1] It is considered to be the same as the Codex Britannicus, on the authority of which Erasmus inserted the disputed words; because there is no other manuscript in the British Isles which contains the passage, and because the words inserted by Erasmus, found in no other manuscript, are the same as those contained in this. The text is as follows: ὅτι τρεῖς εἰσὶν οἱ μαρτυροῦντες ἐν τῷ οὐρανῷ πατὴρ λόγος καὶ πνεῦμα ἅγιον, καὶ οὗτοι οἱ τρεῖς ἕν εἰσι· Καὶ τρεῖς εἰσὶν οἱ μαρτυροῦντες ἐν τῇ γῇ πνεῦμα ὕδωρ καὶ αἷμα. The whole manuscript is Latinized, and this passage in particular is undoubtedly a translation from the Vulgate: it wants the article before the heavenly and earthly witnesses—there being no article in Latin; it places the adjective ἅγιον after πνεῦμα (spiritum sanctum), and it omits the clause καὶ οἱ τρεῖς εἰς τὸ ἓν εἰσίν at the end of ver. 8, —a clause contained in the Greek manuscripts, but wanting

---

[1] For the history of this MS. see Scrivener, *Introduction to the Criticism of the New Testament*, 1st edition, p. 149; 3rd edition, p. 187; and Marsh's *Michaelis*, vol. iii. p. 756 f.

in several of the most recent manuscripts of the Vulgate. Indeed, Porson insinuates that the manuscript was interpolated in this place for the purpose of deceiving Erasmus; a supposition which Scrivener appears to think not improbable, as the leaf on which it is written is the only one which is glazed, as if to protect it from harm.[1] Dr. Adam Clarke supposes that the manuscript was written in the thirteenth century, but all our best critics assign it to the fifteenth or sixteenth century.[2] A second manuscript, containing the passage, is Codex 162, or Codex Ottobonianus, a Greek and Latin copy of the Acts and the Pauline and Catholic Epistles, now in the Vatican. Here also the passage is an evident translation from the Vulgate, as it wants the article before the heavenly witnesses. It differs from all manuscripts in having ἀπὸ τοῦ οὐρανοῦ instead of ἐν τῷ οὐρανῷ, and ἀπὸ τῆς γῆς instead of ἐν τῇ γῇ, the reading which is adopted by the Complutensian editors. The manuscript is probably of the fifteenth century, and consequently is of no value as an authority. A third manuscript is Codex 173, or Codex Neapolitano Regio. The words in this manuscript are on the margin, written by a second and recent hand. The marginal reading is supposed to belong to the sixteenth century, though the manuscript itself may be as early as the eleventh. Besides these manuscripts there are others which can hardly be reckoned as testimonies. There are two manuscripts in Wolfenbüttel: the one, Guelpherbytus C, contains the words in the margin by a recent hand taken from a printed text; and the other, Guelpherbytus D, was written after the invention of printing, as it contains various readings from the Latin translations of Erasmus, Beza, etc.[3] The passage is also found in the Codex Ravianus or Berolinensis in Berlin; but this manuscript is a forgery, chiefly copied from the printed text of the Complutensian edition, containing its errors and mistakes. From all this examination it is evident that the passage in question is entirely wanting

[1] Porson's *Letters to Travis*, p. 117. Scrivener's *Introduction to the Criticism of the N. T.*, 1st edition, p. 149.

[2] Davidson's *Biblical Criticism*, vol. ii. p. 408. Horne's *Introduction to the Scriptures*, vol. iv. p. 450.

[3] For the Wolfenbüttel MSS. see Marsh's *Michaelis*, vol. ii. p. 263. Davidson's *Biblical Criticism*, vol. ii. pp. 408, 409.

in manuscript attestation, as even those few manuscripts which contain it are destitute of all authority.[1]

The testimony of the ancient versions is also adverse to the retention of the passage. The words are found in no ancient version except in the old Latin, where there are possible traces of it, and in the more recent manuscripts of the Vulgate. It is not contained in the Peshito or earliest Syriac, nor in the Philoxenean Syriac, although it is now found in the modern Syriac. Tremellius first translated it from Greek into Syriac, and placed it in the margin, and from that it found its way into the text.

Cardinal Wiseman found the passage in a manuscript preserved in the monastery of Santa Croce at Rome. It bears the title *Libri de speculo*, and consists of a classified series of scriptural passages, containing extracts from nearly all the books of the New Testament. It bears a remarkable resemblance to the work published at Paris in 1655 under the title of *the speculum of St. Augustine*, and which was wrongly attributed to that Father;[2] but with this remarkable difference, that the scriptural quotations are not from the Vulgate, but from the old Latin. In the second chapter of this speculum, which treats of "the distinction of persons" (*De Distinctione Personarum*), the disputed passage is given in the following terms: "Item Johannis in epistola: Item illic tres sunt qui testimonium dicunt in cœlo Pater, Verbum et Spiritus sanctus et hii tres unum sunt." The manuscript itself, according to Westcott and Hort, belongs to the eighth or ninth century; but still if the words are from the old Latin, it is a presumption that they were contained in the Latin version before its emendation in the Vulgate of Jerome.[3]

---

[1] It is absurd to speak, as Cardinal Wiseman does, of its supposed existence in certain manuscripts which have never been examined. *Essays on Various Subjects*, vol. i. pp. 68, 69.

[2] It was rejected as spurious by the Benedictine editors of Augustine's works; and the fact that it contains the disputed passage is adverse to the opinion that it is the work of Augustine, as that Father, in his commentary on St. John's Epistle, omits the passage.

[3] For an account of the Santa Croce MS., see Foster's *Three Heavenly Witnesses*, p. 152 ff.; Davidson's *Biblical Criticism*, vol. ii. p. 409 f.; and especially Wiseman's *Essays on Various Subjects*, vol. i. p. 12 ff.: "Two Letters on 1 John v. 7." Cardinal Wiseman's object was to strengthen the

The great point, however, on which the defenders of this passage insist, is that it appears in the Vulgate. In the Clementine edition of the Vulgate it is as follows : " Quondam tres sunt qui testimonium dant in cœlo ; Pater, Verbum et Spiritus sanctus ; et hi tres unum sunt. Et tres sunt qui testimonium dant in terra: Spiritus et aqua et sanguis ; et hi tres unum sunt." But although now found in most of the manuscripts of the Vulgate, it is wanting in the oldest and best, in the Codex Amiatinus and in the Codex Fuldensis of the sixth century ; in the Codex Harleianus of the seventh century ; in those manuscripts which were used by Alcuin ; in about fifty manuscripts in all. The earliest manuscript of the Vulgate, in which it has been found, is perhaps that mentioned by Cardinal Wiseman, preserved in the monastery of La Cava, situated between Naples and Salerno.[1] The age of this manuscript is doubtful ; whilst Abbé Rozan supposes that it is only a thousand years old, and accordingly belonging to the ninth century, Cardinal Mai has no hesitation in assigning it to the seventh century. There are also numerous variations in the manuscripts which contained the passage. In the oldest of them, as in the La Cava manuscript, the earthly witnesses precede the heavenly.[2] In several of them the passage is an evident insertion by a later hand. In most of them the words, "and these three agree in one," in the eighth verse, are omitted ; while some (as the La Cava manuscript) add to the passage "in Christo Jesu." Some read

argument derived from the Latin testimonies. "These essays pretend to nothing more than the collection of additional evidence in favour of the text from the authority of the Latin MSS." He correctly asserts that "the strongest portion of the evidence in favour of this long-controverted passage consists in the authority of Latin testimonies, the Vulgate and the Latin Fathers." He undertakes to show that it has the testimony of the African recension of the Latin version, and from this he infers the probability that Tertullian and Cyprian, who used that version, cited the passage (see below). Cardinal Wiseman, however, gives no opinion of his own as to the genuineness of the passage, though it may be inferred that he leans to the affirmative side of the question.

[1] Wiseman's *Essays on Various Subjects*, vol. i. pp. 7–12.
[2] The reading of the La Cava MS. is as follows: Quia tres sunt qui testimonium dant in terra, spiritus et aqua et sanguis, et hi tres unum sunt in Christo Jesu : et tres sunt qui testimonium dicunt in cœlo, Pater, Verbum et Spiritus et hi tres unum sunt.

filius instead of *verbum*. And Porson mentions a manuscript where the testimony of the heavenly witnesses is placed both before and after the testimony of the earthly witnesses.[1] All these circumstances go to prove that the Vulgate is rather a witness against than for the passage, and that the words were originally a gloss afterwards introduced into the text.

The passage is omitted in all the Greek Fathers before the sixth century. In their controversies with heretics, while adducing texts in support of the doctrine of the Trinity, the early Greek Fathers, as Irenæus, Hippolytus, Clemens Alexandrinus, and Origen, make no reference to it. So also in the celebrated Arian controversy in the fourth century, where, if the passage did exist, it would undoubtedly be quoted, it was never appealed to by the Nicene Fathers. Nor is it mentioned in any of the acts of the early œcumenical and provincial councils. So also it is cited by none of the Latin Fathers previous to the close of the fifth century, with the possible exceptions of Tertullian and Cyprian. It is not contained in the writings of Hilary, Ambrose, Rufinus, Augustine, Pope Leo, or Bede.[2]

From the works of Tertullian three passages have been adduced, which are supposed to be allusions or references to the disputed passage. In discoursing on the Paraclete as revealed in St. John's Gospel, Tertullian observes: "He shall receive of mine, says Christ, just as He Himself received of the Father. Thus the connection of the Father in the Son, and of the Son in the Paraclete, produces three coherent Persons, the one distinct from the other. These three are one (essence), not one (person), as it is said, 'I and my Father are one,' in respect of unity of substance, not singularity of number."[3] It is argued that the words "which

---

[1] Tischendorf, in his notes on 1 John v. 7, 8, gives a list of the numerous variations in the Vulgate.

[2] Porson gives a list of the Greek and Latin Fathers who do not quote the passage, although they would be naturally led to do so were it extant in their manuscripts. *Letters to Travis*, pp. 363-368.

[3] Tertullian, *Adv. Praxean*, chap. 25: Cæterum de meo sumet, inquit, sicut ipse Patris. Ita connexus Patris in Filio et Filii in Paracleto, tres efficit cohærentes alterum ex altero: qui tres unum sunt, non unus: quomodo dictum est: Ego et Pater unum sumus, ad substantiæ unitatem, non ad numeri singularitatem.

three are one" (tres unum sunt), are an allusion to, or a quotation from, 1 John v. 7. But these words are a statement of the doctrine of the Trinity, and are not given as a quotation; the quotation is not from the Epistle, but from the Gospel of John. Indeed, this quotation from John's Gospel is a proof that Tertullian was ignorant of the passage concerning the heavenly witnesses; for, had he been acquainted with it, he would have quoted it as being more suitable for his purpose than the quotation, "I and my Father are one." The second passage adduced is the following: " The Church itself is properly and chiefly the Spirit Himself in whom is the Trinity of the One Divinity—Father and Son and Holy Ghost. (The Spirit) combines that Church which the Lord has made to consist of three."[1] Here there is an assertion of the doctrine of the Trinity—a doctrine fully recognised in the early Church, but no reference to the disputed passage; indeed, the want of reference to it implies ignorance of it. The third passage is as follows: "For if in three witnesses every word of God shall be established, how much more—when through the benediction we have the same as the authority of the faith—does the number of divine names suffice for the assurance of hope!"[2] But here, as is evident from the context and text, the allusion is to the baptismal formula, and possibly to the apostolic benediction; whereas the silence as to the heavenly witnesses in John's Epistle is rather a proof that Tertullian was unacquainted with any such passage.

Two passages have likewise been adduced from the writings of Cyprian. In his Epistle to Jubaianus, he writes: "If any one could be baptized among the heretics, certainly he could also obtain remission of sins. If he attained remission of sins, he was also sanctified, and was made the temple of God. I ask, Of what God? If of the Creator, he could not be, because he has not believed in Him. If of Christ, he

---

[1] *De Pudicitia*, chap. 23: Ecclesia proprie et principaliter ipse est spiritus in quo est trinitas unius divinitatis Pater et Filius et Spiritus sanctus. Illam ecclesiam congregat quam Dominus in tribus posuit.

[2] *De Baptismo*, chap. vi.: Nam si in tribus testibus stabit omne verbum Dei quanto magis dum habemus per benedictionem eosdem arbitros fidei. . . . Sufficit ad fiduciam spei etiam numerus nominum divinorum.

could not become His temple, since he denies that Christ is God. If of the Holy Ghost, since the three are one (cum tres unum sunt), how can the Holy Ghost be at peace with him who is the enemy either of the Son or of the Father?"[1] The genuineness of the words *cum tres unum* is doubtful, as they are not contained in the edition of Erasmus; but even if genuine, they are merely, like the similar expression in Tertullian, an assertion of the Trinity, but there is no quotation, and no intimation of an acquaintance with the passage in question. The other extract from Cyprian is much more important: "He who gathereth elsewhere than in the Church, scattereth the Church of Christ. The Lord says, 'I and my Father are one;' and again it is written of the Father and of the Son and of the Holy Ghost, 'And these three are one.'"[2] Here undoubtedly there appears to be a direct quotation from the disputed passage, introduced by the formula *scriptum est*; and accordingly it is admitted by some critics, as Ebrard and Scrivener, that Cyprian read the passage in the Latin version which he used, and that at this early period (A.D. 248) the words had gained admission into the Latin text.[3] Others think that the language of Cyprian is better explained on the supposition that he had in view the words " the spirit, the water, and the blood," which, according to the patristic explanation, referred to the Trinity; and that his quotation, "And these three are one" (et hi tres unum sunt), was the concluding words of the eighth verse.[4] This indeed is directly affirmed by Facundus, an African bishop of the sixth century (A.D. 550), who so understood Cyprian.

[1] *Ad Jubaianum*, 72: Oxford ed. Ep. 73: Si baptizari quis apud hæreticum potuit, utique et remissam peccatorum consequi potuit. Si peccatorum remissam consecutus est et sanctificatus est, et templum Dei factus est: quaero, cujus Dei? Si creatoris: non potuit, qui in eum non credidit. Si Christi; non hujus potest fieri templum, qui negat Deum Christum. Si Spiritus Sancti, cum tres unum sint, quomodo Spiritus placatus esse ei potest qui aut Patris aut Filii inimicus est?

[2] *De unitate ecclesiæ*, sec. 6: Dicit Dominus: Ego et Pater unum sumus: iterum de Patre et Filio et Spiritu Sancto scriptum est: Et hi tres unum sunt.

[3] Ebrard, *St. John's Epistles*, p. 325. Scrivener's *Introduction to the Criticism of N. T.*, 1st edition, p. 461; 3rd edition, p. 652.

[4] It must be remembered that the words *et hi tres unum sunt* are in the eighth as well as in the seventh verse.

His words are: "The Apostle John in his Epistle thus speaks of the Father and the Son and the Holy Ghost, There are three who bear witness on earth, the spirit, the water, and the blood, and these three are one: which testimony of the Apostle John St. Cyprian understood to be spoken of the Father and the Son and the Holy Ghost."[1] On the other hand, Fulgentius, bishop of Ruspe, of the same century (A.D. 510), asserts that Cyprian refers to 1 John v. 7;[2] but in doing so he gives only his own opinion. The supposition that Cyprian had in view the testimony of the water, the spirit, and the blood is probable from a remarkable passage of Augustine, who so interprets the eighth verse without the slightest reference to the seventh: "If we will inquire into the things signified by these. Here not unreasonably comes into our thoughts the Trinity itself, which is the one true Supreme God, Father, Son, and Holy Ghost, of whom it could most truly be said, There are three witnesses, and the three are one. So that by the term *spirit*, we understand God the Father, as it was concerning the worshippers of Him that the Lord was speaking when He said, 'God is a Spirit.' By the term *blood*, the Son; because the Word was made flesh. And by the term *water*, the Holy Ghost; as when Jesus speaks of the water which He gave to them that thirst, the evangelist says, 'But this said He of the Spirit, that they which believe on Him were to receive.'"[3] And the truth of this supposition is strengthened when it is observed that Cyprian and Augustine, in speaking of the Second Person of the Trinity, call Him the Son (*filius*), and not the Word (*verbum*), as in the disputed passage of the Epistle of John.

There is no reference to this passage in the numerous writings of Augustine. He frequently refers to the eighth verse in such a manner as proves that he was unacquainted

---

[1] *Defensio trium capitulorum concilii Chalcedonensis*, i. 3, quoted by Düsterdieck, *Johanneische Briefe*, vol. ii. p. 351.

[2] *Responsio ad Arianos* Beatus enim Joannes Apostolus testatus: tres sunt qui testimonium perhibent in cœlo, Pater, Verbum, et Spiritus Sanctus: et tres unum sunt. Quod etiam beatissimus martyr Cyprianus et in epistola De Unitate Ecclesiæ confitetur. All that this proves is that in the opinion of Fulgentius, Cyprian alluded to 1 John v. 7.

[3] Augustine, *Contra Maximin.* ii. 22, 23.

with the seventh, as in the above quotation. At one time it was supposed that Jerome quoted the passage, because it is contained in the prologue frequently affixed to the Vulgate; but it has now been proved that this prologue was not written by him.[1] The first undoubted reference to the passage is in the Confession of Faith drawn up by Eugenius, bishop of Carthage, at a conference of bishops in that town in A.D. 484, and transmitted to us by Victor Vitensis. In this confession the following passage occurs: "That we may further show it to be clearer than the light that the divinity of the Father, the Son, and the Holy Spirit is One, we have the testimony of the Evangelist John, 'There are three which bear testimony in heaven, the Father, the Word, and the Holy Spirit, and these three are one.'"[2] So also Vigilius Tapsensis (A.D. 490) observes: "John the Evangelist, in his Epistle to the Parthians, observes: 'There are three who bear witness on earth, the water, the blood, and the flesh, and these three are in us. And there are three who bear witness in heaven, the Father, the Word, and the Spirit, and these three are one.'"[3] Afterwards it was quoted by Fulgentius, bishop of Ruspi (A.D. 510),[4] and by Cassiodorus[5] (A.D. 550). From this time the words had gained admission into the Latin text.

Whilst the external evidence is strongly against the passage, the internal evidence is not in its favour. Internal or subjective evidence for a passage is of little value, when the external evidence is strongly against it. When the external evidence is doubtful, internal evidence is of importance to ascertain the correct reading, especially to determine what the author could not have written. But when the external evidence is decided, as in the present case, internal evidence is of little value in determining what the apostle did write.

---

[1] This prologue is found in the Codex Fuldensis of the sixth century, though in that codex the passage is not found in the text of the Epistle.
[2] *Historia Persecutionis Vandalicæ*, p. 29. Michaelis' *Introduction to the N. T.*, vol. vi. pp. 426-428. Horne's *Introduction to the Scriptures*, vol. iv. p. 462.
[3] *Adv. Varim.* i. 5. [4] *De Trinitate*, iii. 10.
[5] *Complexiones.* Porson's *Letters to Travis*, 347-349. Davidson's *Biblical Criticism*, vol. ii. p. 417. Westcott's *Epistles of St. John*, p. 194 ff.

It does not even diminish, far less does it outweigh, the force of the opposing external evidence. If the external evidence decidedly testifies against the view that the apostle wrote the passage containing the testimony of the heavenly witnesses, no internal evidence can persuade us that he did. Nevertheless the defenders of the passage put great stress upon the internal evidence. They bring forward the following arguments:—

1. The context, they affirm, requires its insertion. The threefold testimony on earth presupposes a threefold testimony in heaven. But this argument proceeds on the supposition that the words *on earth* (ἐν τῇ γῇ) are genuine, whereas they form part of the disputed passage. The undisputed words are only: "There are three that bear witness, the Spirit, the water, and the blood: and the three agree in one." It is further asserted that the train of thought is in favour of the retention of the passage. But the contrary is the case. That a somewhat reasonable sense can be made out, according to the paraphrases of Bishop Burgess and Bishop Horsley,[1] may be admitted; but undoubtedly the sense is better connected if the passage be omitted. The apostle is adducing the witnesses in favour of the statement that Jesus is the Son of God; he mentions the water, the blood, and the Spirit. "This is He that came by water and blood, even Jesus Christ; not by water only, but by water and blood. And it is the Spirit that beareth witness, because the Spirit is truth" (1 John v. 6). Thus there are three witnesses, the water, the blood, and the Spirit, and a threefold testimony. Now, omitting the seventh verse, we have a continuation of the same thought—an enumeration of the same witnesses. "There are three that bear witness, the Spirit, the water, and the blood; and these three agree in one" (1 John v. 8). Whereas the introduction of the seventh verse disturbs the unity of the context by interpolating other witnesses.[2] The insertion of the heavenly witnesses also creates confusion, and it is difficult to ascertain

---

[1] Burgess, *Tracts on the Divinity of Christ.* Horsley's *Works*, vol. i. p. 123.

[2] "If," observes Lücke, "we look to the meaning and context of the interpolated words, we shall find that when omitted they are missed by nobody; but

what is intended by them. The witness of the Father may be explained by the voice from heaven: "This is my beloved Son, in whom I am well pleased;" but it is difficult to understand what is meant by the witness of the Word, Christ's bearing testimony to His own Sonship; and the witness of the Holy Ghost cannot be distinguished from that of the Spirit in the earthly witnesses. "The whole design of the apostle," observes Sir Isaac Newton, "being to prove to men by witness the truth of Christ's coming, I would ask, How the testimony of the three in heaven makes to this purpose? If their testimony be not given to men, how does it prove to them the truth of Christ's coming? If it be, how is the testimony in heaven distinguished from that on earth? It is the same Spirit which witnesses both in heaven and in earth. If in both cases it witnesses to us men, wherein lies the difference between its witnessing in heaven and its witnessing on earth? If in the first case it does not witness to them, to whom does it witness? And to what purpose? And how does its witnessing make to the design of St. John's discourse? Let them make good sense of it who are able; for my part, I can make none."[1]

2. It is asserted that the grammatical structure of the passage requires the insertion of the clause. The numeral τρεῖς, it is argued, is masculine, whereas, if it only refers to the Spirit, the water, and the blood, it should be neuter, as each of these substantives is neuter: it thus supposes the testimony of the heavenly witnesses. But we cannot see the force of this argument; in any case, this second τρεῖς must refer to the three neuter substantives—the spirit, the water, and the blood: these three are in this passage personified; they are adduced as witnesses that Jesus is the Son of God; and hence the masculine gender is here properly employed. It is further argued that the article τό in the clause καὶ οἱ τρεῖς εἰς τὸ ἓν εἰσίν refers to a unity previously mentioned: an argument insisted on by Bishop Middleton in his work on the Greek

every one, even he who is most favourable to them, feels himself embarrassed when they are retained and have to be interpreted." *Commentary on the Epistles of John*, p. 270.

[1] Sir Isaac Newton's *Paraphrastic Exposition*, *Works*, vol. v. pp. 528, 529.

article.[1] But there is no necessity for this; τὸ ἓν may only express the unity of their testimony, as in Phil. ii. 2, τὸ ἓν φρονοῦντες, "being of one mind."

3. It is suggested that the verse might have been omitted by the carelessness of the transcribers, by what is termed a homœoteleuton; that is, by the eye passing over from the first μαρτυροῦντες in ver. 7 to the second μαρτυροῦντες in ver. 8, and that thus the intervening words "in heaven the Father, the Word, and the Holy Ghost: and these three are one. And there are three that bear witness" were inadvertently omitted. But unfortunately for this explanation, the words ἐν τῇ γῇ, which come after the second μαρτυροῦντες, also form part of the disputed passage, and are in no manuscript, version, or quotation which omits the heavenly witnesses: so that the idea of a homœoteleuton is entirely excluded.[2]

It follows from an examination both of the external and internal evidence that the passage is to be rejected as an interpolation. In a former age, before ancient documents and manuscripts were critically examined, it had some defenders of high scholarly attainments, among whom are to be reckoned Ernesti, Knittel,[3] Horsley, Waterland, Mill, Travis,[4] and Bengel; the last of these scholarly defenders were Bishop Burgess and perhaps Cardinal Wiseman. In the controversy which arose concerning it, it was first attacked by Richard Simon and afterwards by Semler, Bentley, Clarke, Michaelis, Bishop Marsh, Sir Isaac Newton, and especially by Porson in his masterly but somewhat scurrilous "Letters to Archdeacon Travis;" and it is now relinquished by all theologians with any pretensions to scholarship. It is omitted in all modern critical editions of the New Testament, and of this Epistle in particular; by Wetstein, Matthæi, Scholz, Griesbach, Lachmann, Tregelles, Tischendorf, De Wette, Lücke, Huther, Düsterdieck, Haupt, Wolf,[5] Ebrard, Alford, Wordsworth,

---

[1] Bishop Middleton, *On the Greek Article*, pp. 633-653. See also Foster's *Three Heavenly Witnesses*, p. 236 ff.; and in answer, Davidson's *Biblical Criticism*, vol. ii. p. 424.

[2] Porson's *Letters to Travis*, pp. 391-393.

[3] *New Criticism on* 1 John v. 7, published in 1785, answered by Michaelis.

[4] *Letters to Gibbon*, which called forth Porson's celebrated letters.

[5] Wolf's *Die Briefe Johannis:* a Roman Catholic commentator.

Westcott and Hort. It has been rightly expunged without note from the revised edition of the New Testament; and it ought to be expunged from all authorized national versions. It has been affirmed that by the omission of this passage we sensibly weaken the testimony in favour of the great Christian doctrine of the Trinity; but not to mention that it would be injurious to any cause to support it by weak arguments, or to make the fear of consequences a reason why we should not follow after the truth, the remark of Bentley is well worthy of our attention: "If the fourth century knew that text, let it come in in God's name; but if that age did not know it, then Arianism in its height was beat down without the help of that verse; and let the fact prove as it will, the doctrine is unshaken."

We consider that the passage originated by being written on the margin of some Latin manuscript, from which it was at an early period transferred to the text. The gloss arose from the necessity of explaining the mystical eighth verse, as according to the opinion of the Fathers "the Spirit, the water, and the blood" denoted the Father, the Son, and the Holy Ghost. This is the probable meaning of the passage quoted from Cyprian, and is undoubtedly the interpretation given by Augustine. Such a meaning of the eighth verse would naturally be written on the margin of some Latin manuscript as an explanatory note, and was in the course of time transferred to the text of the Latin version. This opinion is favoured by the fact that in all the oldest manuscripts of the Vulgate in which the disputed passage occurs, it is found, not before, but after the testimony of the earthly witnesses.[1] In two manuscripts mentioned by Porson the words are as follows: "Because there are three who bear witness, the Spirit, the water, and the blood: and these three are one; so in heaven there are three, the Father, the Word, and the Holy Ghost: and these three are one." Afterwards in later manuscripts of the Vulgate the verses were transposed, as the heavenly witnesses were considered more important

[1] On the origin of the Latin text, see Westcott's *Epistles of John*, pp. 194-196.

than the earthly. From the Vulgate the words found their way by translation into the Greek text; they are first found in a Greek version of the Acts of the Lateran Council in 1215; and in the few recent manuscripts of the Greek Testament which contain them they are evidently a translation from the Latin.

The passage was first printed in the Complutensian edition of the Greek Testament (A.D. 1514); but here also there is no doubt that the editors did not take it from any Greek manuscript, but translated it from the Vulgate; for when challenged by Erasmus to produce a Greek manuscript containing it, Stunica, the principal editor, replied: "It should be known that the Greek codices are corrupt, but that ours contain the truth,"[1] thus admitting that he knew of no Greek manuscript containing the words. Erasmus in his first (A.D. 1516) and second editions (A.D. 1518) omitted the passage, because he found it in no Greek manuscript; but on being censured for doing so, he rashly promised that if a Greek manuscript could be produced containing the words he would insert them. A sheet of what he calls the Codex Britannicus, and which is now ascertained to be the same with the Codex Montfortianus, containing the words was transmitted to him,—the manuscript itself he did not see,—and he redeemed his promise by inserting the words in his third edition (A.D. 1522). In that edition the words were inserted as they were found in the manuscript sent him, without the articles before the heavenly and earthly witnesses; but in the fourth edition (A.D. 1527) he corrected the construction into pure Greek by the insertion of the articles, but without any manuscript authority. In this corrected form the passage was printed in the editions of Stephens, Beza, and the Elzevir,[2] and in this form it appeared in the *textus receptus*. The *textus receptus* formed the basis of most of the translations of the New Testament in modern languages, and hence the passage is found in all national authorized versions. It is, however, to be observed that Luther had the courage and critical judgment to reject it in

---

[1] Sciendum est Græcorum codices esse corruptos: nostros vero ipsam veritatem continere.

[2] The passage is omitted by Aldus in the Venetian edition, 1518.

his translation, as it was regarded by him as spurious,[1] nor was it inserted in that version until A.D. 1593, nearly fifty years after his death. Calvin, on the other hand, with less critical judgment, regarded the passage as genuine, on the authority of the prologue to the Vulgate, which he wrongly ascribed to Jerome, and its supposed suitableness to the context; he, however, adds: "Inasmuch as all do not receive this reading, I will therefore so expound what follows as though the apostle referred to the witnesses only on earth."

DISSERTATION II.

GNOSTICISM AS REFERRED TO IN JOHN'S EPISTLE.[2]

In the second century there arose a number of sects known by the generic name of Gnostics, who propounded views opposed to the general teaching of the Church; and against whom the Fathers of that and the succeeding century, Irenæus, Hippolytus, Clemens Alexandrinus,[3] Tertullian, Origen, and Epiphanius, employed all their eloquence and learning. Names of celebrated teachers occur, such as Valentinus and Marcion, who were regarded in their days as arch-heretics,

[1] Luther, however, comments upon it in his commentary on the First Epistle of John without questioning its genuineness. This is to be explained by the fact that he founded his commentary on the text of Erasmus.

[2] Gnosticism and the sects of the Gnostics are treated of in Baur's *Die Christliche Gnosis*, Tübingen 1835, and in his *Kirchengeschichte der drei ersten Jahrhunderte*; in Burton's *Bampton Lectures* for 1829 on "The Heresies of the Apostolic Age;" in an article on the Gnostics in the *Encyclopedia Britannica* by Principal Tulloch; in an article on the Gnosis in Herzog's *Real-Encyklopädie* by Jacobi; in a dissertation on the Colossian heretics by Bishop Lightfoot in his *Commentary on the Ep. to the Colossians*; in Mosheim's *Church History*; in Mansel's *Gnostic Heretics*; in Neander's *Church History*, vol. ii.; in Schaff's *History of the Christian Church*; in Harnack's *Zur Quellenkritik der Geschichte des Gnosticismus*; in Matter's *Histoire critique du Gnosticisme*; in Lipsius' *Die Quellen der ältesten Ketzergeschichte*; in Kurtz's *History of the Christian Church*, vol. i. p. 96 ff., E. Tr.

[3] The Gnostic heresies are specially discussed by Irenæus, *Adv. Hær.* lib. v.; Hippolytus, ἔλεγχος κατὰ πασῶν αἱρέσεων; Clemens Alexandrinus, *Stromata*; and Tertullian, *Præscrip. adv. Hær.* and *Adv. Marcionem*.

corrupting the Christian Church and drawing away disciples after them.[1] Nor are the opinions of those Gnostic sects, however alien to our mode of thought, to be regarded as mere caprices; in a great measure they were so, but they were also the natural and inevitable outcome of the contact of Christianity with heathen philosophy. The age of the apostles was pre-eminently a period of transition; the religions of the ancient world were losing their hold upon the people, and the different systems of philosophy were drifting into agnosticism. Christianity affected all that it came in contact with; and although it was at first treated with disdain by the philosophers, as Paul experienced when he preached Christ to the Stoics and Epicureans at Athens, yet, in the next age, it compelled their attention and modified their views. Hence it was inevitable that in the second century religious systems should be formed containing an admixture of Christianity and heathen philosophy; and as heathenism manifested itself in different phases of philosophy, so Gnosticism had its different schools of thought. Hence, also, the Gnostic tenets were not properly heresies in the ordinary acceptation of that term; they were not perversions of Christian doctrine, like Arianism and Pelagianism, but the blending of heathen philosophy with Christianity—a combination of heathen opinions with Christian doctrines, as is the case with the Brahma-somaj of the present day. It is very probable that several of the founders of the Gnostic sects never belonged to the Christian Church; they remained heathen philosophers, engrafting into their philosophy certain ideas taken from Christianity.[2] Others, as Marcion, belonged to the Christian Church before they were expelled from it; and others, as Tatian, Heracleon, and Bardesanes, perhaps never left the Christian community.

Gnosticism is derived from gnosis (γνῶσις), knowledge.[3] There is a true as well as a false gnosis. The writers of the New Testament dwell much upon the true knowledge of God.

[1] We know the opinions of the Gnostics only from the writings of the Fathers. Of all the numerous Gnostic works only one has survived the πίστις σοφία of Valentinus, edited by Petermann, Berlin 1851.

[2] See Bigg's *Bampton Lectures*, Lecture VII. : "The Reformed Paganism."

[3] Gnosticism has been called a philosophy of religion or philosophic Christianity.

To impart this was one of the chief designs of Christ's mission into the world; He came to reveal the Father—to make known the nature and will of God, and His relations toward the human race. "This," says our Lord, "is life eternal, that they should know Thee the only true God, and Him whom thou didst send, even Jesus Christ" (John xvii. 3). And the apostle prays for his converts that they might abound in knowledge and in all discernment (Phil. i. 9). St. Paul also distinguishes between two classes of men—the natural, who were incapable of comprehending this knowledge, and the spiritual, who were able to apprehend it: "The natural man receiveth not the things of the Spirit of God; for they are foolishness unto him; and he cannot know them, because they are spiritually judged. But he that is spiritual judgeth all things" (1 Cor. ii. 14, 15). And in his later Epistles he speaks of a false knowledge, arising from an intrusion into those things which are not seen—"the oppositions of science," literally the antithesis of knowledge, "falsely so called"[1] (1 Tim. vi. 20). The Gnostics viewed Christianity as a revelation of speculative knowledge, whilst moral virtue and Christian duties occupied only a small portion of their systems; according to them, the design of the gospel was not so much to make men *righteous*, as to make them *wise*. They perverted the distinction which Paul makes between the natural and the spiritual man into the wise or initiated and the ignorant or uninitiated, a distinction common to most systems of heathen philosophy.[2] But that which especially distinguished Gnosticism from all heathen schools of philosophy was the admission into its systems of the idea of redemption. The person and work of Christ were recognised by it; Christ, as the Saviour, had

---

[1] ἀντιθέσεις τῆς ψευδωνύμου γνώσεως; rendered in the Revised Version: "oppositions of the knowledge which is falsely so called."

[2] The Gnostics, in general, had in their systems the distinction of an esoteric and an exoteric doctrine. The very meaning of the name which they adopted implied that they were an intellectual class. They divided men into three classes: the spiritual (πνευματικοί), in whom the spiritual element predominates—the true Gnostics; the psychical (ψυχικοί), in whom a religious nature rules—the ordinary Christian; and the carnal (σαρκικοί), in whom matter rules—the world outside of Christianity.

appeared to deliver men from certain evils, and to confer on them certain blessings. "The distinctive feature which marks Gnosticism," observes Mansel, "in all its schools as a religious heresy, and not as a mere philosophical extravagance, is the presence of this idea of a redemption of the world, and the recognition, in a perverted form, of the person and work of Christ, as taking part in this redemption."[1]

The germs of Gnosticism appeared at the earliest contact of philosophy with Christianity. Indeed, the system of Philo is but a species of Jewish Gnosticism,[2] being an admixture of Judaism and Platonism. And when Christianity appeared, it was inevitable that there should be a similar admixture of Christianity and heathenism. The Fathers assert that Simon Magus was the father of Gnosticism and of all heresies; and, in a certain sense, this is true. Simon Magus appears to have been an impostor, who imposed upon the Samaritans with his great pretensions and his magical works. He gave out that he was some great one, and, more specifically, that he was the power of God, which is called Great ($\dot{\eta}$ $\delta\acute{v}\nu\alpha\mu\iota\varsigma$ $\tau o\hat{v}$ $\theta\epsilon o\hat{v}$ $\dot{\eta}$ $\kappa\alpha\lambda o\nu\mu\acute{e}\nu\eta$ $\mu\epsilon\gamma\acute{\alpha}\lambda\eta$, Acts viii. 9, 10). Coming in contact with the apostles, he professed Christianity and was baptized; but he did so only from mercenary motives, and most probably his attachment to the Christian Church was only temporary. He occupies a conspicuous place in the writings of the early Church, especially in the Clementines; but the accounts which we have of him and of his encounters with Peter are doubtless legendary.[3] According to Irenæus, he taught that it was he himself who appeared among the Jews as the Son, but among the Samaritans as the Father, and among other nations as the Holy Ghost.[4] His only claim to be considered as a Gnostic was the name which he applied to himself—"the power of God," being the same name that the Gnostics gave to their æons, whom they regarded as

---

[1] Mansel's *Gnostic Heresies*, p. 5. See also Dorner, *Person of Christ*, vol. i. p. 344, E. Tr.

[2] Ewald considers Philo as the father of Gnosticism.

[3] On the legends connected with Simon Magus, see p. 153 ff.

[4] Irenæus, *Adv. Hær.* i. 23. 1. According to Jerome, he said: "Ego sum Sermo Dei, ego sum speciosus, ego paracletus, ego omnipotens, ego omnia Dei," on Matt. xxiv. 5.

powers of God. The first use of the term Gnostic, as a distinctive appellative, was made by Carpocrates, who lived in the beginning of the second century;[1] and it was probably not until that century that Gnosticism was developed into a system, although its germs were abundant in the apostolic age.[2]

Gnosticism was an eclectic system. The Gnostics appropriated those elements which they considered best in Christianity and in heathen philosophy, and welded them into their various systems; just as the Brahma-somaj, in the present day, is a combination of Christianity, Mahometanism, and Brahmanism. There were especially three principal sources of Gnosticism—Platonism, Zoroasterism, and Buddhism.[3] The chief source was Greek philosophy, and especially Platonism as modified by Philo. From this the Gnostics derived their notion of the superiority of the intellect, and most of their philosophical words and tendencies. So also Dualism, or the philosophy, or rather theosophy, of Zoroaster pervades Gnosticism to a large extent. Like the Persians, the Gnostics regarded matter as inherently evil, and looked upon the creator of the world as different from the true God. The idea of two antagonistic principles, the light and the darkness, the good and the evil, pervades their whole system. Their doctrine of æons, or emanations from God, as filling up the space between the Supreme Being and His creation, seems to be derived from Buddhism[4] as modified by Platonism. To the same source also are to be referred their docetic views, a species of immaterialism which was incorporated in most

---

[1] Irenæus, *Adv. Hær.* i. 25. 6. Euseb. *Hist. Eccl.* iv. 7. According to Hippolytus, the term was first used by the Ophites, *Ref. Hær.* v. 6. "These doctrines," he observes, "the Naasseni (Ophites) attempt to establish, calling themselves Gnostics."

[2] The Gnostics probably did not appear as heretical sects until the beginning of the second century, as, according to the often quoted words of Hegesippus: "The Church continued until the reign of Trajan as a pure and uncorrupt virgin; but when the sacred choir of the apostles became extinct, then combinations of impious error arose by the fraud and delusions of false teachers." Eusebius, *Hist. Eccl.* iii. 32, iv. 22.

[3] Mansel's *Gnostic Heresies*, p. 32.

[4] For the Buddhist doctrines in Gnosticism, see Schmidt, *Ueber die Verwandschaft der Gnostisch-theosoph. Lehren mit d. Religionsystemen des Orients vorzüglich des Buddhæsmus.*

of their systems.[1] The variation of the Gnostic sects arose from the unequal mixture of these tendencies. The Gnosticism of the Alexandrian Gnostics, as Basilides and Valentinus, was chiefly derived from Platonism and Platonic-Buddhism; they regarded Judaism as an imperfect religion which Christianity was designed to complete; whilst the Gnosticism of the Syrian Gnostics, as Saturninus, Marcion, Tatian, and Bardesanes was chiefly derived from Parseeism; they regarded Judaism as a hostile religion, and Christianity as a deliverance from it.

The classification of the Gnostic systems has been made on different principles by different writers: Giescler divides them into two classes, the Alexandrian Gnostics, among whom traces of the Platonic philosophy are most obvious, and Syrian Gnostics, among whom the influence of Parseeism was superadded; among the former the emanation doctrine was pre-eminent, among the latter dualism.[2] Neander distinguishes them into those Gnostics who regarded Judaism as an imperfect preparation for Christianity, and those who regarded it as antagonistic to Christianity. Baur arranges the Gnostic systems into three classes:—1. Such as combine Christianity with Judaism and paganism; 2. Such as oppose Christianity to both; 3. Such as, identifying Judaism and Christianity, oppose them to paganism.

There are certain principles common to Gnosticism, or which at least pervade nearly all its systems, and which principles remove it from pure Christianity. One of these is the antithesis between God and matter. This antithesis is found in almost all the philosophies of the heathen, and forms a distinguishing feature in Gnosticism, indeed it lies at the foundation of the Gnostic system. "The fundamental character of Gnosticism," observes Baur, "in all its forms is dualistic. It is its sharply-defined, all-pervading dualism that, more than anything else, marks it directly for an off-

[1] Some suppose that Gnosticism is chiefly of Jewish origin, derived from the Cabbala of the Jews. There is certainly a great similarity between them; but the date of the Cabbala is very uncertain, and its doctrines are evidently derived from the Parseeism of Zoroaster.

[2] Giescler's *Church History*, vol. i. p. 136. So also Kurtz, *History of the Christian Church*, vol. i. pp. 102, 103.

spring of paganism."[1] Matter was regarded as inherently evil; so that there was a vast space between God and matter which required to be filled up. The supreme God dwelt in a pleroma of inaccessible light. Besides the name Father, the Gnostics called Him Bythus (depth), to denote the unfathomable nature of His perfections. Between God and matter there existed a vast number of spiritual beings or powers called æons, which were considered as emanations from God. These æons deteriorated the farther they were removed from their original source. Various names were given to them; and in many systems, notably in that of Valentinus, their genealogies were traced. In all probability we are to conceive them as the personified archetypes of the world, analogous to the ideas of Plato. Some of the Gnostic sects, especially those of Alexandria, drifted into pantheism;[2] whilst others, especially those of Syria, resembled what was afterwards known as Manicheism.

Another principle, common to nearly all the Gnostic sects, is the idea of the Demiurgus or Creator of the world, as distinct from the supreme God. All Gnostics agree that the Creator of the world is a being different from God. Matter being considered as inherently corrupt, it was impossible for them to suppose that it could be created or moulded into its present condition by a God of infinite purity and holiness, and therefore they substituted another being as the creator. To this creator they gave the name Demiurgus, a name employed in a similar sense by Plato.[3] In general, the Demiurgus was regarded as Jehovah, the God of the Jewish people; because in the Old Testament the Creator is represented as such. From him came the law of Moses. The Demiurgus was an æon or emanation from God, more or less distant

---

[1] *Kirchengeschichte*, vol. i. p. 183 [E. Tr. vol. i. p. 193].

[2] The opinions of Basilides are decidedly pantheistic and indeed atheistic. According to him, God is the Supreme Being whose nature cannot be expressed by any language; He cannot be identified with anything that exists, and therefore may be called absolute non-existence. "Basilides," observes Baur, "places simple nothing at the summit of existence, and thus speaks of God not as the Being, but as the not-being."

[3] Δημιουργός is the former of the world in Plato's *Timæus*, and the word is also similarly employed in Xenophon's *Memorab.* i. 4. 7.

from Him. Different opinions are entertained regarding his nature and character. Those who approached to pantheism regarded him as the soul of the world. Some adopted the notion that the world was made by angels, the chief of whom was the Demiurgus. Some considered him as an imperfect, but upon the whole a good being, who, although ignorant of the true God, yet was by no means hostile to Him. Others, adopting the system of Zoroaster, viewed him as a malignant being, who had revolted from and set himself in opposition to God, and from whose power Christ came to deliver the human race.[1]

A third principle, common to nearly all the Gnostic sects, was the docetic nature of Christ—that His person was an appearance and not a reality. Christ was regarded by most as the highest æon or chief emanation from God. Now, if matter is inherently corrupt, the Gnostics could not assume that Christ actually became incarnate—that He was really manifest in the flesh: the incarnation could form no part of their system. They therefore conceived that Christ had only an apparent body, that His appearances were illusive. There was an apparent, but not a real humanity. Docetism was not a particular heresy, confined to one sect of Gnostics called the Docetæ, but a principle which pervaded Gnosticism in general, and was a necessary consequence arising from the opinion of the evil nature of matter.[2] It assumed two forms. One set of Gnostics distinguished between Jesus and Christ. They granted that there was a man Jesus descended from Jewish parents, pre-eminent among His countrymen for His wisdom and holiness, upon whom the æon Christ descended

---

[1] Two opposite views are thus taken of the Jewish religion; according to the one, it is an imperfect preparation for Christianity; according to the other, it is an antagonistic religion. Hence the classification of Neander into Jewish and anti-Jewish Gnostics. In the Gnosticism of Marcion the antagonism between Judaism and Christianity is carried to its extreme limits. According to him, it was the Demiurgus who accomplished Christ's death. See Neander's *Church History*, vol. ii. p. 20 ff.; Gieseler's *Ecclesiastical History*, vol. i. p. 136 ff.

[2] Confusion has often arisen on this point by regarding the Docetæ as a distinct sect of Gnostics different from the Valentinians and other Gnostic sects: whereas all Gnostics, with the possible exception of Basilides, adopted the principle involved in Docetism.

at His baptism, but left Him before His sufferings.[1] According to this view, Jesus possessed a real body, with which Christ was in a manner united. Another set of Gnostics carried the principle of the inherent evil of matter to its full consequences. According to them, Jesus Christ had no real body —there was only the appearance of a body; He only appeared to eat and drink, like the angels who were entertained by Abraham.[2] Some grounded this view on pure immaterialism, others regarded it as a peculiarity of the Lord Jesus Christ. Of course, according to this view, the resurrection of Christ can have no place in Gnosticism; and the women at the sepulchre were correct in their assumption that they thought they saw a phantom.

There was a twofold ethical tendency in Gnosticism, resulting from the common idea of the evil nature of matter.[3] The Fathers accuse the Gnostics of licentiousness and of leading immoral lives, and are very vehement in their denunciations; but it appears from their own statements that this was only true of a certain class. Some, on the contrary, led ascetic lives, mortified their bodies, and practised various austerities. Considering the body as evil, they thought it their duty to mortify it and keep it in subjection. Hence they discountenanced marriage and inculcated abstinence from meats. Both Marcion and Tatian, from all that appears, were distinguished for the purity of their lives and for the practice of asceticism. Others, proceeding from the same principle of the depravity of matter, ran into the opposite extreme. They taught that, as the body was depraved, it mattered not how they behaved regarding it; the spirit was the real man, and could not be affected by the pollutions of the flesh; if they possessed the true gnosis, that was all that was neces-

[1] Irenæus, *Adv. Hær.* iii. 16, 1. According to this Father, Basilides supposed that Simon the Cyrenian was crucified instead of Christ.

[2] As the angel Raphael is represented as saying to Tobit: "All these days I did appear unto you; but I did neither eat nor drink, but you did see a vision," Tobit xii. 19.

[3] "The Dualism of the Gnostics," observes Lechler, "brought with it in ethics an asceticism that mortifies the body, the rejection of marriage as a demoniacal institution, etc.; or a pronounced antinomianism, inasmuch as the opposites touch and pass over into one another." *Apostolische Zeitalter*, p. 501 [E. Tr. vol. ii. p. 372].

sary.¹ Some went the length of asserting that the moral law was not given by God, but by the Demiurgus, whom they regarded as an evil principle, and that therefore it had no authority over them, and they were at liberty to disobey it.²

Although Gnosticism was not fully developed until the second century, and although certainly until then the name as an appellative was unknown, yet its germs were abundant in the apostolic age. Whenever Christianity came in contact with heathen philosophy, Gnosticism was the result. We find traces of it in the later Epistles of Paul.³ In the Epistle to the Ephesians the Gnostic term *pleroma* or fulness frequently occurs. Thus the Church is spoken of as the body of Christ, the fulness ($\pi\lambda\eta\rho\hat{\omega}\mu\alpha$) of Him who filleth all in all (Eph. i. 23); and the Christian is spoken of as coming to a perfect man, to the measure of the stature of the fulness of Christ (Eph. iv. 13). It is not improbable that the apostle uses this term $\pi\lambda\eta\rho\hat{\omega}\mu\alpha$ with reference to the Gnostic error, to bring out the truth of which it was the perversion, that this pleroma resided in Christ; though it is also possible that the Gnostics borrowed this term from the apostle. In the contemporary Epistle to the Colossians reference is made to heretical teachers, whose opinions bear a close resemblance to the views of the Gnostics. The apostle warns the Colossians from being led astray by a false philosophy: "Beware lest any man spoil you through philosophy and vain deceit, after the traditions of men, after the rudiments of the world, and not after Christ;" and then, with a reference which finds its full significance as a counterpart to Gnostic errors, he adds, "in whom dwelleth all the pleroma of the Godhead bodily" (Col. ii. 8, 9).⁴ He dwells upon Christ as the Creator of the world, a statement which receives its full import when con-

---

¹ So the Carpocratians are described by Irenæus, *Adv. Hær.* i. 25. 4. The Ophites and the Nicolaitans were also infamous for their immoral practices.

² A sect called the Cainites went the length of declaring that the Demiurgus, or God of the Old Testament, being an evil principle, all that is condemned in the Old Testament is to be regarded as good, and all that is approved as evil. Epiphan. *Hær.* xxxviii. 2.

³ Some find a reference to Gnosticism in 1 Cor. viii. 1, when the apostle says, ἡ γνῶσις φυσιοῖ, ἡ δὲ ἀγάπη οἰκοδομεῖ; but the reference there is to the Jewish notion of clean and unclean meats.

⁴ Ἐν αὐτῷ κατοικεῖ πᾶν τὸ πλήρωμα τῆς θεότητος σωματικῶς.

trasted with the Gnostic doctrine of the Demiurgus as different from the supreme God: "For by Him were all things created which are in heaven or in earth, visible or invisible, whether they be thrones, or dominions, or principalities, or powers, all things were created by Him, and for Him: and He is before all things, and by Him all things consist" (Col. i. 16, 17). He adverts to the worship of angels, a form of idolatry which was practised by certain Gnostics who worshipped angels as the æons who constituted the pleroma: "Let no man beguile you of your reward in a voluntary humility and worshipping of angels, intruding into those things which he hath not seen, vainly puffed up by his fleshly mind" (Col. ii. 18). And so also in the Pastoral Epistles there are various expressions which receive an evident meaning when applied to the perversions of the Gnostics. Thus Paul speaks of the antithesis of knowledge falsely so called (1 Tim. vi. 20),[1] which may well apply to the opposing principles recognised in most of the Gnostic systems. He refers to the fables and endless genealogies which may be understood of the successive descents of the æons, peculiar to Gnosticism. He warns Timothy to shun profane and vain babblings, for they will increase unto more ungodliness; and he refers especially to the heresy of Hymeneus and Philetus, who appear to have given a docetic or spiritual interpretation of the resurrection (2 Tim. ii. 16-18). And in the Apocalypse mention is made of the Nicolaitans (Rev. ii. 6), who are mentioned in the works of the Fathers as an early Gnostic sect.[2]

But especially in the First Epistle of John, and probably in his Gospel, there are distinct references to Gnosticism. This Epistle is to a certain extent polemic, and the heresy which it encounters is evidently Docetism: that of those who denied that Jesus Christ came in the flesh. The Ebionites regarded Jesus Christ as a mere man, the son of Joseph and

---

[1] The Fathers with one consent apply this expression to the Gnostics.

[2] The Nicolaitans are mentioned by the Fathers as an impure Gnostic sect. Irenæus informs us that they led lives of unrestrained indulgence, and states that they were the followers of Nicolas, one of the "seven deacons," *Adv. Hær.* ii. 26, 3: a statement which is also made by Tertullian, Epiphanius, and Jerome, but called in question by Clemens Alexandrinus (*Strom.* iii. 4) and Eusebius (*Hist. Eccl.* iii. 29).

Mary; and to this view is here added the docetic notion which separates Jesus from the Christ, regarding Jesus as a man upon whom Christ, as a heavenly æon, descended. Hence these heretical teachers denied that Jesus is the Son of God, and that Jesus as the Christ came in the flesh. Pure Docetism was not developed until the second century; but in the above crude and imperfect state John opposes it in this Epistle: "Hereby know ye the Spirit of God: every spirit that confesseth that Jesus Christ is come in the flesh is of God; and every spirit that confesseth not that Jesus Christ is come in the flesh is not of God: and this is that spirit of antichrist, whereof ye have heard that it should come; and even now already is it in the world" (1 John iv. 2, 3). And in similar terms, in his Second Epistle, he writes: "Many deceivers are entered into the world, who confess not that Jesus Christ is come in the flesh. This is a deceiver and an antichrist" (2 John 7).

The peculiar form of Gnosticism opposed by John is generally supposed to be that taught by Cerinthus; and from what we learn of his tenets as given by the Fathers, and of his encounter with John at Ephesus, this supposition is highly probable. We are informed that Cerinthus lived toward the close of the first century. He was either a Jew or a Jewish proselyte by birth, and a native of Alexandria, the headquarters of Jewish Gnosticism. We are informed by Epiphanius[1] that he was one of the circumcision who troubled the Gentile Christians at Antioch; that he was among those who occasioned the arrest of Paul at Jerusalem; and that he belonged to those Judaizing teachers who continually opposed that apostle in preaching the gospel.[2] These accounts may at once be dismissed as legends. But his encounter with John in the bath at Ephesus, formerly alluded to, rests on a different foundation and on better evidence. The account is given us by Irenæus, who affirms

---

[1] Epiphanius, *Hær.* xxviii.

[2] Although the account of the encounter of Paul with Cerinthus is undoubtedly fabulous, yet there is a resemblance between his views and those of the false teachers at Colosse. Bishop Lightfoot observes that Cerinthus is the proper link between the incipient gnosis of the Colossian heretics and the mature gnosis of the second century. *Epistle to the Colossians*, p. 110.

that he received it from Polycarp, an immediate disciple of the apostle.[1] At all events there is no anachronism in supposing that the docetic views, which John in his Epistle so vehemently opposes, were the views of Cerinthus.

Cerinthus taught the Gnostic doctrine, that the creator of the world was not the supreme God, but some inferior being. Thus Irenæus observes that "Cerinthus, a man educated in the wisdom of the Egyptians, taught that the world was not made by the supreme God, but by a certain power far separate from Him and at a distance from that Principality who is supreme over the universe, and ignorant of Him who is God over all."[2] As a Jew he does not, however, appear to have adopted the notion that the creator of the world was a malevolent being, but merely inferior to and distinct from God: a notion somewhat similar to that adopted by Philo. He appears also to have distinguished the creator from Jehovah, the God of the Jews, and to have identified Jehovah with the angel who delivered the law. His views were more Judaistic than that of any of the other founders of Gnostic sects.

The Christology of Cerinthus was a modified Docetism. He denied the miraculous conception, and, like the Ebionites, held that Jesus was a mere man, the earthly Messiah (ὁ κάτω Χριστός), and that the Holy Ghost, the heavenly Messiah (ὁ ἄνω Χριστός), descended upon Him at His baptism, and withdrew from Him at His crucifixion. "Cerinthus," observes Irenæus, "represented Jesus as having not been born of a virgin, but as being the son of Mary and Joseph, according to the ordinary course of human generation, while he nevertheless was more righteous, prudent, and wise than other men. Moreover, after His baptism, Christ descended upon him in the form of a dove from the supreme Ruler, and that then he proclaimed the unknown Father, and performed miracles. But at last Christ departed from Jesus, and that

---

[1] On the encounter with John in the bath, see p. 271.

[2] *Adv. Hær.* i. 26. 1: Non a primo Deo factum esse mundum docuit, sed a virtute quadam valde separata et distante ab ea principalitate quæ est super universa et ignorante eum qui est super omnia Deum. So also Hippolytus, *Hær.* vii.

then Jesus suffered and rose again, but Christ remained impassible, inasmuch as he was a spiritual being." The same account is given of his views by Hippolytus.[1] The Christology of Cerinthus is evidently not pure Docetism, as it was afterwards developed, but a mixture of Ebionism and Docetism.[2] According to him, the mission of Christ into the world was not to redeem the world from sin, or to deliver it from the power of the Demiurgus, as the Gnostics generally taught, but to impart the true knowledge of God: Christ was a teacher of speculative knowledge rather than of righteousness, and therefore the ethical tendency of the system of Cerinthus was probably subversive of morality.

According to later writers, there were intermingled Judaistic elements with these Gnostic views. Cerinthus was a Jew by birth, and therefore it is natural that Judaism affected his opinions. He maintained the perpetual obligation of the Mosaic law, and entertained chiliastic or millenarian views concerning the establishment of the Messianic kingdom.[3] Thus Caius observes: "Cerinthus, by means of revelations which he pretended were written by a great apostle, also falsely pretended to wonderful things, as if they were shown him by angels, asserting that after the resurrection there would be an earthly kingdom of Christ, and that the flesh, that is men, again inhabiting Jerusalem, would be subject to desires and pleasures."[4] And so also Dionysius of Alexandria observes: "This is the doctrine of Cerinthus, that there will be an earthly reign of Christ: and as he was a lover of the body, and altogether sensual in those things which he so eagerly craved, he dreamed that he would revel in the gratification of his sensual appetites, in eating, and drinking, and marrying; and, to give things a milder aspect and expression, in festivals and sacrifices and the slaying of victims."[5] These chiliastic views are not mentioned by Irenæus and Hippolytus, and they are inconsistent with

---

[1] Irenæus, *Adv. Hær.* i. 26. Hippolytus, *Hær.* vii. 21. Epiphanius, *Hær.* xxviii. 1.
[2] Gloag's *Pauline Epistles*, pp. 292, 293.
[3] Neander's *Church History*, vol. ii. pp. 42-47.
[4] Eusebius, *Hist. Eccl.* iii. 28.   [5] *Ibid.* iii. 28, vii. 25.

the Docetism of Cerinthus. Still it is not improbable that, as a Jew, he may have adopted them in a modified form. They are essentially Jewish in their character, and not Gnostic; and it was a Jewish Gnosticism that Cerinthus promulgated.

Now all these views of Cerinthus, except his chiliastic notions, are opposed by John in his writings; indeed, Irenæus informs us that John composed his Gospel as a direct refutation of Cerinthus. "John," he observes, "the disciple of the Lord, preaches this faith, and seeks, by the proclamation of the gospel, to remove that error which, by Cerinthus, had been disseminated among men."[1] And although this is undoubtedly a mistake, yet there is no reason to deny that there is in the writings of John an occasional reference to the errors of Cerinthus. Cerinthus asserted that Jesus was a mere man, that He was not born of a virgin, but was the son of Joseph and Mary; John insists on the supreme divinity of Christ: "In the beginning was the Word, and the Word was with God, and the Word was God" (John i. 1, 2). Cerinthus distinguished between God and the creator, and asserted that the world was created by a power far separate from God and at a distance from Him; John affirms that Christ as God was the Creator of the world: "All things were made by Him; and without Him was not anything made that was made" (John i. 3). Cerinthus denied that Christ came in the flesh; John insists strongly on the incarnation: "And the Word was made flesh, and dwelt among us; and we beheld His glory, as the glory of the Only-begotten of the Father, full of grace and truth" (John i. 14). Cerinthus distinguished between Jesus and Christ, and taught that Jesus was a mere man upon whom Christ descended at his baptism; John denounces those who thus separate Jesus from the Christ: "Who is a liar but he that denieth that Jesus is the Christ? He is antichrist that denieth both the Father and the Son" (1 John ii. 22). Cerinthus affirmed that although Christ might be called the Son of God, yet Jesus was not the Son of God, but a mere man; John insists upon the confession of the divine Sonship of Jesus: "Whosoever

[1] *Adv. Hær.* iii. 11. 1.

shall confess that Jesus is the Son of God, God dwelleth in him, and he in God" (1 John iv. 15). And toward the conclusion of his Gospel he says: "These are written that ye might believe that Jesus is the Christ, the Son of God; and that believing ye might have life in His name" (John xx. 31).[1]

But whilst Christianity by coming in contact with heathen philosophy gave rise to Gnosticism; on the other hand, heathen philosophy affected Christianity and gave rise to scientific theology. Christianity, when brought in contact with philosophy, was forced to be more exact in its definitions, more clear in its distinctions, and more logical in its statements. Hence, in the third century, arose the Alexandrian school with its great Fathers, Clement and Origen;[2] and, as a further result, in the fourth century arose those memorable controversies which resulted in the Nicene Creed and in the other formulæ of Christian doctrine. "The Gnostics," observes Jacobi, "by their truths and by their errors exercised a powerful reflex influence on Christianity. When the Church was in danger of sinking into formalism, the idealistic speculations of the Gnostics gave her an impulse towards thought and a more comprehensive treatment of doctrine. The consequence was, that those points in which Christianity was distinguished from Judaism and heathen philosophy were investigated and emphasized. A new impetus was given to the study of Christian philosophy; and in consequence of this impetus arose the Alexandrian school of theologians, who more than equalled the Gnostics in depth of speculative thought. It was not free from error in placing too much stress upon knowledge, but its gnosis was of an

---

[1] For an account of Cerinthus and his opinions, see article on Cerinthus by Rev. John Fuller in Smith's *Dictionary of Christian Biography*. Mosheim's *Church History*, vol. i. p. 144 ff., translated by Maclaine. Mansel's *Gnostic Heresies*, pp. 110-117. Gieseler's *Ecclesiastical History*, vol. i. p. 116. Milman's *History of Christianity*, vol. ii. p. 65. Burton's *Bampton Lectures*, pp. 174-176. Lightfoot's *Epistle to the Colossians*, pp. 107-112. Neander's *Church History*, vol. ii. pp. 42-46. Lardner's *Works*, vol. iv. pp. 564-570. Ewald's *History of Israel*, vol. viii. pp. 136-138, E. Tr.

[2] For an account of the Alexandrian theology, see Kingsley's *Alexandria and her Schools*. Neander's *Church History*, vol. ii. pp. 224-266. Bigg's *Bampton Lectures*: "The Christian Platonists of Alexandria."

elevated, pure character, and it was Christian in tone both of doctrine and morality."[1] Of course it may be a matter of dispute whether this reflex influence of Gnosticism on Christianity was upon the whole good and wholesome; but it was the inevitable consequence of these movements of thought.

Nor has Gnosticism yet ceased to operate. Its influence is not extinct. It is a phase of Christian development which must always exist whenever philosophical views and Christian doctrines come into contact. Gnosticism certainly attained its greatest development in the second century, especially in the system inculcated by Valentinus; but we can trace it throughout the Middle Ages, in the views of the Manicheans and the Paulicians,[2] and in the writings of many of the schoolmen; and in modern times the contact of philosophy with Christianity has often given rise to views which bear a close resemblance to the tenets of the ancient Gnostics. The destructive criticism of the Tübingen school was anticipated by Marcion; the Pantheism of modern times bears a close resemblance to the emanation theory of several of the Gnostic sects; the representation given by Hegel of the fall is, according to Mansel, the same as the Ophite theory;[3] the Absolute of Schelling has its counterpart in Basilides' view of the divine nature;[4] and even the Cerinthian notion of the separation of Jesus the Son of man from Christ the Son of God may be found in the speculations of modern theology.[5]

[1] Article by Jacobi on the Gnosis in Herzog's *Encyklopädie*, vol. v. p. 216.

[2] For an interesting and instructive account of this sect and their connection with the Albigenses, see Gibbon's *Decline and Fall of the Roman Empire*, chap. liv. See also Schaff's *Mediæval Christianity*, vol. ii. p. 574 ff.

[3] On the Ophite sects, see Mansel's *Gnostic Heresies*, Lecture vii.

[4] "The theory of Basilides," observes Mansel, "has reappeared with all the advantages of modern philosophical genius and learning in the resuscitated Neoplatonism of Germany; in Schelling, who speaks of the Absolute as neither ideal nor real, neither thought nor being; and in Hegel, who identifies pure existence with pure nothing." *Gnostic Heresies*, p. 147.

[5] Westcott, *Epistles of St. John*, Introduction, p. 36.

THE SECOND EPISTLE OF JOHN.

I. THE AUTHENTICITY OF THE EPISTLE.

CONSIDERING the brevity of this Epistle, the absence of any statement of doctrine, and its address to a private person, we cannot expect frequent allusions to it in the writings of the Fathers; indeed, the only points in it which would attract attention are the allusion to heretical teachers and the prohibition against their reception (vers. 7, 10); nevertheless, we meet with so many quotations and references, that the external evidence in its favour is greater than might *à priori* have been expected. The first reference is in the Muratorian canon (A.D. 170), where we have these words: "The Epistle of Jude, however, and two Epistles bearing the name of John are received in the Catholic Church" (or are reckoned among the Catholic Epistles).[1] The words are certainly ambiguous; they may refer to the Second and Third Epistles of John, as the First had previously been mentioned in the canon, when referring to the Gospel of John; or to the First and Second Epistles, the Third being omitted; but whatever interpretation we put upon the words, they prove at least that John was regarded as having written more than one Epistle. The next witness is Irenæus (A.D. 180), who refers in two places to the Second Epistle, and ascribes it to John: "John, the disciple of the Lord, has intensified their con-

---

[1] Epistola sane Jude et superscriptio Johannis duas in catholica habentur. The passage is corrupt. There afterwards follow: ut (or et) sapientia ab amicis Salomonis in honorem ipsius scripta. So that the testimony is somewhat doubtful. See Huther's *Epistles of John*, p. 490. Braune in Lange's *Commentary*, p. 182, E. Tr.

demnation, when he desires us not even to address to them
(the heretical teachers) the salutation of God speed: for, says
he, 'He that bids them God speed is a partaker with their
evil deeds.'"[1] And again, after quoting the First Epistle, he
says: "And John the disciple of the Lord, in his Epistle
already mentioned, commands us to avoid them when he says,
For many deceivers are entered into the world, who confess
not that Jesus Christ is come in the flesh; this is a deceiver
and an antichrist. Take heed to them, that ye lose not what
ye have wrought."[2] Irenæus here either regards the Second
Epistle as an appendix to the First; or, what is more probable,
quotes it by mistake as if it were the First. Clemens Alexandrinus (A.D. 190), referring to the First Epistle, uses these
words: "John in his larger Epistle manifestly teaches us the
differences of sins;"[3] which shows that he was acquainted
with at least another and smaller Epistle. And in the fragment of the Adumbrationes found in the Latin translation of
Cassiodorus, we have the following remarkable statement, to
which we shall again refer: "The Second Epistle of John,
which is written to virgins, is very simple. It was written to
a Babylonian lady by name Electa, and indicates the election
of the holy Church. He establishes in this Epistle that the
following out of the faith is not without charity; and so that
no one divide Jesus Christ; but to believe that Jesus Christ
has come in the flesh:"[4] and then follows the caution against
the reception of heretical teachers contained in ver. 10. It
is not improbable that "the Adumbrationes" is a fragment
of that work to which Eusebius alludes when he says: "In
the work called Hypotyposes he (Clement) has given us
abridged accounts of all the canonical scriptures, not even

---

[1] Irenæus, *Adv. Hær.* i. 16. 3: 'Ἰωάννης δὲ ὁ τοῦ Κυρίου μαθητής, ἐπέτεινε τὴν καταδικὴν αὐτῶν, μηδὲ χαίρειν αὐτοῖς ὑφ' ἡμῶν λέγεσθαι βουληθείς· ὁ γὰρ λέγων αὐτοῖς φησί, χαίρειν, κοινωνεῖ τοῖς ἔργοις αὐτῶν τοῖς πονηροῖς.

[2] *Ibid.* iii. 16. 8: Et discipulus ejus (Domini) Joannes in prædicta epistola fugere eos præcepit dicens: "Multi seductores exierunt in hunc mundum, qui non confitentur Jesum Christum in carne venisse," etc.

[3] Clement, *Strom.* ii. 15: Φαίνεται Ἰωάννης ἐν τῇ μείζονι ἐπιστολῇ τὰς διαφορὰς τῶν ἁμαρτιῶν ἐκδιδάσκων.

[4] Clement, *Opp.* ed. Potter, p. 1011: Secunda Johannis Epistola, quæ ad virgines scripta est, simplicissima est; scripta vero est ad quandam Babyloniam Electam nomine, significat autem electionem ecclesiæ sanctæ.

omitting those that are disputed, namely the Book of Jude and the other Catholic Epistles:"[1] from which it may be inferred that Clement was acquainted with the seven Catholic Epistles. Origen (A.D. 230) was evidently acquainted with the two shorter Epistles of John, but states that they were not generally acknowledged. "John," he observes, "has left an Epistle consisting of few lines: possibly also a Second and a Third are from him; for all are not agreed that they are genuine, but both together do not contain a hundred lines."[2] Origen does not state his own opinion, but elsewhere he speaks of the Epistles of John, thus indicating that there were more than one.[3] Dionysius of Alexandria (A.D. 245) evidently recognised the Second and Third Epistles, for he appeals to them in support of his opinion concerning the Apocalypse: "But neither in the Second nor Third Epistle ascribed to John, though they are brief, is the name of John affixed. But anonymously it is written, 'The presbyter.'"[4] Cyprian (A.D. 248) does not mention the Second Epistle of John, but in his account of the Synod of Carthage he states that "Aurelius, bishop of Chullabi, said: John the Apostle laid it down in his Epistle saying, If any one come unto you and have not the doctrine of Christ, receive him not into your house, and say not unto him God speed. For he that saith to him God speed participates in his evil deeds."[5] Alexander, bishop of Alexandria (A.D. 324), makes a similar appeal to these words of the Epistle: "It is incumbent on us who are Christians to withdraw ourselves from all those who speak or entertain thoughts against Christ: neither does it

---

[1] Euseb. *Hist. Eccl.* vi. 14.

[2] *Ibid.* vi. 25: Καταλίλοιπι ('Ιωάννης) δὲ καὶ ἐπιστολὴν πάνυ ὀλίγων στίχων· ἔστω δὲ καὶ δευτέραν καὶ τρίτην· ἐπεὶ οὐ πάντες φασὶ γνησίους εἶναι ταύτας· πλὴν οὐκ εἰσὶ στίχων ἀμφότεραι ἑκατόν.

[3] Origen, *In libr. Jesu nave hom.* 8, *Opp.* 12, p. 412: Addit nihilominus atque et Joannes tuba canere per epistolas suas et apocalypsim.

[4] Euseb. *Hist. Eccl.* vii. 25: 'Αλλ' οὐδὲ ἐν τῇ δευτέρᾳ φερομένῃ Ἰωάννου καὶ τρίτῃ, καίτοι βραχείαις οὔσαις ἐπιστολαῖς, ὁ Ἰωάννης ὀνομαστὶ πρόκειται, ἀλλὰ ἀνωνύμως ὁ πρεσβύτερος γέγραπται.

[5] Cyprian, *De hær. baptiz.*: Aurelius a Chullabi dixit: Joannes Apostolus in epistola sua posuit dicens, Si quis ad vos venit, et doctrinam Christi non habet, nolite cum admittere in domum vestram, et ave illi non dixeritis. Qui enim dixerit illi, ave, communicat factis ejus malis.

become us even to salute such men, as the blessed apostle has charged us, lest we should at any time be made partakers of their sins."[1] Eusebius (A.D. 325) mentions the two smaller Epistles of John, but classes them among the antilegomena or the disputed books: "Among the disputed books, although they are well known and approved by many, is reported that called the Epistle of James and that of Jude. Also the Second Epistle of Peter and those called the Second and Third of John, whether they are by the evangelist or by some other of the same name."[2] He, however, elsewhere mentions those Epistles of John without any intimation of their dubiety. "In his Epistles he (John) either mentions not his own name or calls himself only presbyter, but nowhere apostle or evangelist."[3] The Second and Third Epistles of John are omitted in the Peshito or old Syriac, although the Second Epistle is appealed to by Ephraem Syrus (A.D. 370).[4] After the time of Eusebius these two Epistles are incorporated into the canon, and were acknowledged by important Councils of the Church, as the Council of Laodicea (A.D. 343) and the third Council of Carthage (A.D. 397).

The internal evidence in favour of the Second Epistle of John is not without weight. No possible motive can be assigned for its forgery; it contains no doctrinal statement, it supports no particular opinion, it is addressed to no Church. It is an Epistle to a private Christian, whose very name is doubtful. The only clause which was of any special importance, as bearing on the state of parties in the Christian Church, is the prohibition against the reception of heretics (ver. 10); but we cannot suppose that the Epistle was written for the sake of this clause. The simple designation

[1] Socrates, *Hist. Eccl.* i. 6: Μὴ δὲ κἂν χαίρειν τοῖς τοιούτοις λέγειν· ἵνα μήποτε καὶ ταῖς ἁμαρτίαις αὐτῶν κοινωνοὶ γινώμεθα ὡς παρήγγειλεν ὁ μακάριος Ἰωάννης.

[2] Euseb. *Hist. Eccl.* iii. 25.

[3] Euseb. *Demonstratio Evangelica*, iii. 5: Ἐν μὲν ταῖς ἐπιστολαῖς αὐτοῦ οὐδὲ μνήμην τῆς οἰκείας προσηγορίας ποιεῖται, ἢ πρεσβύτερον ἑαυτὸν ὀνομάζει, οὐδαμοῦ δὲ ἀπόστολον οὐδὲ εὐαγγελιστήν.

[4] In the Greek version of Ephræm's works the Second Epistle of John is thus quoted: "This is not my saying, but the words of John the divine, who says, Whosoever transgresseth and abideth not in the doctrine of Christ, has not God." *De Amore Pauperum*, Tom. iii. Gr. p. 52.

of the writer, "the presbyter," is an internal mark of genuineness; for had the Epistle been the work of a forger, the writer would have designated himself by a more exalted name, such as "John the Apostle," in order to give it weight and authority; and the reception of the Epistle into the canon, notwithstanding this designation, is a presumption that those who admitted it had evidence that it was written by John.

The strongest internal evidence, however, is the resemblance which this Epistle bears to the First Epistle of John. As Bleek observes: "Both Epistles (the Second and the Third) present such an affinity with First John, in ideas, exposition, and language, both generally and in particulars, as to lead us to attribute them to the same writer; for this affinity cannot be explained as an imitation. The little that is peculiar to these Epistles as distinct from the First Epistle and the Gospel, is not of a character to warrant the supposition that they have come from a different hand, and is far outweighed by the points of resemblance."[1] There is a remarkable similarity between the style and language of the First and Second Epistles of John. It has been observed that no less than seven or eight out of the thirteen verses in the Second Epistle are found in the First. Lists of these points of resemblance are given by various writers.[2] So also the allusion to the heretics is the same, namely, to the Docetæ. Thus in the First Epistle it is said: "Every spirit that confesseth not that Jesus Christ is come in the flesh is not of God" (1 John iv. 3); and in the Second Epistle: "For many deceivers are entered into the world, who confess not that Jesus Christ is come in the flesh" (2 John 7). And the train of thought and character of the two Epistles is similar; in both the apostle insists on walking in the truth, and on love as the new commandment of the gospel.

In modern times doubts have been expressed of the genuine-

[1] Bleek's *Introduction to the N. T.*, vol. ii. p. 196, E. Tr.

[2] De Wette's *Einleitung in das N. T.*, p. 404 [E. Tr. p. 362]. Braune on "Second John" in Lange's *Bibelwerk*, p. 184, E. Tr. Plummer's *Epistles of St. John*, p. 54. Compare 2 John 1 with 1 John iii. 18; 2 John 4 with 1 John iv. 21; 2 John 5 with 1 John ii. 7; 2 John 6 with 1 John v. 3; 2 John 7 with 1 John iv. 1–3; 2 John 9 with 1 John ii. 23; 2 John 12 with 1 John i. 4.

ness of this Epistle. Its brevity and its address to a solitary individual necessarily weakened its evidence. It has been rejected by Schleiermacher, Credner, Baur, Schwegler, Hilgenfeld, Mangold, and Holtzmann. Schleiermacher supposes the Second Epistle of John to be a compilation from the First; and the Third Epistle to be a poor imitation of other writings, and from a later hand.[1] The Tübingen school, as represented by Baur and Schwegler, suppose the Second and Third Epistles to be of Montanist origin;[2] while Hilgenfeld thinks that the Second Epistle was a letter of excommunication against the Gnostic teachers, and the Third Epistle a letter of commendation to Gaius, inculcating hospitality toward itinerant missionaries as against the practice of Judaizing Christians.[3]

The Epistle has been objected to, because of the injunction in it which prohibits the reception of heretics, and the bestowal upon them of even the common rites of hospitality: "If there come any unto you, and bring not this doctrine, receive him not into your house, neither bid him God speed: for he that biddeth him God speed is partaker of his evil deeds" (2 John 10, 11). It is asserted that these words indicate an intolerant spirit, unlike the loving spirit of the Gospel, so beautifully manifested by John, the apostle of love. It is the part of Christian love to restore the erring to the truth, and not to thrust them away. But there is nothing in this injunction at variance with the benevolent spirit of the Gospel or with the character of John.[4] It is the province of love to hate evil. The more a man loves Christ, the more does he hate Antichrist. We are repeatedly commanded to avoid all unnecessary communication with the wicked. John, in his First Epistle, sternly reproves the heretical teachers who were corrupting the Church; and he justly feared that association with them might lead astray the unwary and pervert their faith. And so far from this injunction being opposed to the character of John, we have here the element

[1] Quoted in Bleek's *Introduction to N. T.*, vol. ii. p. 195.
[2] For the views of Baur and Schwegler, see introduction to 3 John.
[3] Hilgenfeld's *Einleitung*, pp. 686, 693.
[4] In the newly discovered *Teaching of the Twelve Apostles* (the Didaché), rules are laid down for the reception of itinerant missionaries, showing that abuses of this practice had crept into the early Church.

of moral indignation which enters largely into it. His love was not weak and effeminate; but bold and daring, uncompromisingly opposed to evil. It was the same trait of character that made him wish to draw down fire from heaven to consume the inhospitable Samaritans, that obtained for him the name of Boanerges, and that was displayed by him in his encounter with Cerinthus in the bath, according to the not improbable tradition. Besides, the doctrine taught by these heretics—that Jesus Christ had not come in the flesh—was at variance with the whole truth and spirit of Christianity, and, if admitted, would overthrow the religion of Jesus. "This," he observes, "is a deceiver and an antichrist."

II. THE AUTHOR OF THE EPISTLE.

Some writers ascribe the Second and Third Epistles, not to John the Apostle, but to John the Presbyter. In both Epistles the writer designates himself ὁ πρεσβύτερος; and as, in the Ecclesiastical History of Eusebius, a person called "John the Presbyter" is mentioned as resident at Ephesus, these Epistles have been ascribed to him. This opinion was adopted by Jerome, who says: "John wrote one Epistle, which is approved by all ecclesiastics and learned men; but the other two, at the beginning of which is 'the Elder,' are said to have been written by John the Presbyter, whose sepulchre is at this day shown at Ephesus."[1] This opinion was revived by Erasmus at the time of the Reformation, and has been adopted by Grotius,[2] Fritzsche, Bretschneider, Wieseler, and Credner.[3] In recent times it has been supported by Ebrard. "The Presbyter John," he asserts, "was the author of these two Epistles." At the same time, he carefully guards himself against the inference that he thereby denies the canonicity and inspiration of these two Epistles: "We must hold fast that the Presbyter John wrote these words under the in-

---

[1] Jerome, *vir. illustr.* chap. ix. [2] *Annotationes in Ep.* ii.
[3] Credner's *Einleitung in das N. T.*, p. 689 ff. Reuss observes: "An obvious confusion of the son of Zebedee with a contemporary presbyter at Ephesus of the same name is always a possibility." *Geschichte des heil. Schrift. N. T.*, p. 228 [E. Tr. p. 238].

spiration of the Spirit of the Lord Jesus Christ, and in harmony with the teaching of his master, the apostle."[1]

One reason assigned for the above opinion, besides the title "Presbyter" at the commencement of these Epistles, is that we cannot imagine an opposition, such as that which Diotrephes (3 John 9) displayed, to be directed against so exalted a personage as the apostle John. But to this it may be replied that this opposition finds its counterpart in the equally strong opposition that was raised against the apostle Paul in the Church of Corinth and among the Jewish Christians in Jerusalem.[2] The remarkable resemblance of the Second Epistle to the First in style and language, in thought and turns of expression, proves that they were the composition of one author, and refutes the opinion that this author was John the Presbyter.

Indeed, it is doubtful if such a person as John the Presbyter ever existed. Theologians differ greatly on this point; Huther, Westcott, and Bishop Lightfoot admit that such a person lived in Ephesus at the close of the apostolic age; whilst Riggenbach, Farrar, Plummer, Warfield, and Salmon consider his existence as extremely problematical.[3] Our chief, if not our only reason, for believing in his personality, is a statement of Papias (A.D. 120) recorded by Eusebius.[4] Papias, speaking of the care he took in collecting the traditions of the apostolic age, says: "On any occasion when a person came in my way who had been a follower of the presbyters, I would inquire about the discourses of the presbyters, what was said by Andrew, or by Peter, or by Philip, or by Thomas, or by James, or by John, or Matthew, or any other of the Lord's disciples, and what Aristion and the Presbyter John, the disciples of the Lord, say."[5] Eusebius points out that the

---

[1] Ebrard's *Commentary on St. John's Epistles*, pp. 375, 376.

[2] It is also to be observed that the opposition was not directly against John himself, but against those sent by him.

[3] For John the Presbyter, see article by Salmon in Smith's *Dictionary of Christian Biography*, vol. iii. p. 398 ff. Plummer, *On John's Epistles*, pp. 213-216, Appendix E, "John the Presbyter or the Elder."

[4] For an account of Papias and the fragments of his works which have come down to us, see Salmon's *Introduction to the N. T.*, pp. 104-125.

[5] Euseb. *Hist. Eccl.* iii. 39.

name of John is twice mentioned: once along with Andrew, Peter, Philip, Thomas, James, and Matthew, who were apostles; and at another time in company with an unknown disciple called Aristion; hence he infers that Papias mentions two Johns—John the Apostle and John the Presbyter. This inference of Eusebius has, however, been called in question, and it has been supposed that Papias alludes only to one John. It is observed that Papias applies the title "presbyter" to all those above mentioned; in the first clause he speaks of what they said (εἶπεν), and consequently of those traditions which he received at second hand; and in the second clause he speaks of what they say (λέγουσι), and consequently of those traditions which he received from contemporaries. From John he received information of both kinds; reports of what he said when the other apostles were alive, and of what he says now at the time Papias wrote.[1] Such an explanation may not be free from objection; but it is certain that except this statement of Papias, preserved by Eusebius, there is no mention of John the Presbyter by any of the earlier writers who refer to the early Church of Ephesus. But even if such a person did exist, the title presbyter as applied to him must have been an official title, common to others; and hence in writing letters he would have designated himself by his own name to prevent his being mistaken for another;[2] whereas with John the Apostle there was no such necessity on account of the eminence of his position. "While," observes Professor Salmon, "we own the Eusebian interpretation of Papias to be a possible one, we are unable to see that it is the only possible one; and therefore while we are willing to receive the hypothesis of two Johns, if it will help to explain any difficulty, we do not think the evidence for it enough to make us regard it as a proved historical fact. And we frankly own that, if it were not for deference to better judges, we should unite with Keim in relegating, though in a different

---

[1] See Plummer's *Commentary on St. John's Epistles*, p. 213.
[2] Credner, indeed, thinks that this John designated himself ὁ πρεσβύτερος, not on account of his office, but either because he was older than John the Apostle, or had come at an earlier period to Asia Minor. *Einleitung*, p. 697.

way, this Doppelgänger of the apostle to the region of ghost-land."[1]

Two reasons have been assigned why John called himself "the Presbyter." Bleek and Lücke suppose that he did so on account of his age;[2] just as Paul, in his Epistle to Philemon, designates himself by a similar term (πρεσβύτης, Philem. 9). To this it is objected, that he would for this purpose have employed more usual terms, ὁ πρεσβύτης or ὁ γέρων. Accordingly Michaelis, Braune, and Düsterdieck,[3] suppose that he uses the word on account of his official position, taking the lower title *presbyter*, instead of the higher title *apostle*, from a spirit of humility; as Peter used the same title when addressing the Churches to which he wrote: "The elders which are among you I exhort, who am also an elder" (συμπρεσβύτερος, 1 Pet. v. 1). It is also to be recollected that at this time there was no distinction between presbyters and bishops.

III. THE PERSON ADDRESSED.

The Epistle is addressed to ἐκλεκτῇ κυρίᾳ καὶ τοῖς τέκνοις αὐτῆς, translated in our version: "To the elect lady and her children."[4] This lady is several times mentioned in the Epistle. Mention is made of her children "walking in the truth" (ver. 4); she is personally addressed: "I beseech thee, lady" (ver. 5); the apostle intimates his intention of visiting her (ver. 12); and a salutation is sent her from the children of her elect sister (ver. 13).

Some suppose that the Epistle is not addressed to any individual, but to the Church in general, or rather to some particular Church; and that by the title, "the elect lady and her children," the Church addressed is personified. This

---

[1] Smith's *Dictionary of Christian Biography*, vol. iii. p. 401. Another equally mysterious John the Presbyter or Prester John figures off in the twelfth century; see Baring-Gould's *Myths of the Middle Ages*, p. 32.
[2] Bleek's *Introduction to N. T.*, vol. ii. p. 196. Lücke, *On John's Epistles*, pp. 307, 308.
[3] Michaelis' *Introduction to N. T.*, vol. vi. p. 446. Braune's *Epistles of John*: Lange's *Bibelwerk*, p. 183. Düsterdieck's *Johanneische Briefe*, p. 469.
[4] So also in the Revised Version.

opinion is apparently countenanced by Clemens Alexandrinus, when he says that the name Electa indicates the election of the holy Church.¹ It was held by Jerome, and is adopted by Michaelis, Hofmann, Huther, Baur, Hilgenfeld, Ewald, Holtzmann, Wieseler, Wolf, Lightfoot, Weiss,² Wordsworth, and Salmon.³ The reasons assigned for this opinion are that it imparts importance to the Epistle; that the language of the Epistle is inapplicable to an individual or a private family; that the children of the one sister salute those of the other, as if a sister Church saluted another; and that in the First Epistle of Peter (1 Pet. v. 13) there is a similar expression where a Church is referred to.⁴ Michaelis supposes that the term κυρία is used elliptically for κυρία ἐκκλησία, which, among the Greeks, signified an assembly of the people held at a stated time; and that accordingly ἐκλεκτῇ κυρίᾳ, with ἐκκλησίᾳ understood, would signify "the elect Church or community which comes together on Sundays."⁵ This is certainly a very fanciful explanation. The opinion that a Church is here meant is supported by no less an authority than Bishop Lightfoot. In a note to his commentary on the Epistle to Philemon, he observes: "I take the view that the κυρία addressed in the Second Epistle of John is some Church personified, as indeed the whole tenour of the Epistle seems to imply. The salutation to the 'elect lady' from her 'elect sister' will then be a greeting sent to one Church from another; just as in First Peter the letter is addressed at the outset ἐκλεκτοῖς Πόντου κ.τ.λ., and contains at the close a salutation from ἡ ἐν Βαβυλῶνι συνεκλεκτή."⁶ Bishop Wordsworth adopts the same opinion. "It appears," he observes, "more probable that under this title John is addressing a Christian Church. This interpretation is suggested by the words used by John's brother apostle, Peter, at the close of his Epistle: 'The co-elect with you that is in Babylon saluteth you.' There the word 'co-elect' signifies a Church,

---

¹ See *supra*, p. 323.   ² *Einleitung*, p. 470.
³ *Introduction to the N. T.*, p. 338.
⁴ See Hilgenfeld's *Einleitung*, p. 685. Holtzmann's *Einleitung*, pp. 469, 470.
⁵ Michaelis, *Introduction to the N. T.*, vol. vi. p. 450.
⁶ Lightfoot's *Colossians and Philemon*, p. 371, 1st edition.

and it is probable that the word ἐκλεκτή (elect) here used by John has a like meaning. The word Κυρία, *lady*, here used with ἐκλεκτή, elect, is descriptive of a Church. Jesus Christ, the Lord, is Κύριος; His spouse, a Church, is Κυρία. This is declared in the very name Church (Κυριακή)."[1] But if the word κυρία denotes a Church, it is evident that some particular Church must be understood, and not, as Jerome supposes, the Church universal, because John proposes to pay a visit to the elect lady: "I trust to come unto you, and to speak face to face, that our joy may be full" (ver. 12). And although it is idle and fanciful to fix on a particular Church, yet some have carried conjecture to this unwarrantable extent. Serarius supposes it to be the Church of Corinth, because the Third Epistle is addressed to Gaius, whom he identifies with Gaius of Corinth; Whitby and Augusti suppose it to be Jerusalem, because this was the mother Church; Whiston supposes the Church of Philadelphia; Baur, the Church of Rome; and Wordsworth, the Church of Babylon.

Notwithstanding the high authority by which this opinion is supported, we regard it as without foundation. It introduces a mystical meaning into the Epistle. There is nothing whatever in the Epistle itself to lead us to infer that the words are not to be taken in their ordinary sense, and that an individual is not addressed. The elect lady is spoken of throughout as a person; her children are mentioned and described as walking in the truth; and the apostle promises her a visit. It would be straining the letter, and destroying its simplicity, to suppose that there is here a hidden meaning: that a Church and not an individual was the object of address. Besides, although the title κυρία may be appropriate to represent the Church universal—the Church being the Lamb's wife; yet it is not appropriate to denote a particular Church. And, on this supposition, the distinction between the elect lady and her children would vanish, as it is the children themselves, that is, believers, who constitute the Church; the two are identical. Further, this Epistle is similar in its mode of address to the Third Epistle. The Second Epistle begins with the words: "The elder to the elect lady and her

[1] Wordsworth's *Greek Testament:* "The Catholic Epistles," pp. 127, 128.

children, whom I love in the truth" (2 John 1); and the Third Epistle with the words: "The elder unto the well-beloved Gaius, whom I love in the truth" (3 John 1). It is admitted by all that Gaius is the name of an individual, and therefore it is analogous to suppose that "the elect lady" is also the name of an individual. The only plausible argument is that derived from the words of Second Peter: "The Church that is at Babylon, elect together with you (ἡ ἐν Βαβυλῶνι συνεκλεκτή), saluteth you" (1 Pet. v. 13). The meaning of these words is doubtful; it is a question whether a Church or an individual is meant. But admitting, as is probable, that Peter here alludes to the Church of Babylon, yet we cannot infer from this that a Church is alluded to by John, when there is no indication to that effect.[1]

It being admitted that by the words ἐκλεκτῇ κυρίᾳ not a Church but an individual is meant, opinions differ as to the proper translation of the words. Some suppose that ἐκλεκτή, Electa, is the name of the lady; others, that it is κυρία, Kyria; and others, as in the Authorized and Revised Versions, suppose that both ἐκλεκτή and κυρία are appellatives, and translate the phrase, "To the elect lady," the name not being given.

The opinion that Electa is the name is favoured by Clemens Alexandrinus in the passage formerly quoted: "The Second Epistle of John was written to a Babylonian lady by name Electa." It has been adopted in recent times by Wetstein, Grotius, and Bishop Middleton. It is, however, a mere conjecture; no reason has been assigned for it. Electa does not occur as a Greek feminine name,[2] nor does it appear to have been the custom to use the title κυρία (lady) along with feminine names. This meaning is, moreover, grammatically untenable; for, if Electa were a proper name, the words would require to have been written ἐκλεκτῇ τῇ κυρίᾳ. And in the thirteenth verse of the Epistle a salutation is sent from the children of her elect sister τῆς ἀδελφῆς σοῦ τῆς ἐκλεκτῆς, which, if Electa is a name, would require to be translated, "From the children of

[1] Bishop Alexander in *Speaker's Commentary* N. T., vol. iv. pp. 356, 357.
[2] Electus is to be found as a man's name.

your sister Electa," so that both sisters would have borne the same name; an objection which it has been attempted to avoid by conjectural emendations of the text.

The other name, Kyria, has been more generally adopted. The words are rendered: "To the elect Kyria;" and it is supposed that some Christian lady of that name is addressed. This opinion is favoured by Athanasius, who says: "John is writing to Kyria and her children;" and is adopted by Bengel, De Wette, Guericke, Lücke, Bleek, Credner, Neander, Olshausen, Düsterdieck, Ebrard, Davidson, Alford, and Bishop Alexander. It is argued that a definite name must be attached to the letter, and that as this name could not have been Electa, it must be Kyria. "Elect" is the usual epithet which the apostles applied to their converts, so that there is nothing strange in the phrase "the elect Kyria." Besides, Kyria elsewhere frequently occurs as a Greek name; two of the early martyrs were so called; and it is just the Greek rendering of the Roman patrician name Curia.[1] The masculine Κύριος, Cyrus, is of frequent occurrence. To this view, however, the same grammatical objection arises as in the case of the name Electa; if κυρία be a proper name, the words ought to have been written Κυρίᾳ τῇ ἐκλεκτῇ, as in the Third Epistle the words are Γαίῳ τῷ ἀγαπητῷ. The only answer that has been given to this objection is the very unsatisfactory one, that John did not write classical Greek. "If," observes Lücke, "John had been a strict classical author, we undoubtedly would, in this case, have required that he should have written Κυρίᾳ τῇ ἐκλεκτῇ. But John is not a classic, and the prelocation of ἐκλεκτῇ is satisfactorily accounted for, partly by the omission of the article, and partly by the usage of the adjective ἐκλεκτός, which probably at that time had lost much of its emphasis."[2] But John wrote grammatically in the address of the Third Epistle, and therefore it is an unsatisfactory solution to the objection to say that he did not do so in the address of the Second Epistle.

We therefore adopt the opinion that neither word is a

---

[1] Guericke's *Neutestamentliche Isagogik*, p. 477. Lücke, *On John's Epistles*, p. 318.

[2] Lücke, *On John's Epistles*, p. 319, E. Tr.

proper name, but that both are appellatives, and that the words are correctly rendered in the Authorized Version, "the elect lady," or more strictly, "an elect lady." This opinion is adopted by Luther, Beza, Schleiermacher, Mill, Macknight, Lardner, Braune, Farrar, Plummer, Meyrick, and the New Testament Revisers. The name of the lady is not given, just as the name of the writer is wanting; the letter would be conveyed to the person for whom it was intended. The necessity of a definite name being attached is a mere supposition for which there is no adequate reason. Of course it is idle to imagine who is particularly intended; yet such conjectures have been made. Cornelius a Lapide gives the tradition that her name was Drusia; Carpzovius supposes that she was Martha, the sister of Lazarus, as κυρία is the translation of the Chaldaic Martha; and Knauer thinks that she was Mary the mother of our Lord, because to her only was the title *Κυρία* appropriate.

IV. THE DESIGN AND CONTENTS OF THE EPISTLE.

The relation of John to the elect lady and her circumstances is as follows. It would appear that John had met certain sons of hers, probably at Ephesus, and was rejoiced to find that they were adorning the Christian profession by a holy conduct. There were also resident at Ephesus the children of the sister of this lady; in all probability the sister herself was dead. The apostle was also deeply impressed with the danger of certain erroneous opinions, probably those of Cerinthus, that had infected the Asiatic Churches, and he was anxious to warn his disciples against them. He also designed to pay a visit to this lady. These circumstances were the occasion of this friendly Epistle. Its design appears to have been twofold: to testify to "the elect lady" the apostle's approbation that he found her children walking in the truth (ver. 4); and to warn her against the reception of false teachers and countenancing their pernicious errors (ver. 10). The whole Epistle is imbued with the spirit of John. It dwells on the truth, on love as being the spirit of truth, and on obedience as being the effect of love.

It is a precious fragment of the private correspondence of the beloved and loving disciple.

Contents.—The contents of the Epistle are as follows:—After the address and salutation the aged apostle expresses his joy at finding the children of the elect lady walking in the truth, and adorning by their conduct the gospel of Christ; he exhorts her to abound in love as the great commandment of the gospel, the spirit of the religion of Christ; he warns her against those false teachers who had entered into the Church, and denied the reality of the incarnation of Jesus Christ; he admonishes her not to receive them into her house, or to wish them God speed; and he concludes the Epistle by expressing his hope of being able soon to visit her, and by conveying the greetings of her sister's children.

V. THE TIME AND PLACE OF WRITING.

Nothing can be definitely affirmed regarding the date of this Epistle. It was written by John in his old age; but whether before or after the First Epistle cannot be determined. Eichhorn supposes that it was written before the First Epistle, because, he thinks, the language shows a more vigorous spirit, and displays fewer traces of the feebleness of age;[1] whereas Lücke thinks that it was written after, because it indicates fuller information respecting the heretical teachers who in the First Epistle are merely alluded to.[2] In both the Second and Third Epistles it is observed that the apostle announces a journey which he designed to make (2 John 12; 3 John 14), but we cannot tell whether the same journey is intended in both Epistles; in other words, whether "the elect lady" and Gaius resided in the same place. In all probability, the residence of "the elect lady" was not far from Ephesus, the apostle's usual abode. The supposition that the Epistle was written during his exile in the island of Patmos is a baseless conjecture.

[1] Eichhorn's *Einleitung*, vol. ii. p. 319.
[2] Lücke's *Commentary*, p. 324.

The literature on the Second and Third Epistles of John is the same as that on the First Epistle, as in general those who wrote on the First Epistle also wrote on the other two. The Epistles are also treated of by the Rev. Samuel Cox in his work entitled, *The Private Letters of St. Paul and St. John*, London 1867.

THE THIRD EPISTLE OF JOHN.

I. THE AUTHENTICITY OF THE EPISTLE.

IT is admitted that the external evidence in favour of this Epistle is not so strong as that in favour of the Second. There are fewer references to it and quotations from it in the writings of the Fathers; indeed it, with perhaps the exception of the Second Epistle of Peter, is less alluded to than any other book of the New Testament. The comparative want of external testimony in this case was to be expected on account of the brevity of the Epistle, the nature of its contents, and its address to an unknown person. Besides, as Hug remarks, "the Third Epistle has this peculiarity, that it does not explain or recommend certain doctrines of faith, or principles of moral conduct, and consequently is no document for the general instruction of Christians, but it is rather a direction, relative to the private concerns of the apostle. Therefore it did not offer to the ancients any assistance for instruction and refutation, a necessary consequence of which has been the want of testimonies respecting it in their works."[1] This Epistle is recognised by Dionysius of Alexandria, and is mentioned by Origen and Eusebius;[2] and after the time of Eusebius was generally received in the Catholic Church. It is contained in the old Latin, but is omitted in the Peshito, though quoted by Ephræm Syrus in the Greek translation of his

---

[1] Hug's *Introduction to the N. T.*, vol. ii. p. 549.

[2] Eusebius, *Hist. Eccl.* vi. 25, iii. 25. If what Eusebius says of Clemens Alexandrinus is to be taken in its full extent, that Clement has given us abridged accounts of all the canonical Scriptures, not omitting the Antilegomena, namely, the Book of Jude and the other Catholic Epistles (*Hist. Eccl.* vi. 14), then this Epistle was known to Clement.

works.[1] It was recognised by the Councils of Laodicea (A.D. 363) and Hippo (A.D. 393), and the third Council of Carthage (A.D. 397).

But the great argument in favour of the authenticity of this Epistle arises from the internal evidence. It is impossible to assign any adequate motive for forgery. It contains no statement of doctrine; it does not, like the Second Epistle, refer to any heresy; it does not even insist on any definite line of conduct; it purports to be a private letter of the Apostle John to a certain Gaius otherwise unknown, called forth by a mere transitory circumstance. Besides, as has already been remarked with regard to the Second Epistle, had this Third Epistle been the work of a forger, who personated the apostle, the writer would not have designated himself by the simple and ambiguous title "the elder" (ὁ πρεσβύτερος), but would have called himself "John the Apostle," to give weight and authority to the Epistle.

But the strongest argument in favour of this Epistle arises from the resemblance between it and the Second Epistle, a resemblance so close that both must stand or fall together. Indeed, the common authorship of these Epistles has, so far as we know, never been called in question.[2] They are "twin-sisters," as Jerome styles them. Even Baur admits that they must have been written by one author. The resemblance between these two Epistles extends both to their form and contents. The addresses are alike: "The elder (ὁ πρεσβύτερος) to the elect lady and her children, whom I love in the truth" (οὓς ἐγὼ ἀγαπῶ ἐν ἀληθείᾳ, 2 John 1). "The elder (ὁ πρεσβύτερος) to the well-beloved Gaius, whom I love in the truth" (ὃν ἐγὼ ἀγαπῶ ἐν ἀληθείᾳ, 3 John 1). The expression of joy on account of the holy conduct of his converts is the same: "I rejoiced greatly that I found of thy children walking in the truth" (ἐχάρην λίαν ὅτι εὕρηκα ἐκ τῶν τέκνων σου περιπατοῦντας ἐν ἀληθείᾳ, 2 John 4). "I have no greater joy than when I hear that my children walk in the truth" (μειζοτέραν τούτων οὐκ ἔχω χαράν, ἵνα ἀκούω τὰ ἐμὰ τέκνα ἐν τῇ ἀληθείᾳ περιπατοῦντα,

---

[1] Ephraem's *Works: Ad Imitat. Proverb.* Tom. i. Gr. p. 76.

[2] According to Holtzmann, Späth referred them to two separate authors, *Einleitung*, p. 469.

3 John 4). And the Epistles conclude in the same manner: "Having many things to write unto you, I would not write with paper and ink; but I trust to come unto you, and speak face to face" (πολλὰ ἔχω ὑμῖν γράφειν οὐκ ἐβουλήθην διὰ χάρτου καὶ μέλανος, ἀλλὰ ἐλπίζω γενέσθαι πρὸς ὑμᾶς καὶ στόμα πρὸς στόμα λαλῆσαι, 2 John 12). "I had many things to write, but I will not with ink and pen write unto thee; but I trust that I shall shortly see thee, and we shall speak face to face" (πολλὰ εἶχον γράψαι σοι, ἀλλ' οὐ θέλω διὰ μέλανος καὶ καλάμου σοι γράφειν· ἐλπίζω δὲ εὐθέως σε ἰδεῖν, καὶ στόμα πρὸς στόμα λαλήσομεν, 3 John 13, 14).[1] The Epistles then having the same author, it is evident that if we admit the authenticity of the Second Epistle, that of the Third follows as a necessary consequence. It is indeed objected to the Third Epistle, that there are in it certain Pauline words and expressions;[2] but these are few in number, result from the nature of the Epistle, and are to be found elsewhere in the writings of John. The Epistle is Johannine, not Pauline.

The Epistle has been frequently objected to from subjective reasons; but the most singular of these objections are those entertained by the Tübingen school, represented by Baur and Schwegler. Baur supposes that the two Epistles were written by the same person, and addressed to the Church of Rome. He founds his opinion on the words of Clemens Alexandrinus, that the Second Epistle was written to a Babylonian lady Electa, and that by Electa is meant the election of the Church.[3] From this he infers that ἐκλεκτή is a metaphorical designation of a Church, and he understands Babylon as the usual allegorical designation, employed by the early Church, for Rome, as in 1 Pet. v. 13. From

---

[1] The Greek text in these quotations is that of Tischendorf's *Novum Testamentum Græce*, editio septima. Whilst these resemblances show that the Epistles were by the same author, the minute variations prove that the one Epistle was not copied from the other.

[2] The Pauline words adduced are ὑγιαίνειν (ver. 2), εὐοῦσθαι (ver. 2), προπέμπειν (ver. 6), φιλοπρωτεύων (ver. 9), φλυαρῶν (ver. 10). See Lücke on the *Epistles of John*, p. 310. Westcott's *Epistles of John*, p. lv.

[3] Scripta vero est ad quandam Babyloniam Electam nomine, significat autem electionem ecclesiae sanctae. *Opp.* ed. Potter, p. 1011.

these premises he deduces the inference that this Third Epistle was written by a disciple of Montanus to the Church of Rome, with the view of warning the disciples against the hierarchical pretensions of the Roman bishop. According to this view, Diotrephes who thrust out the disciples is a symbolical name for the Roman bishop; and this is indicated by the epithet φιλοπρωτεύων, as the bishop of Rome aimed to be the first among the bishops (*episcopus episcoporum*). According to Schwegler, the bishop of Rome referred to was Victor, a contemporary of Irenæus; but according to Baur, he must have been some earlier bishop, Anicetus, Soter, or Eleatheros, as the Second Epistle is referred to by Irenæus. Both Epistles are considered as controversial writings, wherein the bitterness of controversy is apparent; in the Second Epistle by the injunction given to " the elect lady " not to show hospitality to heretical teachers; and in the Third by the attack on Diotrephes.[1] Such a supposition is the very extravagance of criticism; it is wholly fanciful without a shred of argument. How Epistles, that contain not one word in favour of Montanism, can be assigned to a Montanist, is difficult to conceive.

Hilgenfeld, the ablest living representative of the Tübingen school, and who perhaps excels his master (Baur) in ingenuity and plausibility, gives a different account of the origin of these Epistles. According to him, both were writings of the second century, and were written with a direct reference to Gnosticism. The Second Epistle is one of those excommunicatory writings, which the early Church was accustomed to send for the purpose of denouncing those who were infested with Gnostic errors; similar to the letter now lost which Paul wrote to the Church of Corinth (1 Cor. v. 9); whilst the Third Epistle was one of those letters of recommendation (ἐπιστολὴ συστατική) which Christians were accustomed to receive when they went from one Christian community to another; similar to those recommendatory letters mentioned by Paul in his Second Epistle to the Corinthians (2 Cor. iii. 1). To these Epistles the name " elder " or " presbyter " was affixed, for the purpose of imparting to them official authority, but without

---

[1] See Düsterdieck's *Johanneische Briefe*, vol. ii. pp. 461, 462. Huther's *Epistles of John*, p. 495, E. Tr.

any reference to the Apostle John.[1] These suppositions are ingenious, but are pure inventions without substantial foundation. It is admitted that the Third Epistle was probably "a letter of recommendation," but there is no reason for concluding that it was not written by the Apostle John.

II. THE PERSON ADDRESSED.

The Epistle is addressed to a certain Gaius (3 John 1). There are three of this name mentioned in the New Testament: 1. Gaius of Corinth, who was one of those converts whom Paul himself baptized (1 Cor. i. 14), and who in all probability is the same who is mentioned in the Epistle to the Romans written from Corinth: "Gaius mine host, and of the whole Church, saluteth you" (Rom. xvi. 23); 2. Gaius of Derbe in Lycaonia (Γάϊος Δερβαῖος), who is mentioned in the list of those who accompanied Paul in his last journey to Jerusalem (Acts xx. 4); and 3. Gaius of Macedonia, who was with Paul during the tumult at Ephesus: "Gaius and Aristarchus, men of Macedonia, Paul's companions in travel" (Acts xix. 29). Lücke supposes the Gaius of this Epistle to be the same as Gaius of Derbe,[2] but he assigns no reasons for this opinion. Michaelis and Bishop Alexander suppose him to be the same as Gaius of Corinth, because that Gaius is also praised for his hospitality, and because the place where the Gaius of the Epistle lived was torn with factions, which was then the case with the Church of Corinth.[3] These are purely conjectural suppositions: the name Gaius is the same as the Latin Caius, one of the most common names among the Greeks and Romans. There is a fourth Gaius, mentioned in the *Apostolic Constitutions*, as being appointed bishop of Pergamos by the Apostle John.[4] Mill, Whiston, C. A. Wolf, and Hilgenfeld identify him with this Gaius, on account of his

---

[1] Hilgenfeld's *Einleitung*, p. 693. So also Holtzmann, *Einleitung*, p. 470.
[2] Lücke *On St. John's Epistles*, p. 320. Bleek identifies Gaius of Derbe with Gaius of Macedonia, and observes that "this may probably be the Gaius of our Epistle." *Introduction to N. T.*, vol. ii. p. 198.
[3] Michaelis, *Introduction to N. T.*, vol. vi. p. 455. Bp. Alexander in *Speaker's Commentary*, vol. iv. p. 372.
[4] *Apost. Constit.* vii. 46.

being a disciple of John, and on account of the proximity of Pergamos to Ephesus.[1] Gaius, however, does not appear to have been a bishop or office-bearer of any church; but a Christian layman, a man of position and influence in the Christian community to which he belonged. He is commended for his hospitality toward certain brethren and strangers, and for his charity before the Church: "I rejoiced greatly when the brethren came and testified of the truth that is in thee, even as thou walkest in the truth" (3 John 3).

III. THE DESIGN AND CONTENTS OF THE EPISTLE.

It would appear from the Epistle that John—who seems to have exercised an episcopal oversight of the Churches of Proconsular Asia, as may be seen in his address to "the seven Churches which are in Asia" (Rev. i. 4)—had sent certain members of the Ephesian Church as evangelists to the Church to which Gaius belonged, and along with them a letter of recommendation: "I wrote," says he, "unto the Church" (3 John 9). But in that Church, probably occupying some official position, was a certain Diotrephes, a proud and ambitious man, who not only repudiated the epistle and authority of the apostle, but rejected those brethren sent by him, and prevented, or endeavoured to prevent, their reception by the Church. Gaius, however, a person of influence in the Church, welcomed them into his house, treated them with hospitality, and probably by pecuniary aid brought them on their journey. On the return of these brethren to Ephesus they reported to John the overbearing conduct of Diotrephes, and the Christian and honourable reception which they received from Gaius. In consequence of this the apostle wrote this letter to Gaius, wherein he commends him for his generosity and kindness to the travelling evangelists, and sternly rebukes Diotrephes for his haughty and overbearing conduct. He commends a certain Demetrius, who was perhaps the bearer of this Epistle.

The Third Epistle is more lifelike than the Second. Three persons are brought before us, and their characters delineated

---

[1] Wolf's *Commentar zu den drei Briefen Johannis*, p. 326. Hilgenfeld's *Einleitung*, p. 686.

with master strokes—the hospitable Gaius, the proud and overbearing Diotrephes, and the reputable Demetrius. We have already touched upon Gaius as the person to whom this Epistle is addressed. Diotrephes is thus mentioned: "I wrote unto the Church, but Diotrephes, who loveth to have the preeminence among them, received us not. Wherefore, if I come, I will remember his deeds which he doeth, prating against us with malicious words; and not content therewith, neither doth he himself receive the brethren, and forbiddeth them that would, and casteth them out of the Church" (3 John 9, 10). Diotrephes is not here censured for his heretical teaching; there is no reason for the supposition that he belonged to those heretical teachers, mentioned in the first two Epistles, who called in question Christ's advent in the flesh; it was not his opinions, but his conduct which was blamed. He appears to have possessed some kind of official influence in the Church, and to have had the power of excommunication. Hence then, in all probability, he was the presbyter or bishop of the Church, of which Gaius was a member. He exercised his episcopal power in an imperious manner, and even set at defiance the authority of the apostle, being jealous of his interference. Some suppose that the brethren, whom he cast out of the Church, were the travelling evangelists who had come with a letter of recommendation from John, and whom he regarded with a jealous eye; and others think that they were those who wished to receive and maintain these evangelists. Different reasons have been assigned for his conduct. Grotius represents him as a strict Gentile Christian, who would not receive Jewish Christian brethren; and others think that he was a strict Jewish Christian, who would prevent the gospel being preached to the Gentiles. Ewald supposes that the Second and Third Epistles were addressed to the same Church, that Diotrephes had specially interested himself in those false teachers who are condemned in the Second Epistle, and that John wrote this Epistle to Gaius from fear lest the Second Epistle might have been suppressed by Diotrephes,[1]—a hypothesis which has no foundation, and cannot be proved from a comparison

[1] Huther's *Epistles of John*, p. 498.

of these two Epistles. It has been thought highly improbable that any one could have had the audacity to oppose himself to the authority of the Apostle John, so as to reject those whom he had sent.[1] But the apostolic Church does not appear to have been so obedient to the authority of the apostles, as we are apt to imagine. Hymeneus and Philetus could resist Paul, the Corinthian and Galatian converts could oppose themselves to his authority, and so we need not be surprised that Diotrephes could resist the Apostle John.[2]

Whilst the apostle censures Diotrephes, he commends Demetrius. "Demetrius hath good report of all men, and of the truth itself; yea, and we also bear record: and ye know that our record is true" (3 John 12). Ebrard supposes that Demetrius was one of those who would have received the brethren, but whom Diotrephes prevented.[3] Lücke, Düsterdieck, Huther, and Braune, with greater probability, suppose him to have been a travelling evangelist and the bearer of this Epistle, recommended to the hospitable regards of Gaius.[4] He had a good report of all men, that is, of the Christians at Ephesus. Some strangely imagine that he is the same as Demetrius the silversmith, the opponent of Paul at Ephesus (Acts xix. 24), and who had been converted to Christianity.

In the apostolic times evangelists were sent from the different Churches to diffuse the gospel among the heathen. They appear to have been furnished with letters of recommendation; and there is some ground for the supposition that this Epistle was a letter of recommendation of the evangelist Demetrius, though there is no reason to think that it was not written by John. These travelling evangelists were of different characters, and hence danger arose from their too ready admission into the Churches. Some appear to have diffused pernicious doctrines; and others to have made gain of preaching the gospel. The true missionaries are here described as those who, actuated by a spirit of disinterestedness

---

[1] Ebrard *On John's Epistles*, pp. 371–374. Davidson's *Introduction to the Study of the N. T.*, vol. ii. p. 318, 1st edition; vol. ii. p. 253, 2nd edition.
[2] Ewald's *History of Israel*, vol. viii. p. 159, E. Tr.
[3] Ebrard *On John's Epistles*, p. 405.
[4] Braune on John's Epistles in Lange's *Bibelwerk*, p. 199.

like Paul, would take nothing of the Gentiles (3 John 7); these were to be received and entertained by the Church. The false missionaries were those who were actuated by covetousness and diffused heretical opinions; these were neither to be received nor encouraged (2 John 10). It would appear that regulations were laid down in the early Church for the reception of these travelling evangelists; so that, on the one hand, the Church might not be imposed on, and, on the other hand, the rights of Christian hospitality might be practised. We find a trace of these rules in that remarkable document *The Teaching of the Twelve Apostles*, recently discovered and published (A.D. 1883) by Bryennios, and supposed to belong to the close of the first century.[1] There we read: "Whoever cometh and teacheth you all these things, before spoken, receive him; but if the teacher himself turn aside and teach another teaching, so as to overthrow this, do not hear him; but if he teach so as to promote righteousness and knowledge of the Lord, receive him as the Lord. Every apostle who cometh to you, let him be received as the Lord; but he shall not remain more than one day; if, however, there be need, then the next day; but if he remain three days, he is a false prophet. But when the apostle departeth, let him take nothing except bread enough till he lodge again; but if he ask money, he is a false prophet."[2] But not only the soundness of their doctrine, but also the purity of their motives was to be tested: "Let every one that cometh in the Lord's name be received, but afterward ye shall test and know him. If he who comes is a traveller, help him as much as you can; but he shall not remain with you, unless for two or three days, if there be necessity. But if he will take up his abode among you, being an artisan, let him work and so eat; but if he have no trade, provide, according to your understanding, that no idler live with you as a Christian. But if he will not act according to this, he is one who makes gain out of Christ; beware of such."[3]

[1] Διδαχὴ τῶν δώδεκα ἀποστόλων. The work is referred to by Eusebius, *Hist. Eccl.* iii. 25, called by him τῶν ἀποστόλων αἱ λεγόμεναι διδαχαί. See *supra*, p. 82.

[2] Chap. xi. See Schaff's *Oldest Church Manual*, pp. 199-201.

[3] Chap. xii. Schaff, p. 201.

Mention is made of an epistle which John had written to the Church of which Gaius was a member: "I wrote unto the Church" (3 John 9), or, according to the corrected text: "I wrote somewhat unto the Church"[1] (Revised Version). The purport of this Epistle was evidently to recommend certain travelling brethren, probably evangelists, to the favourable notice of the Church. Some (Storr, etc.) suppose that this writing was the First Epistle of John; whilst others (Besser, Ewald, Lechler, C. A. Wolf, Salmon) think that it was the Second.[2] Neither of these suppositions is correct, because there is nothing in common in these Epistles with the circumstances here alluded to. Others refer it to this letter itself, and translate the verb ἔγραψα, "I would have written;" but this is not the obvious rendering, and involves the incredible supposition that John was deterred from writing through fear of Diotrephes. Some manuscripts read ἔγραψα ἄν, and the Vulgate has *scripsissem forsitan*—"I would have written;" but such a reading is too weakly attested. The words evidently refer to an epistle which John wrote to the Church, but which has not been preserved. And doubtless many of the apostolic Epistles, especially those of a private nature, have been lost. Mention is made of a lost Epistle of Paul to the Laodiceans (Col. iv. 10), and of a lost Epistle of his to the Corinthians (1 Cor. v. 9),[3] and here of a lost Epistle of John. Those Epistles of the inspired apostles have been preserved which were necessary to be a sufficient rule for our faith and practice. What is lost may indeed have been equally valuable with what remains, but not essentially necessary.

Contents. — The Epistle commences with an address to Gaius, expressing the hope that he may prosper and be in health, both in soul and body. The apostle rejoices greatly in the good report which was conveyed to him by certain evangelists; he could experience no greater joy than to hear that his converts walked in the truth. But whilst he praises Gaius for his hospitality toward the travelling

---

[1] ἔγραψά τι τῇ ἐκκλησίᾳ; attested by ℵ A B C.

[2] Wolf's *Briefe Johannis*, p. 339. Salmon's *Introduction to N. T.*, p. 338.

[3] See author's *Introduction to the Pauline Epistles:* "On the Lost Epistles of Paul," pp. 23-36.

evangelists, he gives them also credit for their disinterestedness: "they went forth taking nothing of the Gentiles;" and therefore it was at once the privilege and duty of believers to minister to their wants. He next reflects on the opposite conduct of Diotrephes. He had written a letter with these evangelists, but Diotrephes had set at nought his authority, and refused to receive them. When he comes, he will visit his conduct with merited censure and punishment. The apostle then takes occasion to exhort Gaius to imitate the good and not the evil, for whosoever does good is of God, and whosoever does evil hath not recognised Him. He recommends a certain Demetrius, an evangelist and the bearer of this Epistle. And concludes by announcing a speedy visit, when writing with pen and ink will give place to personal communication.

The Epistle is pervaded throughout with the spirit of John. As in his other two Epistles, he dwells upon the importance of walking in the truth. It also shows the high Christian tone which pervades the private correspondence of the apostolic writers. The Epistle of Paul to Philemon and these two Epistles of John are private letters to individuals which, even more than letters to Churches, disclose the heart of the authors; in these the writers express their inward feelings without restraint or disguise. They are eminently Christian letters, and by their high moral tone and spirituality are distinguished from the celebrated remains of antiquity, the letters of Cicero and Pliny.[1] We have here also in these two Epistles of John a glimpse of the state of the apostolic Churches; the mixed character of the Churches, the prevalence of heretical teaching, the institution of travelling evangelists, and the occasional resistance even to apostolic authority. "In these two short occasional letters," observes Bishop Alexander, "St. John provided two safeguards for the Catholic Church. Heresy and schism are the dangers to which it is perpetually exposed. St. John's condemnation of the spirit of *heresy* is recorded in the Second Epistle; his condemnation of the spirit of *schism* is written in the Third Epistle."[2]

---

[1] See Cox, *The Private Letters of St. Paul and St. John.*
[2] Bishop Alexander in *Speaker's Commentary*, vol. iv. p. 374.

IV. TIME AND PLACE OF WRITING.

In both these Epistles the apostle promises a visit; in the one to "the elect lady" (2 John 12), and in the other to "the well-beloved Gaius" (3 John 14). In all probability, the journeys here alluded to were journeys of episcopal visitation. We learn from Eusebius that John, when aged, settled in Ephesus, and undertook the superintendence of the Churches of Proconsular Asia, and was accustomed to make journeys of visitation. "About this time," he observes, "the beloved disciple of Jesus, John the apostle and evangelist, still surviving, governed the Churches of Asia after his return from exile on the island (of Patmos) and the death of Domitian." And again he observes: "After the tyrant (Domitian) was dead, John, coming from the island of Patmos to Ephesus, went also, when called, to the neighbouring Churches of the Gentiles; in some to appoint bishops, in some to institute entirely new Churches, in others to appoint to the ministry some of those that were pointed out by the Holy Ghost."[1] The Second and Third Epistles were written when John was aged, so that the title "presbyter" which he affixes to them may well refer to his age as well as to his office. There is nothing improbable in the supposition that they were written after his return from the island of Patmos, and consequently about the same time as the Gospel and First Epistle.[2] If John was banished to Patmos in the reign of Domitian, he would not be recalled until A.D. 96, when that tyrant was put to death; and, according to ecclesiastical tradition, he survived even to the reign of Trajan, who ascended the imperial throne A.D. 98. There is no reason to doubt that the place of composition was Ephesus, the usual residence of John in his later years.

---

[1] Eusebius, *Hist. Eccl.* iii. 23.

[2] Dr. Davidson and those belonging to the Tübingen school fix the date of the Epistle at A.D. 130. *Introduction to the Study of the N. T.*, vol. ii. 262, 2nd edition.

THE EPISTLE OF JUDE.

I. THE AUTHENTICITY OF THE EPISTLE.

THE Epistle of Jude, considering its brevity and the nature of its contents, is well authenticated by external evidence. The supposed allusions to it in the writings of the Apostolic Fathers[1] are indeed too vague and uncertain to be insisted on; nor is there any mention of it in the writings of Irenæus. The first notice which we have is in the Muratorian Canon (A.D. 170), where it is mentioned in the following words: "The Epistle of Jude, and the two Epistles bearing the name of John, are received in the Catholic (Church)."[2] The first Father who directly refers to it is Clemens Alexandrinus (A.D. 190), and he does so in several of his works. Thus, in the *Instructor* or *Pædagogus*, he observes: "I would have you know, says Jude, that God having once saved the people from the land of Egypt, afterwards destroyed them that believed not; and the angels which kept not their first estate, but left their own habitation, He hath reserved to the judgment of the great day, in everlasting chains, under darkness" (Jude 5, 6).[3] In the *Miscellanies* or *Stromata* he thus writes: "It was concerning these (namely, the heresies of Carpocrates and his followers) and similar heresies that Jude spoke prophetically."[4] And again: "The greater a man seems to be, the more humble

---

[1] Allusions have been adduced from Barnabas, Hermas, and Polycarp. Charteris' *Canonicity*, p. 331.

[2] *Supra*, p. 322.

[3] *Pædagog.* iii. 8: Εἴδεναι γὰρ ὑμᾶς φησὶν ὁ Ἰούδας, βούλομαι ὅτι ὁ θεὸς ἅπαξ ἐκ γῆς Αἰγύπτου λαὸν σώσας κ.τ.λ.

[4] *Strom.* iii. 2: Ἐπὶ τούτων οἶμαι καὶ τῶν ὁμοίων αἱρέσεων προφητικῶς Ἰούδαν ἐν τῇ ἐπιστολῇ εἰρηκέναι.

should he be, as Clement says in his Epistle to the Corinthians such an one as is capable of complying with the precept: And some plucked from the fire, and on others have compassion, making a difference"[1] (Jude 22, 23). And in the *Adumbrationes* we have a comment on the Epistle of Jude, commencing with these words: "Jude, who wrote the Catholic Epistle, the brother of the sons of Joseph, a very religious man, while knowing his near relationship to the Lord, yet did not say that he was His brother. But what said he? 'Jude, a servant of Jesus Christ, of Him as Lord; but the brother of James.'"[2] The *Adumbrationes* is supposed to be the same as the *Hypotyposes* of Clement, described by Eusebius as an abridgment "of all the canonical Scriptures, not even omitting those that are disputed, namely, the Epistle of Jude and the other Catholic Epistles."[3] Tertullian (A.D. 200) adduces the Epistle of Jude in favour of the inspiration of the Book of Enoch: "To these considerations is added the fact that Enoch possesses a testimony in the Apostle Jude."[4] In a doubtful work ascribed to Hippolytus (A.D. 220) we have the following direct reference to Jude: "Jude, the brother of James, speaks in like manner: In the last days there shall be mockers walking after their own ungodly lusts. These be they who without fear feed themselves" (Jude 18, 12).[5] Origen (A.D. 230) frequently refers to this Epistle, and appears to have set a high value upon it. Thus, in his commentary on Matthew's Gospel, he says: "Jude wrote an Epistle of few lines indeed, but full of the powerful words of heavenly grace; at the beginning of which he says, Jude, the servant of Jesus Christ, and brother of James."[6] "In

---

[1] *Strom.* vi. 8.

[2] Clem. *Opp.* ed. Potter, p. 1007: Judas, qui catholicam scripsit epistolam, frater filiorum Joseph, exstans valde religiosus, quum sciret propinquitatem Domini, non tamen dixit seipsum fratrem ejus esse: Sed quid dixit? Judas servus Jesu Christi, utpote Domini, frater autem Jacobi.

[3] *Hist. Eccl.* vi. 14.

[4] Tertullian, *de cultu fœm.* c. 3: Eo accidit, quod Enoch apud Judam apostolum testimonium possidet.

[5] Hippolytus, *De consummatione sæculi*, c. 10.

[6] Origen, *Comm. on Matt.* xiii. 55: Ἰούδας ἔγραψεν ἐπιστολήν, ὀλιγόστιχον μέν, πεπληρωμένην, δὲ τῶν τῆς οὐρανίου χάριτος ἐῤῥωμένων λόγων, ὅστις ἐν τῷ προοιμίῳ εἴρηκιν· Ἰούδας Ἰησοῦ Χριστοῦ δοῦλος, ἀδελφὸς δὲ Ἰακώβου.

the Epistle of Jude it is written, To them that are beloved in God the Father, and preserved in Christ Jesus, and called."¹ "If any one received the Epistle of Jude, let him consider what will follow from what is there said: And the angels which kept not their first estate, but left their habitation, he has reserved in everlasting chains, under darkness, unto the judgment of the great day."² And in the works of Origen, preserved in the Latin translation of Rufinus, we have frequent references to, and express quotations from, the Epistle of Jude. There is no mention of this Epistle in the writings of Cyprian (A.D. 248); but it is quoted in a treatise preserved in his works by an anonymous writer, who was his contemporary, against the Novatian heresy: "As it is written, Behold, He cometh with many thousands of His messengers, to execute judgment upon all, and to destroy all the wicked"³ (Jude 14, 15). Malchion (A.D. 270), a presbyter of Antioch, in a letter addressed in the name of the bishops, presbyters, and deacons of Asia to the bishops of Rome and Alexandria, condemnatory of the heresy of Paul of Samosata, evidently alludes to the Epistle of Jude. Paul is there described as one "who denied his God and Lord, and kept not the faith which he himself formerly held"⁴ (Jude 4). Eusebius (A.D. 325) places the Epistle among the antilegomena, but observes that it was well known and widely acknowledged: "Among the disputed books, although they are well known by many, is reputed that called the Epistle of James and that of Jude."⁵ And again he observes: "Not many of the ancients have mentioned the Epistle of Jude, which is also one of the seven Catholic Epistles. Nevertheless we know that these, with the rest, are publicly used in most of the churches."⁶ After the time of Eusebius, the Epistle of Jude was generally received by

---

¹ *Comm. on Matt.* xviii. 10: Καὶ ἐν τῇ Ἰούδα ἐπιστολῇ, τοῖς ἐν θεῷ πατρὶ ἠγαπημένοις καὶ Ἰησοῦ Χριστοῦ τετηρημένοις κλητοῖς.
² *Comm. on Matt.* xxii. 23: Εἰ δὲ καὶ τὴν Ἰούδα προσοιτό τις ἐπιστολήν, ὁράτω τί ἕπεται τῷ λόγῳ διὰ τό· ἀγγέλους τε τοὺς μὴ τηρήσαντας τὴν ἑαυτῶν ἀρχὴν κ.τ.λ.
³ *Opp. Cyprian.* vol. iii. p. 35: Sicut scriptum est: Esse venit cum multis, millibus nuntiorum suorum, facere judicium de omnibus, etc.
⁴ Eusebius, *Hist. Eccl.* vii. 30: Τοῦ καὶ τὸν θεὸν τὸν ἑαυτοῦ καὶ Κύριον ἀρνησαμένου καὶ τὴν πίστιν ἣν καὶ αὐτὸς πρότερον εἶχε μὴ φυλάξαντος.
⁵ *Ibid.* iii. 25. ⁶ *Ibid.* ii. 23.

the Church, and its genuineness remained undisputed until the time of the Reformation. It is acknowledged by Athanasius, Cyril of Jerusalem, Epiphanius, Rufinus, Jerome, Augustine, and by the Councils of Laodicea and Carthage. It is contained in the Latin version, but is among the omitted books in the Peshito. It is, however, frequently quoted by Ephræm Syrus, though only in the Greek translation of his works.[1]

The internal evidence is not so strong as the external. The comparative obscurity of the author affords a presumption in favour of its genuineness. Were it a forgery, it would, like almost all the other forgeries in the early Church, be attributed to some leader of the Church, not to one who is almost entirely unknown. Neither can any reason be assigned which could induce any person to forge such an Epistle. The references to heresies are too vague to admit of a particular application; and the design ascribed to it by the Tübingen school, afterwards to be alluded to, is highly fanciful and incapable of proof. Even De Wette, who certainly as a critic was not given to credulity, admits the genuineness of the Epistle. "No important objection," he observes, "to the genuineness of this Epistle can be made good; neither the use of the apocryphal Book of Enoch, nor the resemblance of vers. 24, 25 to Rom. xvi. 25, nor a style of writing which betrays a certain familiarity with the Greek tongue. The Epistle is the less open to suspicion, as the author does not distinctly claim to be an apostle, nor can a pretext for forgery be discerned."[2]

It is no matter of surprise that such an Epistle as that of Jude should be much disputed in the Christian Church. Its genuineness was early questioned; it was classed among the antilegomena by Eusebius, nor is it received without hesitation in the present day. The uncertainty whether the author was the Apostle Jude, surnamed Thaddæus, or some other of the same name, rendered its reception into the canon a matter of hesitation; and the insertion of an apparently apocryphal legend, and the quotation of a prophecy of Enoch,

---

[1] Vol. ii. pp. 153, 161, iii. p. 61.
[2] *Einleitung in das N. T.*, p. 409 [E. Tr. p. 366].

gave rise to suspicions. In modern times doubt has been expressed by the two great Reformers, Luther and Calvin; it has been rejected by Grotius, Michaelis, Semler, Mayerhoff, Schleiermacher, Schenkel, Mangold, and all the writers belonging to the Tübingen school;[1] and has been doubted by Neander and Reuss.[2] Calvin thus expresses his opinion concerning it: "Though there was a dispute among the ancients concerning this Epistle, yet as the reading of it is useful, and as it contains nothing inconsistent with the purity of apostolic doctrine, and was received as authentic formerly by some of the best, I willingly add it to the others."[3] And in commenting on the Epistle, he observes: "I have said that this prophecy of Enoch was known to the Jews by being reported; but if any one think otherwise, I will not contend with him, nor indeed respecting the Epistle itself, whether it be that of Jude or of some other. In things doubtful, I only follow what seems probable."[4] Grotius supposes that this Epistle was written by Jude, the fifteenth bishop of Jerusalem, who, according to Eusebius, lived in the time of Hadrian;[5] whilst he affirms that the words "and brother of James" are an interpolation,—an opinion for which there is not the slightest foundation in the readings of the manuscripts.[6] On the other hand, the genuineness of this Epistle has been maintained by such eminent critics as Bleek, De Wette, Wiesinger, Brückner, Huther, Frommüller, Keil, and Kirchhofer among the Germans; and by Lardner, Alford, Farrar, Salmon, Lumby, Plumptre, Plummer, and Bishop Wordsworth among English theologians.

Those belonging to the Tübingen school object to the Epistle on the grounds that it bears marks of being post-apostolic, and that it was written with a special design to counteract Paulinism. They infer from vers. 17, 18, where the author refers to the "words spoken before of the apostles of our Lord Jesus Christ," that the Epistle belongs to

[1] As Baur, Hilgenfeld, Schwegler, Volkmar, Holtzmann, Lipsius.
[2] Reuss' *Geschichte der heil. Schrift. N. T.*, p. 231 [E. Tr. p. 241].
[3] *Preface to the Epistle of Jude.* [4] Calvin on Jude 15.
[5] Eusebius, *Hist. Eccl.* iv. 5. This opinion is also adopted by Volkmar, *Mose Himmelfahrt*, p. 92.
[6] Grotius, *Annotationes in Epistolam Judae.*

post-apostolic times. The heresies mentioned are said to be those which belonged to the second century. "The heretical teachers here attacked," observes Hilgenfeld, "are evidently the Gnostics of the second century. That it was written by Jude, whether one of the brethren of the Lord or an apostle, is out of the question."[1] And Schwegler affirms that the Epistle was written in the interests of Jewish Christianity in opposition to Paulinism, and that for this reason it was attributed to Jude, the brother of James, the great apostle of the circumcision.[2] But these objections are without weight. Vers. 17, 18 do not point to a post-apostolic age, but rather suppose that the readers of the Epistle had heard the preaching of the apostles, whose words they are called upon to remember, seeing that what they had foretold had now come to pass. The heresies adverted to are described in such general terms that no particular sect of Gnostics can be specified. The Gnosticism alluded to is undeveloped, such as we know to have occurred in apostolic times; licentiousness rather than heresy is condemned in this Epistle. There is absolutely nothing in the Epistle to show an antagonism to Pauline Christianity; and if it were the polemical work of a forger in the interests of Jewish Christianity, it would have been ascribed to some more eminent person, such as Peter or James, the apostles of the circumcision, and not to Jude, a person otherwise so entirely unknown.

The supposed apocryphal references which it contains have been urged as forming an objection to the genuineness of this Epistle.[3] This was the objection which was brought against it in early times, and which caused it to be placed among the antilegomena. Jerome, although he himself received the Epistle, alludes to this objection in his days. "Jude," he observes, "the brother of James, has left us a short Epistle, which is one of the seven so-called Catholic Epistles. But

---

[1] Hilgenfeld's *Einleitung in das N. T.*, p. 744.
[2] Huther's *Judas*, p. 351 [E. Tr. p. 387].
[3] This objection is urged by positive criticism; with rationalism it has no weight; this is only interested in the date of the apocryphal writings used by Jude, and the inquiry into this is not against, but rather in favour of the Epistle.

because of a quotation from the Book of Enoch, which is apocryphal, it is rejected by many. However, at length it has obtained authority from its antiquity and from prescription, so that it is reckoned among the Sacred Scriptures."[1] In this short Epistle there are more apparent apocryphal and legendary allusions than in any other Epistle of the New Testament, or, indeed, in all the writings of the New Testament put together. Among these apocryphal references may be mentioned the allusion to the rebellion of the angels and the nature of their sin, which bears a striking resemblance to the account of the fall of angels given in the book of Enoch; the dispute between Michael the archangel and the devil about the body of Moses; and the prophecy of Enoch concerning the judgment. It has been affirmed that such apocryphal references are inconsistent with the idea of inspiration; because, if the Epistle were inspired, authority would thus be given to apocryphal books, and to what at least closely resemble those rabbinical legends against which Paul warns Titus: "Not giving heed to Jewish fables, and commandments of men that turn from the truth" (Titus i. 14).

The apparent apocryphal references or quotations are chiefly two: the contention between Michael the archangel and the devil about the body of Moses (Jude 9), supposed to be taken from a book entitled The Assumption of Moses, and the prophecy of Enoch (Jude 14, 15), supposed to be taken from the so-called Book of Enoch. These references are so curious and interesting that we reserve them for future consideration.[2] Meanwhile it is to be observed that the reality of these apocryphal references has been questioned by many critics. The reference to the contest between Michael and the devil has been supposed by some to be a reference, not to any apocryphal book, but to the prophecy of Zechariah, where the words occur, "The Lord rebuke thee, O Satan" (Zech. iii. 2); or, according to others, to be an allusion to the mysterious burial of Moses, mentioned in the Book of

---

[1] *Catalog. script. eccles.* c. 4.

[2] See Dissertation I. On the Assumption of Moses; and Dissertation II. On the Book of Enoch.

Deuteronomy, where we are informed that the Lord Himself buried him (Deut. xxxiv. 6). And the prophecy of Enoch is supposed to be not a quotation from the apocryphal Book of Enoch, but a real prophecy of Enoch communicated to the writer by the Holy Spirit. But admitting, as we do, that there are here references either to apocryphal books or rabbinical traditions, yet it is urged that these references are no objection to the genuineness of the Epistle of Jude, but only instances, undoubtedly on a larger scale, similar to the quotations adduced by Paul from heathen writers (Acts xvii. 28; 1 Cor. xv. 33; Titus i. 12), or to the references made by him to the promulgation of the law by the instrumentality of angels (Gal. iii. 19), and the mention of Jannes and Jambres as the disputants with Moses[1] (2 Tim. iii. 8); both of which are mentioned as rabbinical traditions, but neither of which is alluded to in the Old Testament.

II. THE AUTHOR OF THE EPISTLE

The inscription of the Epistle is as follows: "Jude, the servant of Jesus Christ, and brother of James" ('Ιούδας 'Ιησοῦ Χριστοῦ δοῦλος, ἀδελφὸς δὲ 'Ιακώβου, Jude 1). Jude or Judas was a common Jewish name: there are no less than six of this name mentioned in the New Testament.[2] Of these three have, by different writers, been affirmed to be the author of this Epistle; Judas the apostle, surnamed Thaddæus; Judas Barsabas, who, along with Silas, was sent by the Church of Jerusalem to Antioch to confirm the disciples; and Judas, who is mentioned in the Gospels among the brethren of our Lord.

Some suppose that the author of this Epistle was Judas, surnamed Thaddæus and Lebbæus, one of the twelve apostles. This was the evident opinion of Tertullian and Origen, and of the Fathers in general, and is adopted by Bertholdt,

---

[1] On Jannes and Jambres, Origen observes: "This is not found in the Scriptures, but in a secret book, entitled Jannes and Jambres."

[2] Judas Iscariot; Judas the apostle, surnamed Thaddæus; Judas among the brethren of the Lord; Judas, surnamed Barsabas; Judas of Galilee; Judas with whom Paul lodged at Damascus.

Schneckenburger, Winer, Hofmann, Lange, Keil, Tregelles, and Bishop Wordsworth.[1] The chief arguments on which they ground this opinion are the fact that Judas the apostle is styled in the apostolic list "the brother of James" (Luke vi. 16 ; Acts i. 13); and the admission of this Epistle into the canon of the New Testament, which, they affirm, would not have occurred, had it not been written by an apostle. This opinion of the apostolic authorship of the Epistle cannot, however, be maintained. Nowhere in the Epistle does the writer claim to be an apostle. He calls himself "the servant of Jesus Christ, and the brother of James." It is true that the title "the servant of Jesus Christ" does not exclude the apostolic dignity; but the phrase "the brother of James" seems to do so; for, had he been an apostle, he would have called himself "Jude the apostle," rather than have designated himself as the brother of another apostle. It is true that in the catalogue of the apostles we read of "Judas the brother of James;" but, as we formerly remarked, it is doubtful if the words 'Ιούδας 'Ιακώβου are correctly translated; the more exact rendering is "Judas the son of James." It would appear from the Epistle itself that Jude expressly excludes himself from the number of the apostles. Thus he says: "Remember the words which were spoken before of the apostles of our Lord Jesus Christ, how they told you there should be mockers in the last time" (Jude 17, 18). Here he refers his readers to the warnings of the apostles; but he does not include himself among them.

Others suppose that the writer was Judas, surnamed Barsabas, who is called a prophet, and was reckoned "a chief man among the brethren," and who was sent by the Council of Jerusalem along with Silas to settle the dispute at Antioch (Acts xv. 22, 32). This opinion has been adopted by different writers on various grounds. Schott thinks that Barsabas denotes the son of Zebedee, and considers this Jude as the brother of John and James;[2] an opinion for which there is no foundation. Dr. John Light-

---

[1] Wordsworth's *Greek Testament:* "The General Epistles," p. 137.
[2] Schott's *Isagoge*, p. 431.

foot supposes him to be the same as Judas the apostle; and considers the name Barsabas to be not a patronymic, but, like Barnabas, an epithet descriptive of character, denoting "the son of wisdom."[1] Dean Plumptre, though on different grounds, has recently revived this opinion of the identity of Jude with Judas Barsabas. He observes that there are two mentioned in the Acts bearing the name of Barsabas; Joseph or Joses called Barsabas, who was a candidate with Matthias for the apostleship (Acts i. 23), and Judas, surnamed Barsabas, the companion of Silas (Acts xv. 23). These he supposes to be brothers, and agrees with Dr. John Lightfoot in supposing the name Barsabas to be a descriptive appellation. These two, on account of their prominence in the early Christian Church of Jerusalem, he supposes to be identical with the Joses and Judas who are in the Gospels mentioned among the brethren of our Lord (Mark vi. 3).[2] This opinion, however ingenious, is a mere supposition unsupported by adequate reasons.

We accept the third view, that this Jude was the Judas who is mentioned in the Gospels among the brethren of our Lord. This opinion was adopted by Clemens Alexandrinus among the Fathers, and by Bleek, Schmidt, Credner, Brückner, Neudecker, Wiesinger, Jessien, Spitta, Alford, Farrar, Lumby, Plummer, and Salmon. He calls himself "Jude the brother of James," evidently implying that there was a distinguished leader of that name in the early Church; and there is mention in the Acts and in the Epistles of such a distinguished person, one of the three pillars of the Church who exercised a preponderant influence in the apostolic Church, known in ecclesiastical history as the bishop of Jerusalem, who is called by Paul "James the Lord's brother" (Gal. i. 19), and whose martyrdom by the Jews finds a place in the history of Josephus. Now, among the brothers of Jesus, mentioned by the evangelists, the name of Judas occurs along with that of James (Matt. xiii. 55; Mark vi. 3). James, the Lord's brother, then had a brother called Jude, and it is this Jude whom we consider to be the author of

---

[1] Lightfoot's *Works*, ed. Pitman, vol. viii. pp. 38, 39.
[2] Plumptre, *The Epistles of Peter and Jude*, pp. 85, 86.

this Epistle. We do not here inquire into the relationship of James and Jude to our Lord, as we have already done so in the introduction to the Epistle of James. There we came to the conclusion that the preponderance of evidence is in favour of the opinion that James and Judas were the sons of Joseph and Mary. The reason why Jude calls himself "the brother of James" and not "the brother of the Lord" is obvious; it is the same reason that restrained his more distinguished brother James from applying to himself that appellation. When our Lord ascended into glory, His human relationship ceased; and thus, from humility and from a sense of the exalted dignity of the ascended Lord, both these writers call themselves, not "the brothers of the Lord," but "the servants of Jesus Christ;" a reason mentioned long ago by Clemens Alexandrinus: "Jude, whilst knowing his near relationship to the Lord, yet did not say that he himself was His brother; but Jude, a servant of Jesus Christ, of Him as Lord, but brother of James."[1] It was also natural that Jude should style himself the brother of James, of one who had attained a position of more exalted eminence in the Christian Church.

The notices of Jude in Scripture are few and indefinite. It has been inferred that he along with the other brothers of Jesus remained unbelieving during our Lord's lifetime (John vii. 5), but that they were converted and joined themselves to the Church after His resurrection (Acts i. 14). It would also seem from a statement in one of Paul's Epistles that Jude was married (1 Cor. ix. 5); a fact which is supported by ecclesiastical tradition.

The traditionary accounts of the Church are conflicting and uncertain, as we cannot tell whether they refer to Jude the author of this Epistle, or to Jude the apostle. According to the Western tradition, he and his brother Simon preached the gospel to the Persians, and there suffered martyrdom. On the other hand, Nicephorus relates that he preached the gospel in Palestine, Syria, and Arabia, and died a natural death at Edessa.[2] According to the Syrian tradition, Jude left Edessa and went into Assyria, and suffered martyrdom

[1] *Adumbrat. in Ep. Jud.* [2] Nicephorus, *Hist. Eccl.* vol. ii. p. 40.

on his return to Phœnicia.[1] The founding of the Church of
Edessa, the chief seat of Syrian literature, is ascribed, according to ecclesiastical history, to Judas, surnamed Thaddæus,
the apostle. "The apostle Thaddæus," observes Jerome,
"called by the evangelist Luke, Judas, the brother of James,
was sent to Abgarus, king of Edessa." Eusebius, on the
other hand, mentions Thaddæus not as one of the twelve
apostles, but as one of the seventy disciples.[2]

We have, however, an interesting tradition of the family
of this Jude, the brother of the Lord, recorded by Hegesippus,
and preserved by Eusebius in his history. Domitian, alarmed
like Herod by guilty fears, had issued orders that all the
descendants of David should be put to death, and two grandchildren of this Jude were accused. "There were yet living,"
observes Hegesippus, "of the family of our Lord, the grandchildren of Judas, called the brother of our Lord according to
the flesh. These were reported as being of the family of
David, and were brought before Domitian: for this emperor
was as much alarmed at the appearance of Christ as Herod.
He put the question, whether they were of David's race, and
they confessed that they were. He then asked them what
property they had, or how much money they earned. And
both of them answered that they had between them only
nine thousand denarii, not in silver, but in the value of land,
containing thirty-nine acres; from which they raised their
taxes and supported themselves by their labours. When
asked respecting Christ and His kingdom, they replied that
it was not a temporal nor an earthly kingdom, but celestial
and angelic; and that it would appear in the end of the
world, when coming in glory He would judge the quick and
the dead, and give to every one according to his works.
Upon which Domitian, despising them, made no reply; but
treating them with contempt as simpletons, commanded them
to be dismissed, and by a decree ordered the persecution
(against them) to cease. Thus delivered, they ruled the

---

[1] For these legends see Winer's *Biblisches Wörterbuch*, vol. i. p. 745 ff.
Keil's *Comm. über die Briefe Petrus und Judas*, p. 288.

[2] Eusebius, *Hist. Eccl.* i. 13. For the Abgarus legend of Edessa, see Lipsius, *Apostolgeschichten und Apostellegenden*, vol. ii. pp. 154-158.

Churches both as witnesses and relatives of the Lord. When peace was established, they continued living even to the times of Trajan."[1] There is nothing improbable in this account, and Hegesippus may have obtained the story from a reliable source. It would follow from this that Jude himself was not alive when this incident occurred, so that he must have died before A.D. 96, the year when Domitian was murdered.

III. THE READERS OF THE EPISTLE.

The Epistle is addressed "to them that are called, beloved in God the Father, and kept for Jesus Christ." It is catholic in its terms; the readers are described as Christians generally, without any limitation.[2] Accordingly, many suppose that it is addressed to all Christians, whether they are converted Jews or converted Gentiles. Although undoubtedly it displays certain Jewish characteristics, yet it is asserted that this arises, not from the character of the readers addressed, but from the idiosyncrasy of the writer. "Jude," observes Sieffert, "addressed his Epistle not to any local congregation, but to the Church at large. Its circle of readers was even larger than that addressed by James, including not only believing Jews outside of Palestine, but all believers, without distinction of birth or locality."[3] It is argued that if, as will be seen to be most probable, this Epistle belonged to the later period of the apostolic age, it must have been addressed to Christians in general; because, with the possible exception of some districts in Palestine, Jewish Christian churches did not exist; the Gentiles must have constituted the great majority of converts; nor was the distinction between Jewish and Gentile converts maintained: both were united in Christ Jesus, in whom there was neither Jew nor Gentile.

Notwithstanding, it is the opinion of most critics that the

---

[1] Eusebius, *Hist. Eccl.* iii. 19, 20, 32.

[2] Brückner imagines that the readers are designated generally as Christians, because the warning which the writing contains was not to the honour of the particular Church addressed. *Katholische Briefe*, p. 101. Ewald calls it "a pastoral circular, reminding its readers of established Christian truths." *History of Israel*, vol. viii. p. 140.

[3] Herzog's *Real-Encyklopädie*, article "Judasbrief," vol. vii. p. 278.

Epistle of Jude, like that of his brother James, was specially addressed to Jewish Christians; and that, although the address is catholic, it is necessarily limited by its contents. This is the opinion adopted by Estius, Hammond, Eichhorn, Schmidt, Credner, Wiesinger, Spitta, Alford, Arnaud, Lumby, and the generality of expositors. The allusions in the Epistle are all Jewish; the references are to incidents in Jewish history, such as the deliverance of the Israelites from Egypt, the destruction of Sodom and Gomorrah, the rebellion of Korah, the mission of the false prophet Balaam, all of which presuppose an acquaintance with the Old Testament not to be expected from the generality of Gentile Christians; and the traditions are all rabbinical, as the rebellion and sin of the angels, the contention of Michael with the devil, and the prophecy of Enoch, which presuppose a further acquaintance, not only with the Old Testament, but with Jewish tradition and possibly with Jewish literature. And although it is true that outside of Palestine such Jewish Christian churches did not at that time exist, there is nothing to prevent the supposition that the Epistle was addressed to some church or churches in Palestine, in which the majority of converts were still converted Jews. To this Huther objects, that all these features in the Epistle might have arisen from the individuality of the writer, without being conditioned by a regard to the readers.[1] Jude, like his brother James, was a strict Jewish Christian, and his mind was imbued with the incidents of Jewish history and with Jewish ideas. But we do not think that this is a sufficient answer. The Epistle, considering its brevity, not merely contains more allusions to Jewish history than any other Epistle in the New Testament except the Second Epistle of Peter, which so closely resembles it, and the Epistle actually addressed to the Hebrews, but it refers to Jewish traditions which it is extremely improbable could at that time be known to any but to the Jews.

Although the Epistle is in form catholic, addressed to the Christian Church in general without any restriction as to locality, yet from the nature of its contents it is evident that it must have been directed to Christians belonging

---

[1] Huther's *Der Brief des Judas*, p. 247 [E. Tr. p. 383].

to some particular church, or residing in some particular
district. The Epistle was occasioned by the report of
certain perversions from the faith and of the existence of
licentious persons within the Church; "there are certain men
crept in unawares," " these are spots in your feasts of charity;"
which give a particularity to the address. Accordingly
different localities have been fixed upon. Credner, Schmid,
Wiesinger, and Keil place the readers in Palestine, because,
as they suppose, the Epistle was addressed to Jewish readers,
and only in that country could there be churches composed
of Jewish Christians. Olshausen fixes on the churches in the
adjoining country of Syria. Others, as Schneckenburger, suppose
that the readers resided in one of the flourishing and luxurious
cities of Proconsular Asia, as Colosse or Ephesus, because of
the resemblance of the Epistle to the Second Epistle of Peter
addressed to the Asiatic churches, and because the persons
described are similar to the heretics adverted to in the Epistle
to the Colossians. Guericke supposes that the Epistle was
intended specially for the Pauline churches, to which also
Peter directed his Epistle, and that its design was to counteract those antinomian views and practices which arose from a
perversion of the teaching of Paul.[1] Others fix upon Corinth,
because that city was pre-eminent for its luxury and licentiousness, and such a state of morals among Christians as is
described in this Epistle could occur only in a city of this
description. Mayerhoff is singular in fixing on Egypt,
because Clemens Alexandrinus is the first Father who refers
to the Epistle, the physical allusions in the Epistle find their
counterpart in the physical features of Egypt, and the Book of
Enoch was there known and recognised.[2] All these views are
baseless suppositions, except that which fixes on Palestine.

IV. THE DESIGN AND CONTENTS OF THE EPISTLE.

The design of the Epistle is thus stated by its author:
" Beloved, while I was giving all diligence to write unto you
of our common salvation, I was constrained to write unto you,
exhorting you to contend earnestly for the faith which was

[1] *Isagogik*, pp. 437, 438.   [2] *Petrinische Schriften*, p. 195.

once for all delivered to the saints. For there are certain men crept in privily, even they who were of old set forth to this condemnation, ungodly men, turning the grace of our God into lasciviousness, and denying our only Master and Lord, Jesus Christ" (vers. 3, 4).[1] From this it appears that the immediate design of this Epistle was not merely to instruct Christians in the common salvation, and so to confirm them in the faith,[2] but to urge them to stand up for the faith in opposition to those wicked men who were seeking to corrupt the Church by their licentious conduct and impious opinions.

The portrait of these men, who had crept in unawares into the Christian Church, is painted in the blackest colours. Whilst they called themselves Christians, professed to belong to the Christian Church, and joined in the Christian love-feasts, they were openly immoral in their practice; they were "ungodly men, turning the grace of God into lasciviousness, and denying our only Master and Lord, Jesus Christ;" they were filthy dreamers, despising dominion, speaking evil of dignities; they were murmurers, complainers, walking after their own ungodly lusts; they were proud boasters, speaking great swelling words; they resembled the worst characters in the Old Testament—Cain, Korah, and Balaam (vers. 4, 8, 16, 18, 19). And these men were not outside, but inside the Christian Church. From this description we must correct our views as to the supposed purity of the early Church. Men, converted from the pollutions and abominations of heathenism, do not all at once cast off their former nature; the old habits will sometimes reveal themselves. And although the Jews were higher in point of morality than the heathen, yet, as we learn from Josephus, they were infected by their contact with heathen impurity, and were at the time when this Epistle was written sunk in wickedness. Christianity raised its converts from the wickedness in which the whole world was involved, but, especially if discipline were relaxed, "certain

---

[1] Revised Version.

[2] Spitta understands here a reference to another work which Jude was engaged in writing; and consequently the words on "the common salvation" do not give the design of the Epistle. *Der Zweite Brief des Petrus und der Brief des Judas*, p. 306.

men would creep into the Church unawares," who would bring along with them their heathen or Jewish vices. We learn that such was the case in the Church of Corinth; though certainly the wickedness described in Jude's Epistle is more astounding than that mentioned in the First Epistle to the Corinthians.[1] Hence, then, the statement of Hegesippus, that the Church—he is alluding specially to the Church in Palestine—continued as a pure virgin until the reign of Trajan,[2] must be taken with considerable limitation. It must, however, be remembered that the persons described constituted the great exceptions—their entrance into the Church was stealthy —παρεισέδυσαν τινες ἄνθρωποι.

There are different opinions concerning these persons. Some, as Dorner, Ewald, Huther, Fronmüller,[3] Th. Schott, Thiersch, Sieffert, Mangold, Wiesinger, and Holtzmann,[4] suppose that they were heretical teachers who inculcated Gnostic errors, and thus corrupted both the faith and the practice of the Church. "The opponents of Jude," observes Dorner, "are not only corrupt in practice, but also heretical teachers."[5] Others, as Bleek, De Wette, Brückner, Hofmann, Reuss, Ritschl, Spitta, Weiss, Davidson, and Salmon, suppose that they were rather carnally-minded men, practical antinomians who turned the grace of God into lasciviousness, abused the doctrine of justification into the occasion of sin, converted the agapæ into scenes of excess, and were seditious in their words and practice. "From the author's description," observes Bleek, "these men would not seem to have been teachers who threatened to corrupt Christian doctrine by mere theoretical errors, at least the theoretical must with them have been wholly secondary and subordinate."[6] Most probably the truth lies between these views. These persons were heretical

---

[1] Not so if we interpret 1 Cor. xi. 21 literally, that the agapæ and the Lord's Supper were actually converted into scenes of drunkenness.

[2] Eusebius, *Hist. Eccl.* iv. 22.

[3] Ewald's *History of Israel*, vol. viii. p. 141. Huther's *Epistle of Jude*, p. 383. Fronmüller's "Epistle of Jude" in Lange's *Bibelwerk*, pp. 6, 7.

[4] Holtzmann's *Einleitung in das N. T.*, p. 502.

[5] *Entwicklungsgesch. d. Lehre Chr.*, Theil i. p. 104 [E. Tr. vol. i. p. 72].

[6] *Introduction to the N. T.*, vol. ii. p. 153. He identifies them with the Christian rebels in the great Jewish war. "It is," he adds, "very probable that these men were to be found in the author's own neighbourhood in Judea, where

teachers, as is seen in their denial of the only Lord God and of our Lord Jesus Christ (ver. 4); but their teaching was of a licentious tendency, and its effects were seen, not so much in the heretical views, as in the open wickedness and licentiousness of their followers—"turning the grace of God into lasciviousness."

We know that several of the Gnostic sects, who flourished about the middle of the second century, were of this description; as the Ophites, who taught that the fall occasioned by the seduction of the serpent was productive of good;[1] the Cainites, who reversed the teaching of the Old Testament, and made heroes of those who are there condemned;[2] the Antitactæ, or Adversaries of the Creator, who held that it was a duty to the Supreme Being to resist the commands of the Creator, whom they considered as the author of evil;[3] and the Carpocratians, who regarded the Demiurgus, or Creator of the world, as an evil being whose commands were to be disobeyed. Indeed, Clement of Alexandria considers the words of Jude as a prediction of Carpocrates and his followers.[4] Now, although Gnosticism was not fully developed until the post-apostolic age, yet, as we have had frequent occasion to remark, its germs were apparent in apostolic times. There was an early Jewish Gnosticism which preceded the developed Gentile Gnosticism of the second century. The Fathers ascribe the rise of Gnosticism to Simon Magus; and the first Gnostic sects which are mentioned—the Menandrians, the Cerinthians, and the Nicolaitans—were of Jewish origin. The Nicolaitans are mentioned in the Apocalypse (Rev. ii. 15), and we know from the writings of the Fathers that their tenets were of a licentious character. Indeed, several theologians, as Thiersch, Ewald,[5] Huther, Wiesinger,[6] Schott, Burton,[7] and Mansel,

it is quite possible many professed adherents of the Christian Church shared in the political excitement and restless movements of the Jews."

[1] Irenæus, *Adv. Hær.* i. 30.
[2] For the views of the Cainites, see Mansel's *Gnostic Heresies*, p. 100 ff.
[3] Clement, *Strom.* iii. 4.
[4] *Ibid.* iii. 2. Schenkel, Mangold, and Holtzmann consider that it is to the Carpocratians that Jude alludes in his Epistle; consequently they place the date of the Epistle at A.D. 130.
[5] Ewald's *History of Israel*, vol. viii. p. 141.
[6] Wiesinger, *Der Brief des Judas*, p. 172.
[7] Burton's *Bampton Lectures*, p. 152.

suppose that it is the Nicolaitans who are described in this Epistle of Jude. "In the language of Jude," observes Mansel, "as in that of Peter, we may clearly discern a reference to the Gnostic sect of the Nicolaitans, mentioned by name in the Revelation."[1] Whether this sect, which infested the Asiatic churches when John wrote the Apocalypse, was prevalent over the whole Christian Church when Jude wrote his Epistle may be questioned; but similar tendencies would undoubtedly be abroad. In all probability, the evil against which Jude contends is the same as that combated by the apostles Paul, John, and Peter; only in the case of the persons against whom Jude wrote, the evil assumed more of the character of immorality than of heresy.

Contents.—The train of thought is as follows. Jude introduces himself to his readers as the servant of Jesus Christ and brother of James; he states that he felt constrained to address them, and to exhort them to an earnest contention for the faith, on account of the secret entrance of certain wicked men into the church, who had perverted the grace of God into a reason for licentiousness, and who by their impious opinions had denied their Master and Lord, Jesus Christ.[2] These wicked men, he asserts, had sealed their own condemnation; wickedness and ruin were necessarily connected. This he confirms by three examples, the destruction of the rebellious Israelites in the wilderness, the perdition of the fallen angels, and the overthrow of Sodom and Gomorrah. These wicked persons are described as defilers of the flesh and despisers of dignities; and the greatness of their wickedness is prominently brought forward by contrasting it with the conduct of Michael the archangel, in his contest with the devil. A woe is denounced upon them, because they are the imitators of Cain, Balaam, and Korah. They are described by various figurative expressions, denoting the ruin which by their wicked works they bring upon themselves. A prophecy of Enoch is introduced, testifying to the destruction of the ungodly. Having thus described these wicked intruders and pronounced their doom, Jude turns to his readers and exhorts them to be mindful of the words of the apostles who had

---

[1] Mansel's *Gnostic Heresies,* p. 70. [2] Revised Version.

foretold the advent of these mockers. He exhorts them to keep themselves in the love of God, and to wait patiently for the mercy of the Lord Jesus Christ. And, after giving a short direction how they were to deal with those who had already been perverted, he concludes the Epistle with a doxology.

The Epistle was originally written in Greek. There is no reason to assume, with Bertholdt and Schmid, that it is a translation from the Aramaic. The Greek, however, is that of one not trained in Greek literature, to whom Aramaic was the more familiar dialect. The Epistle abounds with a number of peculiar words and phrases not found elsewhere in the New Testament. Its diction is described by Eichhorn as "round, full, and lively."[1] It has also been remarked, and indeed is very obvious, that there is throughout a love of triple arrangements. Thus those whom Jude addresses are sanctified, preserved, and called; the blessings which he invokes for them are mercy, peace, and love; the wicked men who had crept into the church are those who are ordained to condemnation, turned the grace of God into lasciviousness, and denied their only Master and Lord, Jesus Christ; the examples of punishment are the Israelites in the wilderness, the fallen angels, and the cities of the plain; the persons denounced are those who defile the flesh, despise dominions, and speak evil of dignities; their conduct is described as an imitation of that of Cain, Balaam, and Korah; their character is depicted as those who separate themselves, sensual, and not having the Spirit; and the treatment to be observed with reference to those seduced is threefold—those who were hesitating and were in doubt were to be reasoned with, those who had fallen were to be snatched out of the fire, and those who continued in their wickedness were to be pitied, whilst their sins were to be abhorred.[2] The Epistle is vehement in tone and strong in expression, resembling the vehement utterances of the Old Testament prophets, such as Joel and Hosea, when denouncing the wickedness and foretelling the doom of the ungodly.

What especially characterizes this Epistle, and distin-

---

[1] *Einleitung*, vol. iii. p. 651.
[2] According to the correct reading of Jude 22, 23.

guishes it from the other writings of the New Testament, is the partiality of the author for incidents of Jewish history and tradition. Jude not only draws his examples from the Old Testament, such as the references to the deliverance of the Israelites from Egypt, the destruction of Sodom and Gomorrah, the comparison of the ungodly with Cain, Balaam, and the company of Korah,—and in this resembles Peter in his Second Epistle; but he also adduces certain rabbinical legends or traditions which are not contained in the Old Testament nor referred to in Peter's Epistle. For example, he seems to hint at the rabbinical notion of the nature of the sin of the fallen angels; he adverts to the contention of the archangel Michael with the devil; and he introduces a prophecy of Enoch. He mentions, as John also does in the Apocalypse (Rev. xii. 7), and Daniel in his prophecy (Dan. x. 13, 21), Michael as the name of an archangel. Nay, there is reason to suppose that he quotes from two Jewish apocryphal books—the Book of Enoch and the Assumption of Moses.[1]

V. TIME AND PLACE OF WRITING.

Different opinions have been entertained regarding the date of this Epistle. Kirchhofer supposes it to have been written about A.D. 60. Lardner places it between the years 64 and 66, Weiss about A.D. 65, Sieffert between 70 and 80, and Bleek before A.D. 70. Credner,[2] followed by Reuss, Schott, Spitta, and Lumby, fix it as late as A.D. 80.[3] The relation of this Epistle to the Second Epistle of Peter must influence our determination of its date. If the Epistle of Jude is the prior Epistle, then it must have been composed at least before A.D. 64, the year of Peter's martyrdom; but if, on the other hand, Jude makes use of the Epistle of Peter, then it was probably written after that date. There are several

---

[1] See Keil's *Commentar über die Briefe Petrus und Judas*, p. 293. Farrar's *Early Days of Christianity*, vol. i. p. 238.

[2] Credner's *Einleitung*, p. 617.

[3] Volkmar, Mangold, and Schenkel suppose that it was written after A.D. 130, or even A.D. 140; and with them Davidson, in the last edition of his *Introduction to the Study of the N. T.*, vol. ii. p. 271, agrees.

intimations in the Epistle which affect our decision as to its date. 1. We must allow time for the development of error. Error and heresy in the Christian Church had not only sprung up, but had to a certain extent been developed. There were prevalent not only erroneous opinions, but corrupt practices such as we cannot suppose existed in the early stage of the Christian Church. Perhaps the discipline of the early Church had been relaxed; for otherwise the existence of such persons within the Church is hardly intelligible. The state of the Church of Corinth, however, causes us to put less stress on this argument. 2. The teaching of the apostles is spoken of in such a manner as would lead us to think that it had passed its meridian. Jude calls upon his hearers to remember "the words which were spoken before by the apostles of our Lord Jesus Christ" (Jude 17). The teaching of the apostles was rather a thing past, the memory of which was to be recalled, than actually carried on at the time. "These words," observes Alford, "point to a time when the agency of the apostles themselves had passed away from the readers, but the impress of their warning words had not faded from their memories."[1] 3. But, though late in the apostolic age, the Epistle was written before the destruction of Jerusalem. If that event had occurred, we do not see how Jude, as a strict Jewish Christian, could possibly have omitted that awful calamity which made such a powerful impression on all Jews in his examples of the destructions which befell the ungodly; to Jude it must have appeared the most striking of all the instances of divine wrath, and the most appropriate for his purpose. Credner, Sieffert, and Huther affirm that no argument can be drawn from the mere silence of Jude, as he omits other striking judgments, such as the deluge and the first destruction of Jerusalem by Nebuchadnezzar;[2] but the destruction of Jerusalem by Titus would be so recent, so striking, and so appropriate an example that its omission is inexplicable, except on the assumption that the Epistle was written before its occurrence.

[1] Alford's *Greek Testament*, vol. iv. Prolegomena, p. 193.
[2] Credner's *Einleitung*, p. 618. Huther's *Kommentar*, p. 250 [E. T. p. 386]. Sieffert in Herzog's *Encyklopädie*.

Regarding the place of composition there are no grounds to proceed upon. Most expositors fix on Palestine, because it is supposed that the Jewish converts did not forsake that country until the commencement of the Jewish war; so that it is not improbable that the place of composition was Jerusalem. Mayerhoff supposes that it was written in Egypt, from the supposed references to the physical features of that country, such as clouds without water and raging waves of the sea; a reason which is extremely fanciful.

The most important commentaries on the Epistle are those of Witsius (Basil 1739), C. F. Schmid (Leipsic 1768), J. G. Hasse (Jena 1786), Hänlein (Erlangen 1799), Jessien (Leipsic 1821), Schneckenburger (Stuttgard 1832), De Wette (Leipsic 1847), Stier (Berlin 1850), Arnaud (Strasburg 1851), Rampf (Salzburg 1854), Fronmüller (Lange's *Bibelwerk*, Bielefeld 1859; translated by Mombert, New York 1867), Wiesinger, (Olshausen's *Bibelwerk*, 1862), Schott (Erlangen 1863), Brückner (dritte Auflage, Leipsic 1865), Hofmann (Nordlingen 1876), Huther (vierte Auflage, Göttingen 1877; translated, Edinburgh 1881), Plumptre (in the Cambridge series; Cambridge 1880), Lumby (in the *Speaker's Bible*; London 1881), Keil (Leipsic 1883), Plummer (in Ellicott's Commentary), Spitta (Halle 1885).

DISSERTATION I.

THE ASSUMPTION OF MOSES.

We remarked that the chief peculiarity of the Epistle of Jude is the numerous references to apocryphal books or rabbinical legends which it contains. Two of these are especially deserving of consideration; the contention between Michael the archangel and the devil concerning the body of Moses, and the prophecy of Enoch. The first of these is contained in the following passage: "But Michael the archangel, when, contending with the devil, he disputed about the body of Moses, durst not bring against him a railing accusation, but said, The Lord rebuke thee" (Jude 9). We have in this dissertation no concern with the meaning of the passage, or with the nature of the dispute: our only question is, Whence did Jude derive his information? The supposed allusions to the incident in the Old Testament (Zech. iii. 2; Deut. xxxiv. 6) are too vague and indefinite to be relied on; the reference must be either to some rabbinical tradition, or to some apocryphal book. Now we have the statement of Origen, that this incident recorded by Jude was taken from an apocryphal book entitled "The Assumption of Moses" (ἀνάληψις Μωυσέως). In the Latin translation of Origen's works by Rufinus there occurs the following passage: "In the Book of Genesis the serpent is described as having seduced Eve; regarding whom in the work entitled 'The Assumption of Moses'—a little treatise which the Apostle Jude quotes in his Epistle—Michael the archangel, when disputing with the devil regarding the body of Moses, says that the serpent, being inspired by the devil, was the cause of the transgression of Adam and Eve."[1]

Besides this reference to the Assumption of Moses by Origen, the work is referred to by the Greek Fathers down to the tenth century.[2] Hilgenfeld supposes that a reference occurs in the following words from the Epistle of Clemens Romanus (A.D. 96): "Yet he (Moses), though thus greatly honoured, did not adopt lofty language, but said, when the divine oracle came to him out of the bush, Who am I that Thou sendest me? I am a man of a feeble voice and of a slow tongue: and again he said, I am but as the smoke of a pot."[3] The last clause, which is not a scriptural quotation, is supposed to be taken from "the Assumption of Moses." But this is a mere conjecture, as no similar clause has

---

[1] *De Principiis*, iii. 2. 1: In Genesi serpens Evam seduxisse describitur, de quo in Adscensione Mosis, cujus libelli meminit in epistola sua apostolus Judas, Michael Archangelus cum diabolo disputans de corpore Mosis, ait a diabolo inspiratum serpentem causam exstitisse prævaricationis Adæ et Evæ.

[2] For references in the writings of the Fathers to the Assumption of Moses, see Fabricius, *Codex Pseudepigraphus V. T.*, pp. 839-846. Fritzsche, *Libri V. T. Pseudepigraphi selecti*, p. xiv. f.

[3] *Epist.* chap. xvii.: ἐγὼ δέ εἰμι ἀτμὶς ἀπὸ κύθρας.

been found in that work. The following statement of Clemens Alexandrinus (A.D. 190) is much more probably an allusion to "the Assumption:" "Joshua, the son of Nun, saw Moses when he was taken up in a twofold manner: one Moses with the angels and another Moses on the mountains honoured with burial in their ravines. And Joshua saw this spectacle below, being elevated by the Spirit, along with Caleb; but both did not see similarly."[1] The same strange idea of a twofold Moses, as we shall see, is referred to by another Christian writer (Evodius), and is said to be contained in the apocryphal writings of Moses. So also Origen asserts that in a certain uncanonical book mention is made of two Moses': one alive in the spirit, and the other dead in the body.[2] In the *Adumbrationes* preserved by Cassiodorus, Clemens Alexandrinus alludes to the same book when he says, "When Michael the archangel, disputing with the devil, debated about the body of Moses. Here he confirms the Assumption of Moses."[3] In the *Apostolic Constitutions*, a patristic work of uncertain date, mention is made of the apocryphal books of Moses (βιβλία ἀπόκρυφα Μωυσέως).[4] Didymus of Alexandria (A.D. 360) informs us that many objected to the Epistle of Jude and the Assumption of Moses on account of the passage concerning the contest of Michael the archangel and the devil about the body of Moses.[5] Evodius (A.D. 395), in an Epistle to Augustine, writes, "In the Apocrypha and in the mysteries of Moses, a writing which is wholly devoid of authority, it is said that when Moses ascended the mount to die through the power which his body possessed, there was one body which was committed to the earth, and another body which was joined to the angel who accompanied him."[6] In the Acts of the Second Nicene Council (A.D. 786) there is the following reference: "In the book, the ἀνάληψις Μωυσέως, the archangel Michael, disputing with the devil, says, 'Of His Holy Spirit are we all created;' and again,

---

[1] *Strom.* vi. 15.   [2] Origen, *Libr. Jesu Nave*, Hom. ii. 1.

[3] Clem. *Opp.* ed. Potter, p. 1007. Zahn's *Supplementum Clementinum*, p. 84: Hic confirmat assumptionem Moysi.

[4] *Apost. Const.* vi. 16.   [5] In *epist. Judae enarratio*.

[6] *Ep. ad Augustinum: Augustin. Epp.* 158. Translation of the works of St. Augustine: Letters of Augustine, vol. ii. p. 266, Edinburgh 1875.

'From the face of God went forth His Spirit, and the world was made.'"¹ And in another fragment of the same Acts we have the following passage : " Moses, the prophet, when about to depart this life, as it is written in the book of the ἀνάληψις Μωυσεώς, called Joshua the son of Nun and said to him, 'God looked upon me before the foundation of the world that I should be the mediator of His covenant.'"² Nicephorus (A.D. 800) in the Stichometry mentions the Assumption of Moses among the apocryphal books, and states that it contained 1400 lines (στίχοι), and that it equalled in length the Apocalypse of John. Reference is made to it in the so-called *Synopsis* of Athanasius. And Oecumenius (A.D. 950), quoting from the same apocryphal book, explains the nature of the dispute between Michael and the devil. According to this, Michael was employed in burying Moses, but the devil endeavoured to prevent him by alleging that Moses had murdered an Egyptian, and was therefore unworthy of an honourable burial.³

According to Volkmar, we find a free recension of the Assumption of Moses in the later Jewish literature. He observes : " Later Judaism has reproduced this work with some variations in the rabbinical dialect—according to many indications from the Greek or Latin—under the title פטירה של משה (Petirath Mose). The chief of the demons here seeks the life of Moses, but the guardian angel of Israel defends him and puts Satan to flight."⁴ So also Ewald remarks that it was probably this work which, subsequently undergoing repeated modifications, finally assumed the full rabbinical form in the Petirath Mose.⁵ But these works, the Assumption of Moses and the Petirath Mose, do not appear to be the same; at least the legends contained in them of the contest

¹ *Act. Syn. Nic.* ii. 20. Volkmar, *Mose Himmelfahrt*, p. 9. Neither of these quotations is found in the fragments which remain of the Assumption of Moses.
² *Idem*, chap. 18. Fabricius, *Codex Pseudepigraphus V. T.*, vol. i. p. 845. This quotation is found in "the Assumption," see below.
³ In *Ep. Jude*, p. 340 (tom. ii. p. 629). Fabricius, *Codex Pseudepigraphus V. T.*, vol. i. p. 846. Spitta mentions that ninety-eight cursive MSS. have on the margin at Jude 9 : Μωϋσὴ ἀποκρύφου.
⁴ Volkmar, *Mose Himmelfahrt*, p. 10 ; see Gfrörer, *Prophetæ Veteres Pseudepigr.* p. 317.
⁵ Ewald's *History of Israel*, vol. ii. p. 226.

of Michael and Satan about the body of Moses are very different.[1] Among the Jews there are numerous legends concerning the death and burial of Moses, in which both Michael and the devil play important parts; but from what we know of the Assumption of Moses by the fragments which remain, it is doubtful if that work is referred to by Jewish writers at all.

The Assumption of Moses was lost for nearly nine hundred years, and until recently was referred to as a book of whose character, nature, and date we were entirely ignorant. In 1861, however, an important fragment of it was discovered by Ceriani, the learned librarian of the Ambrosian Library of Milan, and was published by him.[2] The manuscript which contained it was found in the monastery of Bobbio,[3] and was a parchment palimpsest. The recent writing upon it was obliterated by a chemical process, and the greater part of the ancient writing rendered legible. The manuscript belonged to the sixth century,[4] and was in Latin; it also contained a considerable fragment of the Book of Jubilees, also in a Latin translation. That part which contained the Assumption of Moses was much disfigured: there were numerous omissions, and several of the leaves were torn. The title and a few lines at the beginning were awanting; and the last portion of the work was lost. If the statement of Nicephorus is correct, that the book was equal in length to the Apocalypse of John, then only a third part of the work has been recovered. Unfortunately the fragment does not contain the account of the burial of Moses, so that the passage in the Epistle of Jude is not contained in it. The work, as we have it, ought rather to be called the Prophecy than the Assumption or Ascension of Moses; but still there is little doubt that it is the same work as that referred to by the Greek writers; inasmuch as a passage mentioned in

---

[1] See Michaelis, *Introduction to N. T.*, by Marsh, vol. vi. pp. 381-385. Wolfii, *Bibliotheca Rabbinica*, tom. ii. p. 1278 f.

[2] Ceriani, *Monumenta sacra et profana ex codicibus praesentim Bibliothecæ Ambrosianæ*.

[3] The famous Muratorian Canon also came from the same monastery.

[4] This is proved from the nature of the writing in uncial letters, the absence of division between words, and the sparing punctuation.

the Acts of the second Council of Nice, concerning Moses as appointed by God before the foundation of the world to be the mediator of His covenant, is contained in it.[1] The passage in the Assumption is as follows: "The Lord prepared me before the foundation of the world to be the mediator of His covenant" (chap. ii.).

We have already stated that the manuscript containing the fragments discovered by Ceriani was in Latin; but there is not the slightest doubt that the Latin is a translation from the Greek. The translation is slavish, as Greek words and constructions are retained; and hence Hilgenfeld could make the attempt to restore the Greek text.[2] Without doubt it was in Greek that the work was known to the early Christian writers. It is, however, a matter of dispute whether the Greek itself is not a translation from the Aramaic. Ewald, Merx, Schmidt, Colani, and Dillmann suppose that it was originally written in Aramaic; whilst Mangold, Hilgenfeld, and Drummond think that the Greek was the original. The latter opinion is in all probability the more correct, as the Old Testament references in the work are more related to the Septuagint than to the Hebrew, and as it is doubtful whether the work was known to the Talmudic writers. The Hebraisms which pervade it may be accounted for from the fact that the author was a Jew, the same cause which accounts for the numerous Hebraisms that are to be found in several of the writings of the New Testament.

It is unnecessary to dwell long upon the contents of the work.[3] The fragment which we possess is divided into two parts: the prophetical address of Moses to Joshua (chaps. i.-xv.), and the answer of Joshua with the encouraging address of Moses (chaps. xvi.-xix.). We possess, with the exception of a few lines at the commencement, the whole of the first part, but only a very small fragment of the second. The work commences in the following terms: "The prophecy

---

[1] Quoted in Fabricius, *Cod. Pseud. V. T.*, vol. i. p. 845.

[2] In his *Messias Judæorum*.

[3] For the Latin text of the work and the translation into German, see Volkmar's *Mose Himmelfahrt*, pp. 137-152. Fritzsche's *Libri Vet. Test. pseudepigraphi selecti*, pp. 132-161.

which Moses made in the Book of Deuteronomy, when he called to himself Joshua the son of Nun, a man well pleasing to the Lord, that he should be his successor for the people and for the tabernacle of the testimony." After a short introduction (chaps. i., ii.), Moses is represented as giving a history of Israel from his own time, in the form of a prophecy, down, evidently, to the time when the author wrote. There are clear references to the kings of Judah and Israel, to Nebuchadnezzar, to Daniel, to Cyrus, and to the Maccabean princes. There is a distinct allusion to Herod the Great in a passage where his character is described in terms too plain to be mistaken: "After them shall succeed an insolent king, not of the family of priests, a man rash and shameless; and he shall judge them according to their deserts. He shall slay their chiefs with the sword, and shall not spare their young men; and he shall execute judgment upon them for the space of four and thirty years" (chap. ix.). It is also generally agreed that there is a reference to the defeat of the Jews by Varus in the reign of Augustus, when he burned part of the temple (A.D. 4).[1] On the other hand, there is no reference to the great Jewish war, or to the destruction of the temple by Titus. The course of events can be tolerably clearly traced to the close of the reign of Herod; but after this follow enigmatical passages which have taxed the ingenuity of critics, and given rise to various suppositions. Mention is made of four hours or periods following the events already related: "When this shall come to pass the times shall end. In a moment the course of events will end, when the four hours (periods) are come" (chap. x.). And then there is a description of the advent of a mysterious person under the name of Taxo: "In that day a man shall arise from the tribe of Levi, whose name shall be called Taxo" (chap. xiii.). He and his seven sons betake themselves to a cave, encouraging themselves with the thought that it is better to die than to transgress the commands of God. Then

[1] The supposed reference is contained in the following words: "A mighty king of the west shall come, and shall utterly defeat the people, lead some away into captivity, crucify others in the city, and burn part of the temple." See Josephus, *Bell. Jud.* ii. 3. 1; *Ant.* xvii. 10. 1.

follows an account of the advent of the Lord Himself, the final defeat of all His enemies, and the establishment of His kingdom. "Then shall the heavenly One arise from the seat of His kingdom, and come forth from His holy habitation with wrath and indignation for the sake of His children. And the earth shall quake to its utmost bounds, and the lofty mountains shall be brought low, and the valleys shall sink. The sun shall give no light and shall be turned into darkness, and the horns of the moon shall be broken, and the host of the stars shall be confounded; for the Most High, the Eternal, the only God shall arise and come to chastise the heathen and to destroy their images" (chap. xiv.). The second part of the Assumption, containing the answer of Joshua and the encouraging address of Moses, requires no remarks (chaps. xvi.–xix.). The concluding and missing portion of the work would contain the remainder of the address of Moses, and would then, it is highly probable, relate the death of Moses and his burial in the lowly valley at the foot of Pisgah.

The author of this strange apocalyptic work was certainly not a Jewish Christian.[1] There is no allusion to Christianity, and no reference to the Person of our Lord; and the idea, that Christ may possibly be mentioned in that portion of the book which is lost, is excluded by the fact that the passage containing the advent of the Lord is fully preserved, and in it there is no reference to the Messiah and little resemblance to the doctrine of the advent as contained in Scripture.[2] Whoever the author was, he was evidently a Jew belonging to the strictest sect, that of the zealots.[3] He regards even the native Maccabean princes as usurpers, because latterly they favoured the Sadducean faction. Thus, with evident reference to John Hyrcanus and his descendants, he says: "And now the days of trial shall draw near, and vengeance shall arise because of the wickedness of princes given for their punishment; for ministers who are no priests, but slaves born

---

[1] Philippi is the only one who ascribes the authorship to a Christian.

[2] Volkmar's *Mose Himmelfahrt*, pp. 85, 86.

[3] See Schürer's *Jewish People in the Time of Jesus Christ*, E. Tr. vol. iii. pp. 79, 80.

of slaves shall defile the altar."¹ There is also a remarkable absence of Messianic expectations. The Messiah is not mentioned, and only obscurely alluded to, unless indeed He be referred to under the name of Taxo.² It is Jehovah Himself who shall appear, and who shall condemn the wicked and reward the righteous. This peculiarity distinguishes the work from other similar apocalyptic works, as the Second Book of Ezra, the early Sibyllines, and the Book of Enoch.

Different opinions have been entertained regarding the age of the book. It must have been written after the death of Herod, the length of whose reign is exactly stated, and after the defeat of the Jews by Varus (A.D. 4). Mention is also made of the sons of Herod: "He shall beget sons who shall reign a shorter time than their father." It is to be observed that this is a mistake, as two of the sons of Herod, Herod Antipas and Philip, reigned longer than their father; and hence some suppose that this is a proof that the work was written before the conclusion of their reigns. Ewald accordingly thinks that the book was written about A.D. 6, after the rebellion of Judas the Gaulonite, because there are no direct historical allusions in the work later than the expedition of Varus against Jerusalem.³ He supposes that by Taxo, who, with his seven sons, stood up for the law of God, is meant Judas the Gaulonite. This early date has also been adopted by Dillmann,⁴ Wieseler, and Schürer,⁵ as the most probable. Hilgenfeld assigns the date to the reign of Claudius, A.D. 44.⁶ His opinion is founded on the interpretation which he gives of the four hours mentioned in the prophecy, as four emperors, and on the ground that the work must have been written before the commencement of the Jewish war, as there is no reference in it to that event. According to him, by Taxo is meant the Messiah. The opinion that the book was written

---

[1] John Hyrcanus was taunted by the Pharisee Eleazar with being the son of a captive woman. Josephus, *Ant.* xiii. 10. 5.

[2] So Hilgenfeld. Schürer regards the enigmatical Taxo as a corruption of the text.

[3] Ewald's *History of Israel*, vol. vi. pp. 55, 60.

[4] Herzog's *Encyclopädie*, vol. xii. p. 353.

[5] Schürer's *Jewish People in the Time of Jesus Christ*, vol. iii. p. 79.

[6] *Mess. Jud.* p. lxxiv.

before the Jewish war is adopted by Mangold, who agrees with Hilgenfeld,[1] by Gutschmid, who fixes on A.D. 54, and by Merx, Schmidt, and Fritzsche, who think that it was written between A.D. 54 and A.D. 64. Davidson remarks in general terms: "Internal evidence points to its composition after the death of Herod the Great and before the destruction of Jerusalem."[2] Langen of Bonn, on the other hand, thinks that the work was written shortly after the destruction of Jerusalem (A.D. 75); and that it is this event, and not the expedition of Varus, that is alluded to. Hausrath fixes on the reign of Domitian.[3] Volkmar supposes that it was written A.D. 137-138, and that the allusion is to the rebellion of Barcocheba in the reign of Hadrian. The calamities mentioned are the persecutions of the Jews under that emperor, and Taxo, the man of the tribe of Levi, is Rabbi Akiba, the great supporter of Barcocheba. According to Volkmar, the four hours are four dynasties, the last of which was the Trajan-Hadrian dynasty.[4] The opinion adopted by the majority of critics is that of Hilgenfeld, that it was written about the middle of the first century, and, if so, it might well be referred to by Jude. On the other hand, Philippi supposes that the book is post-Christian, and posterior to the Epistle of Jude.[5]

The relation of the Assumption of Moses to the Epistle of Jude is, however, a matter of considerable difficulty, and has given rise to a variety of opinions. Unfortunately we do not possess that portion of the work which contains the account of the death and burial of Moses, and consequently cannot tell how far the statement of Origen, that Jude quotes from it, is correct. Philippi asserts that "the Assumption of Moses" was a Christian writing composed in the second century, in consequence of the statement of the burial of Moses contained in the Epistle of Jude; so that the "Assumption of Moses" was derived from the Epistle of Jude, and not conversely.[6]

---

[1] Mangold's *Einleitung*, p. 725.
[2] *Encyclopedia Britannica*, vol. ii. p. 177.
[3] *Das Judenthum in Palästina zur Zeit Christi*.
[4] *Mose Himmelfahrt*, pp. 58-60. This opinion of Volkmar is regarded as extravagant, and is adopted by no other writer.
[5] See *infra*. [6] See Philippi, *Das Buch Henoch*, pp. 166-191.

But whoever has read the fragments which are preserved must be convinced that such an assertion is highly improbable, indeed is wholly untenable. Philippi further supposes that the information contained in Jude's Epistle was derived, not from any apocryphal book or rabbinical legend, but from the direct instruction of Christ. He thinks that Jesus, after His transfiguration, at which Moses and Elijah appeared, communicated to His disciples, in answer to their question, how the dead and buried Moses could appear in bodily form, the account of the burial of Moses, and that this direct teaching of the Lord was the source of the statement in Jude's Epistle; that just as the disciples inquired concerning the appearance of Elijah, they inquired concerning the appearance of Moses. But this ingenious supposition rests on no foundation.

Others, to escape the inference that Jude refers to a Jewish legend found in an apocryphal book, suppose that the reference is to the prophecy of Zechariah, where there is mention of a contest between the angel of the Lord and Satan, and where the Lord, or the angel of the Lord, is represented as saying: "The Lord rebuke thee, O Satan" (Zech. iii. 1, 2). Thus Lardner observes: "To me it is apparent that Jude refers to the vision in Zech. iii. 1–3: 'And he showed me Joshua the high priest, and Satan standing at his right hand to resist him. And the Lord (that is, 'the angel of the Lord' before mentioned) said to Satan, The Lord rebuke thee.' The text of Jude is parallel with 2 Pet. ii. 11 : ' Whereas angels, which are greater in power and might, bring not railing accusation before the Lord.' Here also is a plain reference to the vision in Zechariah. The thing itself and that circumstance 'before the Lord,' answering to the expression in Zechariah, 'standing before the Lord,' or 'before the angel of the Lord,' put it, as seems to me, beyond question."[1] But with the exception of the words, "the Lord rebuke thee," there is here little resemblance to the language of Jude; by " the angel of the Lord " Michael might indeed be meant, but there is no mention of any contention about the body of Moses. Some, in order to avoid this objection, suppose that " the body of Moses " is a figurative expression for the Jewish

[1] Lardner's *Works*, vol. iii. p. 444, quarto edition.

people, as Christians are called "the body of Christ," and that Joshua the high priest is here to be taken as the representative of the Jewish people, so that the context in both passages is in reality the same. But this is a mere subterfuge to escape a difficulty.

Others, as Hofmann, refer the words of Jude to the mysterious burial of Moses as recorded in Deuteronomy, where we read: "And the Lord buried him in a valley in the land of Moab, over against Beth-peor; but no man knoweth of his sepulchre unto this day" (Deut. xxxiv. 6). The probable reason of this mysterious burial was to prevent the Jews worshipping the relics of their great lawgiver. According to the Targum of Jonathan, the sepulchre of Moses was left under the charge of Michael the archangel.[1] Hence it is supposed that the rabbinical legend arose containing an account of a contest between Satan and the guardian angel Michael about the disposal of the body of Moses.

Another opinion is, that the reference, both in the Epistle of Jude and in the Assumption of Moses, was derived from a current rabbinical legend.[2] This opinion is favoured by Calvin,[3] Alford,[4] and Keil.[5] We cannot refuse to credit the statement of Origen, that a narrative similar to that of Jude was contained in the Assumption of Moses, although not extant in the fragments which have come down to us; but it is affirmed that it is by no means improbable that Jude did not copy from the Assumption of Moses, but that both derived their statements from a common source. The Jewish legends concerning the death and burial of Moses are very numerous, and in most of them mention is made of a contest between Michael and Satan, though in the Jewish traditions the stress is laid on the death rather than on the burial of Moses.[6] Hence it is not improbable that we have here a Jewish expansion of the account of the burial of Moses as is contained in Deuteronomy, perhaps modified by the words in

[1] Alford on Jude 9.
[2] Herder thinks that it was taken from the Zendavesta.
[3] Calvin *in loco*. [4] Alford on Jude 9.
[5] Keil's *Commentar über die Briefe Petrus et Judas*, p. 314.
[6] See Baring-Gould's *Legends of Old Testament Characters*, vol. ii. pp. 131-137.

the prophecy of Zechariah.[1] In this form Jude applied the legend for his own purpose, namely, to censure those who were irreverent in thought and word, who "despised dominion and spoke evil of dignities" (Jude 8). At the same time, it must be admitted that the preponderance of evidence is in favour of the words in question being a quotation from, or reference to, the Assumption of Moses.

Admitting that there is here a reference either to an apocryphal book or to a rabbinical tradition, yet this is no objection to the authenticity or authority of the Epistle of Jude. Jude employs it simply as an illustration of the evil of irreverence, and as a rebuke to those against whom he wrote. "It is no more strange," observes Cave, "that Jude should quote an apocryphal book, than that Paul should put down Jannes and Jambres for the two magicians of Pharaoh that opposed Moses, which he must either have derived from tradition or fetched from some uncanonical author of those times, there being no mention of their names in Moses' relation of that matter."[2]

The discovery of the Assumption of Moses by Ceriani attracted much attention in Germany. Hilgenfeld was the first to publish a critical edition, supplying as far as possible the omissions by conjectural emendations. He afterwards turned the Latin text into Greek, from which, as he supposed, it was originally translated.[3] Volkmar, in his *Mose Prophetie und Himmelfahrt*, published at Leipsic in 1867, was the first who translated the work into German, with a learned preliminary dissertation and numerous notes. A third translation was made by Merx and Schmidt,[4] and a fourth by Fritzsche in his *Libri Apocryph. Vet. Test.* Besides these translations and critical editions, the work has been more or less discussed by Ewald in his *Geschichte des Volkes Israel* and in the *Göttinger Anzeiger*, 1862; by Philippi in his *Das Buch Henoch*; by Haupt in the *Zeitschrift für wiss. Theol.* 1867; by Schürer in his *Neutestamentliche Zeitgeschichte*;[5] by Langen of Bonn

---

[1] See Spitta, p. 348.   [2] Cave's *Lives of the Apostles:* Life of Jude.
[3] Hilgenfeld's *Novum Testamentum extra Canon., Messias Judæorum,* and *Zeitschr. für wissen. Theol.* 1868.
[4] *Archiv. für wissen. Erforsch. des A. T.* 1868.
[5] Schürer's *Jewish People in the Time of Jesus Christ*, vol. iii. pp. 73-80, E. Tr., Edinburgh 1886.

in his *Das Judenthum in Palästina zur Zeit Christi*; by Colani in the *Revue de Theol.* 1868; by Dillmann in his article on the "Pseudepigraphen des alten Testaments" in Herzog's *Encyklopädie*; by Wieseler in the *Jahrbuch für deutsche Theol.* 1868; by Rönsch in the *Zeitschrift für wissen. Theol.* 1869; by Hausrath in his *Neutestamentliche Zeitgeschichte*; and by Reuss in his *Geschichte der heiligen Schriften A. T.* In England, on the other hand, the work has received little attention; it is briefly noticed by Davidson in the article on "Apocalyptic Literature" in the *Encyclopædia Britannica*, and more fully treated by Drummond in his *Jewish Messiah*; but the fullest discussion of it is contained in an able article in the *Monthly Interpreter* for 1885 by the Rev. William J. Deane.

DISSERTATION II.

THE BOOK OF ENOCH.[1]

In the Epistle of Jude there is a reference to the prophecy of Enoch, and there has been much discussion concerning the source from which Jude derived his information. The reference is as follows: "And to these also Enoch, the seventh from Adam, prophesied saying, Behold, the Lord came with ten thousands of His holy ones to execute judgment upon all, and to convict all the ungodly of all their works of ungodliness, which they have ungodly wrought, and of all the hard things which ungodly sinners have spoken against Him" (Jude 14, 15: *Revised Version*). Now there are numerous allusions in the Fathers to a Book of Enoch:[2] and it is a remarkable circumstance that, toward the close of last century,

[1] The chief authorities consulted for this dissertation were Ewald's *Abhandlung über des Buches Henokh Entstehung, Sinn und Zusammensetzung*; Dillmann's *Das Buch Henoch*; Drummond's *Jewish Messiah*; Laurence's *Book of Enoch*; and Schodde's *The Book of Enoch translated*, besides the articles in Herzog, Kitto, and Smith's Dictionaries.

[2] For the allusions and references to the Book of Enoch in various writings, see Fabricius' *Codex Pseudepigraphus Vet. Test.*, vol. i. pp. 161-224, and Philippi, *Das Buch Henoch*, pp. 102-118.

a book, written in Ethiopic, was discovered in the distant land of Abyssinia, purporting to be this Book of Enoch, and containing words similar to this prophecy quoted by Jude.

The earliest allusion to the Book of Enoch, with the exception of these words of Jude, is in the so-called Epistle of Barnabas (A.D. 100), where we read : " The source of danger approaches, concerning which it is written, as Enoch says : For this end the Lord hath cut short the times, that His Beloved may hasten." [1] There is, however, no such passage in the Book of Enoch, and it is doubtful whether Enoch here is not an erroneous reading for Daniel, which is the text of the Latin version. In the Testament of the Twelve Patriarchs, a Christian work of uncertain date, but probably belonging to the first half of the second century, the Book of Enoch is repeatedly referred to.[2] Justin Martyr (A.D. 150) has no direct allusion to it, but in his account of the fall of the angels, of the nature of their sin, and of the evil influence which they exerted on the human race, he had in all probability the Book of Enoch in view, because his description coincides with the account contained in that work.[3] Athenagoras (A.D. 178) has a similar statement concerning the fall and sin of "the ruler of the world and its various forms."[4] Irenæus (A.D. 180) makes reference to this work when he states that Enoch was employed in a mission to the fallen angels. " Enoch," he observes, " pleasing God without circumcision, discharged the office of God's legate to the angels, although he was a man and was translated, and is preserved until now as a witness of the just judgment of God."[5] But the most important testimony is that of Tertullian (A.D. 200),

[1] Barnabas, *Epist.* ch. 4. It is now generally agreed that this Epistle was not by Barnabas, but was written about the commencement of the second century.

[2] For example, in Reuben 5, Simeon 5, Levi 10, 14, 16, Judah 18, Dan 5, Naphtali 4, and Benjamin 9. For these references see Fabricius, *Codex Pseudepigraph.*, vol. i. pp. 161-166. The Testament of the Twelve Patriarchs is given in Fabricius, vol. i. pp. 496-759. A translation of it by the Rev. Robert Skinner, Cambridge, is contained in Clark's *Ante-Nicene Fathers*, and strangely inserted at the end of the second volume of the writings of Lactantius.

[3] Justin, *Apol.* ii. 5.   [4] Athenagoras, *Legatio p. Chr.*, ch. 24.
[5] *Adv. Hær.* iv. 16. 2 ; comp. Enoch, chs. xiv., xv.

who not only repeatedly quotes from the Book of Enoch, but asserts its inspiration. "These things," he observes, "the Holy Ghost, foreseeing from the beginning, foretold through the most ancient prophet Enoch."[1] And, in a still more remarkable passage, he thus meets the objections made to the authenticity and consequent inspiration of this book: "I am aware that the scripture of Enoch, which has assigned this office to the angels, is not received by some, because it is not admitted into the Jewish canon. I suppose, having been published before the deluge, they did not think that it could have survived that universal calamity." Tertullian then proceeds to show that, notwithstanding the deluge, the preservation of the prophecy of Enoch was quite possible; and then goes on to say: "But since Enoch in the same scripture has preached likewise concerning the Lord, nothing at all must be rejected by us which is useful to us; for we read that every scripture, suitable for edification, is divinely inspired. By the Jews it seems to have been rejected because it testified of Christ. Nor is it wonderful that they did not receive some scriptures which spake of Him whom even in person, speaking in their presence, they rejected. To these considerations is added this fact, that Enoch possesses a testimony in the Apostle Jude."[2] The Book of Enoch is also frequently referred to by Origen (A.D. 230), though, differing from Tertullian, he does not assert its inspiration. Thus he mentions the names and particular offices of the angels in terms similar to those used in the Book of Enoch : "A particular office is assigned to a particular angel; as to Raphael, the work of curing and healing; to Gabriel, the conduct of wars; to Michael, the duty of attending to the prayers and supplications of mortals."[3] And in another part of the same work Origen observes: "Enoch, in his book, speaks as follows: I have walked on even to imperfection' (Enoch xxi. 1): which expression I

---

[1] *De Idol.* ch. 15.

[2] *De Cultis fem.* i. 3. See also *De Idol.* ch. iv. *De Cultis fem.* ii. 10.

[3] *De Principiis*, i. 8; comp. with this Enoch, ch. xl. 9 : "The first is Michael, the long-suffering and patient; the second is Raphael, who is placed over all the diseases and wounds of mortals; and the third is Gabriel, who is placed over all the powers."

consider may be understood to mean that the mind of the prophet proceeded in its scrutiny and investigation of all visible things, until it arrived at that first beginning, in which it beheld imperfect matter without qualities: for it is written in the same Book of Enoch, 'I beheld the whole of matter'"[1] (Enoch xix. 3). In his refutation of Celsus, Origen observes: "Celsus, in a confused manner, adduces, when examining the subject of the visits of angels to men, what he has derived, without seeing its meaning, from the contents of the Book of Enoch; for he does not appear to have read the passages in question, nor to have been aware that the books which bear the name of Enoch do not at all circulate in the churches as inspired."[2] Anatolius, bishop of Laodicea (A.D. 269), quotes the Book of Enoch as proving that the first month of the Hebrews is about the equinox.[3] Augustine (A.D. 395) frequently refers to it, but asserts that the writings of Enoch and Noah are not held to be of divine authority, either by the Jews or by the Christians.[4] The Book of Enoch is also reckoned among the apocryphal books in the *Apostolical Constitutions*,[5] in the *Synopsis Athanasii*, and in the catalogue of Nicephorus, the patriarch of Constantinople;[6] this latter writer states that it contains 4800 lines ($\sigma\tau\iota\chi o\iota$).

The knowledge of the Book of Enoch gradually died out, and appears in the fifth century to have been lost in the Latin Church. The investigations of the learned Scaliger discovered some traces of it in the Greek Church toward the end of the eighth century. In the Chronographia of Georgius Syncellus (A.D. 790), a chronology extending from Adam to Diocletian, then an unpublished manuscript, he found considerable fragments, purporting to be from the Book of Enoch, referring chiefly to the fall of the angels. Scaliger printed these fragments, and called the attention of the learned to them.[7]

The researches of Archbishop Laurence, which have since

---

[1] *De Principiis*, iv. 1. 35.   [2] *Contra Celsum*, v. 54.
[3] Eusebius, *Hist. Eccl.* vii. 32.
[4] *De civitate Dei*, xviii. 38. See also *ibid*. xv. 23. It is also referred to by Jerome and Epiphanius.
[5] *Apost. Const.* vi. 16.   [6] Nicephorus, *Hist. Eccl.* (ed. Dindorf) i. 787.
[7] These fragments, preserved by Syncellus, are given in Fabricius, *Codex*

been confirmed by Dillmann and Jellinek,[1] have shown that the Book of Enoch was not unknown to the mediæval Jewish Church. He adduces two references to it in that remarkable cabbalistic book, the Zohar, a work which, though first known in Europe in the thirteenth century through Spanish Jews, is generally supposed to belong to the sixth or seventh century. These references are as follows: "The holy and the blessed One raised Enoch from the world to serve Him, as it is written, 'For God took him.' From that time a book was delivered down, which was called the Book of Enoch. In that hour God took him, and showed him all the repositories above. He showed him the tree of life in the midst of the garden, its leaves and its branches; we see all this in his book." And the other passage is still more direct: "We find in the Book of Enoch, that the holy and blessed One caused him to ascend, and showed him all the repositories of the superior and inferior kingdom. He showed him the tree of life, and the tree respecting which Adam had received a commandment; and he showed him the habitation of Adam in the garden of Eden."[2] The investigations of the learned have discovered other traces of the Book of Enoch in Rabbi Menahem, in Parasha Bereshit, and in other Jewish writings. It is referred to in the Book of Jubilees, a Jewish work supposed to be written about the beginning of the Christian era.[3]

Such was all that was known of the Book of Enoch until near the close of last century. The importance assigned to it by the Fathers, and the supposed quotation from it by Jude, had attracted the attention of the learned; but the Book itself was regarded as irrecoverably lost. In the

Pseudepigraphus V. T., vol. i. pp. 179-199, in Laurence's *Book of Enoch*, p. 203, and in Dillmann's *Das Buch Henoch*, pp. 82-86.

[1] Dillmann's *Das Buch Henoch*, Introduction, p. 57, and Jellinek, *Zeitschrift der deutschen morgenländischen Gesellschaft*, vol. vii. p. 249 ff.

[2] Laurence's *Book of Enoch*, preliminary dissertation, pp. 29, 30.

[3] See article on the Book of Jubilees, or the Little Genesis, by the Rev. W. J. Deane, in the *Monthly Interpreter*, vol. i. p. 268 ff. Rönsch, *Das Buch der Jubiläen oder die kleine Genesis*, p. 403 ff. There are several Midrashim in existence published by Jellinek containing legends similar to those found in the Book of Enoch. Dr. Kalisch has also some remarks on this book in his *Commentary on Genesis*.

beginning of the seventeenth century it was supposed to have been discovered in Abyssinia; but the manuscript brought from that country was proved by the Ethiopic scholar Ludolph to be a worthless rabbinical production.[1] In 1773, however, the illustrious Abyssinian traveller Bruce astonished the theological world by the assertion, that he had brought back with him from Abyssinia three copies of the Book of Enoch written in the Ethiopic language. "Among the articles," he states, "which I consigned to the Library of Paris was a very beautiful and magnificent copy of the prophecies of Enoch in large quarto. Another is among the books of Scripture which I brought home, standing immediately before the Book of Job, which is its proper place in the Abyssinian canon; and a third copy I presented to the Bodleian Library at Oxford by the hands of Dr. Douglas, Bishop of Carlisle."[2] Since that time several more copies have been brought from Abyssinia, all of them written in the Ethiopic language. After this discovery by Bruce, a fragment of the Book of Enoch was found by Cardinal Mai among the manuscripts of the Vatican, and was published by him in facsimile. This fragment must have been brought earlier to Europe than the manuscripts of Bruce.[3]

Notwithstanding the importance which one would think would be assigned to the discovery of an apocryphal book which was supposed to be quoted by a sacred writer, such was the decadence of theological learning toward the close of last century, that it was suffered to remain on the shelves of the libraries of Oxford and Paris. In 1800, Silvestre de Sacy in the *Magazine Encyclopédique* published an account of the work, with a Latin translation of a few chapters from the

---

[1] See Laurence's *Enoch*, preliminary dissertation, pp. 12, 13. Ludolf, *Commentarius in Hist. Æthiop.* p. 347. Fabricius, *Codex Pseudep.* vol. i. pp. 209–214.

[2] Bruce's *Travels*, vol. ii. p. 412, octavo ed. 1813. Laurence's *Book of Enoch*, preliminary dissertation, p. 14. The second copy was also purchased for the Bodleian Library after Bruce's death. It is marked MS. Bruce, 74. It consists of five volumes; vol. iv. consists of Enoch, followed by Job, Isaiah, the twelve minor prophets, etc.

[3] See Kitto's *Encyclopedia of Biblical Literature*, vol. i. p. 792. Schodde, *The Book of Enoch*, p. 3. Published by Mai in *Patrum Nova Bibliotheca*, vol. ii. The fragment is in Greek, not in Ethiopic.

Paris manuscript.¹ But it was not until 1821 that the attention of theologians was called to the value of its contents by a publication of an English translation of the whole work from the Oxford manuscript by Laurence, afterwards Archbishop of Cashel, under the title: *The Book of Enoch, the prophet, an apocryphal production supposed for ages to have been lost; but discovered at the close of last century in Abyssinia, now first translated from an Ethiopic manuscript in the Bodleian Library.* A second edition appeared in 1833, and a third in 1838; and in the same year the Ethiopic text itself was printed under the superintendence of Laurence.² The Book of Enoch was introduced to the notice of German theologians by Hoffmann of Jena. He published a German version with a running commentary in two parts; the first part containing the first fifty-seven chapters, published in 1833, was a translation of Laurence's version with the help of De Sacy's extracts; and the second part, published in 1838, was an independent translation of the remainder from another Ethiopic manuscript in the library of Frankfort-on-the-Maine.³ In 1840 Gfrörer made a Latin translation from the German and English versions, and published it in his *Prophetæ Veteres Pseudepigraphi*. But these translations have all been superseded by the praiseworthy labours of Professor Dillmann, now of Berlin, who first

---

[1] *Notice sur le Livre d'Enoch.* De Sacy's translation is inserted in Laurence's *Enoch*, p. 191. The chapters which De Sacy selected for translation were the first three, the sixth to the sixteenth inclusive, and the twenty-second and thirty-second.

[2] *Libri Enoch Propheta versio Æthopica.* Dillmann writes in disparaging terms of Laurence's translation: he observes, "It is to be regretted that the first publication of this book did not fall into the hands of a more learned man than Laurence appears to have been, both from this and from his other writings;" a remark that has been repeated by Schodde, p. 6. But such a depreciatory remark is unwarranted. The translation may be defective, but it must be recollected that the study of Ethiopic was then comparatively rare, and that Laurence had only one manuscript before him; indeed there is no essential difference between his version and that of Dillmann. And so far are his other writings from showing him to be a man of defective learning, that they rather entitle him to occupy a high place among the most erudite theologians of the Church of England.

[3] *Das Buch Henoch in Vollständiger Uebersetzung mit fortlaufendem Commentar*, 2 vols., Jena 1833-1838.

published in 1851 the Ethiopic text from a collation of five manuscripts, and then in 1853 gave to the world his German translation, furnished with a learned and exhaustive introduction, and with copious notes.[1] Recently a new translation was published by Professor Schodde of America, founded chiefly on Dillmann's translation.[2] It is to be observed that the arrangement of chapters and verses in the various manuscripts is different, and is also different in the versions of Laurence and Dillmann; in Laurence's version the chapters number 105, whereas in Dillmann's they number 108. In the references made in this dissertation the arrangement of Dillmann is adopted.

There is no reason to doubt that the book discovered by Bruce in Abyssinia is the same as that quoted by Jude, and mentioned or cited by the Fathers. The passage contained in the Epistle of Jude is found in almost similar terms: the references and quotations by the Fathers have their counterparts in this book; and the long extract of Syncellus, with the exception of one paragraph,[3] and the fragment in the Vatican manuscript,[4] are also found in the Ethiopic Book of Enoch.

The Book of Enoch is now only known to us in the Ethiopic language; all the manuscripts which we possess have been brought from Abyssinia. The Ethiopic is doubtless a version, probably made from the Greek about the fourth century, when the Bible was translated into Ethiopic, as, according to Bruce, the Book of Enoch formed part of the Abyssinian canon.[5] The fragments of Syncellus and those in the Vatican manuscript are in Greek, and the Fathers

[1] *Das Buch Henoch, übersetzt und erklärt*, Leipzig 1853.
[2] *The Book of Enoch, translated from the Ethiopic with Introduction and Notes*, Andover 1882.
[3] The fragments preserved by Syncellus answer to ch. vi. 1 to ch. ix. 4, ch. viii. 4 to ch. x. 14, and ch. xv. 8 to ch. xvi. 1, and a paragraph not found in the extant Book of Enoch.
[4] The fragments preserved in the Vatican MS. are chs. xlii.-xlix. and ch. lxxxix.
[5] This is the case in the MS. of the Book of Enoch in the Bodleian Library. How the Book of Enoch found entrance into the Abyssinian canon is unknown; that canon also includes, according to Dillmann, the Book of the Jubilees and the Ascension of Isaiah. No MS. in the Bodleian Library contains an Ethiopic Book of Jubilees; the MS. Huntingdon, 626 (Ethiopic), contains, I am informed, the Ascension of Isaiah and the Apocalypse of Ezra.

without doubt in their quotations cited from the Greek. But the Greek itself is a translation from the Hebrew or Aramaic. Learned critics have observed that the names of the angels, of the sun, of the winds, and of the conductors of the months are all from Hebrew, or at least from Semitic roots. The Ophanim, who are mentioned along with the Cherubim and Seraphim, is just the Hebrew word for the "wheels" in Ezekiel. And besides the work, as Laurence, Dillmann, and Jellinek show, was known and used by Jewish writers until the sixth century. It is generally agreed that the Ethiopic version gives a tolerably correct transcript of the original, at least so far as we can judge by testing the accuracy of the Ethiopic version of the Bible and of other books,[1] and by comparing the Ethiopic text with the Greek of Syncellus with which it generally agrees. It must, however, be remembered that it is a translation of a translation; and consequently the English and German versions are thrice removed from the original Hebrew.

The Book of Enoch is divided into four parts or books, each of which has its own introduction and conclusion, so that the work is frequently cited by the Fathers as "the Books of Enoch."[2] The following is a brief statement of the contents of the work. It commences as follows: "The word of the blessing of Enoch, with which he blessed the elect and the righteous, who will exist in the time of trouble, when the wicked and ungodly shall be rejected. Enoch, a righteous man, whose eyes God had opened, so that he saw a holy vision in the heavens which the angels showed, answered, and said." Then follows a general introduction, in which the nature of the whole work is stated (chs. i.–viii.). In the first book there is an account of the fall of the angels, and of

---

[1] See Dillmann's article in Herzog's *Encyclopædia*, 2nd edition. Article "Æthiopische Bibelübersetzung," vol. i. p. 203 ff. On the Ethiopic version of the Bible, Dillmann remarks: "It is very faithful, being for the most part a verbal rendering of the Greek, yet readable and fluent."

[2] So Origen. Augustine speaks of it as "the Books of Noah and Enoch." The following is the general arrangement:—Introduction (chs. i.–v.); Part I.: The Book of Travels (chs. vi.–xxxvi.); Part II.: The Book of Similitudes (chs. xxxvii.–lxxi.); Part III.: The Book of the Luminaries (chs. lxxii.–lxxxii.); Part IV.: The Book of Visions (chs. lxxxiii.–xci.); Part V.: The Book of Exhortation (chs. xcii.–cv.); two Appendices (chs. cvi.–cviii.).

the origin of the giants, containing many rabbinical extravagances (chs. vi.–xvi.).[1] To this historical narrative is attached an account of the journeys of Enoch under the guidance of an angel, in which he describes what he saw on earth, in heaven, and in hell (chs. xvii.–xxxvi.). The second book, styled "The Second Book of Wisdom which Enoch saw," is divided into three sections, called in the text parables or similitudes. The first parable (chs. xxxvii.–xliv.) is a continuation of Enoch's journey, containing an eloquent description of the heavenly world. The second parable (chs. xlv.–lvii.) is by far the most important part of the work, and is a very elevated description of the kingdom of the Messiah, of the destruction of all His enemies, of the universal establishment of peace, and of the glories of the Messianic reign. In the third parable (chs. lviii.–lxiv.) there is a vision of the New Jerusalem, and of the exaltation of the Messiah, surrounded with myriads of angels. Inserted in this parable there occurs, in an entirely disconnected manner, the vision of Noah, which is evidently out of place, and is almost universally regarded as an interpolation (chs. lxv.–lxix.). Then follows a suitable conclusion to the parables (chs. lxx., lxxi.). The third book, styled "The book of the courses of the luminaries of heaven," contains a statement of the laws of the sun, moon, and stars, a description of the winds and seasons of the year, treated rather in a religious than in a scientific spirit (chs. lxxii.–lxxxii.). The fourth book contains two visions which were imparted to Enoch in early youth. The first vision (chs. lxxxiii., lxxxiv.) is that of the coming deluge; and the second (chs. lxxxv.–xc.) is a history of the world, supposed to be foretold to Enoch from his time down to the establishment of the Messianic kingdom; the whole is carried on in the form of an allegory, wherein the righteous are represented as sheep attacked by ravenous beasts and birds of prey. The book closes with an admonition of Enoch to his children (ch. xci.). The fifth book contains the advice of Enoch "to his children who will dwell upon the earth and to all future generations who will practise righteousness and peace." The history of the world is again

---

[1] This is the part which is most frequently referred to by the Fathers.

given in a different form; it is divided into ten weeks, and it was at the end of the first of these weeks that Enoch himself lived (chs. xcii.–cv.). To the whole work are attached two appendices, evidently interpolations: the one containing an account of the miraculous birth of Noah (chs. cvi., cvii.); and the other, styled "another book that Enoch wrote for his son Methuselah," containing a concluding summary and exhortation (ch. cviii.).

It need hardly be stated that the book is undoubtedly apocryphal. The Fathers generally asserted its spuriousness.[1] The only one who defended its authenticity and inspiration was Tertullian, and that on the most untenable grounds; an extravagance which has since been repeated in recent times by the Rev. W. Aldis, who asserts that the book was written by the pen of inspiration.[2] How far such a fictitious use of the name of Enoch was excusable may admit of a question: certain it is that, in the century before and in that after Christ, such a practice of publishing works under the fictitious names of illustrious saints was not uncommon among Jewish and Christian writers, and does not appear to have been regarded in the same moral point of view as that in which it would be looked upon in our days. But perhaps, after all, the author did not intend to impose his work upon his readers as a forgery, as if it actually contained the visions and revelations of Enoch, but merely used the name of that patriarch as the vehicle for the communication of certain important truths which he wished to inculcate. The work may be regarded as a romance, a species of fiction in those early times, not unlike in kind to Gessner's once celebrated but now almost forgotten *Death of Abel*.[3]

It is hardly a matter of dispute among critics, whether the Book of Enoch is a single work or a compilation. It is almost universally admitted that there are in it interpolations: as, for example, the vision of Noah inserted at the close of the

---

[1] Origen, Augustine, and Jerome describe it as apocryphal, and it is ranked among the apocryphal books in the *Apostolical Constitutions*.

[2] *The Holy Prophecies, Visions, and Life of the Prophet Enoch*, by the Rev. W. Aldis, Edinburgh 1839. This work is full of extravagances.

[3] So also the *Clementine Recognitions* is a species of early Christian romance.

third similitude, and the account of the birth of Noah at the close of the work. Archbishop Laurence observes that different parts of the book may have been composed at different periods; they may have been different tracts, as well as tracts composed by different authors.[1] Philippi stands almost alone in maintaining that the book is to all intents and purposes one work.[2] But although it is admitted that the book is a compilation, yet very different views are entertained concerning the number, extent, and age of the separate works of which it is composed.[3]

Dillmann, in the introduction to his translation, asserts that the work is formed on a unity of plan, and substantially proceeds from one author, though certain additions have been inserted. "We distinguish," he observes, "(1) the proper and original Book of Enoch, comprehending by far the greater part of the work as we now have it; (2) historical additions, for the elucidation of certain doctrines and ideas occurring in the parent book; (3) the Noachian document and the interpolations connected with it."[4] He has since modified his view in his article on the pseudepigraphic writings, in the first edition of Herzog's *Encyclopædia*. "Partly," he observes, "further consideration, and partly the dissertation of Ewald, which has appeared since my translation, has convinced me that my former view cannot be maintained, and I now recognise that, after the withdrawal of the historical additions and of the Noachian document, the remainder of the book must have been made up of two if not three writings."[5] And in his recent article in the new edition of Herzog, he considers that the Book of Enoch is composed chiefly of three writings,[6] an opinion which accords with that of Schürer afterwards to be mentioned.

[1] Laurence's *Book of Enoch*, preliminary dissertation, p. 58.
[2] Philippi's *Das Buch Henoch, sein Zeitalter und sein Verhältniss zum Judasbrief*, 1868. Hofmann held that the interpolations were few and of a trifling character. Lücke at one time adopted the same view, but afterwards abandoned it.
[3] For the views of different scholars concerning the authorship of the book, see Schodde's *Book of Enoch*, pp. 20-26; Schürer's *Jewish People in the Time of Christ*, vol. iii. p. 59 ff.
[4] *Das Buch Henoch*, Introduction, p. 9.
[5] Herzog's *Encyclopädie* (1st edition), vol. xii. p. 309.
[6] *Ibid.* (2nd edition) vol. xii. p. 351.

Ewald supposes that the Book of Enoch is a compilation of the works of four different authors, but artificially united with additions and omissions by a fifth author who was the compiler. According to him, "the Book of Similitudes," with the abstraction of the Noachian document, constitutes the first or original work. The author of this work directs his attacks against the external enemies of his people. The second work contains the account of the fall of the angels and the origin of the giants, and the so-called "Book of Exhortations." This second author is chiefly engaged in combating internal foes. The third work contains the greater part of the "Book of the Luminaries," and the two dreams or visions of Enoch concerning the deluge and the history of the world. This third author explains the secrets of nature and providence. The fourth book is the vision of Noah, which, however, is not confined to the Noachian portion, but is interwoven by the compiler throughout the whole work. And, lastly, there is the fifth author, or the compiler, who joined together the four above-mentioned works, omitting portions of them and making certain additions of his own.[1]

Schürer supposes that the Book of Enoch is composed of at least three distinct parts, written by different authors: 1. The groundwork (chs. i.-xxxvi. and lxxii.-cv.). 2. The Book of Similitudes (chs. xxxvii.-lxxi.), with the exception of the Noachian portions. 3. The Noachian portions (chs. liv. 7-lv. 2, lxv.-lxix., cvi.-cvii.). The last chapter (ch. cviii.) is an independent addition.[2] This opinion, in its general features, is that of Lücke,[3] Köstlin,[4] and Schodde;[5] and to it Dillmann has given in his adhesion. The book, however, it is to be observed, is substantially a unity, pervaded by the same spirit, and enunciating the same views.

[1] Ewald, *Abhandlung über des äthiopischen Buches Henokh*, etc. The criticism of Ewald is extremely fanciful, a fault which is characteristic of the writings of this great theologian. It is difficult to trace the process of reasoning by which he rearranges the Book of Enoch, and assigns certain portions to certain authors.

[2] Schürer, *Neutestamentliche Zeitgeschichte*, p. 521 ff. [E. Tr. vol. iii. pp. 61-69].

[3] Lücke, *Einleit. in die Offenb. Johannes*, 1852, pp. 89-144.

[4] *Theol. Jahrbücher*, 1856, pp. 240-279.

[5] Schodde, *Book of Enoch*, pp. 28, 32.

Different opinions have also been entertained with regard to the age of the book generally, and of its separate parts in particular. Whilst the general opinion is that it was written before the Christian era, some critics suppose it to be post-Christian. This is the view adopted by Credner,[1] Philippi, Hofmann of Erlangen,[2] Volkmar, Böttcher, and Moses Stuart of America.[3] Hilgenfeld and Colani[4] think that the greater part is pre-Christian, but that the Messianic portions, especially those contained in the "Book of Similitudes," were composed in the reign of Titus, and are pervaded with Gnostic ideas.[5] Dr. Pusey, in his *Lectures on Daniel*, assigns it to the early Maccabean age, perhaps to the time of Judas Maccabeus.[6] Dillmann, Anger, Hausrath, Keim,[7] Oehler, Schenkel, Lücke, Sieffert, Kuenen,[8] Köstlin, and Dean Stanley[9] assign at least the greater part of the work to the reign of John Hyrcanus; whilst Laurence, Hoffmann of Jena, Wieseler, and Gieseler[10] consider that it was written in the commencement of the reign of Herod the Great (A.D. 40). Lücke,[11] Schürer,[12] and Schodde suppose that the first part or groundwork was written in the early Maccabean age, whilst the "Book of Similitudes" belongs to the age of Herod. Ewald and Lipsius[13] suppose that the different works were all composed in the period intervening between Jonathan Maccabeus and the early days of Herod.

In this diversity of opinion it is impossible to arrive at a definite conclusion. The opinion of Dillmann, that the greater portion of it was written in the reign of John Hyrcanus, appears to be best supported. The struggles

---

[1] Credner's *Einleitung in das N. T.*, p. 618.
[2] Hofmann's *Schriftbeweis*, i. 420 ff.   [3] *American Bibl. Report.* 1840.
[4] Colani's *Croyances Messianiques*, p. 31.
[5] Hilgenfeld finds in the work a reference to the eruption of Vesuvius, Enoch lxvii. 5, 6.
[6] Pusey's *Lectures on Daniel*, p. 392.
[7] Keim's *Jesus of Nazara*, vol. i. p. 317.
[8] Kuenen's *History of Israel*, vol. iii. p. 265.
[9] Stanley's *Jewish Church*, vol. iii. p. 374.
[10] Gieseler's *Church History*, vol. i. p. 94.
[11] Lücke's *Einleitung in die Offenbarung Johannis*, pp. 52-78; 1852, p. 89 ff.
[12] Schürer's *Jewish People in the Time of Christ*, vol. iii. p. 68, E. Tr.
[13] See Lipsius's article on the apocryphal Book of Enoch in Smith's *Dictionary of Christian Biography*, vol. ii. p. 124 ff.

of the Maccabean age are distinctly alluded to in the allegory of the sheep attacked by birds of prey. The sheep become blind and are attacked by the ravenous birds. Little lambs are born who begin to open their eyes and see; and horns grow upon them, evidently representing the Maccabean heroes. They cry to the sheep, but the sheep remain blind and deaf. The ravens flew down and destroyed many of them. At length there arose a ram with a great horn, and the eyes of the sheep were opened, and when they cried they all ran to him; and the recording angel came to the assistance of the ram, so that all the attacks of the ravens and other birds of prey were in vain; and at length the Lord of the sheep Himself came, and all the birds of prey fled away. "And I saw that a great sword was given to the sheep who went forth against all the beasts of the field to slay them. But all the beasts and birds of heaven fled away from before their face."[1] Now, certainly, as Dillmann shows, the description of the ram with the great horn best suits John Hyrcanus, under whom the Maccabean struggle with the Syrian kings came to an end, and Judea recovered its freedom and was recognised as an independent kingdom.[2]

There is one objection to so early a date, namely, the mention of the Parthians, as already a warlike and conquering race: "In those days the angels will assemble and turn their heads toward the east, toward the people of Parthia and Media."[3] Now, as Archbishop Laurence argues, it was not until the first years of the reign of Herod that the Parthians could be thus spoken of by a Jewish writer. It was shortly before this, B.C. 54, that they defeated and destroyed the army of Crassus, and a few years afterwards, B.C. 40, that they took Jerusalem and drove Herod from his dominion.[4] Dillmann,[5] however, asserts that the Parthians were well

---

[1] Enoch xc. 19.

[2] Dillmann's *Das Buch Henoch*, Introduction, p. 43. A similar conclusion is drawn by Dillmann from the consideration of the ten weeks of the world's history given in the fifth part of the Book of Enoch.

[3] Enoch lvi. 5.

[4] So also Schürer argues from this that the Book of Similitudes was composed "at the very soonest in the time of Herod."

[5] *Das Buch Henoch*, p. 45.

known to the Jews in the time of John Hyrcanus, for that prince assisted Antiochus Sidetes, the king of Syria, in his campaign against them, and indeed they then formed the mightiest empire in the East.[1]

Volkmar considers that the whole work is post-Christian, written about A.D. 132 in the defence of the impostor Barcocheba, after Rabbi Akiba had given in his adhesion to the revolt, and that therefore it is Jewish and anti-Christian in its teaching.[2] There is nothing in the whole book to countenance such a view. The whole description of the attacks of the enemies refers to the struggle between the Jews and the Syrians, and not to that between the Jews and the Romans. Whilst the destruction of the temple by Nebuchadnezzar is mentioned, there is no allusion to the comparatively recent (if Volkmar's view be correct) and more awful destruction of it by Titus.

One important point appears to be demonstrated, that at least the greater portion of the Book of Enoch was composed before the Christian era. There is no allusion to Christianity in the book. It abounds with Messianic passages, but there is no reference to any incident in the life of Jesus. Nor is there any opposition in it to the doctrines of Christianity or to the persons of Christians. Nor is there any reference to the Romans. It would seem to have been written before the Roman empire gained its ascendency, and before it came into direct contact with Judea. The description of the enemies of God's people suits the Syrians, but not the Romans. The conclusion, then, that we arrive at is that this Book of Enoch was composed by a Jewish writer before the Christian era and before the Romans came into collision with the Jews, most probably in the time of John Hyrcanus.[3]

What imparts to it peculiar value are the Messianic

---

[1] Arsaces, king of Parthia, is mentioned in the time of Simon, 1 Macc. xiv. 2, 3, xv. 22; he is there called "the King of Persia and Media."

[2] *Zeitschrift der deutschen morgenländischen Gesellschaft* for 1860. For the view of Volkmar, see Drummond's *Jewish Messiah*, pp. 43, 44. This extravagant opinion hardly deserves mention, had it not been partially adopted by Dean Alford, *Greek Testament*, vol. iv., Prolegomena, p. 196.

[3] The Book of Enoch, according to Hausrath, was written some forty years before the first appearance of the Romans in Palestine. *New Testament Times*, vol. i. p. 192.

statements which it contains.[1] The Messiah is directly represented without symbol or type. He is the Son of man, who is not merely the Ruler, but the Judge of the world, the King of kings, exalted above all dominion and power. He is the elect One, the Messiah, the Anointed of the Lord. His pre-existence is distinctly assumed. He was chosen before the world was created, and His name was invoked before the Lord of the spirits, before the sun and stars were called into existence.[2] Kings fall down before Him; the mighty of the world do homage to Him as their sovereign Lord; and all the nations of the world worship before Him, and are converted into obedient subjects. War and strife are abolished, and peace is universally established. A new Jerusalem is built, and a new temple is erected for the worshippers of the Lord. Wisdom is poured out like water, glory ceases not before Him from eternity to eternity, and the fountain of righteousness shall be inexhaustible. In Him dwells the spirit of wisdom and power, and He shall sit on the throne of His glory. "And he answered and said to me, This is the Son of man, who has righteousness, with whom righteousness dwells, and who reveals all the treasures of that which is concealed, because the Lord of the spirits has chosen Him, and His lot before the Lord of the spirits has surpassed all by righteousness for ever. And this Son of man, whom thou hast seen, will expel the kings and mighty from their seats, and the powerful from their thrones, and shall break the teeth of sinners. And He shall hurl kings from their thrones and their dominions, because they will not exalt or praise Him, nor humble themselves before Him, by whom their kingdoms were bestowed."[3]

It has been asserted that these Messianic statements prove a Christian origin, and that the book, though originally pre-Christian, has been tampered with by Christian hands. This is the view advocated by Hilgenfeld,[4] Keim,[5] Kuenen,[6]

---

[1] See Dorner, *Doctrine of the Person of Christ*, vol. i. pp. 152-154.
[2] Enoch xlviii. 2-6.   [3] Enoch xlvi. 3-5.
[4] Hilgenfeld's *Die jüd. Apokalyptik*, pp. 91-184.
[5] Keim's *Jesus of Nazara*, vol. i. p. 317 ff.
[6] Kuenen's *Religion of Israel*, vol. iii. p. 265.

Oehler,[1] Drummond,[2] and recently by Davidson.[3] The reason given is that the character of the Messiah, and especially the conception of a mysterious pre-existing Being, is too much developed; and that the titles "the Son of God," "the Son of man," and "the Son of the woman," by which He is designated, could hardly be applied to Him by a pre-Christian Jew. But there is nothing in the Messianic views contained in this book which could not have been derived from the prophecies of Isaiah and Daniel; and there are clear intimations that the book is wholly pre-Christian, or at least that there are in it no Christian additions. Not only is there no reference to the life and sufferings of Jesus, but there is no reference to a suffering Messiah, which would undoubtedly have been the case had it been composed in part by a Christian writer. "To whatever cause," says Row, "we may assign the absence of this conception of Him, the fact is beyond dispute. This alone places a profound gulf between the conception of Him as entertained by this writer and that of the Jesus of the Gospels."[4] The Messiah is throughout an exalted Being, a mighty Conqueror, a supreme Ruler. Nor is the view of the Messiah here given the Christian view. His pre-existence is indeed asserted, but not His divine nature; He is not removed from created beings. Only once is the name "the Son of God" applied to Him, and that not directly, but by inference, as when it is said: "I and my Son will unite ourselves with them for ever and ever in the paths of righteousness in their lives."[5] And as to the expression "the Son of the woman,"[6] there is nothing unreasonable in the supposition that the author, for the sake of variety, used it as equivalent to the Son of man. In short, as Dillmann observes: "That there are Christian portions in the book, whether of short interpolations or of long pieces, has often been supposed

---

[1] Oehler, in his article on "the Messias" in Herzog's *Encyklopädie*, 2nd ed. vol. ix. p. 657.

[2] Drummond's *The Jewish Messiah*, p. 59 ff.

[3] Davidson in his article on "Apocalyptic Literature" in the new edition of the *Encyclopedia Britannica*. He denies it in his article in Kitto's *Encyclopedia*.

[4] Row's *The Jesus of the Evangelists*, p. 189.

[5] Enoch cv. 2. [6] Enoch lxii. 5.

and maintained, but this assertion is proved, on a close examination, to be without foundation. If one objects to such frequently occurring expressions as 'believers,' 'to deny God and His anointed,' etc., it is to be considered that those expressions are frequently used in the Ethiopic Old Testament for the corresponding Greek and Hebrew words. The Christology of the book is indeed high, but not so high that its individual features cannot be perfectly explained from Old Testament premises."[1]

There is an intimate relation between the "Book of Enoch" and the "Prophecies of Daniel;" the former is formed after the model of the latter. Many expressions are the same in both. God is described as the "Ancient of days," with His head as white as wool, seated on His throne.[2] The Messiah is represented, not as the ideal King, but as the Son of man. The visions which Enoch saw are modelled on the visions of Daniel. An angel accompanies Enoch on his journeys as his interpreter, and explains to him the mysteries of the future. The doctrine of the angels, as unfolded in the Book of Enoch, is in several respects similar to that contained in the prophecies of Daniel. The angels are employed as the ministers of the divine vengeance, or else as the defenders and helpers of the righteous. They are known by distinctive names, as Gabriel and Michael (Dan. viii. 16, x. 13). Daniel's celebrated prophecy of the Seventy Weeks is twice imitated by the author of the Book of Enoch. The seventy shepherds who ruled over Israel from the period of the captivity to the advent of the Messiah, and the ten weeks or seventy days of the world's history, are evidently mere imitations of Daniel's prophecy.

Different opinions have been formed of the nature and character of this book. Dean Plumptre stands alone in the strong depreciatory judgment which he pronounces. He asserts that it leaves on the mind an impression like that of a delirious dream with endless repetitions, and scarcely the

---

[1] Herzog's *Encyklopädie* (1st ed.), vol. xii. pp. 309, 310. See also Schürer's *Jewish People*, etc. vol. iii. p. 68.

[2] Comp. Enoch xlvi. 1: "And there I saw the Ancient of days, whose head was as white as wool, and with Him another, whose countenance resembled that of a man." Comp. with Dan. vii. 9, 13.

vestige of a plan or purpose; and that it belongs to that class of writings, on which St. Paul seems to pass a final sentence when he speaks of them as "old wives' fables."[1] But very different are the estimates of other eminent critics who have devoted time and learning to the study of this work. Thus Row observes: "The aspirations of the author after holiness are deep, his desire for close communion with God intense, and he represents the happiness of the future world as consisting in the most intimate communion with Him. On these points the book stands almost on a level with the Revelation. The morality of the book is pure, and will bear a favourable comparison with that of the Old Testament. Equally holy are the views which it presents of the Divine character. Its religion is spiritual, with scarcely a trace of Pharisaism, externalism, or casuistry. Those forms of moral and spiritual degeneracy, on account of which our Lord so vehemently denounced the hollow hypocrites of the day, are nowhere to be found in it. Compared with the general aspect of religion as it appears in the Apocrypha, it stands incomparably higher."[2] Similar opinions on its merits are expressed by Davidson, Plummer, and Westcott.[3] The work is pervaded throughout with a religious spirit. Though not free from rabbinical fancies,[4] it is by no means to be classed with those fantastic apocalyptic books which were so common in the early days of Christianity, and whose religious tendency is very doubtful. Its moral tendency is unmistakeable. Not only are the most stern rebukes and threatenings denounced

---

[1] Plumptre's *Commentary on Jude*, the Cambridge Bible, p. 217. "The reader of the English Apocrypha," he observes, "may find the nearest accessible approach to the class of literature which it represents in the Second Book of Esdras, but that, in its profound and plaintive pessimism, has at least the elements of poetry and unity of purpose."

[2] *The Jesus of the Evangelists*, p. 170.

[3] Davidson in Kitto's *Encyclopedia of Biblical Literature*, vol. ii. p. 793; Plummer's *Commentary on Jude*, p. 290; and Westcott's *Introduction to the Study of the Gospels*, p. 92. Westcott remarks: "No apocryphal book is more remarkable for eloquence and poetic vigour; and the range of subjects which it includes is as noble as its style. In its present form the book aims at little else than a comprehensive vindication of the action of Providence, both in the physical and in the moral world."

[4] Several of these rabbinical fancies—as, for example, the miraculous birth of Noah—are interpolations.

against all idolaters and persecutors of the righteous, but the wicked in Israel are denounced in the strongest terms. The terrors of the Lord are displayed against all the workers of iniquity without exception; and the wrath to come is described with the spirit and in the language of an Old Testament prophet. The doctrine of retribution lies at the foundation of the teaching of the Book of Enoch; and the future blessedness of the righteous is described in terms free, in a great measure, from those sensuous descriptions of heaven which are so common in other apocryphal books and in the writings of the Fathers.

It only remains that we should examine the relation of Jude to this Book of Enoch. The passage quoted is found near the commencement of the book, in that portion which is nearly universally admitted to be pre-Christian, and although not word for word, is as close a citation as many of those which are made from the Old Testament by the sacred writers in the New, or from the New Testament by the Fathers. And, besides, it is to be remembered that as Jude quoted from a Greek version (or from the Hebrew original), the translation of the Greek into the Ethiopic must have unavoidably caused some verbal difference. The following is the passage as given in Dillmann's version: "Behold, He (God) cometh with myriads of His holy ones to pass judgment on them, and will destroy the ungodly and reckon with all flesh for everything which the sinners and the ungodly have done and committed against Him."[1] Some affirm that other references are to be found in Jude's description of the nature of the sin of the fallen angels and of the punishment which was inflicted on them[2] (Jude 6, 7).

Some, in order to escape the inference that Jude quotes from a book confessedly apocryphal, and which contains many rabbinical extravagances, affirm that this prophecy of Enoch was communicated to Jude by direct revelation.

---

[1] Enoch i. 9. Dillmann's *Das Buch Henoch*, p. 1. The following is Laurence's translation: "Behold, He (God) comes with ten thousand of His saints to execute judgment upon them and destroy the wicked, and reprove all the carnal, for everything which the sinful and ungodly have done and committed against Him."

[2] Stanley's *Jewish Church*, vol. iii. p. 377.

Others, as Cave, Witsius, Simon, and Lardner,[1] suppose that Jude cited a traditionary prophecy or saying of Enoch; but those theologians wrote before the discovery of the Book of Enoch by Bruce. Others, as Keil, suppose that the passage in Jude was interpolated into the Greek version of the Book of Enoch;[2] but the passage is not there in a disconnected form, but is entirely suitable to the context. Such and similar suppositions[3] cannot be met by a distinct denial; but when we consider that the Book of Enoch was written before the Christian era, and was well known to the early Christians, and especially to Jewish Christians; that words, or at least similar words to those which Jude uses are to be found in that book; the conclusion appears to be almost unavoidable, that Jude quoted from this Book of Enoch. In doing so he imparted no authority to the book itself, but merely quotes it for the sake of illustration, as Paul quoted the heathen poets, Epimenides, Aratus, and Menander.

Of late years the Book of Enoch has attracted much attention among learned theologians in England and America, but especially in Germany. We have in the course of this dissertation had occasion to refer to the early labours of De Sacy, Laurence, Hoffmann of Jena, and Gfrörer. After its translation by Laurence an attempt was made by the Rev. Edward Murray, in a work entitled *Enoch restitutus*,[4] to prove that it was a compilation, and to exhibit the original book quoted by Jude. The attempt was a failure, and excited but little interest. There are valuable articles on the Book of Enoch by Dr. Davidson in Kitto's *Encyclopedia* and in the *Encyclopedia Britannica*, and by Professor Westcott in Smith's *Dictionary of the Bible*. The subject has been treated more or less fully in Drummond's *Jewish Messiah*; Pusey's *Lectures*

---

[1] Lardner's *Works*, quarto edition, vol. iii. pp. 443, 444.
[2] Keil, *Commentar über die Briefe des Petrus und Judas*, pp. 322, 323.
[3] Philippi thinks that Jude, by reason of a deeper understanding of Gen v., could speak of a prophecy of Enoch, the reality of which was confirmed to him by the testimony of the Holy Ghost. *Das Buch Henoch*, p. 151.
[4] This is a work of great ingenuity and research; there is a long and valuable introductory dissertation; and opposite the translation of the Book of Enoch there is placed a list of scriptural parallels.

on *Daniel*; Row's *Jesus of the Evangelists*; Stanley's *Lectures on the Jewish Church*; and Westcott's *Introduction to the Study of the Gospels*. In America the Book of Enoch has been discussed by Bissell in his *Apocrypha of the Old Testament*, and by Schodde in his *Book of Enoch, translated with Introduction and Notes*. In France the subject has been treated by Colani in his *Les Croyances Messianiques*, and by Vernes in his *Histoire des idées Messianiques*. But it is in Germany and by German theologians that this book has been most fully discussed; a rich theological literature has gathered around it. The following are the most important German works on the subject:—Dillmann's *Translation of the Book of Enoch*, frequently adverted to, and three important articles by him, two in the two editions of Herzog's *Encyklopädie* and one in Schenkel's *Bibellexicon*; Ewald's *Abhandlung über des æthiopischen Buches Henokh, Entstehung, Sinn und Zusammensetzung*; Hilgenfeld's *Die jüdische Apokalyptik*, pp. 81–184; Lücke's *Einleitung in die Offenbarung Johannis*; Schürer's *Neutestamentliche Zeitgeschichte*, p. 521 ff.; Anger's *Vorlesungen über die Geschichte des Messianischen Idee*, p. 83 ff.; Philippi's *Das Buch Henoch, sein Zeitalter und sein Verhältniss zum Judasbrief*; an article on the apocryphal Book of Enoch by Lipsius in Smith's *Dictionary of Christian Biography*; one by Volkmar in the *Zeitschrift der deutschen morgenländischen Gesellschaft* for 1860; and one by Köstlin in the *Theol. Jahrbücher* for 1856.

INDEX.

Abbott's articles in the Expositor on Second Peter, 215, 221, 222.
Abraham's justification, 77, 78.
Abyssinian canon, the, 393.
Acts of Peter and Paul, 155, 156.
Aldis' Prophecies, Visions and Life of Enoch, referred to, 396.
Alexander, bishop of Alexandria, his testimony to 2 John, 324.
Alexander, bishop of Derry, his commentary on the Epistle of John, referred to, 259, 278, 334, 343, 349.
Alford, on the Curetonian Syriac, 17; on the Greek of the Epistle of James, 58; on the style of 1 Pet., 156; on Peter's residence in Rome, 158; on the preaching to the spirits in prison, 185, 190; on 1 Pet. iv. 6, 193; on the intermediate state, 206; on the readers of 2 Pet., 225; the priority of Jude's Epistle to 2 Pet., 248; identity of the authorship of the Gospel of John and 1 John, 260; date of Jude, 372.
Anatolius, bishop of Laodicea, quotes from the Book of Enoch, 389.
Anicetus, bishop of Rome, referred to, 342.
Anointing used as a medicinal remedy, 95-97; anointing of the dead, 99; of the sick, 100-108.
Antitactæ, the, 368.
Apostolical Constitutions, referred to, 42, 98, 154, 375.
Asiatic Churches, 1 John addressed to them, 276.
Assumption of Moses, dissertation on, 373-386.
Athenagoras, reference to the Book of Enoch, 387.
Augustine, his view of purgatorial fire, 197; his interpretation of 1 John v. 8, 298.
Aurelius, bishop of Challabi, his testimony to 2 John, 324.

Authenticity of the Catholic Epistles in general, 14-22; Epistle of James, 23-39; First Epistle of Peter, 109-121; Second Epistle of Peter, 204-226; First Epistle of John, 254-266; Second Epistle of John, 322-328; Third Epistle of John, 339-343; Epistle of Jude, 351-358.

Babylon, mentioned in 1 Pet. v. 12, 140-144.
Barcocheba's rebellion referred to, 50, 382, 401.
Baring-Gould's Myths of the Middle Ages, 331; Legends of Old Testament Characters, 384.
Barnabas, his testimony to 2 Pet., 206; supposed to refer to the Book of Enoch, 387.
Basilides, referred to, 311, 321.
Bassett on the Epistle of James, 31, 45, 58.
Baur supposes a contradiction between Paul and James, 66; his objections to 1 Pet., 116; on Peter's residence in Rome, 145; his objections to 1 John, 263; considers 1 John to be Montanistic, 265; classification of the Gnostic systems, 310; the origin of 2 and 3 John, 341.
Bengel's Gnomon, 183, 191, 192, 273, 282.
Bertholdt, his objections to 1 Pet., 115; his view of 2 Pet., 222; on the heretics mentioned in 2 Pet., 230; supposes Jude to be a translation from the Aramaic, 370.
Beyschlag, der Brief des Jakobus, 56, 80.
Beza on Christ's preaching to the spirits in prison by Noah, 188.
Bigg's Bampton Lectures for 1886, 195, 200, 306.
Bingham's Christian Antiquities, on Unction, 97.

Bleek's Introduction to the New Testament. The omitted Epistles in the Peshito, 20; authenticity of the Epistle of James, 27; objection to the authenticity of 2 Pet., 215, 218, 225; the priority of Jude to 2 Pet., 245; resemblance of 1 John to John's Gospel, 260; resemblance of 2 John to 1 John, 326; on the heretics referred to by Jude, 367.
Branne on the Epistles of John, 289, 326, 346.
Bretschneider's objections to 1 John, 262, 264.
Brother, the Lord's, meaning of, 32–40.
Brown's Exposition of the Thirty-Nine Articles, 182.
Bruce's discovery of the Book of Enoch, 391.
Brückner, Brief des Jakobus, 68; Der Erste Brief des Petrus, 185, 194, 226; Der Zweite Brief des Petrus, 250; Brief des Judas, 363.
Buddhism, an element in Gnosticism, 309.
Bunsen, his view of 2 Pet., 223.
Burgess, Tracts on the Divinity of Christ, 300.
Burnet on the Thirty-Nine Articles, 107, 188.
Burton's Bampton Lectures, 230, 305, 368.

CAINITES, their opinions, 314.
Caius on the trophies of Peter and Paul at Rome, 148.
Calvin on the Epistle of James, 28; on James' view of justification, 70; his view of Hades, 198; on 2 Pet., 213; on the want of arrangement in 1 John, 282; on 1 John v. 7, 8, 305; on the Epistle of Jude, 355.
Carpocratians, the, 368.
Cassiodorus, de institutione divinarum literarium, 7, 25, 274.
Catalogues of the Catholic Epistles, 15, 16.
Catholic Epistles, meaning of the term, 1–7; their authors, 7–10; relation to the Pauline Epistles, 8; number and order, 10, 11; interpretation, 11–14; authenticity, 14–22.
Cave's Lives of the Apostles, referred to, 385.
Ceriani's Monumenta sacra, 377.
Cerinthus, John's encounter with him, 271; his Gnostic views, 316–319; opposition of John to him, 320.
Charteris' Canonicity, 25, 351.
Christ's preaching to the spirits in prison, 180–191.

Christianity, its relation to Judaism, 162–164.
Christology of Peter, 165–171.
Clemens Alexandrinus, his testimony to the Epistle of James, 25; to 1 Pet., 111; preaching of the gospel in Hades, 294, 296; his testimony to 2 Pet., 207; to 1 John, 257; John's residence at Ephesus, 270; his testimony to 2 John, 323; to Jude, 351; allusion to the Assumption of Moses, 375.
Clemens Romanus, testimony to Epistle of James, 25; on the death of Peter and Paul, 147; testimony to 2 Pet., 205; supposed allusion to the Assumption of Moses, 374.
Clementine Homilies, referred to, 42, 154, 158.
Clopas supposed to be the same as Alphæus, 33, 35.
Codex Montfortianus or Britannicus, 291.
Codex Neapolitano Regio, 292.
Codex Ottobonianus, 292.
Colani's Croyances Messianiques, 399.
Coleridge on conditional immortality, 199.
Colossian heretics, their Gnostic character, 314.
Complutensian edition of the Greek Testament, 304.
Conditional immortality, 199.
Cook's commentary on 1 Pet., 133, 185, 194; article on 2 Pet. in Smith's Dictionary, 215.
Cornelius a Lapide, referred to, 336.
Cox, Salvator Mundi, 200; Private letters of Paul and John, 338, 349.
Credner on the readers of the Epistle of James, 45; views of Paul combated by James, 67; objections to 2 Pet., 214, 219; on the date of 2 Pet., 234; age of the book of Enoch, 399.
Cureton's Syriac Gospels, 16.
Curetonian Syriac, 16, 17.
Cyprian on anointing at baptism, 98; testimony to 1 Pet., 112; to 1 John, 257; supposed reference to 1 John v. 7, 8, 296; testimony to Jude, 353.

DAVIDSON, Dr. Samuel, Biblical Criticism, 21, 292.
Davidson, Dr. Samuel, Introduction to the N. T., 36, 67, 119, 161.
Davidson, Dr. Samuel, Introduction to the Study of the N. T.; objection to Epistle of James on account of the purity of its Greek, 58; assertion that the Pauline doctrine of justification is combated by James, 67;

INDEX OF AUTHORS AND SUBJECTS. 411

objections to 2 Pet., 218, 220; date of 2 Pet., 235; priority of the Epistle of Jude, 245.
Deane, Rev. W. J., commentary on the Book of Wisdom, 265; article on the Assumption of Moses, 386; article on the Book of Jubilees, 390.
Demetrius mentioned in 3 John, 346.
Demiurgus, the, 311.
Descensus ad inferos, 175–179.
De Wette, objections to the Epistle of James, 28, 29; on the readers of that Epistle, 44; objections to 1 Pet., 116; priority of the Epistle of Jude, 250–252; asserts the genuineness of 1 John, 258; and of Jude, 354.
Diaspora, the, 46, 47.
Didaché, resemblance to the Epistle of James, 82; reference to 1 Pet., 110; on travelling evangelists, 347.
Didymus of Alexandria, reference to the Assumption of Moses, 375.
Diffusion of Christianity, 131.
Dillmann's Buch Henoch, 393; its authorship, 397; its date, 400; not interpolated by Christians, 403.
Diognetus, Epistle to, reference to 1 Pet., 110.
Diotrephes, mentioned in 3 John, 345.
Docetism, referred to in John's Epistles, 264, 281: its nature, 312.
Domitian, banished John to Patmos, 271; Jude's grandchildren brought before him, 362.
Dorner's Entwicklungsgeschichte der Lehre von der Person Christi, 162, 163, 308, 367, 402.
Drummond's Jewish Messiah, 378, 401.
Düsterdieck on the epistolary character of 1 John, 274; its arrangement, 283; its profundity, 286.

EADIE'S article on 1 Pet. in Kitto's Encyclopedia, 118.
Ebionites, the, 51, 52.
Ebrard's commentary on 1 John, 264, 278, 297, 328, 346.
Edward VI., his prayer book, 105.
Eichhorn's Einleitung in das N. T., objections to 1 Pet., 115; to 2 Pet., 214; relation between 2 Pet. and Jude, 244; priority of 2 John to 1 John, 337; the diction of Jude, 370.
Elect Lady, the, 331–336.
Ellendorf disputes the fact of Peter's Roman residence, 146.

Encyclopedia Britannica referred to, 158, 191, 382, 386.
Enoch, the Book of, dissertation on, 386–408.
Ephesus, John's residence in, 270.
Ephraem Syrus, 18, 19.
Epiphanian theory regarding the Lord's brother, 36, 37.
Epistle, lost, of John, 348.
Erasmus' editions of the Greek Testament, 304.
Erdmann's Brief des Jakobus, 61.
Eschatology of Peter, 172–203.
Eugenius, bishop of Carthage, referred to, 299.
Eusebius, Historia Ecclesiastica, *passim*.
Evangelists, travelling, 346, 347.
Evodius' reference to the death of Moses, 375.
Ewald's Abhandlung über das Buch Henoch, 398.
Ewald's Geschichte des Volkes Israel, 59, 218, 234, 279, 376.
Ewald's Sieben Sendschreiben des neuen Bundes, 134, 215, 229.
Expositor, the, Dr. Lumby's articles, 211; Dr. Abbott's articles, 220.
Extreme unction, 100–108.

FABRICIUS, Codex Pseudepigraphus V. T., the Assumption of Moses, 374, 378; the Book of Enoch, 386, 391.
Facundus, an African bishop, referred to, 297.
Faith, Paul's view of, 76; James' view of, 77.
Farrar's Early Days of Christianity, 10, 114, 130, 141, 168, 186, 212, 221, 224, 371.
Farrar's Eternal Hope, 199.
Farrar's Mercy and Judgment, 195, 199, 201.
Firmilian, testimony to 2 Pet., 208.
Form of the First Epistle of John, 272–274.
Foster, Rev. Charles, "The Three Heavenly Witnesses," 290.
Foster, John, his belief in universal restoration, 200.
Fritzsche's Libri V. T. Pseudepigraphi, Assumption of Moses, 374, 378.
Frohschammer's Romance of Romanism, 147, 156.
Fronmüller on 1 Pet., 128, 198, 201; on 2 Pet., 254; on Jude, 367.

GAIUS, Third John addressed to, 343.
German Bible, arrangement of the Catholic Epistles in it, 11.
Gfrörer, Prophetæ veteris Pseudepigr., 376, 392.

INDEX OF AUTHORS AND SUBJECTS.

Gibbon, Travis' letters to, 302.
Gieseler affirms that Peter suffered martyrdom at Rome, 146; origin of the opinion that First John was addressed to the Parthians, 275; classification of the Gnostic systems, 310; age of the Book of Enoch, 399.
Gloag, Pauline Epistles, 12; article on the early Syrian versions, 20; Exegetical Studies, 34, 191.
Gnosticism, its spread, 305; its nature, 306; its origin, 308; its sources, 309; its classification, 310; its principles, 310-313; its ethical tendency, 313; allusions to it in N. T., 314; its effects on Christianity, 320.
Greek Church, its ceremony of anointing, 105.
Gregory of Nyssa, his belief in universal restoration, 195.
Grotius' Annotationes, 222, 230, 234, 328, 345, 358.
Guericke's Neutestamentliche Isagogik, 254, 259, 365.

HADES, nature of, 177-179.
Hatch's article on Peter in Encyclopedia Britannica, 158, 214, 222.
Haupt's commentary on 1 John, 278, 288.
Hausrath's New Testament Times, 154, 382, 401.
Heavenly Witnesses, dissertation on, 289-305.
Hegesippus' account of James, 41; account of Jude's grandchildren, 362.
Heidegger supposes 1 John to be a treatise, 273.
Hengstenberg's view of justification, 71.
Herder on the Epistle of Jude, 243.
Heretical teachers referred to in 2 Pet., 229; in the Epistle of Jude, 367.
Herod the Great, referred to, 381.
Herzog's Encyklopädie, Sieffert's article on James, 35; on Peter, 157; Dillmann's article on Henoch, 397.
Heydenreich on the design of 2 Peter, 228.
Hieronymian view of James' relation to Christ, 33-35.
Hilgenfeld's Einleitung in das N. T., 18, 44, 133, 258, 327, 342, 356.
Hilgenfeld's Evangelium und die Briefe Johannis, 261, 263.
Hilgenfeld's Messias Judæorum, 378.
Hilvidian view of James' relation to Christ, 38.

Hippolytus' testimony to Second Peter, 207; to Jude, 352.
Hoffmann of Jena, Das Buch Henoch, 392.
Hofmann of Erlangen, Der Erste Brief des Petrus, 141.
Hofmann's Schriftbeweis, referred to, 64, 68, 189, 193, 399.
Hollaz, Christ's announcement of condemnation in Hades, 184.
Holtzmann's Einleitung in das N. T., 28, 30, 220, 282, 332.
Horne's Introduction to the Scriptures, 3, 292, 299.
Horsley, Christ's preaching to the spirits in prison, 182, 183; supposes First John to be a treatise, 273; his defence of 1 John v. 7, 8, 300.
Hug's Introduction to the N. T., 4, 18, 63, 66, 229, 249, 275, 339.
Huther, his distinction between justification and salvation, 71; on First Peter, 165; Christ's preaching to the spirits in prison, 181, 187; denies the authenticity of Second Peter, 283; the readers of Jude's Epistle, 366; date of that Epistle, 372.

IGNATIUS' testimony to Peter's presence in Rome, 147.
Innocent I., his letter to Decentius on anointing, 101.
Integrity of Second Peter, 222, 223.
Intermediate state supposed to be a state of probation, 200-203.
Interpretation of the Catholic Epistles, 10-14.
Irenæus's testimony to Epistle of James, 25; description of the Ebionites, 51; the anointing of the dead, 99; testimony to First Peter, 111; to Peter's residence at Rome, 148; Christ's descent into Hades, 196; testimony to Second Peter, 206; to First John, 256; John's residence in Ephesus, 270; John's encounter with Cerinthus, 271; testimony to Second John, 322; reference to the Book of Enoch, 387.

JACOBEAN doctrine of justification, 69-77.
Jacobi, influence of Gnosticism on Christianity, 320.
James, Epistle of, authenticity, 23-30; author, 31-43; readers, 43-53; design and contents, 53-59; date, 59-63.
James, the Lord's brother, the author of the Epistle of James, 32; not

INDEX OF AUTHORS AND SUBJECTS. 413

identical with James the son of Alphæus, 33-36; not the son of Joseph by a previous marriage, 36, 37; the son of Joseph and Mary, 38-40; notices in Scripture, 40, and in ecclesiastical history, 41, 42; his relation to Judaism, 43.

James, the son of Zebedee, the Epistle of James ascribed to him, 31, 32.

Jellinck on the references by Jewish writers to the Book of Enoch, 390.

Jerome on the Epistle of James, 24; his view of the relation of James to Christ, 33; on Second Peter, 209, 214; legend concerning John, 272; on the Epistle of Jude, 356; mission of Thaddæus to Edessa, 362.

Jewish Christians, the, 47-53.

John, First Epistle of, authenticity, 256-266; author, 266-272; readers, 272-277; design and contents, 278-286; date, 287.

John, Second Epistle of, authenticity, 322-328; author, 328-331; person addressed, 331-336; design and contents, 336, 337; date, 337.

John, Third Epistle of, authenticity, 339-343; person addressed, 343; design and contents, 344-349; date, 350.

John, references to him in Scripture, 266-269; notices in ecclesiastical history, 269-272.

John Hyrcanus, reference to him, 380, 400.

John the Presbyter, 2 and 3 John ascribed to him, 328; statement of Papias concerning him, 329; his existence doubtful, 329.

Jones' Canon of the N. T., 16.

Josephus on the martyrdom of James, 41; the Jews in Babylon, 142, 143; Peter is supposed to quote from him, 221.

Judas Barsabas, the Epistle of Jude assigned to him, 359.

Jude, Epistle of, relation to Second Peter, 236-255; authenticity, 351-358; author, 358-363; readers, 363-365; design and contents, 365-371; date, 371, 372.

Jude, the brother of the Lord, 358-360; notices in Scripture, 361; in ecclesiastical history, 361-363.

Justification as taught by Paul and James, 64-79.

Justin Martyr on the Jewish Christians, 50; his mistake concerning Simon Magus, 126; Christ's descent into Hades, 195; testimony to Second Peter, 206; reference to the Book of Enoch, 387.

KEIL, Briefe des Petrus, 157, 181; Brief des Judas, 362, 371, 384, 407.

Keim's Jesus of Nazara, 399, 402.

Kern, Brief des Jakobus, 54, 69, 96.

Kirchhofer's Quellensammlung, referred to, 3, 16, 26, 205, 371.

Kitto's Encyclopedia, 118, 121, 391, 405.

Köstlin, Lehrbegriff des Evangelium und der Briefe Johannis, 263.

Kuenen's Religion of Israel, 399, 402.

Kurtz' History of the Apostolic Church, 101, 305.

LA CAVA, manuscript, 294.

Lactantius' account of the martyrdom of Peter, 148.

Lange, Der Brief des Jakobus, 10, 44, 53, 70; Das Apostolische Zeitalter, 223.

Lange, S. G., his objections to First John, 263.

Langen, Das Judenthum in Palästina zur Zeit Christi, 382, 386.

Language, original, of First Peter, 137; of Second Peter, 234; of Jude, 370.

Lardner's Works, 19, 241; supposes that Peter and Jude wrote independently, 241; supposes that Jude refers to Zech. iii., 383.

Laurence's Book of Enoch, 389-392, 397, 400, 406.

Lechler's Das Apostolische Zeitalter, 53, 61, 68, 161, 216, 313.

Leontius Byzanticus' view of the term Catholic, 5.

Lightfoot, Dr. John, cited, 97, 276, 359.

Lightfoot, Bishop, his "Epistles of Clement" referred to, 25, 49; supposes James to be the son of Joseph by a previous marriage, 37; reference to his commentary on the Galatians, 37; and to his commentary on the Colossians, 332.

Lipsius, Apostelgeschichten und Apostellegenden, 269, 271, 362.

Lipsius, Quellen der römischen Petrussage, 145, 154, 156.

Love, the keynote of John's Epistle, 285.

Lücke on the Epistles of John, 18, 258, 282, 300, 335.

Lücke's Offenbarung Johannis, 398, 399.

Lumby, commentary on Second Peter in the Speaker's Bible, 210, 243,

247; article on Second Peter in the Expositor, 211, 243.
Luther, the necessity of candour, 13; his attack on the Epistle of James, 27, 66; his view of Christ's descent into Hades, 197; supposes that Jude borrowed from Peter, 245; his view of 1 John v. 7, 8, 304.

MACKNIGHT supposes that First John was addressed to Jewish Christians, 275.
Mai, Cardinal, referred to, 294, 391.
Malchion, presbyter of Antioch, 19, 353.
Maugold's Einleitung in das N.T. von Bleek, 61, 79, 116, 133, 220, 382.
Mansel's Gnostic heresies, 230, 308, 369.
Marcionites reject First John, 258.
Martensen, Bishop, his views of a future state, 203.
Martyrdom of James, 41, 42; of Peter, 125.
Maurice, Frederick, his view of a future state, 198, 202.
Mayerhoff, Einleitung in die petrinischen Schriften, 118, 137, 150, 215, 217, 229, 234, 248, 365.
Melito, testimony to 2 Peter, 206.
Merivale's History of the Romans, cited, 142.
Messianic statements in the Book of Enoch, 401-404.
Methodius, Bishop of Tyre, his testimony to Second Peter, 208.
Meyer on anointing the sick, 106; reference to the descent into Hades in Eph. iv. 9, 10, 179.
Michael the archangel, 383-385.
Michaelis' Introduction to the N.T. by Marsh, 3, 16, 31, 45, 59, 70, 118, 129, 273, 343.
Middleton (Bishop) on the Greek article, referred to, 301, 334.
Montanus, First John supposed to be written by one of his disciples, 265.
Monthly Interpreter: article on the early Syriac versions, 20; article on the Assumption of Moses, 386.
Moses' death and burial, 384.
Müller, Julius, his view of a future state, 200.
Muratorian canon, 15, 112, 257, 322, 351.
Murray, Enoch restitutus, 407.

NAZARENES and Ebionites distinguished, 52, 53.
Neander on the absence of doctrine in James' Epistle, 56; Pauline phraseology in James' Epistle, 60; Peter's residence in Rome doubtful, 151; objections to Second Peter, 226, 233; classification of the Gnostic system, 310.
Nestorian Christians, reference to them, 53.
Newton, Sir Isaac, on the testimony of the heavenly witnesses, 301.
Nice, the second Council of, 375.
Nicephorus, Hist. Eccl., 361, 339.
Nicolaitans, the, 315, 368, 369.
Nitzsch, quoted, 10.

OBJECTIONS to the authenticity of the Epistle of James, 27-30; to First Peter, 115-121; to Second Peter, 213-224; to First John, 262-266; to Second John, 327, 328; to Third John, 341-343; to the Epistle of Jude, 354-358.
Oecumenius, his view of the term Catholic, 5; on the contest between Michael and Satan, 376.
Oehler's article on the "Messias" in Herzog's Encyklopädie, 403.
Olshausen asserts Peter's residence at Rome, 146; opuscula theologica, 244.
Ophites, the, 368.
Origen, his use of the term Catholic, 1; testimony to the Epistle of James, 26; on the Ebionites, 51; testimony to 1 Peter, 112; Christ's preaching in Hades, 196; testimony to 2 Peter, 207; to 1 John, 257; to 2 John, 324; to Jude, 352; states that Jude quoted from the Assumption of Moses, 374; refers to the Book of Enoch, 388.

PAPIAS, referred to, 147; testimony to 1 John, 256; on John the Presbyter, 329.
Parallels, table of, between Epistle of James and Sermon on the Mount, 81, 82; between Epistle of James and 1 Peter, 89; between 1 Peter and the Pauline Epistles, 117; between First and Second Peter, 211; between Second Peter and Jude, 238, 239; between the Gospel of John and First John, 259; between First and Second John, 326.
Parthians, John's Epistle supposed to be addressed to, 274; mentioned in Book of Enoch, 400.
Patmos, John's residence there, 269.
Paul's Epistles mentioned in Second Peter, 218.
Pauline doctrine of justification, 64, 75-77.

Pearson on the perpetual virginity of Mary, 38.
Peshito, the books omitted in it, 14; its relation to the Curetonian Syriac, 16-19; contains the Epistle of James, 26.
Peter, First Epistle of, authenticity, 108-121; author, 121-127; readers, 127-133; design and contents, 133-138; date, 138-144.
Peter, Second Epistle of, authenticity, 204-224; readers, 224-227; design and contents, 227-234; date, 234-236; relation to Jude, 236-255.
Peter, notices of him in Scripture, 121-124; in ecclesiastical tradition, 125; legends concerning him, 125-127; residence in Rome, 144-160.
Petirath Mose, 376.
Petrine Theology, 160-174.
Pfleiderer's Paulinism, 116, 135, 161, 163, 166.
Philippi, Das Buch Henoch, 382, 397, 407.
Philo, his system a species of Jewish Gnosticism, 308.
Pliny's letter to Trajan, 132.
Plummer's commentary on Jude, 237, 254; on the Epistles of John, 259, 283, 326.
Plumptre, apocryphal references in James' Epistle, 92-94; on the spirits in prison, 201; priority of Jude's Epistle, 248, 253; identifies Jude with Judas Barsabas, 360; his opinion of the Book of Enoch, 404.
Polycarp, his testimony to First Peter, 110; to First John, 256.
Porson's letters to Travis, 292, 295.
Prettyman's Elements of Christian Theology, quoted, 46.
Purgatory, 197.
Pusey: What is faith in everlasting punishment? 184, 201; lectures on Daniel, referred to, 399.

Rawlinson's Bampton lectures, referred to, 22.
Redemption a distinguishing feature of Gnosticism, 307.
Relation between the Catholic and Pauline Epistles, 8; between Second Peter and Epistle of Jude, 236-255.
Renan acknowledges First Peter, 108; affirms Paul's residence in Rome, 151, 158.
Resemblances in the Epistle of James, 79-94; between Second Peter and Jude, 238-240.
Resurrection of Christ, importance assigned to it by Peter, 170.

Reuss' Geschichte der heiligen Schriften N. T., 30, 68, 115, 204, 216, 273.
Reuss' Theology of the Apostolic Age, 54, 129, 161, 282.
Ritschl's Entstehung der alte Kirche, 50, 118.
Rome supposed to be the Babylon in 1 Pet. v. 13, 140-142; Peter's residence there, 144-160.
Row, Rev. C. A., Jesus of the Evangelists, quoted, 403, 405.

Salmasius calls in question Peter's residence in Rome, 145.
Salmon, his Introduction to the N. T., 22, 56, 209, 222, 262; his article on John the Presbyter in Smith's Dict. of Christian Biography, 330.
Santa Croze MS., the, 293.
Scaliger objects to First John, 262.
Schaff on the relation of James to Judaism, 43; Paul and James' view of justification, 79; Peter's view of Judaism, 163; on Petrinism, 174.
Schaff's Oldest Church Manual, 347.
Schegg's opinion that James is the son of Clopas, 35.
Schelling, his Gnosticism, 221.
Schleiermacher's objection to the Epistle of James, 28; to Second and Third John, 327.
Schmid's Biblical Theology of N. T., 70, 181.
Schmidt, Lehrgehalt des Jacobus Briefes, 59, 63, 69.
Schodde's Book of Enoch, 393, 398.
Schott's Der erste Brief Petri, 141, 146, 184; Der zweite Brief Petri, 254.
Schürer's Jewish People in the Time of Christ; the Assumption of Moses, 380; the Book of Enoch, 393, 399.
Schwegler's Das Nachapostolische Zeitalter, 116, 119, 120, 228, 235, 356.
Scott's commentary on the Epistle of James, 72.
Scrivener's Introduction to the Criticism of the N. T., 17, 291, 297.
Sheol, its derivation, 177; its nature, 178.
Sherlock on the relation between 2 Peter and Jude, 242-244.
Sick, anointing of the, 95-108.
Sieffert's article on Peter in Herzog's Encyklopädie, 249; article on Jude, 363, 371.
Simon Magus legend, 126, 153, 158, 308.
Smith's Biblical Dictionary, 179, 205, 216.

Smith's Dictionary of Antiquities, 101.
Smith's Dictionary of Christian Biography, 19, 329, 399.
Spanheim's Dissertatio de ficta profectione Petri in urbem Romam, 145, 150.
Speculum, the, of St. Augustine, 293.
Spitta, Der zweite Brief des Petrus und Brief des Judas, 236, 245-253, 366.
Stanley's Jewish Church, 399, 406.
Stanley's Sermons and Essays on the Apostolic Age, 144, 271, 272.
Steiger's commentary on First Peter, 119.
Stier's commentary on Epistle of James, 63.
Style and diction of the Epistle of James, 57-59; of First Peter, 136; of Second Peter, 214 ; of First John, 285, 286.
Sufferings of Christ, Peter's view of them, 166-168.
Syncellus, Georgius, referred to, 389.
Syriac versions, e r y, 16-20.
Syrian Church, its reception of the Epistle of James, 26.

TARTARUS, 178.
Tatian, Diatessaron of, 16.
Taxo, meaning of the name, 381.
Tennyson's In Memoriam, quoted, 200.
Tertullian on the Ebionites, 51 ; anointing at baptism, 98 ; testimony to 1 Peter, 111 ; Peter at Rome, 148 ; Christ's preaching in Hades, 196 ; testimony to 1 John, 257 ; the heretics against whom John wrote, 280 ; supposed reference to 1 John v. 7, 8, 295; testimony to Jude, 352 ; the Book of Enoch, 387.
Testimony of the Twelve Patriarchs, 387.
Themison, a Marcionite, 4, 5.
Tischendorf's N. T. Græce, 341.
Tregelles on the Curetonian Syriac, 11.
Tremellius, edition of the Peshito, 32.
Trench on the Parables, referred to, 179.
Trent, Council of, its decree on extreme unction, 102, 103.
Trollope's Liturgy of James, 42.
Tulloch, Principal, his article on the Gnostics, 305.

ULLMANN's view of 2 Peter, 223.
Universalism, on, 199.

VALENTINIANS, the, 311.

Varus, his victory over the Jews, 379, 381.
Vetus Latina, 20.
Vigilius Tapsus mentions 1 John as written *ad Parthos*, 274 ; quotes 1 John, v. 7, 8, 299.
Volkmar's Mose Himmelfahrt, 373, 378, 382, 385 ; on the age of the Book of Enoch, 401.
Vulgate, the, contains 1 John v. 7, 8, 294.

WACE's article on Tatian's Diatessaron in the Expositor, 16.
Warfield, Professor B., on the old Syriac version, 18 ; refutation of Abbott's views, 222 ; on the canonicity of 2 Peter, 224.
Watzel on the difference between Alphæus and Clopas, 35.
Weiss' Biblical Theology of the N. T., 138, 165, 194.
Weiss' Einleitung in das N. T., 128, 211, 216, 224, 249.
Weiss' Der Petrinische Lehrbegriff, 117, 137, 163, 181.
Westcott on the Canon, 16, 209.
Westcott's commentary on the Epistles of John, 259, 261, 273, 299, 303, 341.
Westcott's Introduction to the Study of the Gospels, 405.
Westcott and Hort's Greek Testament, 17.
Whately's Bacon's Essays, referred to, 267.
White's Life in Christ ; on conditional immortality, 199, 202.
Widmanstad, his edition of the Peshito, 31, 32.
Wieseler's Chronologie des apost. Zeitalter, 142.
Wiesinger, Brief des Jakobus, 62 ; der erste Brief des Petrus, 133, 159, 182 ; der zweite Brief des Petrus, 246, 249 ; Brief des Judas, 365.
Windischmann's Vindiciæ Petrinæ, 160.
Winer's Biblisches Wörterbuch, referred to, 33, 362.
Wisdom of Solomon, James supposed to quote from, 93.
Wiseman's Essays on Various Subjects, 21.
Wolf's Die Briefe Johannes, 302, 343.
Wordsworth's Greek Testament, 53, 105, 107, 185, 192, 206, 332.

ZAHN on Tatian's Diatessaron, 16 ; Supplementum Clementinum, 375.
Zeller's Acts of the Apostles, 155.
Zohar, quotations from, 390.

Will shortly be published, in demy 4to,

A

GREEK-ENGLISH LEXICON

OF THE

NEW TESTAMENT

BEING

GRIMM'S WILKE'S CLAVIS NOVI TESTAMENTI

TRANSLATED, REVISED, AND ENLARGED

BY

JOSEPH HENRY THAYER, D.D.

BUSSEY PROFESSOR OF NEW TESTAMENT CRITICISM AND INTERPRETATION IN THE
DIVINITY SCHOOL OF HARVARD UNIVERSITY

EDINBURGH
T. & T. CLARK, 38 GEORGE STREET
LONDON: HAMILTON, ADAMS, & CO.

a

T. and T. Clark's Publications.

Just published, in demy 8vo, price 12s.,

AN INTRODUCTION TO THEOLOGY:
Its Principles, Its Branches, Its Results, and Its Literature.
By ALFRED CAVE, B.A.,
PRINCIPAL, AND PROFESSOR OF THEOLOGY, OF HACKNEY COLLEGE, LONDON.

'We can most heartily recommend this work to students of every degree of attainment, and not only to those who will have the opportunity of utilizing its aid in the most sacred of the professions, but to all who desire to encourage and systematise their knowledge and clarify their views of Divine things.'—*Nonconformist and English Independent.*

'We know of no work more likely to prove useful to divinity students. Its arrangement is perfect, its learning accurate and extensive, and its practical hints invaluable.'—*Christian World.*

'Professor Cave is a master of theological science. He is one of the men to whose industry there seems no limit. . . . We can only say that we have rarely read a book with more cordial approval.'—*Baptist Magazine.*

Just published, in crown 8vo, price 4s. 6d.,

THE BIBLE
AN OUTGROWTH OF THEOCRATIC LIFE.
By D. W. SIMON,
PRINCIPAL OF THE CONGREGATIONAL COLLEGE, EDINBURGH.

'A book of absorbing interest, and well worthy of study.'—*Methodist New Connexion Magazine.*

'We heartily recommend every one who desires a better understanding of the true character of the Book of Books to procure it at once and make a study of it. . . . A more completely satisfactory book we have not had through our hands for a long time.'—*Aberdeen Journal.*

Just published, in crown 8vo, price 3s. 6d.,

THE RELIGIOUS HISTORY OF ISRAEL.
A Discussion of the Chief Problems in Old Testament History, as opposed to the Development Theorists.
By Dr. FRIEDRICH EDUARD KÖNIG,
THE UNIVERSITY, LEIPZIG.
TRANSLATED BY REV. ALEXANDER J. CAMPBELL, M.A.

'An admirable little volume. . . . By sincere and earnest minded students it will be cordially welcomed.'—*Freeman.*

'Every page of the book deserves study.'—*Church Bells.*

Just published, in crown 8vo, price 6s.,

NEW TESTAMENT TEACHING IN PASTORAL THEOLOGY.
By J. T. BECK, D.D.,
PROF. ORD. THEOL., TÜBINGEN.
EDITED BY PROFESSOR B. RIGGENBACH.
TRANSLATED BY REV. JAS. M'CLYMONT, B.D., AND REV. THOS. NICOL, B.D.

'The volume contains much which any thoughtful and earnest Christian minister will find helpful and suggestive to him for the wise and efficient discharge of his sacred functions.'—*Literary World.*

T. and T. Clark's Publications.

Just published, in Two Vols., 8vo, price 21s.,

NATURE AND THE BIBLE:

LECTURES ON THE MOSAIC HISTORY OF CREATION IN ITS RELATION TO NATURAL SCIENCE.

By Dr. FR. H. REUSCH.

REVISED AND CORRECTED BY THE AUTHOR.

TRANSLATED FROM THE FOURTH EDITION BY KATHLEEN LYTTELTON.

'Other champions much more competent and learned might have been placed in the field; I will only name one of the most recent, Dr. Reusch, author of "Nature and the Bible."'—The Right Hon. W. E. GLADSTONE.

Just published, in demy 4to, price 14s.,

CREMER'S LEXICON.
SUPPLEMENT
TO
BIBLICO-THEOLOGICAL LEXICON
OF
NEW TESTAMENT GREEK.

By HERMANN CREMER, D.D.

TRANSLATED AND ARRANGED FROM THE LAST GERMAN EDITION
By WILLIAM URWICK, M.A.

The Complete Work, including Supplement, is now issued at 38s.

Will shortly be published, in demy 4to,

GRIMM'S LEXICON.
A GREEK-ENGLISH LEXICON
OF THE
NEW TESTAMENT.

BEING GRIMM'S 'WILKE'S CLAVIS NOVI TESTAMENTI.'

Translated, Revised, and Enlarged
By JOSEPH HENRY THAYER, D.D.,
OF HARVARD UNIVERSITY.

Just published, in Two Vols., crown 8vo, price 16s.,

THE APOSTOLIC
AND
POST-APOSTOLIC TIMES.

THEIR DIVERSITY AND UNITY IN LIFE AND DOCTRINE.

By G. V. LECHLER, D.D.

THIRD EDITION, THOROUGHLY REVISED AND RE-WRITTEN.

TRANSLATED BY A. J. K. DAVIDSON.

T. and T. Clark's Publications.

HISTORY OF THE CHRISTIAN CHURCH.

By PHILIP SCHAFF, D.D., LL.D.

APOSTOLIC CHRISTIANITY, A.D. 1–100. In Two Divisions. Ex. demy 8vo, price 21s.
ANTE-NICENE CHRISTIANITY, A.D. 100–325. In Two Divisions. Ex. demy 8vo, price 21s.
NICENE and POST-NICENE CHRISTIANITY, A.D. 325–600. In Two Divisions. Ex. demy 8vo, price 21s.
MEDIÆVAL CHRISTIANITY, A.D. 590–1073. In Two Divisions. Ex. demy 8vo, price 21s.

'No student, and indeed no critic, can with fairness overlook a work like the present, written with such evident candour, and, at the same time, with so thorough a knowledge of the sources of early Christian history.'—*Scotsman.*

'I trust that this very instructive volume will find its way to the library table of every minister who cares to investigate thoroughly the foundations of Christianity. I cannot refrain from congratulating you on having carried through the press this noble contribution to historical literature. I think that there is no other work which equals it in many important excellences.'—Rev. Prof. FISHER, D.D.

'In no other work of its kind with which I am acquainted will students and general readers find so much to instruct and interest them.'—Rev. Prof. HITCHCOCK, D.D.

In demy 4to, Third Edition, **with Supplement,** *price 38s.,*

BIBLICO-THEOLOGICAL LEXICON OF NEW TESTAMENT GREEK.

By HERMANN CREMER, D.D.,
PROFESSOR OF THEOLOGY IN THE UNIVERSITY OF GREIFSWALD.

TRANSLATED FROM THE GERMAN OF THE SECOND EDITION
By WILLIAM URWICK, M.A.

THE SUPPLEMENT, WHICH IS INCLUDED IN THE ABOVE, MAY BE HAD SEPARATELY, price 14s.

'Dr. Cremer's work is highly and deservedly esteemed in Germany. It gives with care and thoroughness a complete history, as far as it goes, of each word and phrase that it deals with. . . . Dr. Cremer's explanations are most lucidly set out.'—*Guardian.*

'It is hardly possible to exaggerate the value of this work to the student of the Greek Testament. . . . The translation is accurate and idiomatic, and the additions to the later edition are considerable and important.'—*Church Bells.*

'We cannot find an important word in our Greek New Testament which is not discussed with a fulness and discrimination which leaves nothing to be desired.'—*Nonconformist.*

In demy 8vo, price 9s.,

GREEK AND ENGLISH LEXICON OF THE NEW TESTAMENT.

By PROF. EDWARD ROBINSON, D.D.

'We regard this Lexicon as a valuable addition to philological science, and, on the whole, *the best Lexicon* upon the New Testament which a student could purchase.'—*Baptist Magazine.*

T. and T. Clark's Publications.

Just published, in demy 8vo, price 7s. 6d.

SERMONS TO THE SPIRITUAL MAN.
By WILLIAM G. T. SHEDD, D.D.

'A uniform excellence pervades the tone, style, and thought of this volume. . . . We express our gratitude to the author for his able and helpful book.'—*Methodist Recorder.*

BY THE SAME AUTHOR.
In demy 8vo, price 7s. 6d.,

SERMONS TO THE NATURAL MAN.

'Characterized by profound knowledge of divine truth, and presenting the truth in a chaste and attractive style, the sermons carry in their tone the accents of the solemn feeling of responsibility to which they owe their origin.'—*Weekly Review.*

In One Volume, crown 8vo, price 5s., Third Edition,

LIGHT FROM THE CROSS.
SERMONS ON THE PASSION OF OUR LORD.
TRANSLATED FROM THE GERMAN OF A. THOLUCK, D.D.

'With no ordinary confidence and pleasure, we commend these most noble, solemnizing and touching discourses.'—*British and Foreign Evangelical Review.*

In crown 8vo, price 6s.,

THE INCARNATE SAVIOUR.
A LIFE OF JESUS CHRIST.
By REV. W. R. NICOLL, M.A.

'It commands my warm sympathy and admiration. I rejoice in the circulation of such a book, which I trust will be the widest possible.'—Canon LIDDON.

'There was quite room for such a volume. It contains a great deal of thought, often penetrating and always delicate, and pleasingly expressed. The subject has been very carefully studied, and the treatment will, I believe, furnish much suggestive matter both to readers and preachers.'—Rev. Principal SANDAY.

In crown 8vo, Eighth Edition, price 6s.,

THE SUFFERING SAVIOUR;
OR, MEDITATIONS ON THE LAST DAYS OF THE SUFFERINGS OF CHRIST.
By F. W. KRUMMACHER, D.D.

BY THE SAME AUTHOR.
In crown 8vo, Second Edition, price 6s.,

DAVID, THE KING OF ISRAEL.
A PORTRAIT DRAWN FROM BIBLE HISTORY AND THE BOOK OF PSALMS.

T. and T. Clark's Publications.

PROFESSOR GODET'S WORKS.

In Three Volumes, 8vo, price 31s. 6d.,
A COMMENTARY ON
THE GOSPEL OF ST. JOHN.
By F. GODET, D.D.,
PROFESSOR OF THEOLOGY, NEUCHATEL.

'This work forms one of the battle-fields of modern inquiry, and is itself so rich in spiritual truth that it is impossible to examine it too closely; and we welcome this treatise from the pen of Dr. Godet. We have no more competent exegete, and this new volume shows all the learning and vivacity for which the Author is distinguished.'—*Freeman.*

In Two Volumes, 8vo, price 21s.,
THE GOSPEL OF ST. LUKE.
Translated from the Second French Edition.

'Marked by clearness and good sense, it will be found to possess value and interest as one of the most recent and copious works specially designed to illustrate this Gospel.'—*Guardian.*

In Two Volumes, 8vo, price 21s.,
ST. PAUL'S EPISTLE TO THE ROMANS.

'We have looked through it with great care, and have been charmed not less by the clearness and fervour of its evangelical principles than by the carefulness of its exegesis, its fine touches of spiritual intuition, and its appositeness of historical illustration.'—*Baptist Magazine.*

In crown 8vo, Second Edition, price 6s.,
DEFENCE OF THE CHRISTIAN FAITH.
TRANSLATED BY THE
HON. AND REV. CANON LYTTELTON, M.A.,
RECTOR OF HAGLEY.

'This volume is not unworthy of the great reputation which Professor Godet enjoys. It shows the same breadth of reading and extent of learning as his previous works, and the same power of eloquent utterance.'—*Church Bells.*

'Professor Godet is at once so devoutly evangelical in his spirit, and so profoundly intelligent in his apprehension of truth, that we shall all welcome these contributions to the study of much-debated subjects with the utmost satisfaction.'—*Christian World.*

In demy 8vo, Fourth Edition, price 10s. 6d.,
MODERN DOUBT AND CHRISTIAN BELIEF.
A Series of Apologetic Lectures addressed to Earnest Seekers after Truth.
By THEODORE CHRISTLIEB, D.D.,
UNIVERSITY PREACHER AND PROFESSOR OF THEOLOGY AT BONN.

Translated, with the Author's sanction, chiefly by the Rev. H. U. WEITBRECHT, Ph.D., and Edited by the Rev. T. L. KINGSBURY, M.A.

'We recommend the volume as one of the most valuable and important among recent contributions to our apologetic literature. . . . We are heartily thankful both to the learned Author and to his translators.'—*Guardian.*

'We express our unfeigned admiration of the ability displayed in this work, and of the spirit of deep piety which pervades it; and whilst we commend it to the careful perusal of our readers, we heartily rejoice that in these days of reproach and blasphemy so able a champion has come forward to contend earnestly for the faith which was once delivered to the saints.'—*Christian Observer.*

T. and T. Clark's Publications.

Just published, in demy 8vo, price 10s. 6d.,

THE LORD'S PRAYER:
A PRACTICAL MEDITATION.
By Rev. NEWMAN HALL, LL.B.

'Short, crisp sentences, absolute in form and lucid in thought, convey the author's meaning and carry on his exposition. . . . He is impatient of dim lights; his thoughts are sharply cut, and are like crystals in their clearness.'—*British Quarterly Review*.

'A new volume of theological literature, by Rev. Newman Hall, is sure to be eagerly welcomed, and we can promise its readers that they will not be disappointed. . . . Upon every subject Mr. Hall writes with clearness and power.'—*Nonconformist*.

Just published, in crown 8vo, price 6s.,

STUDIES IN THE CHRISTIAN EVIDENCES.
By ALEXANDER MAIR, D.D.

'Dr. Mair has made an honest study of Strauss, Renan, Keim, and "Supernatural Religion," and his book is an excellent one to put into the hands of doubters and inquirers.'—*English Churchman*.

'Will in every way meet the wants of the class for whom it is intended, many of whom are "wayworn and sad," amid the muddled speculations of the current day.'—*Ecclesiastical Gazette*.

Just published, in demy 8vo, price 9s.,

LECTURES ON PAUL'S EPISTLES TO THE THESSALONIANS.
By Rev. Dr. HUTCHISON.

'We have not—at least amongst modern works—many commentaries on these epistles in which the text is at once treated with scholarly ability, and turned to popular and practical account. Such is the character of Dr. Hutchison's work—his exegesis of crucial passages strikes us at once as eminently clear.'—*Baptist*.

'Certainly one of the ablest and best commentaries that we have ever read. The style is crisp and clear, and the scholarship is in no sense of a superficial or pretentious order.'—*Evangelical Magazine*.

Just published, in crown 8vo, price 6s.,

CHRISTIAN CHARITY IN THE ANCIENT CHURCH.
By G. UHLHORN, D.D.

'A very excellent translation of a very valuable book.'—*Guardian*.

'The historical knowledge this work displays is immense, and the whole subject is wrought out with great care and skill. It is a most readable, delightful, and instructive volume.'—*Evangelical Christendom*.

'The facts are surprising, many of them fresh, and the truths to be deduced are far more powerful as weapons for warring against infidelity than scores of lectures or bushels of tracts.'—*Ecclesiastical Gazette*.

Just published, in demy 8vo, price 10s. 6d.,

THE PARABLES OF JESUS.
A METHODICAL EXPOSITION.
By SIEGFRIED GOEBEL,
COURT CHAPLAIN IN HALBERSTADT.
TRANSLATED BY PROF. J. S. BANKS, HEADINGLEY COLLEGE.

'This ought to be one of the most helpful of all the volumes in the "Foreign Theological Library." . . . Such expositions as those of the Good Samaritan and the Prodigal Son are as full of human feeling as others are of ripe learning. The volume is quite a treasury of original exposition on a subject on which preachers constantly need help, and on which little that is new has appeared in recent years.'—*Methodist Recorder*.

T. and T. Clark's Publications.

Just published, in crown 8vo, price 6s.,

OLD AND NEW THEOLOGY:
A CONSTRUCTIVE CRITIQUE.
By Rev. J. B. HEARD, M.A.

'We can promise all real students of Holy Scripture who have found their way out of some of the worst of the scholastic byelanes and ruts, and are striving to reach the broad and firm high road that leads to the Eternal City, a real treat from the perusal of these pages. Progressive theologians, who desire to find "the old in the new, and the new in the old," will be deeply grateful to Mr. Heard for this courageous and able work.'—*Christian World.*

'Among the many excellent theological works, whether English or German, published by Messrs. Clark, there are few that deserve more careful study than this book. . . . It cannot fail to charm by its grace of style, and to supply food for solid thought.'—*Dublin Express.*

'We predict an earnest welcome for this volume. . . . We could wish that the principles and sentiments of this book were widely diffused among Christian people, in all Churches.'—*Literary World.*

BY THE SAME AUTHOR.
Fifth Edition, in crown 8vo, price 6s.,

THE TRIPARTITE NATURE OF MAN:
SPIRIT, SOUL, AND BODY.

Applied to Illustrate and Explain the Doctrines of Original Sin, the New Birth, the Disembodied State, and the Spiritual Body.

'The author has got a striking and consistent theory. Whether agreeing or disagreeing with that theory, it is a book which any student of the Bible may read with pleasure.'—*Guardian.*

'An elaborate, ingenious, and very able book.'—*London Quarterly Review.*

'The subject is discussed with much ability and learning, and the style is sprightly and readable. It is candid in its tone, and original both in thought and illustration.'—*Wesleyan Methodist Magazine.*

Just published, in demy 8vo, price 9s.,

THE DOCTRINE OF THE HOLY SPIRIT.
(NINTH SERIES OF THE CUNNINGHAM LECTURES.)
By Rev. GEO. SMEATON, D.D.,
Professor of Exegetical Theology, New College, Edinburgh.

'A valuable monograph. . . . The masterly exposition of doctrine given in these lectures has been augmented in value by the wise references to current needs and common misconceptions.'—*British and Foreign Evangelical Review.*

BY THE SAME AUTHOR.
Second Edition, in demy 8vo, price 10s. 6d.,

THE DOCTRINE OF THE ATONEMENT
AS TAUGHT BY CHRIST HIMSELF;
Or, The Sayings of Jesus Exegetically Expounded and Classified.

'We attach very great value to this seasonable and scholarly production. The idea of the work is most happy, and the execution of it worthy of the idea. On a scheme of truly Baconian exegetical induction, he presents us with a complete view of the various positions or propositions which a full and sound doctrine of the atonement embraces.'—*British and Foreign Evangelical Review.*

'The plan of the book is admirable. A monograph and exegesis of our Lord's own sayings on this greatest of subjects concerning Himself, must needs be valuable to all theologians. And the execution is thorough and painstaking—exhaustive as far as the completeness of range over these sayings is concerned.'—*Contemporary Review.*

PUBLICATIONS OF

T. & T. CLARK,
38 GEORGE STREET, EDINBURGH.
LONDON: HAMILTON, ADAMS, & CO.

Adam (J., D.D.)—AN EXPOSITION OF THE EPISTLE OF JAMES. 8vo, 9s.
Alexander (Dr. J. A.)—COMMENTARY ON ISAIAH. Two vols. 8vo, 17s.
Ante-Nicene Christian Library—A COLLECTION OF ALL THE WORKS OF THE FATHERS OF THE CHRISTIAN CHURCH PRIOR TO THE COUNCIL OF NICÆA. Twenty-four vols. 8vo, Subscription price, £6, 6s.
Augustine's Works—Edited by MARCUS DODS, D.D. Fifteen vols. 8vo, Subscription price, £3, 19s.
Bannerman (Prof.)—THE CHURCH OF CHRIST. Two vols. 8vo, 21s.
Baumgarten (Professor)—APOSTOLIC HISTORY. Three vols. 8vo, 27s.
Beck (Dr.)—OUTLINES OF BIBLICAL PSYCHOLOGY. Crown 8vo, 4s.
—— PASTORAL THEOLOGY IN THE NEW TESTAMENT. Crown 8vo, 6s.
Bengel—GNOMON OF THE NEW TESTAMENT. With Original Notes, Explanatory and Illustrative. Five vols. 8vo, Subscription price, 31s. 6d. *Cheaper Edition, the five volumes bound in three*, 24s.
Besser's CHRIST THE LIFE OF THE WORLD. Price 6s.
Bible-Class Handbooks. Crown 8vo.
  BINNIE (Prof.)—The Church, 1s. 6d.
  BROWN (Principal)—The Epistle to the Romans, 2s.
  CANDLISH (Prof.)—The Christian Sacraments, 1s. 6d.
  —— The Work of the Holy Spirit, 1s. 6d.
  DAVIDSON (Prof.)—The Epistle to the Hebrews, 2s. 6d.
  DODS (MARCUS, D.D.)—The Post-Exilian Prophets, 2s.
  —— The Book of Genesis, 2s.
  DOUGLAS (Principal)—The Book of Joshua, 1s. 6d.
  —— The Book of Judges, 1s. 3d.
  HAMILTON (T., M.A.)—Irish Presbyterian Church History, 2s.
  HENDERSON (ARCHIBALD, M.A.)—Palestine, with Maps. *The maps are by Captain Conder, R.E., of the Palestine Exploration Fund.* Price 2s. 6d.
  LINDSAY (Prof.)—The Gospel of St. Mark, 2s. 6d.
  —— The Reformation, 2s.
  —— The Acts of the Apostles, Two vols., 1s. 6d. each.
  MACGREGOR (Prof.)—The Epistle to the Galatians, 1s. 6d.
  MACPHERSON (JOHN, M.A.)—Presbyterianism, 1s. 6d.
  —— The Westminster Confession of Faith, 2s.
  —— The Sum of Saving Knowledge, 1s. 6d.
  MURPHY (Prof.)—The Books of Chronicles, 1s. 6d.
  SCRYMGEOUR (WM.)—Lessons on the Life of Christ, 2s. 6d.
  STALKER (JAMES, M.A.)—The Life of Christ, 1s. 6d.
  —— The Life of St. Paul, 1s. 6d.
  SMITH (GEORGE, LL.D.)—A Short History of Missions, 2s. 6d.
  WALKER (NORMAN L., M.A.)—Scottish Church History, 1s. 6d.
  WHYTE (ALEXANDER, D.D.)—The Shorter Catechism, 2s. 6d.
Bible-Class Primers. Paper covers, 6d. each; free by post, 7d. In cloth, 8d. each; free by post, 9d.
  CROSKERY (Prof.)—Joshua and the Conquest.
  GIVEN (Prof.)—The Kings of Judah.
  GLOAG, (PATON J., D.D.)—Life of Paul.
  IVERACH (JAMES, M.A.)—Life of Moses.
  PATERSON (Prof. J. A.)—Period of the Judges.
  ROBSON (JOHN, D.D.)—Outlines of Protestant Missions.
  SALMOND (Prof.)—Life of Peter.
  SMITH (H. W., D.D.)—Outlines of Early Church History.
  THOMSON (PETER, M.A.)—Life of David.
  WALKER (W., M.A.)—The Kings of Israel.

Bible-Class Primers—*continued.*
    WINTERBOTHAM (RAYNER, M.A.)—Life and Reign of Solomon.
    WITHEROW (Prof.)—The History of the Reformation.
Bleek's INTRODUCTION TO THE NEW TESTAMENT. Two vols. 8vo, 21s.
Bowman (T., M.A.)—EASY AND COMPLETE HEBREW COURSE. 8vo.
    Part I., 7s. 6d. ; Part II., 10s. 6d.
Briggs (Prof.)—BIBLICAL STUDY: Its Principles, Methods, and
    History. Second Edition, post 8vo, 7s. 6d.
—— AMERICAN PRESBYTERIANISM : Its Origin and Early History,
    together with an Appendix of Letters and Documents. Post 8vo, 7s. 6d.
—— MESSIANIC PROPHECY. Post 8vo, 7s. 6d.
Brown (David, D.D.)—CHRIST'S SECOND COMING : Will it be Pre-
    Millennial? Seventh Edition, crown 8vo, 7s. 6d.
Bruce (A. B., D.D.)—THE TRAINING OF THE TWELVE ; exhibiting the
    Twelve Disciples under Discipline for the Apostleship. 3rd Ed., 8vo, 10s. 6d.
—— THE HUMILIATION OF CHRIST, in its Physical, Ethical, and
    Official Aspects. Second Edition, 8vo, 10s. 6d.
Buchanan (Professor)—THE DOCTRINE OF JUSTIFICATION. 8vo, 10s. 6d.
—— ON COMFORT IN AFFLICTION. Crown 8vo, 2s. 6d.
—— ON IMPROVEMENT OF AFFLICTION. Crown 8vo, 2s. 6d.
Bungener (Felix)—ROME AND THE COUNCIL IN THE NINETEENTH
    CENTURY. Crown 8vo, 5s.
Calvin's INSTITUTES OF THE CHRISTIAN RELIGION. Translated by
    HENRY BEVERIDGE. Two vols. 8vo, 14s.
Calvini Institutio Christianæ Religionis. Curavit A. THOLUCK.
    Two vols. 8vo, Subscription price, 14s.
Candlish (Prof. J. S., D.D.)—THE KINGDOM OF GOD, BIBLICALLY AND
    HISTORICALLY CONSIDERED. 8vo, 10s. 6d.
Caspari (C. E.)—A CHRONOLOGICAL AND GEOGRAPHICAL INTRODUC-
    TION TO THE LIFE OF CHRIST. 8vo, 7s. 6d.
Caspers (A.)—THE FOOTSTEPS OF CHRIST. Crown 8vo, 7s. 6d.
Cave (Prof.)—THE SCRIPTURAL DOCTRINE OF SACRIFICE. 8vo, 12s.
—— AN INTRODUCTION TO THEOLOGY : Its Principles, its Branches,
    its Results, and its Literature. 8vo, 12s.
Christlieb (Dr.)—MODERN DOUBT AND CHRISTIAN BELIEF. Apologetic
    Lectures addressed to Earnest Seekers after Truth. 8vo, 10s. 6d.
Cotterill — PEREGRINUS PROTEUS : Investigation into De Morte
    Peregrini, the Two Epistles of Clement to the Corinthians, etc. 8vo, 12s.
—— MODERN CRITICISM : Clement's Epistles to Virgins, etc. 8vo, 5s.
Cremer (Professor)—BIBLICO-THEOLOGICAL LEXICON OF NEW TESTA-
    MENT GREEK. Third Edition, with Supplement, demy 4to, 38s. SUPPLE-
    MENT, separately, 14s.
Crippen (Rev. T. G.)—A POPULAR INTRODUCTION TO THE HISTORY
    OF CHRISTIAN DOCTRINE. 8vo, 9s.
Cunningham (Principal)—HISTORICAL THEOLOGY. Review of the
    Principal Doctrinal Discussions since the Apostolic Age. Two vols. 8vo, 21s.
—— DISCUSSIONS ON CHURCH PRINCIPLES. 8vo, 10s. 6d.
Curtiss (Dr. S. I.)—THE LEVITICAL PRIESTS. Crown 8vo, 5s.
Dabney (R. L., D.D.)—THE SENSUALISTIC PHILOSOPHY OF THE
    NINETEENTH CENTURY CONSIDERED. Crown 8vo, 6s.
Davidson (Professor)—AN INTRODUCTORY HEBREW GRAMMAR. With
    Progressive Exercises in Reading and Writing. Eighth Edition, 8vo, 7s. 6d.
Delitzsch (Prof.)—A SYSTEM OF BIBLICAL PSYCHOLOGY. 8vo, 12s.
—— COMMENTARY ON JOB. Two vols. 8vo, 21s.

T. and T. Clark's Publications.

Delitzsch (Prof.)—COMMENTARY ON PSALMS. Three vols. 8vo, 31s. 6d.
—— ON THE PROVERBS OF SOLOMON. Two vols. 8vo, 21s.
—— ON THE SONG OF SOLOMON AND ECCLESIASTES. 8vo, 10s. 6d.
—— OLD TESTAMENT HISTORY OF REDEMPTION. Cr. 8vo, 4s. 6d.
—— COMMENTARY ON ISAIAH. Two vols. 8vo, 21s.
—— ON THE EPISTLE TO THE HEBREWS. Two vols. 8vo, 21s.
Doedes—MANUAL OF NEW TESTAMENT HERMENEUTICS. Cr. 8vo, 3s.
Döllinger (Dr.)—HIPPOLYTUS AND CALLISTUS; or, The Roman Church in the First Half of the Third Century. 8vo, 7s. 6d.
Dorner (Professor)—HISTORY OF THE DEVELOPMENT OF THE DOCTRINE OF THE PERSON OF CHRIST. Five vols. 8vo, £2, 12s. 6d.
—— SYSTEM OF CHRISTIAN DOCTRINE. Four vols. 8vo, £2, 2s.
—— SYSTEM OF CHRISTIAN ETHICS. *In preparation.*
Eadie (Professor)—COMMENTARIES ON ST. PAUL'S EPISTLES TO THE EPHESIANS, PHILIPPIANS, COLOSSIANS. New and Revised Editions, Edited by Rev. WM. YOUNG, M.A. Three vols. 8vo, 10s. 6d. each; or *set*, 18s. *nett.*
Ebrard (Dr. J. H. A.)—THE GOSPEL HISTORY. 8vo, 10s. 6d.
—— COMMENTARY ON THE EPISTLES OF ST. JOHN. 8vo, 10s. 6d.
—— APOLOGETICS. 3 vols. 8vo (vol. I. now ready, 10s. 6d.).
Elliott—ON THE INSPIRATION OF THE HOLY SCRIPTURES. 8vo, 6s.
Ernesti—BIBLICAL INTERPRETATION OF NEW TESTAMENT. Two vols., 8s.
Ewald (Heinrich)—SYNTAX OF THE HEBREW LANGUAGE OF THE OLD TESTAMENT. 8vo, 8s. 6d.
—— REVELATION: ITS NATURE AND RECORD. 8vo, 10s. 6d.
Fairbairn (Principal)—TYPOLOGY OF SCRIPTURE, viewed in connection with the series of Divine Dispensations. Sixth Edition, Two vols. 8vo, 21s.
—— THE REVELATION OF LAW IN SCRIPTURE, 8vo, 10s. 6d.
—— EZEKIEL AND THE BOOK OF HIS PROPHECY. 4th Ed., 8vo, 10s. 6d.
—— PROPHECY VIEWED IN ITS DISTINCTIVE NATURE, ITS SPECIAL FUNCTIONS, AND PROPER INTERPRETATIONS. Second Edition, 8vo, 10s. 6d.
—— NEW TESTAMENT HERMENEUTICAL MANUAL. 8vo, 10s. 6d.
—— THE PASTORAL EPISTLES. The Greek Text and Translation. With Introduction, Expository Notes, and Dissertations. 8vo, 7s. 6d.
—— PASTORAL THEOLOGY: A Treatise on the Office and Duties of the Christian Pastor. With a Memoir of the Author. Crown 8vo, 6s.
Forbes (Prof.)—SYMMETRICAL STRUCTURE OF SCRIPTURE. 8vo, 8s. 6d.
—— ANALYTICAL COMMENTARY ON THE ROMANS. 8vo, 10s. 6d.
Frank (Prof. F. H.)—SYSTEM OF CHRISTIAN EVIDENCE. 8vo, 10s. 6d.
Gebhardt (H.)—THE DOCTRINE OF THE APOCALYPSE, AND ITS RELATION TO THE DOCTRINE OF THE GOSPEL AND EPISTLES OF JOHN. 8vo, 10s. 6d.
Gerlach—COMMENTARY ON THE PENTATEUCH. 8vo, 10s. 6d.
Gieseler (Dr. J. C. L.)—A COMPENDIUM OF ECCLESIASTICAL HISTORY. Four vols. 8vo, £2, 2s.
Gifford (Canon)—VOICES OF THE PROPHETS. Crown 8vo, 3s. 6d.
Given (Rev. Prof. J. J.)—THE TRUTHS OF SCRIPTURE IN CONNECTION WITH REVELATION, INSPIRATION, AND THE CANON. 8vo, 6s.
Glasgow (Prof.)—APOCALYPSE TRANSLATED AND EXPOUNDED. 8vo, 10s. 6d.
Gloag (Paton J., D.D.)—A CRITICAL AND EXEGETICAL COMMENTARY ON THE ACTS OF THE APOSTLES. Two vols. 8vo, 21s.
—— THE MESSIANIC PROPHECIES. Crown 8vo, price 7s. 6d.
—— INTRODUCTION TO THE PAULINE EPISTLES. 8vo, 12s.
—— INTRODUCTION TO THE CATHOLIC EPISTLES. *In preparation.*

Gloag (P. J., D.D.)—EXEGETICAL STUDIES. Crown 8vo, 5s.
Godet (Prof.)—COMMENTARY ON ST. LUKE'S GOSPEL. Two vols. 8vo, 21s.
———— COMMENTARY ON ST. JOHN'S GOSPEL. Three vols. 8vo, 31s. 6d.
———— COMMENTARY ON EPISTLE TO THE ROMANS. Two vols. 8vo, 21s.
———— COMMENTARY ON EPISTLES TO THE CORINTHIANS. 2 vols. 8vo, 21s.
———— LECTURES IN DEFENCE OF THE CHRISTIAN FAITH. Cr. 8vo, 6s.
Goebel (Siegfried)—THE PARABLES OF JESUS. 8vo, 10s. 6d.
Gotthold's Emblems; or, INVISIBLE THINGS UNDERSTOOD BY THINGS THAT ARE MADE. Crown 8vo, 5s.
Grimm's GREEK-ENGLISH LEXICON OF THE NEW TESTAMENT. Translated, Revised, and Enlarged by JOSEPH H. THAYER, D.D. Demy 4to, 36s.
Guyot (Arnold, LL.D.)—CREATION; or, The Biblical Cosmogony in the Light of Modern Science. With Illustrations. Crown 8vo, 5s. 6d.
Hagenbach (Dr. K. R.)—HISTORY OF DOCTRINES. Edited, with large additions from various sources. Three vols. 8vo, 31s. 6d.
———— HISTORY OF THE REFORMATION IN GERMANY AND SWITZERLAND CHIEFLY. Two vols. 8vo, 21s.
Hall (Rev. Newman, LL.B.)—THE LORD'S PRAYER. 8vo, 10s. 6d.
Harless (Dr. C. A.)—SYSTEM OF CHRISTIAN ETHICS. 8vo, 10s. 6d.
Harris (Rev. S., D.D.)—THE PHILOSOPHICAL BASIS OF THEISM. 8vo, 12s.
Haupt (Erich)—THE FIRST EPISTLE OF ST. JOHN. 8vo, 10s. 6d.
Hävernick (H. A. Ch.)—INTRODUCTION TO OLD TESTAMENT. 10s. 6d.
Heard (Rev. J. B., M.A.)—THE TRIPARTITE NATURE OF MAN—SPIRIT, SOUL, AND BODY. Fifth Edition, crown 8vo, 6s.
———— OLD AND NEW THEOLOGY. A Constructive Critique. Cr. 8vo, 6s.
Hefele (Bishop)—A HISTORY OF THE COUNCILS OF THE CHURCH. Vol. I., to A.D. 325; Vol. II., A.D. 326 to 429. Vol. III., A.D. 431 to the close of the Council of Chalcedon, 451. 8vo, 12s. each.
Hengstenberg (Professor)—COMMENTARY ON PSALMS. 3 vols. 8vo, 33s.
———— COMMENTARY ON THE BOOK OF ECCLESIASTES. Treatises on the Song of Solomon, Job, and on Isaiah, etc. 8vo, 9s.
———— THE PROPHECIES OF EZEKIEL ELUCIDATED. 8vo, 10s. 6d.
———— DISSERTATIONS ON THE GENUINENESS OF DANIEL, AND THE INTEGRITY OF ZECHARIAH. 8vo, 12s.
———— HISTORY OF THE KINGDOM OF GOD. Two vols. 8vo, 21s.
———— CHRISTOLOGY OF THE OLD TESTAMENT. Four vols. 8vo, £2, 2s.
———— ON THE GOSPEL OF ST. JOHN. Two vols. 8vo, 21s.
Hermes Trismegistus—THEOLOGICAL AND PHILOSOPHICAL WORKS. Translated from the original Greek by J. D. CHAMBERS, M.A. 8vo, 6s.
Herzog—ENCYCLOPÆDIA OF BIBLICAL, HISTORICAL, DOCTRINAL, AND PRACTICAL THEOLOGY. *Based on the Real-Encyklopädie of Herzog, Plitt, and Hauck.* Edited by Prof. SCHAFF, D.D. In Three vols., price 24s. each.
Hutchison (John, D.D.)—COMMENTARY ON THESSALONIANS. 8vo, 9s.
Janet (Paul)—FINAL CAUSES. By PAUL JANET, Member of the Institute. Translated from the French. Second Edition, demy 8vo, 12s.
———— THE THEORY OF MORALS. Demy 8vo, 10s. 6d.
Jouffroy—PHILOSOPHICAL ESSAYS. Fcap. 8vo, 5s.
Kant—THE METAPHYSIC OF ETHICS. Crown 8vo, 6s.
———— PHILOSOPHY OF LAW. *In preparation.*
Keil (Prof.)—COMMENTARY ON THE PENTATEUCH. 3 vols. 8vo, 31s. 6d.
———— COMMENTARY ON JOSHUA, JUDGES, AND RUTH. 8vo, 10s. 6d.
———— COMMENTARY ON THE BOOKS OF SAMUEL. 8vo, 10s. 6d.
———— COMMENTARY ON THE BOOKS OF KINGS. 8vo, 10s. 6d.

T. and T. Clark's Publications.

Keil (Prof.)—COMMENTARY ON CHRONICLES. 8vo, 10s. 6d.
—— COMMENTARY ON EZRA, NEHEMIAH, ESTHER. 8vo, 10s. 6d.
—— COMMENTARY ON JEREMIAH. Two vols. 8vo, 21s.
—— COMMENTARY ON EZEKIEL. Two vols. 8vo, 21s.
—— COMMENTARY ON DANIEL. 8vo, 10s. 6d.
—— ON THE BOOKS OF THE MINOR PROPHETS. Two vols. 8vo, 21s.
—— MANUAL OF HISTORICO-CRITICAL INTRODUCTION TO THE CANONICAL SCRIPTURES OF THE OLD TESTAMENT. Two vols. 8vo, 21s.
Keymer (Rev. N., M.A.)—NOTES ON GENESIS. Crown 8vo, 1s. 6d.
Killen (Prof.)—THE OLD CATHOLIC CHURCH; or, The History, Doctrine, Worship, and Polity of the Christians, traced to A.D. 755. 8vo, 9s.
—— THE IGNATIAN EPISTLES ENTIRELY SPURIOUS. Cr. 8vo, 2s. 6d.
König (Dr. F. E.)—THE RELIGIOUS HISTORY OF ISRAEL. A Discussion of the Chief Problems in Old Testament History as opposed to the Development Theorists. Crown 8vo, 3s. 6d.
Krummacher (Dr. F. W.)—THE SUFFERING SAVIOUR; or, Meditations on the Last Days of the Sufferings of Christ. Eighth Edition, crown 8vo, 6s.
—— DAVID, THE KING OF ISRAEL: A Portrait drawn from Bible History and the Book of Psalms. Second Edition, crown 8vo, 6s.
—— AUTOBIOGRAPHY. Crown 8vo, 6s.
Kurtz (Prof.)—HANDBOOK OF CHURCH HISTORY. Two vols. 8vo, 15s.
—— HISTORY OF THE OLD COVENANT. Three vols. 8vo, 31s. 6d.
Ladd (Prof. G. T.)—THE DOCTRINE OF SACRED SCRIPTURE: A Critical, Historical, and Dogmatic Inquiry into the Origin and Nature of the Old and New Testaments. Two vols. 8vo, 1600 pp., 24s.
Laidlaw (Prof.)—THE BIBLE DOCTRINE OF MAN. 8vo, 10s. 6d.
Lange (J. P., D.D.)—THE LIFE OF OUR LORD JESUS CHRIST. Edited, with additional Notes, by MARCUS DODS, D.D. Second Edition, in Four vols. 8vo, Subscription price 28s.
—— COMMENTARIES ON THE OLD AND NEW TESTAMENTS. Edited by PHILIP SCHAFF, D.D. OLD TESTAMENT, 14 vols.; NEW TESTAMENT, 10 vols.; APOCRYPHA, 1 vol. Subscription price, nett, 15s. each.
—— ON ST. MATTHEW AND ST. MARK. Three vols. 8vo, 31s. 6d.
—— ON THE GOSPEL OF ST. LUKE. Two vols. 8vo, 18s.
—— ON THE GOSPEL OF ST. JOHN. Two vols. 8vo, 21s.
Lechler (Prof. G. V., D.D.)—THE APOSTOLIC AND POST-APOSTOLIC TIMES. Their Diversity and Unity in Life and Doctrine. 2 vols. cr. 8vo, 16s.
Lehmann (Pastor)—SCENES FROM THE LIFE OF JESUS. Cr. 8vo, 3s. 6d.
Lewis (Tayler, LL.D.)—THE SIX DAYS OF CREATION. Cr. 8vo, 7s. 6d.
Lisco (F. G.)—PARABLES OF JESUS EXPLAINED. Fcap. 8vo, 5s.
Lotze (Hermann)—MICROCOSMUS: An Essay concerning Man and his Relation to the World. Second Edition, two vols. 8vo (1450 pages), 36s.
Luthardt, Kahnis, and Brückner—THE CHURCH. Crown 8vo, 5s.
Luthardt (Prof.)—ST. JOHN THE AUTHOR OF THE FOURTH GOSPEL. 7s. 6d.
—— ST. JOHN'S GOSPEL DESCRIBED AND EXPLAINED ACCORDING TO ITS PECULIAR CHARACTER. Three vols. 8vo, 31s. 6d.
—— APOLOGETIC LECTURES ON THE FUNDAMENTAL (*Sixth Edition*), SAVING (*Fourth Edition*), MORAL TRUTHS OF CHRISTIANITY (*Third Edition*). Three vols. crown 8vo, 6s. each.
M'Cosh (Dr. Jas.)—PHILOSOPHIC SERIES. Part I. (Didactic). Part II. (Historical). In Eight Parts, price 2s. each.
Macdonald—INTRODUCTION TO PENTATEUCH. Two vols. 8vo, 21s.
—— THE CREATION AND FALL. 8vo, 12s.

M'Lauchlan (T., D.D., LL.D.)—THE EARLY SCOTTISH CHURCH. To the Middle of the Twelfth Century. 8vo, 10s. 6d.
Mair (A., D.D.)—STUDIES IN THE CHRISTIAN EVIDENCES. Cr. 8vo, 6s.
Martensen (Bishop)—CHRISTIAN DOGMATICS: A Compendium of the Doctrines of Christianity. 8vo, 10s. 6d.
—— CHRISTIAN ETHICS. (GENERAL ETHICS.) 8vo, 10s. 6d.
—— CHRISTIAN ETHICS. (INDIVIDUAL ETHICS.) 8vo, 10s. 6d.
—— CHRISTIAN ETHICS. (SOCIAL ETHICS.) 8vo, 10s. 6d.
Matheson (Geo., D.D.)—GROWTH OF THE SPIRIT OF CHRISTIANITY, from the First Century to the Dawn of the Lutheran Era. Two vols. 8vo, 21s.
—— AIDS TO THE STUDY OF GERMAN THEOLOGY. 3rd Edition, 4s. 6d.
Meyer (Dr.)—CRITICAL AND EXEGETICAL COMMENTARY ON ST. MATTHEW'S GOSPEL. Two vols. 8vo, 21s.
—— ON MARK AND LUKE. Two vols. 8vo, 21s.
—— ON ST. JOHN'S GOSPEL. Two vols. 8vo, 21s.
—— ON ACTS OF THE APOSTLES. Two vols. 8vo, 21s.
—— ON THE EPISTLE TO THE ROMANS. Two vols. 8vo, 21s.
—— ON CORINTHIANS. Two vols. 8vo, 21s.
—— ON GALATIANS. 8vo, 10s. 6d.
—— ON EPHESIANS AND PHILEMON. One vol. 8vo, 10s. 6d.
—— ON PHILIPPIANS AND COLOSSIANS. One vol. 8vo, 10s. 6d.
—— ON THESSALONIANS. (*Dr. Lünemann.*) One vol. 8vo, 10s. 6d.
—— THE PASTORAL EPISTLES. (*Dr. Huther.*) 8vo, 10s. 6d.
—— THE EPISTLE TO THE HEBREWS. (*Dr. Lünemann.*) 8vo, 10s. 6d.
—— ST. JAMES' AND ST. JOHN'S EPISTLES. (*Huther.*) 8vo, 10s. 6d.
—— PETER AND JUDE. (*Dr. Huther.*) One vol. 8vo, 10s. 6d.
Michie (Charles, M.A.)—BIBLE WORDS AND PHRASES. 18mo, 1s.
Monrad (Dr. D. G.)—THE WORLD OF PRAYER; or, Prayer in relation to Personal Religion. Crown 8vo, 4s. 6d.
Morgan (J., D.D.)—SCRIPTURE TESTIMONY TO THE HOLY SPIRIT. 7s. 6d.
—— EXPOSITION OF THE FIRST EPISTLE OF JOHN. 8vo, 7s. 6d.
Müller (Dr. Julius)—THE CHRISTIAN DOCTRINE OF SIN. An entirely New Translation from the Fifth German Edition. Two vols. 8vo, 21s.
Murphy (Professor)—COMMENTARY ON THE PSALMS. 8vo, 12s.
—— A CRITICAL AND EXEGETICAL COMMENTARY ON EXODUS. 9s.
Naville (Ernest)—THE PROBLEM OF EVIL. Crown 8vo, 4s. 6d.
—— THE CHRIST. Translated by Rev. T. J. DESPRÉS. Cr. 8vo, 4s. 6d.
—— MODERN PHYSICS: Studies Historical and Philosophical. Translated by Rev. HENRY DOWNTON, M.A. Crown 8vo, 5s.
Nicoll (W. R., M.A.)—THE INCARNATE SAVIOUR: A Life of Jesus Christ. Crown 8vo, 6s.
Neander (Dr.)—GENERAL HISTORY OF THE CHRISTIAN RELIGION AND CHURCH. Nine vols. 8vo, £3, 7s. 6d.
Oehler (Prof.)—THEOLOGY OF THE OLD TESTAMENT. 2 vols. 8vo, 21s.
Oosterzee (Dr. Van)—THE YEAR OF SALVATION. Words of Life for Every Day. A Book of Household Devotion. Two vols. 8vo, 6s. each
—— MOSES: A Biblical Study. Crown 8vo, 6s.
Olshausen (Dr. H.)—BIBLICAL COMMENTARY ON THE GOSPELS AND ACTS. Four vols. 8vo, £2, 2s. *Cheaper Edition*, four vols. crown 8vo, 24s.
—— ROMANS. One vol. 8vo, 10s. 6d.
—— CORINTHIANS. One vol. 8vo, 9s.
—— PHILIPPIANS, TITUS, AND FIRST TIMOTHY. One vol. 8vo, 10s. 6d.

T. and T. Clark's Publications.

Orelli—OLD TESTAMENT PROPHECY REGARDING THE CONSUMMATION OF THE KINGDOM OF GOD. 8vo, 10s. 6d.

Owen (Dr. John)—WORKS. *Best and only Complete Edition.* Edited by Rev. Dr. GOOLD. Twenty-four vols. 8vo, Subscription price, £4, 4s. The '*Hebrews*' may be had separately, in Seven vols., £2, 2s. nett.

Philippi (F. A.)—COMMENTARY ON THE EPISTLE TO THE ROMANS. From the Third Improved Edition, by Rev. Professor BANKS. Two vols. 8vo, 21s.

Piper—LIVES OF LEADERS OF CHURCH UNIVERSAL. Two vols. 8vo, 21s.

Popular Commentary on the New Testament. Edited by PHILIP SCHAFF, D.D. With Illustrations and Maps. Vol. I.—THE SYNOPTICAL GOSPELS. Vol. II.—ST. JOHN'S GOSPEL, AND THE ACTS OF THE APOSTLES. Vol. III.—ROMANS TO PHILEMON. Vol. IV.—HEBREWS TO REVELATION. In Four vols. imperial 8vo, 12s. 6d. each.

Pressensé (Edward de)—THE REDEEMER: Discourses. Crown 8vo, 6s.

Räbiger (Prof.)—ENCYCLOPÆDIA OF THEOLOGY. Two vols. 8vo, 21s.

Rainy (Principal) — DELIVERY AND DEVELOPMENT OF CHRISTIAN DOCTRINE. (*The Fifth Series of the Cunningham Lectures.*) 8vo, 10s. 6d.

Reusch (Professor) — NATURE AND THE BIBLE: Lectures on the Mosaic History of Creation in its Relation to Natural Science. Two vols. 8vo, 21s.

Reuss (Professor)—HISTORY OF THE SACRED SCRIPTURES OF THE NEW TESTAMENT. 640 pp. 8vo, 15s.

Riehm (Dr. E.)—MESSIANIC PROPHECY: Its Origin, Historical Character, and Relation to New Testament Fulfilment. Crown 8vo, 5s.

Ritter (Carl)—THE COMPARATIVE GEOGRAPHY OF PALESTINE AND THE SINAITIC PENINSULA. Four vols. 8vo, 26s.

Robinson (Rev. S., D.D.)—DISCOURSES ON REDEMPTION. 8vo, 7s. 6d.

Robinson (Edward, D.D.)—GREEK AND ENGLISH LEXICON OF THE NEW TESTAMENT. 8vo, 9s.

Rothe (Prof.)—SERMONS FOR THE CHRISTIAN YEAR. Cr. 8vo, 4s. 6d.

Saisset—MANUAL OF MODERN PANTHEISM. Two vols. 8vo, 10s. 6d.

Sartorius (Dr. E.)—DOCTRINE OF DIVINE LOVE. 8vo, 10s. 6d.

Schaff (Professor)—HISTORY OF THE CHRISTIAN CHURCH. (New Edition, thoroughly Revised and Enlarged.)
—— APOSTOLIC CHRISTIANITY, A.D. 1–100. In Two Divisions. Ex. 8vo, 21s.
—— ANTE-NICENE CHRISTIANITY, A.D. 100–325. In Two Divisions. Ex. 8vo, 21s.
—— POST-NICENE CHRISTIANITY, A.D. 325–600. In Two Divisions. Ex. 8vo, 21s.
—— MEDIÆVAL CHRISTIANITY, A.D. 590–1073. In Two Divisions. Ex. 8vo, 21s.
—— THE TEACHING OF THE TWELVE APOSTLES. The Didaché and Kindred Documents in the Original. Second Edition, ex. 8vo, 9s.

Schmid's BIBLICAL THEOLOGY OF THE NEW TESTAMENT. 8vo, 10s. 6d.

Schürer (Prof.)—HISTORY OF THE NEW TESTAMENT TIMES. Div. II. Three vols. 8vo, 31s. 6d.

Scott (Jas., M.A., D.D.)—PRINCIPLES OF NEW TESTAMENT QUOTATION ESTABLISHED AND APPLIED TO BIBLICAL CRITICISM. Cr. 8vo, 2nd Edit., 4s.

Shedd—HISTORY OF CHRISTIAN DOCTRINE. Two vols. 8vo, 21s.
—— SERMONS TO THE NATURAL MAN. 8vo, 7s. 6d.
—— SERMONS TO THE SPIRITUAL MAN. 8vo, 7s. 6d.

Simon (Rev. Prof. D. W.)—THE BIBLE; An Outgrowth of Theocratic Life. Crown 8vo, 4s. 6d.

T. and T. Clark's Publications.

Smeaton (Professor)—THE DOCTRINE OF THE ATONEMENT AS TAUGHT BY CHRIST HIMSELF. Second Edition, 8vo, 10s. 6d.
—— ON THE DOCTRINE OF THE HOLY SPIRIT. 8vo, 9s.
Smith (Professor Thos., D.D.)—MEDIÆVAL MISSIONS. Cr. 8vo, 4s. 6d.
Stalker (Rev. Jas., M.A.)—THE LIFE OF JESUS CHRIST. New Edition, in larger Type. Crown 8vo, 3s. 6d.
—— LIFE OF ST. PAUL. Large Type Edition. Crown 8vo, 3s. 6d.
Stanton (V. H., M.A.).—THE JEWISH AND THE CHRISTIAN MESSIAH. A Study in the Earliest History of Christianity. 8vo, 10s. 6d.
Steinmeyer (Dr. F. L.)—THE MIRACLES OF OUR LORD: Examined in their relation to Modern Criticism. 8vo, 7s. 6d.
—— THE HISTORY OF THE PASSION AND RESURRECTION OF OUR LORD, considered in the Light of Modern Criticism. 8vo, 10s. 6d.
Stevenson (Mrs.)—THE SYMBOLIC PARABLES: The Predictions of the Apocalypse in relation to the General Truths of Scripture. Cr. 8vo, 3s. 6d.
Steward (Rev. G.)—MEDIATORIAL SOVEREIGNTY: The Mystery of Christ and the Revelation of the Old and New Testaments. Two vols. 8vo, 21s.
—— THE ARGUMENT OF THE EPISTLE TO THE HEBREWS. 8vo, 10s. 6d.
Stier (Dr. Rudolph)—ON THE WORDS OF THE LORD JESUS. Eight vols. 8vo, £4, 4s. Separate volumes may be had, price 10s. 6d.
In order to bring this valuable Work more within the reach of all Classes, both Clergy and Laity, Messrs. Clark continue to supply the Eight-volume Edition bound in FOUR *at the Original Subscription price of £2, 2s.*
—— THE WORDS OF THE RISEN SAVIOUR, AND COMMENTARY ON THE EPISTLE OF ST. JAMES. 8vo, 10s. 6d.
—— THE WORDS OF THE APOSTLES EXPOUNDED. 8vo, 10s. 6d.
Tholuck (Professor)—COMMENTARY ON GOSPEL OF ST. JOHN. 8vo, 9s.
—— THE EPISTLE TO THE ROMANS. Two vols. fcap. 8vo, 8s.
—— LIGHT FROM THE CROSS. Third Edition, crown 8vo, 5s.
—— COMMENTARY ON THE SERMON ON THE MOUNT. 8vo, 10s. 6d.
Tophel (Pastor G.)—THE WORK OF THE HOLY SPIRIT. Cr. 8vo, 2s. 6d.
Uhlhorn (G.)—CHRISTIAN CHARITY IN THE ANCIENT CHURCH. Cr. 8vo, 6s.
Ullmann (Dr. Carl)—REFORMERS BEFORE THE REFORMATION, principally in Germany and the Netherlands. Two vols. 8vo, 21s.
—— THE SINLESSNESS OF JESUS: An Evidence for Christianity. Fourth Edition, crown 8vo, 6s.
Urwick (W., M.A.)—THE SERVANT OF JEHOVAH: A Commentary upon Isaiah lii. 13-liii. 12; with Dissertations upon Isaiah xl. lxvi. 8vo, 6s.
Vinet (Professor)—STUDIES ON BLAISE PASCAL. Crown 8vo, 5s.
—— PASTORAL THEOLOGY. Second Edition, post 8vo, 3s. 6d.
Watts (Professor)—THE NEWER CRITICISM AND THE ANALOGY OF THE FAITH. Third Edition, crown 8vo, 5s.
Weiss (Prof.)—BIBLICAL THEOLOGY OF NEW TESTAMENT. 2 vols. 8vo, 21s.
—— LIFE OF CHRIST. Three vols. 8vo, 31s. 6d.
White (Rev. M.)—SYMBOLICAL NUMBERS OF SCRIPTURE. Cr. 8vo, 4s.
Williams—SELECT VOCABULARY OF LATIN ETYMOLOGY. Fcap. 8vo, 1s. 6d.
Winer (Dr. G. B.)—A TREATISE ON THE GRAMMAR OF NEW TESTAMENT GREEK, regarded as the Basis of New Testament Exegesis. Third Edition, edited by W. F. MOULTON, D.D. Ninth English Edition, 8vo, 15s.
—— A COMPARATIVE VIEW OF THE DOCTRINES AND CONFESSIONS OF THE VARIOUS COMMUNITIES OF CHRISTENDOM. 8vo, 10s. 6d.
Wright (C. H., D.D.)—BIBLICAL ESSAYS; or, Exegetical Studies. Crown 8vo, 5s.
Wuttke (Professor)—CHRISTIAN ETHICS. Two vols. 8vo, 12s. 6d.

www.ingramcontent.com/pod-product-compliance
Lightning Source LLC
Chambersburg PA
CBHW022143300426
44115CB00006B/329